Fast & Easy ECGs

A Self-Paced Learning Program

Bruce Shade, EMT-P, EMS-I, AAS

Keith Wesley, MD, FACEP

Higher Education

Boston Burr Ridge, IL Dubuque, IA Madison, WI New York San Francisco St. Louis
Bangkok Bogotá Caracas Kuala Lumpur Lisbon London Madrid Mexico City
Milan Montreal New Delhi Santiago Seoul Singapore Sydney Taipei Toronto

Higher Education

FAST & EASY ECGS: A SELF-PACED LEARNING PROGRAM

Published by McGraw-Hill, a business unit of The McGraw-Hill Companies, Inc., 1221 Avenue of the Americas, New York, NY 10020.

This book is printed on recycled, acid-free paper containing 10% postconsumer waste.

1 2 3 4 5 6 7 8 9 0 QPD/QPD 0 9 8 7 6 5

ISBN–13 978–0–07–294811–0
ISBN–10 0–07–294811–6

Publisher, Career Education: *David T. Culverwell*
Senior Sponsoring Editor: *Claire Merrick*
Editorial Coordinator: *Michelle L. Zeal*
Outside Managing Editor: *Kelly Trakalo*
Marketing Manager: *Lynn M. Kalb*
Senior Project Manager: *Sheila M. Frank*
Senior Production Supervisor: *Kara Kudronowicz*
Lead Media Project Manager: *Audrey A. Reiter*
Media Technology Producer: *Janna Martin*
Senior Coordinator of Freelance Design: *Michelle D. Whitaker*
Cover/Interior Designer: *Rokusek Design*
(USE) Cover Image: © *Karl Weatherly/CORBIS*
Senior Photo Research Coordinator: *John C. Leland*
Compositor: *Carlisle Communications, Ltd.*
Typeface: *11.5/13 Minion*
Printer: *Quebecor World Dubuque, IA*

Library of Congress Cataloging-in-Publication Data

Shade, Bruce R.
Fast & easy ECGs : a self-paced learning program / Bruce R. Shade, Keith Wesley. — 1st ed.
p. cm.
Includes index.
ISBN–13 978–0–07–294811–0—ISBN–10 0–07–294811–6
1. Electrocardiography—Interpretation. I. Title: Fast and easy ECGs. II. Wesley, Keith. III. Title.

FC683.5.E5S44 2007 2005050511
CIP

Medicine is an ever-changing science. As new research and clinical experience broaden our knowledge, changes in treatment and drug therapy are required. The authors and the publisher of this work have checked with sources believed to be reliable in their efforts to provide information that is complete and generally in accord with the standards accepted at the time of publication. However, in view of the possibility of human error or changes in medical sciences, neither the authors nor the publisher nor any other party who has been involved in the preparation or publication of this work warrants that the information contained herein is in every respect accurate or complete, and they are not responsible for any errors or omissions or for the results obtained from use of such information. Readers are encouraged to confirm the information contained herein with other resources. For example and in particular, readers are advised to check the product information sheet included in the package of each drug they plan to administer to be certain that the information contained in this book is accurate and that changes have not been made in the recommended dose or in the contradictions for administration. This recommendation is of particular importance in connection with new or infrequently used drugs.

www.mhhe.com

This book is dedicated to my wife Cheri, my daughter Katherine, and my son Christopher. Their love and support gave me the strength to carry this good idea from concept to text even when the days dragged into weeks, months, and then years.

Bruce Shade

To my loving and devoted wife Karen who gives me the strength and encouragement to accomplish the impossible, I love you.

And to the dedicated members of the Chippewa Fire District. Thank you for striving to be excellent. You are the best.

Keith Wesley

About the Authors

Bruce Shade

Bruce Shade is an Assistant Public Safety Director for the City of Cleveland, Cleveland, OH. He is also a part-time paramedic/firefighter for the City of Willoughby, OH and a paramedic instructor at Cuyahoga Community College.

Bruce has been involved in emergency services since 1972. He started as a volunteer firefighter/EMT and has served as paramedic, educational supervisor, paramedic training program director, and commissioner for the City of Cleveland's Division of Emergency Medical Service. He has also served as executive administrator and the City of Cleveland's Disaster and Emergency Coordinator.

Bruce is a past President, Vice President and Treasurer of the National Association of EMTs and chairperson of the Instructor Coordinator Society. He has served as president of several local associations and chairperson of many committees and task forces. Bruce has authored several EMS textbooks and written many EMS-related articles. He has lectured extensively at local, regional, state, and national EMS conferences.

Keith Wesley

Keith Wesley is an emergency medicine physician. He has been an active EMS medical director for 20 years and is a frequent speaker at state and national EMS conferences. He has authored several EMS textbooks and numerous articles on EMS. Dr. Wesley is active in both state and national EMS organizations and says, "Teaching the healthcare provider of tomorrow is my greatest passion."

Though originally from Texas, he currently lives in Eau Claire, Wisconsin. When not working, writing, or speaking, Dr Wesley dreams of sailing to faraway lands.

Contents

Preface

This book, as its title implies, is meant to serve as a self-learning program. The original idea was to create a practical textbook that could dynamically teach healthcare professionals how to interpret electrocardiograms. It occurred to me at the time that we needed to write a text in the same way an instructor might present the information to you in a classroom: with lots of illustrations, clinical tidbits of information and instructional notes, questions to prompt critical thinking, and lots of practice strips to allow application of concepts.

The first two chapters of the book look at the underlying concepts of the anatomy and electrophysiology of the heart and the electrocardiogram itself. Chapters 3 through 7 have been designed to follow the five-step process of ECG interpretation. Each chapter provides an in-depth look at one of the steps, and while it begins to introduce names of dysrhythmias, its focus is to understand why we interpret ECGs in this way and understanding the alterations in electrophysiology that are occurring. Chapters 8 through 11 lead you through dysrhythmias of the sinus node, the atria, the AV junction, and the ventricles. Chapter 12 introduces the concept of electrical axis. Chapters 13 through 15 introduce concepts important to 12-lead ECG interpretation and recognizing myocardial injury, ischemia, and infarction. Finally, Chapter 16 discusses other cardiac conditions and their effect on the ECG.

The *ECG Mentor: Presentations and Demonstrations* provides a professor who is available at your fingertips to help review and reinforce the key concepts of the book. Lectures narrated by co-author, Dr. Keith Wesley, provide instruction on important and difficult-to-understand topics. Dr. Wesley also demonstrates how to actually go through the five-step process of ECG interpretation. Also included are narrated animations of anatomy and electrophysiology to help you understand what goes on inside the heart.

For the instructor we have provided an *Instructor's CD-ROM* containing PowerPoint slides, a test bank of questions, and a bank of animations.

We hope this learning program is beneficial to both students and instructors. Greater understanding of ECG interpretation can only lead to better patient care everywhere.

Features to Help You Study and Learn

Brief Contents

Learn it Like You Practice!

The text is organized according to the 5-step approach of interpreting ECGs.

A basic introduction to 12-lead ECG interpretation is covered in Chapters 13, 14, and 15.

x Fast & Easy ECGs

Regularity

4

Case History

An 85-year-old woman presents to her family physician's office for her yearly checkup. She has a history of atherosclerotic heart disease and non-insulin-dependent diabetes. She has been careful to follow her doctor's advice and takes her medications regularly. She denies any new complaints.

While taking her vital signs, the nurse notes that the woman's heart rate is irregular. He examines the patient's medical record to see if this condition has been previously recorded. He finds no evidence that the patient has ever had an irregular heart rhythm and calls the physician into the room to examine the patient. A cardiac monitor is attached to the patient and a rhythm strip is run. The nurse and physician examine the strip and observe that the rate is within normal limits but is irregularly irregular, meaning there is no pattern to the irregularity.

Chapter Preview

- Analyzing the ECG
- Step 2: Determining the Regularity
- Methods of Determining Regularity
- Types of Irregularity

Chapter Previews

Provide an overview of the major chapter topics.

A Case History

Starts each chapter providing real-life scenarios involving ECG interpretation. Follow up questions at the end of the chapter refer back to the scenario to assess understanding.

Fill-in-the-Blank

Areas are integrated throughout each chapter. They reinforce and review information that has been presented to the reader.

Easy to Read

Clear, concise and to-the-point coverage of key information.

The Electrocardiogram 59

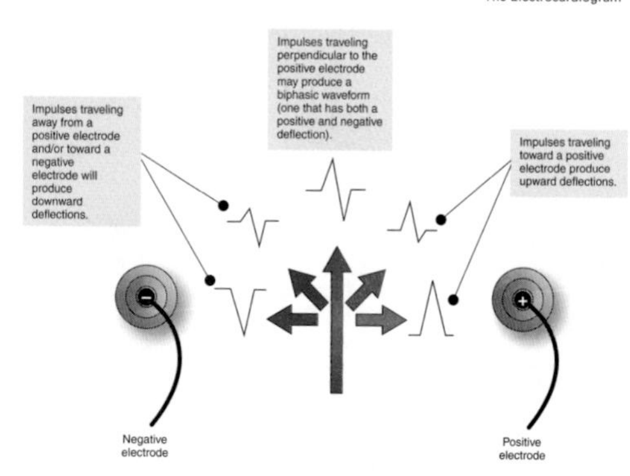

Figure 2-13
The direction the electrical impulse takes toward or away from a positive electrode causes the waveform to deflect either upward or downward.

Electrical currents traveling toward a positive electrode produce a waveform that takes an ____________ deflection while those traveling away from a ____________ electrode or toward a negative electrode produce a waveform with a ____________deflection. A ____________ waveform is composed of both positive and negative deflections.

[upright] [positive] [downward] [biphasic]

Planes of the Heart

Electrodes are placed at specific spots on the patient's chest wall and extremities to view the heart's electrical activity from different angles or planes (Figure 2-14). Planes provide a cross-sectional view of the heart. The frontal plane is essentially a vertical cut through the middle of the heart. The leads arranged on the frontal plane view the inferior,

Stimulating Sidebars

Questions

Ask the reader about important concepts and information. This reinforces what the reader "needs to know" and ensures understanding. Answers are found at the end of each chapter.

Key Concepts

Provide the reader with a concise look of what they "need to know".

Clinical Moments

Provide the reader with extra clinical information.

Instructional Moments

Provide the reader with an "instructor" who gives hints and clarifications about the concepts being presented.

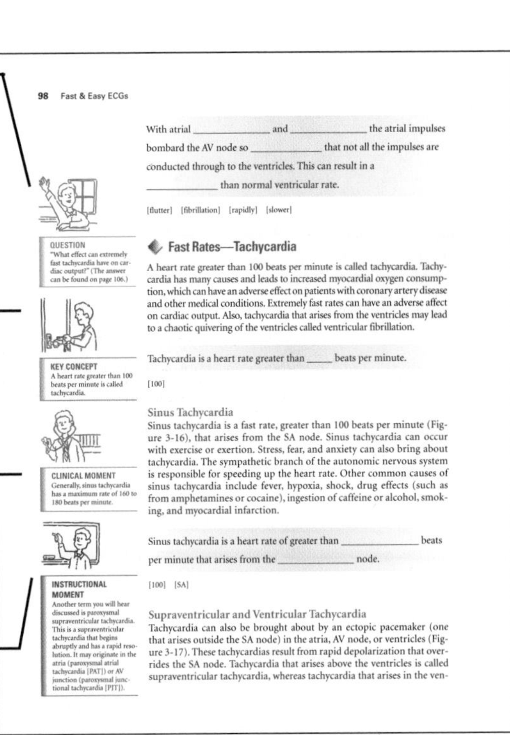

98 Fast & Easy ECGs

With atrial ______ and ______ the atrial impulses bombard the AV node so ______ that not all the impulses are conducted through to the ventricles. This can result in a ______ than normal ventricular rate.

[flutter] [fibrillation] [rapidly] [slower]

QUESTION
"What effect can extremely fast tachycardia have on cardiac output?" (The answer can be found on page 106.)

Fast Rates—Tachycardia

A heart rate greater than 100 beats per minute is called tachycardia. Tachycardia has many causes and leads to increased myocardial oxygen consumption, which can have an adverse effect on patients with coronary artery disease and other medical conditions. Extremely fast rates can have an adverse affect on cardiac output. Also, tachycardia that arises from the ventricles may lead to a chaotic quivering of the ventricles called ventricular fibrillation.

KEY CONCEPT
A heart rate greater than 100 beats per minute is called tachycardia.

Tachycardia is a heart rate greater than ____ beats per minute.

[100]

Sinus Tachycardia

Sinus tachycardia is a fast rate, greater than 100 beats per minute (Figure 3-16), that arises from the SA node. Sinus tachycardia can occur with exercise or exertion. Stress, fear, and anxiety can also bring about tachycardia. The sympathetic branch of the autonomic nervous system is responsible for speeding up the heart rate. Other common causes of sinus tachycardia include fever, hypoxia, shock, drug effects (such as from amphetamines or cocaine), ingestion of caffeine or alcohol, smoking, and myocardial infarction.

CLINICAL MOMENT
Generally, sinus tachycardia has a maximum rate of 160 to 180 beats per minute.

Sinus tachycardia is a heart rate of greater than ______ beats per minute that arises from the ______ node.

[100] [SA]

INSTRUCTIONAL MOMENT
Another term you will hear discussed is paroxysmal supraventricular tachycardia. This is a supraventricular tachycardia that begins abruptly and has a rapid resolution. It may originate in the atria (paroxysmal atrial tachycardia [PAT]) or AV junction (paroxysmal junctional tachycardia [PJT]).

Supraventricular and Ventricular Tachycardia

Tachycardia can also be brought about by an ectopic pacemaker (one that arises outside the SA node) in the atria, AV node, or ventricles (Figure 3-17). These tachycardias result from rapid depolarization that overrides the SA node. Tachycardia that arises above the ventricles is called supraventricular tachycardia, whereas tachycardia that arises in the ven-

Table 11-1 Premature Ventricular Complex

Causes of PVCs	Examples
Cardiac disorders	Myocardial ischemia and infarction, enlargement of the ventricular chambers, congestive heart failure, myocarditis
Use of certain drugs	Drug intoxication, particularly cocaine, amphetamines, tricyclic antidepressants; use of stimulants, such as alcohol, caffeine, tobacco; sympathomimetic drugs, such as phencyclidine (PCP), cocaine, epinephrine, isoproterenol
Other	Hypoxia, electrolyte imbalance, such as hypokalemia, hyperkalemia, hypomagnesemia, and hypocalcemia; metabolic acidosis, increased sympathetic stimulation

Informative Tables

Detail causes of dysrhythmias.

Boxes

Review characteristics of dysrhythmias.

Review of key characteristics associated with PVCs

Rate:	Depends on the underlying rhythm
Regularity:	May be occasionally irregular or frequently irregular (depends on the number of PVCs present)
P waves:	Not preceded by a P wave (if seen, they are dissociated)
QRS complexes:	Wide, large, and bizarre looking
PR interval:	Not measurable
QT interval:	Usually prolonged with the PVC

Outstanding Art Package

The text and its companion DVD are highly visual. Approximately 500 pieces of full-color art uniquely illustrate important concepts, anatomical causes of dysrhythmias and lots of practice ECG strips.

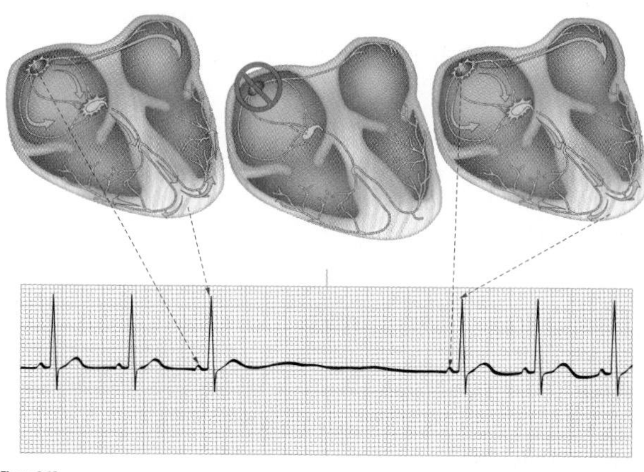

Figure 3-13
Sinus arrest occurs when the SA node fails to initiate an impulse. Because of the dropped beat(s) it can result in bradycardia.

Figure 4-4
With the calipers open they are moved across the tracing from the point of one R wave or P wave to the next consecutive R wave or P wave (the R-R or P-P interval).

Practice Makes Perfect

Exercises are located throughout the chapters. They provide the reader with real ECG strips to practice the techniques of ECG interpretation. There are approximately 200 Practice Makes Perfect exercises. Answers to the exercises are found in Appendix A.

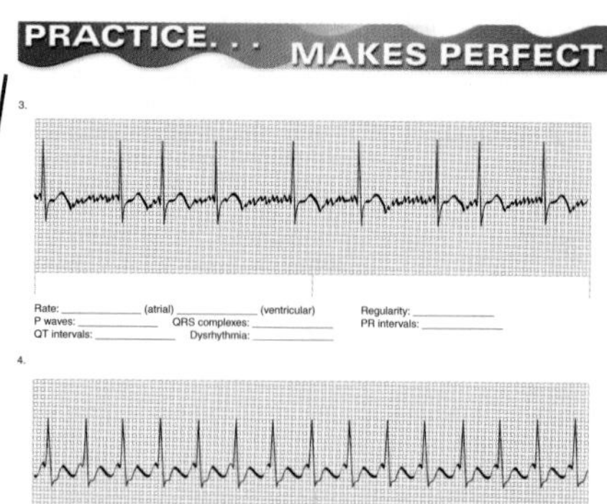

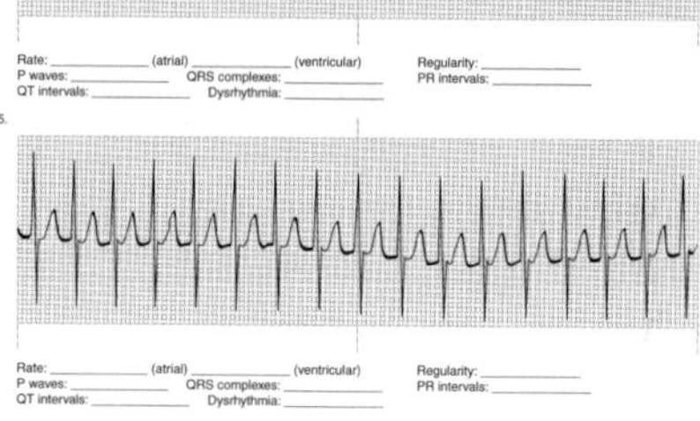

Key Points

At the end of each chapter provide an "at a glance" look at the need to know and understand concepts of the chapter.

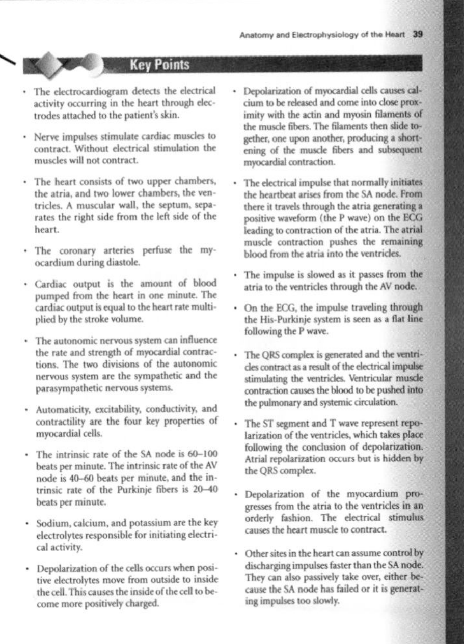

Anatomy and Electrophysiology of the Heart 39

Key Points

- The electrocardiogram detects the electrical activity occurring in the heart through electrodes attached to the patient's skin.
- Nerve impulses stimulate cardiac muscles to contract. Without electrical stimulation the muscles will not contract.
- The heart consists of two upper chambers, the atria, and two lower chambers, the ventricles. A muscular wall, the septum, separates the right side from the left side of the heart.
- The coronary arteries perfuse the myocardium during diastole.
- Cardiac output is the amount of blood pumped from the heart in one minute. The cardiac output is equal to the heart rate multiplied by the stroke volume.
- The autonomic nervous system can influence the rate and strength of myocardial contractions. The two divisions of the autonomic nervous system are the sympathetic and the parasympathetic nervous systems.
- Automaticity, excitability, conductivity, and contractility are the four key properties of myocardial cells.
- The intrinsic rate of the SA node is 60–100 beats per minute. The intrinsic rate of the AV node is 40–60 beats per minute, and the intrinsic rate of the Purkinje fibers is 20–40 beats per minute.
- Sodium, calcium, and potassium are the key electrolytes responsible for initiating electrical activity.
- Depolarization of the cells occurs when positive electrolytes move from outside to inside the cell. This causes the inside of the cell to become more positively charged.
- Depolarization of myocardial cells causes calcium to be released and come into close proximity with the actin and myosin filaments of the muscle fibers. The filaments then slide together, one upon another, producing a shortening of the muscle fibers and subsequent myocardial contraction.
- The electrical impulse that normally initiates the heartbeat arises from the SA node. From there it travels through the atria generating a positive waveform (the P wave) on the ECG leading to contraction of the atria. The atrial muscle contraction pushes the remaining blood from the atria into the ventricles.
- The impulse is slowed as it passes from the atria to the ventricles through the AV node.
- On the ECG, the impulse traveling through the His-Purkinje system is seen as a flat line following the P wave.
- The QRS complex is generated and the ventricles contract as a result of the electrical impulse stimulating the ventricles. Ventricular muscle contraction causes the blood to be pushed into the pulmonary and systemic circulation.
- The ST segment and T wave represent repolarization of the ventricles, which takes place following the conclusion of depolarization. Atrial repolarization occurs but is hidden by the QRS complex.
- Depolarization of the myocardium progresses from the atria to the ventricles in an orderly fashion. The electrical stimulus causes the heart muscle to contract.
- Other sites in the heart can assume control by discharging impulses faster than the SA node. They can also passively take over, either because the SA node has failed or it is generating impulses too slowly.

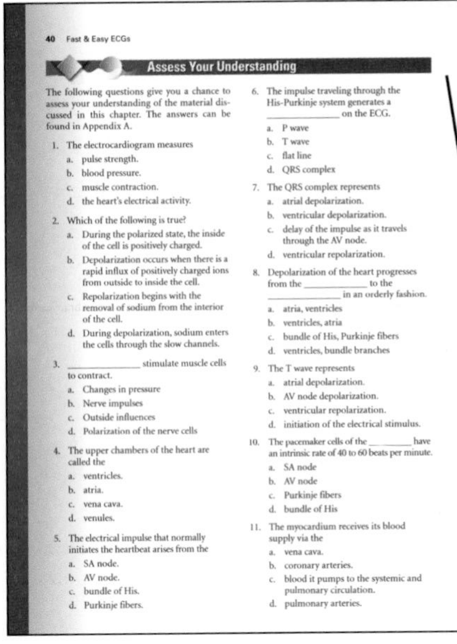

40 Fast & Easy ECGs

Assess Your Understanding

The following questions give you a chance to assess your understanding of the material discussed in this chapter. The answers can be found in Appendix A.

1. The electrocardiogram measures
   a. pulse strength.
   b. blood pressure.
   c. muscle contraction.
   d. the heart's electrical activity.
2. Which of the following is true?
   a. During the polarized state, the inside of the cell is positively charged.
   b. Depolarization occurs when there is a rapid influx of positively charged ions from outside to inside the cell.
   c. Repolarization begins with the removal of sodium from the interior of the cell.
   d. During depolarization, sodium enters the cells through the slow channels.
3. ____________ stimulate muscle cells to contract.
   a. Changes in pressure
   b. Nerve impulses
   c. Outside influences
   d. Polarization of the nerve cells
4. The upper chambers of the heart are called the
   a. ventricles.
   b. atria.
   c. vena cava.
   d. venules.
5. The electrical impulse that normally initiates the heartbeat arises from the
   a. SA node.
   b. AV node.
   c. bundle of His.
   d. Purkinje fibers.
6. The impulse traveling through the His-Purkinje system generates a ____________ on the ECG.
   a. P wave
   b. T wave
   c. flat line
   d. QRS complex
7. The QRS complex represents
   a. atrial depolarization.
   b. ventricular depolarization.
   c. delay of the impulse as it travels through the AV node.
   d. ventricular repolarization.
8. Depolarization of the heart progresses from the ____________ to the ____________ in an orderly fashion.
   a. atria, ventricles
   b. ventricles, atria
   c. bundle of His, Purkinje fibers
   d. ventricles, bundle branches
9. The T wave represents
   a. atrial depolarization.
   b. AV node depolarization.
   c. ventricular repolarization.
   d. initiation of the electrical stimulus.
10. The pacemaker cells of the ____________ have an intrinsic rate of 40 to 60 beats per minute.
    a. SA node
    b. AV node
    c. Purkinje fibers
    d. bundle of His
11. The myocardium receives its blood supply via the
    a. vena cava.
    b. coronary arteries.
    c. blood it pumps to the systemic and pulmonary circulation.
    d. pulmonary arteries.

Assess Your Understanding

Is a review section at the end of each chapter. A variety of questions and practice strips allow the reader to assess their understanding of chapter material. Answers are found in Appendix A.

On the DVD

Is a section at the end of each chapter. It provides the reader with an outline of the lecture topics, demonstrations and animations which appear on the DVD for this chapter.

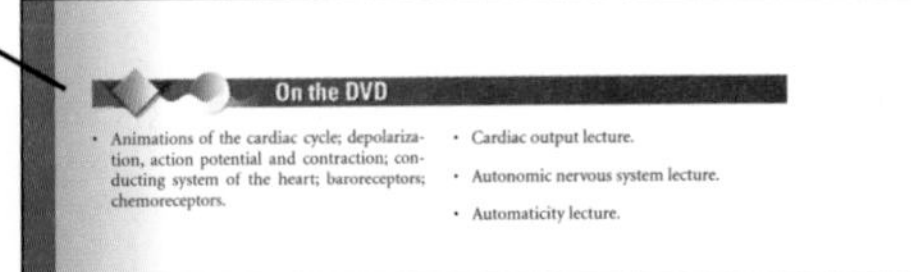

On the DVD

- Animations of the cardiac cycle; depolarization, action potential and contraction; conducting system of the heart; baroreceptors; chemoreceptors.
- Cardiac output lecture.
- Autonomic nervous system lecture.
- Automaticity lecture.

The ECG Mentor

Presentations, demonstrations and animations on the DVD assist in retention and understanding of material.

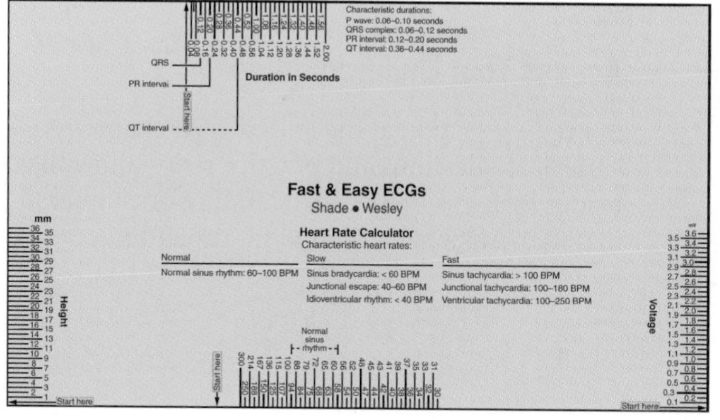

Heart Rate Calculator!

Included as part of the back cover, the heart rate calculator is an easy tool to use!

Acknowledgments

We would first like to thank Claire Merrick, our editor. It was discussions with her that lead to the idea of this book, and her strength and wisdom that pulled us through it. We would like to thank Dave Culverwell, Publisher at McGraw-Hill. Dave embraced the idea of this book with great enthusiasm. He stood by the project even when things were behind schedule and we struggled to carry the concept fully into text pages. We would like to thank Kelly Trakalo the project's managing editor. Kelly is nothing short of phenomenal. Her tireless work on the book shaped its wonderful look and style as well as helped ensure the accuracy of the content. She was also the "task master" who kept us on track to get the material turned around in a timely manner.

This book, because of our dynamic, visual approach, required huge effort on the part of our production project manager, Sheila Frank. She stuck with us through thick and thin, no matter how many changes and additions we requested. Without her efforts the book would be just bare pages with text and stick figures instead of the warm, stimulating tapestry that surrounds our words and dynamic pictures. Rod Wiese was our artist for the project. He had no way of knowing what he was getting into when we first spoke. While I told him there would be lots of figures and that I wanted them to be vibrant and dynamic, none of us really knew how much work would be required. Rod did great work and produced figures that are unparalleled in other textbooks. Cindy Sweeney also put up with our many requests of "Hey, can you just change this?"

Other members of the McGraw-Hill team who we proudly acknowledge include Janna Martin (electronic publishing) and Michelle Whitaker (design). Finally, we wish to acknowledge the efforts of Denny Hare and Russ Doran at Complete Project Management. They shot the video and produced the DVD that accompanies this text. The talents of Denny and Russ become readily apparent as you view the DVD.

Bruce Shade and Keith Wesley

I also wish to acknowledge my co-author Keith Wesley. Keith is a thoughtful and extremely talented practicing emergency physician. This project has benefited from his years of teaching healthcare professionals, as well as his newly discovered "on screen persona." I further wish to acknowledge my father, Elmer Shade, Jr. who taught me the value of working hard and my mother Lucille who was herself an aspiring author. Last, I want to acknowledge some of the many people who profoundly influenced me throughout my career in public safety and healthcare education including Granger Township Fire Chief Richard Alber who taught me to be a "stand up" person; Copley Township Fire Chief Joseph Ezzie who taught me the value of presenting information to students visually; City of Columbus, Ohio public safety director Mitchell Brown who mentored me as I developed my instructional and management skills; and former City of Cleveland, Ohio public safety director James Draper who restored my confidence and showed me the meaning of leadership and the value of humor.

Bruce Shade

Publisher's Acknowledgments

Rhonda J. Beck, NREMT-P
Central Georgia Tech
Hawkinsville, GA

Christopher Black
Eastern Arizona College
Safford, AZ

Angel Clark Burba, MS, NREMT-P
Associate Professor, Program Director
Emergency Medical Services
Howard Community College
Columbia, MD

Gary D. Clark, EdD, CRNA
Webster University
Godfey, IL

Paula Byrne Davis, MS, FNP-C
Glendale Community College
Glendale, AZ

Glen Garwood
Oakland Community College
Macomb Twp. MI

Michael Galluci, MS, PT
Assistant Professor
Physical Therapy, School of Public Health
New York Medical College
Pearl River, NY

Kevin Johnson, BS, NREMT-P
Emergency Health Services Faculty
Inver Hills Community College
Inver Grove Heights, MN

Deborah E Kortyna, MMS, PA-C
Physician Assistant Studies, Academic Coordinator
Chatham College
Pittsburgh, Pennsylvania

Brenda J. Mister, MS, RN
Assistant Professor of Nursing
Wor-Wic Community College
Salisbury, MD

Cynthia M. Parsons, RN, MSN, CCRN
Caldwell Community College and Technical Institute
Hickory, NC

Randall Perkins, ALS Program Director
Scottsdale Community College
Scottsdale, AZ

Debra M. Redfearn, BGS, NREMT-P,
Program Director, Department of EMS Education
Delgado Community College
Paramedic, West Jefferson Medical Center
New Orleans, LA

Julie A. Stone, EdD, CRNA
Webster University
Fairview Heights, IL

Rachel Yeater, Ph.D.
Professor and Chair
Division of Exercise Physiology
School of Medicine
West Virginia University

Anatomy and Electrophysiology of the Heart

1

Case History

Emergency medical services (EMS) responds to the home of a 46-year-old man complaining of a dull ache in his chest for the past two hours which came on while mowing his lawn. He also complains of a "fluttering" in his chest and "shortness of breath." He has a history of hypertension, elevated cholesterol, and a one-pack-a-day smoking habit.

After introducing themselves, the paramedics begin their assessment, which finds the patient's blood pressure to be 160/110, pulse 120 and irregular, respirations of 20, and oxygen saturation of 92% on room air. The patient is awake and alert, his airway is open, his breathing slightly labored, and his pulses are strong.

The paramedics apply oxygen by nasal cannula and attach the patient to a cardiac monitor by applying electrodes to his chest. The monitor shows a fast, narrow complex rhythm with frequent wide and bizarre appearing extra complexes.

Based on what they observe, the paramedics obtain a 12-lead electrocardiogram (ECG) to determine if signs of a heart attack are present. The 12-lead ECG confirms their suspicions. The patient is having a myocardial infarction.

The paramedics then administer aspirin, nitroglycerin, and morphine to the patient and transport him to the nearest appropriate facility. En route to the hospital, the patient states his pain is less and the paramedics notice that the extra complexes are gone from his heart rhythm.

Chapter Preview

- The Electrocardiogram
- How Does the ECG Work?
- Structure of the Heart
- Blood Flow Through the Circulatory System
- How the Heart Works
- Influences on the Heart and Circulatory System
- The Heart's Electrical System
- How Nerve Impulses Are Generated and Muscles Contract
- How It All Works Together

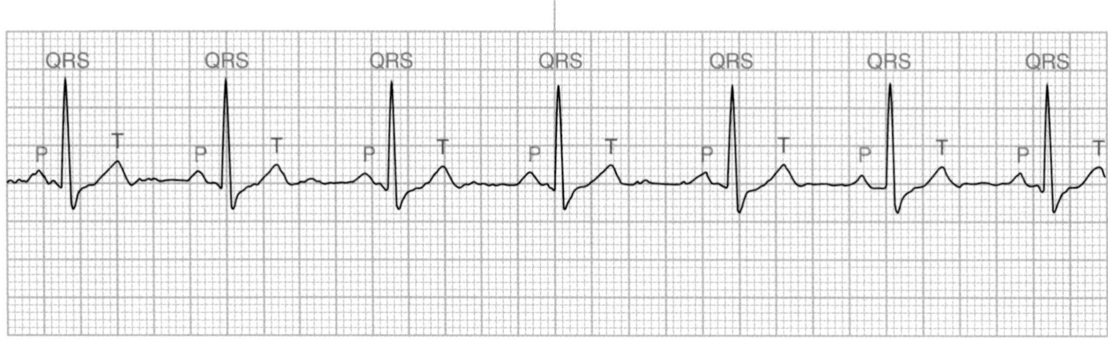

Figure 1-1
The electrocardiogram is a tracing or graphic representation of the heart's electrical activity.

The Electrocardiogram

The **electrocardiogram,** often referred to as an ECG or EKG, is a tracing or graphic representation of the heart's electrical activity (Figure 1-1). The device that detects, measures, and records the ECG is called an **electrocardiograph.**

KEY CONCEPT
The ECG is a tracing or graphic representation of the heart's electrical activity.

The ECG provides healthcare professionals with valuable information. The ECG is used to identify irregularities in the heart rhythm (called **dysrhythmias**) and to reveal the presence of injury, death, or other physical changes in the heart muscle. It is used in the prehospital, hospital, and other clinical settings as both an assessment and diagnostic tool. It can also provide continuous monitoring of the heart's electrical activity during transport or in the coronary care unit. The ECG does not, however, tell us how well the heart is pumping. The presence of electrical activity on the cardiac monitor does not guarantee that the heart is contracting or producing a blood pressure. To determine that, we must assess the patient's pulse and blood pressure, as well as perform an appropriate physical examination.

CLINICAL MOMENT
It is the electrical activity that causes the heart muscle to contract and pump blood. However, the presence of electrical activity does not guarantee muscle contraction.

A tracing or graphic representation of the heart's electrical activity is an _______________. It is used to identify _______________ in the heart rhythm and to reveal the presence of _______________, death, or other _______________ changes in the heart muscle.

[electrocardiogram] [irregularities] [injury] [physical]

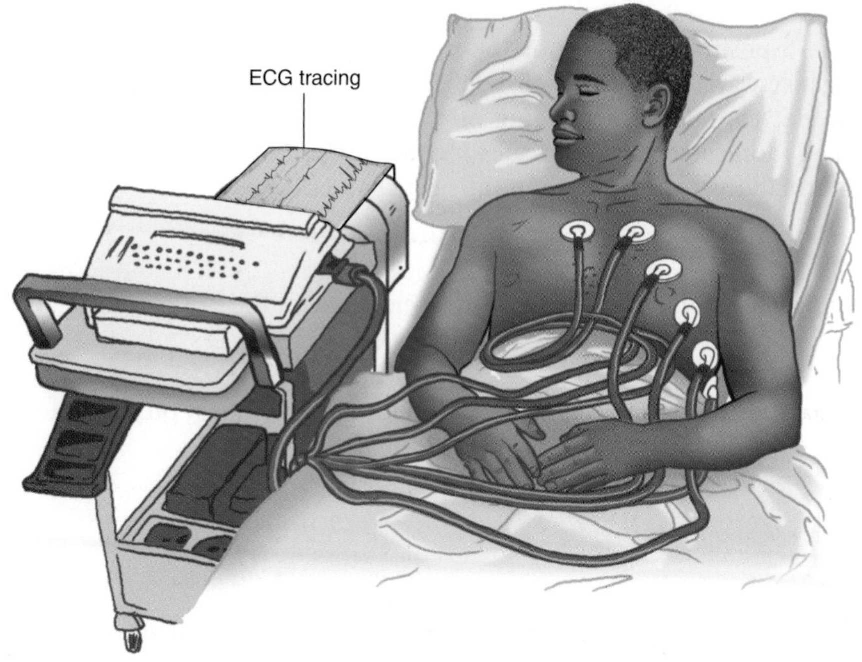

Figure 1-2
The ECG detects electrical activity in the heart.

How Does the ECG Work?

In simple terms, the electrocardiograph or ECG machine detects the electrical current activity occurring in the heart (Figure 1-2). It does this through electrodes placed on the patient's skin. These impulses, which appear as a series of upward (positive) and downward (negative) deflections (waveforms), are then transferred to the ECG machine and displayed on a screen (called the **oscilloscope** or monitor), or they are printed onto graph paper (often referred to as an ECG tracing or strip).

KEY CONCEPT
The ECG machine detects electrical current activity occuring in the heart.

The electrical activity of the heart produces ________________ that radiate through the surrounding tissues to the ________________. The ECG detects this electrical activity through ________________ placed on the skin.

[currents] [skin] [electrodes]

As the impulse moves toward a positive electrode of the ECG it produces a positive waveform (upright deflection). Refer to Figure 1-1. In this ECG tracing all the waveforms (P, QRS, and T) are positive, meaning the impulses are traveling toward a positive electrode. When it moves away from a positive electrode or toward a negative electrode, it produces a negative waveform (downward deflection). The sites for the placement of the electrodes vary depending on which view of the heart's activity is being monitored. Different sites provide different views. We discuss this information in more depth in the next chapter.

Impulses that move toward a positive electrode of the ECG produce a _______________ waveform (upright deflection). When it moves away from a positive electrode or toward a negative electrode it produces a _______________ waveform.

[positive] [negative]

This book is designed to teach you how to interpret what you see on an ECG. To do this, you must first understand the anatomy and physiology of the heart. We begin by discussing its location and structure, how it works mechanically, and the influence of the autonomic nervous system on the heart. Then we talk about how the generation and conduction of nerve impulses leads to contraction of cardiac muscle. Finally, we put it all together to show you how the electrical event leads to contraction of the chambers of the heart, which then pumps blood throughout the body.

CLINICAL MOMENT
Perfusion describes the circulatory system's delivery of oxygen and nutrients to the tissues and the removal of waste products. Perfusion is necessary for the body's cells to function and survive. The body's cells die if there is insufficient blood supply to meet their needs.

Structure of the Heart

Let's begin by discussing the structure of the heart. The heart is an amazing organ. It is the pump of the circulatory system. Each time it contracts it pushes blood throughout the body. The typical adult heart beats an average of 75 times a minute, 24 hours a day, 365 days a year, never stopping to take a rest. In an average day it pumps between 7000 and 9000 liters of blood! This circulates enough blood to deliver needed oxygen and nutrients to the tissues and to remove waste products. Depending on the requirements of the body, the heartbeat can either be sped up (during exercise) or slowed down (while resting or sleeping). Try this experiment: count your pulse rate while sitting or lying comfortably reading this book. Then, if you are physically able, go for a brisk walk (or perhaps run) and then recheck your pulse rate. It should be beating faster; you may even feel the sensation of your heart pounding in your chest. Your body increases the heart rate and strength of contractions to circulate more blood (and oxygen and nutrients) to your cells and to remove the waste products that have been produced by those working cells.

The heart is the _______________ of the circulatory system. It circulates enough blood to deliver the needed _______________ and _______________ to the tissues and to remove _______________ products.

[pump] [oxygen] [nutrients] [waste]

KEY CONCEPT
The heart continually circulates enough blood to deliver needed oxygen and nutrients to the tissues and to remove waste products.

Shape and Position of the Heart

Make a fist. Your heart is about the same size as your closed fist (Figure 1-3a). It is shaped like an inverted blunt cone. Its top (called the base) is the larger, flat part while its inferior end (called the apex) tapers to a blunt, rounded point. The heart is located between the two lungs in the **mediastinum** behind the sternum (Figure 1-3b). It lies on the diaphragm in front of the trachea, esophagus, and thoracic vertebrae. About two-thirds of the heart is situated in the left side of the chest cavity. Its base is directed posteriorly and slightly superiorly at the level of the second intercostal space. Its **apex** is directed anteriorly and slightly inferiorly at the level of the fifth intercostal space in the left midclavicular line. This gives it a front-to-back (anterior-posterior) orientation. In this position the right ventricle is closer to the front of the left chest while the left ventricle is closer to

KEY CONCEPT
The heart is located between the two lungs in the mediastinum behind the sternum. It rests on the diaphragm with a front-to-back (anterior-posterior) orientation.

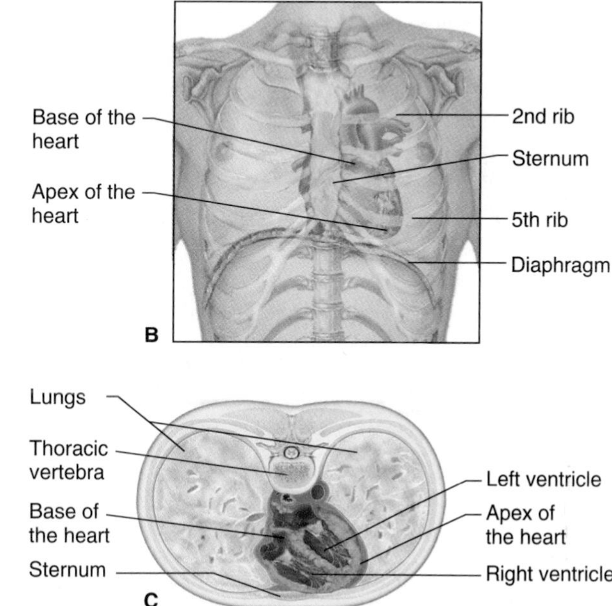

Figure 1-3
(a) The heart is about the size of a closed fist. (b) The position of the heart in the chest. (c) Cross section of the thorax at the level of the heart.

INSTRUCTIONAL MOMENT
Knowing the position and orientation of the heart will help you to understand why certain ECG waveforms appear as they do when the electrical impulse moves toward a positive or negative electrode. The location of the various ECG leads permits us to look at the heart from several different directions.

the side of the left chest (Figure 1-3c). This information will be particularly useful to you when we discuss placement of the various leads in Chapter 2.

The heart is shaped like a _______________ cone. It is located in the mediastinum behind the _______________. The heart's base is at the level of the _______________ intercostal space while its apex is at the level of the _______________ intercostal space in the left midclavicular line.

[blunt] [sterAnum] [second] [fifth]

The Pericardial Sac

CLINICAL MOMENT
The accumulation of additional fluid in the pericardial space can restrict the heart's ability to contract. This leads to a condition called **pericardial tamponade.** Pericardial tamponade can be life threatening.

The heart is surrounded by the pericardial sac (also called the **pericardium**), a double-walled closed sac (Figures 1-4 and 1-5). The tough, fibrous, outer layer is called the fibrous pericardium while the inner, thin, transparent lining is called the serous pericardium. Above the heart, the fibrous pericardium is continuous with the connective tissue coverings of the great vessels, and below, the heart is attached to the surface of the diaphragm. This anchors the heart within the mediastinum. The serous pericardium has two parts: the parietal pericardium, which lines the fibrous pericardium; and the visceral pericardium, which covers the surface of the heart. The pericardial cavity, located between the parietal pericardium and the visceral pericardium, holds a small amount of clear lubricating fluid that allows the heart to contract and expand within the chest cavity with minimal friction.

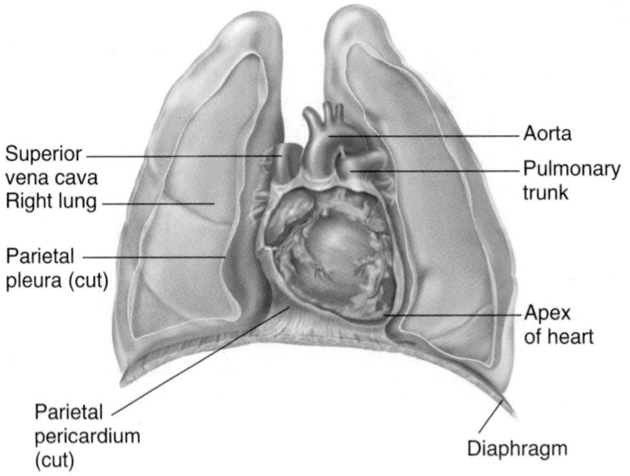

Figure 1-4
The pericardium is the protective sac that surrounds the heart.

The ______________ is a protective sac that encloses the heart. The inner lining is called the ______________ pericardium. It has two layers with a space in-between that contains pericardial ______________. This acts as a ______________.

[pericardium] [serous] [fluid] [lubricant]

The Heart Wall

The heart wall is comprised of three layers (Figure 1-5). The middle layer, the muscular layer, is called the **myocardium.** It is the thickest of the three layers and is composed of cylindrical cells that look similar to skeletal

INSTRUCTIONAL MOMENT
Myo means muscle, while cardia means heart. The heart muscle is called the myocardium.

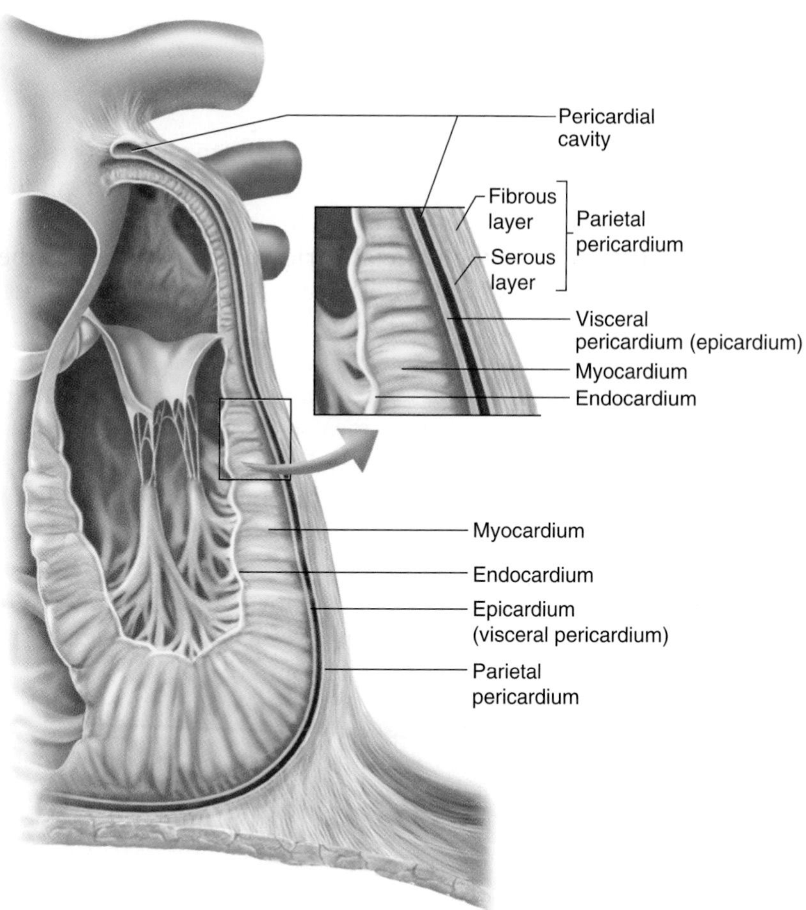

Figure 1-5
This cross section shows the structure of the heart. The enlarged section shows that the wall of the heart has three distinct layers of tissue: the endocardium, myocardium, and epicardium. Also note its relationship to the pericardium.

CLINICAL MOMENT
The outer layer of the heart wall is called the epicardium when referring to the layers of the heart but as the visceral pericardium when referring to the pericardium.

muscle. The innermost layer of the heart wall is called the **endocardium,** while the outermost is the **epicardium.** The endocardium is a serous membrane that lines the four chambers of the heart and its valves. It has a smooth surface and is continuous with the lining of the arteries and veins. It is watertight to prevent leakage of blood into the other layers. The epicardium is a thin serous membrane that constitutes the smooth outer surface of the heart.

The three layers of the heart wall are the ________________, the thickest layer; the ________________, the innermost layer; and the ________________, the outside layer.

[myocardium] [endocardium] [epicardium]

Myocardial Cells (Myocytes)

CLINICAL MOMENT
The heart consists of two syncytium, the atrial syncytium and the ventricular syncytium. The atrial syncytium consists of the walls of the right and left atria, while the ventricular syncytium consists of the walls of the right and left ventricles.

KEY CONCEPT
The structure of the myocardial cells permits the rapid conduction of electrical impulses from one cell to another. This results in the cardiac muscle cells acting as a single unit, permitting coordinated contraction of a whole group of cells.

There are two basic types of cells in the heart—the myocardial cells (also referred to as the working cells), which contract to propel blood out of the heart's chambers, and the specialized cells of the electrical conduction system, which initiate and carry impulses throughout the heart. In this section we will talk about the working cells. Later in this chapter we discuss the specialized cells of the electrical conduction system.

Structurally, the working cells **(myocytes)** are cylindrical branching cells that usually contain only one centrally located nucleus (Figure 1-6). They are enclosed in a plasma membrane called a **sarcolemma.** The individual myocytes are made up of a small latticework of intricate strands composed of two protein filaments referred to as **actin** and **myosin.** These filaments lay side by side and are connected by cross bridges. These contractile elements permit the muscle fiber to shorten itself and then return to its original length. Their organization gives cardiac muscle a striated (banded) appearance when viewed under a microscope. The process of contraction requires a plentiful supply of energy. This is supplied by the mitochondria, interspersed within the cell.

The myocytes are bound together with adjoining cells both end to end and laterally forming a branching and anastomosing network of cells called a **syncytium.** Specialized cellular contacts called **intercalated disks** are located where the branches join. The intercalated disks fit together to form electrical connections. **Gap junctions** permit the rapid conduction of electrical impulses from one cell to another. This results in the myocytes acting as a single unit, permitting coordinated contraction of a whole group of cells. This characteristic allows the walls of the

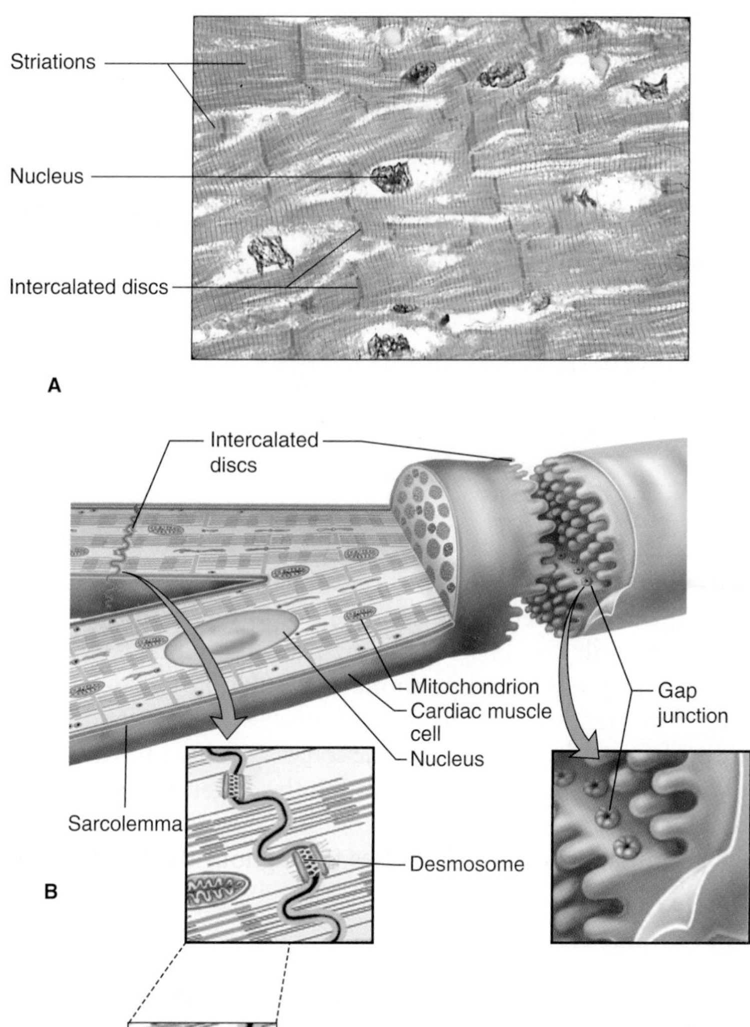

Figure 1-6
Myocardial cells. (a) Cells seen through a light microscope. (b) Myocytes and intercalated disks. (c) Actin and myosin filaments.

myocardium to contract almost simultaneously when stimulated by an electrical impulse. The highly coordinated contractions of the heart depend on this characteristic. Specialized structures in the cellular membrane called **desmosomes** hold the myocytes together to prevent them from pulling apart when the heart contracts.

The myocytes are cylindrical and branching at their ________________.

________________ disks, found where the branches join, act as electrical connections. Electrical impulses move rapidly from one cell to adjacent cells by means of ________________ junctions. This results in the myocytes acting as a single ________________.

________________ hold the cells together.

[ends] [Intercalated] [gap] [unit] [Desmosomes]

 The Internal Heart

CLINICAL MOMENT
The left ventricle is frequently referred to as the workhorse of the heart.

The heart is a muscular, hollow, inverted cone-shaped organ (Figure 1-7). It has two upper chambers, the **atria,** and two lower chambers, the **ventricles.** The thin-walled atria serve as low-pressure containers that collect blood from the systemic and pulmonary circulation and deliver it to the ventricles. The larger, more muscular ventricles pump blood to the pulmonary and systemic circulation. The left ventricle is thicker and more muscular because it pumps blood through the larger, higher pressure systemic circulation.

The four chambers of the heart are the thin-walled ________________, which collect blood from the systemic and pulmonary circulation and deliver it to the ventricles, and the ________________, which pump blood to the pulmonary and systemic circulation. The ________________ ventricle is thicker and more muscular because it pumps blood through the systemic circulation.

[atria] [ventricles] [left]

INSTRUCTIONAL MOMENT
You can also think of the heart as having two upper pumps (the atria) and two lower pumps (the ventricles).

Two Functional Pumps

The heart is separated into two functional units by the **septum** (see Figure 1-7). The interatrial septum is a thin membranous wall that separates the two atria, while the more muscular wall, the interventricular septum, separates the two ventricles. For this reason the heart is referred to as a double pump.

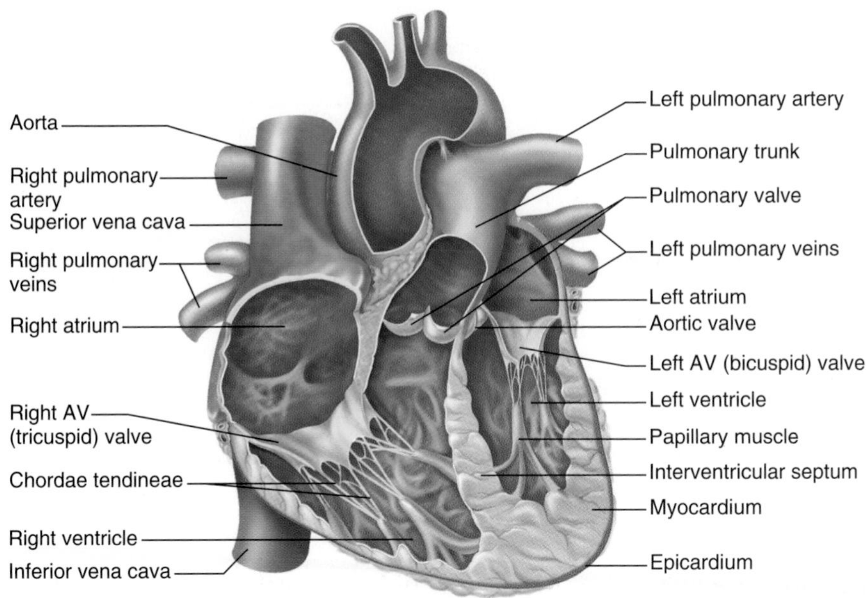

Figure 1-7
Internal anatomy of the heart.

The ________________separates the heart into two functional units. The right side consists of the right ________________ and right ________________ while the left side consists of the left ________________ and left ________________.

[septum] [atrium] [ventricle] [atrium] [ventricle]

KEY CONCEPT
The heart consists of two upper chambers, the atria, and two lower chambers, the ventricles. A muscular wall, the septum, separates the right side from the left side of the heart.

The Heart Valves

Two atrioventricular (AV) valves are located between the atria and ventricles, while two semilunar valves are located between the ventricles and major arteries (Figure 1-8). The two AV valves include the **tricuspid valve,** situated between the right atrium and right ventricle, and the **bicuspid** (or **mitral**) valve located between the left atrium and left ventricle. These valves prevent blood from flowing backward into the atria when the ventricles contract resulting in the ejection of blood forward from the ventricles and into the pulmonary and systemic circulation. The mitral valve has two cusps, while the tricuspid valve has three. The cusps are connected to **papillary muscles** in the floor of the ventricle by thin, strong strings of connective tissue called **chordae tendineae.** These cords prevent the cusps from bulging (prolapsing) backward into the atria during ventricular contraction.

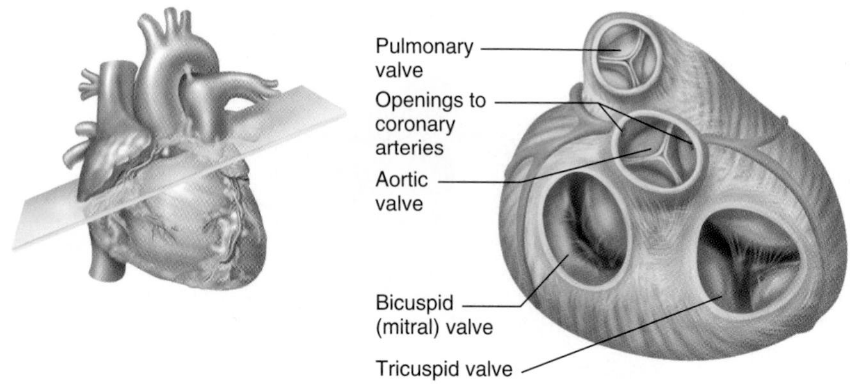

Figure 1-8
Superior view of the heart with the atria removed and four heart valves exposed. (Note the location of the openings to the coronary arteries.)

KEY CONCEPT
The AV valves prevent blood from flowing backward into the atria when the ventricles contract. The semilunar valves prevent blood from flowing backward into the ventricles.

The two semilunar valves include the **pulmonic valve,** found at the base of the pulmonary artery, and the **aortic valve,** situated at the base of the aorta, just as they arise from the right and left ventricles, respectively. They prevent the backward flow of blood after the ventricles have contracted and propelled blood into the pulmonary arteries and aorta. Each valve has three cusps that look somewhat like shirt pockets.

Four heart valves permit blood to flow through the heart in only one direction. These include the ________________ valve, situated between the right atrium and right ventricle; the ________________ valve, located between the left atrium and left ventricle; the ________________ valve, found at the base of the pulmonary artery; and the ________________ valve, situated at the base of the aorta.

[tricuspid] [mitral] [pulmonic] [aortic]

KEY CONCEPT
The skeleton of the heart forms fibrous rings around the AV and semilunar valves. It provides firm support for them and acts to separate the atria from the ventricles.

The Skeleton of the Heart

Between the atria and ventricles is a plate of fibrous connective tissue called the skeleton of the heart (Figure 1-9). This plate forms fibrous rings around the AV and semilunar valves providing firm support. It also acts to separate the atria from the ventricles. This has two important functions. First, it allows the top and bottom parts of the heart to act as separate, sequential pumps. Second, it electrically insulates the atria from the ventricles. This insulation allows the atria to be depolarized without depolarizing the ventricles and allows the ventricles to be depolarized without depolarizing the atria.

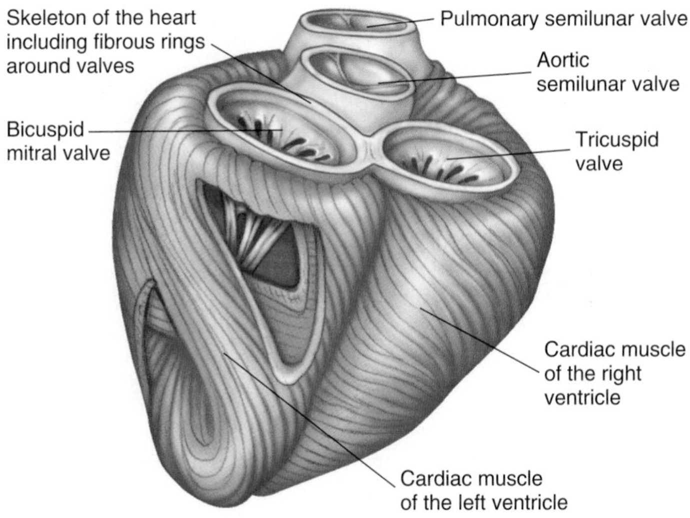

Figure 1-9
The skeleton of the heart consists of fibrous connective tissue rings that surround the heart valves and separate the atria from the ventricles. Cardiac muscle tissue attaches to the fibrous connective tissue.

The cardiac muscles are attached to the fibrous connective tissue and arranged in such a way that when the ventricles contract they do so in a wringing motion, which shortens the distance between the base and the apex of the heart. This results in the most efficient ejection of blood out of the ventricles.

The skeleton of the heart provides firm support for the ______________ and ______________ valves and acts to ______________ the atria from the ventricles. Because of how the cardiac muscles are attached and arranged, the ventricles contract with a ______________ motion, which ______________ the distance between the base and the apex of the heart.

[atrioventricular] [semilunar] [separate] [wringing] [shortens]

INSTRUCTIONAL MOMENT
The important role the skeleton of the heart plays will become more apparent as we move through the rest of the book so you should mark this page for future reference.

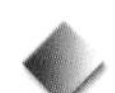 The Heart's Blood Supply

The heart receives most of its blood supply via the **coronary arteries** (Figure 1-10). These arteries originate from the base of the ascending aorta immediately above the leaflets or cusps of the aortic valve. The two major coronary arteries are the right main coronary artery and the left main coronary artery. After passing through the capillaries in the myocardium, blood flows into the **coronary veins.** It then empties into the coronary venous sinus, which in turn drains into the right atrium.

QUESTION
"Where is the aortic valve located?" (The answer can be found on page 41.)

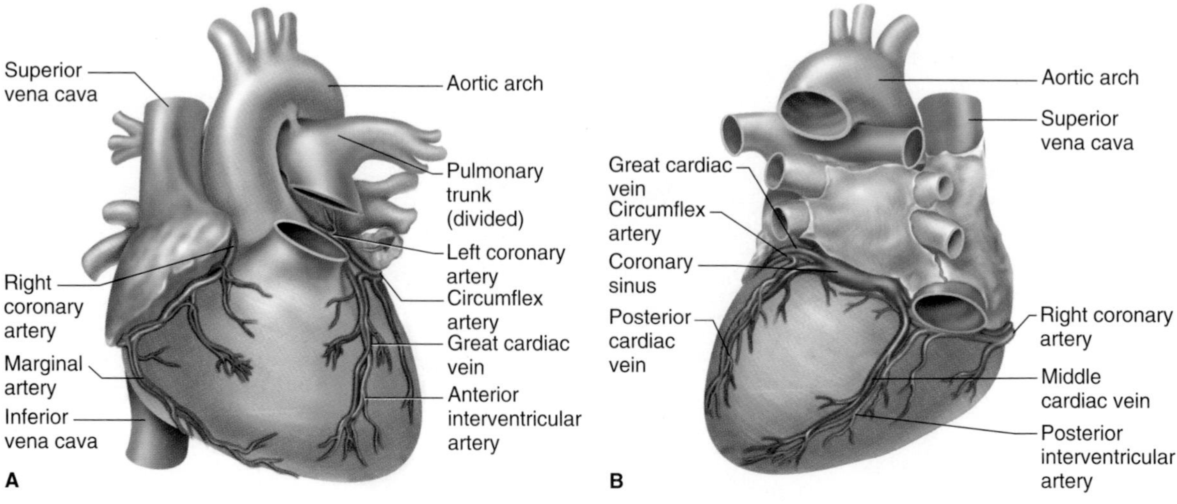

Figure 1-10
The coronary blood vessels supply the heart with oxygen and nutrients and remove waste products. (a) Anterior aspect. (b) Posterior aspect.

QUESTION
"Why are they called the coronary arteries?" (The answer can be found on page 41.)

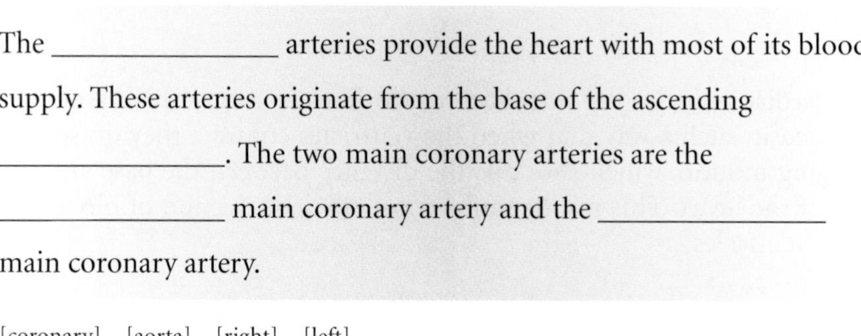

The ______________ arteries provide the heart with most of its blood supply. These arteries originate from the base of the ascending ______________. The two main coronary arteries are the ______________ main coronary artery and the ______________ main coronary artery.

[coronary] [aorta] [right] [left]

KEY CONCEPT
The coronary arteries provide the heart muscle with most of its blood supply.

If the flow of blood in the coronary arteries is diminished, myocardial ischemia may result. When severe ischemia occurs, necrosis or death of muscle tissue can occur.

CLINICAL MOMENT
The heart has a protective mechanism. Interconnections or anastamoses between the coronary arteries, called coronary collateral vessels, can act to protect the heart by enlarging to provide blood flow to regions of the heart where blood supply is decreased as a result of occlusion of any of the coronary arteries.

Blood Flow Through the Circulatory System

Deoxygenated blood is returned to the right atrium via the superior and inferior vena cava. Blood then flows into the right ventricle. Contraction of the right atrium completes the ventricular filling. The right ventricle pumps deoxygenated blood into the pulmonary artery, which branches to each lung (Figure 1-11). There it is oxygenated and carbon dioxide is removed. Freshly oxygenated blood is returned to the left atrium via the pulmonary veins. Blood then flows into the left ventricle. Contraction of the left atrium completes the ventricular filling. The left ventricle then pumps it through the systemic circulation to deliver oxygen and nutrients to the tissues. After passing through the tissues, deoxygenated blood is returned to the right side of the heart via the venous circulation.

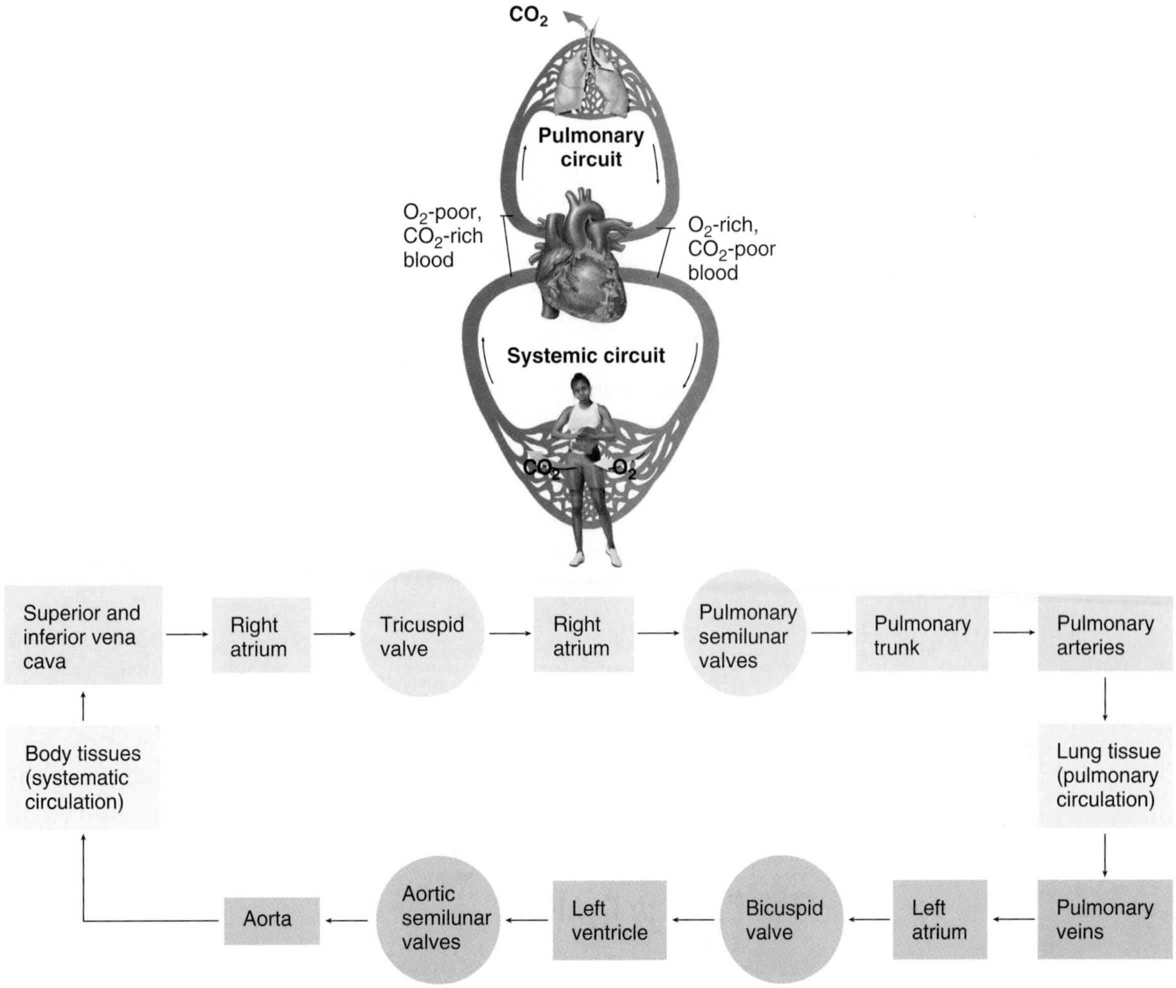

CO_2

Pulmonary circuit

O_2-poor, CO_2-rich blood

O_2-rich, CO_2-poor blood

Systemic circuit

CO_2 O_2

Superior and inferior vena cava → Right atrium → Tricuspid valve → Right atrium → Pulmonary semilunar valves → Pulmonary trunk → Pulmonary arteries → Lung tissue (pulmonary circulation) → Pulmonary veins → Left atrium → Bicuspid valve → Left ventricle → Aortic semilunar valves → Aorta → Body tissues (systematic circulation) → Superior and inferior vena cava

Figure 1-11
Blood flow through the heart and systemic and pulmonary circulations.

Deoxygenated blood is returned to the right _______________ where it flows into the right _______________. Contraction of the right ventricle pumps the deoxygenated blood into the _______________ circulation where it is oxygenated and carbon dioxide is removed. Blood is then returned to the _______________ atrium and ventricle. The blood is then pumped through the systemic circulation to deliver oxygen to the tissues.

[atrium] [ventricle] [pulmonary] [left]

KEY CONCEPT

The arteries of the systemic circulation carry oxygenated blood while the veins carry deoxygenated blood. The reverse is true in the pulmonic circulation where the pulmonary artery carries deoxygenated blood to the lungs and the pulmonary veins carry oxygenated blood back to the heart.

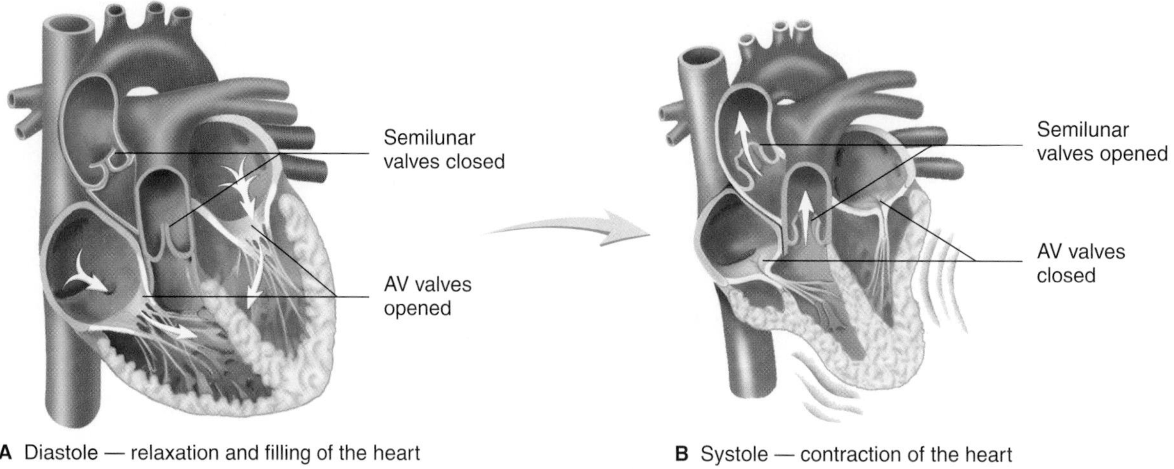

Figure 1-12
The two phases of the cardiac cycle are (a) diastole: the relaxation and filling of both the atria and ventricles (b) systole: contraction of the atria and ventricles.

How the Heart Works

Now let's apply what we have learned so far to the pumping action of the heart as it works to circulate blood throughout the body.

The Cardiac Cycle

The cardiac cycle is the repetitive process of pumping blood that starts with the beginning of cardiac muscle contraction and ends with the start of the next contraction. Pressure changes within the cardiac chambers are produced by myocardial contraction. This causes movement of blood from areas of higher pressure to areas of lower pressure.

Diastole and Systole

There are two phases of the cardiac cycle: **diastole** and **systole** (Figure 1-12). Diastole is the relaxation and filling of both the atria and ventricles. However, clinically it is most often used to describe ventricular relaxation and filling. It is during this time that the heart receives most of its blood supply from the coronary arteries as during systole the myocardium compresses the coronary arteries and restricts blood flow. Thus, in addition to the diastolic blood pressure reflecting the pressure in the heart during the relaxation phase, it also tells us about the perfusion of the heart.

Contraction of the atria and ventricles is referred to as systole. Again, clinically it is most often used to describe ventricular systole. The systolic blood pressure is the pressure within the systemic arteries during ventricular contraction.

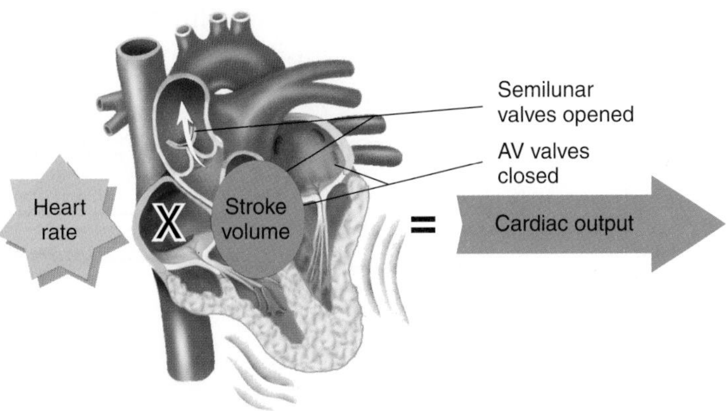

Figure 1-13
Cardiac output is the amount of blood pumped from the heart in one minute.

There are _______________ phases of the cardiac cycle. _______________ is said to be the relaxation and filling of both the atria and ventricles. _______________ is the contraction of the atria and ventricles.

[two] [Diastole] [Systole]

Cardiac Output

Contraction of the ventricles normally results in 60–100 milliliters of blood being ejected into both the pulmonary and systemic circulation. The amount of blood ejected from the ventricles is referred to as the **stroke volume.** It is dependent on **preload** (stretching force exerted on the ventricular muscle at end diastole), contractile force of the myocardium, and **afterload** (workload against which the heart must pump).

The stroke volume is the amount of blood _______________ from the ventricles. It is dependent on _______________, the contractile force of the myocardium, and _______________.

[ejected] [preload] [afterload]

The amount of blood pumped from the heart in one minute is called the cardiac output (Figure 1-13). It is expressed in liters per minute. The cardiac output is the equivalent of the heart rate multiplied by the stroke volume: **Heart Rate × Stroke Volume = Cardiac Output.**

KEY CONCEPT
Cardiac output is the amount of blood pumped from the heart in one minute.

Cardiac output for the right and left ventricles is normally equal. Decreases in either the heart rate or stroke volume result in decreased cardiac output, whereas increases in either result in increased cardiac output.

Factors that influence the heart rate, the stroke volume, or both will influence cardiac output and thus, tissue perfusion.

Cardiac _______________ is the amount of blood pumped from the heart in one minute. It is the product of the heart _______________ multiplied by the _______________ volume.

[output] [rate] [stroke]

Blood Pressure

The blood pressure is the force that blood exerts against the walls of the arteries as it passes through them. This pressure causes blood to flow. The blood pressure is the equivalent of the cardiac output multiplied by the peripheral vascular resistance: **Cardiac Output × Peripheral Vascular Resistance = Blood Pressure.**

A decrease in cardiac output or peripheral vascular resistance results in a decrease in the blood pressure whereas increases in either result in increased blood pressure.

INSTRUCTIONAL MOMENT
You should be familiar with the terms chronotropic, dromotropic, and inotropic. **Chronotropic** refers to the heart rate. *Dromotropic* refers to the rate of impulse conduction through the heart's conduction system. **Inotropic** refers to the contractility of the heart.

Influences on the Heart and Circulatory System

Regulation of the heart rate, speed of electrical conduction, and strength of contraction are influenced by the brain (via the autonomic nervous system), hormones of the endocrine system, and the heart tissue (Figure 1-14). Receptors in the blood vessels, kidneys, brain, and heart constantly monitor the adequacy of the cardiac output. **Baroreceptors** detect changes in pressure, usually within the heart or the main arteries. **Chemoreceptors** have the job of sensing changes in the chemical composition of the blood. If abnormalities are identified, nerve signals are sent to the appropriate target organs, generating the release of hormones or **neurotransmitters** to fix the situation. Once conditions are normal, the receptors stop firing and the signals cease.

QUESTION
"What is the average heart rate in the adult?" (The answer can be found on page 41.)

_______________ in the blood vessels, kidneys, brain, and heart constantly keep an eye on changes occurring in the body. _______________ detect pressure, while _______________ sense changes in the chemical composition of the blood.

[Receptors] [Baroreceptors] [chemoreceptors]

1. Baroreceptors are responsible for detecting changes in pressure, usually within the heart or the main arteries.
   Chemoreceptors sense changes in the chemical composition of the blood. This information is transmitted to the cardioregulatory center in the medulla oblongata.
2. When the blood pressure is elevated, the cardiorespiratory center may activate the parasympathetic nervous system, which acts to slow the heart rate and lower the blood pressure.
3. If the blood pressure is low the cardiorespiratory center will activate the sympathetic nervous system, which acts to increase the heart rate and contractility. This increases cardiac output and raises the blood pressure.
4. The cardioregulatory center causes the release of epinephrine and some norepinephrine from the adrenal medulla into the general circulation. Epinephrine and norepinephrine increase the heart rate and stroke volume.

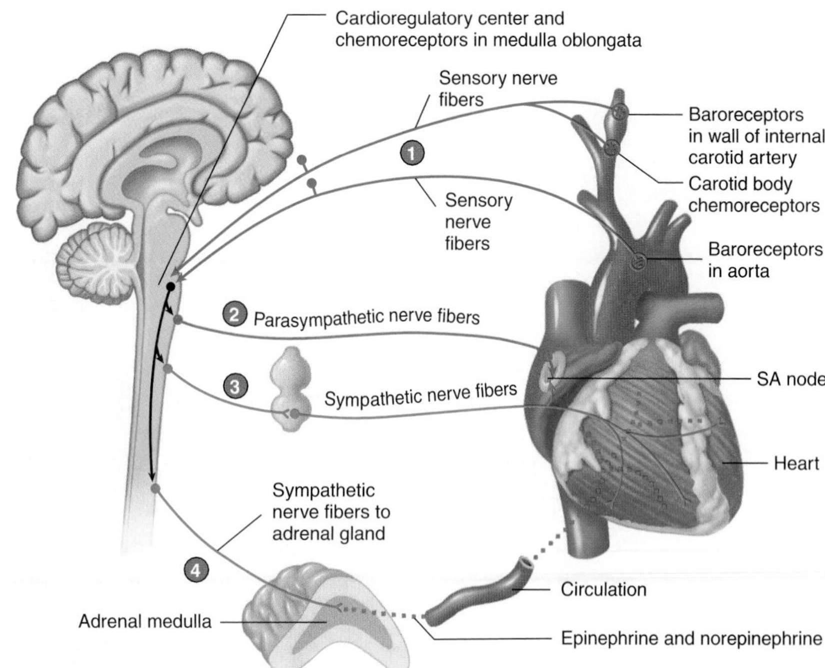

Figure 1-14
Baroreceptor and chemoreceptor reflexes. Sensory (green) nerves carry information from sensory receptors to the medulla oblongata and extend to the heart to regulate its function. Epinephrine and norepinephrine from the adrenal gland also help regulate the heart's action.

 The Autonomic Nervous System

While the myocardial cells can generate electrical impulses on their own, the autonomic nervous system can influence the rate and strength of myocardial contractions (Figure 1-15). This is needed as the cardiovascular system must continually adjust the blood supply to meet demands at the cellular level.

KEY CONCEPT
The autonomic nervous system can influence the rate and strength of myocardial contractions.

Nervous control of the heart originates from two separate nerve centers located in the medulla oblongata, a part of the brainstem. One of these centers, the cardioaccelerator, is part of the sympathetic nervous system while the other, the cardioinhibitor, is part of the parasympathetic nervous system. Both systems exert their effects via neurotransmitters that bind to specific receptors. Impulses from the cardioaccelerator center are transmitted to the heart by way of the sympathetic nerves. Impulses from the cardioinhibitor center are transmitted to the heart by way of the vagus nerve.

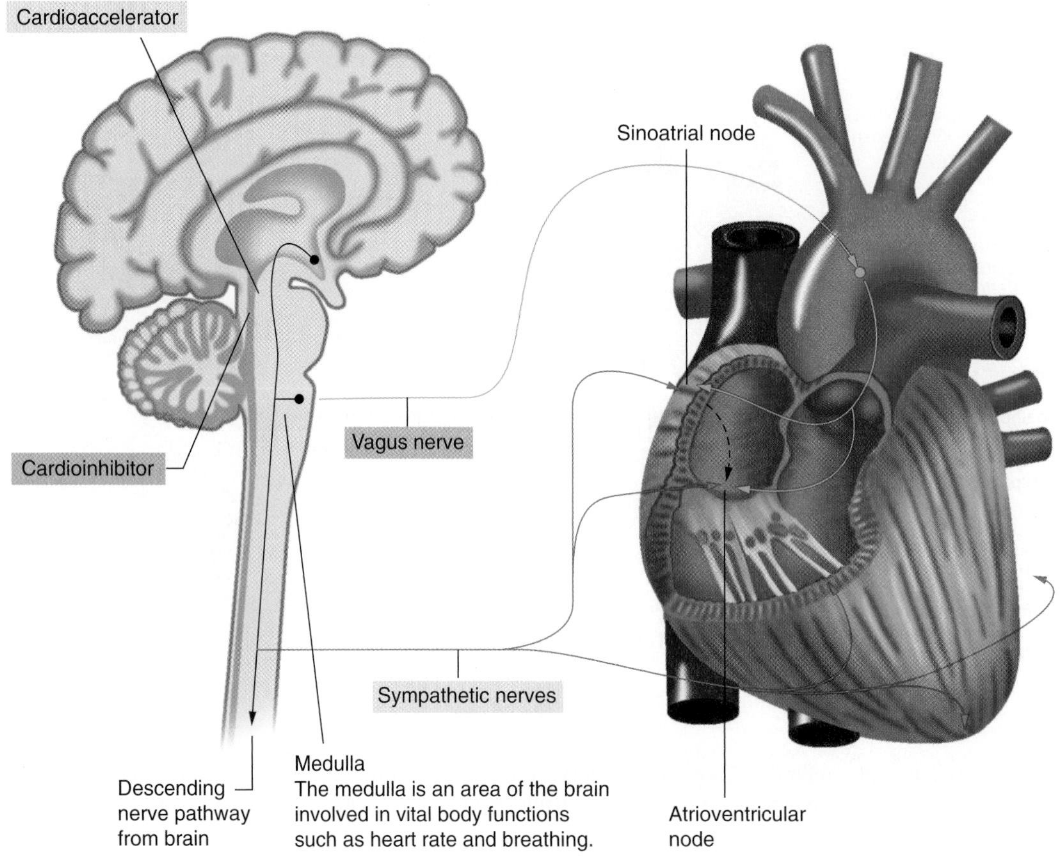

Figure 1-15
Parasympathetic and sympathetic innervation of the heart.

INSTRUCTIONAL MOMENT
The sympathetic and parasympathetic nervous systems work in opposition to one other. The parasympathetic branch dominates during custodial or basal functions, while the sympathetic system dominates during stress. For example, during physical exertion the sympathetic system causes the heart to beat faster, whereas during rest the heart beats slower.

The ____________ nervous system helps regulate the rate and strength of myocardial contractions. Its two divisions are the ____________ and the ____________ nervous systems. Both branches exert their effects via ____________ that bind to specific receptors.

[autonomic] [sympathetic] [parasympathetic] [neurotransmitters]

The Sympathetic Nervous System

The sympathetic branch of the autonomic nervous system is carried through nerves in the thoracic and lumbar ganglia causing the release of the neurotransmitter **norepinephrine** (Figure 1-16). **Epinephrine (adrenalin),** released from the adrenal glands, also functions as a sympathetic branch neurotransmitter. For this reason, the sympathetic branch is called the **adrenergic** system. Stimulation of the sympathetic nervous system produces what we describe as the "fight-or-flight" response—constriction of blood vessels, enhancement of myocardial cell excitability,

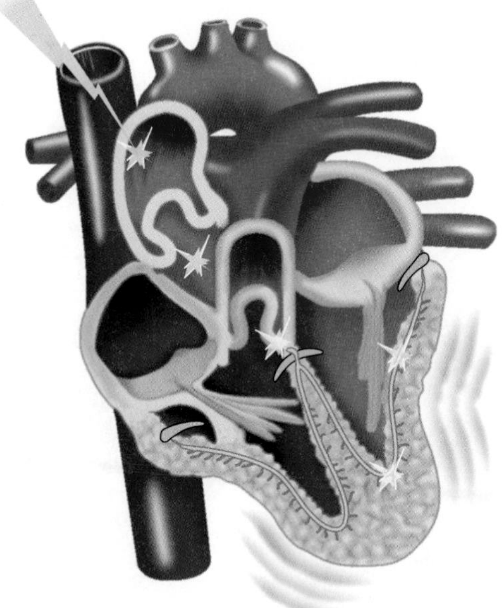

Figure 1-16
Activation of the sympathetic nervous system stimulates the heart to beat faster and stronger.

increased rate of pacemaker firing, increased conduction speed, increased contractility, coronary vasodilation, and a feeling of nervousness. Sympathetic fibers exert their effect by stimulating special receptors. These receptors are divided into categories depending on their response. The two major categories are alpha and beta receptors. The primary sympathetic receptors in the heart are beta receptors—they affect all areas of the heart.

KEY CONCEPT
In the heart, stimulation of the sympathetic nervous system produces enhancement of myocardial cell excitability, increased rate of pacemaker firing, increased conduction speed, increased contractility, and coronary vasodilation.

Effects produced by the sympathetic nervous system include _______________ heart rate and _______________ contractility. Along with these effects one can expect to see increased myocardial oxygen demand. The heart is primarily stimulated by _______________ receptors.

[increased] [increased] [beta]

KEY CONCEPT
Stimulation of the parasympathetic nervous system slows the heart rate and AV conduction.

The Parasympathetic Nervous System

The parasympathetic branch of the autonomic nervous system is carried through the vagus nerve and releases the neurotransmitter, acetylcholine

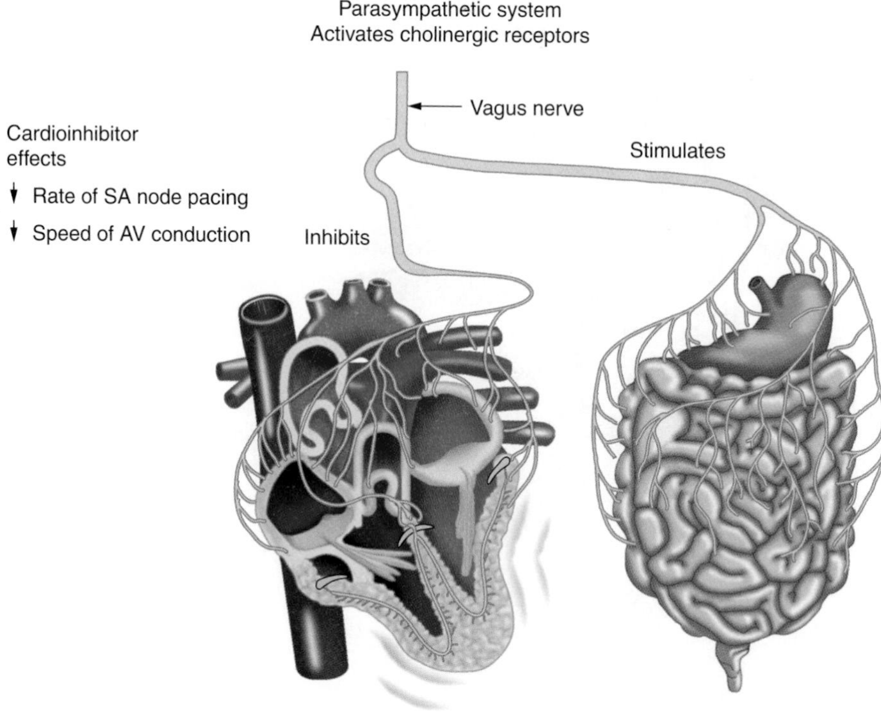

Figure 1-17
Activation of the parasympathetic nervous system causes the heart to beat slower.

CLINICAL MOMENT
The parasympathetic nervous system may also have a modest effect on myocardial contractility by slowing the rate of contraction. In extreme instances, excess stimulation of the parasympathetic nervous system can lead to cardiac arrest.

(Figure 1-17). It is therefore referred to as the **cholinergic** system. The parasympathetic nervous system works just the opposite of the sympathetic branch causing a slowing of the heart rate and atrioventricular (AV) conduction. It also controls intestinal activity and affects pupillary responses. The areas of the heart most affected by the parasympathetic fibers are the sinoatrial (SA) node; atria; AV junction; and to a small extent, the ventricles.

The ______________ nerve carries the parasympathetic branch through the release of the neurotransmitter ______________. Parasympathetic stimulation causes ______________ of the heart rate and AV conduction. In the heart, the parasympathetic fibers mostly affect the ______________ and ______________ nodes.

[vagus] [acetylcholine} [slowing] [SA] [AV]

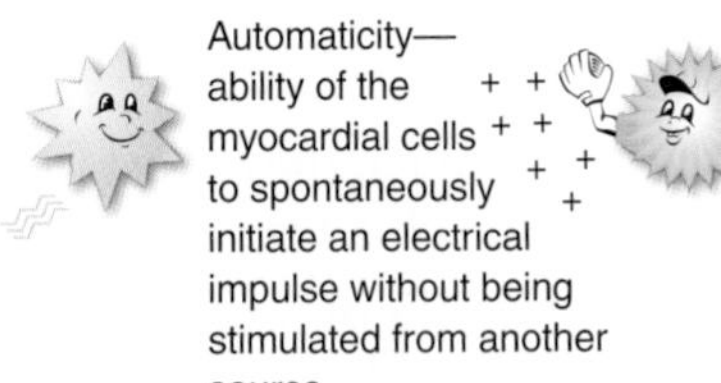

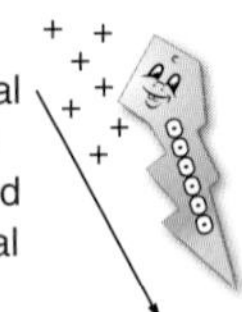

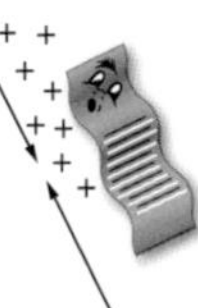

Figure 1-18
The key properties of myocardial cells are automaticity, excitability, conductivity, and contractility.

The Heart's Electrical System

Key Properties of Myocardial Cells

The cells of the heart possess four key properties that allow it to generate, respond to, and conduct impulses resulting in contraction of the heart muscle. These properties are automaticity, excitability, conductivity, and contractility (Figure 1-18).

KEY CONCEPT
Automaticity, excitability, conductivity, and contractility are the four key properties that allow the myocardial cell to generate impulses, respond to them, and conduct them throughout the heart resulting in contraction of the muscle.

Automaticity is the ability of certain myocardial cells to produce an electrical impulse without the need for outside nerve stimulation. This property is associated with the cells of the heart's conduction system, specifically the pacemaker cells. Normally, nonpacemaker myocytes do not possess this property but under certain conditions (as will be discussed later in this textbook) can acquire it. **Excitability** is the ability to respond to an electrical stimulus, while **conductivity** is the ability to transmit an electrical stimulus from cell to cell throughout the myocardium. These three properties—automaticity, excitability, and conductivity are associated with the specialized cells of the heart's electrical conduction system. **Contractility** is the ability of the myocardial cell to contract when stimulated by an electrical impulse. This property is associated with the myocytes, which we referred to earlier as the heart's working cells.

________________ is the ability of certain myocardial cells to produce electrical activity without the need for outside nerve stimulation.

________________ is the ability to respond to an electrical stimulus.

________________ is the ability to transmit an electrical stimulus from cell to cell throughout the myocardium. ________________ is the ability of the myocardial cell to contract when stimulated by an electrical stimulus.

[Automaticity] [Excitability] [Conductivity] [Contractility]

QUESTION
"What device detects, measures, and records the heart's electrical activity?" (The answer can be found on page 41.)

INSTRUCTIONAL MOMENT
The wave of depolarization is carried throughout the heart via the heart's conduction system. The conduction system is a grouping of specialized tissues that form a network of connections, much like an electrical circuit.

The Heart's Conductive Pathway

As we pointed out earlier, for the heart muscles to contact, they must first be electrically stimulated. The specialized cells responsible for generating and carrying impulses throughout the heart form the conductive pathway. These cells differ from the working cells as they lack myofibrils and cannot contract. Also, these cells contain more gap junctions than do the working cells. This allows them to conduct electrical impulses extremely fast. The conductive pathway has two types of cells—the pacemaker cells and the electrical conducting cells. The pacemaker cells have the ability to spontaneously depolarize over and over at a particular rate (in other words, the property of automaticity).

QUESTION
"What does the term intrinsic mean?" (The answer can be found on page 41.)

SA Node

The electrical event that normally initiates the heartbeat is produced by a group of specialized electrical tissues called the **SA node.** The SA node is located high on the posterior wall of the right atrium (Figure 1-19), just below the opening of the superior vena cava and just under the epicardium. The event or impulse is generated automatically. The SA node serves as the heart's primary pacemaker and has an intrinsic rate of 60 to 100 beats per minute.

CLINICAL MOMENT
The term node means a knot or lump.

The _______________ node produces the impulse that initiates the heartbeat. It is located high on the posterior wall of the right _______________ and serves as the primary _______________ having an intrinsic rate of _______________ beats per minute.

[SA] [atrium] [pacemaker] [60 to 100]

It is thought that the impulse is carried to the left atrium by way of the intraatrial conductive pathway (Bachmann's Bundle) and through the right atrium by way of the anterior, middle, and posterior internodal tracts.

CLINICAL MOMENT
The presence of the intraatrial and internodal tracts has not been conclusively proven as they cannot be distinguished structurally from the rest of the atrium. However, the rapid speed at which the impulse moves through the atria strongly supports the belief that these conductive pathways exist.

AV Node

Following their path through the right atrium, the impulses reach the **atrioventricular (AV) node.** The AV node lies on the floor of the right atrium just medial to the mitral valve and just above the ventricle (see Figure 1-19). It is the only pathway (unless there are accessory pathways as described later in this text) for impulses to move from the atria to the ventricles. Conduction through the AV node is slower allowing time for the atria to contract and finish filling the ventricles with blood. It also allows the ventricular muscle to stretch to its fullest for peak cardiac output. You

1. Electrical impulses originate in the SA node and travel across the wall of the atrium (*arrows*) from the SA node to the AV node.
2. Electrical impulses pass through the AV node and along the bundle of His, which extends from the AV node, through the fibrous skeleton, into the interventricular septum.
3. The bundle of His divides into right and left bundle branches, and electrical impulses descend to the apex of each ventricle along the bundle branches.
4. Electrical impulses are carried by the Purkinje fibers from the bundle branches to the ventricular walls.

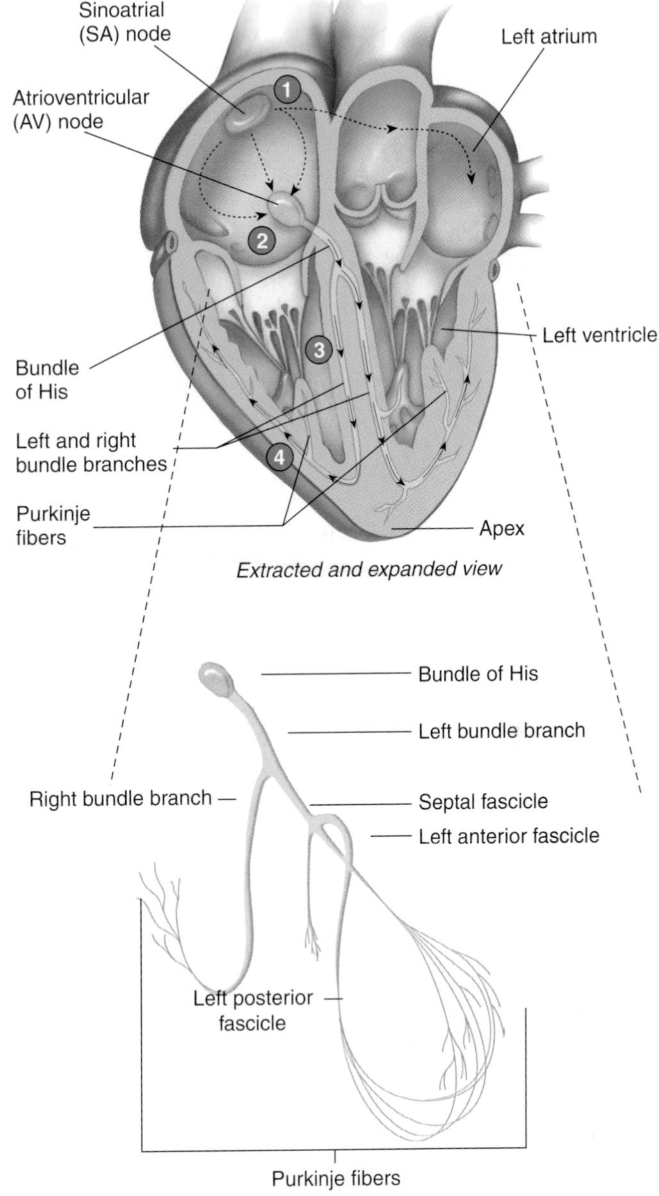

Figure 1-19
The heart's conduction system generates and carries electrical impulses throughout the heart. The enlarged section shows the His-Purkinje system.

can think of the AV node as being a gatekeeper. The impulse travels through the AV node more slowly because the myocytes are thinner in this area, but more importantly, they have fewer gap junctions over which the impulse can be conducted.

INSTRUCTIONAL MOMENT
The AV node is like highway traffic that slows down going through a small town.

The AV node is anatomically less well-defined than the SA node. It is composed of 3 layers: the upper, middle, and lower, which have unique conduction characteristics.

CLINICAL MOMENT
When the AV junction is bypassed by an abnormal pathway, the abnormal route is called an accessory pathway.

Like the SA node, the upper and lower AV nodal tissue has pacemaker cells that allow it to initiate the heartbeat if conditions warrant. The AV node has an intrinsic heart rate of 40 to 60 beats per minute. The nodal tissue in the middle lacks automaticity and is slow to depolarize giving the ventricles time to fill as described previously. The AV node, its atrial pathways, and the bundle of His make up the conductive tissue of the AV junction.

The upper and lower AV nodal tissue has ________ cells that allow it to initiate the heartbeat at an intrinsic rate of ________ beats per minute.

[pacemaker] [40 to 60]

QUESTION
"What is the intrinsic rate of the SA node?" (The answer can be found on page 42.)

Bundle of His and Right and Left Bundle Branches

The AV node gives rise to a conducting bundle to the heart, the **bundle of His.** The bundle of His is also called the AV bundle (see Figure 1-19). This bundle passes from the walls of the right atrium through a small opening in the fibrous skeleton to reach the interventricular septum. In the interventricular septum the bundle divides into the left and right bundle branches. The bundle branches extend beneath the endocardium on either side of the interventricular septum to the apex of each ventricle. The right bundle branch goes to the right ventricle. The left bundle branch goes to the left ventricle. The left bundle branch divides further into three divisions—the septal fascicle, the anterior fascicle, and the posterior fascicle (see Figure 1-19). The septal fascicle carries the impulse to the interventricular septum in a right-to-left direction. The anterior and posterior fibers spread to their respective sides of the heart. The bundle of His, bundle branches, and Purkinje fibers are referred to as the His-Purkinje system.

CLINICAL MOMENT
Remember, the fibrous skeleton acts as an insulator to prevent electrical impulses from getting to the ventricles by any other route than that described.

The bundle of His penetrates the fibrous skeleton then, in the interventricular septum, immediately splits into the ______________ bundle branch and the ______________ bundle branch.

[right] [left]

QUESTION
"What is the intrinsic rate of the AV node?" (The answer can be found on page 42.)

Purkinje Fibers

The right and left bundle branches terminate in the **Purkinje fibers.** The Purkinje fibers consist of countless tiny fibers that extend widely like tiny tree branch twigs extending just underneath the endocardium and terminate in the endocardial cells. These fibers conduct impulses rapidly through the muscle to assist in its depolarization and contraction. This results in ventricular depolarization starting in the endocardium and proceeding outward to the epicardium.

The small terminal ____________ fibers take the stimulus from the bundle branches to the individual ______________ cells. Ventricular depolarization starts at the ______________ and proceeds outward to the ______________.

[Purkinje] [endocardial] [endocardium] [epicardium]

KEY CONCEPT
If the primary pacemaker site were to fail, one of the other pacemaker sites can initiate the heart's electrical impulses.

Like the SA node and AV junction, the ventricles, including the bundle branches and Purkinje fibers, can also serve as the heart's pacemaker, discharging impulses at a rate of 20 to 40 beats per minute. The ventricular tissue is usually called upon to act as the pacemaker. If the SA node or AV junction fail to initiate a heartbeat or there is a blockage of conduction through the AV node or bundle of His, the Purkinje fibers will fire as the last resort.

Intrinsic Rates

Normal depolarization of the myocardium progresses from the atria to the ventricles in an orderly fashion (Figure 1-20). However, other sites in the heart can assume control by discharging impulses faster than the SA node. They can also passively take over, either because the SA node has failed or it is generating impulses too slowly.

INSTRUCTIONAL MOMENT
Pacemaker cells in the lower areas of the heart, such as the junctional tissue and Purkinje fibers, do not normally initiate the heartbeat because they receive impulses from the SA node.

While the ______________ node is the primary pacemaker site, other cardiac cells ______________ in the conduction pathway can play a back-up role. The farther from the SA node, the ______________ its intrinsic rate.

[SA] [lower] [slower]

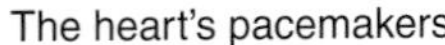

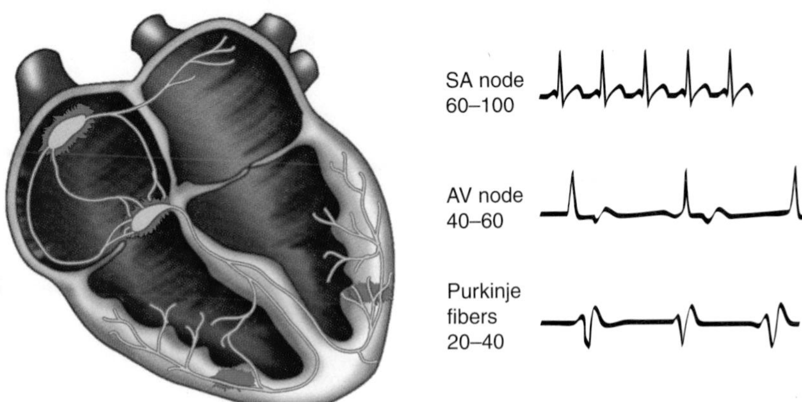

Figure 1-20
Intrinsic rates of pacemaker sites in the heart's conduction system.

How Nerve Impulses Are Generated and Muscles Contract

To better understand how nerve impulses are generated and conducted and how they cause muscles to contract, let's review some basic concepts.

CLINICAL MOMENT
The difference between the electrical charge of the inside and outside of the cell is the resting membrane potential.

Polarized State

As previously stated, for any muscle to contract, it must first be electrically stimulated. Myocardial cells, like all other cells in the body, are bathed in electrolyte solution. The primary electrolytes responsible for initiating electrical charges are sodium (Na+), potassium (K+), and calcium (Ca++). In the resting, or **polarized,** state (meaning no electrical activity takes place) the cells have a high concentration of negatively charged ions, proteins, and organelles on the inside of the cell. On the outside, there is a high concentration of positively charged ions (Figure 1-21). This difference in electrical charge between the inside and the outside of the cell creates a **resting membrane potential** (RMP). In the polarized state the RMP is negative indicating that the cell is ready to fire or discharge. This negative RMP is sustained by the cell membrane's ability to prevent positively charged ions, such as sodium, from entering the cell and the negatively charged ions from leaving the cell.

KEY CONCEPT
For any muscle to contract, it must first be electrically stimulated.

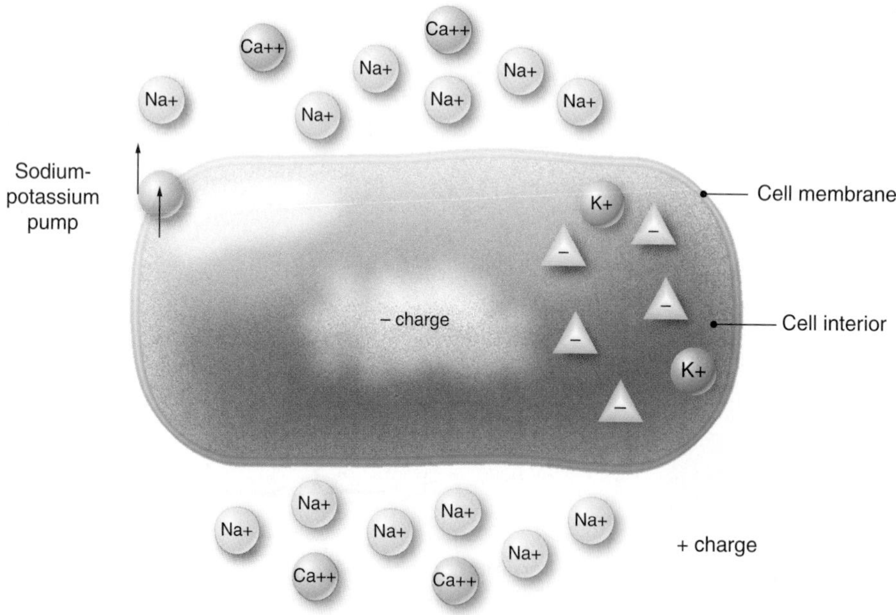

Figure 1-21
In the polarized or resting state the outside of the cell has a high concentration of positively charged ions while the inside of the cell has a high concentration of negatively charged ions with reference to its positively charged exterior. Under these conditions a negative electrical potential exists across the cell membrane.

During the __________ state, the inside of the myocardial cells is more __________ charged relative to the outside of the cells, where it is more __________ charged. This difference in electrical charge between the inside and the outside of the cell creates a __________ membrane potential.

[polarized] [negatively] [positively] [resting]

CLINICAL MOMENT
Even though there are positively charged ions on the inside of the cell, such as potassium (a key ion that facilitates repolarization), there are also an abundance of negatively charged ions, proteins, and organelles needed to sustain the cell. This keeps the inside of the cell negatively charged (in relationship to the outside of the cell) during the polarized state.

Depolarization

Impulses are generated and subsequently transmitted when positively charged ions, such as sodium, rapidly move inside the cells causing the interior to become positively charged (Figure 1-22). This is called **depolarization.** Calcium, another positively charged ion, also enters the cell but more slowly. This change in electrical charge over time is referred to as the **action potential** (or voltage) of the cell and reflects its ability to depolarize. The action potential is measured in millivolts (mV). Different cells in the heart have different action potentials depending on what function they play in the generation and/or conduction of nerve impulses. The way this process occurs differs between the pacemaker cells of the SA node, the AV node, and the nonpacemaker cells. The positively charged ions move through the cell membrane by way of voltage-gated channels. These channels open and close based on the voltage changes in the cell membrane.

INSTRUCTIONAL MOMENT
The term action potential refers to the rapid voltage change during which the myocytes briefly reverse electrical polarity (i.e., going from a negative to positive charge).

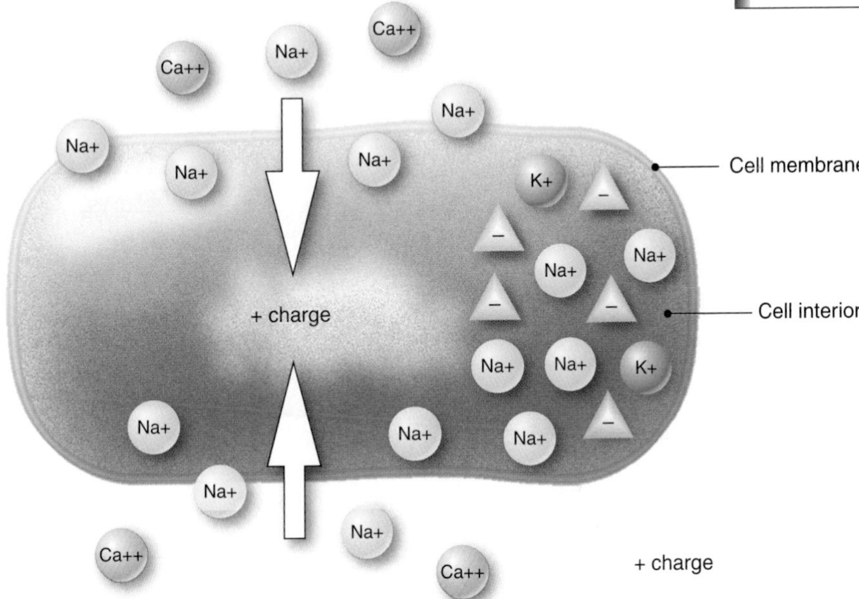

Figure 1-22
Depolarization begins when an electrical stimulus causes the cell membrane to become permeable to positively charged sodium ions. Sodium rushes into the cell followed by a slower influx of positively charged calcium ions. This causes the inside of the cell and the cell membrane potential to rapidly become positive.

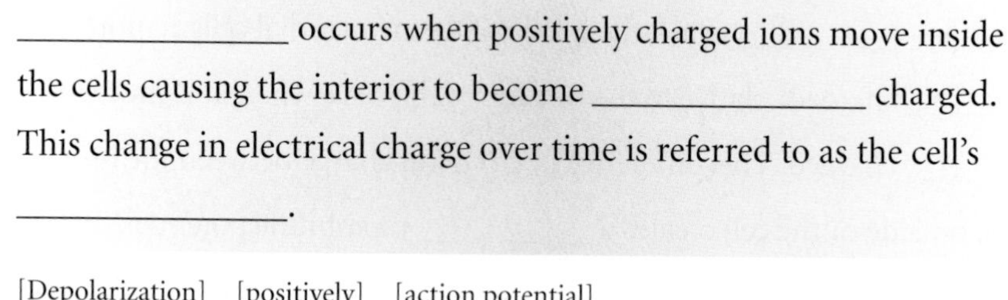

[Depolarization] [positively] [action potential]

KEY CONCEPT
Impulses are generated and subsequently transmitted when positively charged ions, such as sodium and calcium, move inside the cells.

Repolarization

Depolarization is followed by positively charged ions, such as potassium, leaving the cell causing the positive charge to lower. Then the other positively charged ions, such as sodium, are removed by special transport systems, such as the sodium-potassium pumps, until the electrical potential inside the cell reaches its original negative charge. This is called **repolarization** (Figure 1-23).

KEY CONCEPT
Repolarization occurs when positively charged ions, such as potassium, leave the cell and sodium and calcium are transported out of the cell.

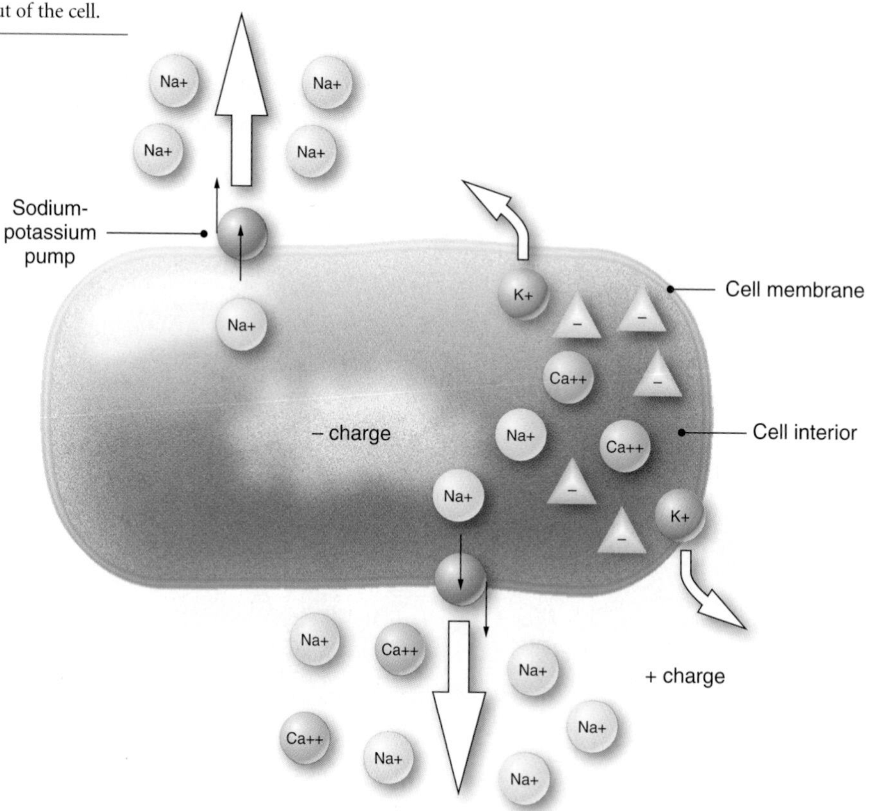

Figure 1-23
As soon as the cell depolarizes, positively charged potassium ions flow out of the cell initiating a process in which the cell returns to its original, polarized state. This is called repolarization. Aside from the flow of potassium, repolarization involves sodium and calcium being transported from the inside to the outside of the cell by special ion transport systems (i.e., sodium-potassium pumps).

_______________ occurs when certain positively charged ions leave the inside of the cell and others are transported out until the electrical potential inside the cell reaches its original _______________ charge.

[Repolarization] [negative]

The action potential of the myocytes consists of five phases: phase 0 (rapid depolarization), phase 1 (early repolarization), phase 2 (plateau), phase 3 (rapid repolarization), and phase 4 (resting).

QUESTION
"How soon can the cell respond to its next electrical stimulus?" (The answer can be found on page 42.)

Refractory Periods

During the **absolute refractory period** (Figure 1-24), no stimulus, no matter how strong, will depolarize the cell. This prevents spasm-producing (tetanic) contractions in the cardiac muscle. During the later phase of repolarization, the **relative refractory period,** a sufficiently strong stimulus *will* depolarize the myocardium.

KEY CONCEPT
During the absolute refractory period, no stimulus, no matter how strong, will depolarize the cell.

During the _____________ refractory period, no stimulus, no matter how strong, will depolarize the cell. During the ____________ refractory period, a sufficiently strong stimulus will depolarize the cell.

[absolute] [relative]

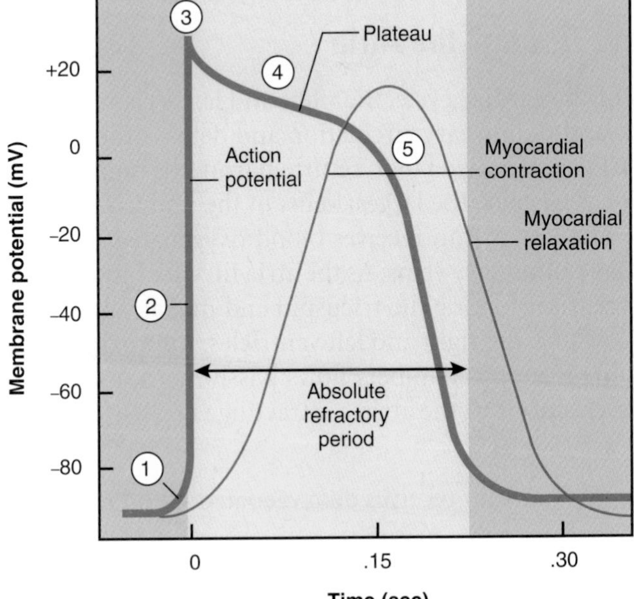

1. Voltage-gated sodium channels open.
2. Na^+ inflow depolarizes the membrane and triggers the opening of still more Na^+ channels, creating a positive feedback cycle and a rapidly rising membrane voltage.
3. Na^+ channels close when the cell depolarizes, and the voltage peaks at nearly +30 mV.
4. Ca^{2+} entering through slow calcium channels prolongs depolarization of membrane, creating a plateau. Plateau falls slightly because of some K^+ leakage, but most K^+ channels remain closed until end of plateau.
5. Ca^{2+} channels close and Ca^{2+} is transported out of cell. K^+ channels open, and rapid K^+ outflow returns membrane to its resting potential.

Figure 1-24
During the absolute refractory period, no stimulus will depolarize the cell. This figure represents where the absolute and relative refractory periods are in relation to the movement of electrolytes during depolarization and repolarization.

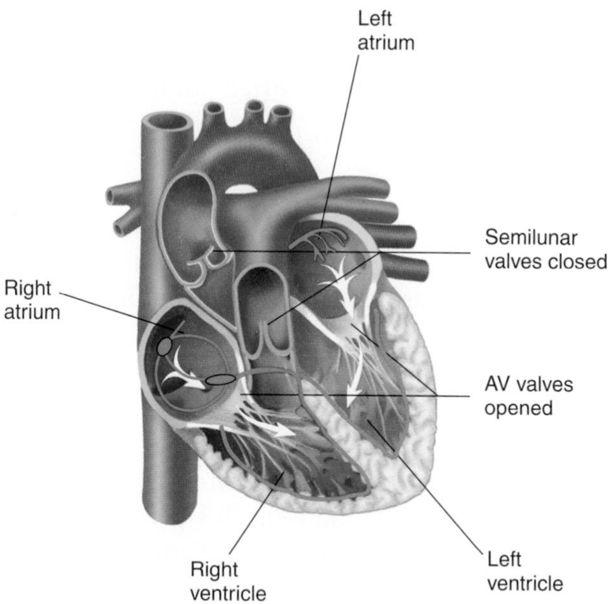

Figure 1-25
At the beginning of the cardiac cycle blood flows into the right and left atria forcing the AV valves open and allowing blood to flow into the right and left ventricles.

How It All Works Together

Blood Flow Through the Atria

At the beginning of the cardiac cycle, the right and left atria receive blood from the systemic and pulmonary circulation and deliver it to the ventricles (Figure 1-25). Deoxygenated blood returned from the body via the superior and inferior vena cava, the largest veins in the body, is delivered to the right atrium. The left atrium receives blood oxygenated in the lungs and returned via the pulmonary veins. As the atria fill with blood, the pressure within the atria rises forcing the tricuspid and mitral valves open allowing blood to flow into the right and left ventricles. Approximately 70% of the blood coming into the chambers flows passively through the atria and into the ventricles prior to the atria contracting.

QUESTION
"What is it that stimulates the heart muscle to contract?" (The answer can be found on page 42.)

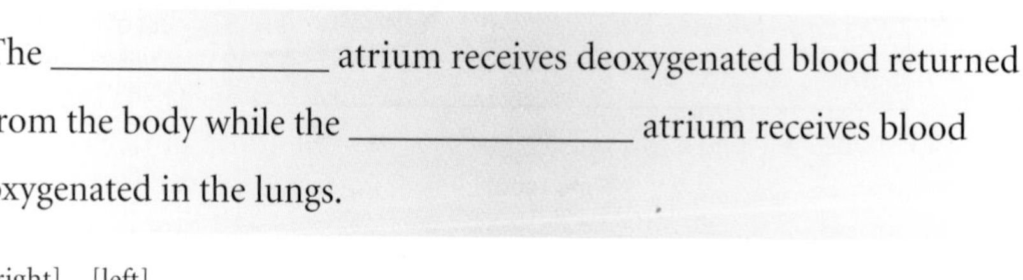

The ________________ atrium receives deoxygenated blood returned from the body while the ________________ atrium receives blood oxygenated in the lungs.

[right] [left]

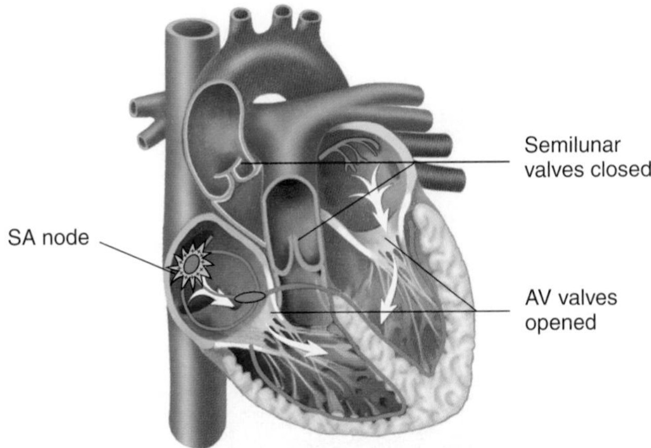

Figure 1-26
Normally, the electrical activity that initiates the heartbeat originates from the SA node.

Initiation of Impulse in the SA Node

The SA node initiates the electrical event that normally causes the heartbeat (Figure 1-26). As described earlier, the ability of certain myocardial cells to discharge electrically (action potential) without the need for external stimulus is called automaticity. The heart is unique in this property. All other muscles in the body require stimulation from nerve impulses supplied by the nervous system. If nerves supplying the voluntary muscles are cut, these muscles cease to function; in other words, they are paralyzed. In contrast, if the nerves supplying the heart are severed, the heart will continue to beat. The cells that possess the property of automaticity are called pacemaker cells.

INSTRUCTIONAL MOMENT
The other myocytes, under certain circumstances, also have the property of automaticity.

The _______________ node initiates the electrical event that normally causes the heartbeat.

[SA]

Atrial Depolarization and Contraction

From the SA node, the electrical impulse spreads from cell to cell in a wavelike manner across the atrial muscle, depolarizing the right atrium, the interatrial septum, and then the left atrium (Figure 1-27). This electrical current produces a waveform called the **P wave.** Remember, the structure of the cardiac muscles (which forms the atrial and ventricular syncytium) permits the rapid conduction of electrical impulses from one cell to another making it possible for impulses to move quickly throughout the

QUESTION
"What do the terms excitability and conductivity mean?" (The answer can be found on page 42.)

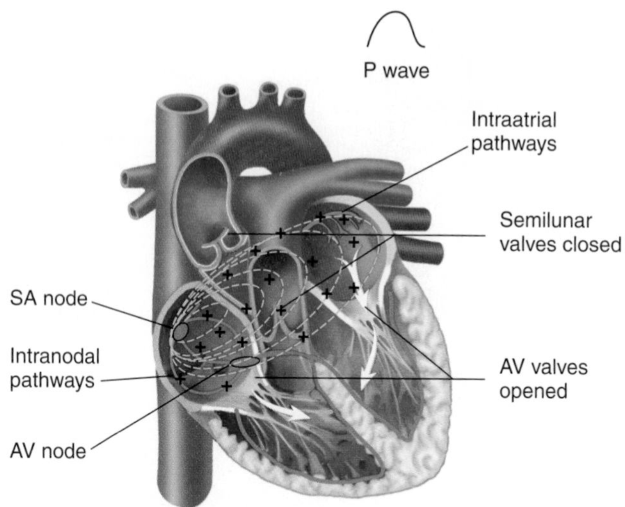

Figure 1-27
From the SA node the electrical impulse moves in a wavelike manner across the atria. This causes the atria to contract, pushing the remaining atrial blood into the ventricles.

CLINICAL MOMENT
Contraction of the atria pushes the remaining 30% of the blood (remember, up to 70% of the blood flows passively through the atria) into the ventricles. This is referred to as the **atrial kick.**

heart. The two key properties of the myocardial cells responsible for moving the impulses from cell to cell are excitability and conductivity. This brings about nearly simultaneous contraction of the right and left atria, squeezing the blood in the chambers and forcing it forward into the ventricles. Following contraction of the atria, the pressure in the atria and ventricles equalizes, and the tricuspid and mitral valves close. At the same time, the impulse is carried through the atria by the intranodal pathways to the AV node.

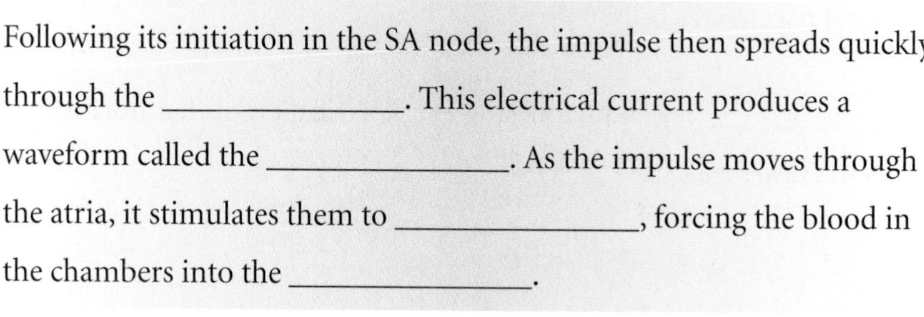

Following its initiation in the SA node, the impulse then spreads quickly through the ______________. This electrical current produces a waveform called the ______________. As the impulse moves through the atria, it stimulates them to ______________, forcing the blood in the chambers into the ______________.

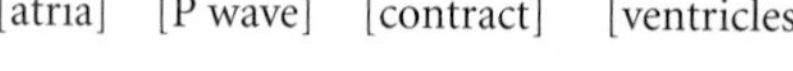

[atria] [P wave] [contract] [ventricles]

KEY CONCEPT
The impulse arising from the SA node, traveling through the atria, generates a positive waveform on the ECG and contraction of the atria. The muscle contraction causes the atria to push the remaining blood (in their chambers) into the ventricles.

Conduction Through the AV Node

The internodal pathways carry impulses through the atria to the AV node (Figure 1-28). It is the only pathway (unless there are accessory pathways as described later in this text) for impulses to move from the atria to the ventricles. The impulse travels slowly through the AV node creating a slight delay that allows the atria to finish pushing any remaining blood

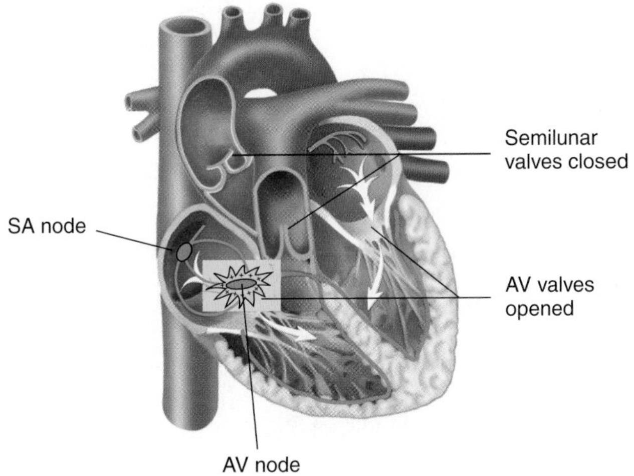

Figure 1-28
The wave of depolarization slows as it passes through the AV node. This allows the atrial contraction to finish filling the ventricles. This electrical activity occurs simultaneously with the P wave.

into the ventricles. On the ECG this electrical stimulation occurs during the P wave. As discussed earlier, the heart skeleton (the plate of fibrous connective tissue) that lies between the atria and the ventricles and includes the heart valves insulates the atrial myocardium from the ventricular myocardium. This allows the electrical stimulus to stimulate the atria as it travels through the upper portion of the heart permitting the upper chambers of the heart to contract as a unit pumping blood to the ventricles. Likewise, once the impulse travels through the ventricles, it causes them to contract as a unit, pumping blood to the lungs and to the body.

KEY CONCEPT
The impulse traveling through the AV node is delayed as it travels from the atria to the ventricles.

The ______________ node serves as the primary pathway for impulses to travel from the atria to the ______________. The impulse travels ______________ through the AV node to allow the atria to finish emptying. The electrical currents travel through the AV node at the same time as the ______________ wave is generated.

[AV] [ventricles] [slowly] [P]

KEY CONCEPT
The impulse traveling through the bundle of His, left and right bundle branches, and the terminal Purkinje fibers is seen as a flat line on the ECG.

Conduction Through the His-Purkinje System

After slowly moving through the AV node, the impulse then rapidly shoots through the bundle of His, the left and right bundle branches, and the terminal Purkinje fibers (the His-Purkinje system) (Figure 1-29). On the ECG this produces a flat line that follows the P wave. This is because the

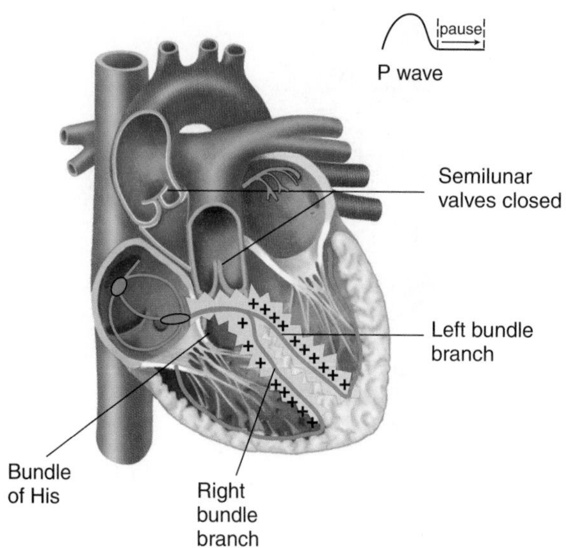

Figure 1-29
After slowly passing through the AV node, depolarization rapidly shoots through and activates the His-Purkinje system. This is represented on the ECG as a flat line called the PR segment.

electrical currents are so small they are not seen on the ECG. This part of the ECG is called the **PR segment.** The His-Purkinje system is responsible for initiating the contraction of the ventricles.

From the AV node, the stimulus passes into the _______________, then into the _______________ bundle branch and the _______________ bundle branch. The _______________ line that follows the P wave represents this activity. And finally, very small terminal _______________ fibers take the stimulus from the bundle branches to the individual myocardial cells.

[bundle of His] [right] [left] [flat] [Purkinje]

QUESTION
"How can both ventricles contract simultaneously when the left ventricle has more mass than the right?" (The answer can be found on page 42.)

Ventricular Depolarization and Contraction

Depolarization of the whole ventricular myocardium produces contraction of the ventricles and a waveform called the **QRS complex** on the ECG. Ventricular depolarization initiates vigorous contraction of the ventricles causing the ventricular pressure to rise sharply, up to about

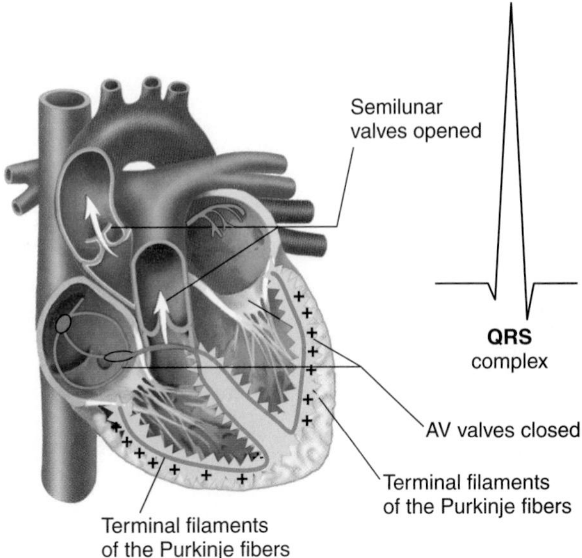

Figure 1-30
The wave of depolarization passing through the whole ventricular myocardium produces contraction of the ventricles and a QRS complex on the ECG.

120 mm Hg in the left ventricle and 26 mm Hg in the right ventricle (Figure 1-30). When the ventricular pressure exceeds the pressure in the aorta and pulmonary artery, the tricuspid and mitral valves close completely and the pulmonic and aortic valves snap open. This allows the blood to be forcefully ejected from the right ventricle into the pulmonary artery where it is carried to the lungs. The blood from the left ventricle is ejected into the aorta where it is circulated to the tissues of the body. At the end of the contraction, the ventricles relax and back pressure in the aorta and pulmonary artery causes the aortic and pulmonic valves to close.

CLINICAL MOMENT
The size of the P wave and the QRS complex, is considerably different due to how much thicker the ventricles are when compared to the atria. The ventricles, a much bigger mass, produce a bigger waveform.

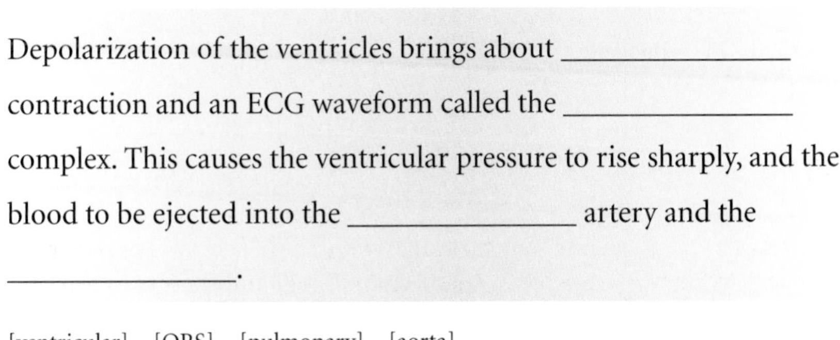

Depolarization of the ventricles brings about _______________ contraction and an ECG waveform called the _______________ complex. This causes the ventricular pressure to rise sharply, and the blood to be ejected into the _______________ artery and the _______________.

[ventricular] [QRS] [pulmonary] [aorta]

KEY CONCEPT
The impulse traveling through the His-Purkinje system generates a positive waveform on the ECG and contraction of the ventricles. The muscle contraction causes the ventricles to push the blood into the pulmonary and systemic circulation.

INSTRUCTIONAL MOMENT
The difference we see in how the atria and ventricles move blood is important as we talk about various cardiac dysrhythmias. Dysrhythmias originating from the atria are generally not life threatening whereas dysrhythmias that arise from the ventricles can be. This is because the ventricles are responsible for pushing blood throughout the body; if they fail, blood circulation throughout the body is compromised.

KEY CONCEPT
Normal depolarization of the myocardium progresses from the atria to the ventricles in an orderly fashion. The electrical stimulus causes the heart muscle to contract. The ECG shows the electrical stimuli as it travels through the heart. The heart performs its pumping action over and over in a rhythmic sequence circulating blood through the pulmonary and systemic circulation.

QUESTION
"Which of the pacemaker sites is the primary pacemaker?" (The answer can be found on page 42.)

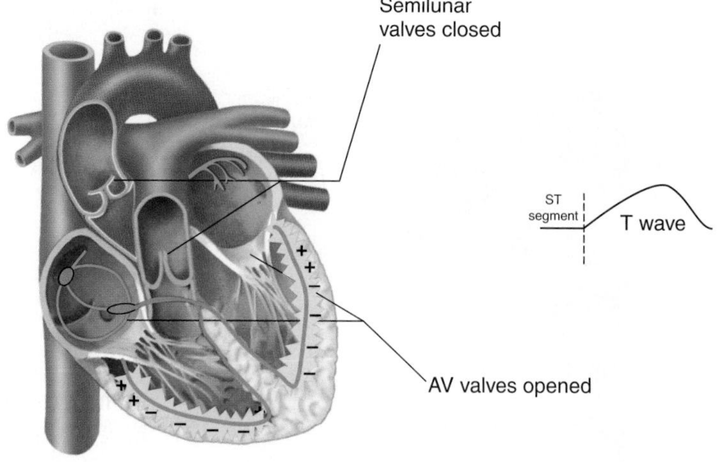

Figure 1-31
Repolarization of the ventricles, which occurs following the conclusion of depolarization, is represented on the ECG by the ST segment and the T wave.

Ventricular Repolarization

Repolarization of the ventricles, which occurs following the conclusion of depolarization, is represented on the ECG by the **ST segment** and the **T wave** (Figure 1-31). Atrial repolarization occurs during ventricular depolarization and is therefore hidden, or obscured, by the QRS complex.

Following depolarization, the cells of the ventricles undergo ________________. This produces the ST segment and the ________________ wave, which follows the QRS complex. The same thing occurs with the atria; however, their repolarization is ________________ by the depolarization of the ventricles.

[repolarization] [T] [hidden]

Key Points

- The electrocardiogram detects the electrical activity occurring in the heart through electrodes attached to the patient's skin.
- Nerve impulses stimulate cardiac muscles to contract. Without electrical stimulation the muscles will not contract.
- The heart consists of two upper chambers, the atria, and two lower chambers, the ventricles. A muscular wall, the septum, separates the right side from the left side of the heart.
- The coronary arteries perfuse the myocardium during diastole.
- Cardiac output is the amount of blood pumped from the heart in one minute. The cardiac output is equal to the heart rate multiplied by the stroke volume.
- The autonomic nervous system can influence the rate and strength of myocardial contractions. The two divisions of the autonomic nervous system are the sympathetic and the parasympathetic nervous systems.
- Automaticity, excitability, conductivity, and contractility are the four key properties of myocardial cells.
- The intrinsic rate of the SA node is 60–100 beats per minute. The intrinsic rate of the AV node is 40–60 beats per minute, and the intrinsic rate of the Purkinje fibers is 20–40 beats per minute.
- Sodium, calcium, and potassium are the key electrolytes responsible for initiating electrical activity.
- Depolarization of the cells occurs when positive electrolytes move from outside to inside the cell. This causes the inside of the cell to become more positively charged.
- Depolarization of myocardial cells causes calcium to be released and come into close proximity with the actin and myosin filaments of the muscle fibers. The filaments then slide together, one upon another, producing a shortening of the muscle fibers and subsequent myocardial contraction.
- The electrical impulse that normally initiates the heartbeat arises from the SA node. From there it travels through the atria generating a positive waveform (the P wave) on the ECG leading to contraction of the atria. The atrial muscle contraction pushes the remaining blood from the atria into the ventricles.
- The impulse is slowed as it passes from the atria to the ventricles through the AV node.
- On the ECG, the impulse traveling through the His-Purkinje system is seen as a flat line following the P wave.
- The QRS complex is generated and the ventricles contract as a result of the electrical impulse stimulating the ventricles. Ventricular muscle contraction causes the blood to be pushed into the pulmonary and systemic circulation.
- The ST segment and T wave represent repolarization of the ventricles, which takes place following the conclusion of depolarization. Atrial repolarization occurs but is hidden by the QRS complex.
- Depolarization of the myocardium progresses from the atria to the ventricles in an orderly fashion. The electrical stimulus causes the heart muscle to contract.
- Other sites in the heart can assume control by discharging impulses faster than the SA node. They can also passively take over, either because the SA node has failed or it is generating impulses too slowly.

Assess Your Understanding

The following questions give you a chance to assess your understanding of the material discussed in this chapter. The answers can be found in Appendix A.

1. The electrocardiogram measures
   a. pulse strength.
   b. blood pressure.
   c. muscle contraction.
   d. the heart's electrical activity.
2. Which of the following is true?
   a. During the polarized state, the inside of the cell is positively charged.
   b. Depolarization occurs when there is a rapid influx of positively charged ions from outside to inside the cell.
   c. Repolarization begins with the removal of sodium from the interior of the cell.
   d. During depolarization, sodium enters the cells through the slow channels.
3. _______________ stimulate muscle cells to contract.
   a. Changes in pressure
   b. Nerve impulses
   c. Outside influences
   d. Polarization of the nerve cells
4. The upper chambers of the heart are called the
   a. ventricles.
   b. atria.
   c. vena cava.
   d. venules.
5. The electrical impulse that normally initiates the heartbeat arises from the
   a. SA node.
   b. AV node.
   c. bundle of His.
   d. Purkinje fibers.
6. The impulse traveling through the His-Purkinje system generates a _______________ on the ECG.
   a. P wave
   b. T wave
   c. flat line
   d. QRS complex
7. The QRS complex represents
   a. atrial depolarization.
   b. ventricular depolarization.
   c. delay of the impulse as it travels through the AV node.
   d. ventricular repolarization.
8. Depolarization of the heart progresses from the _____________ to the _______________ in an orderly fashion.
   a. atria, ventricles
   b. ventricles, atria
   c. bundle of His, Purkinje fibers
   d. ventricles, bundle branches
9. The T wave represents
   a. atrial depolarization.
   b. AV node depolarization.
   c. ventricular repolarization.
   d. initiation of the electrical stimulus.
10. The pacemaker cells of the __________ have an intrinsic rate of 40 to 60 beats per minute.
    a. SA node
    b. AV node
    c. Purkinje fibers
    d. bundle of His
11. The myocardium receives its blood supply via the
    a. vena cava.
    b. coronary arteries.
    c. blood it pumps to the systemic and pulmonary circulation.
    d. pulmonary arteries.

12. Cardiac output is equal to
    a. afterload multiplied by preload.
    b. contractility multiplied by the stroke volume.
    c. heart rate divided by the contractility.
    d. stroke volume multiplied by the heart rate.

13. The sympathetic branch of the autonomic nervous system
    a. is mediated by the neurotransmitter, acetylcholine.
    b. is often called the cholinergic system.
    c. produces the fight-or-flight response.
    d. works the same as the parasympathetic branch.

14. All of the following are true regarding the parasympathetic nervous system EXCEPT
    a. it is mediated through the vagus nerve.
    b. its fibers mostly affect the SA and AV nodes of the heart.
    c. it is sometimes referred to as the adrenergic system.
    d. it works just the opposite of the sympathetic branch.

Referring to the scenario at the beginning of this chapter, answer the following questions.

15. If the flow of blood in the coronary arteries is diminished what will likely occur?
    a. Myocardial ischemia.
    b. Hypertension.
    c. Increased cardiac output.
    d. Decreased diastole.

16. The patient's initial heart rate is fast because of
    a. the effects of nicotine.
    b. sympathetic nervous system stimulation.
    c. hypertension.
    d. parasympathetic nervous system stimulation.

17. Which of the following will likely occur if the patient experiences severe myocardial ischemia and it is not corrected?
    a. Blood flow through the coronary veins increases.
    b. The heart extracts more oxygen from the blood it pumps through its chambers.
    c. The heart beats erratically.
    d. The affected myocardial tissue becomes necrotic.

Answers to Sidebar Questions

"Where is the aortic valve located?"

Answer: The aortic valve is situated at the base of the aorta just as it arises from the left ventricle.

"Why are they called the coronary arteries?"

Answer: They are called the coronary arteries because they encircle the heart like a crown.

"What is the average heart rate in the adult?"

Answer: The average heart rate in the adult is 72 beats per minute.

"What device detects, measures, and records the heart's electrical activity?"

Answer: The device that detects, measures, and records the electrical activity of the heart, or ECG, is an electrocardiograph, or ECG, machine.

"What does the term intrinsic mean?"

Answer: Intrinsic means the range of impulses the pacemaker site can naturally generate per minute.

"What is the intrinsic rate of the SA node?"

Answer: The intrinsic rate of the SA node is 60 to 100 beats per minute.

"What is the intrinsic rate of the AV node?

Answer: The intrinsic rate of the AV node is 40 to 60 beats per minute.

"How soon can the cell respond to its next electrical stimulus?"

Answer: Once the cell has returned to its polarized state it can be stimulated again, but during the relative refractory period, a sufficiently strong stimulus will depolarize the myocardium. This aspect of depolarization will become important later when we discuss ventricular ectopy.

"What is it that stimulates the heart muscle to contract?"

Answer: The electrical activity of the heart causes the heart muscle to contract.

"What do the terms excitability and conductivity mean?"

Answer: Excitability is the ability to respond to an electrical stimulus while conductivity is the ability to transmit an electrical stimulus from cell to cell throughout the myocardium.

"How can both ventricles contract simultaneously when the left ventricle has more mass than the right?"

Answer: While the left ventricle is thicker and more muscular, the impulse is quickly carried to the myocardial cells by the three divisions of the left bundle branch—the septal fascicle depolarize, anterior fascicle and posterior fascicle. This helps to depolarize both ventricles at the same time and produce simultaneous contraction.

"Which of the pacemaker sites is the primary pacemaker?"

Answer: The primary pacemaker of the heart is the SA node.

On the DVD

- Animations of the cardiac cycle; depolarization, action potential and contraction; conducting system of the heart; baroreceptors; chemoreceptors.
- Cardiac output lecture.
- Autonomic nervous system lecture.
- Automaticity lecture.

The Electrocardiogram

2

Case History

It is a busy morning in the cardiac rehabilitation unit where patients, after undergoing cardiac bypass surgery, come to exercise under observation of trained therapists. A 65-year-old man is on the stationary bike when he begins to feel lightheaded and then passes out, falling off the bike onto the floor. A therapist rushes to his side to find him slowly regaining consciousness. The therapist is able to print out a continuous recording of his heart rhythm before, during, and after the incident because the patient was on a cardiac monitor during his exercise routine.

EMS is summoned to transport the patient to the emergency department, and the therapist provides the paramedics with the ECG printout, which shows that the patient was in a slightly fast but otherwise normal heart rhythm before exercise. The rhythm became very slow with pauses up to 10 seconds long during exercise and then returned to normal after he fainted.

Chapter Preview

- The Electrocardiogram
- Components of the Normal Adult ECG
- ECG Machines
- ECG Leads

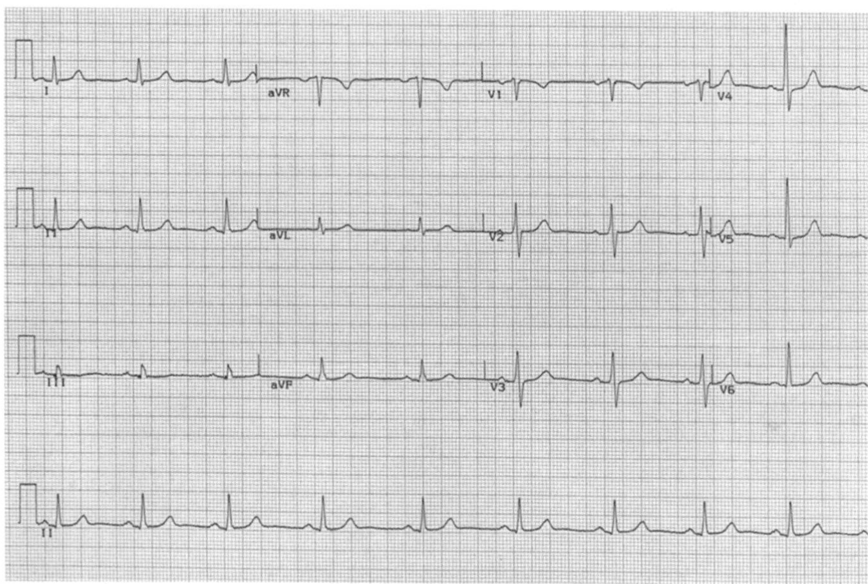

Figure 2-1
The ECG is a graphic record of the heart's electrical activity.

INSTRUCTIONAL MOMENT
The EKG was so named because the earliest machines were German and "kardio" is German for heart.

The Electrocardiogram

As discussed in Chapter 1, the electrocardiogram is a tracing or graphic record of the heart's electrical activity (Figure 2-1). It is often referred to as an ECG or EKG. The device that measures and records the ECG is called an electrocardiograph, although you will probably hear it called the "ECG," "monitor," or "12 lead." To avoid confusion, we will use ECG machine when referring to the electrocardiograph.

INSTRUCTIONAL MOMENT
Static ECG tracings are printed on ECG paper, while the dynamic mode is the real time movement seen across the oscilloscope.

A tracing of the heart's electrical activity is called an ______________,

while the machine that measures and records the ECG is called an

______________.

[electrocardiogram] [electrocardiograph]

QUESTION
"How are the electrical impulses of the heart produced and conducted?" (The answer can be found on page 75.)

Displays and Printouts

Electrodes placed on the patient's skin detect the heart's electrical activity or impulses. These impulses are then transferred to the ECG machine by color-coded wires (lead wires) and displayed on a screen (oscilloscope) or printed onto graph paper. These impulses appear as a series of waves or "blips." Those shown on the oscilloscope are called dynamic ECGs and represent real time electrical activity, while those printed on graph paper are called

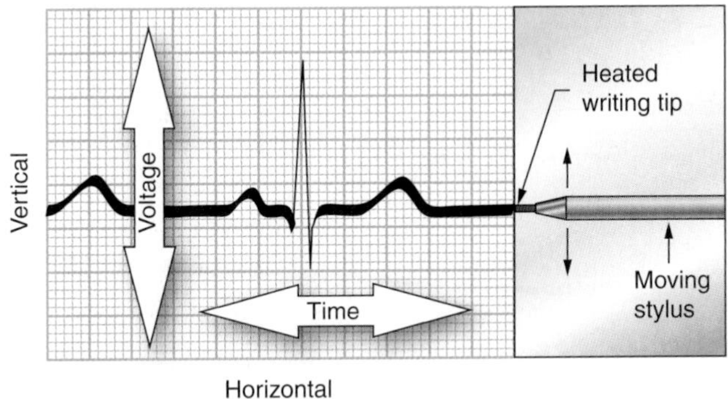

Figure 2-2
ECG paper with stylus generating waveforms. Vertical lines represent amplitude in electrical voltage in millivolts (mV) or millimeters (mm) while horizontal lines represent time or duration.

ECG tracings or static ECGs (also referred to as rhythm strips or printouts) and show what has already occurred. Each type has different purposes. It is much easier to analyze a static ECG to determine abnormalities than it is to examine an image moving across a screen. On the other hand, the static ECG tracing is "past news," so it is also necessary to look at the ECG monitor to see what is presently occurring. ECG machines are typically capable of producing a tracing, whereas not all are equipped with an oscilloscope.

CLINICAL MOMENT
Electrodes commonly used in electrocardiography are disposable and consist of a round adhesive ring with conductive electrolyte gel in the middle. It is the electrolyte gel that conducts skin surface voltage changes through the lead wires to the cardiac monitor.

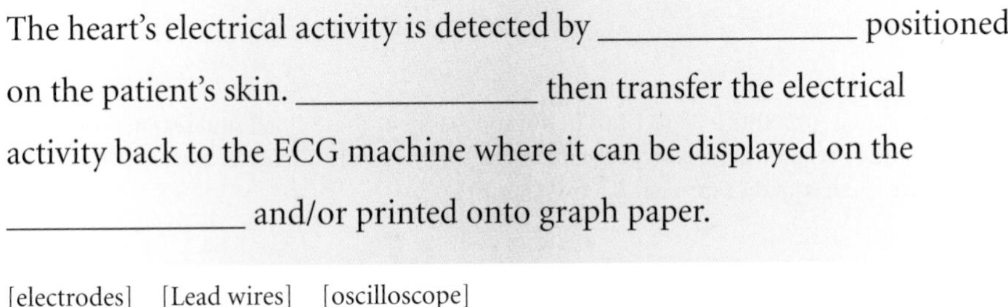

The heart's electrical activity is detected by ______________ positioned on the patient's skin. ______________ then transfer the electrical activity back to the ECG machine where it can be displayed on the ______________ and/or printed onto graph paper.

[electrodes] [Lead wires] [oscilloscope]

INSTRUCTIONAL MOMENT
Remember, it is the electrical impulse that depolarizes the heart and causes the muscle to contract. The muscle contraction propels the blood out of its chambers and throughout the body.

ECG Tracings

A special type of paper is used to record the heart's electrical activity (Figure 2-2). The paper, made of thermally sensitive material, consists of horizontal and vertical lines that form a grid. A heated stylus that responds to the electrical stimulus detected through the ECG electrodes moves up and down and produces markings on the paper. When no electrical stimulus is flowing through the electrode, or it is too small to detect, the stylus burns a straight line (isoelectric) in the paper. Some devices use the same technology as personal computer printers using various inks to produce the waveform.

QUESTION
"What ECG waveforms are generated as a result of the heart's electrical activity?" (The answer can be found on page 75.)

The narrow lines that run vertically and horizontally intersect to form squares. There are five of these squares between heavier (thicker) lines (that run vertically and horizontally). The distance between the lines, or boxes, running horizontally represents time or duration. The distance

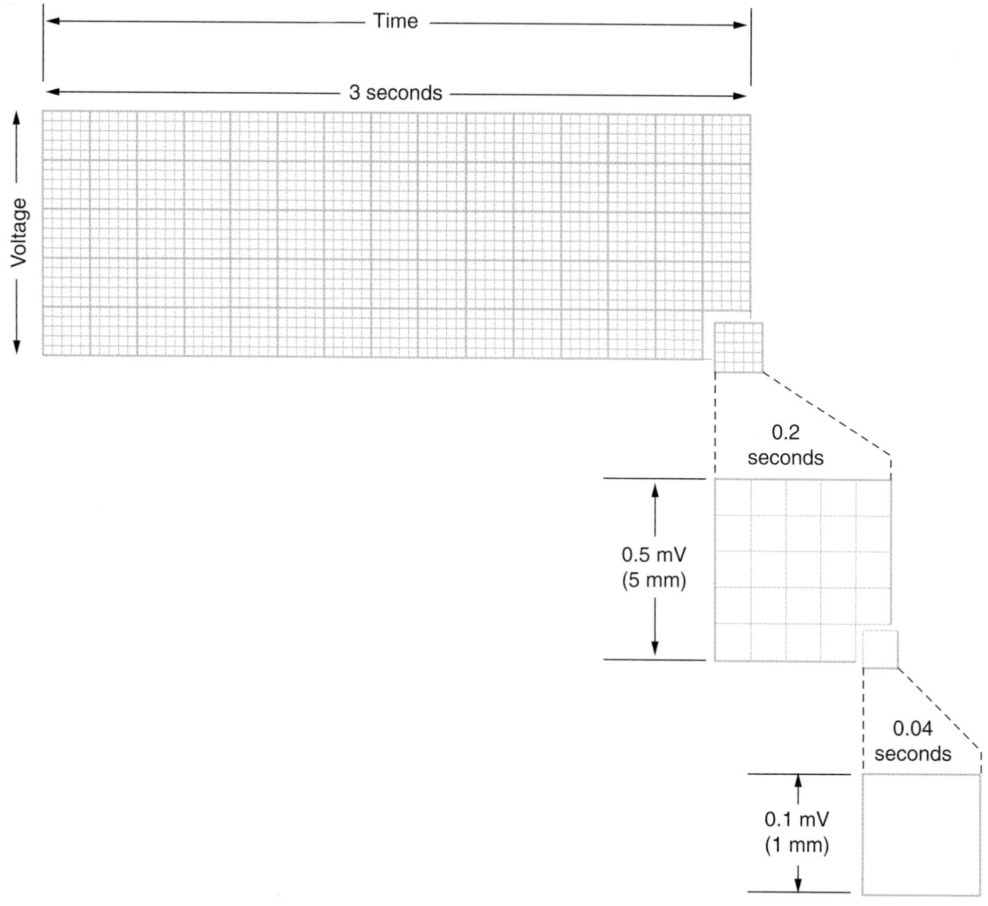

Figure 2-3
From right to left: horizontally each small square represents 0.04 seconds in duration. Five of these small squares (making up a larger box) represent 0.20 seconds in duration. Fifteen of these larger squares represent 3 seconds. Vertically each small square represents 0.1 mV (1 mm) while five of these small squares represent 0.5 mV (5 mm).

KEY CONCEPT
The horizontal axis on the ECG tells us about rate and duration, while the vertical axis tells us about electrical voltage or strength of the impulses.

between the lines, or boxes, running vertically represents **amplitude** in millimeters (mm) or electrical voltage in millivolts (mV).

The grid layout of the ECG paper is made up of ________________ and ________________ lines. This background pattern allows you to quickly determine the ________________ or duration and ________________ of waveforms, intervals, and segments.

[horizontal] [vertical] [time] [amplitude]

Each small square running horizontally represents 0.04 seconds in duration (Figure 2-3). Five of these small squares (making up a larger box) represent 0.20 seconds in duration. Five of these larger boxes represent 1 second. Fifteen larger boxes equal a 3-second interval. Horizontal measurements are used to determine the heart rate. You can also use these standardized distances to determine the length of any portion of an ECG complex. On the top or bottom (and sometimes both) of the printout there are often vertical slashes or markings to represent 3-second intervals (depending on the manufacturer there may be shorter or longer time frames). These markings can help you quickly determine the approximate heart rate. The ECG recorder is set to a standard speed of 25 mm per second so that tracings made from different machines may be uniformly compared.

Each small square running vertically represents 1 mm or 0.1 mV. The larger boxes are made up of five small squares and represent 5 mm or 0.5 mV. To determine the amplitude of a wave, segment, or interval, count the number of small boxes from the baseline to its highest or lowest point.

Each small square represents _______________ seconds in duration and _______________ mV in amplitude. Five of these small squares make up each larger box and represent _______________ seconds in duration. Horizontal measurements are used to determine the heart _______________. Vertical markings on the top or bottom of the ECG paper represent _______________ second intervals and can help you quickly determine the heart _______________.

[0.04] [0.1] [0.20] [rate] [3-] [rate]

INSTRUCTIONAL MOMENT
If the ECG paper doesn't have vertical lines to allow you to quickly determine the heart rate, count out fifteen boxes and place a vertical mark. Then repeat the step to give you two 3-second sections or a full 6-second section of the tracing.

CLINICAL MOMENT
Some ECG machines are equipped with a feature that allows you to speed up the printout to pass 50 mm of paper per second. This effect stretches out the tracings, which can make it easier to diagnose fast rhythms when it is difficult to see the P wave.

QUESTION
"Thirty larger boxes on the ECG paper represent how many seconds?" (The answer can be found on page 75.)

Components of the Normal Adult ECG

As discussed in Chapter 1, depolarization and repolarization of the atria and ventricles are electrical events. The path of the electrical activity through the heart is displayed in a series of waves and complexes, commonly known as the P wave, QRS complex, and T wave. **Morphology** describes the shape of the various waves on the ECG. The morphology may be normal, wide, short, tall, flat, spiked, jagged, or bizarre (meaning its shape is far from normal).

KEY CONCEPT
Each small square represents 0.04 seconds in duration, while one large square represents 0.20 seconds.

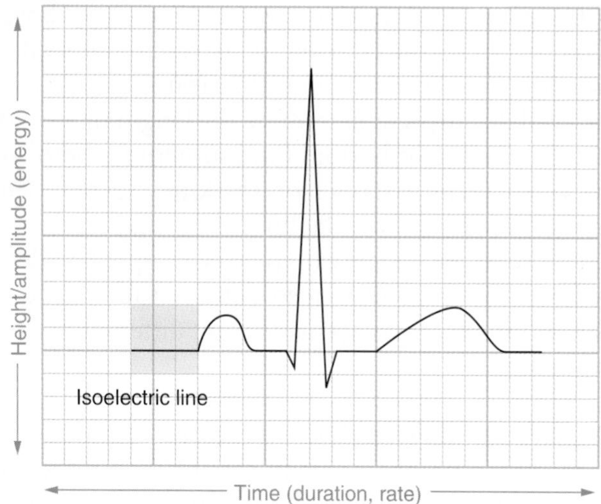

Figure 2-4
Anytime there is no electrical activity occurring or it is too weak to be detected it is represented on the ECG as a flat line called the isoelectric line.

For the purposes of our discussion we will refer to how the waveforms should look in lead II. If another lead is used the appearance of the waveforms may be different. Later, throughout the book, we will discuss how the waveforms should appear in the other leads.

KEY CONCEPT
When referring to the shape of any particular wave on the ECG, we use the term morphology.

 Isoelectric Line

You can expect to see a flat line any time no electrical activity is occurring (usually representing the polarized state of the cells) or it is too weak to be detected (Figure 2-4). This flat line is also called the **isoelectric** line. We use this line as a baseline or reference point to identify the changing electrical amplitude.

QUESTION
"For what purpose do we use the isoelectric line?" (The answer can be found on page 75.)

The flat line of the ECG is called the ______________ line.

[isoelectric]

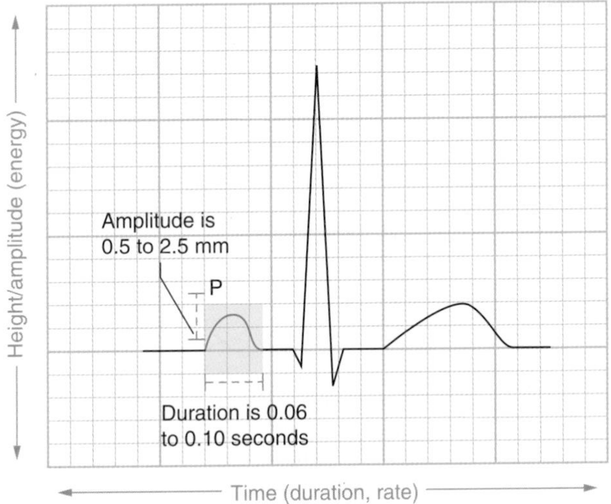

Figure 2-5
The initiation of the impulse in the SA node and its movement (depolarization) through the atria produces a P wave. Conduction of the impulse through the AV node also occurs during the P wave.

P Wave

The initiation of the impulse in the SA node and its movement through the atria produces a **P wave** (Figure 2-5). Depolarization results in contraction in the atrial muscle. The movement of the impulse through the AV node also occurs during the P wave.

Characteristically, the P wave appears as an upright and round waveform. There is one P wave preceding each QRS complex. Its amplitude is 0.5 to 2.5 mm and its duration is 0.06 to 0.10 seconds. If the P wave meets all of the characteristics described previously, it has most likely originated from the SA node. P waves that originate from the SA node are referred to as sinus P waves.

QUESTION
"The amplitude of the normal P wave is represented by how many small squares? Also, the normal duration of the P wave is represented by how many small squares?" (The answer can be found on page 75.)

A ________________ wave is produced by initiation of the impulse in the SA node and depolarization of the ________________. This waveform is upright and ________________.

[P] [atria] [round]

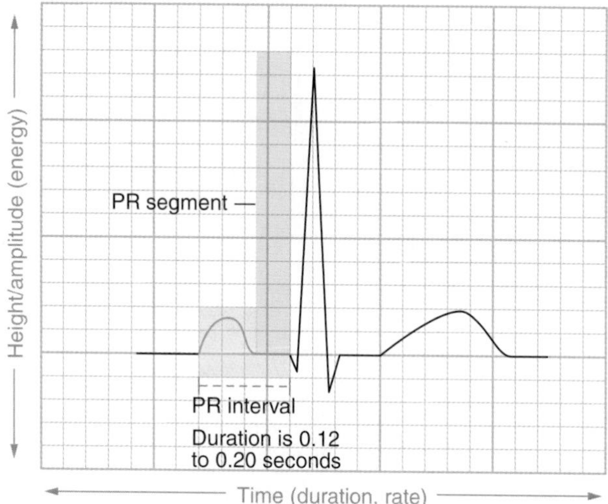

Figure 2-6
The PR segment is a flat line that extends from the end of the P wave to the beginning of the Q wave. The PR interval extends from the beginning of the P wave to the beginning of the Q wave.

PR Segment and PR Interval

CLINICAL MOMENT
With some conditions we may see a PR interval shorter or longer than normal. This tells us that something abnormal is occurring in or around the AV junction. A short PR interval (less than 0.12 seconds in duration) is seen when the electrical impulse arises close to or in the AV junction. A longer PR interval (greater than 0.20 seconds in duration) indicates there is an even greater delay in conduction of the impulse through the AV junction. It is often associated with a condition called AV heart block. Both shorter and longer PR intervals will be discussed in later chapters.

The impulse traveling through the His-Purkinje system is seen as a flat (isoelectric) line called the **PR segment** (Figure 2-6). The PR segment has this appearance because the electrical currents are so small they are not seen on the ECG. The His-Purkinje system is responsible for carrying the impulse to the ventricles.

As part of interpreting the ECG we measure the **PR interval.** This interval is the distance from the beginning of the P wave to the beginning of the Q wave. The PR interval represents depolarization of the heart from the SA node through the atria, AV node, and His-Purkinje system. A normal PR interval indicates the impulse originated from the SA node and traveled through the atria, the AV node, and the His-Purkinje system in a regular, unobstructed course. A normal PR interval is 0.12 to 0.20 seconds in duration; in other words, it extends across three to five small squares.

The flat line seen after the P wave is called the ________________ segment. It represents the movement of the electrical impulse through the ________________ system. The distance from the beginning of the P wave to the beginning of the QRS complex is called the PR ________________; it is normally ________________ seconds in duration.

[PR] [His-Purkinje] [interval] [0.12 to 0.20]

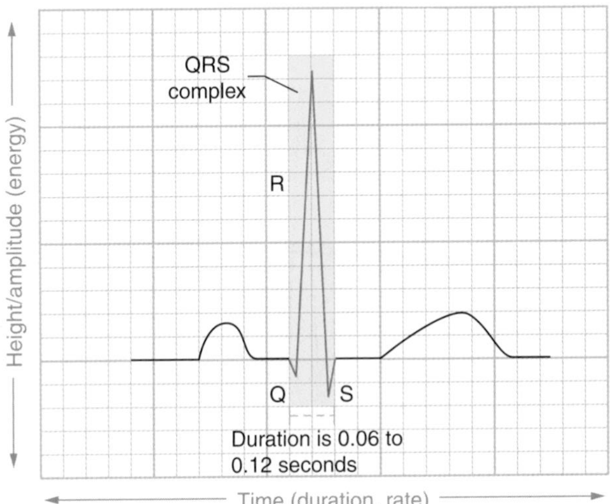

Figure 2-7
The QRS complex consists of the Q wave, R wave, and S wave. It represents movement of the electrical impulse (depolarization) through the ventricles, causing their contraction.

QRS Complex

Following the P wave and PR segment, the next waveform encountered in a sinus rhythm is the QRS complex (Figure 2-7). It is larger in appearance than the P wave and consists of three parts: the Q wave, the R wave, and the S wave. The waves of the QRS complex are generally narrow and sharply pointed. The Q wave is the first downward deflection from the baseline. Its duration is less than 0.04 seconds (1 mm or one small square) and its amplitude is less than 25% of the R wave in that lead. The Q wave is not always present. The R wave is the first upward deflection after the P wave, and the S wave is the first negative deflection after the R wave that extends below the baseline. The QRS complex is normally 0.06 to 0.12 seconds (one and a half to three small boxes) in duration. The duration is measured from the beginning of the Q wave to the end of the S wave or the beginning of the R wave if the Q is not present. The amplitude of the QRS complex is 5 to 30 mm high (but differs with each lead selected). The QRS complex represents movement of the electrical impulse through the ventricles, causing their contraction.

CLINICAL MOMENT
The Q wave is not always present.

Following the PR segment we should see a ________________ complex. It consists of the Q wave, the first ________________ deflection following the PR segment. A ________________ deflection should follow the Q wave. This is called the ________________ wave. The next deflection, which takes a ________________ direction, is called the ________________wave.

[QRS] [negative] [positive] [R] [negative] [S]

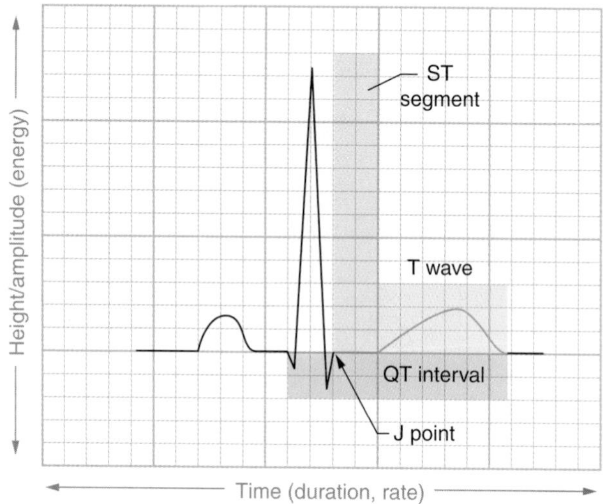

Figure 2-8
A flat line (pause) called the ST segment follows the QRS complex. Following the ST segment is the T wave. It represents ventricular repolarization.

 ST Segment and T Wave

Following the QRS complex there is a pause referred to as the ST segment (Figure 2-8). It appears as a flat or isoelectric line. During this period, the ventricles are preparing to repolarize. The point at which the QRS complex meets the ST segment is called the junction or **J point.** Following the ST segment we should see the T wave. It is larger than the P wave and slightly asymmetrical. The peak of the T wave is closer to the end of the wave than the beginning and the first half has a more gradual slope than the second half. Normally, the T wave is not more than 5 mm in height in the limb leads or 10 mm in any precordial lead. The T wave is normally oriented in the same direction as the preceding QRS complex. It represents ventricular repolarization.

CLINICAL MOMENT
The waveform that represents atrial repolarization is usually hidden by the QRS complex and for this reason is not seen.

Sometimes, a small upright (except in lead aV_L) waveform called the U wave is seen following the T wave, but before the next P wave. Its voltage is so low, however, that the U wave often goes unnoticed.

After the QRS complex, we should see a flat line referred to as the _______________ segment, followed by a larger, slightly asymmetrical waveform called the _______________ wave.

[ST] [T]

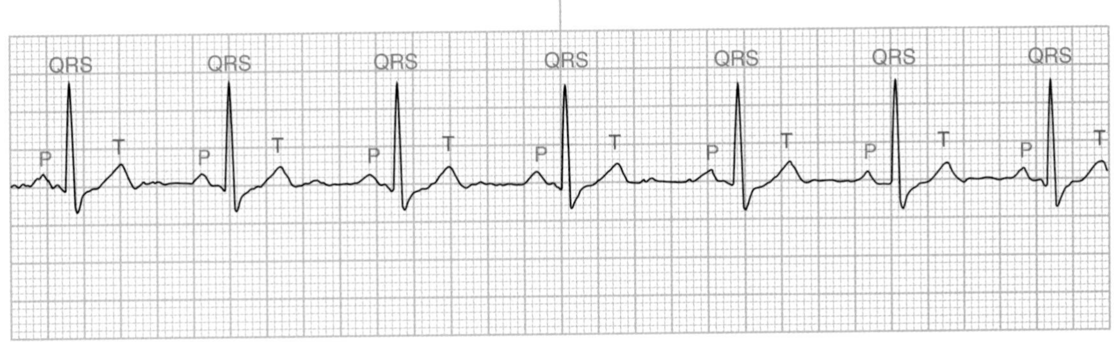

Figure 2-9
The typical ECG representing the normal cardiac rhythm includes a P wave, QRS complex, and T wave. These waveforms repeat themselves over and over.

QT Interval

Another measurement on the ECG rhythm is the **QT interval.** It is the distance from the onset of the QRS complex until the end of the T wave. This interval measures the time of ventricular depolarization and repolarization. It varies according to age, sex, and heart rate. The faster the heart rate, the shorter the QT interval. The QT interval has a normal duration of 0.36 to 0.44 seconds. It shouldn't be greater than half the distance between consecutive R waves when the rhythm is regular. Alterations in the QT interval can indicate numerous conditions (i.e., drug toxicity, electrolyte abnormalities, arsenic poisoning).

The Typical ECG

The typical ECG (Figure 2-9), representing the normal cardiac rhythm (referred to as sinus rhythm) consists of the following:

- Upright and round P waves occurring at regular intervals at a rate of 60 to 100 beats per minute (each is followed by a QRS complex).
- A PR interval of normal duration (0.12 to 0.20 seconds) followed by a QRS complex of normal upright contour, duration (0.06 to 0.12 seconds), and configuration.
- A flat ST segment followed by an upright and slightly asymmetrical T wave.

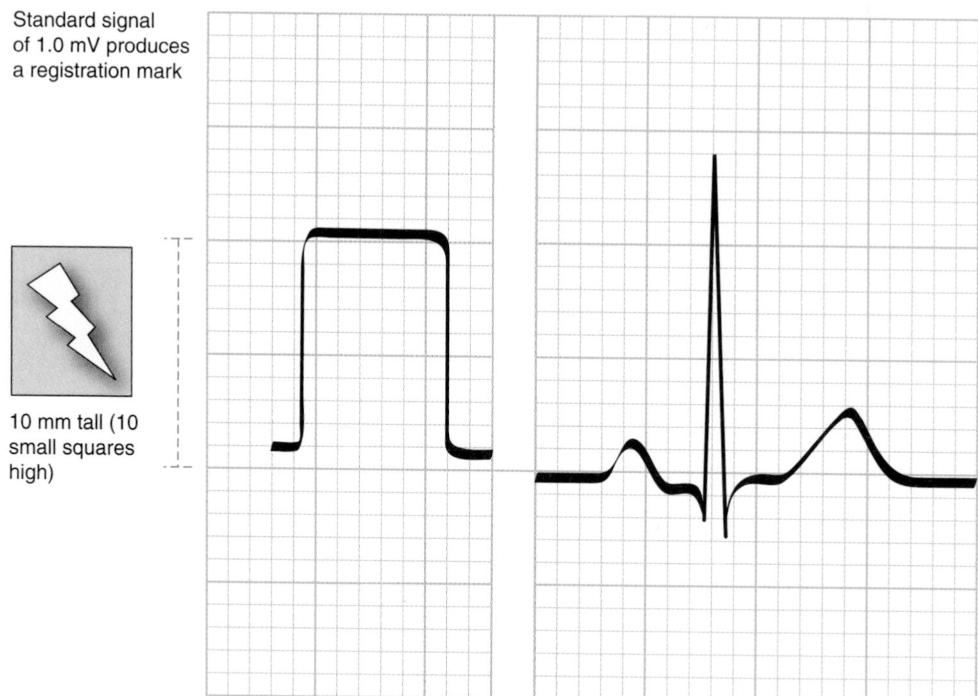

Figure 2-10
Calibration of the ECG.

Calibrating the ECG

Provided the ECG machine is properly calibrated, the height of the P waves, QRS complexes, and T waves can provide you with certain information. For example: small complexes can indicate conditions such as pericardial effusion, whereas tall R waves may point to the presence of left ventricular hypertrophy (both these conditions are discussed in later chapters). To help assure the ECG machine is properly calibrated, you can place a registration or calibration mark as a reference point on the ECG tracing. This is sometimes called calibrating the ECG machine. A standard signal of 1.0 mV will produce a registration point 10 mm tall (ten small squares high). On some ECG machines this mark is created automatically while with others it is necessary to manually place this registration point. This registration mark should be included on every ECG tracing (Figure 2-10).

Artifact

Sometimes we see markings on the ECG tracing that have no relationship to the electrical activity of the heart (Figure 2-11). This makes it hard to accurately interpret the ECG. These markings, called **artifact,** can be caused by such things as the patient moving, shivering, or experiencing muscle tremors; electrodes that are loose or improperly placed; worn out lead wires; a malfunctioning ECG machine; or the presence of 60-cycle

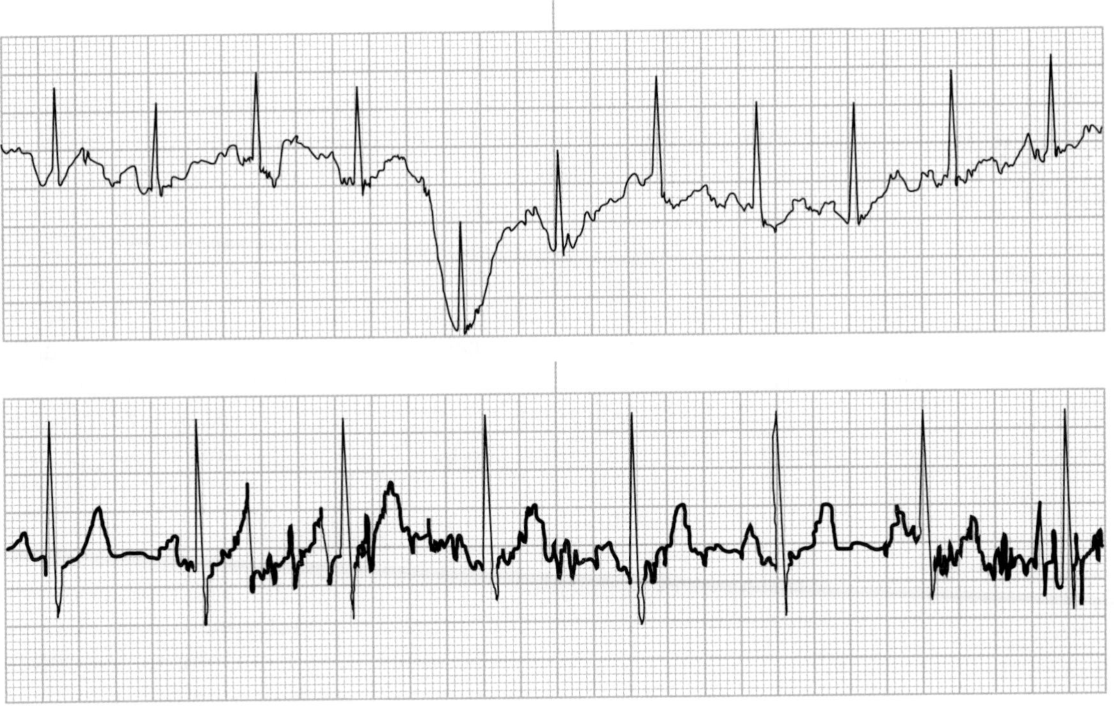

Figure 2-11
Artifact is markings on the ECG caused by such things as the patient moving, shivering, or experiencing muscle tremors; electrodes that are loose or improperly placed; worn out lead wires; a malfunctioning ECG machine; or the presence of 60-cycle current interference.

current interference (caused by improperly grounded electrical equipment or electrical interference). The way you can differentiate artifact from waveforms produced by the heart is that there is usually little consistency to the artifact whereas electrical activity produced by the heart usually looks the same (or at least similar) across the rhythm strip. As you will learn throughout the rest of this text, some dysrhythmias produce chaotic looking waveforms (such as atrial and ventricular fibrillation) but even those waveforms generally repeat themselves. In some cases artifact can mimic life-threatening dysrhythmias. For this reason always compare your rhythm interpretation with the clinical status of the patient. If the patient is awake and alert but the ECG shows a rhythm inconsistent with life you know you are dealing with artifact.

Markings on the ECG tracing that are not a product of the electrical activity of the heart are called ________________. These markings can be caused by such things as the patient ________________ and can mimic ________________ dysrhythmias.

[artifact] [moving] [life-threatening]

ECG Machines

INSTRUCTIONAL MOMENT
Learning about ECGs can be intimidating. For this reason we discuss how to interpret dysrhythmias in the next several chapters and then learn how to analyze the other, more complex, aspects of the ECG.

ECG machines have many uses in both the hospital and out-of-hospital settings. Examples include providing continuous monitoring to check for abnormalities in the heart rate and/or rhythm (called dysrhythmias); performing assessments and testing; diagnosing various cardiac conditions; evaluating response to medications used to treat cardiac, as well as other types of emergencies; and obtaining a baseline recording before, during, and after a medical procedure. The ECG machine can also provide information about how the electrical impulses are being carried through the heart's conduction system, the orientation of the heart in the chest, electrical effects of medications and electrolytes, the mass of the cardiac muscle, as well as identifying changes in the heart muscle due to cardiac conditions, and evaluating the function of artificial implanted pacemakers (a device used to initiate or control the heart rate).

KEY CONCEPT
Dysrhythmias are abnormalities or disturbances in the heart rhythm. Many are insignificant and have no effect on cardiac output, while others may be life threatening.

A variety of ECG machines are available for use. The type used to provide continuous cardiac monitoring is often referred to as an ECG monitor. Some are simple devices, monitoring from one to five different leads, while others are more complex, capable of monitoring up to 12 or more leads simultaneously. Many are equipped with a defibrillator (a device used to deliver an electrical shock to the heart) and pacemaker (a device used to stimulate the heart to beat at a desired rate). Some ECG monitors are portable and used in the prehospital care setting where patients are to be transported from one point to another, while others are fixed in place such as in the coronary care or intensive care units. The devices that monitor only one lead at a time are used primarily to diagnose the heart's rhythm while the 12-lead ECG machine is used to look for evidence of injury to the heart. Both types may be used to interpret cardiac rhythms by selecting the appropriate lead.

ECG Leads

To be skilled at ECG analysis you need to understand the term ECG leads (Figure 2-12). Think of each lead as being a different view or picture of the heart. Earlier we described the characteristics of the waveforms generated as the electrical impulse travels through the heart. Therefore, we only showed how the waveforms appear in one lead (lead II). However, the information obtained through just one lead is limited and only views the area of the heart that the lead is capable of showing.

Think about this for a minute. You are trying to determine whether a fast heart rate (tachycardia) is originating from above the ventricles (referred to as supraventricular tachycardia) or from within the ventricles (referred to as ventricular tachycardia). You have the patient attached to the ECG monitor and are using lead II. This lead is particularly helpful

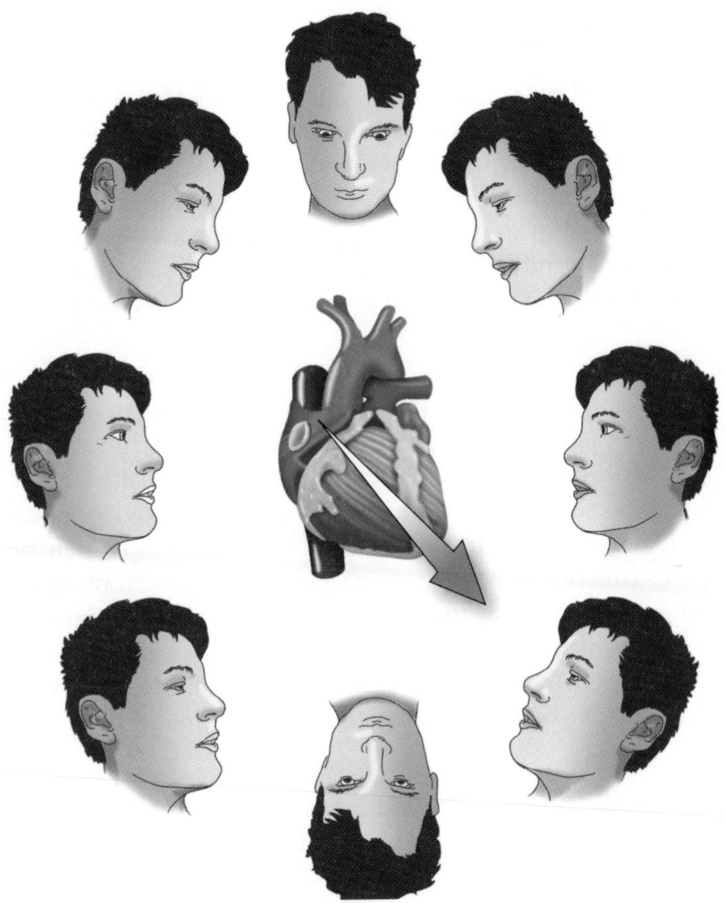

Figure 2-12
Each ECG lead provides a different view of the heart.

in identifying sinus node and atrial dysrhythmias but will not likely provide the information you need in this case. Instead, you should switch to a modified chest lead (described later in this chapter). The modified chest leads are particularly well suited for differentiating between supraventricular and ventricular tachycardia.

The use of several different leads is often required to gain the needed information when you are trying to identify ischemia, infarction, physical changes in the heart muscle, conduction defects, electrical effects of medications and electrolytes, and evaluating pacemaker function.

INSTRUCTIONAL MOMENT
Memorizing what view(s) of the heart each lead will provide will help you decide which lead to use to gain the information you need to make a proper assessment or diagnosis.

Each lead provides a different ________________ of the heart. The information obtained through just one lead is ________________. Therefore multiple leads can help identify ________________ information.

[view] [limited] [needed]

 Views of the ECG

To help understand the concept of ECG leads, think about taking pictures of a house. From the front you get one picture and from the side of the house you get another picture. If there is damage on the back of the house, you should be able to see it in pictures taken at the rear of the house. The different leads work in the same way; they provide a view that the other leads do not. The location or sites where the electrodes are placed vary depending on which view of the heart's activity is being assessed.

Because the electrodes positioned on the patient's skin detect the heart's electrical activity, placing them in a different location changes the lead or view. Think of each electrode used with the ECG machine as being an electrical pole; in other words, representing either a positive or negative charge. A lead presents a view of the heart's electrical activity between one positive pole (electrode) and one negative pole (electrode). Then, between the two poles (the positive and negative electrodes) lies an imaginary line representing the lead's axis, the direction the current is moving through the heart. The concept of the heart's axis will be discussed in more detail in Chapter 13. Settings on most ECG machines allow electrodes to be made either positive or negative, depending on the required lead.

KEY CONCEPT
The location where the electrodes are placed determines the view of the heart or lead. Electrodes are placed on the chest, arms, and legs.

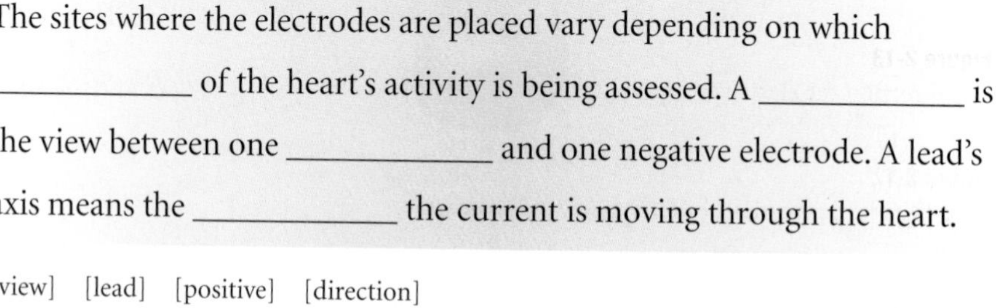

The sites where the electrodes are placed vary depending on which ____________ of the heart's activity is being assessed. A ____________ is the view between one ____________ and one negative electrode. A lead's axis means the ____________ the current is moving through the heart.

[view] [lead] [positive] [direction]

 Electrical Current Flow and ECG Waveform Direction

The direction the electrical current takes, toward a positive or negative electrode, determines the direction a waveform points on an ECG (Figure 2-13). An electrical current traveling toward a positive electrode produces a waveform that points upward. A current traveling away from a positive electrode or toward a negative electrode produces a waveform that points downward. A biphasic waveform (one that has both a positive and negative deflection) is recorded when the impulse travels perpendicular to where the electrode is positioned.

KEY CONCEPT
The ECG shows a positive deflection as the impulse travels toward the positive electrode but downward as it travels away from it.

Depending on which lead is used (where the electrodes are placed) different ECG patterns will be produced. In other words, the waveforms seen in each lead can be expected to look different because each views the heart differently. When discussing the shape of a waveform we take the perspective of the positive electrode of that lead.

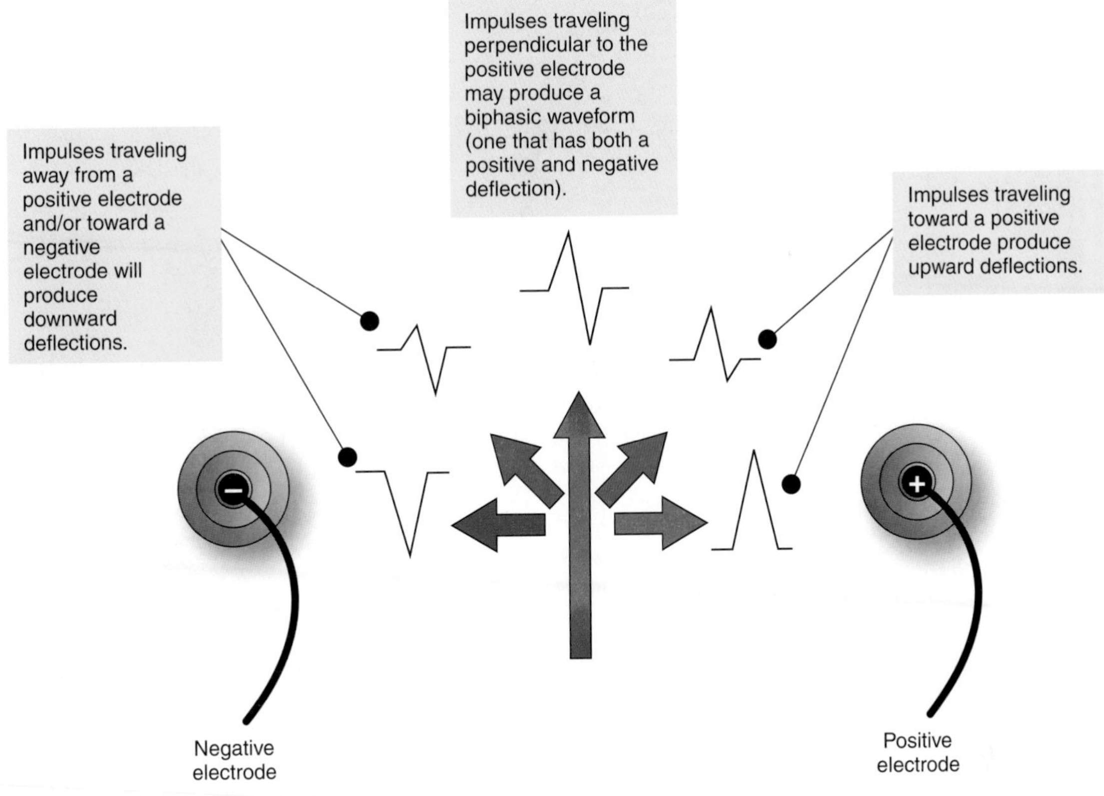

Figure 2-13
The direction the electrical impulse takes toward or away from a positive electrode causes the waveform to deflect either upward or downward.

Electrical currents traveling toward a positive electrode produce a waveform that takes an _______________ deflection while those traveling away from a _______________ electrode or toward a negative electrode produce a waveform with a _______________deflection. A _______________ waveform is composed of both positive and negative deflections.

[upright] [positive] [downward] [biphasic]

Planes of the Heart

Electrodes are placed at specific spots on the patient's chest wall and extremities to view the heart's electrical activity from different angles or planes (Figure 2-14). Planes provide a cross-sectional view of the heart. The frontal plane is essentially a vertical cut through the middle of the heart. The leads arranged on the frontal plane view the inferior,

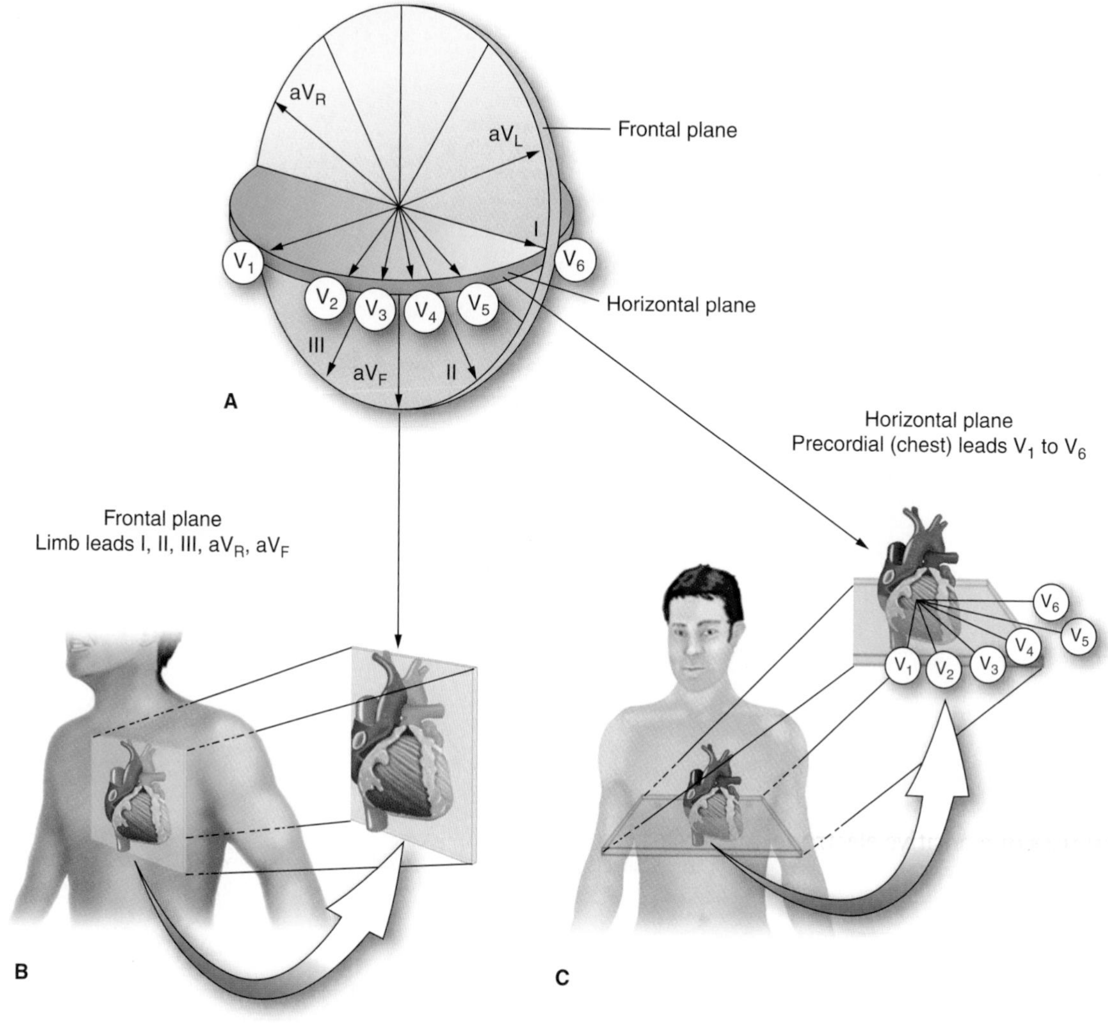

Figure 2-14
The 12-lead ECG views the heart's electrical activity along two planes. (a) Shows a graphic representation of frontal and horizontal planes and the leads which view each. (b) Limb leads provide a view of the frontal plane. (c) Precordial leads provide a view of the horizontal plane.

INSTRUCTIONAL MOMENT
As you will see from our discussion throughout the text, the leads we discuss cannot view all areas of the heart. Later, as we talk about how to locate ischemia and infarction in the posterior area of the heart, we will describe ways to accommodate for this and other types of ECG leads that can be selected.

superior, and lateral aspects of the heart. These are called the limb leads and include leads I, II, III, aV_R, aV_L, and aV_F. The horizontal plane is a transverse cut through the middle of the heart, and leads arranged on this plane provide us with anterior, lateral, and posterior views. These leads are called the precordial leads and include V_1, V_2, V_3, V_4, V_5, and V_6. We will discuss the limb and precordial leads in greater depth shortly.

The limb leads view the ______________ plane. The precordial leads view the heart's electrical activity on the ______________ plane.

[frontal] [horizontal]

Bipolar/Unipolar Leads

ECG leads are either bipolar or unipolar (Figure 2-15). Bipolar leads require two electrodes of opposite polarity (positive and negative). A bipolar lead records the flow of the electrical impulse between the two selected electrodes. Bipolar leads have a third electrode called a ground. The ground is used to help prevent electrical interference from appearing on the ECG and has zero electrical potential when compared to the positive and negative electrodes. The bipolar leads include leads I, II, and III. The axes of these three bipolar leads form a triangle around the heart referred to as **Einthoven's triangle;** this will be discussed in more detail in later chapters.

CLINICAL MOMENT
The color coding on electrodes is meant to help you remember where each electrode is placed. However, do not rely on the color of the wires for proper placement of the electrodes as the colors may vary among different manufacturers. Instead, use the lettering commonly located on the top of the lead wire connector for each lead. LL stands for left leg, LA stands for left arm, and RA stands for right arm.

Unipolar leads use only one positive electrode and a reference point calculated by the ECG machine. The reference point (with zero electrical potential) lies in the center of the heart's electrical field located left of the interventricular septum and below the AV junction. Unipolar leads include leads V_1, V_2, V_3, V_4, V_5, and V_6.

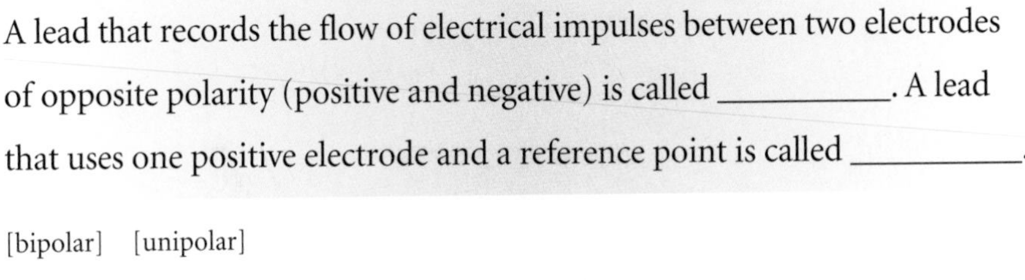

A lead that records the flow of electrical impulses between two electrodes of opposite polarity (positive and negative) is called __________. A lead that uses one positive electrode and a reference point is called __________.

[bipolar] [unipolar]

Different leads are used for different purposes. Some (typically leads I, II, and III or MCL leads) are used for continuous cardiac monitoring (typically to identify the presence of and/or developing cardiac dysrhythmias) while others (such as a 12-lead ECG) are used to obtain specific diagnostic information. A lead may be selected for the purpose of highlighting a specific part of the ECG complex; the electrical events of a specific cardiac cycle; and/or conditions, such as an enlargement of the heart muscle.

12-Lead ECG

A 12-lead ECG provides a more complete picture of the heart's electrical activity, giving 12 different views (Figure 2-16). These views are obtained by placing electrodes on the patient's extremities (called limb leads) and chest (called chest or precordial leads). As previously mentioned, the limb leads provide information about electrical activity of the heart on the frontal plane, while the precordial leads provide information about electrical activity of the heart on the horizontal plane.

CLINICAL MOMENT
There are now ECG machines, such as 15-lead technology, that employ more leads. Coverage on this topic is beyond the scope of this text.

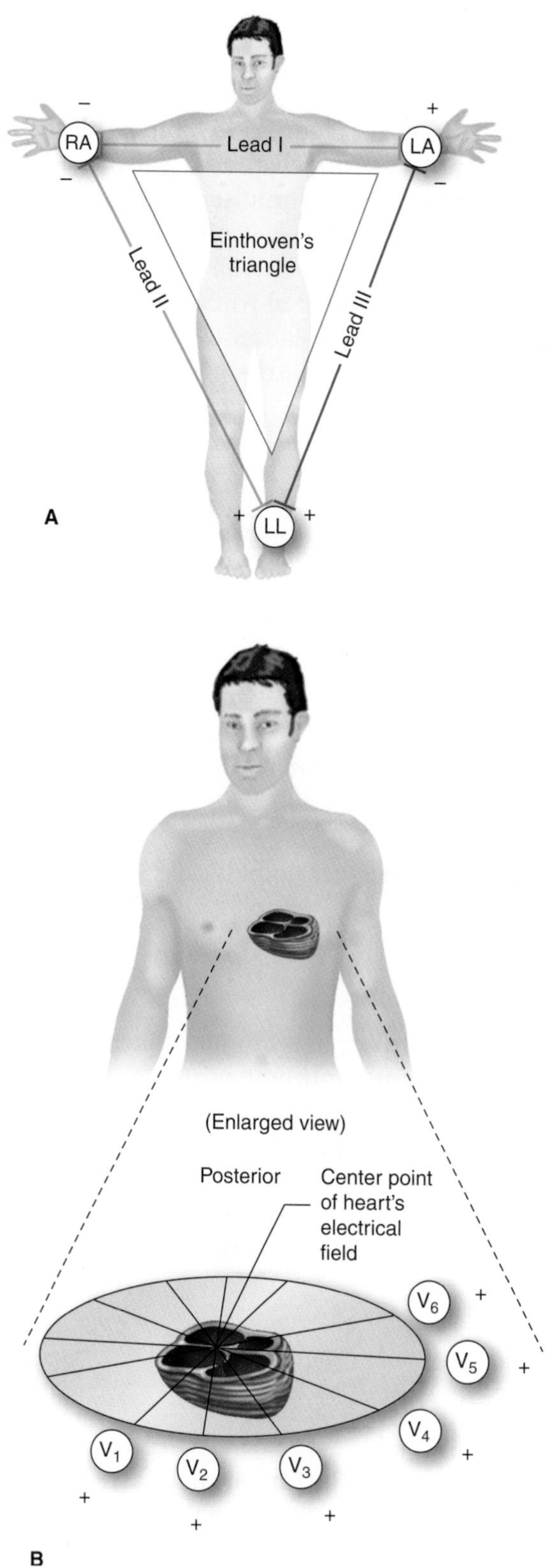

Figure 2-15
Bipolar and unipolar leads. (a) Bipolar lead requires a positive and negative electrode. (b) Unipolar lead has just a positive electrode and a reference point which is calculated by the ECG.

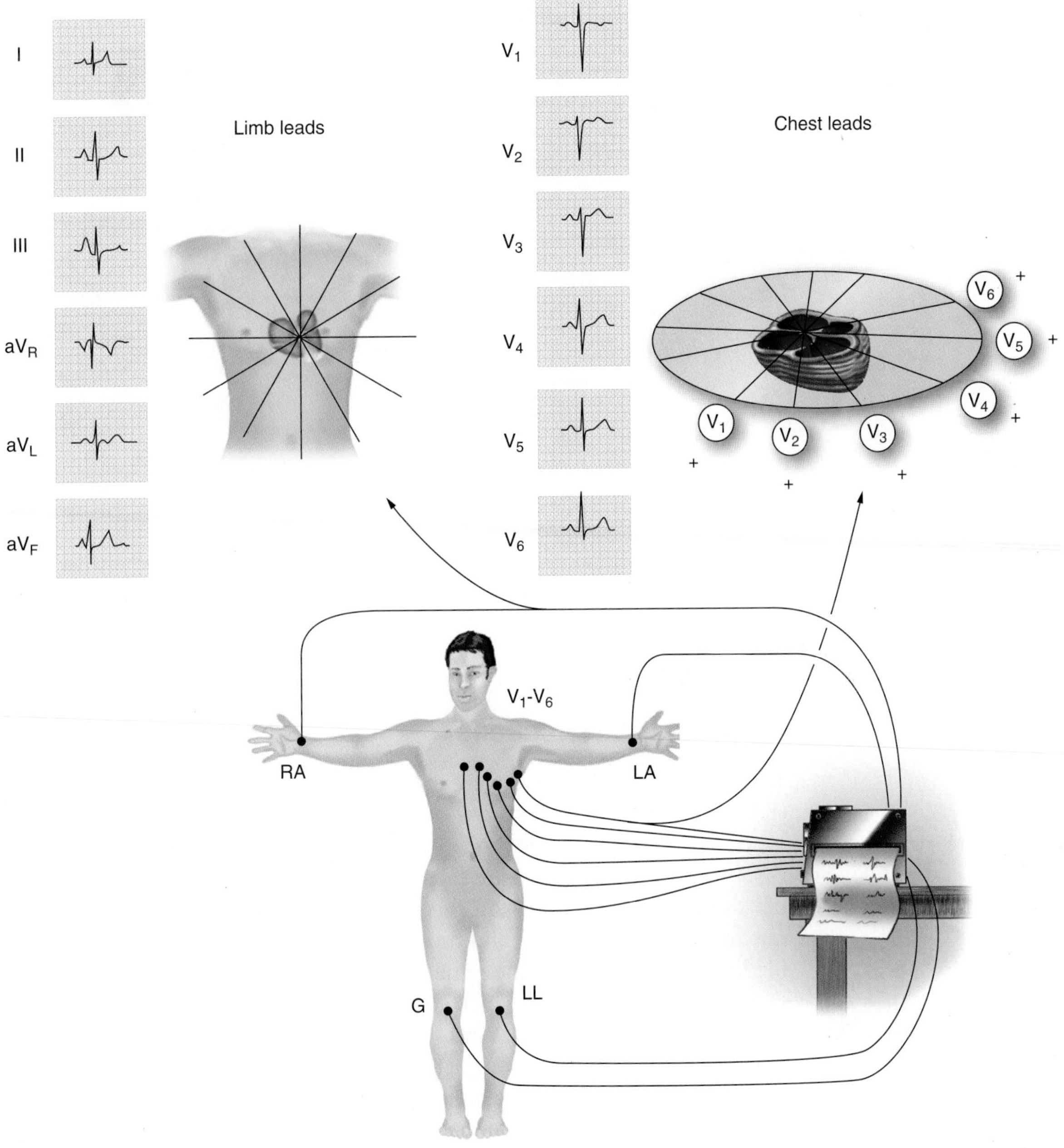

Figure 2-16
The 12-lead ECG provides a more complete picture of the heart's electrical activity; it provides 12 different views.

The ________________ leads are obtained by placing electrodes on the patient's extremities. The ________________ leads are obtained by placing electrodes on the patient's chest.

[limb] [precordial]

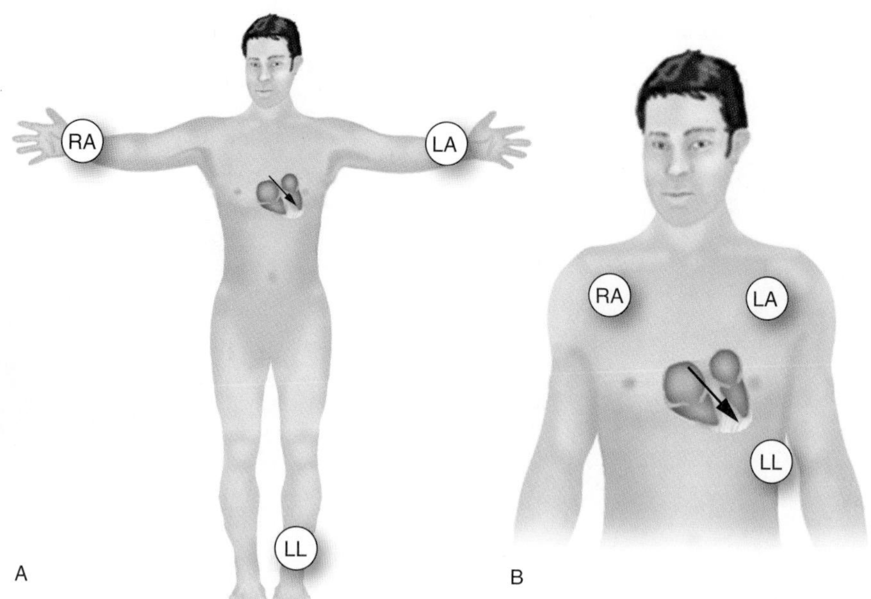

Figure 2-17
Limb leads. (a) Location of electrodes applied to the extremities and (b) location of electrodes applied to the chest.

Limb Lead Locations

To view the limb leads, we place electrodes on the right arm (RA), left arm (LA), and left leg (LL) (Figure 2-17a) at least 10 centimeters (cm) from the heart. Alternatively, the electrodes can be placed on the person's chest (Figure 2-18b), provided that they are each at least 10 cm from the heart. The electrodes are typically placed on the chest during continuous monitoring to maximize patient comfort and minimize muscle artifact. The electrodes for the limb leads remain in the same place no matter which lead we view. The ECG machine will change which electrode is positive (and negative) depending on which lead we select. With some ECG machines this is done manually (by turning a dial or depressing a button), whereas with others it is done automatically. The limb leads include leads I, II, and III; augmented voltage right (aV_R); augmented voltage left (aV_L); and augmented voltage foot (aV_F).

KEY CONCEPT
The limb leads include leads I, II, and III; augmented voltage right (aV_R); augmented voltage left (aV_L); and augmented voltage foot (aV_F).

To view the limb leads, we place electrodes on the ______________ arm, ______________ arm, and ______________ leg.

[right] [left] [left]

Leads I, II, and III

Leads I, II, and III are referred to as the standard limb leads. Again, they are bipolar leads. The electrodes for these leads may be placed on the patient's arms and legs or chest (Figure 2-18). With lead I the positive electrode is

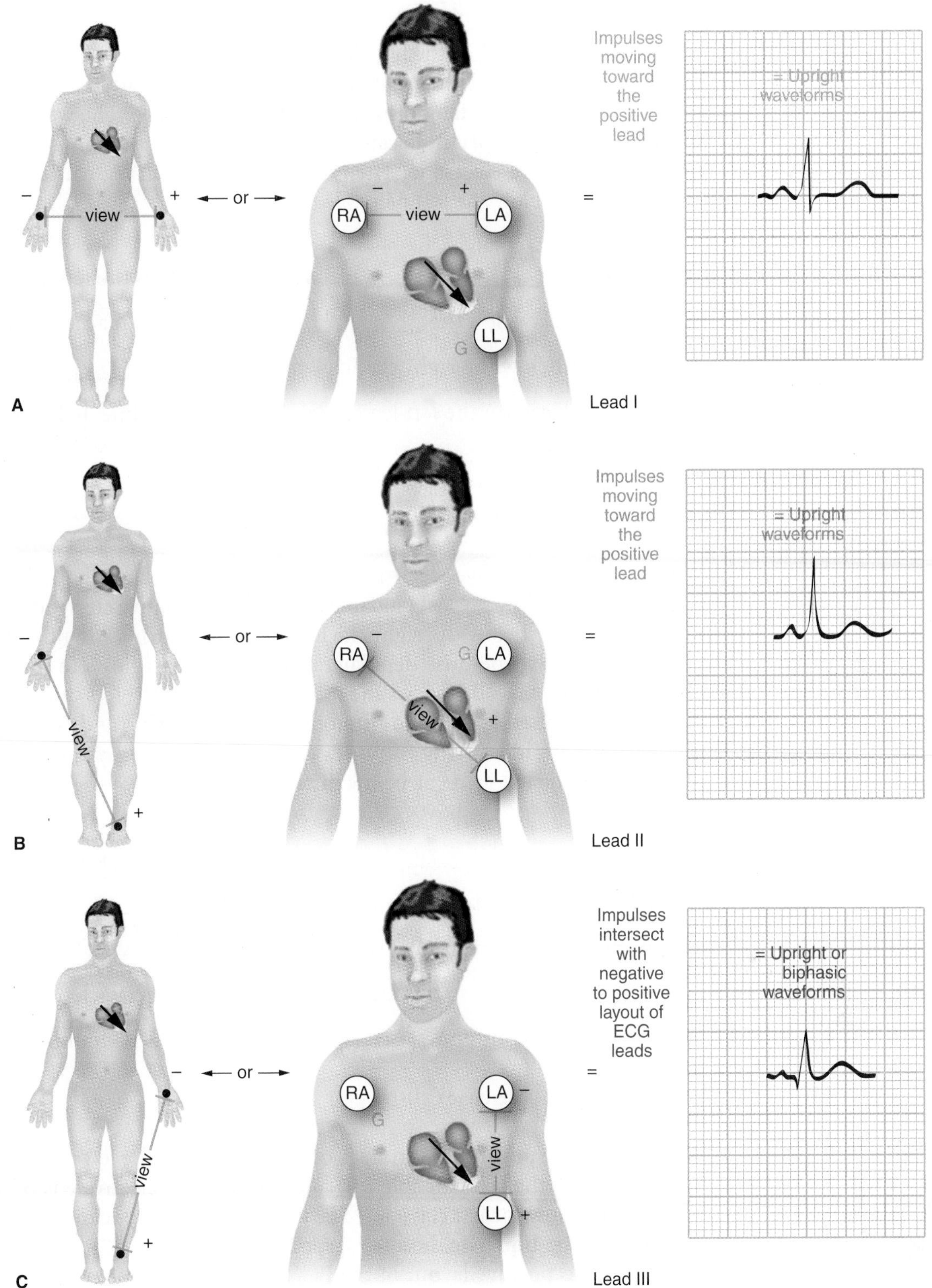

Figure 2-18

Limb lead locations on extremities or chest. (a) In lead I the positive electrode is placed on the left arm or just below the left clavicle while the negative electrode is positioned just below the right clavicle or on the right arm. (b) In lead II the positive electrode is located on the left foot or left midclavicular line, below the last palpable rib while the negative electrode is positioned just below the right clavicle or on the right arm. (c) In lead III the positive electrode is located on the left foot or left midclavicular line, below the last palpable rib while the negative electrode is positioned just below the left clavicle or on the left arm.

QUESTION
"What are bipolar leads?"
(The answer can be found on page 76.)

on the left arm (or below the left clavicle) and the negative electrode is on the right arm (or below the right clavicle). The axis of lead I is from right to left. Lead I views the lateral surface of the left ventricle. The waveforms in lead I are mostly upright because the wave of depolarization is moving toward the positive electrode. The ground is on the left leg (or left midclavicular line, below the last palpable rib).

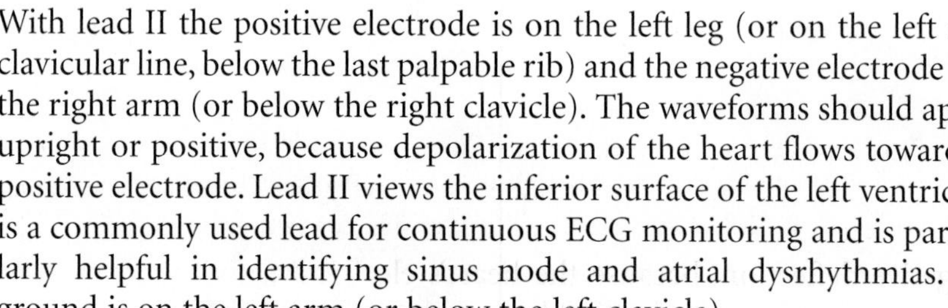

With lead I the _______________ electrode is placed on the left arm (or below the left clavicle), the ______________ electrode is placed on the right arm (or below the right clavicle), and the ______________ electrode is placed on the left leg (or left midclavicular line, below the last palpable rib).

[positive] [negative] [ground]

KEY CONCEPT
Lead II is a commonly used lead for providing continuous ECG monitoring.

With lead II the positive electrode is on the left leg (or on the left midclavicular line, below the last palpable rib) and the negative electrode is on the right arm (or below the right clavicle). The waveforms should appear upright or positive, because depolarization of the heart flows toward the positive electrode. Lead II views the inferior surface of the left ventricle. It is a commonly used lead for continuous ECG monitoring and is particularly helpful in identifying sinus node and atrial dysrhythmias. The ground is on the left arm (or below the left clavicle).

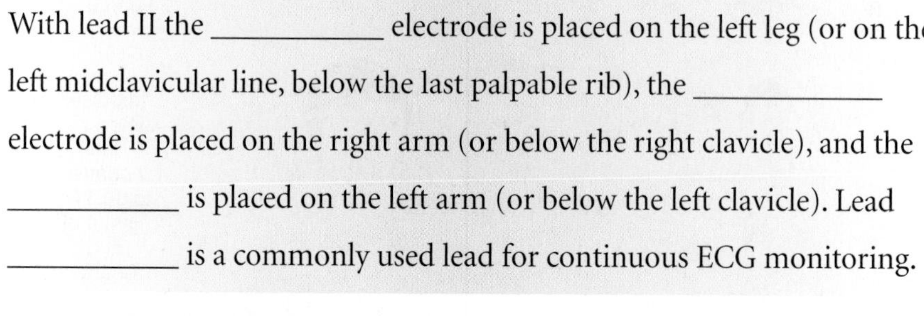

With lead II the ___________ electrode is placed on the left leg (or on the left midclavicular line, below the last palpable rib), the ____________ electrode is placed on the right arm (or below the right clavicle), and the ___________ is placed on the left arm (or below the left clavicle). Lead ___________ is a commonly used lead for continuous ECG monitoring.

[positive] [negative] [ground] [II]

QUESTION
"Which leads are referred to as the standard limb leads?"
(The answer can be found on page 76.)

With lead III the positive electrode is on the left leg (or the left midclavicular line, below the last palpable rib) and the negative electrode is on the left arm (or below the left clavicle). The waveforms may appear to go both directions or be **biphasic,** because depolarization of the heart intersects the negative to positive layout of the ECG electrodes. In other words, the complexes appear as though they are half above and half below the ECG baseline. Alternatively, the QRS complex may be mostly positive although the R wave is not as tall as in lead II. Lead III views the inferior wall of the left ventricle. The ground is on the right arm (or below the right clavicle).

With lead III the ______________ electrode is placed on the left leg (or left midclavicular line, below the last palpable rib), the ______________ electrode is placed on the left arm (or below the left clavicle), and the ______________ is placed on the right arm (or below the right clavicle).

[positive] [negative] [ground]

Leads aV_R, aV_L, and aV_F

The ECG waveforms produced by the augmented leads, aV_R, aV_L, and aV_F ("a" means augmented, "V" means voltage, "R" means right, "L" means left, and "F" means foot), are small. For this reason the ECG machine enhances or augments them by 50% so their amplitude is comparable to other leads. Again, the augmented leads are unipolar. Each uses only one positive electrode on the body surface. The other two limb leads serve as a common ground, which has no charge (Figure 2-19).

QUESTION
"What does the term augmented mean?" (The answer can be found on page 76.)

In lead aV_R the positive electrode is on the right arm. The waveforms take a negative deflection, because the heart's electrical activity moves away from the positive electrode. This lead views the base of the heart, primarily the atria and great vessels. However, it doesn't view any part of the ventricles.

In lead aV_L the positive electrode is placed on the left arm. The waveforms take a positive or biphasic deflection, because the heart's electrical activity moves toward the positive electrode. This lead views the lateral wall of the left ventricle.

Finally, in lead aV_F the positive electrode is located on the left leg. The waveforms take a positive deflection, because the heart's electrical activity moves toward the positive electrode. This lead views the inferior wall of the left ventricle.

In lead aV_R the positive electrode is placed on the right ____________. With lead aV_L the positive electrode is placed on the left ____________, and in lead aV_F the positive electrode is located on the left ___________.

[arm] [arm] [leg]

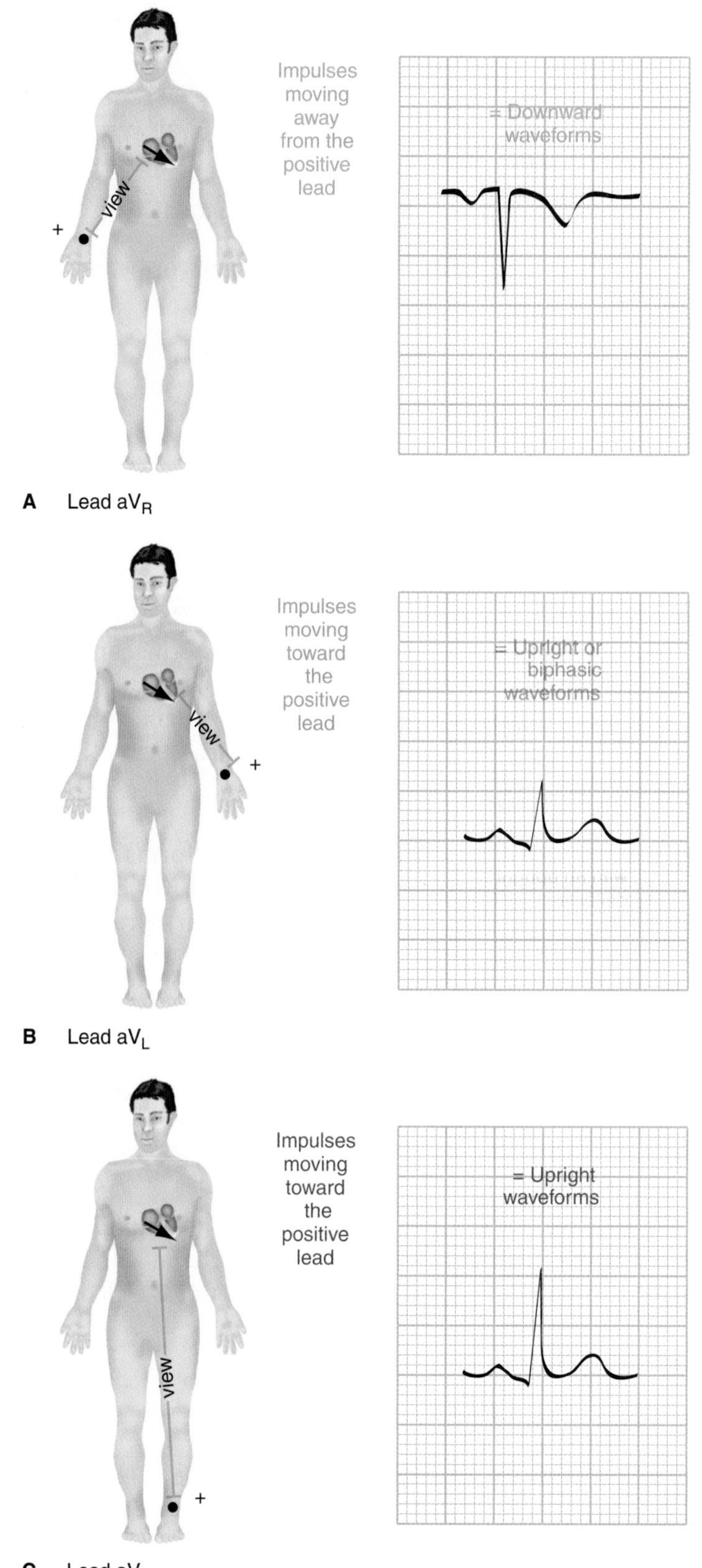

Figure 2-19

Electrode locations for aV_R, aV_L, and aV_F limb leads. (a) In lead aV_R the positive lead is located on the right arm. (b) In lead aV_L the positive lead is located on the left arm. (c) In lead aV_F the positive lead is located on the left leg.

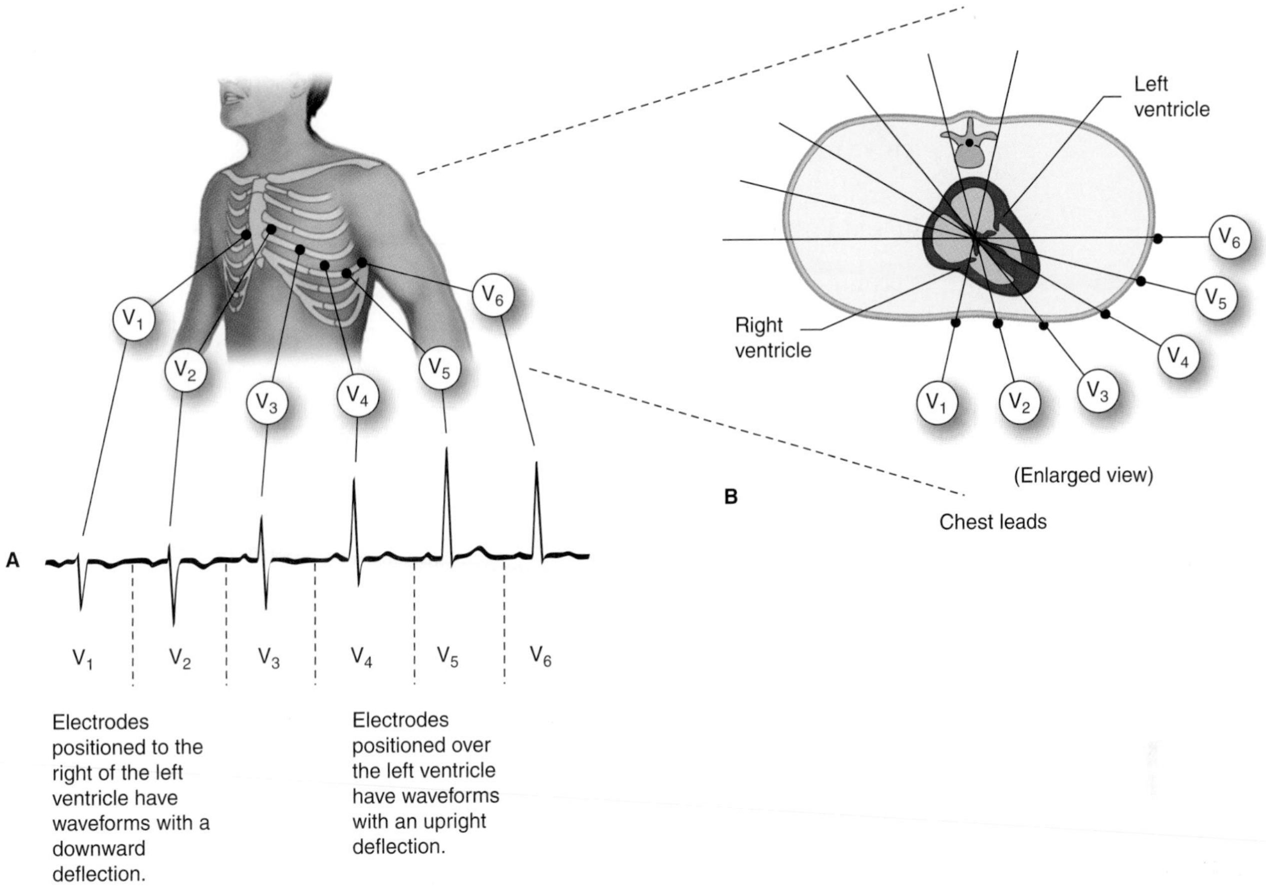

A

B

Chest leads

(Enlarged view)

Left ventricle

Right ventricle

V_1 V_2 V_3 V_4 V_5 V_6

Electrodes positioned to the right of the left ventricle have waveforms with a downward deflection.

Electrodes positioned over the left ventricle have waveforms with an upright deflection.

Figure 2-20
Electrode locations for precordial leads. (a) Leads V_1 through V_6. (b) Enlarged cross-section view of the thorax at the level of the heart showing location of chest leads and what area of the heart they view.

Precordial Lead Locations

The precordial leads (also called the V leads)—V_1, V_2, V_3, V_4, V_5, and V_6—provide information along the horizontal plane of the heart (Figure 2-20). The precordial leads are unipolar, requiring only a single positive electrode. The opposing pole of those leads is the center of the heart as calculated by the ECG. The six precordial leads are positioned in order across the chest.

The precordial lead V_1 electrode is placed on the right side of the sternum in the fourth intercostal space. Lead V_1 is particularly effective at showing the P wave, QRS complex, and the ST segment. It is also helpful in identifying ventricular dysrhythmias, ST segment changes, and bundle branch blocks. Lead V_2 is positioned on the left side of the sternum in the fourth intercostal space. Lead V_3 is located between leads V_2 and V_4. Lead V_1 views the interventricular septum, and along with V_2 and V_3 views the

CLINICAL MOMENT
Leads V_1 and V_2 are essentially in the same location on opposite sides of the chest.

anterior wall of the left ventricle. Lead V_4 is positioned at the fifth intercostal space at the midclavicular line. Lead V_5 is placed in the fifth intercostal space at the anterior axillary line. Lead V_6 is located level with V_4 at the midaxillary line. Leads V_4 through V_6 view the lateral wall of the left ventricle.

In lead V_1 the electrode is placed on the ________________ side of the sternum in the ________________ intercostal space. In lead V_2 the electrode is positioned on the ________________ side of the sternum in the ________________ intercostal space. Lead ________________ is located between leads V_2 and V_4. Lead V_4 is positioned at the ________________ intercostal space at the ________________ line. Lead V_5 is positioned at the fifth intercostal space at the anterior ________________ line. Lead V_6 is located level with V_4 at the ________________ line.

[right] [fourth] [left] [fourth] [V_3] [fifth] [midclavicular] [axillary] [midaxillary]

Modified Chest Leads

Two additional leads commonly used to provide continuous cardiac monitoring (employed primarily to detect dysrhythmias) are MCL_1 (modified chest lead) and MCL_6 (Figure 2-21). To acquire a modified chest lead select lead III, and place the positive electrode in the same position as V_1 (for MCL_1) or V_6 (for MCL_6).

MCL_1

With MCL_1, the positive electrode is positioned in the fourth intercostal space in the right sternal border, the negative electrode is below the left clavicle, and the ground is below the right clavicle. As we discussed earlier the positive electrode is the V_1 lead position to the right of the left ventricle. The waveforms should appear downward or in a negative direction, because depolarization of the heart flows toward the left ventricle (and away from the positive electrode). The lead is effective for monitoring QRS complex dysrhythmias, P wave changes, AV bundle-branch defects, and premature ventricular beats. It is helpful in differentiating between the different types of tachycardia (supraventricular versus ventricular).

CLINICAL MOMENT
With the MCL leads we change the positive electrode from the V_1 position to the V_6 position; the negative electrode and ground remain the same.

MCL_6

With MCL_6, the positive lead is placed at the fifth intercostal space at the midaxillary line, the negative electrode remains positioned below the left clavicle, and the ground remains positioned below the right shoulder. The waveforms are upright, because the depolarization current travels toward the positive electrode. This lead is particularly effective at monitoring ventricular conduction changes.

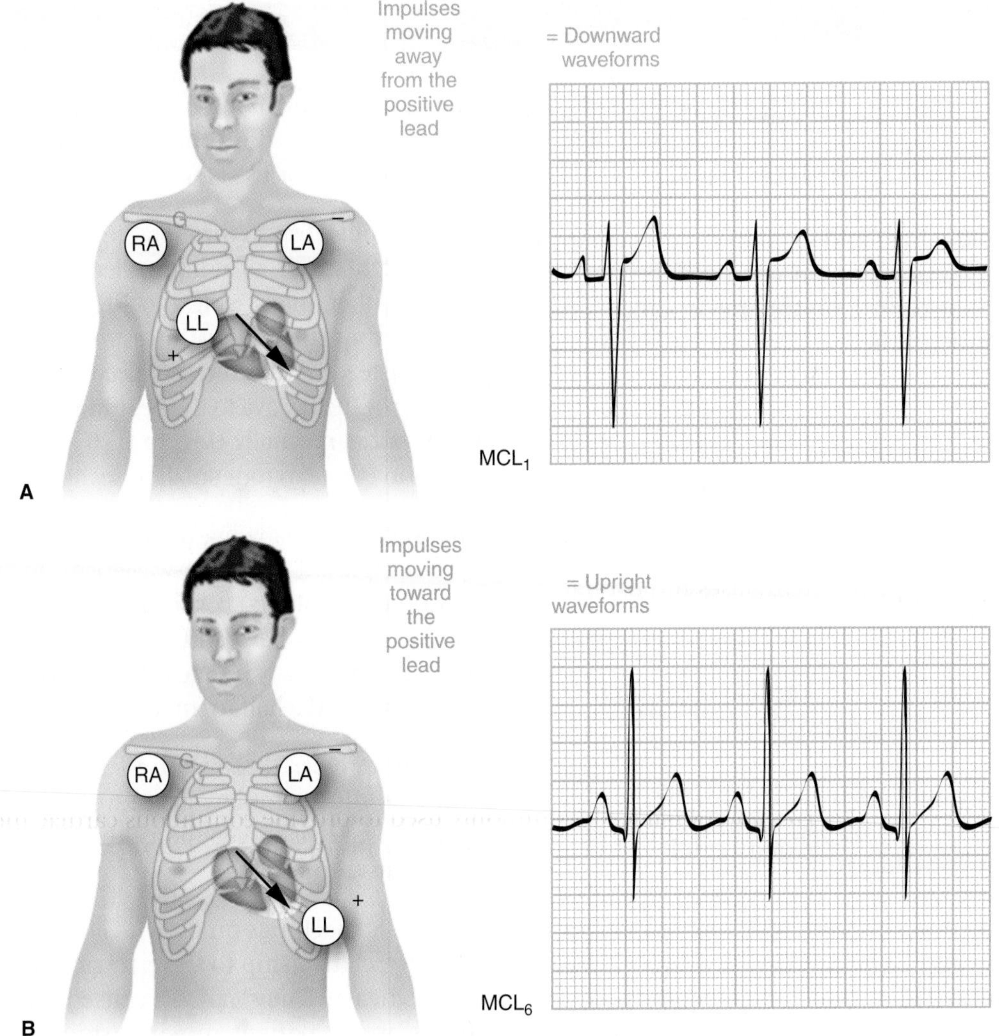

Figure 2-21
Electrode locations for MCL$_1$ and MCL$_6$ leads. (a) In lead MCL$_1$ the positive lead is placed at the 4th intercostal space. (b) In lead MCL$_6$ the positive lead is placed at the 5th intercostal space.

With MCL$_1$, the positive electrode is positioned in the __________ intercostal space in the right __________ border. With MCL$_6$, the positive lead is placed at the _________ intercostal space at the __________ line.

[fourth] [sternal] [fifth] [midaxillary]

Key Points

- Electrodes placed on the patient's skin detect the heart's electrical activity. The electrical activity is then transferred to the electrocardiograph (ECG) by color-coded wires (called lead wires) and displayed on a screen (oscilloscope) or printed onto graph paper. The graphic record or tracing is called an electrocardiogram.
- ECG rhythms shown on the oscilloscope are called dynamic ECGs, while those printed on graph paper are called ECG tracings or static ECGs.
- The ECG machine has many uses in hospital and out-of-hospital settings.
- Abnormalities in the cardiac rate and/or rhythm are called dysrhythmias.
- The ECG paper used to record the heart's electrical activity consists of horizontal and vertical lines that form a grid. The smallest of the squares represents 0.04 seconds in duration. Five of the small boxes represent 0.20 seconds in duration and make up the larger boxes denoted by a heavier line. Fifteen larger boxes equal a 3-second interval. You can use the horizontal measurements to determine the heart rate.
- Vertically on the ECG paper, the distance between the lines, or boxes, represents amplitude in millimeters (mm) or electrical voltage in millivolts (mV). Each small square represents 1 mm or 0.1 mV while the larger boxes, made up of five small squares, represent 5 mm or 0.5 mV.
- The flat line that precedes the electrical impulses is called the isoelectric line.
- The path of the electrical activity through the heart is displayed in a series of waves and complexes known as the P wave, QRS complex, and T wave.
- The first waveform, the P wave, appears as an upright and round waveform and represents depolarization of the atria.
- As the impulse travels through the His-Purkinje system it is seen as a flat line, called the PR segment. Rather than using the PR segment to identify abnormalities we measure the PR interval instead. This is the distance from the beginning of the P wave to the beginning of the Q wave and is normally 0.12 to 0.20 seconds in duration (three to four small boxes).
- The waveform following the PR interval is the QRS complex. It is a larger waveform (in comparison to the others) consisting of three parts: the Q wave, the R wave, and the S wave. The QRS complex is normally 0.06 to 0.12 seconds in duration (one and a half to three small boxes).
- A flat line referred to as the ST segment follows the QRS complex. Next, we should see the T wave. It is larger than the P wave and slightly asymmetrical.
- Artifact is markings on the ECG tracing that have no relationship to the electrical activity of the heart. They can be caused by such things as the patient moving, shivering, or experiencing muscle tremors; electrodes that are loose or improperly placed; worn out lead wires; a malfunctioning ECG machine; or the presence of 60-cycle current interference.
- Each lead provides a different view of the heart.
- Impulses that travel toward a positive electrode are recorded on the electrocardiogram as upward deflections. Impulses traveling away from a positive electrode or toward a negative electrode are recorded as downward deflections.
- The shape of the waveform is described from the perspective of the positive electrode of the selected lead.

- The limb leads are produced by placing electrodes on the right arm (RA), left arm (LA), and left leg (LL). The limb leads include leads I, II, and III; augmented voltage right (aV_R); augmented voltage left (aV_L); and augmented voltage foot (aV_F). They provide a view of the electrical activity along the heart's frontal plane.
- The precordial leads include leads V_1, V_2, V_3, V_4, V_5, and V_6. They provide information along the electrical activity along the horizontal plane of the heart.

Assess Your Understanding

The following questions give you a chance to assess your understanding of the material discussed in this chapter. The answers can be found in Appendix A.

1. An electrocardiogram is a/an
   a. graphic record of the heart's electrical activity.
   b. device that measures and records the ECG.
   c. irregular rhythm.
   d. device that measures the heart's mechanical activity.

2. ____________ positioned on the patient's skin detect the heart's electrical activity.
   a. Electrodes
   b. Lead wires
   c. Tracings
   d. Leads

3. Each small square on the ECG paper running horizontally represents ____________ seconds in duration.
   a. 0.01
   b. 0.04
   c. 0.12
   d. 0.20

4. The larger box on the ECG paper, made up of five small squares, represents ______________ seconds in duration.
   a. 0.12
   b. 0.15
   c. 0.20
   d. 0.32

5. On the top or bottom of the ECG paper there may be vertical slashes or markings to represent ___________ second intervals.
   a. 1
   b. 3
   c. 5
   d. 10

6. Each small square on the ECG paper running vertically represents
   a. 0.1 mV.
   b. 5 mm.
   c. 10 mm.
   d. 2.0 mV.

7. The reference point used to identify the changing electrical amplitude on the ECG is called the
   a. isoelectric line.
   b. ST segment.
   c. PR interval.
   d. QT interval.

8. Impulses that travel toward a positive electrode and away from a negative electrode are recorded on the electrocardiogram as ______________ deflections.
   a. downward
   b. perpendicular
   c. neutral
   d. upward

9. During the ______________ initiation of the impulse in the SA node, its movement through the atria and activation of the AV node occurs
   a. P wave
   b. PR interval
   c. QRS complex
   d. ST segment

10. The normal PR interval is ____________ seconds in duration.
    a. 0.12 to 0.20
    b. 0.04 to 0.08
    c. 0.36 to 0.44
    d. 0.06 to 0.12

11. The PR interval represents
    a. repolarization of the ventricles.
    b. depolarization of the heart from the SA node through the atria, AV node, and His-Purkinje system.
    c. depolarization of the atria.
    d. movement of the electrical impulse through the ventricles.

12. The Q wave is the first __________ deflection after the PR segment.
    a. biphasic
    b. positive
    c. negative
    d. none of the above

13. Artifact is
    a. a normal part of each ECG tracing.
    b. an indication of decreased cardiac output.
    c. sometimes caused by muscle tremors.
    d. consistently the same across the ECG tracing.

14. The frontal plane gives us a/an ______________ view of the heart's electrical activity.
    a. anterior and posterior
    b. superior and inferior
    c. anterior and superior
    d. lateral and inferior

15. The limb leads are obtained by placing electrodes on the
    a. right arm, left arm, and left leg.
    b. chest and back.
    c. right arm, left leg, and right leg.
    d. left arm and left leg.

16. Leads ______________ are referred to as the standard limb leads.
    a. I, II, and III
    b. aV_R, aV_L, and aV_F
    c. V_1, V_2, V_3, V_4, V_5, and V_6
    d. MCL_1 and MCL_6

17. Leads ______________ are referred to as the precordial leads.
    a. MCL_1 and MCL_6
    b. aV_R, aV_L, and aV_F
    c. I and II
    d. V_1, V_2, V_3, V_4, V_5, and V_6

18. With lead II the positive electrode is placed on the
    a. right arm.
    b. left leg.
    c. left arm.
    d. right leg.

19. Lead ______________ is commonly used for continuous ECG monitoring.
    a. V_1
    b. aV_L
    c. II
    d. V_6

20. With the MCL_1 lead, the positive electrode is positioned in/on the
    a. right arm.
    b. left leg.
    c. fourth intercostal space in the right sternal border.
    d. fifth intercostal space in the left midaxillary border.

Referring to the scenario at the beginning of this chapter, answer the following questions.

21. Examination of the ECG by EMS and healthcare personnel provides which of the following?
    a. The patient's pulse rate.
    b. The patient's heart rate.
    c. The patient's blood pressure.
    d. The patient's cardiac output.

22. The patient fainted because
    a. he overexerted himself.
    b. his sympathetic nervous system was over stimulated.
    c. his blood pressure medications are too strong.
    d. his cardiac output dropped too low.

23. Which of the following nerves controls heart rate?
    a. Phrenic.
    b. Aortic.
    c. Vagus.
    d. Diaphragmatic.

Answers to Sidebar Questions

"How are the electrical impulses of the heart produced and conducted?"

Answer: Impulses are generated and subsequently conducted through the heart when positively charged ions, such as sodium, rapidly but briefly move inside the cells causing the interior to become positively charged. This is called depolarization.

"What ECG waveforms are generated as a result of the heart's electrical activity?"

Answer: Each cycle of depolarization and repolarization of the heart produces a P wave, QRS complex, and T wave.

"Thirty larger boxes on the ECG paper represent how many seconds?"

Answer: Thirty larger boxes on the ECG paper represent 6 seconds.

"For what purpose do we use the isoelectric line?"

Answer: We use this line as a baseline or reference point to identify the changing electrical amplitude.

"The amplitude of the normal P wave is represented by how many small squares? Also, the normal duration of the P wave is represented by how many small squares?"

Answer: The P wave should extend no more than two to three small boxes in height and one and a half to three small boxes in duration.

"What are bipolar leads?"

Answer: A bipolar lead requires two electrodes of opposite polarity (positive and negative).

"Which leads are referred to as the standard limb leads?"

Answer: Leads I, II, and III are referred to as the standard limb leads.

"What does the term augmented mean?"

Answer: In the context of the ECG, waveforms produced by the aV_R, aV_L, and aV_F leads are normally small. The ECG machine enhances or augments the leads to make them easier to see, because of this. It magnifies it by 50%. The augmented leads are a combination of the two limb leads angled 30 degrees from it.

On the DVD

- ECG leads lecture.
- Lead location demonstration.

Heart Rate

3

Case History

A 36-year-old woman presents to the emergency department complaining of a rapid heartbeat. She was recently diagnosed with hyperthyroidism for which she has begun treatment. She states that after a heated argument with her husband over finances she noticed that her heart was "pounding out of her chest." She feels lightheaded but denies chest pain.

The patient is promptly brought back to the major medical room and placed on a cardiac monitor while her vital signs are assessed. Her blood pressure is 105/60, pulse 160, respiratory rate is 24, and oxygen saturation is 99% on room air. The emergency physician examines the cardiac monitor and observes that the rhythm is fast, with narrow QRS complexes. The heart rate readout on the monitor appears to be malfunctioning indicating a rate of 320 beats per minute. The physician runs a printout of the rhythm and, using the skills she learned in ECG rhythm recognition, is able to measure the rate using a few rules of thumb. She determines that the patient's heart rate is actually 160 beats per minute.

Chapter Preview

- Analyzing the Electrocardiogram
- Step 1: Determining the Heart Rate
- Counting Both the Atrial and Ventricular Rates
- Normal, Slow, and Fast Rates

KEY CONCEPT
Use a logical and systematic manner to analyze ECG tracings.

INSTRUCTIONAL MOMENT
Students often compare sample or practice ECG tracings to examples provided in various textbooks. Instructors may hear their students remark "It can't be sinus bradycardia because it doesn't look like the example on page ___." It is never a good idea to do "pattern matching." Rather than trying to memorize what each ECG might look like, take the time to learn the **characteristics** of the normal ECG, the various dysrhythmias, and other cardiac conditions you are likely to encounter. Then use the five-step process described later in the chapter to analyze the ECG tracing. This process will allow you to effectively identify any ECG dysrhythmia.

Analyzing the Electrocardiogram

As discussed in Chapter 2, the electrocardiogram (ECG) has many uses. One application is to provide continuous cardiac monitoring to identify existing or emerging irregularities in the heart rate or rhythm (dysrhythmias). We do this by observing the rhythm directly on the ECG monitor screen or by printing an ECG tracing so that the specific waveforms, segments, and intervals can be measured and examined. In this chapter and the next several chapters we focus on the steps used to analyze the ECG.

To analyze an ECG tracing you should approach it in a logical and systematic manner. If a dysrhythmia or abnormality is present, this finding should always be compared with your complete assessment of the patient. This will determine the significance of the dysrhythmia or abnormality and assist in any decision regarding patient treatment.

Analyzing ECG tracings involves approaching each in a __________ and __________ manner. The presence of dysrhythmias should cause you to compare your findings with your patient __________.

[logical] [systematic] [assessment]

Characteristics of the Normal ECG

The key to successfully analyzing ECGs is learning the characteristics or features of each normal and abnormal ECG, then comparing what you see on the ECG tracing to those characteristics (Figure 3-1). Using an algorithmic approach and deductive reasoning you can rule out the dysrhythmias or abnormalities that do not have the same characteristics you see on the ECG tracing.

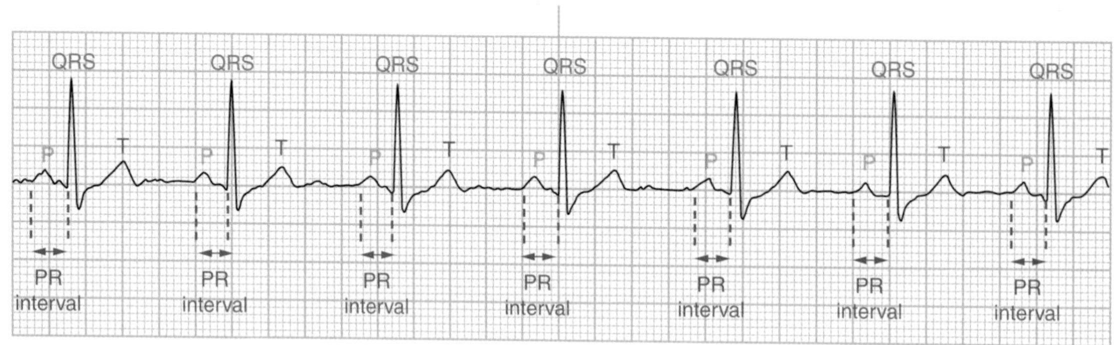

Figure 3-1
Normal sinus rhythm.

A key to successful ECG interpretation is memorizing the ______________ of the normal ECG and the various ______________ and abnormalities.

[characteristics] [dysrhythmias]

QUESTION
"The normal QRS complex will extend over how many small boxes?" (The answer can be found on page 105.)

As a baseline we often use the characteristics of normal (regular) sinus rhythm to which we compare other ECGs. The following are the key characteristics of normal sinus rhythm:

Rate:	60 to 100 beats per minute
Regularity:	Regular
P waves:	Upright and round, one preceding each QRS complex
QRS complexes:	Narrow, 0.06 to 0.12 seconds in duration
PR Interval:	0.12 to 0.20 seconds in duration
T waves:	Upright and slightly asymmetrical

KEY CONCEPT
Learning the characteristics of the normal ECG and the various dysrhythmias and using a systematic process to analyze the ECG tracings is key to successful ECG interpretation.

The Five-Step Process

To perform analysis of ECG tracings use a logical, systematic process (Figure 3-2). The following is a basic five-step process that can be used with any ECG tracing:

1. Determine the rate. (Is it normal, fast, or slow?)
2. Determine the regularity. (Is it regular or irregular?)
3. Assess the P waves. (Is there a uniform P wave preceding each QRS complex? Do they appear normal?)
4. Assess the QRS complexes. (Are the QRS complexes within normal limits? Do they appear normal?)
5. Assess the PR intervals. (Are the PR intervals identifiable? Within normal limits? Constant in duration?)

KEY CONCEPT
The first step to analyzing an ECG rhythm is to determine the heart rate.

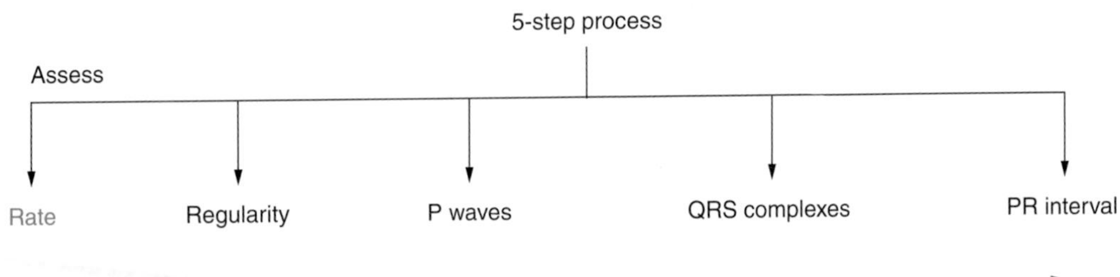

Figure 3-2
Five-step process for analyzing ECGs.

Step 1: Determining the Heart Rate

The first step in analyzing an ECG rhythm is to determine the heart rate. Begin by quickly checking the ECG monitor or tracing to see if the rate is slow, normal, or fast. For this initial look don't be concerned about calculating the exact heart rate, rather identify which group it fits in—slow, normal, or fast. Some ECG rhythms may be profoundly slow or fast in which case you should quickly assess the patient for adequate cardiac output. If cardiac output is compromised, immediate treatment is necessary.

A quick assessment of the heart rate can be done by looking at the space between QRS complexes (Figure 3-3). More space indicates a slower heart rate while less space indicates a faster heart rate.

You can practice determining whether a heart rate is slow, normal, or fast with the following *Practice Makes Perfect* exercises. Answers to these exercises can be found in Appendix A.

Step one in analyzing an ECG is determining the heart ____________.
Begin by determining if the rate is ____________, normal, or ____________. A quick assessment of the heart rate can be done by looking at the ____________ between the ____________ complexes.

[rate] [slow] [fast] [space] [QRS]

QUESTION
"What is the range of the normal heart rate in the adult?" (The answer can be found on page 105.)

CLINICAL MOMENT
Remember the discussion in Chapter 1: Heart rate × stroke volume = cardiac output. A very slow or fast heart rate can cause cardiac output to decrease by lowering the rate or decreasing the stroke volume.

CLINICAL MOMENT
The heart rate seen on the ECG tracing should always be compared with the pulse rate (obtained by palpation). The pulse rate should be counted for 15 seconds in regular rhythms and 30 to 60 seconds in irregular rhythms. It is important to palpate a pulse as some impulses may fail to generate contraction of the heart.

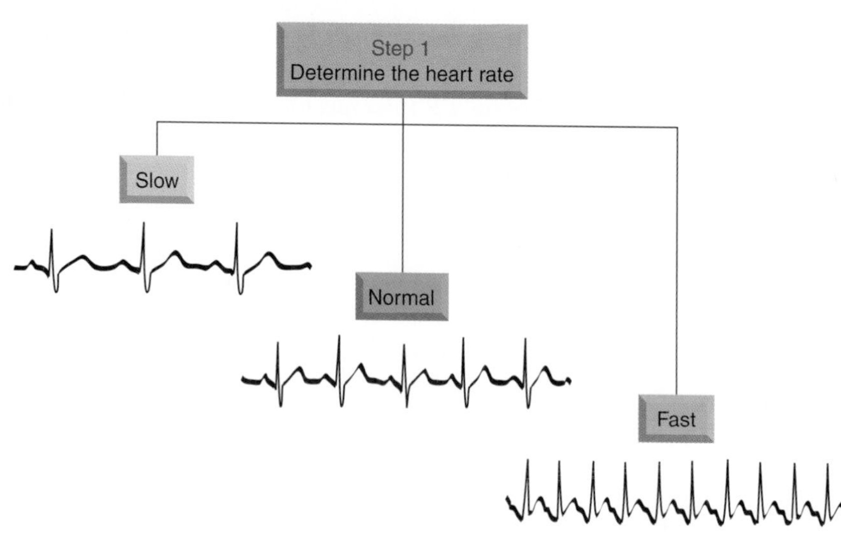

Figure 3-3
The first step in analyzing an ECG rhythm is to determine if the heart rate is slow, normal, or fast.

PRACTICE. . . MAKES PERFECT

1.

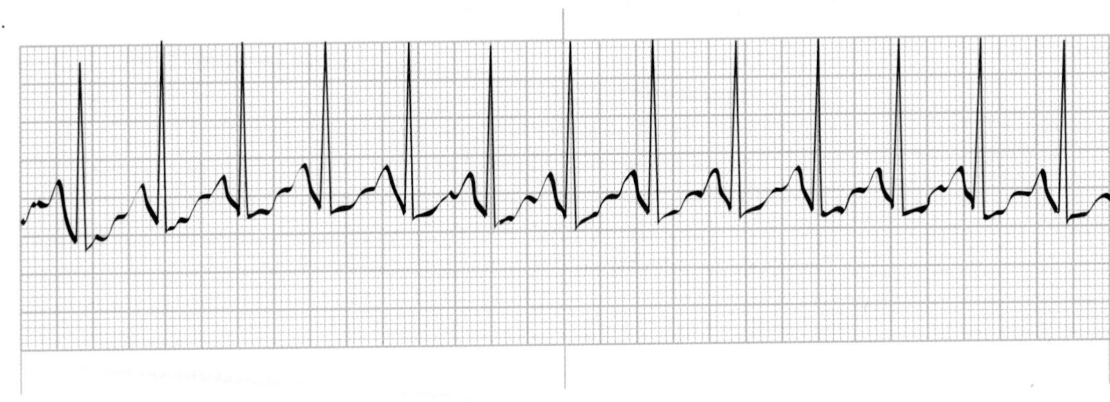

Is this rate slow, normal, or fast ______________ ?

2.

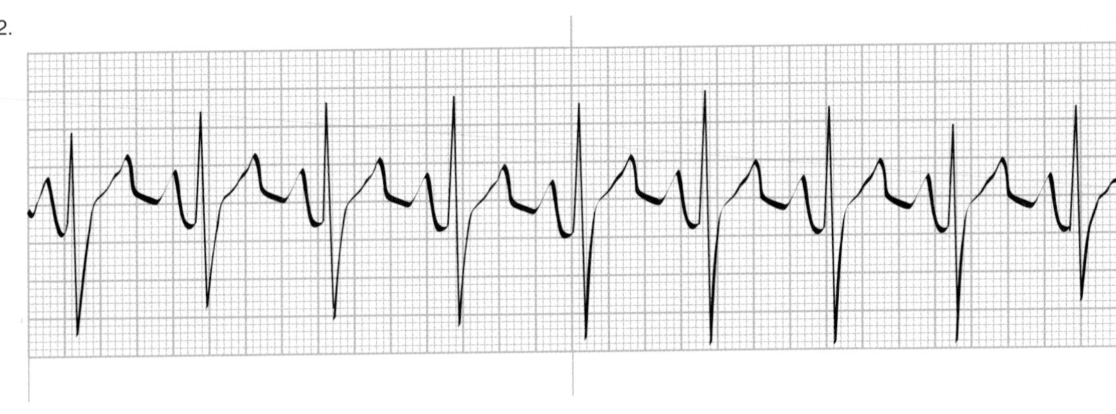

Is this rate slow, normal, or fast ______________ ?

3.

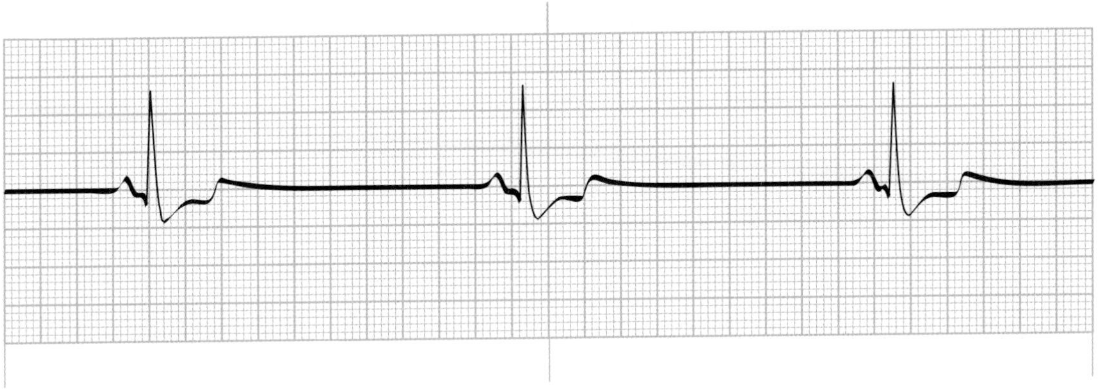

Is this rate slow, normal, or fast ______________ ?

INSTRUCTIONAL MOMENT
The names given the following methods for calculating the heart rate may differ from those found in other references. This was done intentionally to make it easier to remember them as they are descriptive of how they are done.

INSTRUCTIONAL MOMENT
Here are some examples of calculating heart rates using this method: (1) Eight QRS complexes in the 6-second block—the patient has a heart rate of 80 beats per minute; (2) Twelve QRS complexes in the 6-second block—the patient has a heart rate of 120 beats per minute; (3) Four QRS complexes in the 6-second block—the patient has a heart rate of 40 beats per minute.

Following the quick assessment, analyze the rhythm to determine the approximate or actual heart rate. Any one of several methods can be used to calculate the heart rate. Each method has its advantages and disadvantages.

6-Second Interval × 10 Method

The *6-second interval × 10* method involves multiplying by 10 the number of QRS complexes found in a 6-second portion of the ECG tracing (Figure 3-4). Remember that ECG paper typically has markings on the top and/or bottom indicating each 3-second block of time (see Chapter 2). Two of these successive (adjacent to each other) blocks of time equal 6 seconds. When you multiply that amount of time by 10, it represents 60 seconds or 1 minute. Therefore to calculate the heart rate:

1. Identify two successive 3-second marks.
2. Count the number of QRS complexes in that 6-second section.
3. Multiply that number by 10.

This final number is the approximate heart rate per minute.

Because the QRS complexes are measured over 6 seconds, it is an effective means for assessing the rate of an irregular rhythm. Advantages of the 6-second interval × 10 method are that it is quick, easy, and does not require any tools or devices. A disadvantage is that it does not calculate the heart rate as accurately as other methods. In other words, the heart rate might actually be 54 beats a minute instead of 50. Also, if the rhythm is too irregular you may count eight R waves (and/or P) waves in one 6-second section and 11 R waves (and/or P) waves in another making it difficult to obtain an accurate heart rate.

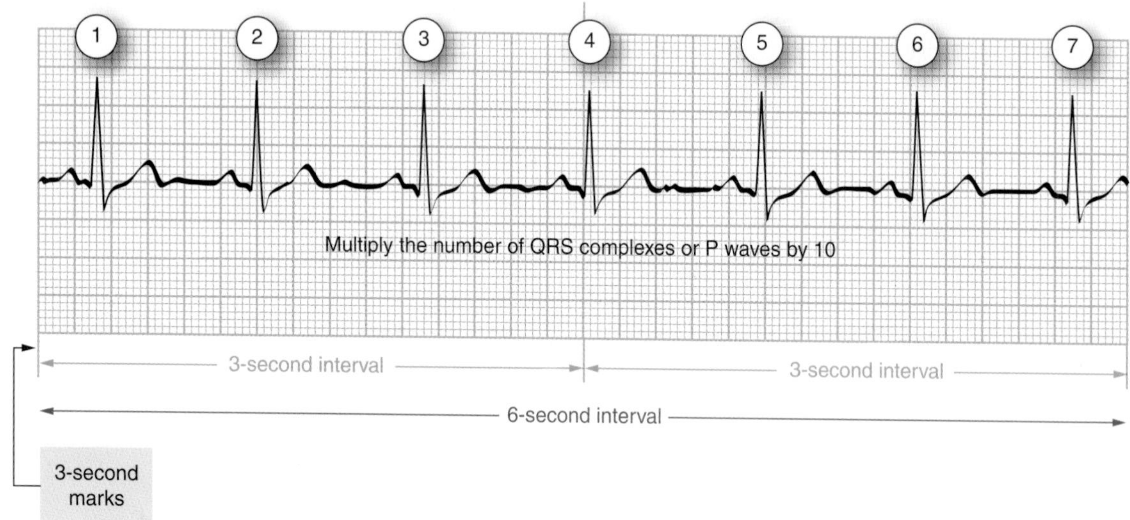

Figure 3-4
To employ the 6-second interval × 10 method, multiply by 10 the number of QRS complexes (for the ventricular rate) or P waves (for the atrial rate) found in a 6-second portion of the ECG tracing. The rate shown in the ECG tracing above is 70.

The 6-second interval × 10 method involves multiplying by ________ the number of QRS complexes found in a ________ -second portion of the ECG tracing. A 6-second portion of the ECG tracing is equal to ________ 3-second blocks of time as identified by markings on the ECG paper. The 6-second × 10 method can be used to measure ________ rhythms.

[10] [6] [two] [irregular]

INSTRUCTIONAL MOMENT
While the 6-second interval × 10 rule is effective for calculating the heart rate in irregular rhythms, there are some dysrhythmias in which the degree of irregularity makes it difficult to find enough consistent tracing to determine an average. In these cases try using a 12-second area of the tracing. Count the number of QRS complexes (and/or P waves) and multiply them by 5 (instead of 10).

This method can also be used to calculate the atrial rate. Multiply by 10 the number of P waves found in a 6-second portion of the ECG tracing.

You can practice determining heart rate using the 6-second interval × 10 method with the *Practice Makes Perfect* exercises on page 89. Answers to these exercises can be found in Appendix A.

KEY CONCEPT
You can quickly determine the heart rate by multiplying by 10 the number of QRS complexes found in a 6-second portion of the ECG tracing.

 300, 150, 100, 75, 60, 50 Method

The *300, 150, 100, 75, 60, 50* method, also called the countdown, sequence, or triplicate method, involves locating an R wave on a bold line on the ECG paper (Figure 3-5). Let's refer to that as the "start point." Each bold line to the right of the start point has a value that denotes

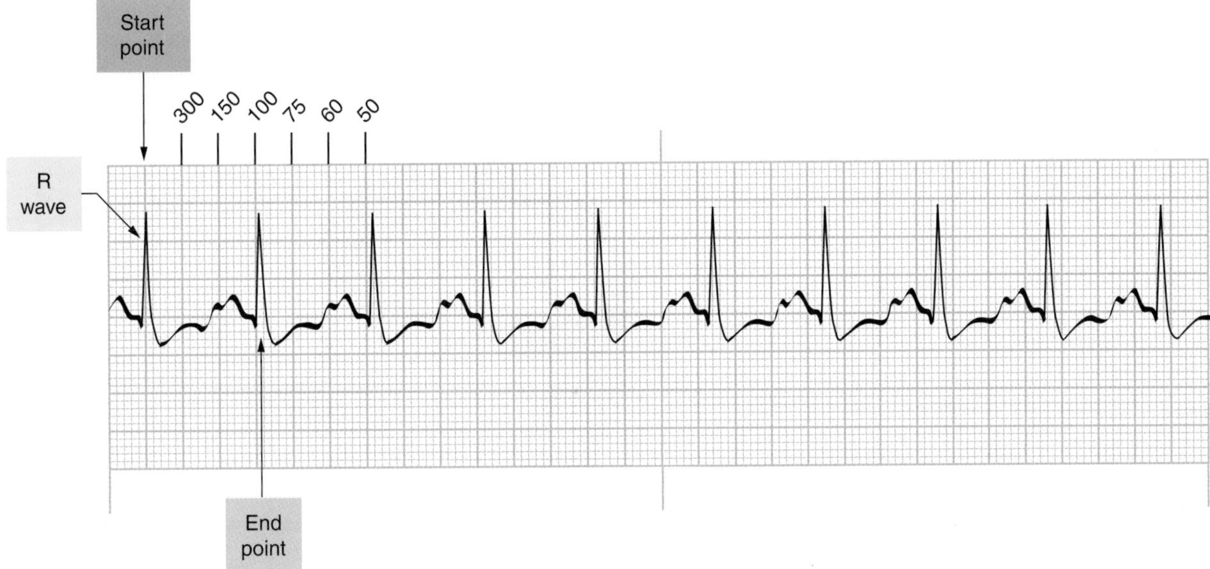

Figure 3-5
The 300, 150, 100, 75, 60, 50 method involves locating an R wave (or P wave) on a bold line on the ECG paper (the **start point**). Each bold line to the right of the start point has a value that denotes the heart rate. The **end point** is where the next R wave (or P wave) is located. The rate shown in this ECG tracing is just under 100 beats per minute.

INSTRUCTIONAL MOMENT
We sometimes use the terms "R" and "QRS" complex interchangeably. This is because when you are trying to line up the waveform to a bold line, it is much easier to use the tallest of the three waveforms (of the QRS complex), the R wave. While we say to look for an R wave, we mean look for the most prominent deflection of the QRS complex. In some cases the S wave may be the most prominent.

INSTRUCTIONAL MOMENT
To determine the heart rate using the 300, 150, 100, 75, 60, 50 method, it is acceptable to move either right or left of the start point. Sometimes you can find better alignments of the R waves and the bold lines looking to the left instead of to the right.

INSTRUCTIONAL MOMENT
An easy way to determine the rate when the R wave does not fall on a bold line is to place a piece of paper over the ECG tracing, then mark it where the first R falls. Next, mark it where the second R wave falls. Slide the paper to the right or left until the first mark lines up with a bold line. Use the second mark to identify the heart rate.

the heart rate. The first bold line is the 300 line. The bold line after that is the 150 line, the one after that is the 100 line, the next line is 75, the line after that is 60, and the next line is 50. Assume for a minute that you are assessing the heart rate. You have located an R wave that falls on a bold line. If the next R wave falls on the second bold line the heart rate is 150 beats per minute. If the next R wave falls on the fourth bold line then the heart rate is 75 beats per minute. Therefore, to calculate the heart rate:

1. Find an R wave located on a bold line, and then
2. Find the next consecutive R wave. If it is on a bold line then the heart rate is the value of that line (300, 150, 100, 75, 60, 50).

An advantage of the 300, 150, 100, 75, 60, 50 method is that it is quick; fairly accurate; and requires no special tools, calculations, or rulers (Figure 3-6). A disadvantage is that this method can only be used if the rhythm is regular.

If the heart rate is less than 50 beats per minute, then the next bold line (following the 50 line) has a value of 43, and the line following that has a value of 37. If it is slower than 37, then it is necessary to use the 6-second interval × 10 method to determine the heart rate.

If the second R wave falls between two bold lines, you can more precisely determine the heart rate if you use identified values for each of the thin lines (Figure 3-7). This set of values is not as easy to remember as the 300, 150, 100, 75, 60, 50 method, so having a cheat sheet or rate calculator is a good idea.

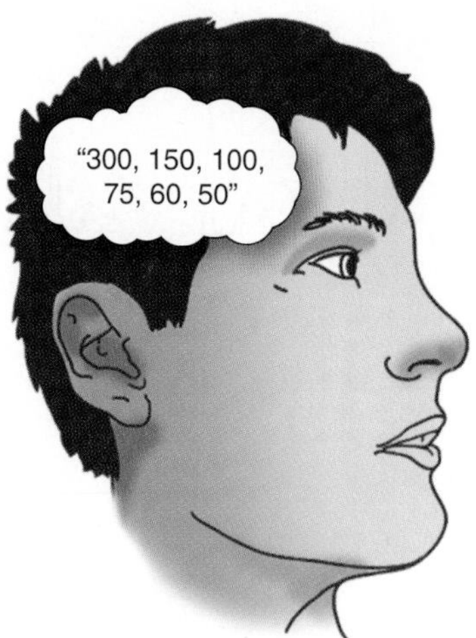

Figure 3-6
The key to using the 300, 150, 100, 75, 60, 50 method is memorizing the value for each of the lines.

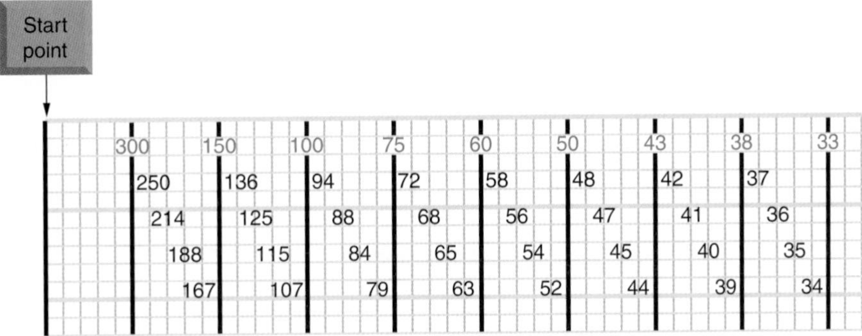

Figure 3-7
Using the identified values shown above for each of the thin lines allows you to more precisely determine the heart rate.

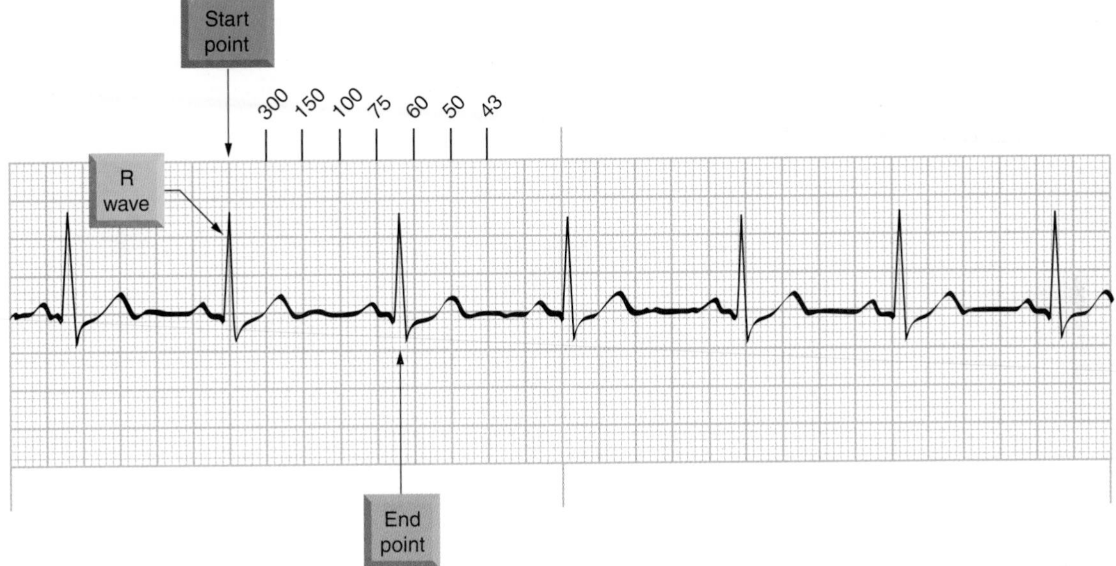

Figure 3-8
When the second R wave doesn't fall on a bold line, we can approximate the heart rate. The heart rate of this tracing is between 60 and 75 beats per minute.

INSTRUCTIONAL MOMENT
Here are some examples of calculating heart rates using this method: (1) A QRS falls on the start point while the next QRS falls on the third bold line to the right—the patient has a heart rate of 100; (2) a QRS falls on the start point while the next QRS falls on the fifth bold line to the right—the patient has a heart rate of 60; (3) a QRS falls on the start point while the next QRS falls on the second bold line to the right—the patient has a heart rate of 150.

Alternatively, when the second R wave does not fall on a bold line you can approximate the heart rate (Figure 3-8). For example, if it falls between the third and fourth lines you can say the heart rate is "between 75 and 100 beats per minute."

This method can also be used to calculate the atrial rate. Begin by finding the peak of a P wave that falls on a bold line. Then locate the next consecutive P wave. The values for each bold (and thin) line are the same as previously described.

KEY CONCEPT

You can quickly determine the heart rate by locating an R wave that falls on a bold line on the ECG paper, then locating the next R wave. Each bold line to the right of the start point has a value that denotes the approximate heart rate (300, 150, 100, 75, 60, 50).

The 300, 150, 100, 75, 60, 50 method involves locating an ____________ wave on a ____________ line on the ECG paper. This is referred to as the ____________ point. The bold lines to the right of the start point have values that denote the heart ____________. From highest to lowest, the values for these next lines are ____________, ____________, ____________, ____________, ____________, ____________.

[R] [bold] [start] [rate] [300] [150] [100] [75] [60] [50]

INSTRUCTIONAL MOMENT

The two quickest methods for determining the heart rate are the 6-second interval × 10 method and the 300, 150, 100, 75, 60, 50 method.

You can practice determining heart rate using the 300, 150, 100, 75, 60, 50 method with the *Practice Makes Perfect* exercises on page 90. Answers to these exercises can be found in Appendix A.

1500 Method

Another way to calculate the heart rate is to use the *1500* method, so named because 1500 small squares on the ECG paper are equal to 1 minute (Figure 3-9). To use this method, count the number of small squares between two consecutive R waves and divide 1500 by that number. For example, if you have 20 small squares (equal to four large boxes) the heart rate is 75 beats per minute (1500 ÷ 20 = 75). This can be used to calculate the atrial rate as well by measuring the number of small squares between the peaks of two consecutive P waves.

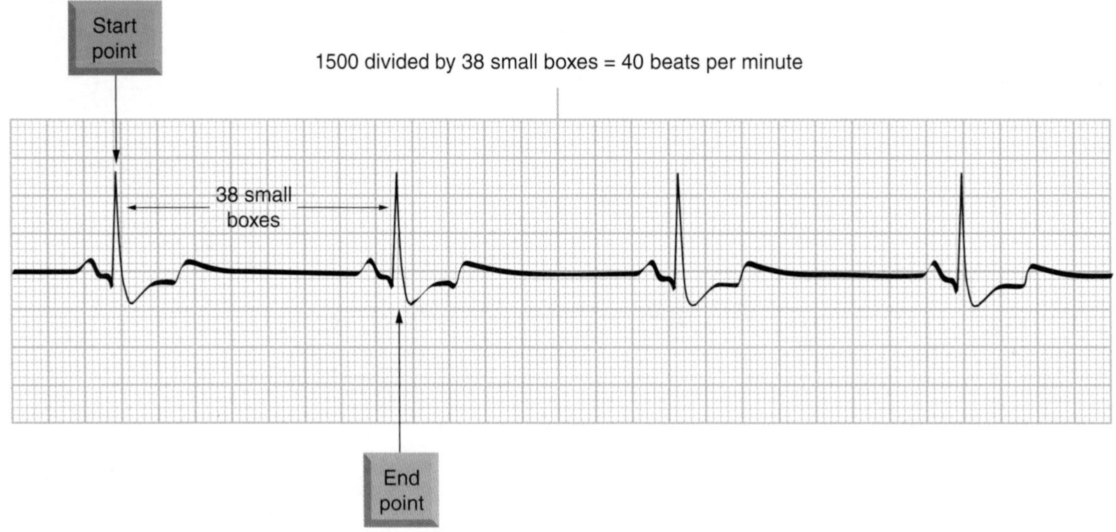

Figure 3-9

To use the 1500 method, count the number of small squares between two consecutive R waves and divide 1500 by that number.

An advantage of the 1500 method is that it is the most accurate and requires no special tools or rulers. Disadvantages of this method are that it requires you to do math at a time when things may be extremely hectic, and you cannot use it if the rhythm is irregular.

The 1500 method involves counting the number of ______________ squares between two consecutive ______________ waves and dividing ______________ by that number.

[small] [R] [1500]

You can practice determining heart rate using the 1500 method with the *Practice Makes Perfect* exercises on page 91. Answers to these exercises can be found in Appendix A.

Rate Calculators

Rate calculators are easy to use (Figure 3-10). They typically have a start mark at one end and numbers indicating the rate along the bottom. Begin by placing the calculator over the ECG tracing. Position the start mark on an R wave. Find the next consecutive R wave. Where the next R wave lines up, is the approximate heart rate.

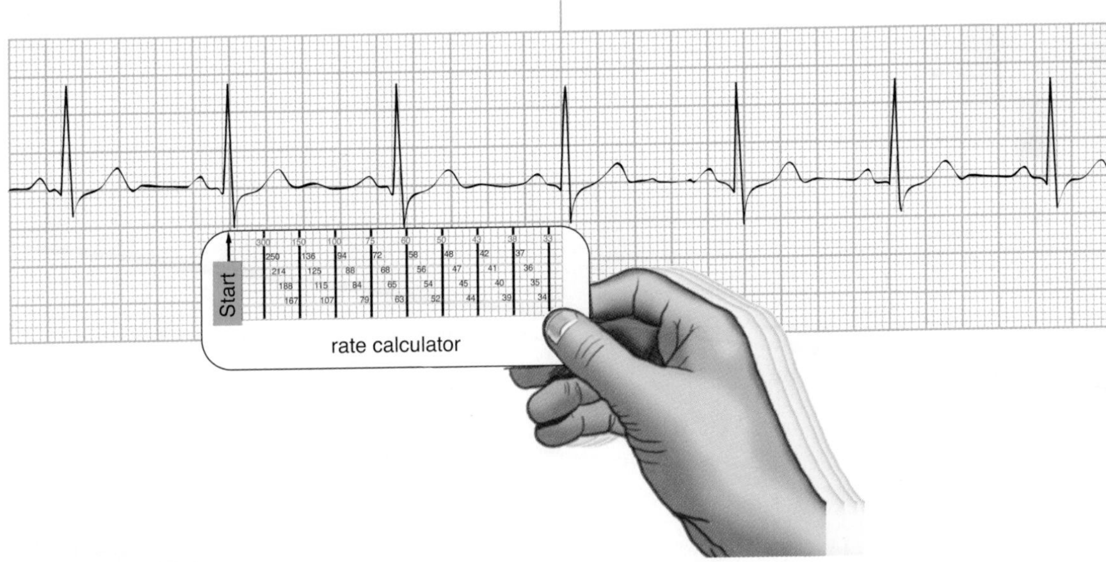

Figure 3-10
To use a heart rate calculator, begin by placing the calculator over the ECG tracing. Position the start mark on an R wave, then find the next consecutive wave. Where that next R wave lines up is the approximate heart rate.

The advantage of these devices is that they allow you to quickly identify the heart rate. The disadvantages are that you must have it available any time you need to calculate a patient's heart rate, and they cannot be used on irregular rhythms.

A heart rate calculator is included on the back cover of this book. You can practice determining heart rate using the rate calculator with the *Practice Makes Perfect* exercises on page 92. Answers to this exercise can be found in Appendix A.

KEY CONCEPT
You count the P waves to determine the atrial rate and the QRS complexes to determine the ventricular rate.

Counting Both the Atrial and Ventricular Rates

While we talk about counting the QRS complexes to determine the ventricular rate, we also count the P waves to determine the atrial rate (Figure 3-11). In some dysrhythmias, the atrial rate may be less than or greater than the ventricular rate. The rate calculating methods previously discussed can also be used to identify the atrial rate.

QUESTION
"Which of the heart's pacemaker sites is considered the 'primary pacemaker'?" (The answer can be found on page 105.)

We count the ______________ to determine the ventricular rate. To determine the atrial rate, we count the ______________.

[QRS complexes] [P waves]

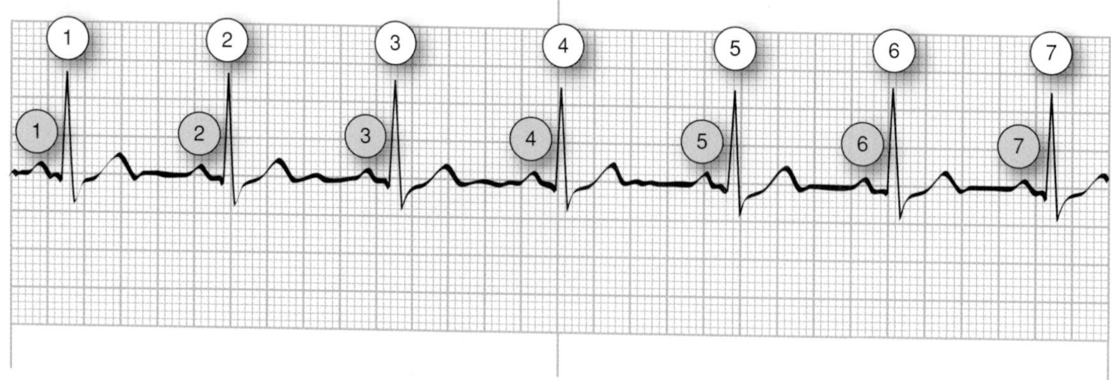

Figure 3-11
When calculating the heart rate, count the number of QRS complexes (for the ventricular rate) and P waves (for the atrial rate). They should be the same. In this 6-second ECG tracing, there are 7 QRS complexes and 7 P waves. Using the 6-second interval × 10 method, the ventricular and atrial rate are 70 beats per minute.

PRACTICE. . . MAKES PERFECT

4. Determine the heart rate using the 6-second interval × 10 method.

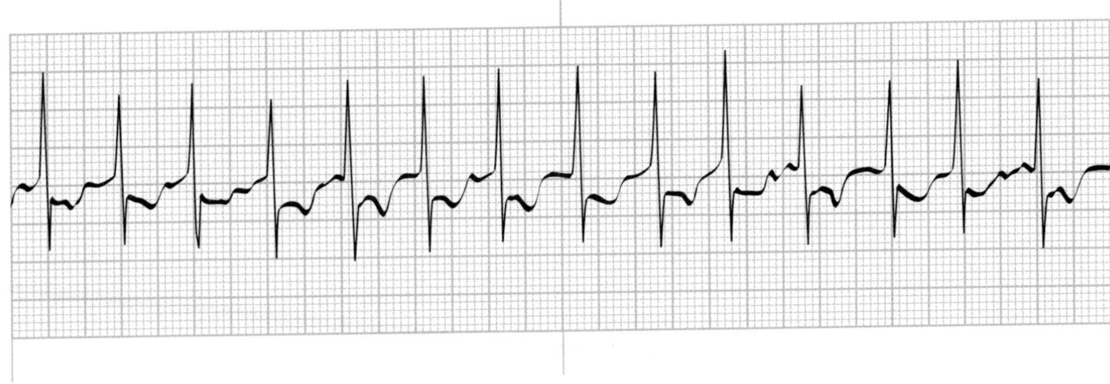

Heart rate _______________ .

5. Determine the heart rate using the 6-second interval × 10 method.

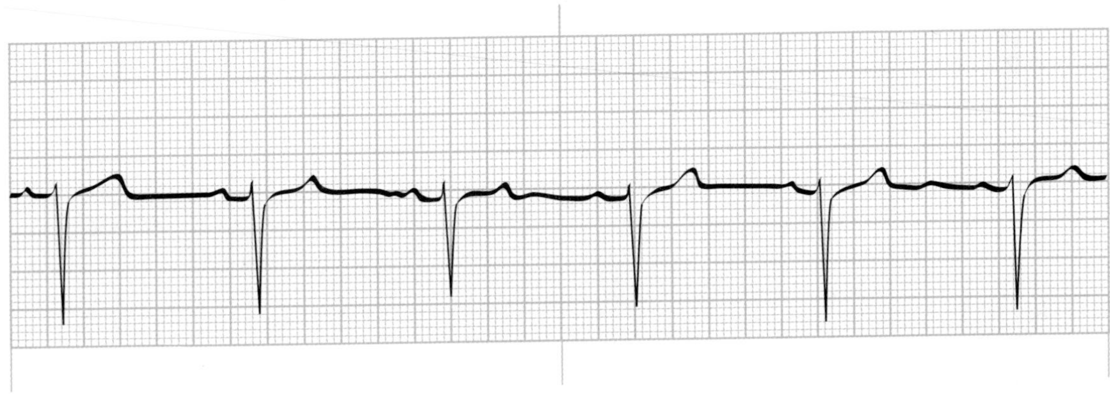

Heart rate _______________ .

6. Determine the heart rate using the 6-second interval × 10 method.

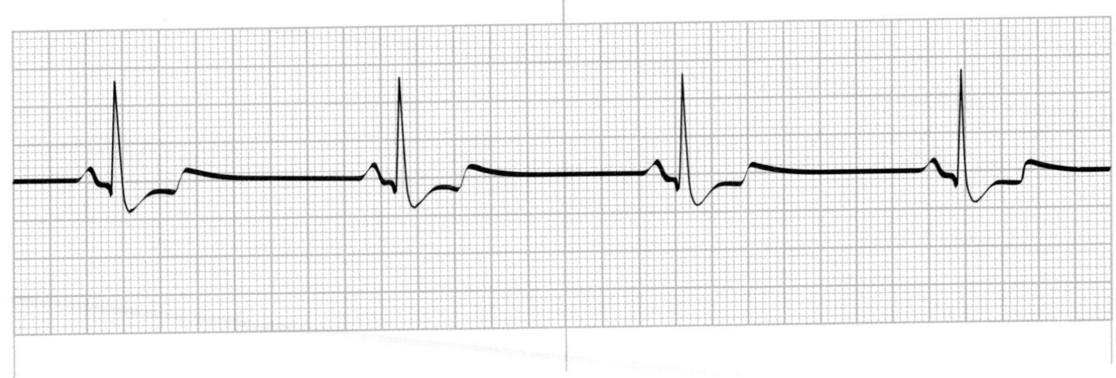

Heart rate _______________ .

PRACTICE. . . MAKES PERFECT

7. Determine the heart rate using the 6 second interval ×10 method.

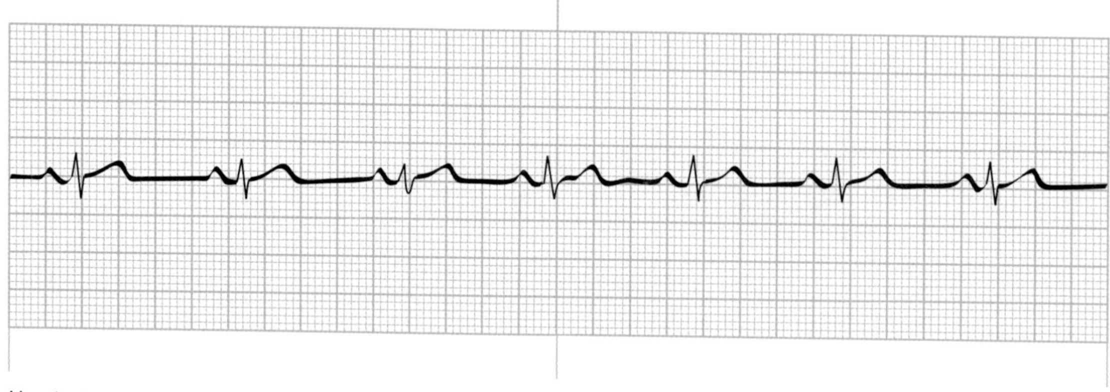

Heart rate ______________ .

8. Determine the heart rate using the 300, 150, 100, 75, 60, 50 method.

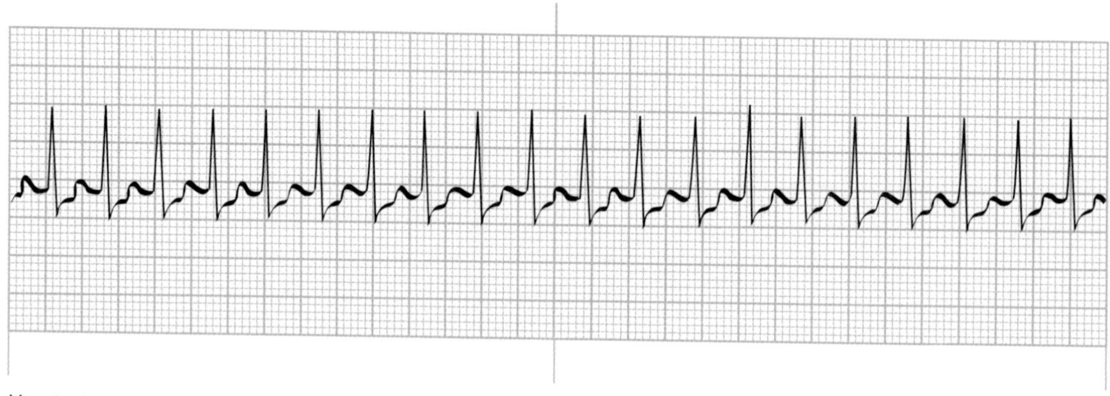

Heart rate ______________ .

9. Determine the heart rate using the 300, 150, 100, 75, 60, 50 method.

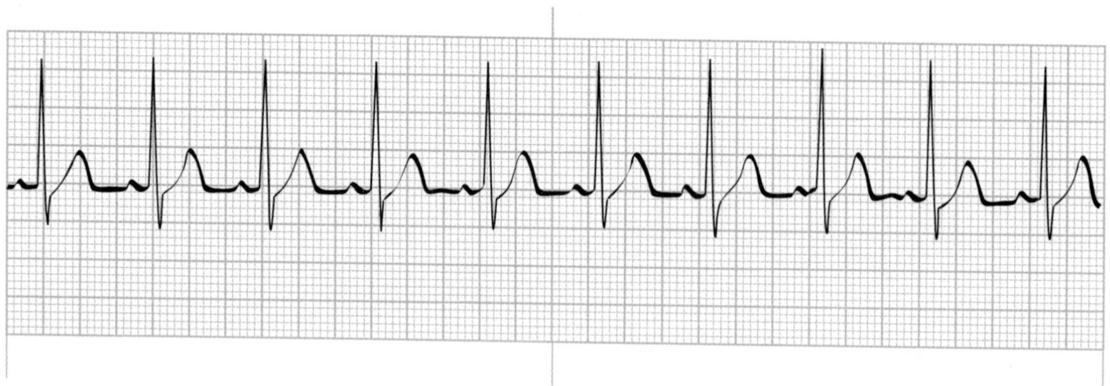

Heart rate ______________ .

PRACTICE. . . MAKES PERFECT

10. Determine the heart rate using the 1500 method.

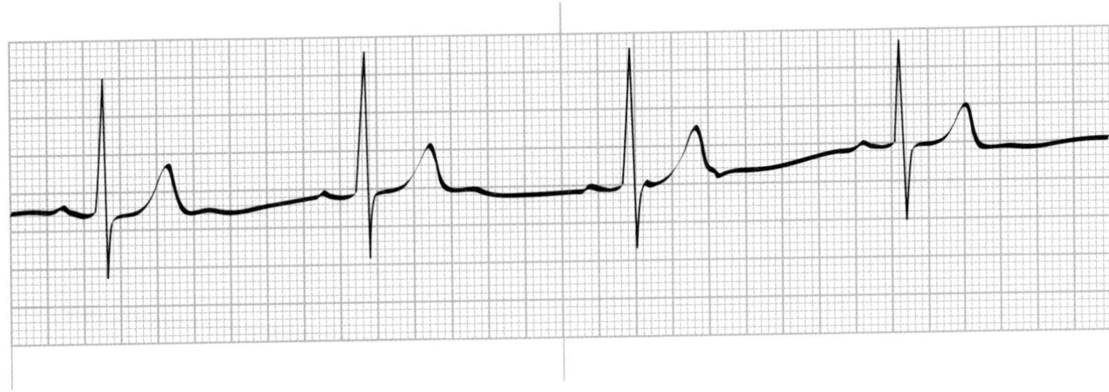

Heart rate ______________ .

11. Determine the heart rate using the 1500 method.

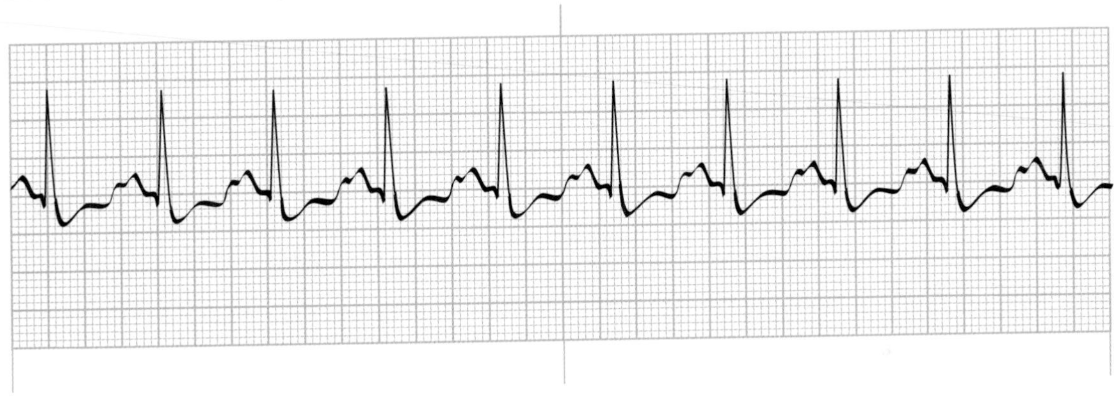

Heart rate ______________ .

12. Determine the heart rate using the 1500 method.

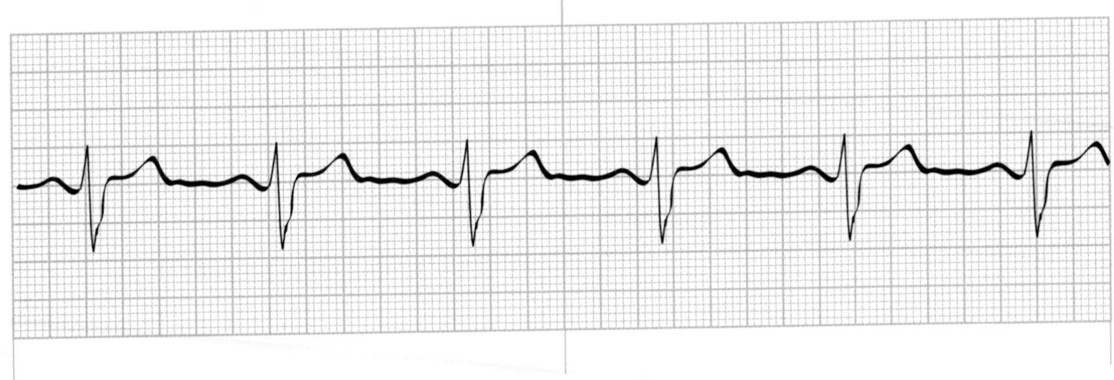

Heart rate ______________ .

PRACTICE. . . MAKES PERFECT

13. Determine the heart rate using the heart rate calculator.

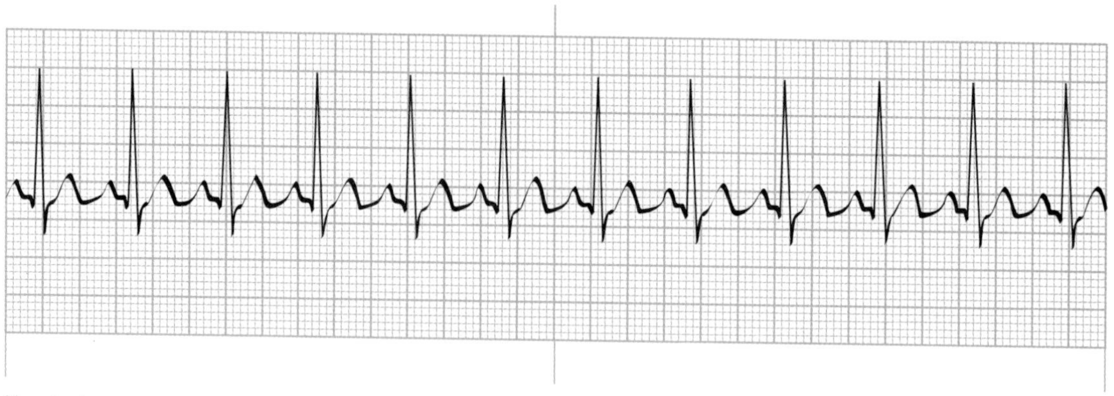

Heart rate ______________ .

INSTRUCTIONAL MOMENT
In the following, we discuss the types of dysrhythmias that lead to slow and fast heart rates. Don't worry about knowing any more about the dysrhythmias than what we discuss. We will review these dysrhythmias in more depth later in the book.

Normal, Slow, and Fast Rates

In the average adult, the normal heart rate is 60 to 100 beats per minute. Normal sinus rhythm, as well as many dysrhythmias (to be discussed in later chapters), characteristically have a normal rate.

Rates above 100 beats per minute or below 60 beats per minute are considered abnormal. When we say abnormal we don't necessarily mean it is a bad thing, but rather it is outside the normal range.

Slow Rates—Bradycardia

A heart rate less than 60 beats per minute is called **bradycardia** and can occur for many reasons. It may or may not have an adverse affect on cardiac output. In the extreme it can lead to severe reductions in cardiac output and eventually deteriorate into asystole (an absence of heart rhythm).

KEY CONCEPT
A heart rate less than 60 beats per minute is called bradycardia.

________________ is a heart rate less than 60 beats per minute.

[Bradycardia]

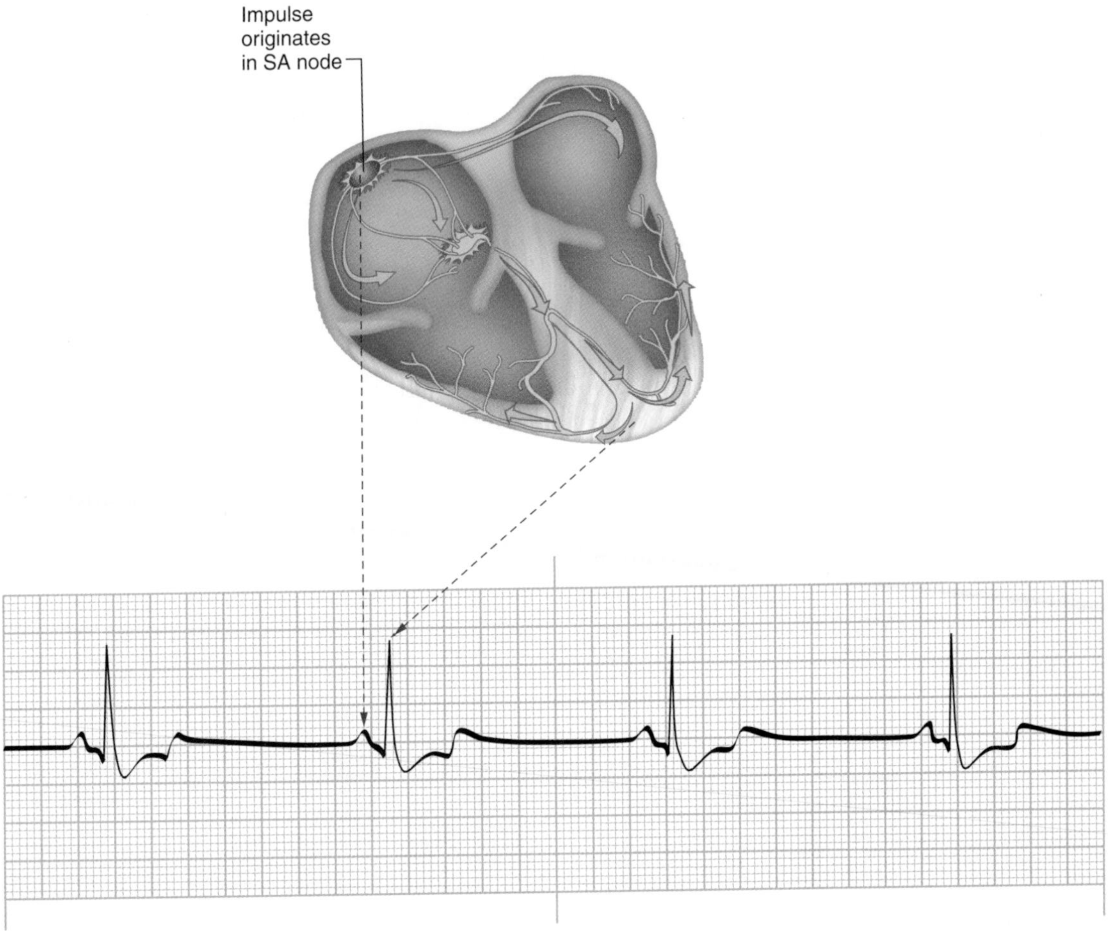

Impulse originates in SA node

Figure 3-12
Sinus bradycardia is a slow rate that arises from the SA node.

Sinus Bradycardia

Sinus bradycardia is a slow rate that arises from the SA node (Figure 3-12). Sometimes it occurs because the patient is at rest. Remember, the parasympathetic branch of the autonomic nervous system slows the heart rate. In some cases, a person's normal heart rate may be slower than 60 beats per minute. An athlete's heart, for example, doesn't beat as fast because his or her body is more efficient and does not require as much oxygen. Other causes of slow heart rate include increased parasympathetic (vagal) tone, intrinsic sinus node disease, hypothermia, hypoxia, drug effects (e.g., digitalis, beta blockers, calcium channel blockers), myocardial infarction, and others.

QUESTION
"What effect may bradycardia have on cardiac output?" (The answer can be found on page 105.)

The ______________ branch of the autonomic nervous systems slows the heart rate. ______________ bradycardia is a slow rate that arises from the SA node.

[parasympathetic] [Sinus]

QUESTION
"Using the 6-second interval × 10 method to determine the heart rate, bradycardia is present if there are less than how many QRS complexes?" (The answer can be found on page 105.)

SA Node Arrest

Bradycardia can also be brought about by failure of the SA node, the heart's primary pacemaker (Figure 3-13). When this occurs, either the SA node will initiate an impulse or an escape pacemaker from either the AV node or the ventricles should take over and initiate the heartbeat. Remember, the intrinsic rate of the AV node is 40 to 60 beats per minute, while the ventricle's is 20 to 40 beats per minute (see Chapter 1). Whether the escape pacemaker arises from the AV node (called junctional escape) or ventricles (called ventricular escape or idioventricular rhythm), it is likely to produce bradycardia.

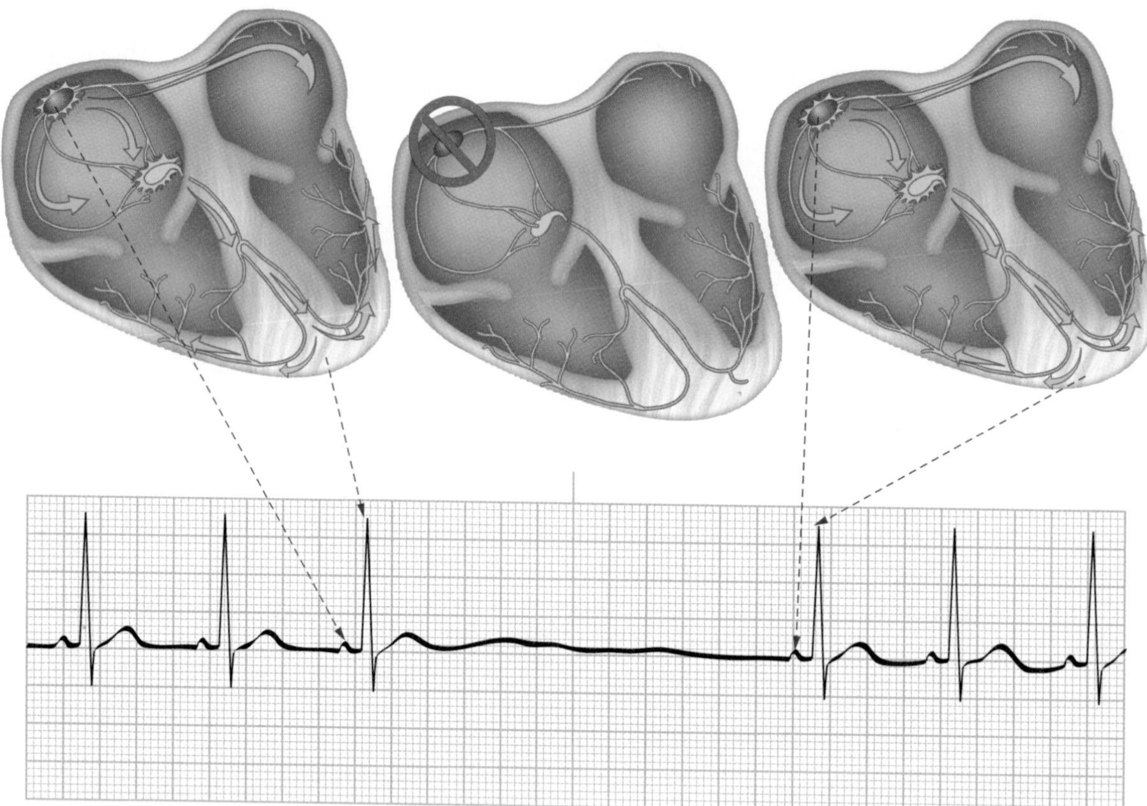

Figure 3-13
Sinus arrest occurs when the SA node fails to initiate an impulse. Because of the dropped beat(s) it can result in bradycardia.

When the heart's primary pacemaker fails, an ______________ pacemaker from either the ______________ or the ______________ should take over and initiate the heartbeat. Both sites have a ______________ intrinsic rate than the SA node.

[escape] [AV node] [ventricles] [slower]

QUESTION
"What is the intrinsic rate of the SA node?" (The answer can be found on page 106.)

Blockage of the AV Node With Slow Ventricular Rates

Blockage of the impulse traveling through the AV node can also be a cause of bradycardia (Figure 3-14). In one type, called 2nd-degree AV heart block, not all the sinus beats are conducted through to the ventricles; this results in a slower ventricular rate (as such, there are more P waves than QRS complexes). With a more severe form of AV heart block, called 3rd-degree AV heart block, there is complete blockage of the AV node. The atria are stimulated to contract by the impulse that originates from the SA node. For this reason the atrial rate should be within a normal range. But because the atrial impulse doesn't reach the ventricles, an escape pacemaker arises from somewhere below the AV node. This results in a slower ventricular rate. The location of the pacemaker site determines the ventricular rate. The closer the escape pacemaker is to the AV node the faster the ventricular rate.

______________ heart blocks can cause a slow heart rate.

[Atrioventricular (AV)]

Rapid Atrial Rates With Slow Ventricular Rates

We may also see slower than normal ventricular rates in conditions where the atria fire and bombard the AV node so rapidly that not all the impulses are conducted through to the ventricles. If the number of atrial impulses reaching the ventricles falls to less than normal, it results in a slower than normal ventricular rate. Two dysrhythmias—atrial flutter and atrial fibrillation (Figure 3-15)—can result in an atrial rate far faster than normal. Atrial flutter produces 250 to 350 atrial impulses per minute while atrial fibrillation produces greater than 350 atrial impulses per minute. When the number of impulses reaching the ventricles falls below normal, it results in bradycardia. We call these conditions atrial flutter or atrial fibrillation with a slow ventricular response.

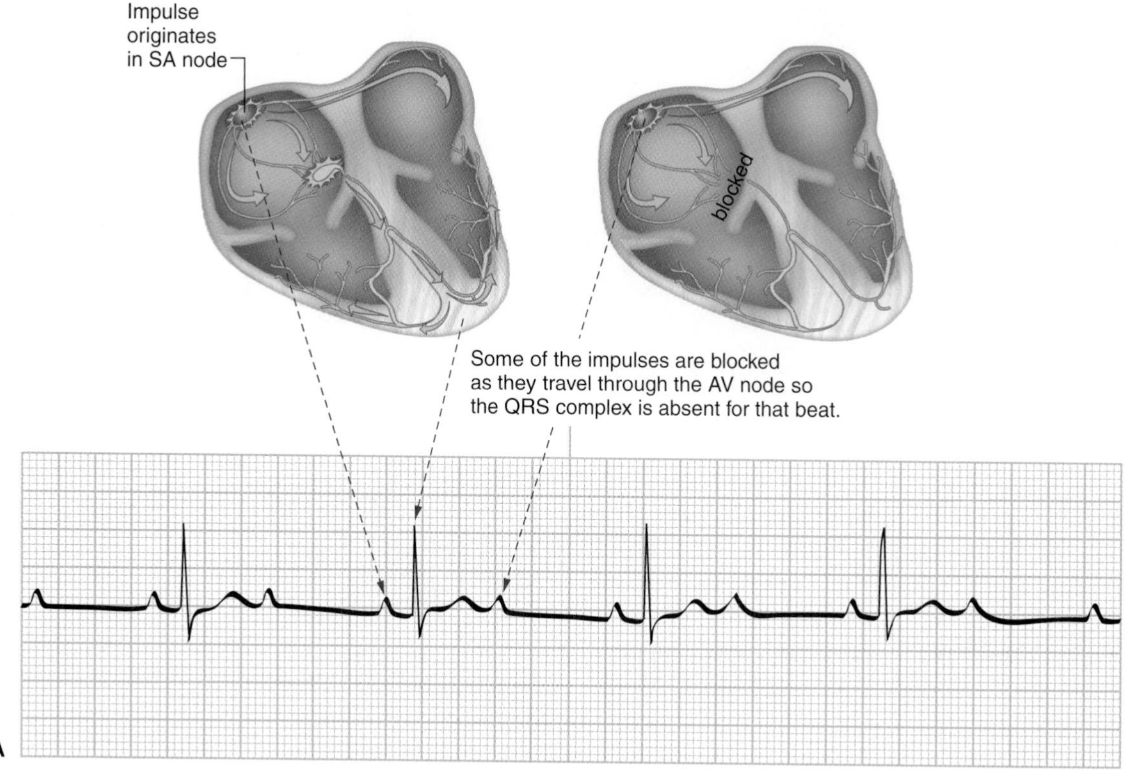

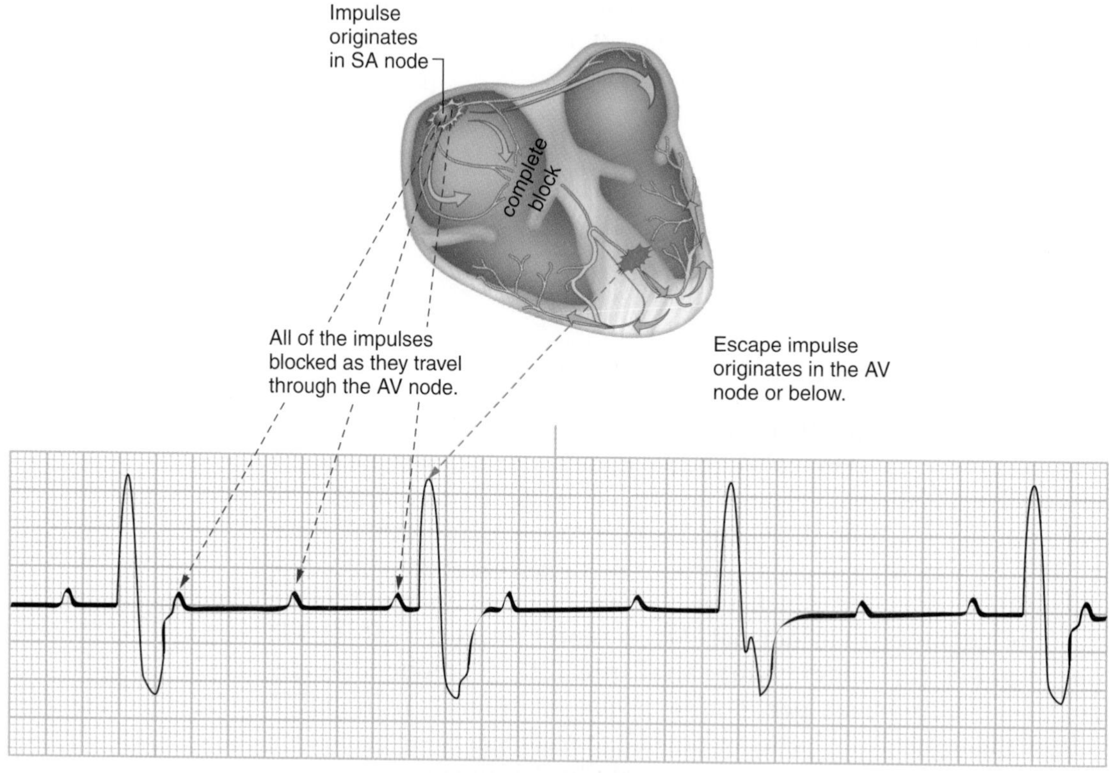

Figure 3-14

(a) In 2nd-degree AV heart block not all the sinus beats are conducted through to the ventricles resulting in a slower ventricular rate. (b) With 3rd-degree AV heart block there is a complete blockage of the AV node resulting in a slower ventricular rate.

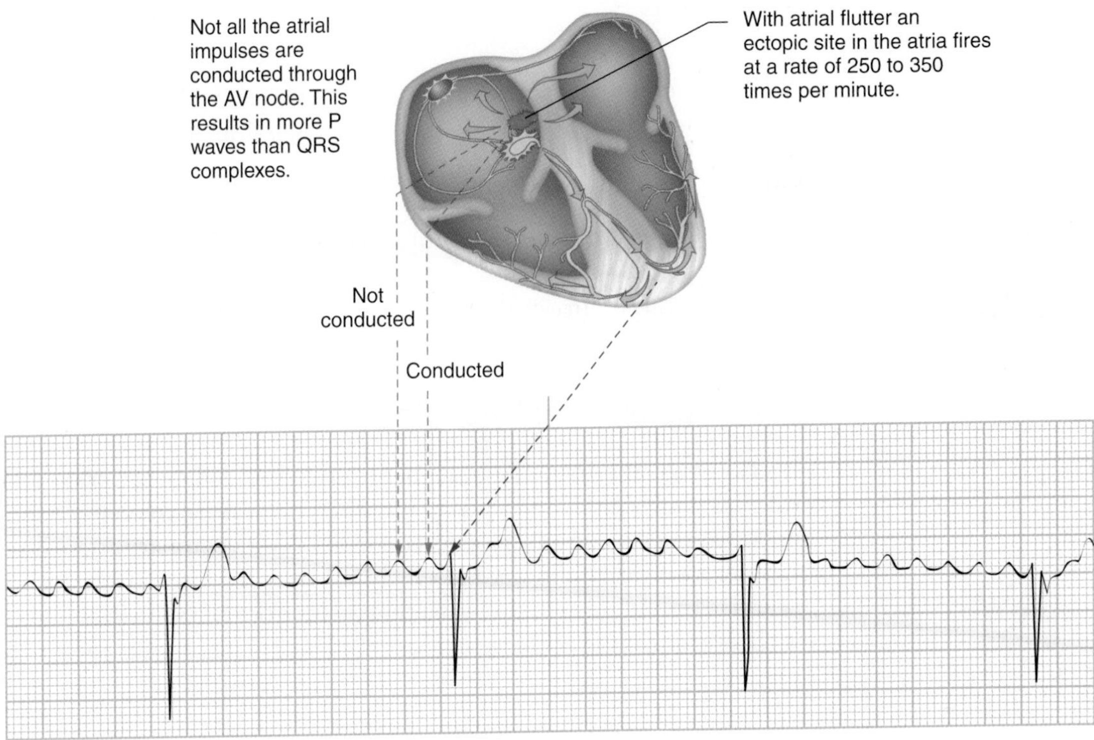

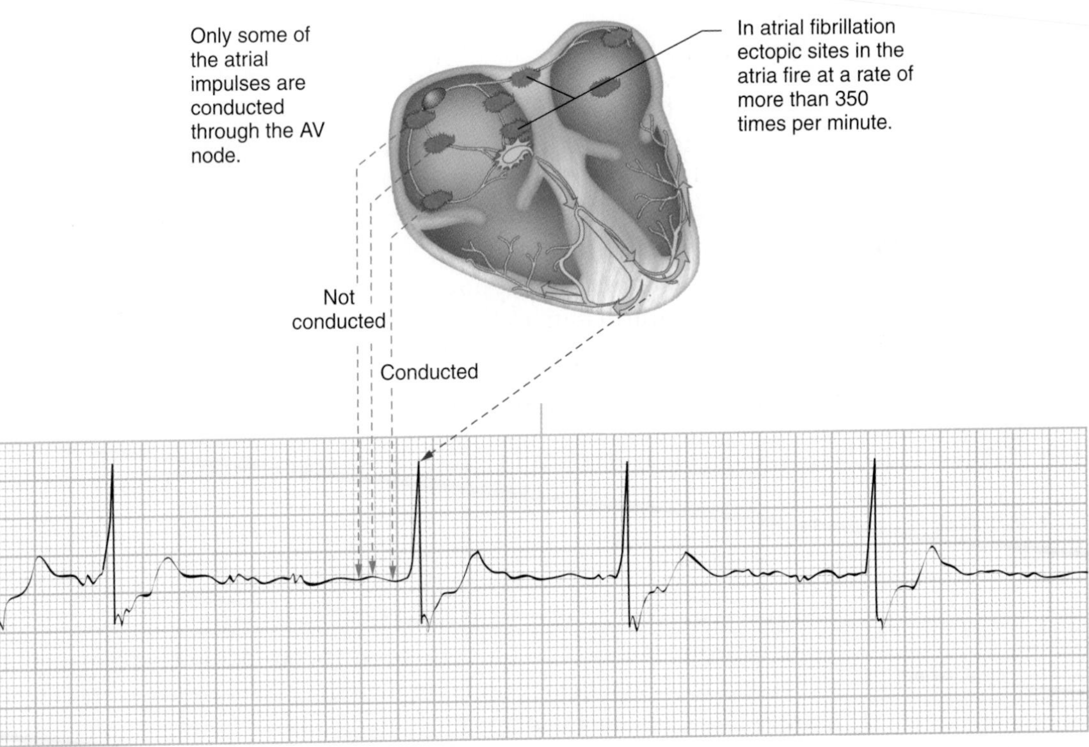

Figure 3-15
With atrial flutter and atrial fibrillation the number of impulses actually reaching the ventricles can fall below normal resulting in a slow ventricular rate.

With atrial ______________ and ______________ the atrial impulses bombard the AV node so ______________ that not all the impulses are conducted through to the ventricles. This can result in a ______________ than normal ventricular rate.

[flutter] [fibrillation] [rapidly] [slower]

QUESTION
"What effect can extremely fast tachycardia have on cardiac output?" (The answer can be found on page 106.)

KEY CONCEPT
A heart rate greater than 100 beats per minute is called tachycardia.

CLINICAL MOMENT
Generally, sinus tachycardia has a maximum rate of 160 to 180 beats per minute.

INSTRUCTIONAL MOMENT
Another term you will hear discussed is paroxysmal supraventricular tachycardia. This is a supraventricular tachycardia that begins abruptly and has a rapid resolution. It may originate in the atria (paroxysmal atrial tachycardia [PAT]) or AV junction (paroxysmal junctional tachycardia [PJT]).

Fast Rates—Tachycardia

A heart rate greater than 100 beats per minute is called tachycardia. Tachycardia has many causes and leads to increased myocardial oxygen consumption, which can have an adverse effect on patients with coronary artery disease and other medical conditions. Extremely fast rates can have an adverse affect on cardiac output. Also, tachycardia that arises from the ventricles may lead to a chaotic quivering of the ventricles called ventricular fibrillation.

Tachycardia is a heart rate greater than _____ beats per minute.

[100]

Sinus Tachycardia

Sinus tachycardia is a fast rate, greater than 100 beats per minute (Figure 3-16), that arises from the SA node. Sinus tachycardia can occur with exercise or exertion. Stress, fear, and anxiety can also bring about tachycardia. The sympathetic branch of the autonomic nervous system is responsible for speeding up the heart rate. Other common causes of sinus tachycardia include fever, hypoxia, shock, drug effects (such as from amphetamines or cocaine), ingestion of caffeine or alcohol, smoking, and myocardial infarction.

Sinus tachycardia is a heart rate of greater than ______________ beats per minute that arises from the ______________ node.

[100] [SA]

Supraventricular and Ventricular Tachycardia

Tachycardia can also be brought about by an ectopic pacemaker (one that arises outside the SA node) in the atria, AV node, or ventricles (Figure 3-17). These tachycardias result from rapid depolarization that overrides the SA node. Tachycardia that arises above the ventricles is called supraventricular tachycardia, whereas tachycardia that arises in the ven-

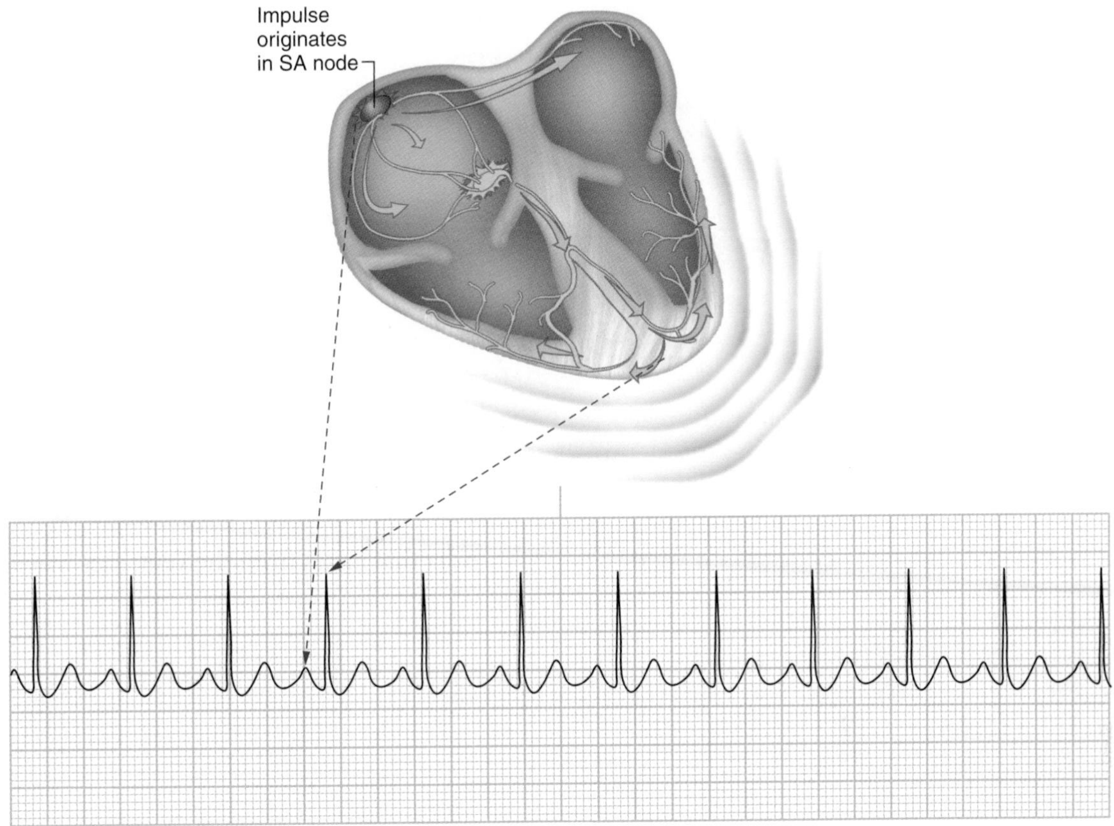

Figure 3-16
Sinus tachycardia is a fast rate that arises from the SA node.

tricles is called ventricular tachycardia. Atrial tachycardia and junctional tachycardia are supraventricular tachycardias (again, as they arise from above the ventricles). The term supraventricular is also used if the origin of the tachycardia cannot be determined as atrial or junctional (often due to the P waves being hidden in the T wave of the preceding beat in faster rates). The heart rate for atrial tachycardia is generally between 150 to 250 beats per minute, junctional tachycardia is generally 100 to 180 beats per minute, and ventricular tachycardia is between 100 to 250 beats per minute.

QUESTION
"What type of tachycardia arises from a site above the ventricles?" (The answer can be found on page 106.)

Tachycardia can also be brought about by an ectopic pacemaker in the

________________, ________________, or ________________.

[atria] [AV node] [ventricles]

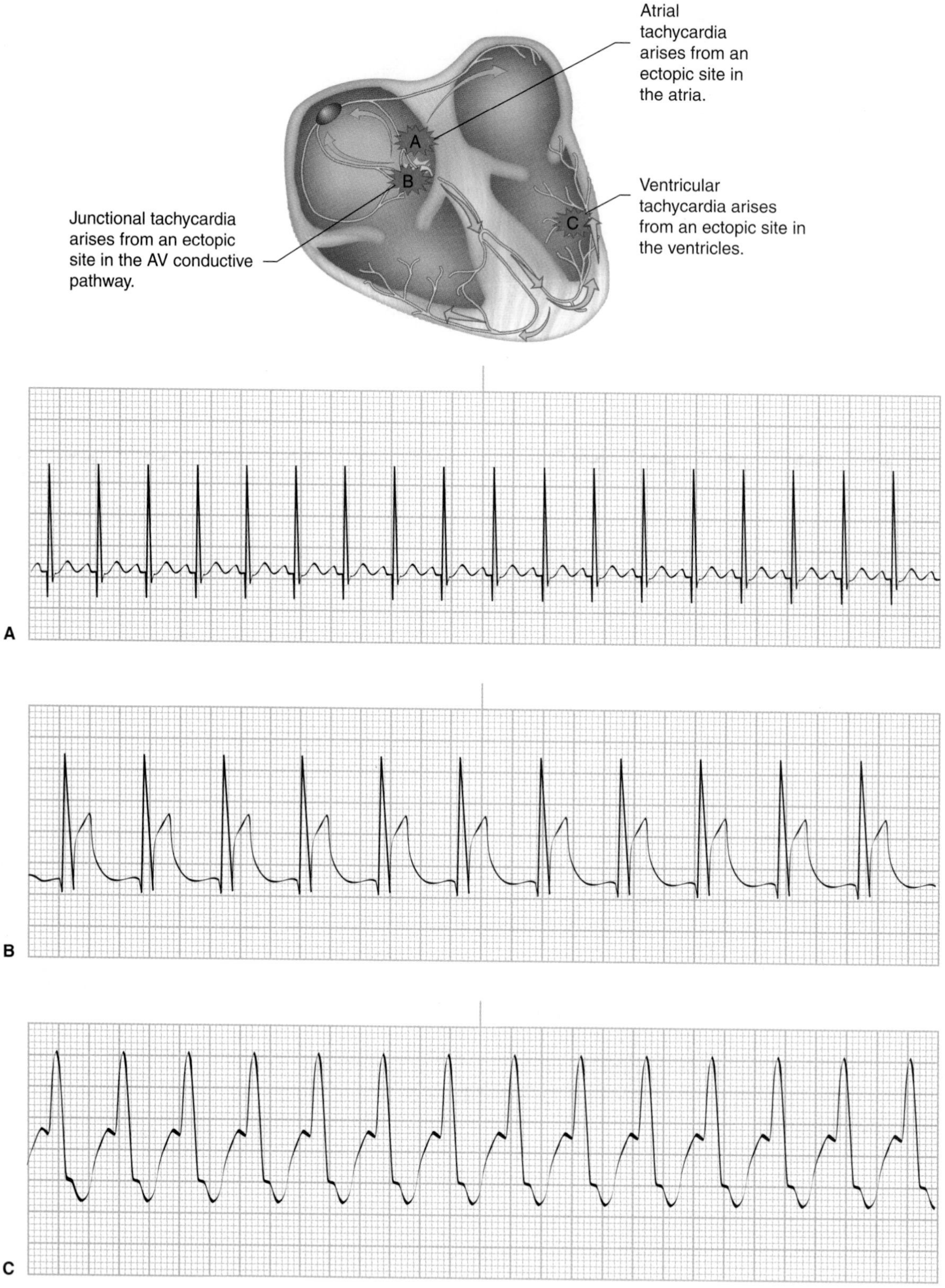

Figure 3-17
Tachycardias from an ectopic site.

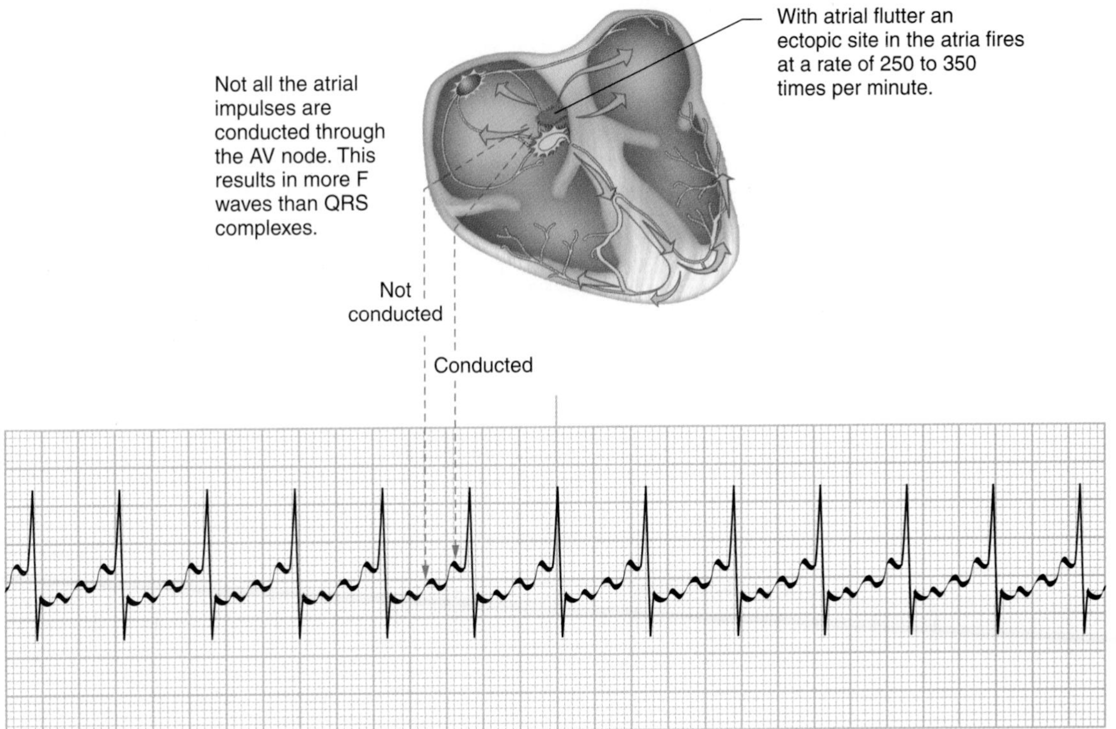

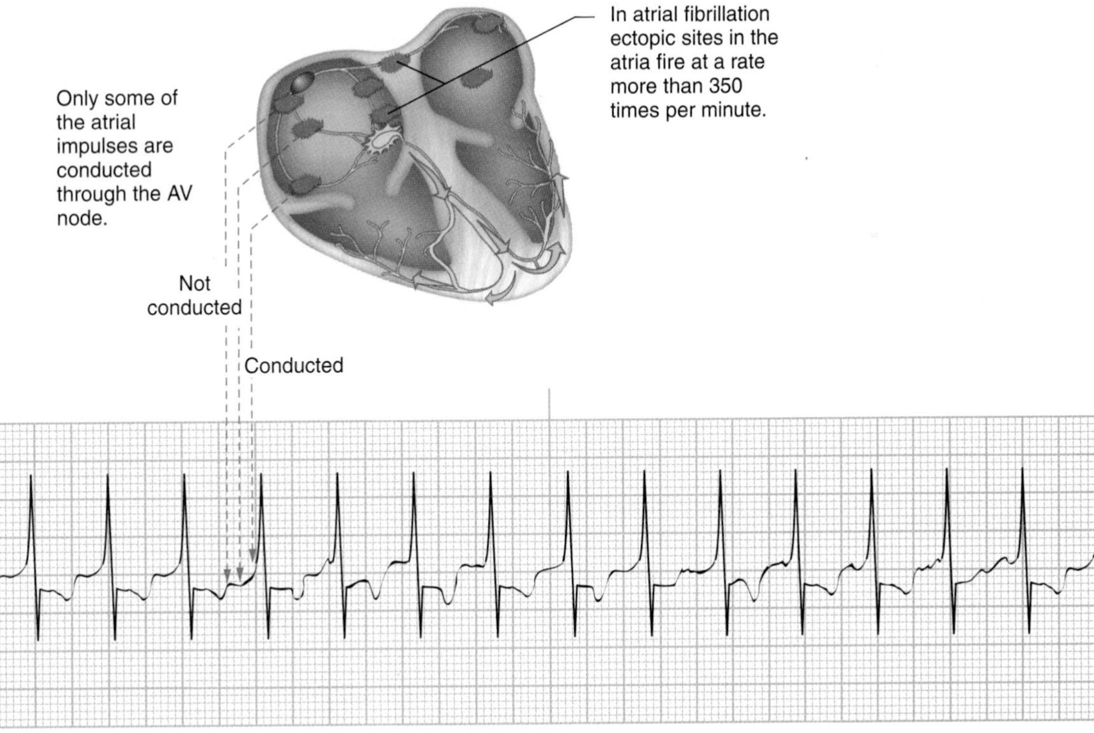

Figure 3-18
With atrial flutter and atrial fibrillation the number of impulses actually reaching the ventricle can be greater than normal resulting in a fast ventricular rate.

Rapid Atrial Rates With Fast Ventricular Rates

In atrial flutter and atrial fibrillation, the ventricular rate can also be faster than normal (Figure 3-18). As discussed earlier, in both of these conditions the atrial rate is far faster than normal. In some cases, the number of atrial impulses actually reaching the ventricles is greater. This results in a faster than normal ventricular rate. We call these conditions atrial flutter with a rapid ventricular response or atrial fibrillation with rapid ventricular response.

With atrial ________________ and ________________, the atrial impulses bombard the AV node ________________ than normal and can result in a ________________ than normal ventricular rate.

[flutter] [fibrillation] [faster] [faster]

Key Points

- Approach each ECG tracing analysis in a logical and systematic manner. If a dysrhythmia is present, compare your finding with your assessment of the patient.
- Some dysrhythmias are no problem to the patient, whereas others are life threatening.
- Successful analysis of ECGs is based on learning the characteristics of each normal and abnormal ECG, then comparing what you see on the ECG tracing to those characteristics.
- The five steps to analyzing an ECG rhythm are determining the (1) heart rate, (2) regularity, (3) presence of and characteristics of P waves, (4) presence of and characteristics of QRS complexes, and (5) presence of and characteristics of the PR intervals.
- Start assessing the heart rate by quickly checking the ECG monitor or tracing to see if the rate is slow, normal, or fast.
- The 6-second interval × 10 method of calculating the heart rate involves multiplying by 10 the number of QRS complexes found in a 6-second portion of the ECG tracing. Because the QRS complexes are measured over 6 seconds, this method is the most effective means for assessing irregular rhythms.
- The 300, 150, 100, 75, 60, 50 method for calculating the heart rate is also called the countdown or sequence method. It involves locating an R wave on a bold line on the ECG paper, then finding the next consecutive R wave and using the 300, 150, 100, 75, 60, 50 values for subsequent bold lines to determine the rate.
- To use the 1500 method, you count the number of small squares between two consecutive R waves and divide 1500 by that number.
- Rate calculators are easy to use and can effectively determine the heart rate.

- We count the QRS complexes to determine the ventricular rate and count the P waves to determine the atrial rate.
- Rates above or below 60 to 100 beats per minute in the typical adult are considered abnormal.
- A heart rate less than 60 beats per minute is called bradycardia. The dysrhythmias that will or are likely to have slow heart rates are sinus bradycardia, junctional escape rhythm, idioventricular rhythm, AV heart block and atrial flutter, or fibrillation with slow ventricular response.
- A heart rate greater than 100 beats per minute is called tachycardia. The dysrhythmias that will or are likely to have fast heart rates are sinus tachycardia, atrial tachycardia, junctional tachycardia, ventricular tachycardia and atrial flutter, or fibrillation with rapid ventricular response.
- Both extremely slow and fast heart rates can result in decreased cardiac output.

Assess Your Understanding

The following questions give you a chance to assess your understanding of the material discussed in this chapter. The answers can be found in Appendix A.

1. To analyze an ECG tracing you should
   a. count the QRS complexes, but not the P waves.
   b. compare it to examples of ECGs found in various textbooks.
   c. use a logical and systematic approach.
   d. begin by assessing the QRS complexes.
2. Which of the following is true regarding dysrhythmias?
   a. All dysrhythmias are life threatening.
   b. Each dysrhythmia has specific characteristics.
   c. Dysrhythmias are normal rhythms.
   d. Dysrhythmias typically lead to reduced cardiac output.
3. The first step in analyzing an ECG is
   a. checking the regularity.
   b. looking at the P waves.
   c. assessing the PR intervals.
   d. determining the heart rate.
4. The 6-second interval × 10 method
   a. can be used to estimate the heart rate in irregular rhythms.
   b. involves multiplying by 25 the number of QRS complexes found in a 6-second portion of the ECG tracing.
   c. is the most accurate method of determining the heart rate.
   d. can only be used to determine the ventricular rate.
5. The 300, 150, 100, 75, 60, 50 method
   a. can be used to measure the heart rate in irregular rhythms.
   b. involves identifying a T wave that falls on a bold line.
   c. requires the use of a rate calculator to determine the heart rate.
   d. requires you to identify a start point from which to identify where the next R wave falls.
6. To use the 1500 method,
   a. count the number of small squares between two consecutive R waves and divide 1500 by that number.
   b. find an R wave that falls on a bold line and begin counting the small squares.
   c. count the number of QRS complexes in a 6-second section of the ECG tracing.
   d. divide by 1500 the number of QRS complexes in a 3-second section of the ECG tracing.

7. Which one of the following methods for determining the heart rate in a regular rhythm is the most accurate?
   a. 6-second interval × 10 method
   b. 300, 150, 100, 75, 60, 50 method
   c. 1500 method
   d. Quick assessment method
8. A rhythm that arises from the SA node and has a heart rate of less than 60 beats per minute is called
   a. junctional escape.
   b. idioventricular rhythm.
   c. sinus bradycardia.
   d. normal sinus rhythm.
9. Tachycardia
   a. is a dysrhythmia that has a heart rate greater than 80 beats per minute.
   b. leads to decreased myocardial oxygen consumption.
   c. can be produced by stimulation of the parasympathetic nervous system.
   d. may be brought about by exercise or exertion.

10. Identify the heart rate of the following ECG.

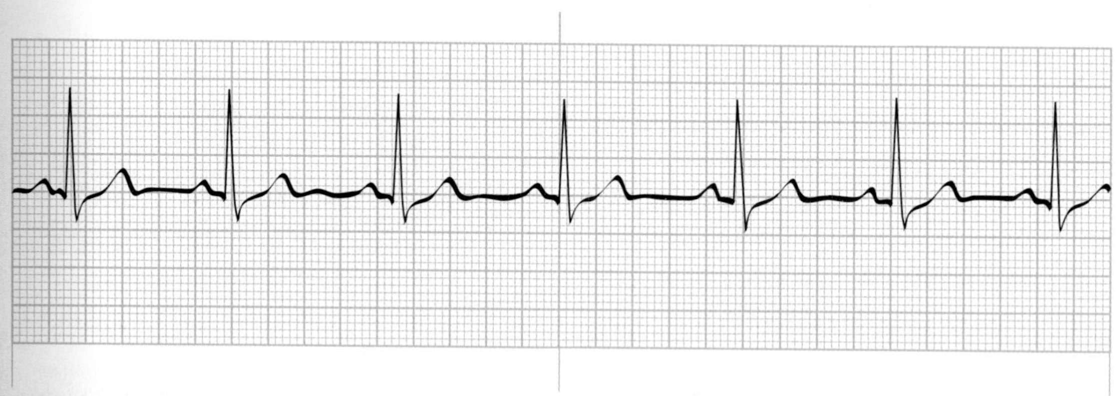

Heart rate ______________.

11. Identify the heart rate of the following ECG.

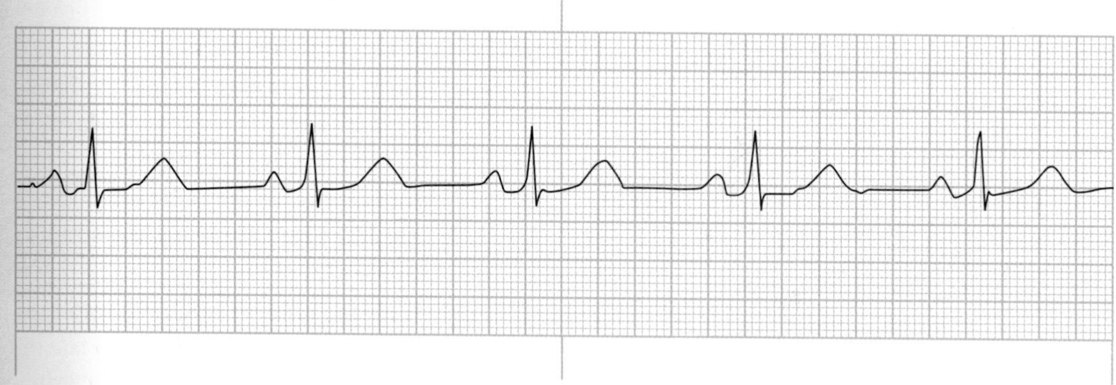

Heart rate ______________.

12. Identify the heart rate of the following ECG.

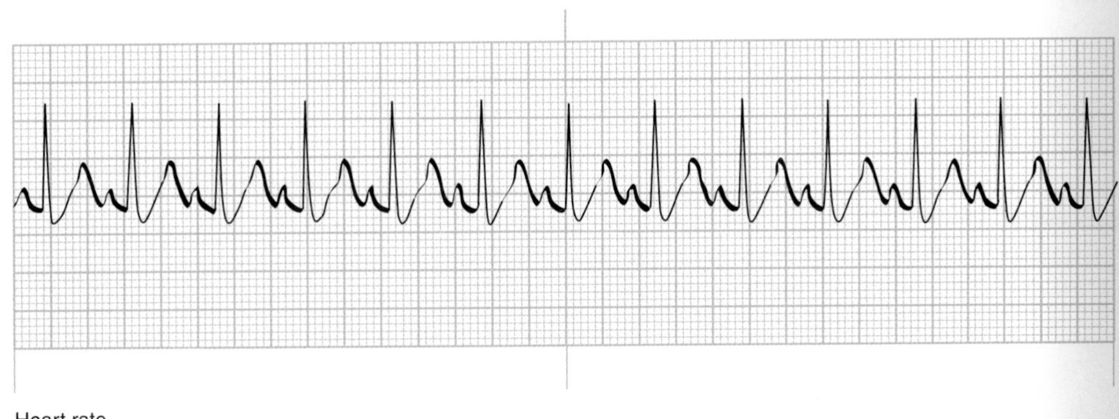

Heart rate _______________ .

Referring to the scenario at the beginning of this chapter, answer the following questions.

13. It is unlikely that the patient's heart rate was actually 320 because
    a. she was awake.
    b. her blood pressure was not low.
    c. she was able to answer questions.
    d. All of the above.

14. The most likely cause of the patient's fast heart rate was
    a. anxiety.
    b. hypoxia.
    c. hyperthyroidism.
    d. amphetamine use.

Answers to Sidebar Questions

"The normal QRS complex will extend over how many small boxes?"

Answer: The normal QRS complex extends over one-and-one-half to three boxes.

"What is the range of the normal heart rate in the adult?"

Answer: The normal heart rate range in the adult is 60 to 100 beats per minute.

"Which of the heart's pacemaker sites is considered the primary pacemaker?"

Answer: The SA node is the primary pacemaker of the heart.

"What effect may bradycardia have on cardiac output?"

Answer: Cardiac output is a product of heart rate × stroke volume. If we reduce the heart rate, it may reduce cardiac output.

"Using the 6-second interval × 10 method to determine the heart rate, bradycardia is present if there are less than how many QRS complexes?"

Answer: In bradycardia there are less than six QRS complexes in the 6-second portion of the ECG tracing.

"What is the intrinsic rate of the SA node?"

Answer: The SA node has an intrinsic rate of 60 to 100 beats per minute.

"What effect can extremely fast tachycardia have on cardiac output?"

Answer: Cardiac output is a product of heart rate × stroke volume. Extremely fast heart rates reduce stroke volume by not allowing enough time between heartbeats for the ventricles (and coronary arteries) to refill with blood. A reduction in stroke volume can lead to decreased cardiac output.

"What type of tachycardia arises from a site above the ventricles?"

Answer: Tachycardia that arises from a site above the ventricles is called supraventricular tachycardia.

On the DVD

- Introduction to the Five-Step Process lecture.
- Demonstration of the methods used to determine heart rate.

Regularity

4

Case History

An 85-year-old woman presents to her family physician's office for her yearly checkup. She has a history of atherosclerotic heart disease and non-insulin-dependent diabetes. She has been careful to follow her doctor's advice and takes her medications regularly. She denies any new complaints.

While taking her vital signs, the nurse notes that the woman's heart rate is irregular. He examines the patient's medical record to see if this condition has been previously recorded. He finds no evidence that the patient has ever had an irregular heart rhythm and calls the physician into the room to examine the patient. A cardiac monitor is attached to the patient and a rhythm strip is run. The nurse and physician examine the strip and observe that the rate is within normal limits but is irregularly irregular, meaning there is no pattern to the irregularity.

Chapter Preview

- Analyzing the ECG
- Step 2: Determining the Regularity
- Methods of Determining Regularity
- Types of Irregularity

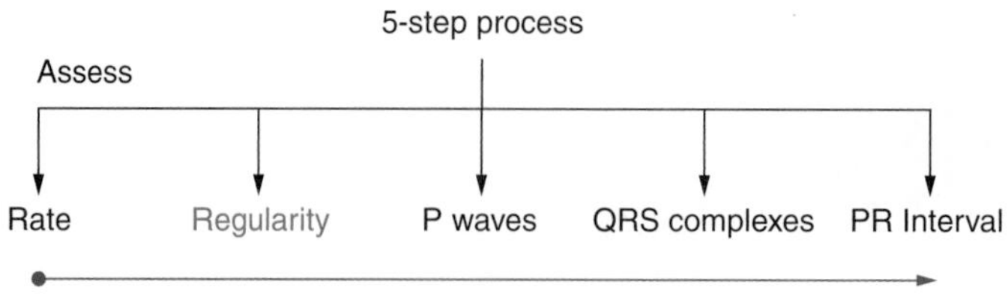

Figure 4-1
Evaluating the regularity is the second step of analyzing an ECG tracing.

Analyzing the ECG

QUESTION
"What does the term dysrhythmia mean?" (The answer can be found on page 138).

As we discussed in Chapter 3, one of the uses of the ECG is to identify existing or emerging dysrhythmias. We do this by observing the rhythm directly on the ECG monitor screen or by printing an ECG tracing so that the specific waveforms, segments, and intervals can be measured and examined.

Five-Step Process

As described earlier, to perform analysis of ECG tracings we can use a logical, systematic process that includes the following five steps:

1. Determine the rate. (Is it normal, fast or slow?)
2. Determine the regularity. (Is it regular or irregular?)
3. Assess the P waves. (Is there a uniform P wave preceding each QRS complex? Do they appear normal?)
4. Assess the QRS complexes. (Are the QRS complexes within normal limits? Do they appear normal?)
5. Assess the PR intervals. (Are the PR intervals identifiable? Within normal limits? Constant in duration?)

KEY CONCEPT
The second step in analyzing an ECG rhythm is to determine if it is regular or irregular.

This chapter examines the second step in ECG interpretation, evaluating the regularity of the rhythm to determine the presence of abnormalities (Figure 4-1).

QUESTION
"What is the first step in analyzing an ECG rhythm?" (The answer can be found on page 138.)

Step two in analyzing an ECG is determining the ______________ of the heart rhythm.

[regularity]

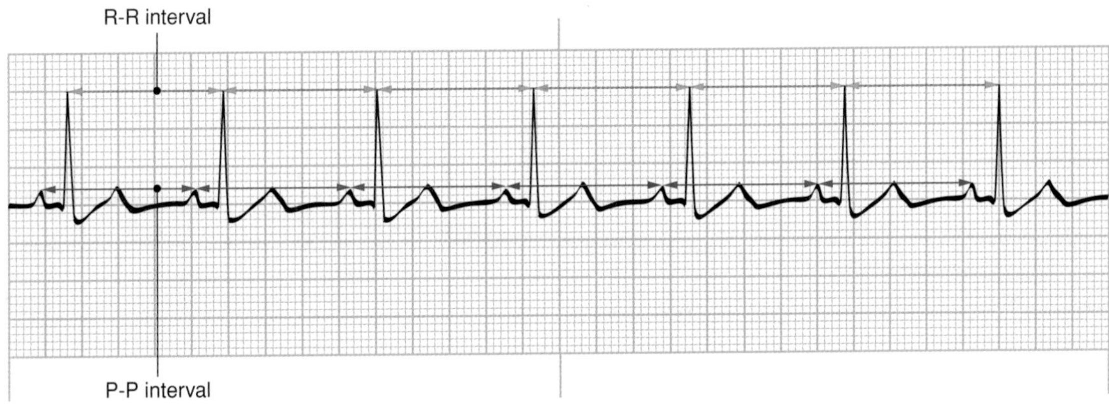

Figure 4-2
The distance between consecutive R waves is called the R-R interval; the distance between consecutive P waves is called the P-P interval.

INSTRUCTIONAL MOMENT
As described in Chapter 3, we use the R wave to measure the distance between QRS complexes as it is typically the tallest waveform of the QRS complex.

Step 2: Determining the Regularity

Normally the heart beats in a regular, rhythmic fashion, producing a P wave, QRS complex, and T wave with each heartbeat. This cycle repeats itself over and over again. The distance between the consecutive P waves should be the same, just as the distance between the consecutive QRS complexes should be the same throughout the tracing. We call these distances the P-P interval and the R-R interval (Figure 4-2).

An irregular rhythm is considered abnormal. A variety of conditions can produce irregularities of the heartbeat.

QUESTION
"What single rhythm is considered normal?" (The answer can be found on page 138.)

As with determining the heart rate, when assessing the regularity of the rhythm it is important to choose a lead, or view, that contains easily identifiable waveforms. Lead II is commonly used to determine regularity, because the majority of electrical activity flows from the right upper chest to the left lower chest. For this reason, lead II is the default monitoring lead on most ECG machines.

INSTRUCTIONAL MOMENT
Many dysrhythmias have a regular rhythm. That doesn't mean they are normal, it just means their rhythm is regular.

Lead ______________ is commonly used to determine regularity.

[II]

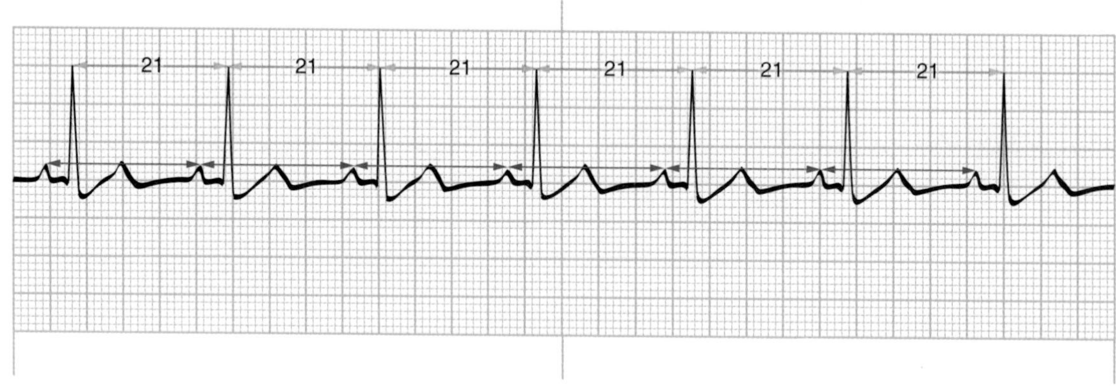

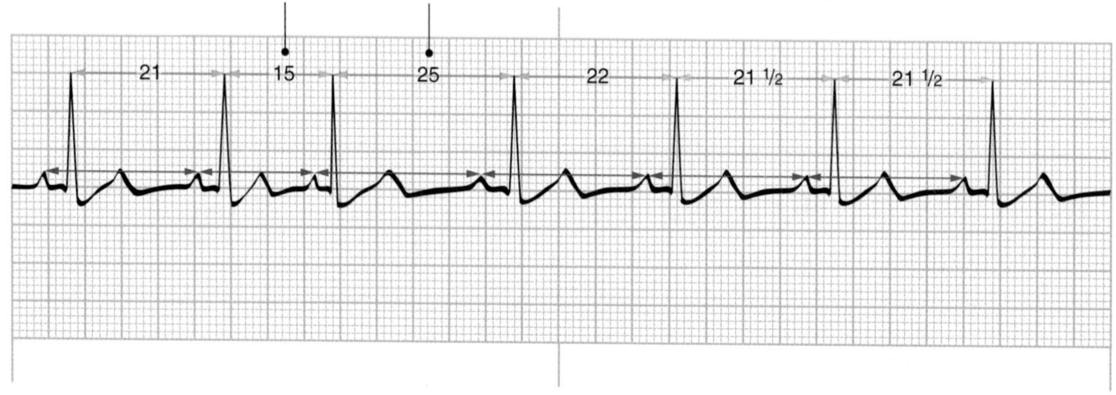

Figure 4-3
The rhythm is regular if the distance between consecutive R waves and P waves is the same. If it changes, the rhythm is irregular.

INSTRUCTIONAL MOMENT
Typically, you will know the patient has an irregular rhythm by checking his or her pulse. This may prompt you to order an ECG when the patient's condition might not otherwise call for it.

Using R-R Intervals and P-P Intervals to Determine Regularity

To assess atrial regularity we analyze the P-P intervals (Figure 4-3). If the distance remains the same between the P-P intervals, then the atrial rhythm is regular. If the distance differs, the atrial rhythm is irregular. To assess the ventricular regularity, we analyze the R-R intervals. If the distance remains the same between the R-R intervals, then the ventricular rhythm is regular. If the distance differs, the ventricular rhythm is irregular. You should compare the intervals in several cycles. Consistently similar intervals represent a regular rhythm, while dissimilar intervals indicate an irregular rhythm.

The final step is to compare the P-P interval with the R-R interval to determine whether they are the same and appear to be associated with each other. In other words, determine if there is a P wave before every QRS complex and a QRS complex after every P wave.

INSTRUCTIONAL MOMENT
If an R wave is not present, then you can use either the Q wave or the S wave of consecutive QRS complexes. You should use the uppermost or lowermost (tallest) point of the QRS for consistency in measurement.

To determine regularity we compare the _______________ intervals. We also compare the _______________ intervals. The rhythm is regular if the interval remains the _______________ and irregular if the distance _______________. Last, we can compare the P-P interval with the R-R interval to determine whether they are the _______________ and appear to be _______________ with each other.

[R-R] [P-P] [same] [changes] [same] [associated]

KEY CONCEPT
The R-R intervals or P-P intervals on the ECG tracing are analyzed to determine if the heart rhythm is regular or irregular. If the distance between the R-R or P-P intervals remains the same, the rhythm is regular. If the distance differs, the rhythm is irregular.

Methods of Determining Regularity

A number of methods can be used to determine the regularity of a rhythm including using calipers, marking a paper with a pen (or pencil), and counting the number of small squares between each R-R interval.

Caliper Method

The calipers typically used to analyze ECGs are hinged at the top with two legs that extend downward (Figure 4-4). The hinged top allows the legs to be extended away from each other to establish the distance between various waveforms. The legs are pointed at the bottom to allow them to be positioned over even the smallest waveform. To assess the regularity of a rhythm with calipers, do the following:

INSTRUCTIONAL MOMENT
Rhythms are considered regular even if there is a slight variance in the R-R or P-P interval. A good rule to follow is one small square (0.04 seconds) difference is still considered normal.

1. Place the ECG tracing on a flat surface.
2. Place one point of the caliper on a starting point. Most often the starting point is the peak of an R wave or P wave.
3. Open the calipers by pulling the other leg until the point is positioned on the next R wave or P wave.
4. With the calipers open in that position, and keeping the point positioned over the second P wave or R wave, rotate the calipers across to the peak of the next consecutive (the third) P wave or R wave. Alternatively, you can move them so they are lined up on the next consecutive R wave.

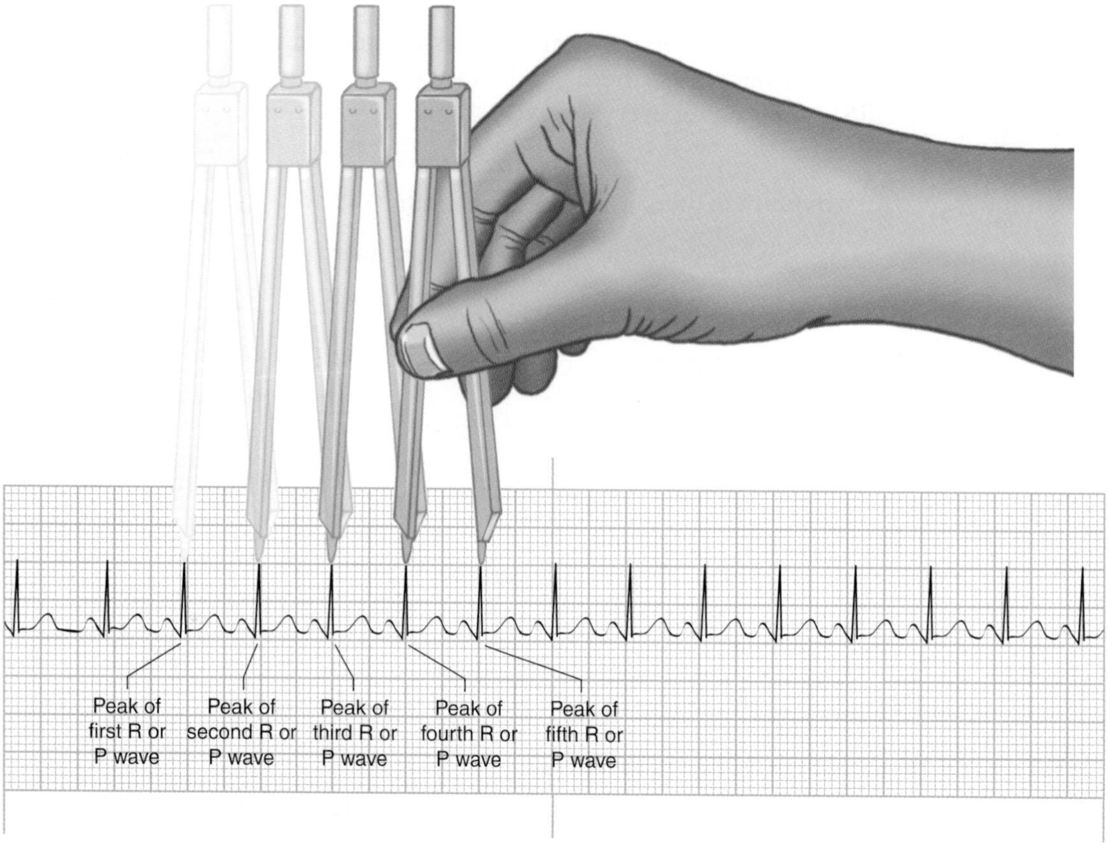

Figure 4-4
With the calipers open they are moved across the tracing from the point of one R wave or P wave to the next consecutive R wave or P wave (the R-R or P-P interval).

If the R-R interval or P-P interval is the same, the point will be above the next R wave or P wave. If the R-R interval or P-P interval is different, the point will be either before or after the identified waveform. Next, either slide or rotate the calipers across to the next R wave or P wave, then the next, and so on. If the rhythm is regular, the distance of each interval should be the same. If the rhythm is irregular, the distances of the intervals will differ.

QUESTION
"Which method may be used to calculate the heart rate in irregular rhythms?" (The answer can be found on page 138.)

To use calipers, place one point on a ____________ point, such as the peak of an ____________ wave or ____________ wave, and the other point on the peak of the next consecutive ____________ wave or ____________ wave. With the calipers in an ____________ position, they are rotated across to the peak of the next R waves or P waves. If the rhythm is regular, the distance of each interval should be the ____________.

[starting] [R] [P] [R] [P] [open] [same]

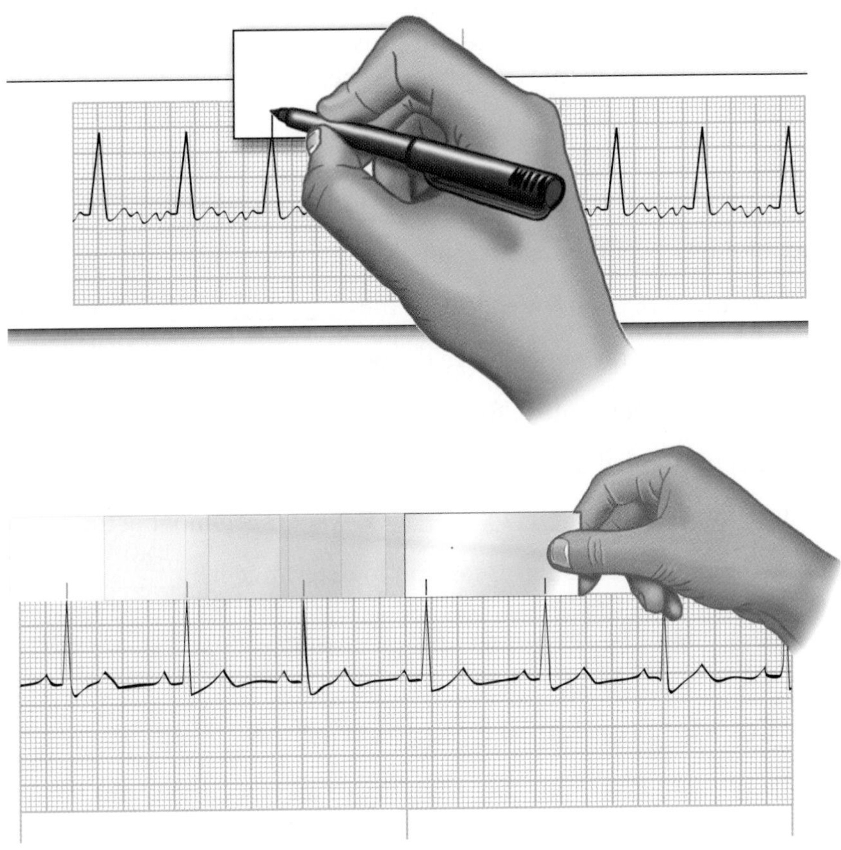

Figure 4-5
The paper and pen method.

Paper and Pen Method

Using paper and a pen (or pencil) is simple, quick, and requires no special tools (Figure 4-5). To assess the regularity of a rhythm with paper and a pen, do the following:

1. Place the ECG tracing on a flat surface.
2. Place the straight edge of a piece of paper above or over the ECG tracing so that the intervals are still visible.
3. Identify a starting point, the peak of an R wave or P wave, and place a mark on the paper in the corresponding position above it (let's call this mark 1).
4. Find the peak of the next consecutive R wave or P wave, and place a mark on the paper in the corresponding position above it (let's call this mark 2).
5. Move the paper across the ECG tracing, aligning the two marks with succeeding R-R intervals or P-P intervals.

KEY CONCEPT
The paper and pen method is a quick and simple way to determine the regularity of an ECG tracing.

If the two marks line up with the following intervals, the rhythm is regular. If the distance between the intervals differs, the rhythm is irregular. You can tell this when mark 2 either falls before or after the second P wave or R wave.

INSTRUCTIONAL MOMENT
An additional method similar to the paper marking method is to use the tip of a pen or pencil to determine regularity. Place the tip of the pen or pencil on an R or P wave. Slide your fingernail back along the pen to the next wave. Keep your fingernail on this spot and then use this mark to check along the ECG strip.

To use the paper and pen method to measure _______________, place a piece of paper over the ECG tracing. Identify a starting point by placing a mark on the paper above the peak of the _______________ R wave or P wave. Then mark the paper above the peak of the _______________ R wave or P wave. Next, move the paper across the ECG tracing so that mark 1 is positioned over the _______________ R wave and mark 2 is positioned over the _______________ R wave. Keep moving the paper across the ECG tracing in this fashion to determine its _______________.

[regularity] [first] [next] [second] [third] [regularity]

QUESTION
"How do you know a heart rhythm is irregular using either the calipers method or paper and pen method?" (The answer can be found on page 138.)

◆ Counting the Small Squares Method

Another way to determine the regularity of an ECG is to count the number of small squares on the ECG paper between the peaks of two consecutive R waves (or P waves) and then compare that to the other R-R (or P-P) intervals (Figure 4-6). You can speed up the process by using the larger boxes (made up of five small squares) for all but the last portion.

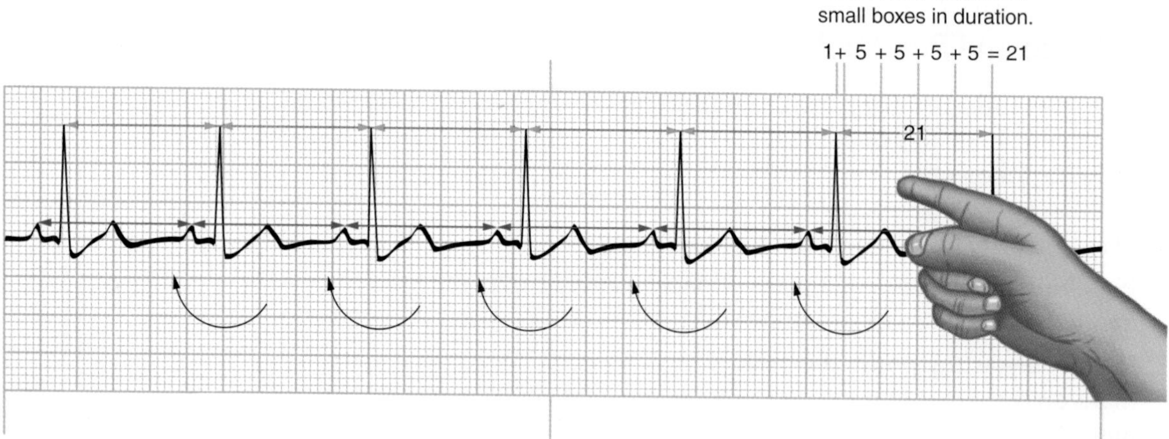

For this figure, we started counting from the last R wave because it fell on the bold line making counting of the small squares easier.

Figure 4-6
Count the number of small boxes between consecutive R and/or P waves (each R-R and P-P interval) and then compare them to each other. If they are the same, the rhythm is regular; if they differ, the rhythm is irregular.

The counting small squares method involves counting the number of ________________ squares between two consecutive ________________ waves.

[small] [R]

INSTRUCTIONAL MOMENT
Rate calculators can also be used to determine regularity. Begin by placing the calculator over the ECG tracing. Position the start mark on the peak of an R wave. Then find the next consecutive R wave. Where that next R wave lines up is then noted (this is the heart rate for that ECG). Next, move the calculator over other R-R intervals and compare your findings to what you found in the first R-R interval.

You can practice determining regularity and heart rate with the following *Practice Makes Perfect* exercises. Answers to these exercises can be found in Appendix A.

Types of Irregularity

If the rhythm is irregular, we can further analyze it to determine the type of irregularity (Figure 4-7).

INSTRUCTIONAL MOMENT
The names given here for the types of irregularity may differ from those found in other references. This was done intentionally to make them more descriptive.

An irregularity in the rhythm can range from being occasionally irregular to being very irregular. It is important to have a general sense of the difference as a very irregular rhythm can be a warning that the heart is extremely irritable and may deteriorate to a worse condition. You might also see the rhythm as being slightly irregular. It is not necessary to remember each term, but be aware that the irregularity may appear this way.

INSTRUCTIONAL MOMENT
This chapter is not intended to be an in-depth discussion of any dysrhythmia but rather a description of how it produces irregularity in the rhythm. Don't worry about memorizing the names of the dysrhythmias at this point.

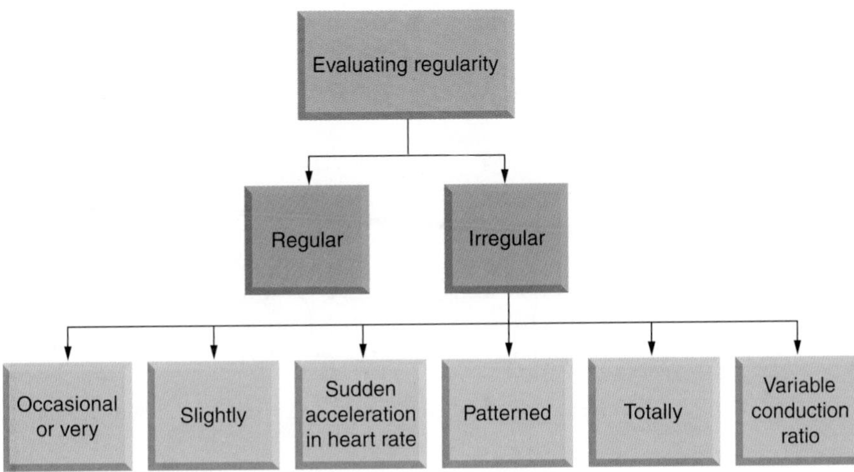

Figure 4-7
Algorithm for regular and irregular rhythms.

PRACTICE. . . MAKES PERFECT

1.

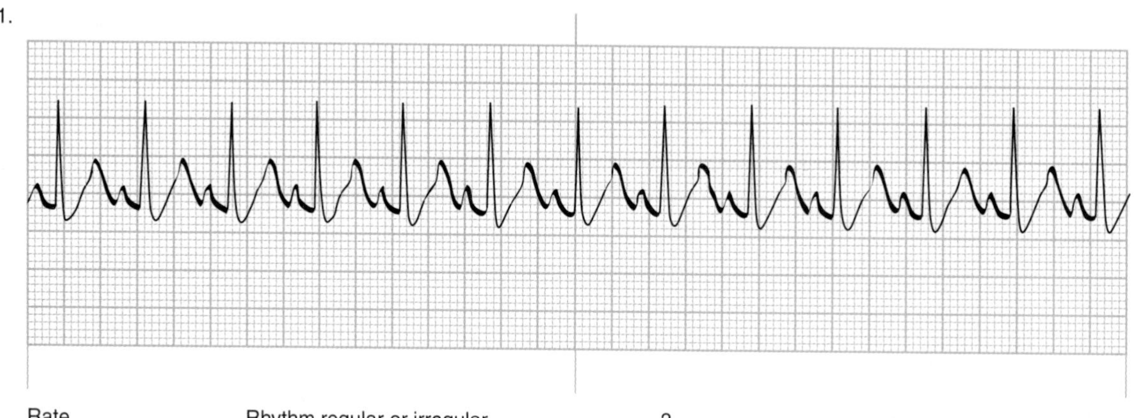

Rate ______________. Rhythm regular or irregular ______________?

2.

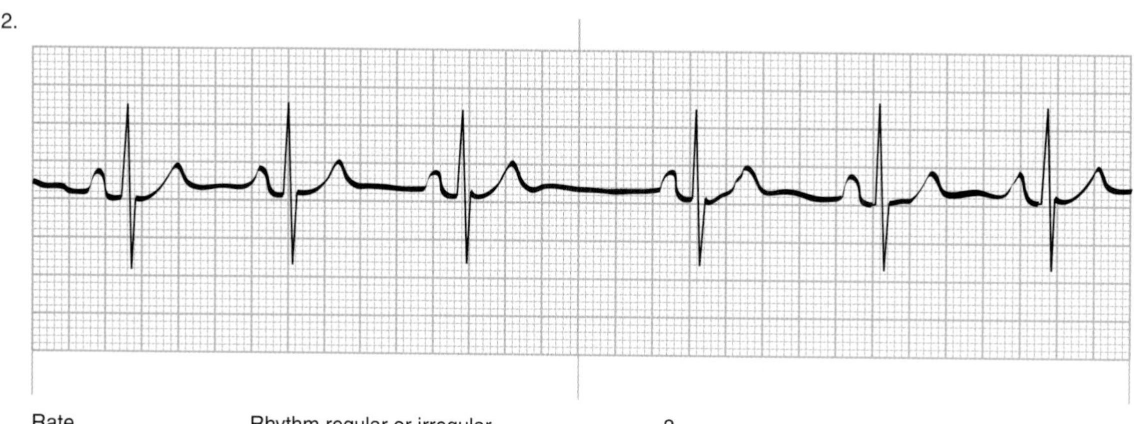

Rate ______________. Rhythm regular or irregular ______________?

3.

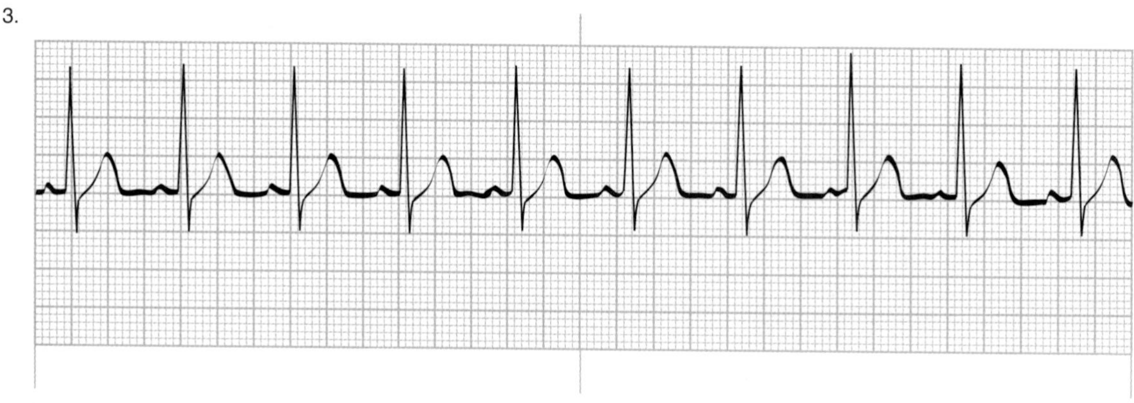

Rate ______________. Rhythm regular or irregular ______________?

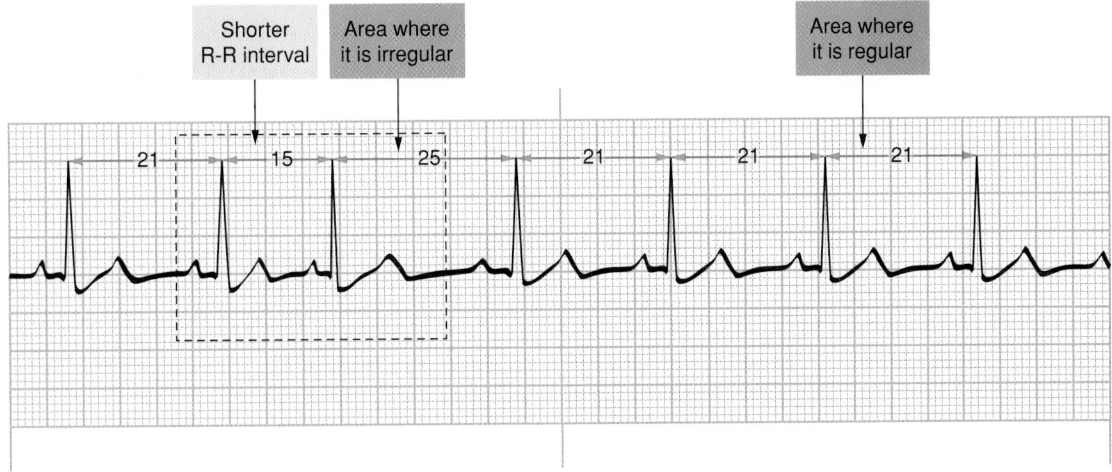

Figure 4-8
An occasionally irregular rhythm appears mostly regular but from time to time it is irregular.

Occasionally or Very Irregular

When it is occasionally irregular, the rhythm appears mostly regular but from time to time you see an area where it is irregular (Figure 4-8). The irregularity may be so infrequent that you might not see it at first.

A rhythm may also look very irregular. Looking at the ECG tracing in Figure 4-9 you see areas where the distance of the R-R intervals appears to be the same and areas where the distance differs. The areas that are the same are considered the underlying rhythm. We compare the underlying rhythm to the other R-R intervals. We need to be concerned with a very irregular rhythm as it suggests that the heart is extremely irritable.

QUESTION
"What is the heart's primary pacemaker site?" (The answer can be found on page 138.)

Premature Complexes

KEY CONCEPT
If the R-R interval is shorter than normal, it is typically due to a premature beat.

An impulse that appears early, called a premature complex or ectopy, is a common cause of irregularity (Figure 4-10). As implied by its name, a premature complex fires early, before the SA node has a chance to initiate the impulse. These premature complexes can arise from any of the cells of the heart including the atria, AV junction, or ventricles. The R-R interval between the normal complex and the premature complex is shorter than the interval between normal complexes. This makes the rhythm irregular. If premature beats occur only a few times a minute, we can describe it as occasionally irregular. If they occur often, it can be described as very or frequently irregular. Frequent premature beats are

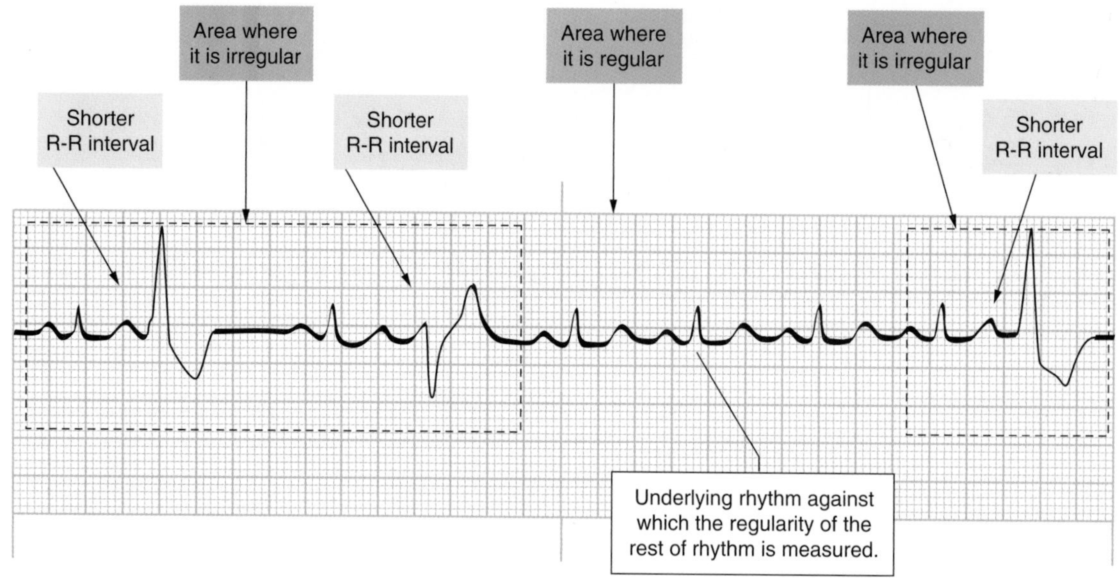

Figure 4-9
A very irregular rhythm has many areas of irregularity.

more likely to progress to very fast atrial, junctional, or ventricular rates (tachycardia). Worse, the rhythm may deteriorate into a quivering of the heart muscle called ventricular fibrillation.

CLINICAL MOMENT
Ectopic means arising from any site other than the SA node.

An irregular rhythm can be caused by ______________ complexes. These impulses come early in the cycle causing the R-R interval to be ______________ than in others. This makes the rhythm ______________.

[premature] [shorter] [irregular]

CLINICAL MOMENT
The most common cause of ectopic beats is hypoxia (lack of oxygen).

Sinus Arrest

A rhythm can also appear irregular when the SA node fails to initiate an impulse (Figure 4-11). This is called sinus arrest and is seen as a pause in the ECG rhythm. Typically, the rhythm leading up to the pause looks normal. Then there is suddenly an absence of a P wave, QRS complex, and T wave. This creates a gap or pause. Usually with this condition the SA node recovers and fires another impulse. If the SA

Normally, the SA node initiates impulses, resulting in a repetitive cycle of P, QRS, and T waveforms.

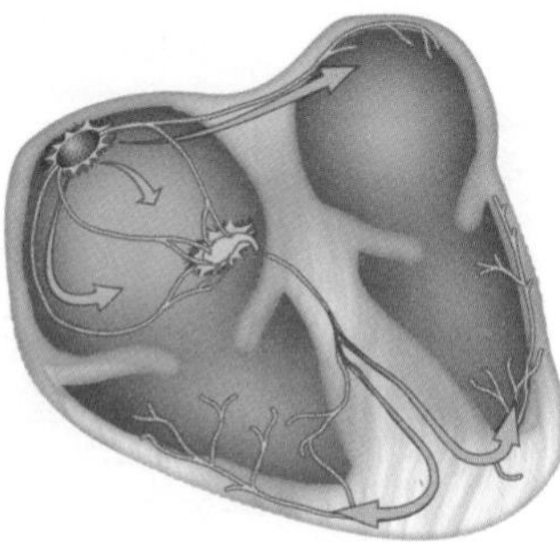

A premature beat occurs when a site in the a) atria, b) AV junction, or c) ventricles fires before the SA node is able to initiate an impulse.

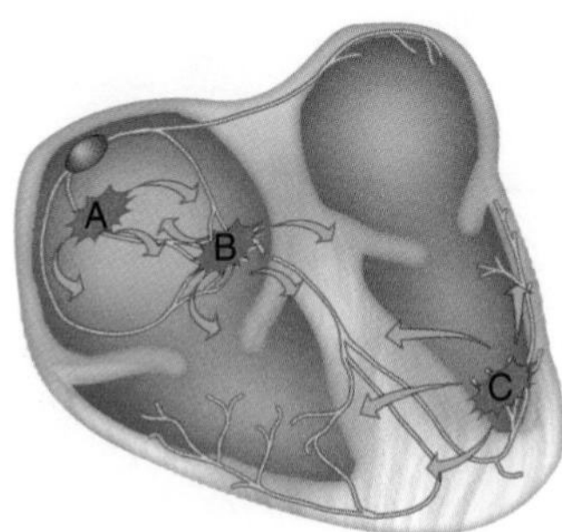

Following the premature beat, the SA node typically reinitiates impulses in the normal manner.

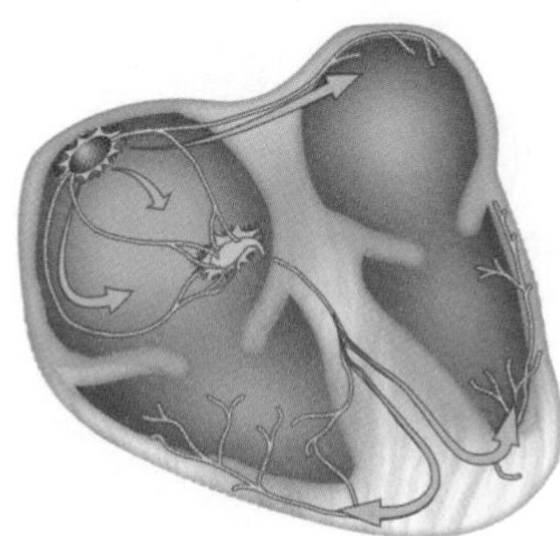

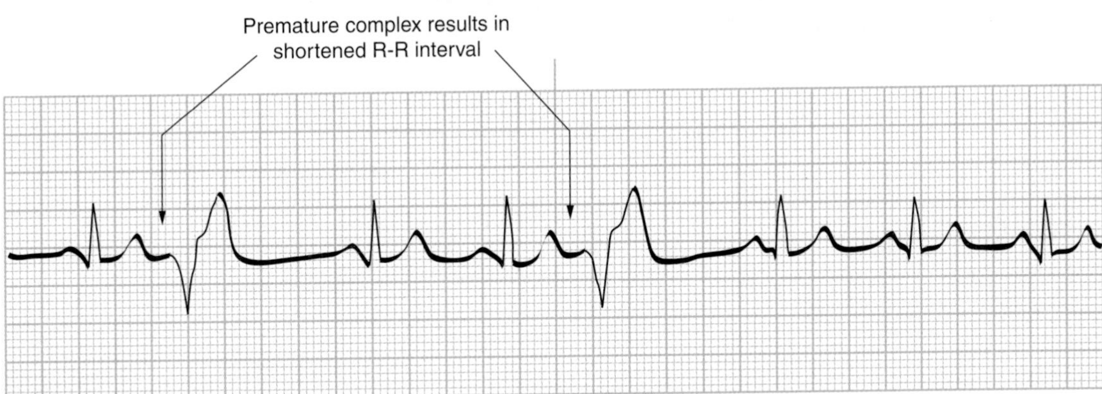

Figure 4-10
Irregularity can be caused by premature complexes that can arise from (a) atria, (b) AV node, or (c) ventricles.

node fails to fire, then an escape pacemaker from the atria, AV junction, or ventricles initiates an impulse. The prominent characteristic you see is a longer than normal R-R interval that occurs because of the dropped beat. If the SA node frequently fails to fire, there will be many pauses causing the rhythm to look very or frequently irregular.

KEY CONCEPT
Irregularity can also be brought about by a longer than normal R-R interval that results from failure of the SA node to initiate an impulse. This results in the absence of a P, QRS, and T wave.

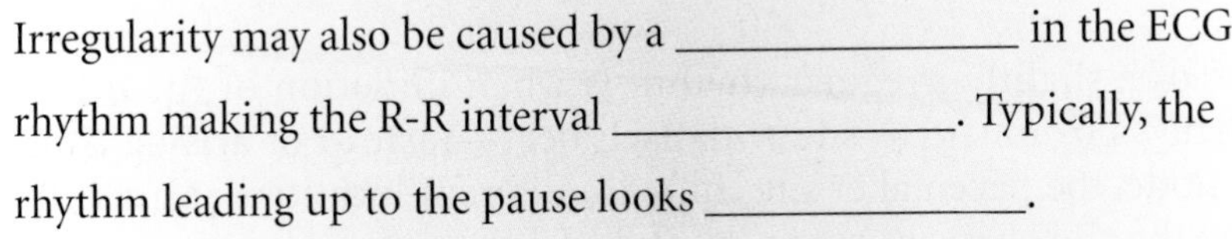
Irregularity may also be caused by a ______________ in the ECG rhythm making the R-R interval ______________. Typically, the rhythm leading up to the pause looks ______________.

[pause] [longer] [normal]

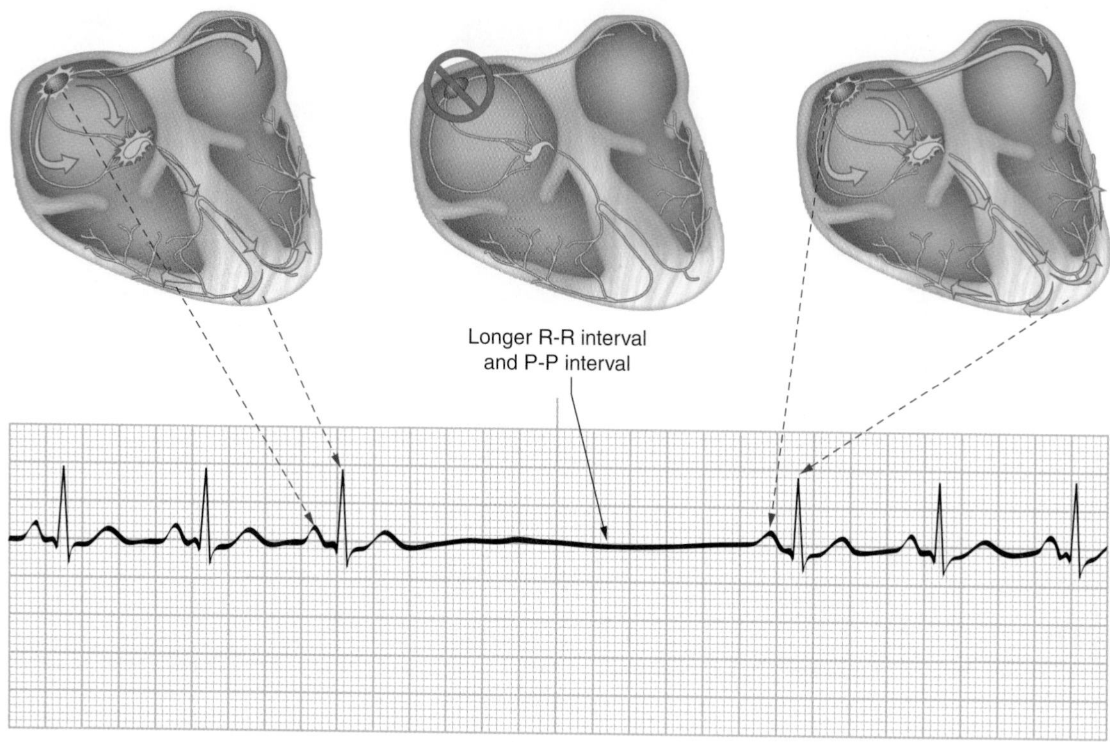

Figure 4-11
Rhythm irregularity due to sinus arrest.

CLINICAL MOMENT
Frequent pauses in the firing of the sinus node may cause so many dropped beats that the heart rate becomes bradycardic and cardiac output is reduced.

Slight Irregularity

A rhythm may also appear to change only slightly with the P-P intervals and R-R intervals varying somewhat (Figure 4-12). It might be so slight that you don't easily see it, but you detect it when you measure the R-R or P-P intervals. The difference between slightly irregular and occasionally irregular rhythms is that with slightly irregular rhythms it is continuous throughout the ECG tracing; with occasional irregularity, the rhythm is mostly regular but there are periods of irregularity.

A cause of a slightly irregular rhythm is when initiation of the heartbeat changes from site to site with each beat—instead of arising from the SA node, the pacemaker site shifts to different locations around the atria. As the site changes, so do the P-P and R-R intervals. Again, these differences can be slight. This dysrhythmia is referred to as wandering atrial pacemaker.

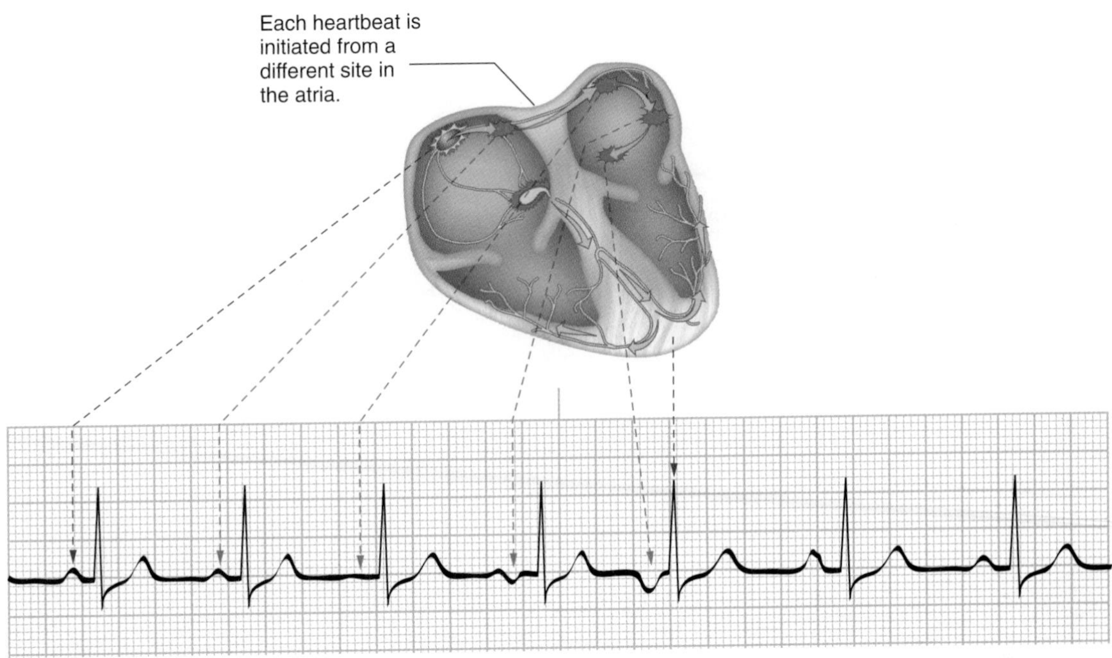

Figure 4-12
A slightly irregular rhythm can occur when instead of arising from the SA node, the heart's pacemaker shifts from site to site throughout the atria. The number of small boxes for each R-R and P-P interval varies slightly throughout the ECG strip.

A _______________ irregular rhythm is where the P-P intervals and R-R intervals vary somewhat. Changes in the _______________ site from site to site can lead to this type of irregularity.

[slightly] [pacemaker]

Irregularity Caused by Sudden Changes in the Heart Rate

A rhythm may also appear irregular when the heart rate suddenly accelerates (Figure 4-13). We use the term **paroxysmal** to describe a dysrhythmia that has a sudden, rapid onset (and resolution). Because the R-R intervals or P-P intervals go from normal distances to shorter distances, it creates an irregular looking rhythm. Any of the types of tachycardia that arise outside the SA node (as we discussed in Chapter 3) can occur suddenly. To know this type of irregularity is present, we would have to observe its onset or resolution.

QUESTION
"In what sites outside the SA node does tachycardia arise?" (The answer can be found on page 138.)

Normally, the SA node initiates impulses, resulting in a repetitive cycle of P, QRS, and T waveforms.

An ectopic site from above the ventricles fires rapidly and takes over as pacemaker.

Figure 4-13
Irregularity can also result from sudden rapid acceleration of the heart rate.

INSTRUCTIONAL MOMENT
Fast rhythms have short R-R or P-P intervals making it difficult to identify the presence of irregularity. Take your time while identifying regularity in fast rates.

Irregularity will be seen when the heart rate suddenly ______________.
The rapid rate causes the R-R intervals or P-P intervals to go from ______________ distances to ______________ distances producing an ______________ looking rhythm.

[accelerates] [normal] [shorter] [irregular]

CLINICAL MOMENT
Remember, cardiac output is the product of heart rate and stroke volume. If we reduce the heart rate due to an irregular rhythm, it may reduce cardiac output.

Patterned Irregularity

Patterned irregularity, also called regularly irregular, is where the irregularity repeats over and over in a cyclic fashion. Premature complexes occurring at regular intervals, a condition where the heart rate speeds up and slows down in a cyclical way and one type of AV node blockage, are characterized as being regularly irregular (Figure 4-14).

Normally, the SA node initiates impulses, resulting in a repetitive cycle of P, QRS, and T waveforms.

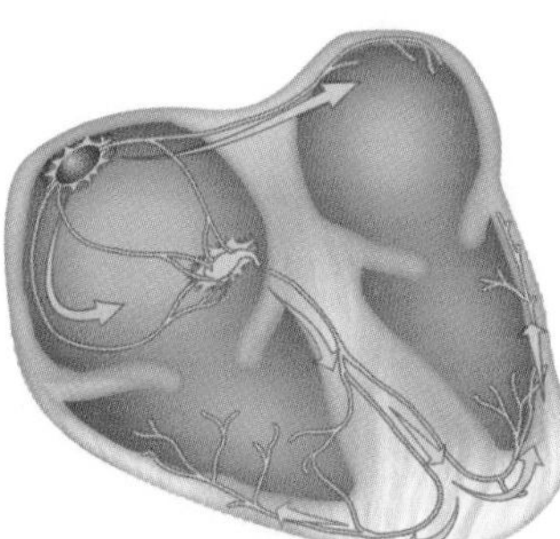

Premature beats occur when a site in the atria, AV node, or ventricles fires before the SA node is able to initiate an impulse.

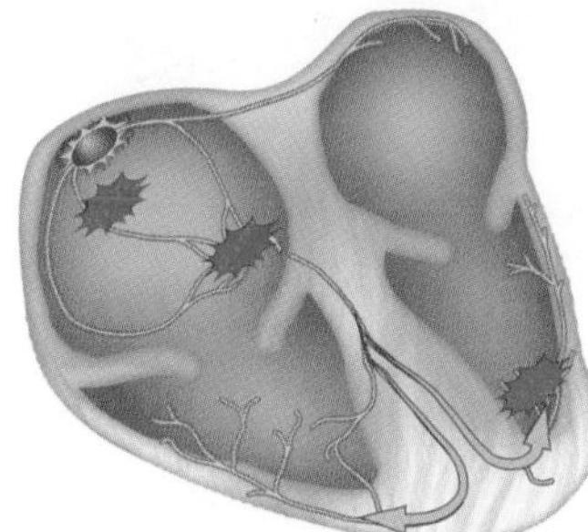

Following the premature beat, the SA node typically reinitiates impulses in the normal manner.

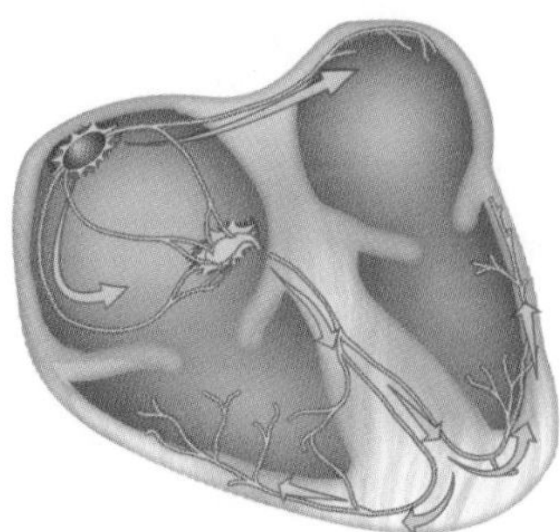

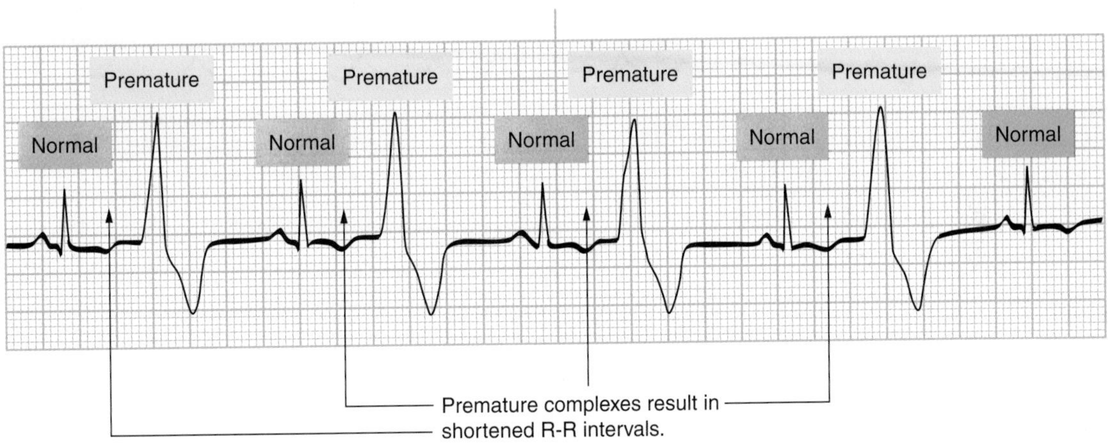

Figure 4-14
The premature beats disrupt the regularity of the rhythm. Patterned irregularity can be caused by bigeminal, trigeminal, or quadrigeminal premature complexes.

Premature complexes seen in a given pattern, such as those occurring every other (second) complex, every third complex, or every fourth complex, produce patterned irregularity. These premature complexes can arise from the atria, AV node, and ventricles.

CLINICAL MOMENT
Premature beats that occur every other beat are called bigeminal complexes, every third complex are called trigeminal, and every fourth complex are called quadrigeminal—bi=2, tri=3, quad=4.

We may also see patterned irregularity when the rhythm speeds up and slows down in a rhythmic fashion (Figure 4-15). The speeding up and slowing down of the heart rate often corresponds with the respiratory cycle and changes in intrathoracic pressure. The heart rate increases during inspiration and decreases during expiration. As a result of the speeding up and slowing down of the heart, you see a narrowing and then a widening of the R-R intervals. This cycle continually repeats. This dysrhythmia is called sinus dysrhythmia.

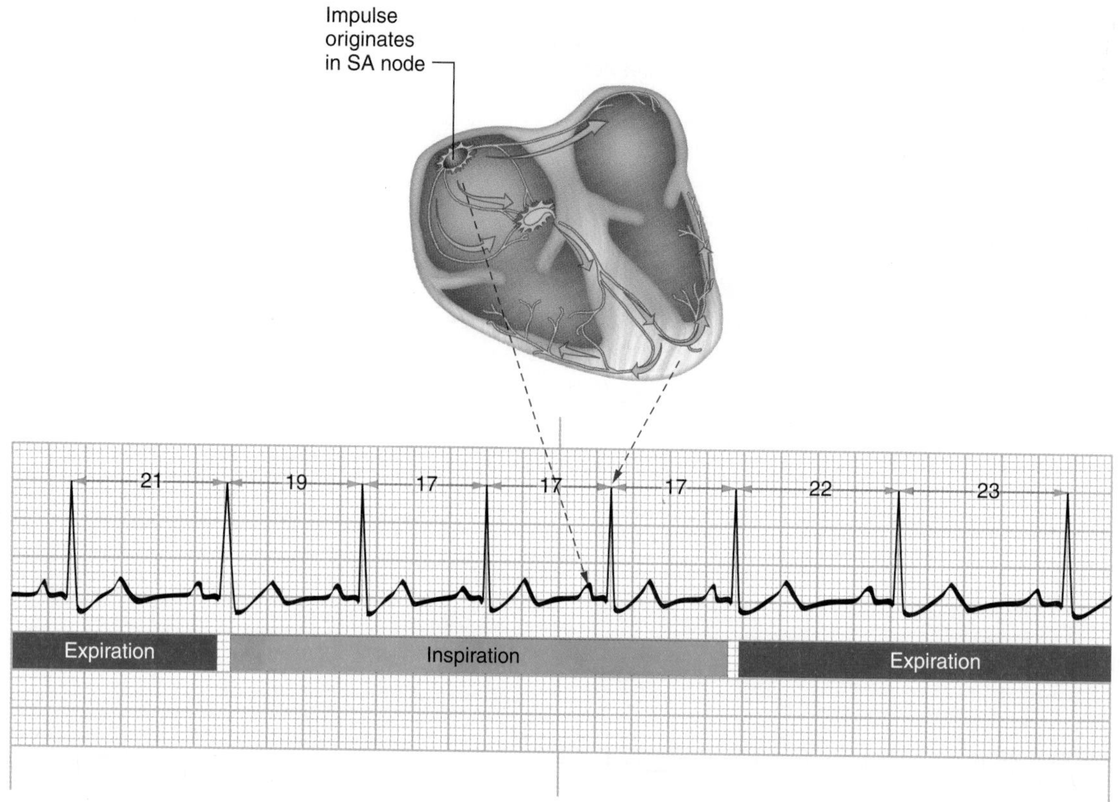

Figure 4-15
With sinus dysrhythmia patterned irregularity can be caused by the speeding up and slowing down of the heart rate in a rhythmic fashion.

QUESTION
"What is role of the AV node?" (The answer can be found on page 138.)

KEY CONCEPT
With patterned irregularity, the irregularity repeats over and over in a cyclic fashion.

Patterned irregularity can also occur in one type of AV heart block where the AV node is weakened and tires more with each conducted impulse until finally it is so tired that it fails to conduct the impulse through to the ventricles (Figure 4-16). This results in a dropped ventricular beat. This causes the R-R intervals to be longer wherever there is a dropped ventricular beat. With the dropped ventricular beat, the AV node has a chance to rest. The next impulse conducting through the AV node will be carried through faster but each subsequent impulse will be delayed until finally another ventricular beat is dropped. This cycle repeats over and over producing a recognizable pattern. This dysrhythmia is called 2nd-degree AV heart block Type I (it is also referred to as Wenckebach).

With ________________ irregularity, the irregularity repeats over and over in a ________________ fashion.

[patterned] [cyclic]

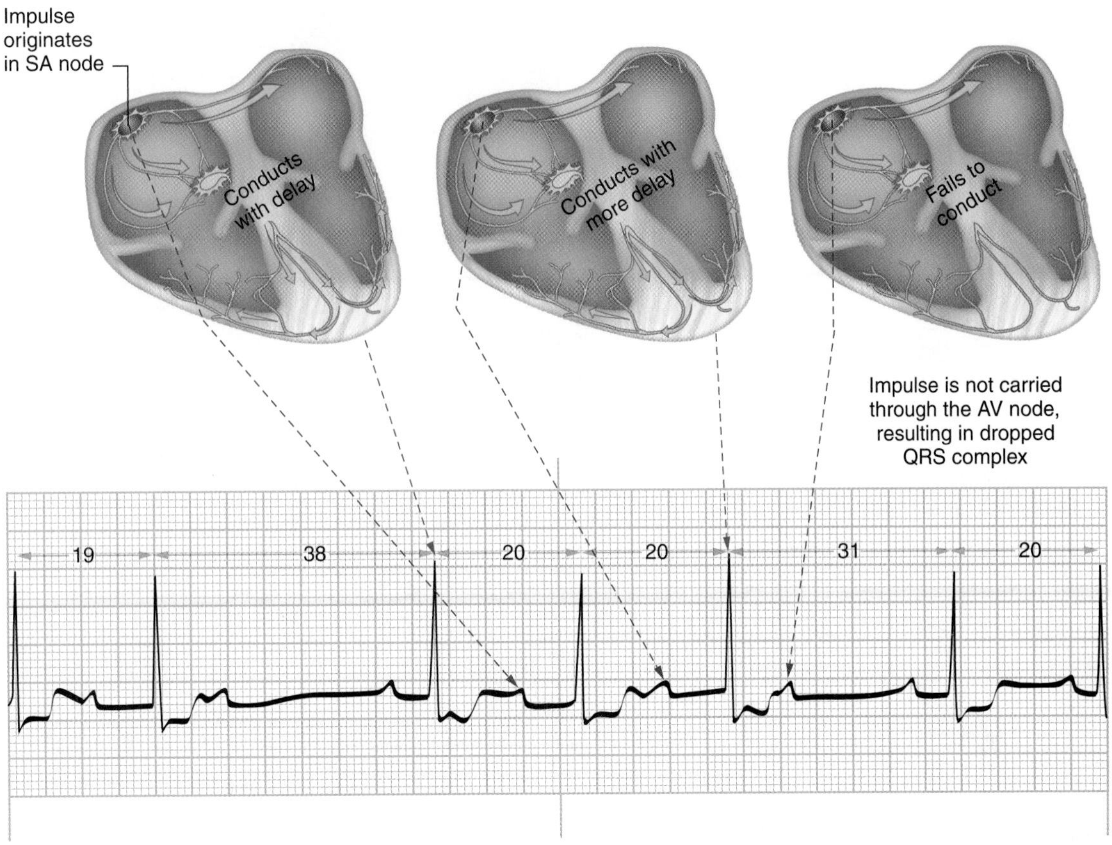

Figure 4-16
With 2nd-degree AV heart block Type I patterned irregularity is caused by a weakened AV node which tires more and more with each conducted impulse until finally it fails to conduct the impulse through to the ventricles. The number of small boxes for the R-R and P-P intervals increases and decreases in ccyclical manner..

Irregularly (Totally) Irregular

An irregularly irregular or totally irregular rhythm, also called a chaotically or grossly irregular rhythm, is one in which there is no consistency to the irregularity. Looking across the tracing, it is hard to find an R-R interval that is the same as others (Figure 4-17).

Totally irregular rhythms are typically atrial fibrillation. Remember, what we said in Chapter 3 about atrial fibrillation—the atria fire at a rate in excess of 350 beats per minute and from multiple sites. These impulses bombard the AV node so rapidly that it cannot respond to all the impulses, allowing only some to get through to the ventricles. The R-R intervals vary from interval to interval, because it is so haphazard as to which impulses are conducted (as many are being generated). This creates the appearance of an irregularly irregular rhythm.

INSTRUCTIONAL MOMENT
Whenever you see a totally irregular rhythm, it is considered atrial fibrillation until you can prove otherwise.

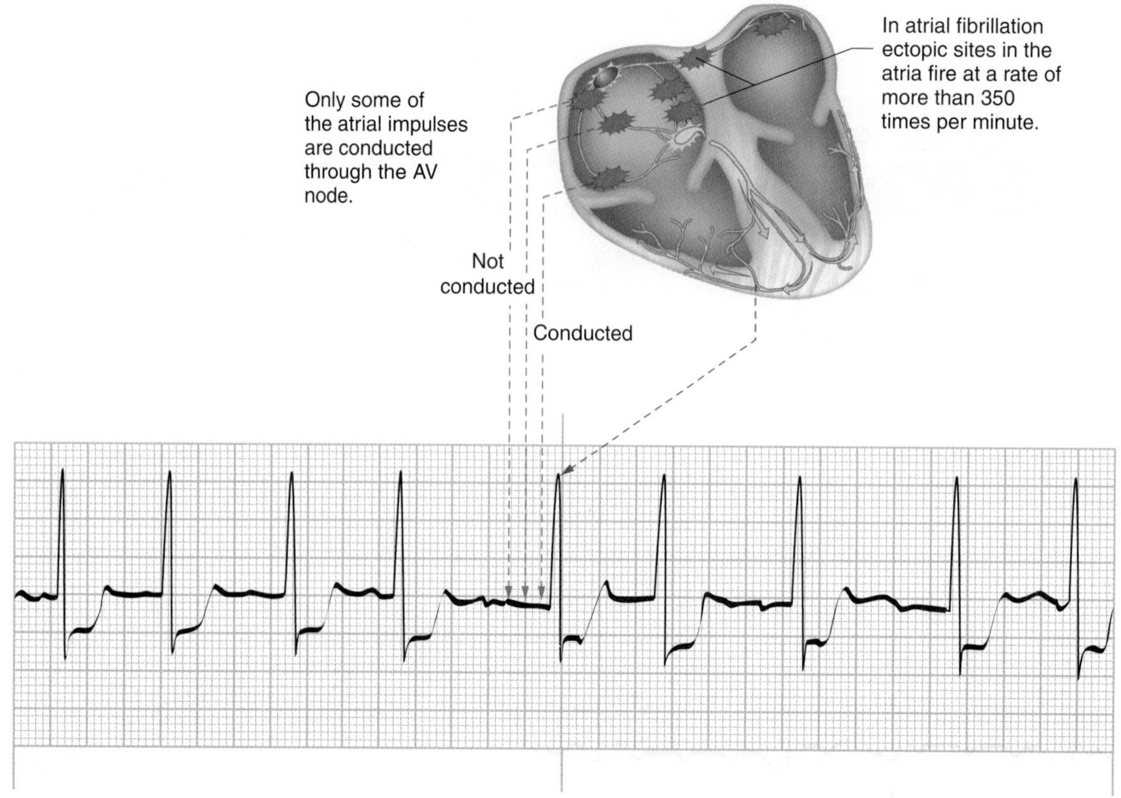

Figure 4-17
An irregularly irregular rhythm can be caused by the rapid firing of the atria, which haphazardly bombard the AV node resulting in only some impulses being conducted to the ventricles.

KEY CONCEPT
A totally irregular rhythm is one in which there is no consistency to the irregularity.

A ________________ irregular rhythm is one in which there is no consistency to the irregularity. With this type of irregularity, the R-R intervals ________________ from interval to interval. The dysrhythmia that typically produces this characteristic total irregularity is called ______________ fibrillation.

[totally] [vary] [atrial]

Irregularity Due to Varying Conduction Ratios

Another cause of irregularity is when the number of impulses reaching the ventricles changes (Figure 4-18). This can occur with atrial flutter and AV heart block, two other dysrhythmias we discussed in Chapter 3.

With atrial flutter, the atria fire at a rate of between 250 and 350 beats a minute. The ventricular rate is dependent on how many impulses conduct through the AV node. We call this the atrial-to-ventricular conduction

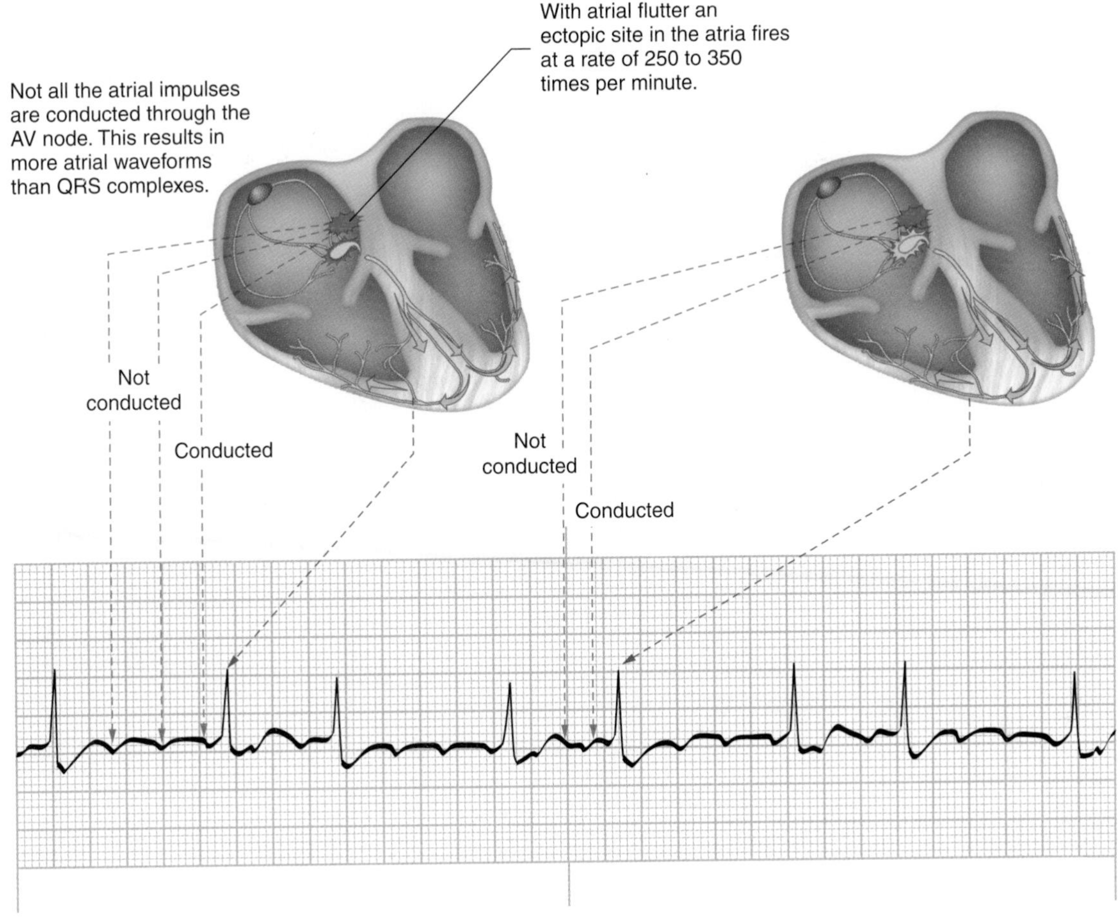

Figure 4-18
Varying conduction ratios cause the duration of the R-R intervals to change, producing an irregular rhythm.

ratio. Often this ratio is constant, such as two atrial impulses to one ventricular beat. To keep it simple, we will refer to just the numbers, for example, 2:1, 3:1, 4:1, and so on. This results in the rhythm being regular. Conversely, if the conduction ratio varies, the rhythm will be irregular. An example is if the atrial-to-ventricular conduction ratio changes from 3:1 to 4:1 and then back again, then the distance between the R-R intervals changes, producing an irregular rhythm. We call this atrial flutter with varying conduction ratio.

This varying conduction ratio (number of P waves to each QRS complex) can also occur in another type of 2nd-degree AV heart block, called Type II (Figure 4-19). This form of AV heart block is more serious than the type we described earlier and is more likely to progress to complete AV heart block. Type II can either have a steady atrial-to-ventricular conduction ratio or the conduction ratio can change (e.g., from 2:1 to 3:1 and then back). When the conduction ratio changes, the distance between the R-R intervals will change, thus producing an irregular rhythm.

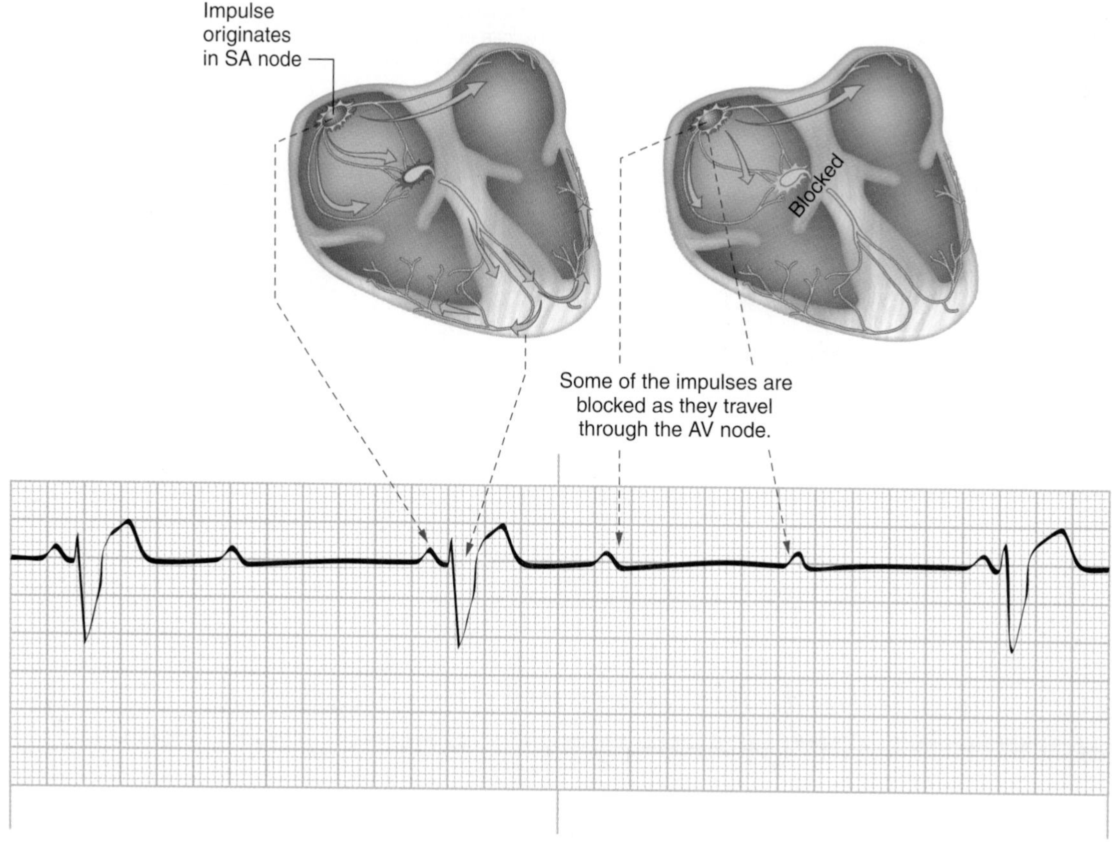

Figure 4-19
Where the atrial to ventricular conduction ratio varies in 2nd-degree AV heart block, the distance between the R-R intervals changes, producing an irregular rhythm.

Atrial flutter will produce irregular R-R intervals if the conduction ratio _______________. We call this atrial flutter with a _______________ conduction _______________. 2nd-degree AV heart block can also have a _______________ conduction ratio.

[varies] [varying] [ratio] [varying]

You can practice determining regularity, type of irregularity and heart rate with the following *Practice Makes Perfect* exercises. Answers to these exercises can be found in Appendix A.

PRACTICE. . . MAKES PERFECT

4.

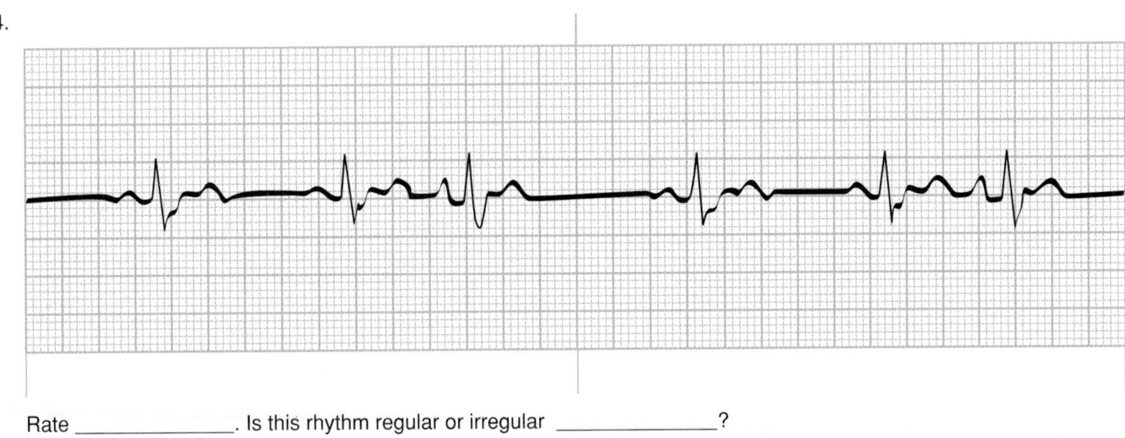

Rate ______________. Is this rhythm regular or irregular ______________?
If irregular, type of irregularity ______________ .

5.

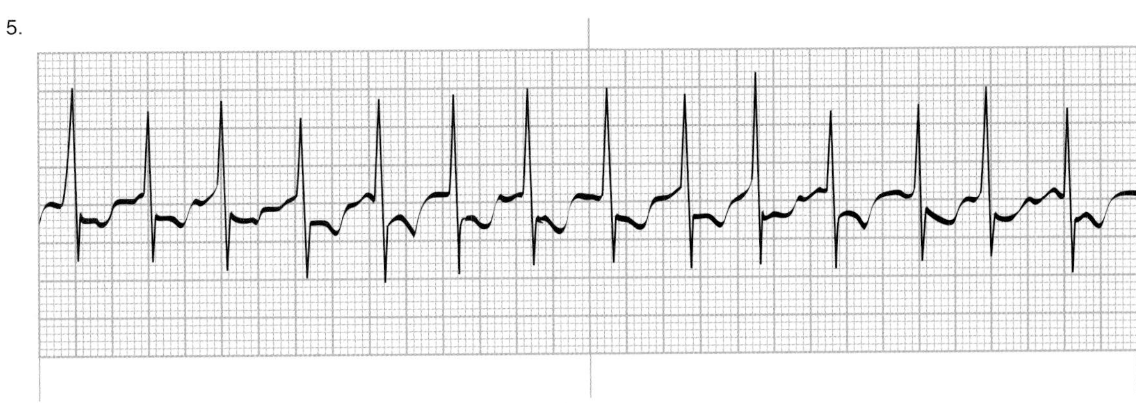

Rate ______________. Is this rhythm regular or irregular ______________?
If irregular, type of irregularity ______________ .

6.

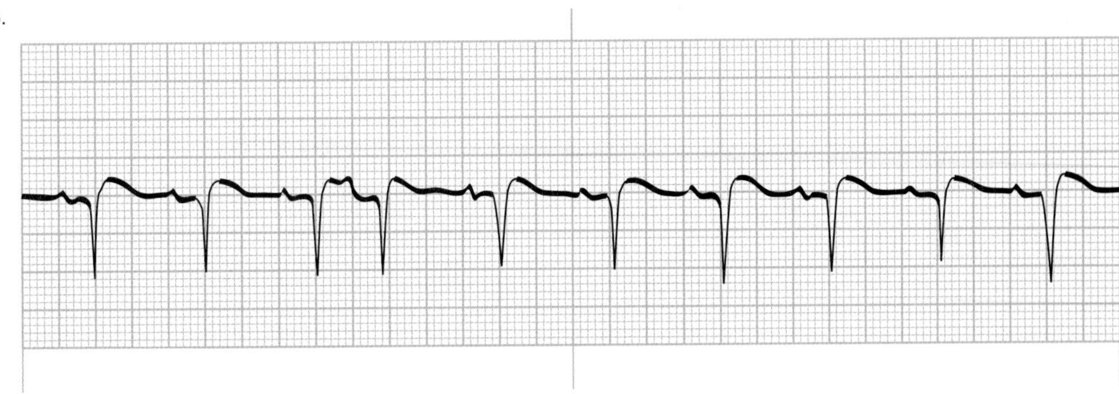

Rate ______________. Is this rhythm regular or irregular ______________?
If irregular, type of irregularity ______________ .

PRACTICE. . . MAKES PERFECT

7.

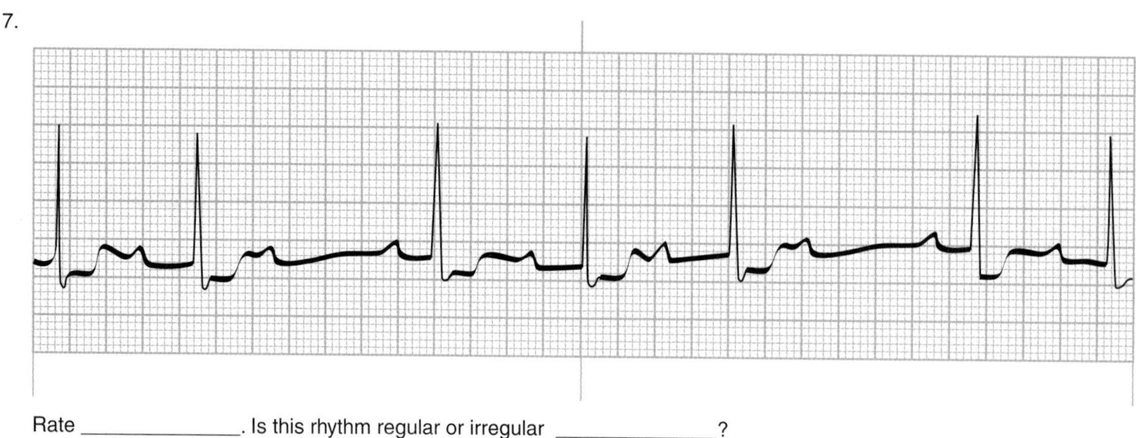

Rate ______________. Is this rhythm regular or irregular ______________?
If irregular, type of irregularity ______________.

8.

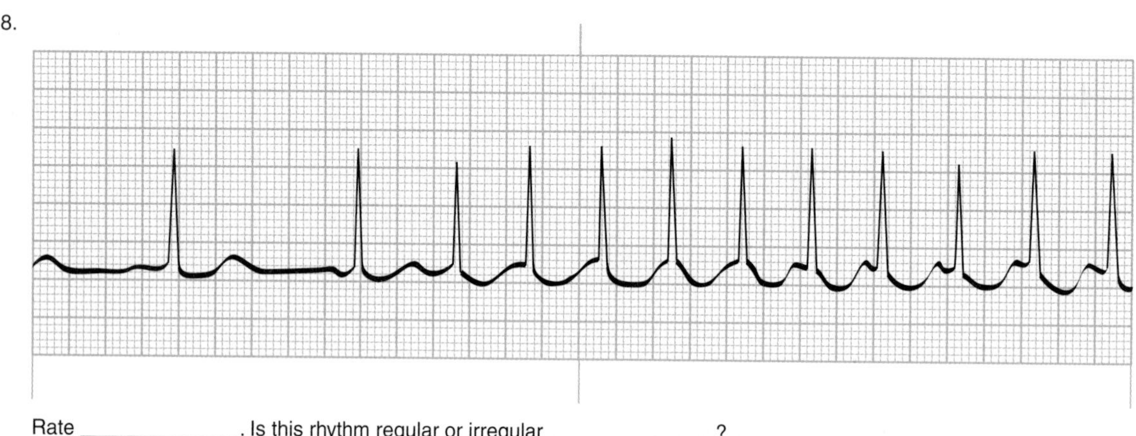

Rate ______________. Is this rhythm regular or irregular ______________?
If irregular, type of irregularity ______________.

9.

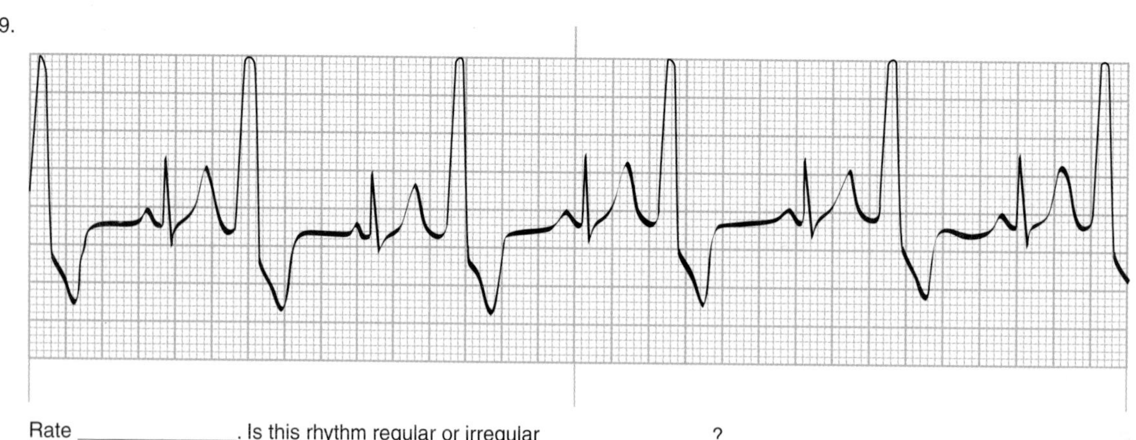

Rate ______________. Is this rhythm regular or irregular ______________?
If irregular, type of irregularity ______________.

PRACTICE. . . MAKES PERFECT

10.

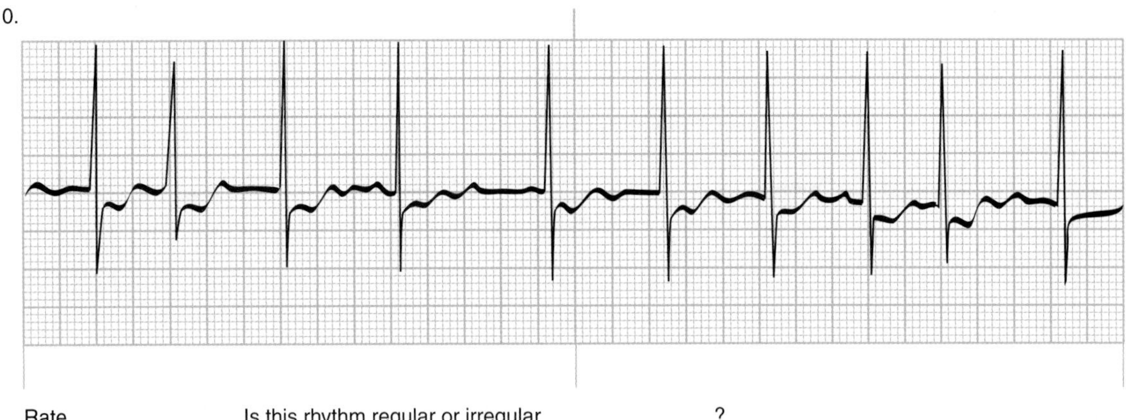

Rate ______________. Is this rhythm regular or irregular ______________?
If irregular, type of irregularity ______________ .

11.

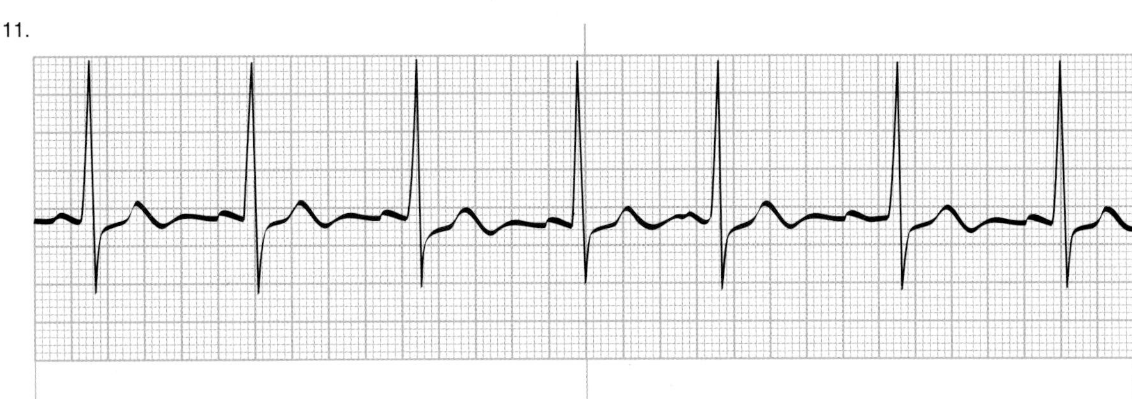

Rate ______________ Is this rhythm regular or irregular? ______________ .
If irregular, type of irregularity ______________ .

12.

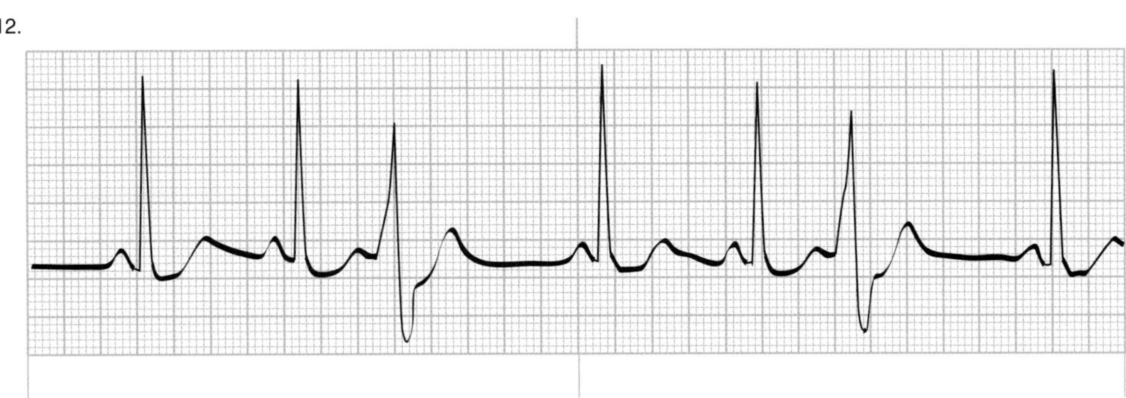

Rate ______________ Is this rhythm regular or irregular? ______________ .
If irregular, type of irregularity ______________ .

PRACTICE. . . MAKES PERFECT

13.

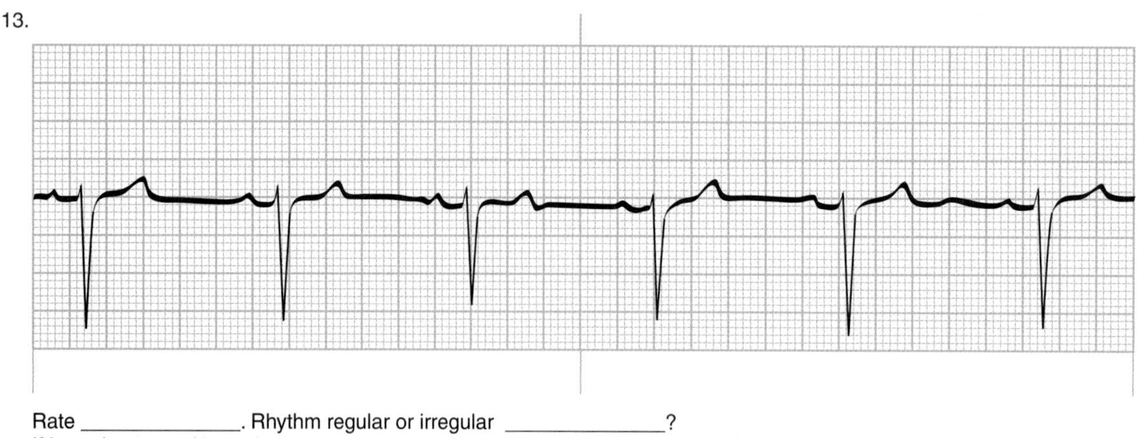

Rate _______________. Rhythm regular or irregular _______________?
If irregular, type of irregularity _______________ .

14.

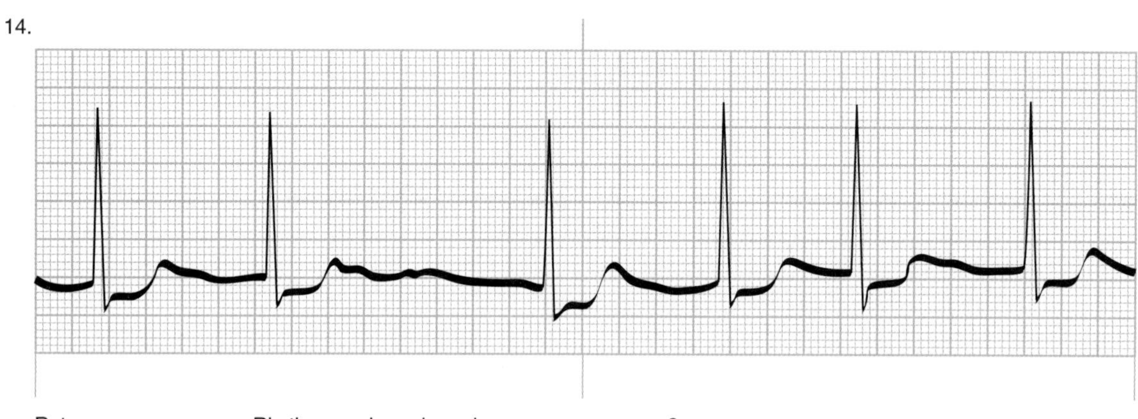

Rate _______________. Rhythm regular or irregular _______________?
If irregular, type of irregularity _______________ .

15.

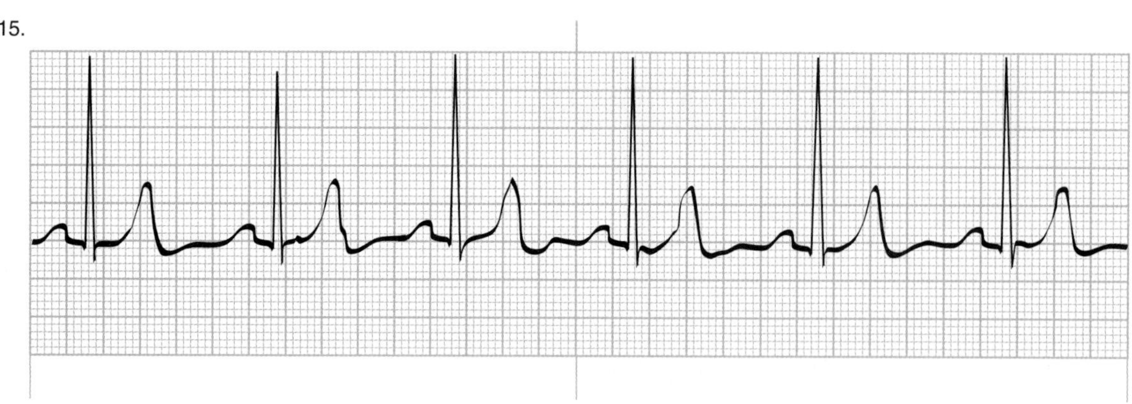

Rate _______________. Rhythm regular or irregular _______________?
If irregular, type of irregularity _______________ .

PRACTICE. . . MAKES PERFECT

16.

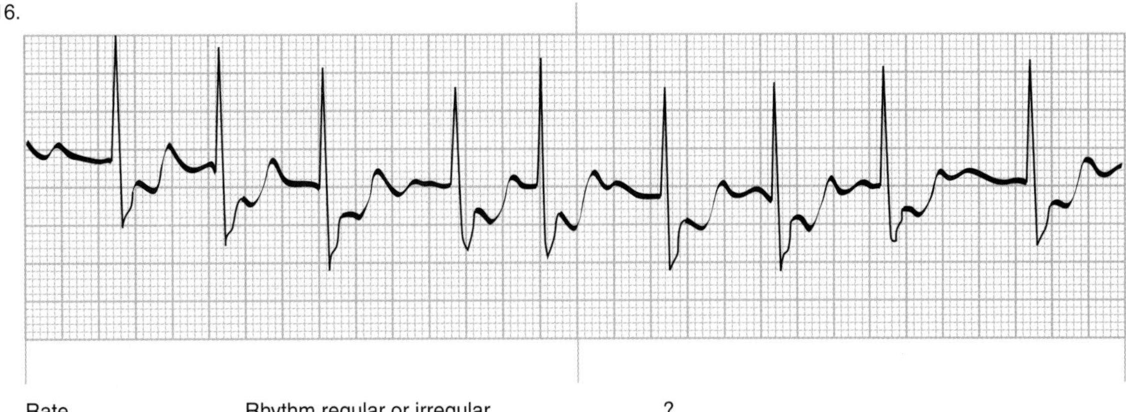

Rate ______________. Rhythm regular or irregular ______________?
If irregular, type of irregularity ______________ .

17.

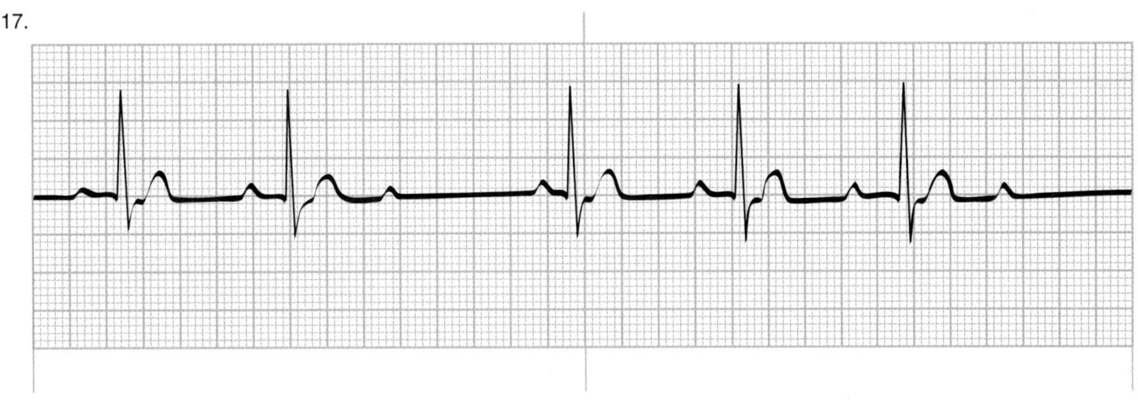

Rate ______________. Rhythm regular or irregular ______________?
If irregular, type of irregularity ______________ .

18.

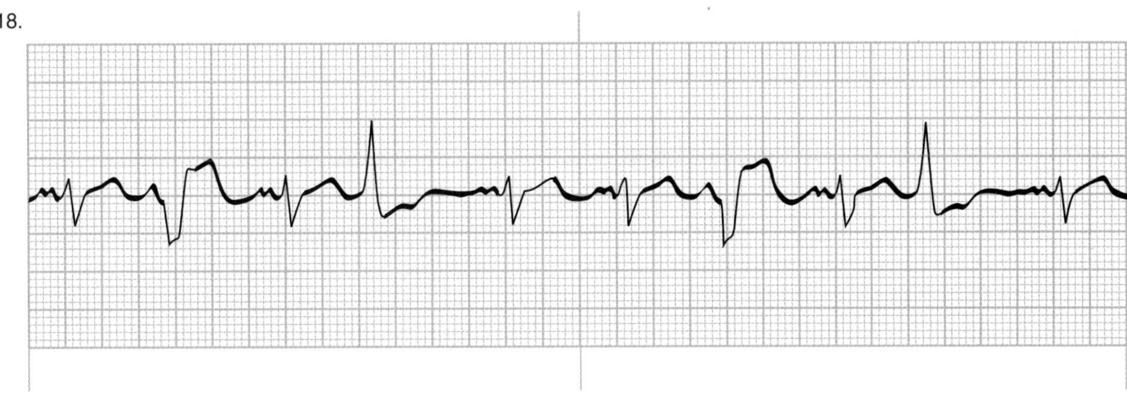

Rate ______________. Rhythm regular or irregular ______________?
If irregular, type of irregularity ______________ .

Key Points

- The second step of analyzing an ECG rhythm is determining its regularity.
- Irregular rhythms are considered abnormal. A variety of conditions can produce irregular rhythms.
- If the distance of the R-R intervals or P-P intervals is the same, the rhythm is regular. If the distance differs, the rhythm is irregular.
- Several methods can be used to determine rhythm regularity, including using calipers, marking a paper with a pen, and counting the small squares between each R-R interval.
- Irregularity may be occasionally irregular or very irregular. It may also be slightly irregular. It can result when the heart rate suddenly accelerates. Irregularity can also be patterned or irregularly (totally) irregular.
- A pacemaker that changes location from site to site may produce a slightly irregular rhythm.
- A very irregular rhythm is one that has many areas of irregularity. A common cause is frequent premature beats.
- A normal rate that suddenly accelerates to a rapid rate produces irregularity in the rhythm.
- Patterned irregularity is where the irregularity repeats over and over in a cyclic fashion.
- A totally irregular rhythm is one in which there is no consistency to the irregularity. Atrial fibrillation and ventricular fibrillation are characterized as totally irregular dysrhythmias.
- Irregularity can also be seen in dysrhythmias that have a varying atrial-to-ventricular conduction ratio.

Assess Your Understanding

The following questions give you a chance to assess your understanding of the material discussed in this chapter. The answers can be found in Appendix A.

1. Normally, the heart beats in a
   a. slightly irregular manner, producing a series of waveforms with each heartbeat.
   b. regularly irregular, rhythmic fashion, producing a P wave, QRS complex, and T wave with each heartbeat.
   c. regular, rhythmic fashion with periods of sudden heart rate acceleration and slowing.
   d. regular, rhythmic fashion, producing a P wave, QRS complex, and T wave with each heartbeat.
2. The distance between two consecutive R waves is called the
   a. R-R interval.
   b. RR segment.
   c. PR interval.
   d. ST segment.
3. The second step in analyzing an ECG is
   a. checking the regularity.
   b. looking at the P waves.
   c. assessing the PR intervals.
   d. determining the heart rate.
4. Calipers can be used to analyze an ECG by
   a. placing one leg on a starting point and extending the second leg four large boxes to the right.

b. establishing the distance between the first R-R or P-P interval and then adjusting the width of the calipers as you assess each consecutive interval.

c. placing one leg on a starting point and extending the second leg to the next consecutive waveform being assessed, then comparing this distance across the ECG strip.

d. moving the calipers across the tracing from each P wave to the next consecutive R wave.

5. The paper and pen method

a. can only be used to measure regular rhythms.

b. involves identifying an R wave that falls on a bold line.

c. requires placing a mark over each R wave on the ECG tracing and then using calipers to determine the distance between them.

d. involves placing two marks on the paper, the first above one of the R waves on the ECG tracing and the second above the next consecutive R wave.

6. To use the counting the small square method, you

a. count the number of small squares between the peaks of two consecutive R waves and then compare that to the other R-R intervals.

b. find an R wave that falls on a bold line and begin counting small squares.

c. count the number of small squares in a 6-second section of the ECG tracing.

d. divide by 1500 the number of QRS complexes in each 6-second section of the ECG tracing.

7. Which of the following methods for determining heart rhythm regularity is the easiest and for which you can use readily available supplies?

a. Counting small squares method.

b. Caliper method.

c. Paper and pen method.

d. Rate calculator method.

8. A/an ______________ irregular rhythm is one that appears mostly regular but from time to time you see an area where it is irregular.

a. occasionally

b. patterned

c. frequently

d. slightly

9. Premature beats

a. arise from the atria but not the other areas of the heart.

b. are also called ectopy.

c. cause the R-R intervals between the normal and premature beat to be longer than normal.

d. cause the rhythm to be chaotically irregular.

10. Failure of the SA node to initiate an impulse causes the

a. rhythm to be irregularly irregular.

b. R-R interval between the normal and the beat following the dropped beat to be shorter than normal.

c. rhythm to have patterned irregularity.

d. R-R interval that occurs because of the dropped beat to be longer than normal.

11. A/an ______________ irregular rhythm is one where the P-P intervals and R-R intervals vary somewhat.

a. slightly

b. patterned

c. occasionally

d. frequently

12. The term we use to describe sudden onset is
    a. transient.
    b. ectopy.
    c. paroxysmal.
    d. chaotic.
13. Patterned irregularity is
    a. transient.
    b. an absence of consistency between the R-R intervals.
    c. a chaotically or grossly irregular rhythm.
    d. the irregularity repeating over and over in a cyclic fashion.
14. Which of the following produces a totally irregular rhythm?
    a. Paroxysmal atrial tachycardia.
    b. Wenckebach.
    c. Atrial fibrillation.
    d. Atrial flutter with varying conduction ratio.
15. A patterned irregular rhythm is seen when
    a. the heart rate suddenly accelerates.
    b. there are many early beats.
    c. initiation of the heartbeat changes from site to site with each heartbeat.
    d. premature complexes occur every other (second) complex, every third complex, or every fourth complex.
16. Is the following rhythm regular or irregular? If it is irregular, what type of irregularity? What is the rate?

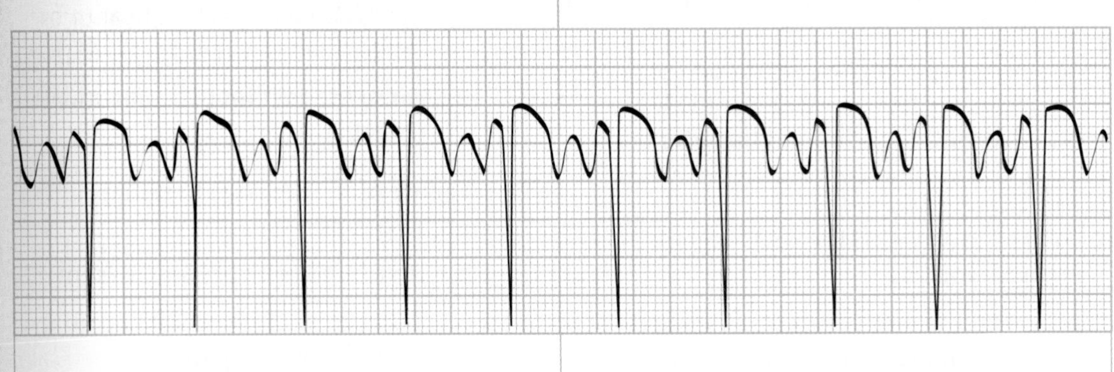

17. Is the following rhythm regular or irregular? If it is irregular, what type of irregularity? What is the rate?

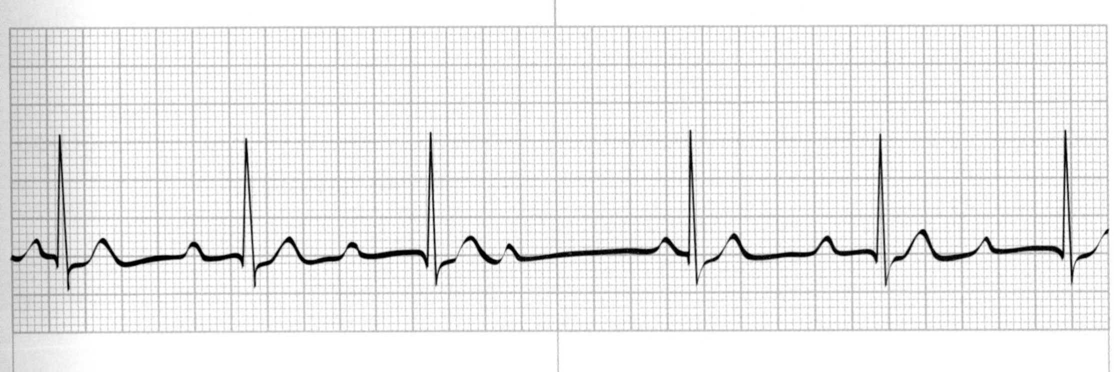

18. Is the following rhythm regular or irregular? If it is irregular, what type of irregularity? What is the rate?

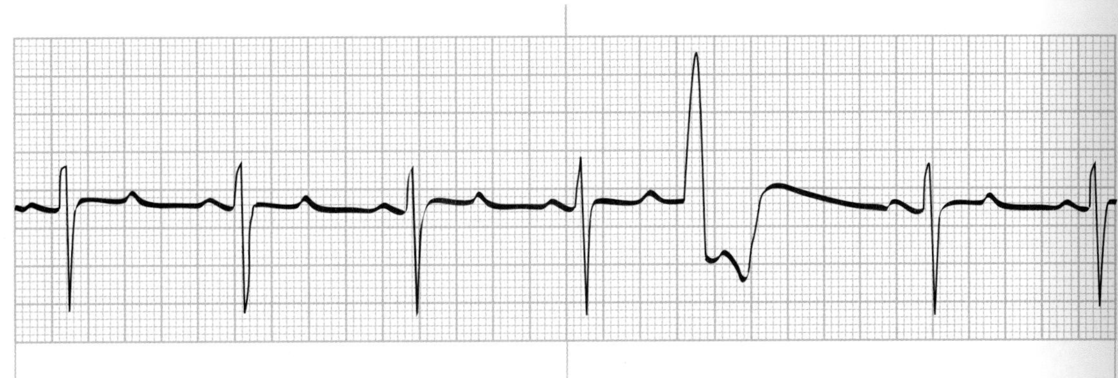

19. Is the following rhythm regular or irregular? If it is irregular, what type of irregularity? What is the rate?

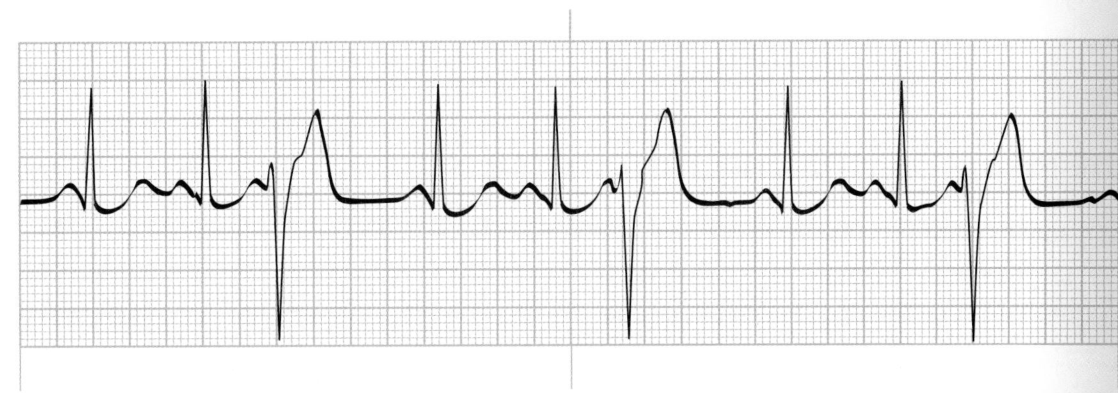

20. Is the following rhythm regular or irregular? If it is irregular, what type of irregularity? What is the rate?

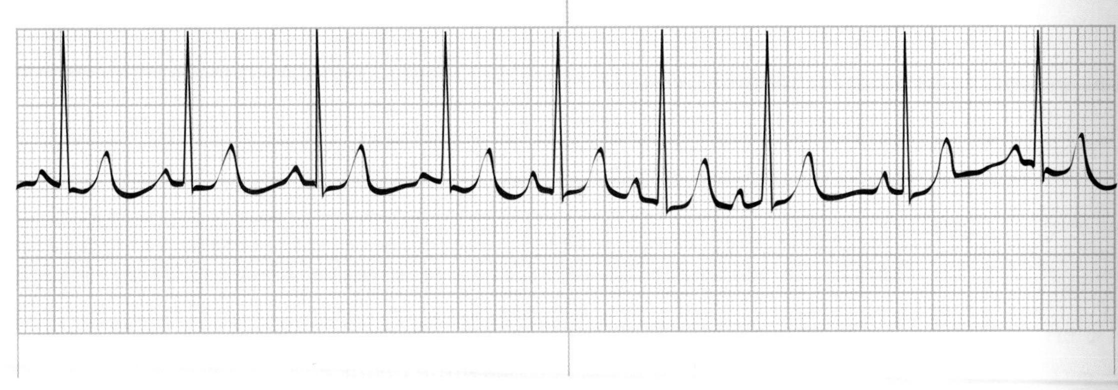

Referring to the scenario at the beginning of this chapter, answer the following questions.

21. Which rhythm does the patient most likely have?
    a. Ventricular fibrillation.
    b. Atrial flutter.
    c. Atrial fibrillation.
    d. Sinus dysrhythmia.
22. The patient's rhythm is caused by increased automaticity in which of the following?
    a. SA node.
    b. Atria.
    c. AV node.
    d. Bundle of His.
23. Which of the following represents the most common long-term complication from this rhythm?
    a. Ventricular fibrillation.
    b. Atherosclerosis.
    c. Complete heart block.
    d. Stroke.

Answers to Sidebar Questions

"What does the term dysrhythmia mean?"

Answer: A dysrhythmia is any deviation in the heart rate or rhythm from normal.

"What is the first step in analyzing an ECG rhythm?"

Answer: The first step in analyzing an ECG rhythm is to determine the heart rate.

"What single rhythm is considered normal?"

Answer: Normal or regular sinus rhythm is the only rhythm considered normal. It is what we measure everything else against.

"Which method may be used to calculate the heart rate in irregular rhythms?"

Answer: The 6-second interval × 10 method is used to calculate the heart rate in irregular rhythms. Regular rhythms can be assessed using the 300, 150, 100, 75, 60, 50 method; 1500 method; or rate calculators.

"How do you know a heart rhythm is irregular using either the calipers method or paper and pen method?"

Answer: The distances between the intervals differs; in other words, from the location you identify as the starting point and where the second caliper point or pen mark falls is either before or after the second P wave or R wave in one or more P-P intervals or R-R intervals.

"What is the heart's primary pacemaker site?

Answer: The SA node is the primary pacemaker of the heart.

"In what sites outside the SA node does tachycardia arise?"

Answer: Tachycardia arises from the atria, AV junction, and ventricles.

"What is the role of the AV node?"

Answer: The AV node is the only pathway for impulses to move from the atria to the ventricles. The impulse travels through the AV node slowly creating a slight delay that allows the atria to finish pushing any remaining blood into the ventricles.

On the DVD

- Determining Regularity lecture.
- Demonstration of the Methods Used to Determine Regularity.

P Waves

5

Case History

EMS is dispatched for a 75-year-old man residing in a nursing home complaining of "nonspecific weakness." Upon arrival the paramedics note that the patient is ashen and diaphoretic, lying on the floor next to his bed. After introducing themselves, the paramedics perform an initial assessment and obtain a history of the events leading up to the patient's collapse. They learn that he apparently felt fine when he went to bed but after rising he went to the bathroom, began to feel weak, and slumped to the floor.

The patient is now awake and alert but feels light-headed when he tries to sit up. Vital signs show a BP of 140/90, pulse 36, and respirations of 18 and unlabored. His oxygen saturation is 94% on room air. The cardiac monitor is attached and reveals a slow rhythm with a narrow QRS complex. One paramedic examines the strip more closely while her partner establishes an intravenous line. The rhythm strip reveals the absence of normal P waves and instead has saw-toothed F waves. A QRS complex occurs after every fourth F wave.

The patient is promptly transported to the hospital for definitive treatment.

Chapter Preview

- Analyzing the ECG
- Step 3: Examining the P Waves

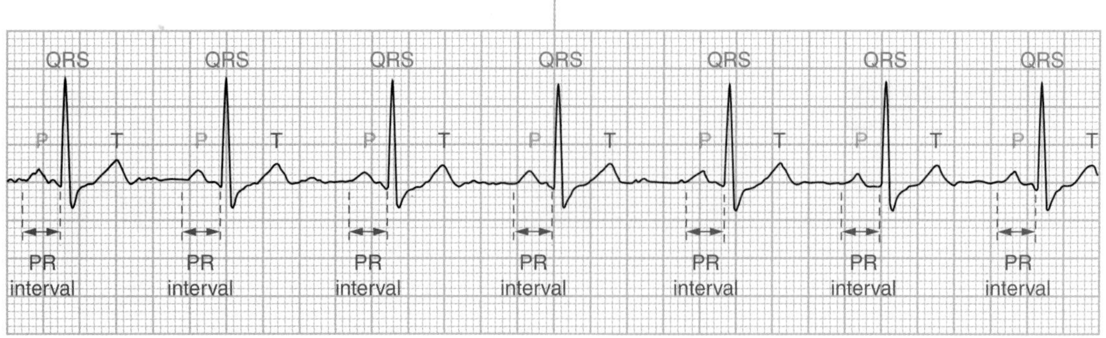

Figure 5-1
The heart beats in a regular, rhythmic fashion.

Analyzing the ECG

Normally, the heart beats in a regular, rhythmic fashion, producing a P wave, QRS complex, and T wave with each heartbeat (Figure 5-1). This cycle repeats over and over.

KEY CONCEPT
The heart normally beats in a regular, rhythmic fashion, producing a P wave, QRS complex, and T wave with each heartbeat.

Five-Step Process

As described earlier, to perform analysis of ECG tracings we can use a logical, systematic process that includes the following five steps:

1. Determine the rate. (Is it normal, fast, or slow?)
2. Determine the regularity. (Is it regular or irregular?)
3. Assess the P waves. (Is there a uniform P wave preceding each QRS complex? Do they appear normal?)
4. Assess the QRS complexes. (Are the QRS complexes within normal limits? Do they appear normal?)
5. Assess the PR intervals. (Are the PR intervals identifiable? Within normal limits? Constant in duration?)

As part of analyzing an ECG we examine and measure the specific waveforms, segments, and intervals. In Chapter 3 we focused on determining the heart rate (Step 1), while in Chapter 4 we addressed identifying regularity (Step 2). In Steps 1 and 2, the lead (or view) used does not affect how the ECG tracing is analyzed. With the next steps of analyzing an ECG rhythm, however, lead selection does affect the appearance of the waveforms, so you need to be familiar not only with how normal waveforms look, but also with how the waveforms look in the different leads.

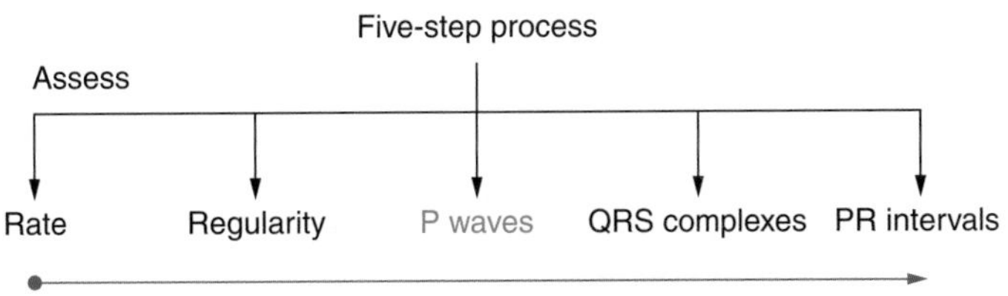

Figure 5-2
Evaluating the P waves is the third step of analyzing an ECG tracing.

INSTRUCTIONAL MOMENT
Remember, our discussion regarding dysrhythmias in this chapter is to give you a sense of the normal P wave and how changes occur. This is not intended to be an in-depth discussion of any dysrhythmia but rather a description of how it produces the P waves you see. Don't worry about memorizing the names of the dysrhythmias at this point.

Normally, the heart beats in a ______________, rhythmic fashion, producing a ______________ wave, ______________ complex, and ______________ wave with each heartbeat.

[regular] [P] [QRS] [T]

INSTRUCTIONAL MOMENT
The term morphology means the appearance of a waveform.

Step 3: Examining the P Waves

The third step of analyzing an ECG rhythm is to examine the P waves (Figure 5-2). As discussed, the P wave is the first waveform at the start of the cardiac cycle. It begins with its movement away from the baseline and ends on its return to the baseline. To examine the P waves we look closely at their characteristics, especially their location and morphology (configuration and deflection).

The following are characteristic features of normal P waves (Figure 5-3):

- *Location.* One P wave precedes each QRS complex
- *Amplitude.* 0.5 to 2.5 mm
- *Duration.* 0.06 to 0.10 seconds
- *Morphology.* Usually rounded and upright (or inverted or biphasic in certain leads)

QUESTION
"What does a sinus P wave represent?" (The answer can be found on page 168.)

Step 3 of analyzing an ECG rhythm is to examine the ______________ waves. Normally, P waves are ______________ and ______________ (in certain leads) with an amplitude of ______________ mm and a duration of ______________ seconds.

[P] [rounded] [upright] [0.5 to 2.5] [0.06 to 0.10]

KEY CONCEPT
The third step to analyzing an ECG rhythm is to assess the P waves.

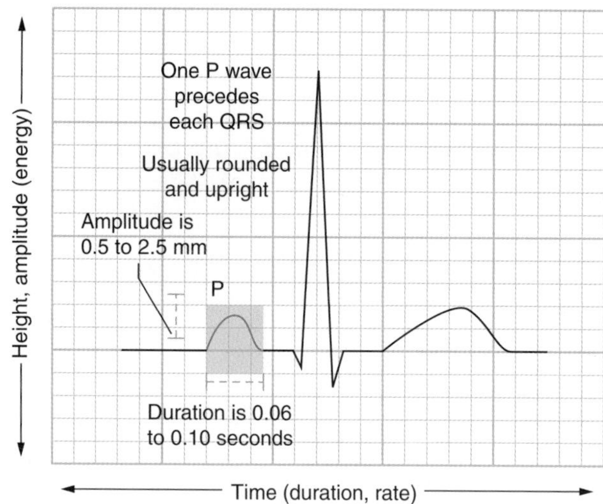

Figure 5-3
The normal P wave.

If the morphology of a P wave is normal—as an example, in lead II it is upright and round—and if the P wave precedes each QRS complex, it is likely that this electrical impulse originated in the SA node and was carried through the atria and AV node in a normal manner. Normal (regular) sinus rhythm is the rhythm against which we compare all others. In the previous two chapters we described several dysrhythmias that originated from the SA node including sinus bradycardia, sinus tachycardia, sinus dysrhythmia, and sinus arrest. These dysrhythmias should have normal looking P waves. However, in faster sinus tachycardias, the P wave can sometimes be buried in the T wave of the preceding beat.

P Wave Configuration in Different Leads

In leads I, II, aV_F, and V_2 through V_6, the deflection of the P wave is characteristically upright or positive. In leads III, and aV_L, and V_1, the P wave is usually upright but may be negative or biphasic (both positive and negative). In lead aV_R, the P wave is negative or inverted (Figure 5-4).

INSTRUCTIONAL MOMENT
One way of analyzing the relationship between the P waves and QRS complexes is to ask two questions: "Is there a P wave preceding each QRS complex?" "Are there any P waves without a QRS complex?"

The P wave is characteristically positive or upright in leads __________, __________, __________, and V_2 through V_6. The P wave is negative or inverted in lead __________.

[I] [II] [aV_F] [aV_R]

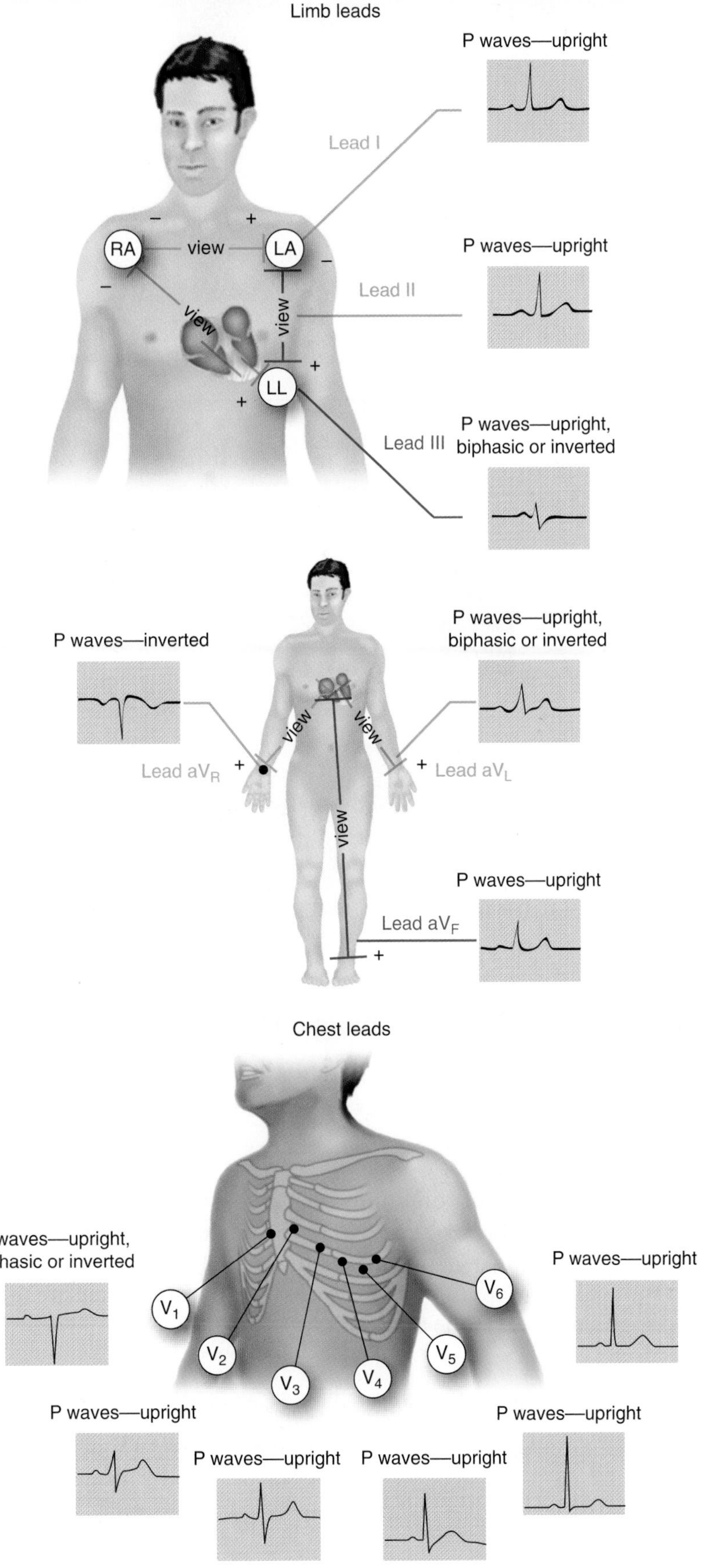

Figure 5-4
Direction of P waves in various leads.

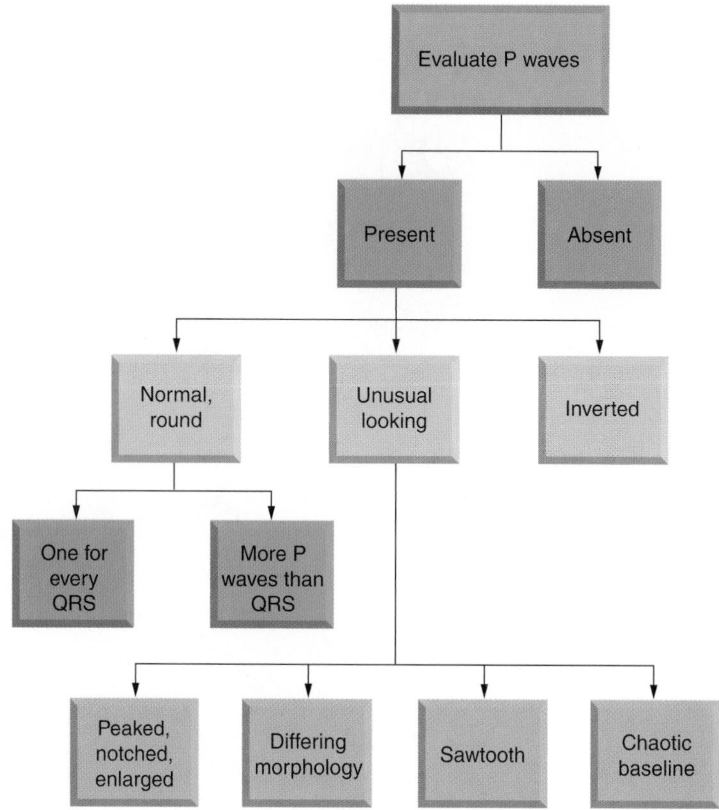

Figure 5-5
Algorithm for normal and abnormal P waves.

QUESTION
"Which rhythm has a characteristic heart rate of 60 to 100 beats a minute, a regular rhythm, and a P wave preceding each QRS complex?" (The answer can be found on page 168.)

P Waves Having a Different Appearance

Abnormal P waves are those that look different, are inverted, absent, follow the QRS complex, or where there are P waves not followed by a QRS complex (Figure 5-5).

A variety of conditions can cause P waves to look different. In some cases, the P wave originates in the SA node but the atria are altered, or damaged resulting in abnormal conduction of the atrial impulse. In other cases, the P wave appears different because the pacemaker site originates from a site other than the SA node.

P waves look different if they originate in the SA node, but the _______________ are altered, damaged, abnormal, or the pacemaker does not originate in the _______________ node.

[atria] [SA]

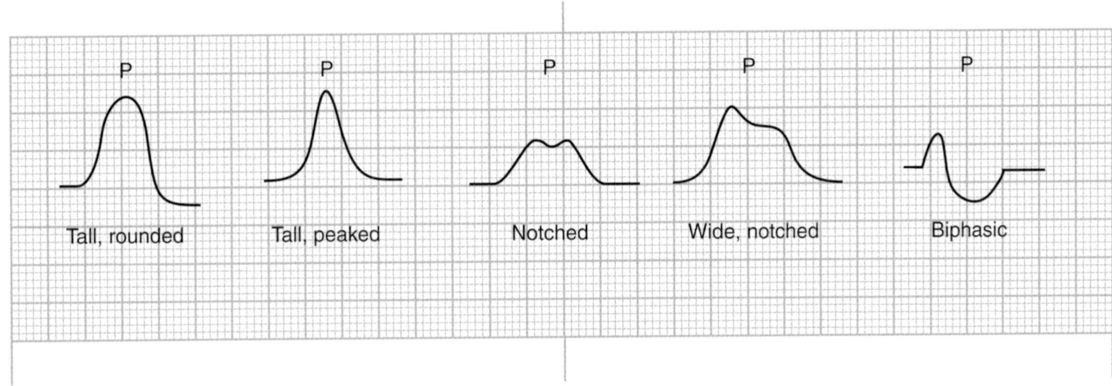

Figure 5-6
Types of abnormal atrial waveforms include: Tall, peaked, notched, wide, or biphasic sinus P waves.

Peaked, Notched, or Enlarged Sinus P Waves

Tall and symmetrically peaked P waves may be seen with increased right atrial pressure and right atrial dilation (Figure 5-6). This is called **P pulmonale.** We may also see abnormally tall P waves in sinus tachycardia.

Notched or wide (prolonged) P waves may be seen in increased left atrial pressure and left atrial dilation. This is called **P mitrale.** In Chapter 14 we discuss these conditions in further detail.

KEY CONCEPT
Tall and symmetrically peaked P waves suggest increased right atrial pressure and right atrial dilation. Notched or wide (enlarged) P waves indicate increased left atrial pressure and left atrial dilation.

These types of P waves may also be seen when there is a delay or block in the movement of electrical impulses through the interatrial conduction tract between the right and left atria resulting in one atrium depolarizing before the other.

Biphasic P waves can occur with both right and left atrial dilation. These waves typically appear in leads V_1 and V_2 and have an initial positive deflection (reflecting right atrial depolarization) followed by a negative deflection (reflecting left atrial depolarization).

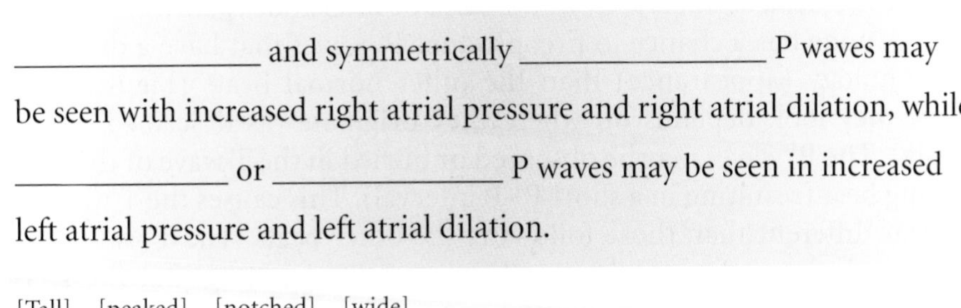

________________ and symmetrically ________________ P waves may be seen with increased right atrial pressure and right atrial dilation, while ______________ or ______________ P waves may be seen in increased left atrial pressure and left atrial dilation.

[Tall] [peaked] [notched] [wide]

INSTRUCTIONAL MOMENT
Waveforms (such as P waves) that look alike from beat to beat are coming from the same location (foci). Waveforms that look different are coming from a different location(s).

INSTRUCTIONAL MOMENT
The term retrograde means that the impulse conducts upward (backward) through the heart instead of downward.

Atrial P Waves

Some dysrhythmias originate outside the SA node. Those that arise from the atrial tissue or in the internodal pathways are referred to as atrial dysrhythmias. The impulses produce P waves (called P prime or P′) that look different than the sinus P waves because the impulses arise from outside the SA node. Premature atrial complexes and atrial tachycardia are two examples of dysrhythmias that arise from the atria.

How the P′ wave looks depends on where it originates and the direction the electrical impulse travels through the atria. As a rule, the closer the site of origin is to the SA node, the more it looks like a normal P wave. If the ectopic pacemaker arises from the upper- or middle-right atrium, depolarization occurs in a normal direction—from right to left and then downward. If it is initiated from the upper-right atrium, the P′ wave should be upright in lead II, resembling a normal sinus P wave. If it is initiated from the middle of the right atrium, the P′ wave is less positive than one that originates from the upper-right atrium.

If the impulse arises from the lower-right atrium near the AV node or in the left atrium, depolarization occurs in a **retrograde** direction—from left to right and then upward resulting in the P′ wave being inverted in lead II.

The ______________ the site of origin is to the SA node, the more the ______________ wave looks like a normal P wave. If the impulse is initiated from the ______________ of the right atrium, the P′ wave is ______________ positive than one that originates from the ______________ right atrium.

[closer] [P′] [middle] [less] [upper]

P′ Waves Seen With Premature Atrial Complexes (PACs)

Premature beats that arise from the atria or internodal pathways, before the SA node has a chance to fire, produce P′ waves that have a different morphology (appearance) than the other normal beats (Figure 5-7). How they look depends on where they originate (as described previously). The P′ waves may be obscured or buried in the T wave of the preceding beat (resulting in a short P′-P interval). This causes the T wave to appear different than those following the other beats. The T wave may look peaked, notched, or larger than normal suggesting that the P′ is buried in the T wave.

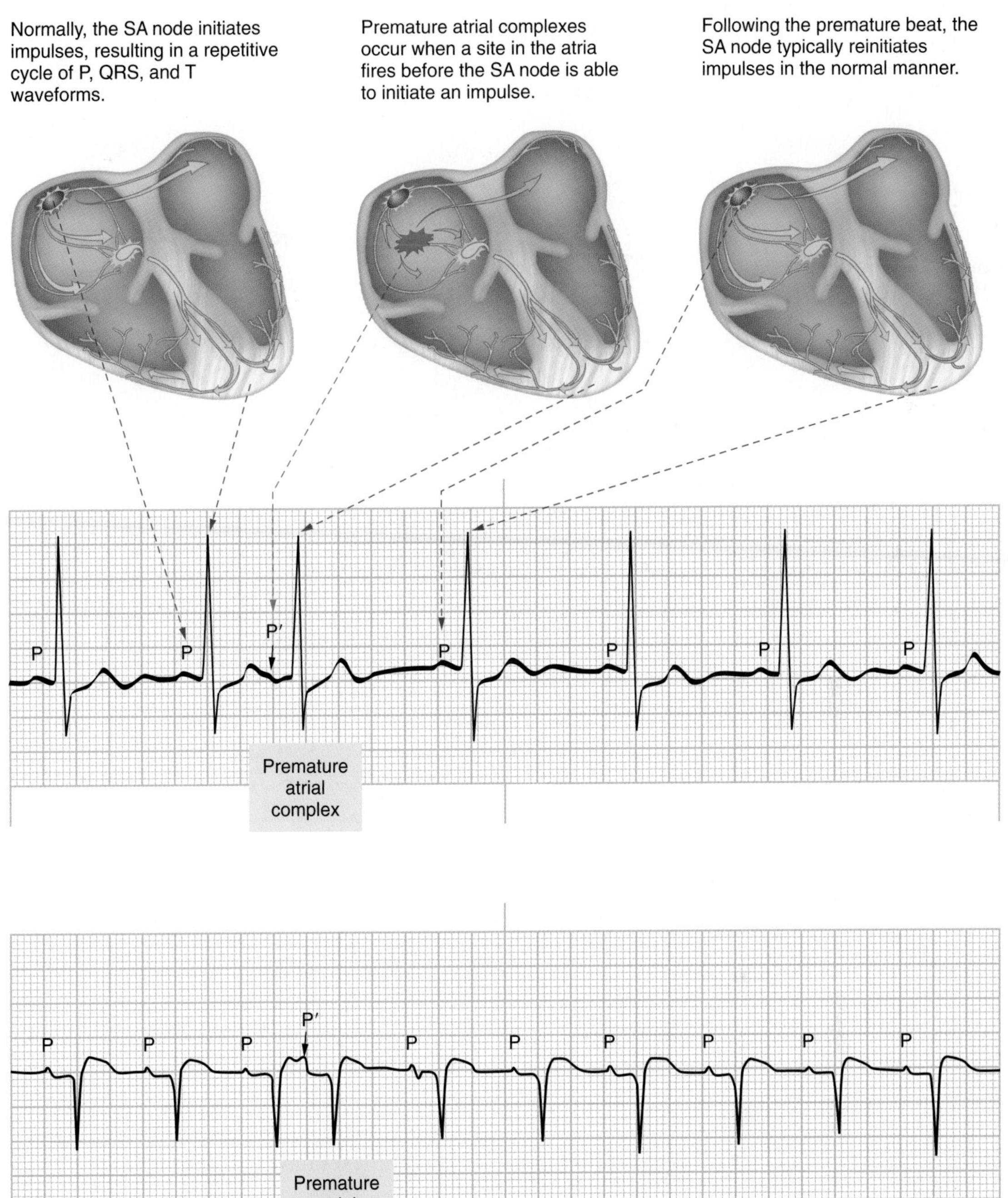

Figure 5-7
P′ waves seen with premature atrial complexes differ from sinus P waves, and may be buried in the preceding T wave.

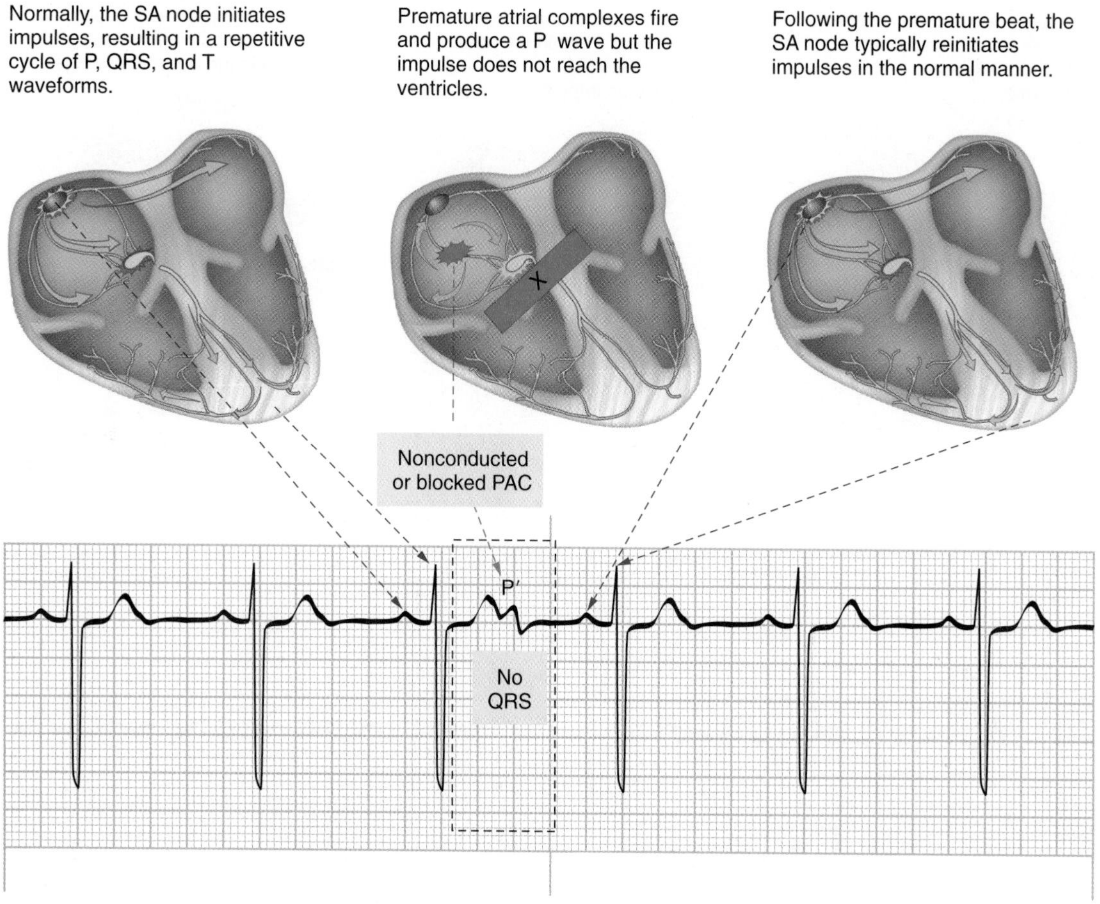

Normally, the SA node initiates impulses, resulting in a repetitive cycle of P, QRS, and T waveforms.

Premature atrial complexes fire and produce a P wave but the impulse does not reach the ventricles.

Following the premature beat, the SA node typically reinitiates impulses in the normal manner.

Nonconducted or blocked PAC

P′

No QRS

Figure 5-8
With a blocked premature atrial complex there is a P′ wave but no QRS complex.

KEY CONCEPT
PACs are early ectopic beats preceded by a P′ wave that have different morphology than the other normal beats.

The P′ wave in premature atria complexes have a different ___________ than the other normal beats. Also, the P′ waves may be ___________ in the T wave of the preceding beat.

[morphology] [buried]

P′ Waves Seen With Nonconducted or Blocked PACs You may see an atrial P′ wave which is not followed by a QRS complex. This is due to a nonconducted or blocked premature atrial complex (Figure 5-8). This can be confused with AV heart block (described later in this chapter). A key dif-

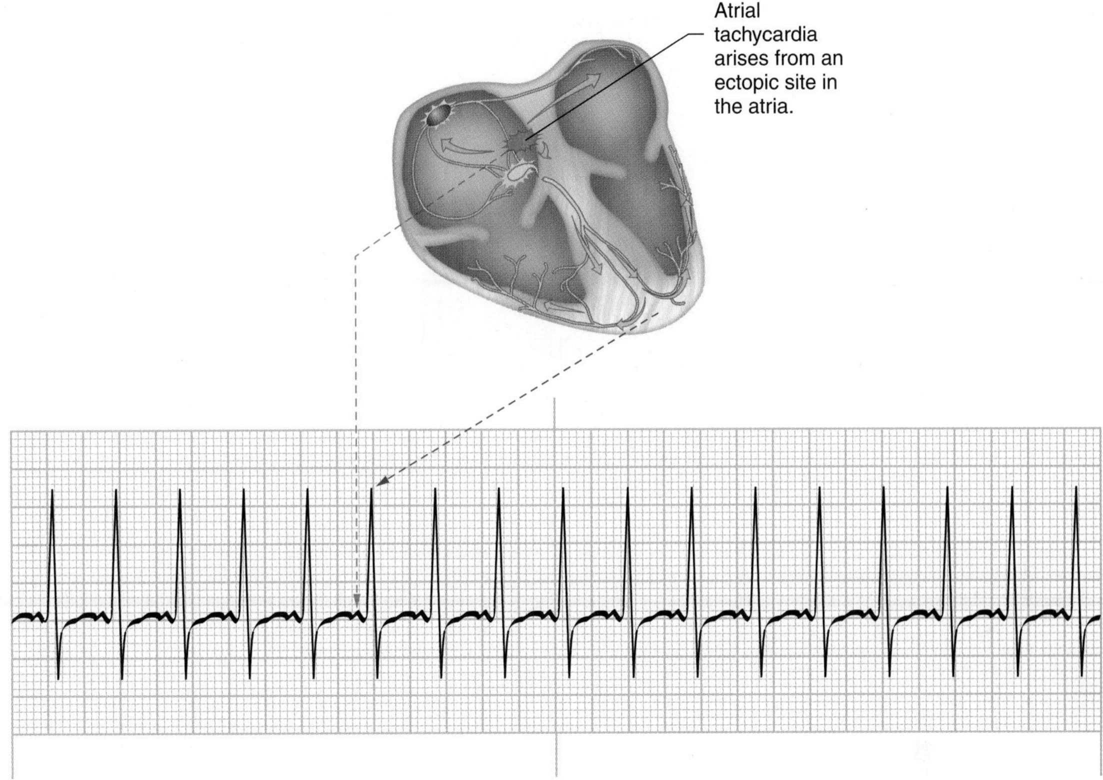

Figure 5-9
If seen, the morphology of the P' waves associated with atrial tachycardia is different from normal beats.

ference between the two is that with premature beats, the P′-P interval is shorter, whereas with AV heart block, the P-P interval remains constant. With premature beats the P′ wave also looks different than the other P waves, whereas with AV heart block, the P waves look alike.

INSTRUCTIONAL MOMENT
Remember, in atrial tachycardia the P waves may also be buried in the T wave of the preceding beat due to the short P-P intervals.

P′ Waves Seen With Atrial Tachycardia

Tachycardia can arise from the atria resulting in rapid depolarization that overrides the SA node (Figure 5-9). It produces a heart rate of between 150 to 250 beats per minute. The P′ wave in atrial tachycardia has a different morphology than normal P waves. The P′ wave is likely to be buried in the T wave of the preceding beat. For this reason, we refer to tachycardias with normal QRS complexes and no discernable P waves as supraventricular tachycardia.

KEY CONCEPT
Atrial tachycardia is a fast dysrhythmia with P waves that have a different morphology than normal beats.

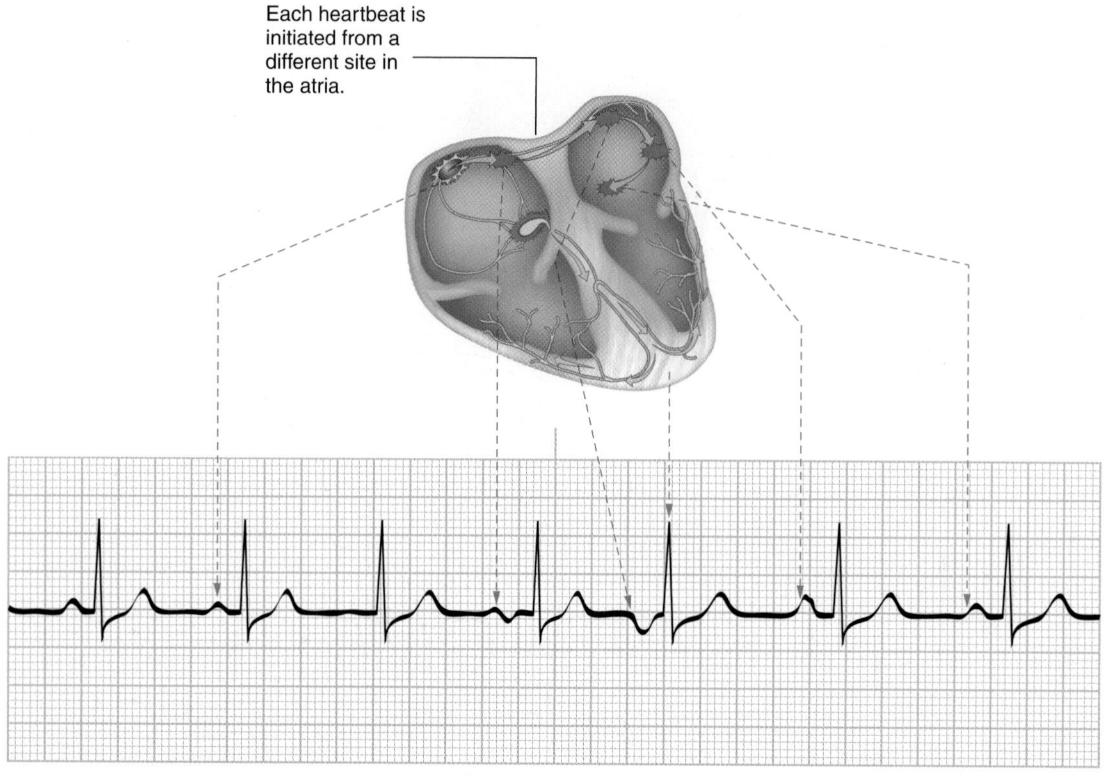

Figure 5-10
Varying P' waves occur when, instead of arising from the SA node, the heart's pacemaker shifts from site to site throughout the atria.

QUESTION
"What type of irregularity is characteristic of wandering atrial pacemaker?" (The answer can be found on page 168.)

KEY CONCEPT
A change in P′ wave morphology from beat to beat is the most distinguishing characteristic of wandering atrial pacemaker.

 Varying Atrial P Waves

P waves coming from one site will look similar. P' waves that continuously change in appearance indicate that the impulse is arising from different locations in the atria (Figure 5-10). This dysrhythmia is called wandering atrial pacemaker. In this dysrhythmia the pacemaker site shifts transiently from beat to beat from the SA node to other latent (hidden) pacemaker sites in the atria and AV junction. This produces its most distinguishing characteristic—a change in P' wave morphology from beat to beat.

A key characteristic of wandering atrial pacemaker are P′ waves that ________________ change in appearance.

[continuously]

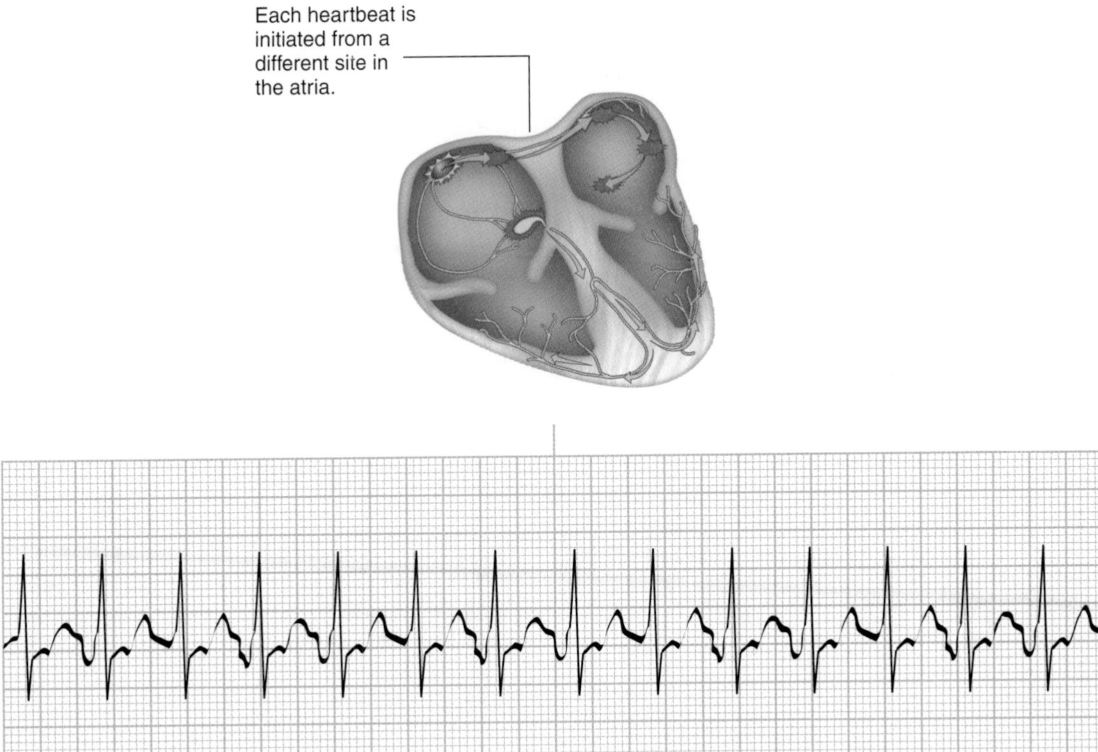

Figure 5-11
The changing pacemaker site in multifocal atrial tachycardia produces dissimilar P' waves.

P′ Waves Seen With Multifocal Atrial Tachycardia

A variation of wandering atrial pacemaker is a dysrhythmia that has dissimilar P′ waves but is associated with rates in the range of 120 to 150 beats per minute (Figure 5-11). It is commonly misdiagnosed as atrial fibrillation with rapid ventricular response. However, if you look closely, you see distinct, but clearly different, P′ waves. In atrial fibrillation there are no P waves. This dysrhythmia is called multifocal (meaning from many different focuses) atrial tachycardia. It is abbreviated as MAT.

Flutter and Fibrillatory Waves

Two other dysrhythmias resulting from very fast atrial rates produce significantly different looking atrial waveforms. Atrial flutter is associated with characteristic flutter waveforms, while atrial fibrillation is associated with a characteristic chaotic-looking baseline.

QUESTION
"How fast is the atrial rate in atrial flutter?" (The answer can be found on page 168.)

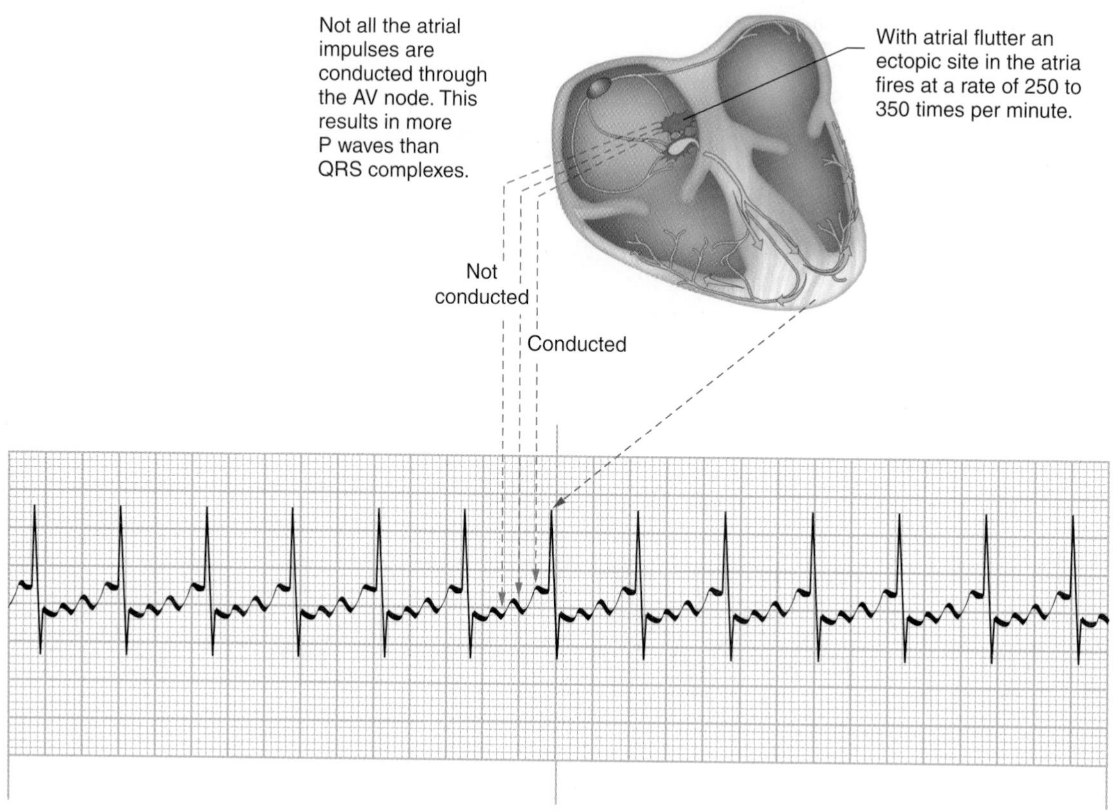

Figure 5-12
Rapid atrial rate from one site produces a saw-toothed pattern of F waves.

INSTRUCTIONAL MOMENT
One of the diagnostic tricks that can be used to identify atrial flutter is to turn the tracing upside down. Atrial flutter has the appearance of a "handsaw blade" used to cut wood.

KEY CONCEPT
Atrial flutter produces atrial waveforms that appear as a saw-toothed pattern.

Saw-Toothed Waveforms

If you recall our discussion in Chapters 3 and 4, we said that in atrial flutter the atria fire at a rate of between 250 and 350 beats per minute (Figure 5-12). Normal P waves are absent, and instead, we see flutter waves (F waves). They are often described as a saw-toothed pattern.

The atrial-to-ventricular conduction ratio of impulses is usually 2:1, 3:1, or 4:1. An atrial to ventricular conduction ratio of 1:1 is rare because the ventricles are unable to repolarize quickly enough to respond to each of the atrial impulses. The conduction ratios may be constant or variable, meaning that over the course of minutes the conduction ratio changes.

With atrial flutter, the normal P waves are ________________; instead there are ______________ waves.

[absent] [flutter]

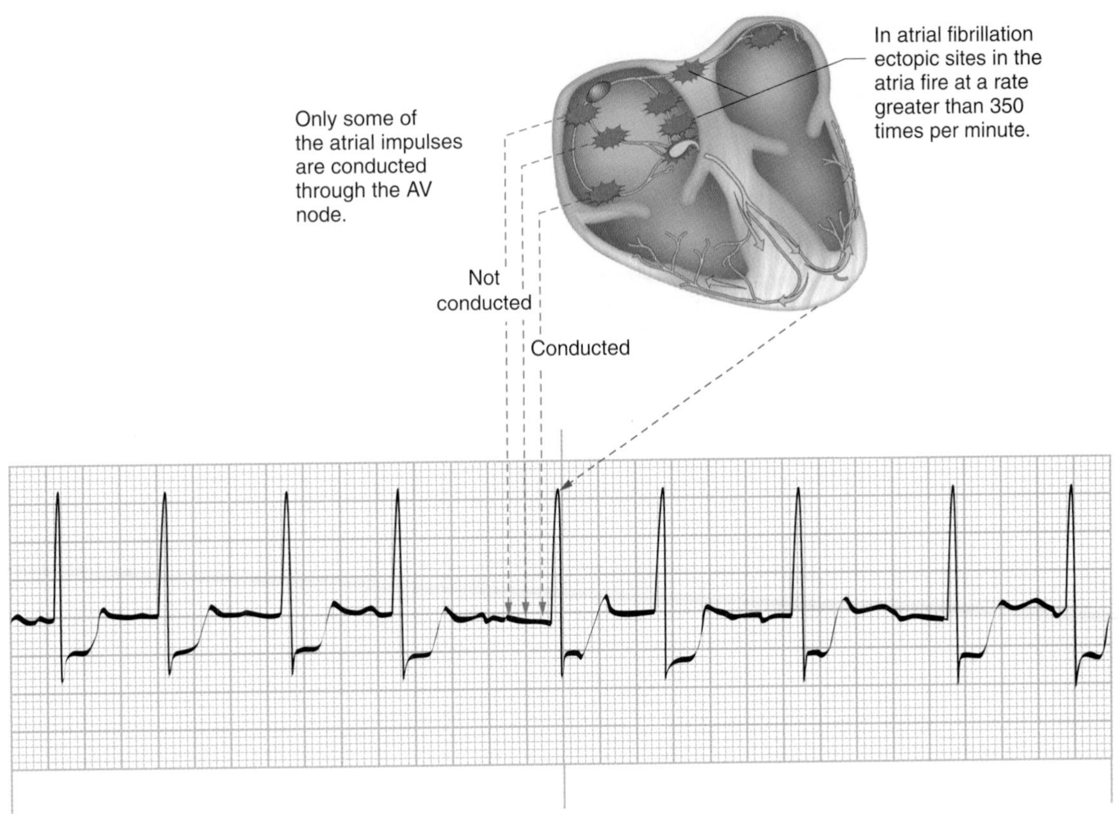

Figure 5-13
With atrial fibrillation, the atria fire at a rate in excess of 350 beats per minute from multiple sites causing a chaotic-looking baseline with no discernable P waves.

Chaotic-Looking Baseline

In atrial fibrillation, the atria fire faster than 350 beats per minute (Figure 5-13). This produces a fibrillatory waveform, reflective of what is occurring with the atrial muscle. This is best described as a chaotic-looking baseline with no discernable P waves (in other words an absence of P waves). Instead of P waves, we see uneven baseline of "f" waves. In some areas along the baseline you may see what looks like a P wave or two but nothing that really appears the same along the tracing.

QUESTION
"What type of irregularity is characteristic of atrial fibrillation?" (The answer can be found on page 168.)

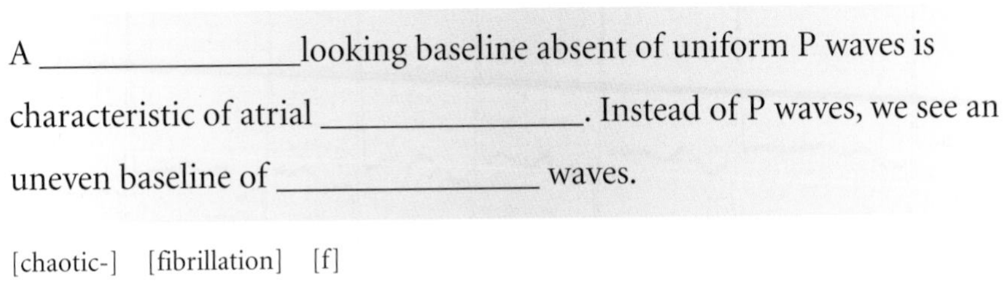

A ________________ looking baseline absent of uniform P waves is characteristic of atrial ________________. Instead of P waves, we see an uneven baseline of ________________ waves.

[chaotic-] [fibrillation] [f]

You can practice determining heart rate, regularity, and type of atrial waveform with the following *Practice Makes Perfect* exercises. Answers to these exercises can be found in Appendix A.

PRACTICE. . . MAKES PERFECT

1.

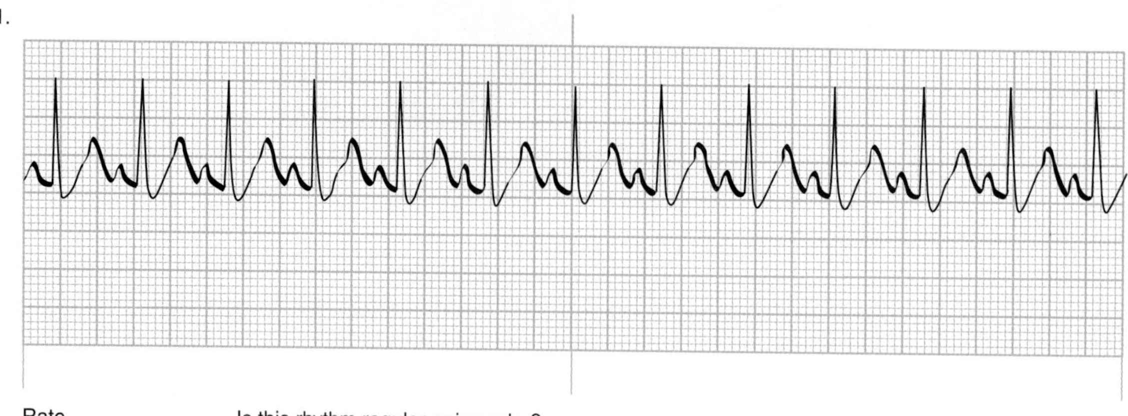

Rate ______________ Is this rhythm regular or irregular? ______________ .
What type of atrial waveform is present? ______________

2.

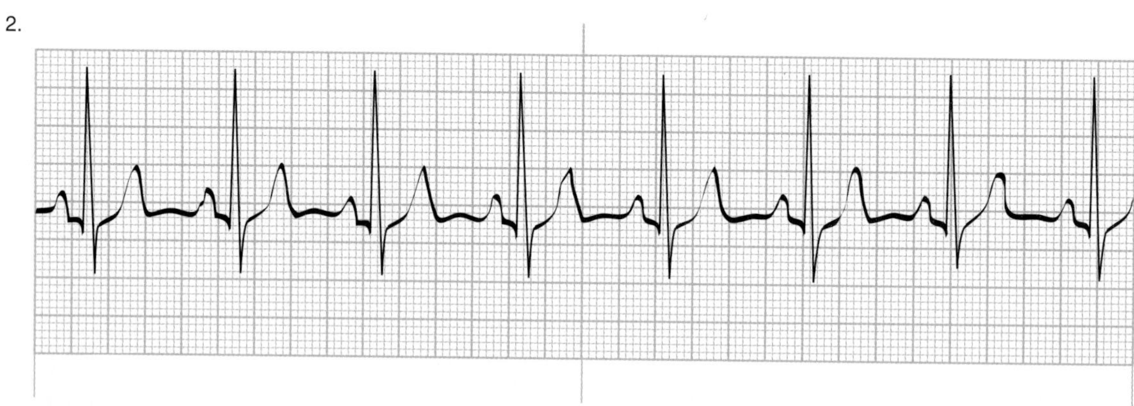

Rate ______________ Is this rhythm regular or irregular? ______________ .
What type of atrial waveform is present? ______________

3.

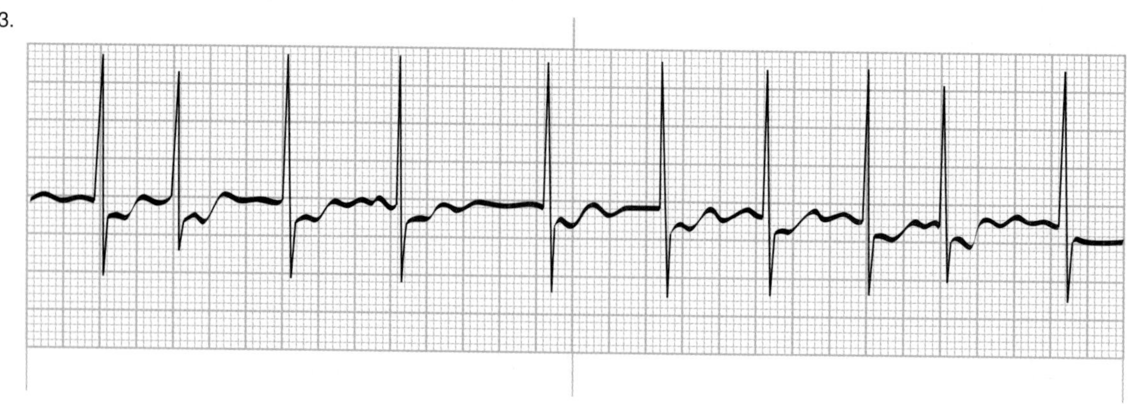

Rate ______________ Is this rhythm regular or irregular? ______________ .
What type of atrial waveform is present? ______________

PRACTICE. . . MAKES PERFECT

4.

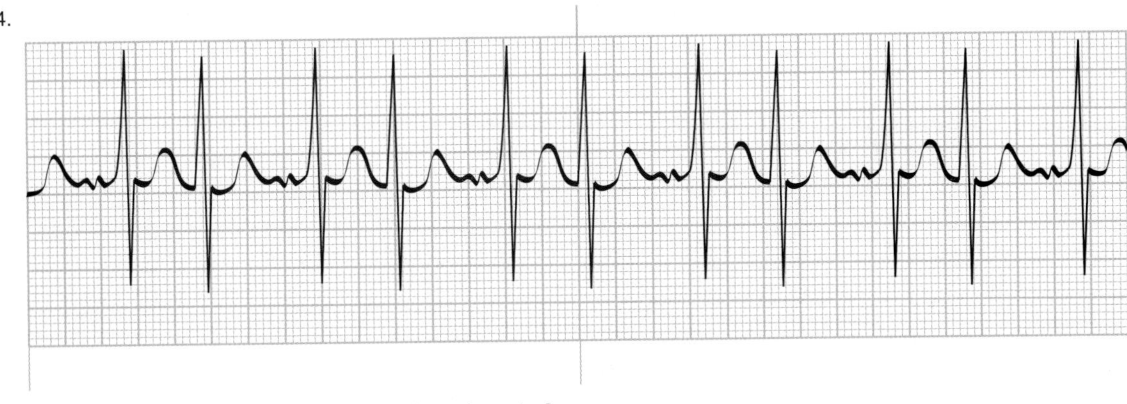

Rate _______________ Is this rhythm regular or irregular? _______________.
What type of atrial waveform is present? _______________

5.

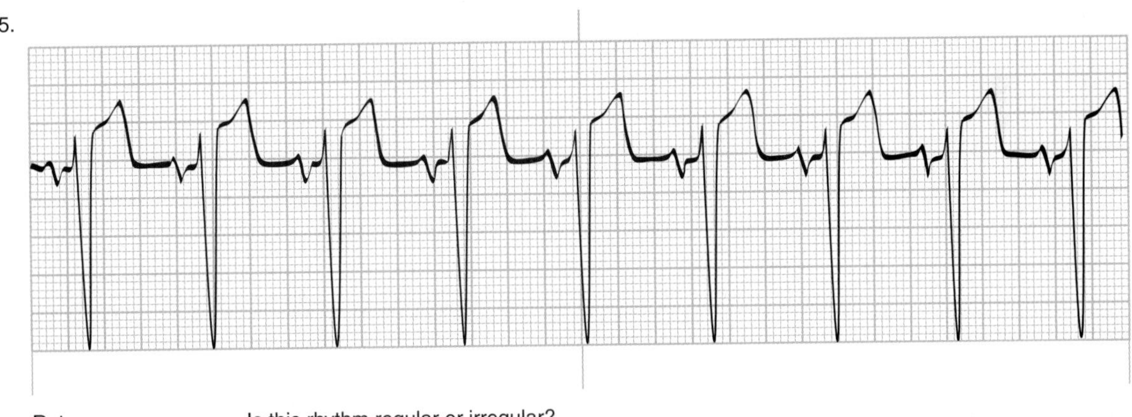

Rate _______________ Is this rhythm regular or irregular? _______________.
What type of atrial waveform is present? _______________

Inverted and Absent P Waves

In addition to the inverted P′ waves arising from the lower-right atrium near the AV node or in the left atrium, they can also arise from the AV junction (Figure 5-14). The inverted P' wave occurs when the electrical impulse travels upward through the AV junction into the atria causing retrograde (backward) atrial depolarization. It can occur before, during (buried in QRS), or after the QRS complex. We describe those buried in the QRS complex as absent. This may change the morphology of the QRS complex. The four junctional dysrhythmias that arise from the AV junction are premature junctional complexes (PJCs), junctional escape rhythm, accelerated junctional rhythm, and junctional tachycardia.

KEY CONCEPT
Junctional dysrythmias have inverted P waves (in lead II) immediately in front of, or that occur during or following, the QRS complex.

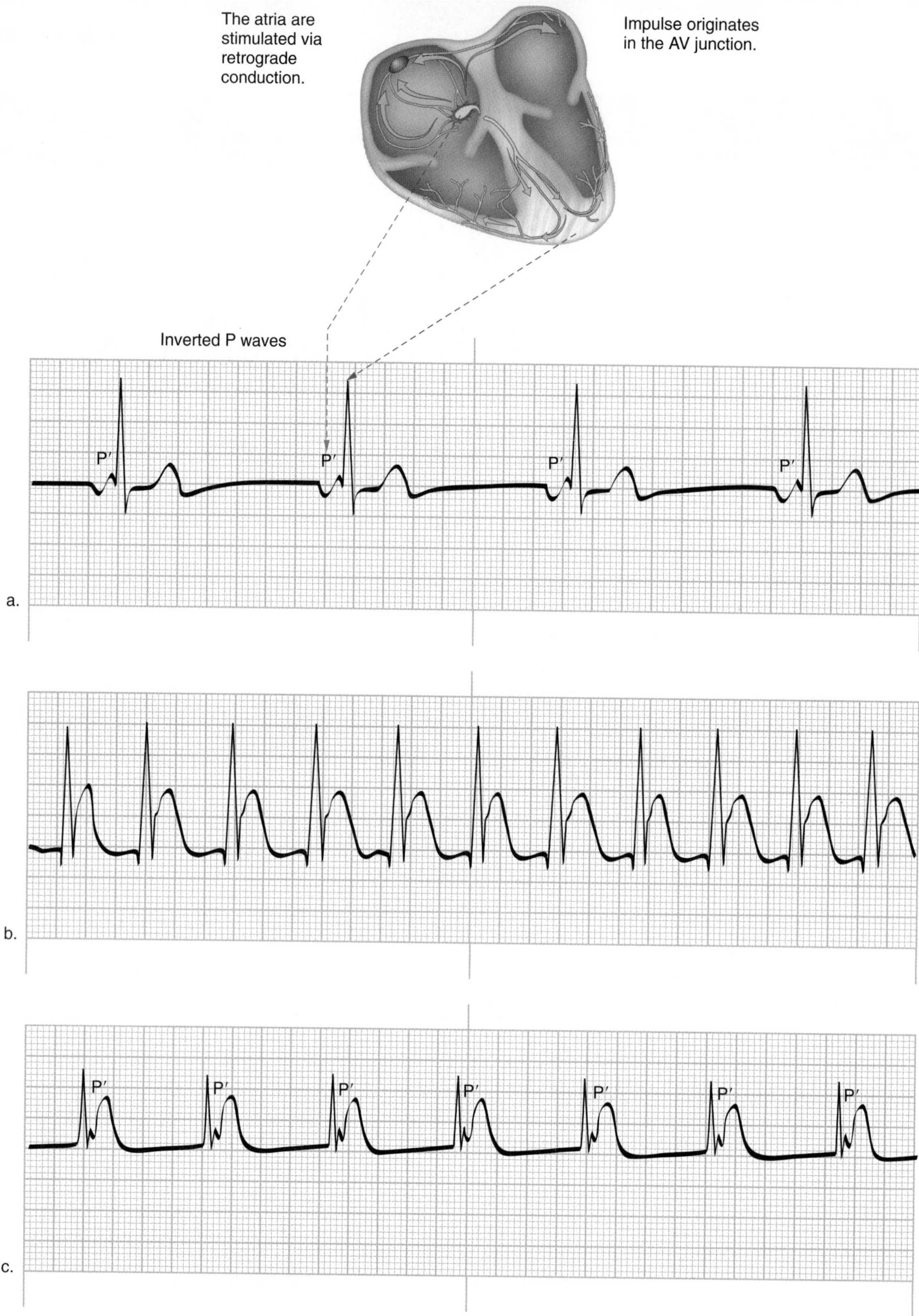

Figure 5-14

Impulses arising from the lower-right atrium near the AV node, in the left atrium, or from the AV junction have inverted P' waves that can occur before, during (buried in QRS), or after the QRS complex. (a) Inverted P waves preceding the QRS complexes. (b) Absent P waves. (c) P waves that follow the QRS complexes.

In junctional dysrhythmias, the P′ wave should be ________ (in lead II) and come immediately ________, during, or ________ the QRS complex.

[inverted] [before] [after]

INSTRUCTIONAL MOMENT

As we discussed earlier, because the P′ waves seen with atrial tachycardia (and PACs) can be buried in the T wave of the preceding beat, it may be hard to separate some junctional dysrhythmias from atrial dysrhythmias. For this reason we use the term supraventricular when referring to narrow QRS complex tachycardias where we aren't sure if they arise from the AV junction or atria.

More P Waves Than QRS Complexes

Normally, there is only one P wave preceding each QRS complex. However, in some dysrhythmias we may see more P waves than QRS complexes. This indicates that the impulse was initiated in the SA node or other ectopic sites in the atria but was blocked and did not reach the ventricles. The most common cause for this is AV heart block. We can also see this with blocked PACs.

P Waves Seen With 2nd-Degree AV Heart Block

In Chapter 4 we described how in 2nd-degree AV heart block, Type I (Wenckebach), the weakened AV node fatigues more with each conducted impulse until finally it is so tired that it fails to conduct an impulse through to the ventricles (Figure 5-15). This results in a P wave, but the QRS complex is dropped. With the dropped ventricular beat the AV node has a chance to rest. The next impulse conducting through the AV node will be carried through faster but each subsequent impulse will be delayed until finally another ventricular beat is dropped. This cycle repeats over and over producing a rhythm that has more P waves than QRS complexes. The P waves should all be normal because the impulses are initiated from the SA node. They just aren't all followed by a QRS complex.

QUESTION

"What type of irregularity is characteristic of Wenckebach?" (The answer can be found on page 168.)

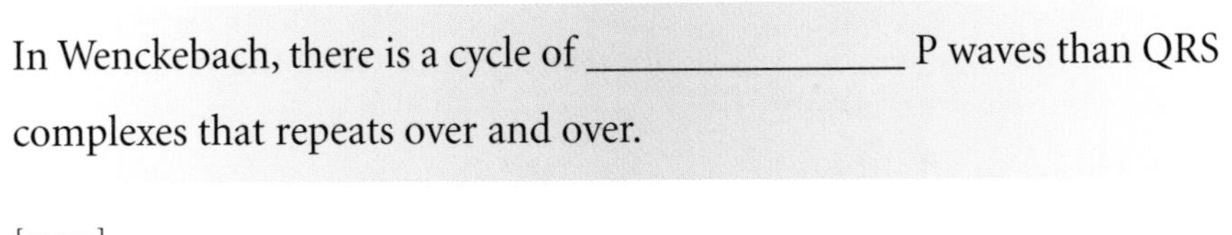

In Wenckebach, there is a cycle of ____________ P waves than QRS complexes that repeats over and over.

[more]

More P waves than QRS complexes can also be seen with 2nd-degree AV heart block, Type II. This occurs because some of the sinus beats are blocked in the AV node and do not reach the ventricles (Figure 5-16). The atrial-to-ventricular conduction ratio is usually 2:1, 3:1, or 4:1 atrial to ventricular beats. The conduction ratios may be constant or variable (changing ratios or starting and stopping). The P waves should all be normal because the impulses are initiated from the SA node. They just aren't all followed by a QRS complex.

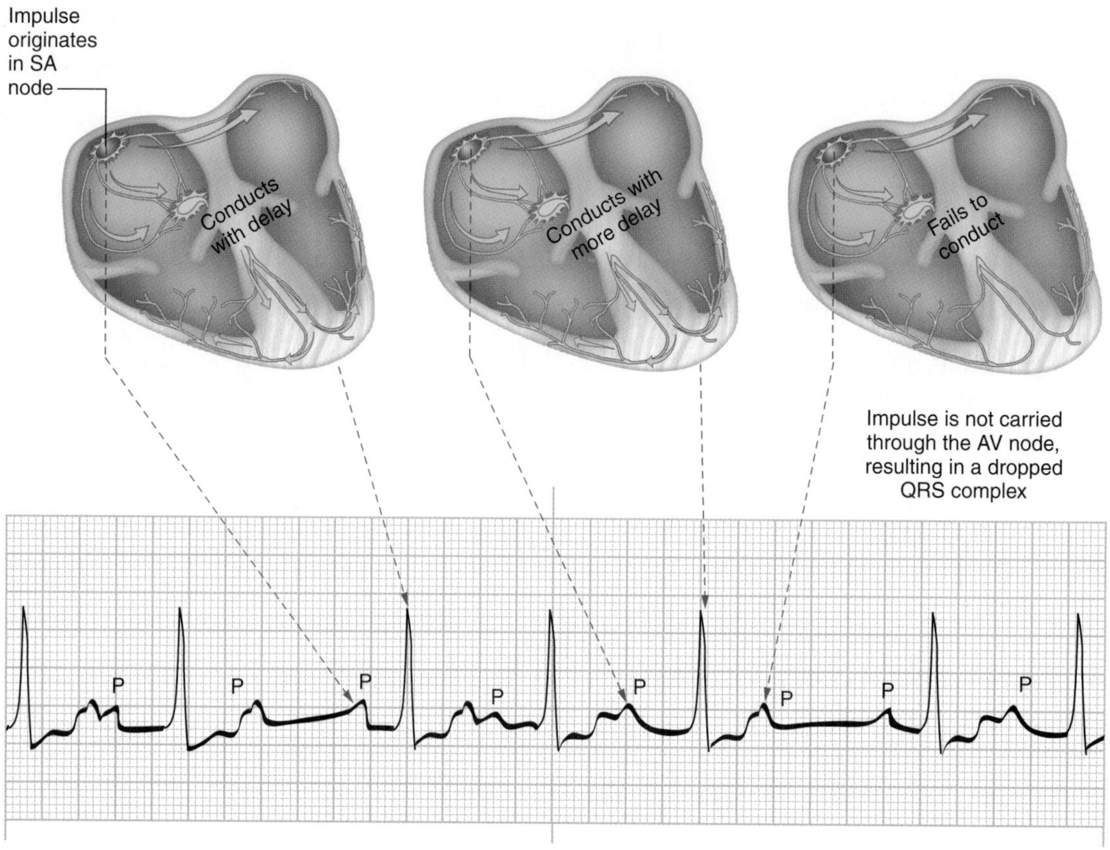

Figure 5-15
Impulses are initiated in the SA node but when the AV node tires it fails to carry the impulse to the ventricles. This results in there being more P waves than QRS complexes.

QUESTION
"What type of ventricular heart rate is characteristic of 3rd-degree AV block?" (The answer can be found on page 168.)

With Type II, 2nd-degree AV heart block, there are more ____________ waves than QRS complexes as some of the ____________ beats are blocked in the ____________ node and do not reach the ventricles.

[P] [sinus] [AV]

P Waves Seen With 3rd-Degree AV Heart Block

In a more severe form of AV heart block, called 3rd-degree AV block, there is complete blockage of the AV node (Figure 5-17). The atria are stimulated to contract by an impulse that originates in the SA node. For this reason the atrial rate should be within a normal range. The ventricles are stimulated to contract by an escape pacemaker that arises from somewhere below the AV node resulting in a slower heart rate. The location of the pacemaker site determines the heart rate. There should be more P waves than QRS complexes, because the SA node has an inherently faster rate than the AV junction or ventricles. Also, because the pacemaker sites (SA

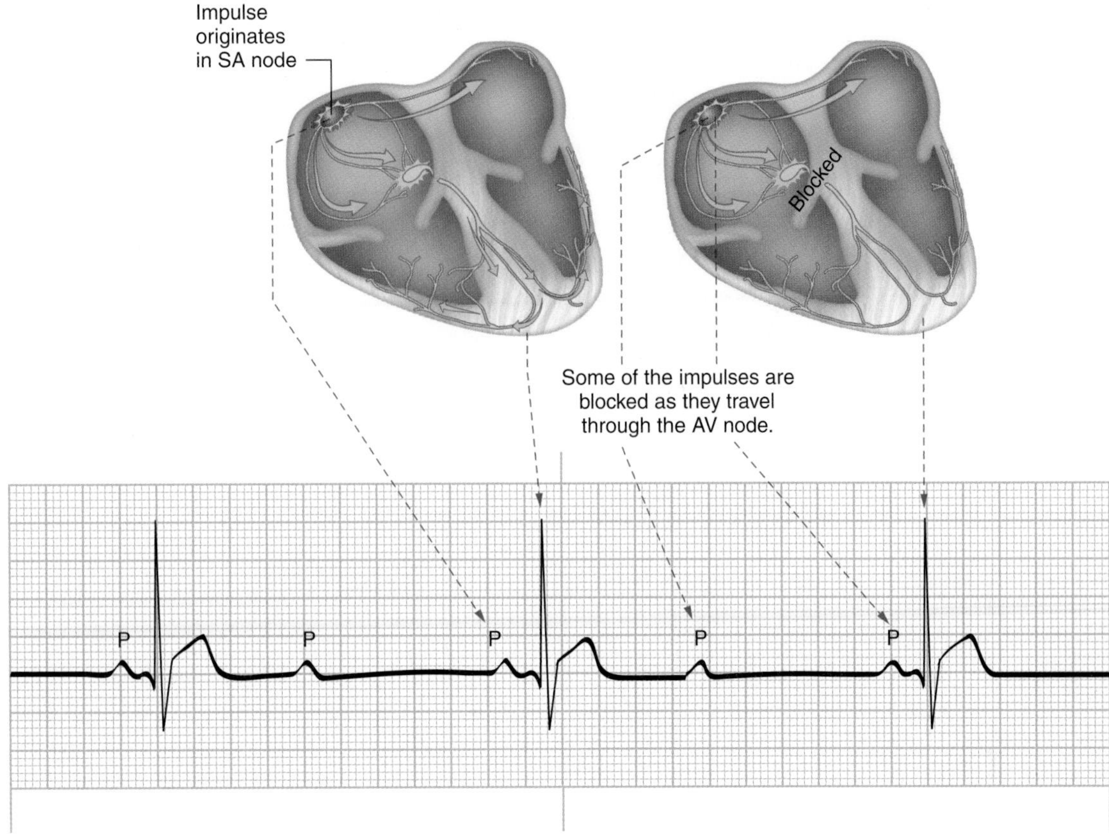

Figure 5-16
Impulses are initiated in the SA node but do not all reach the ventricles. This results in more P waves than QRS complexes.

node and ventricles) are firing independently of each other, the P waves seem to "march through" the QRS complexes. Another key to distinguishing 3rd-degree heart block is to examine the P-P interval and the R-R interval. Each interval is constant but does not correlate with the other.

CLINICAL MOMENT
Remember, heart rate × stroke volume = cardiac output. AV heart blocks, which result in dropped QRS complexes, can cause decreased cardiac output by lowering the heart rate.

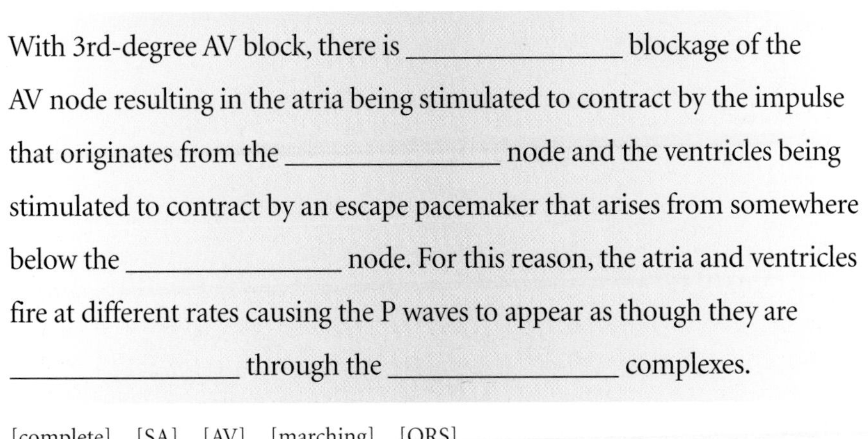

With 3rd-degree AV block, there is ______________ blockage of the AV node resulting in the atria being stimulated to contract by the impulse that originates from the ______________ node and the ventricles being stimulated to contract by an escape pacemaker that arises from somewhere below the ______________ node. For this reason, the atria and ventricles fire at different rates causing the P waves to appear as though they are ______________ through the ______________ complexes.

[complete] [SA] [AV] [marching] [QRS]

KEY CONCEPT
More P waves than QRS complexes indicate that the impulse was initiated in the SA node or other ectopic sites in the atria but was blocked and did not reach the ventricles.

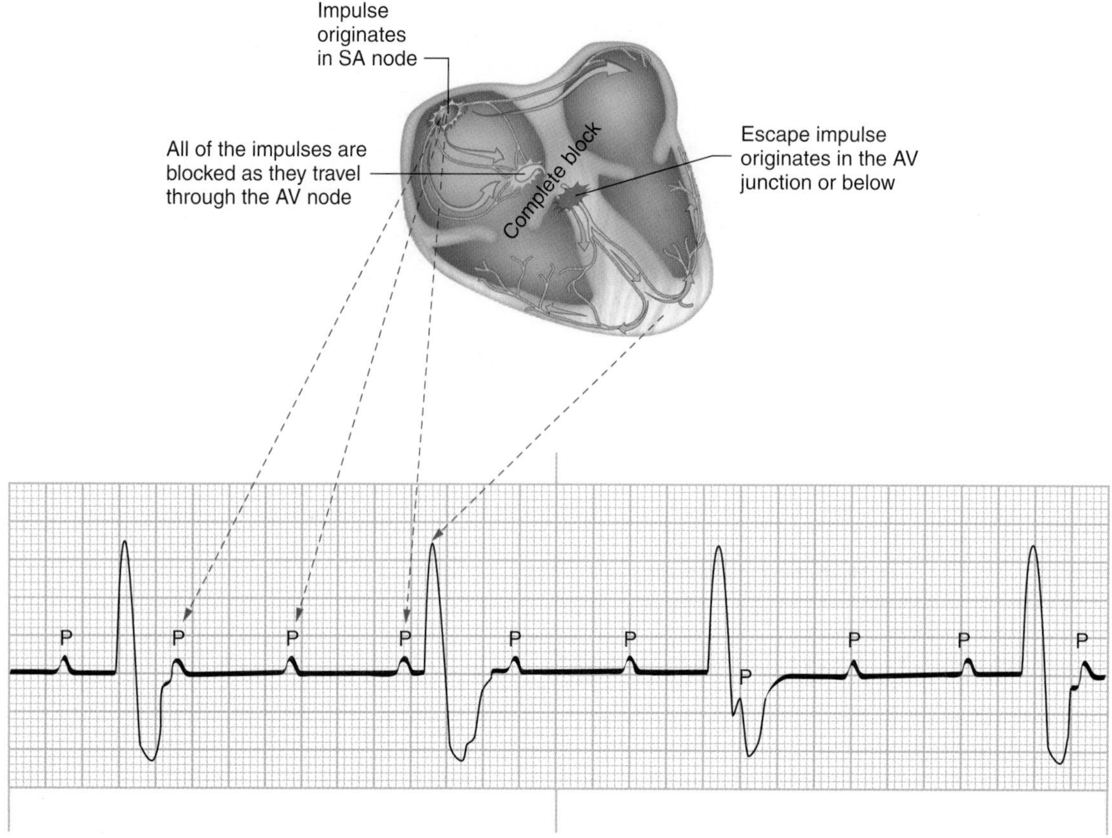

Figure 5-17
With complete blockage of the AV node there are more P waves than QRS complexes. Further, the P waves appear to march through the QRS complexes.

You can practice determining heart rate, regularity, and type of atrial waveform with the following *Practice Makes Perfect* exercises. Answers to these exercises can be found in Appendix A.

PRACTICE. . . MAKES PERFECT

6.

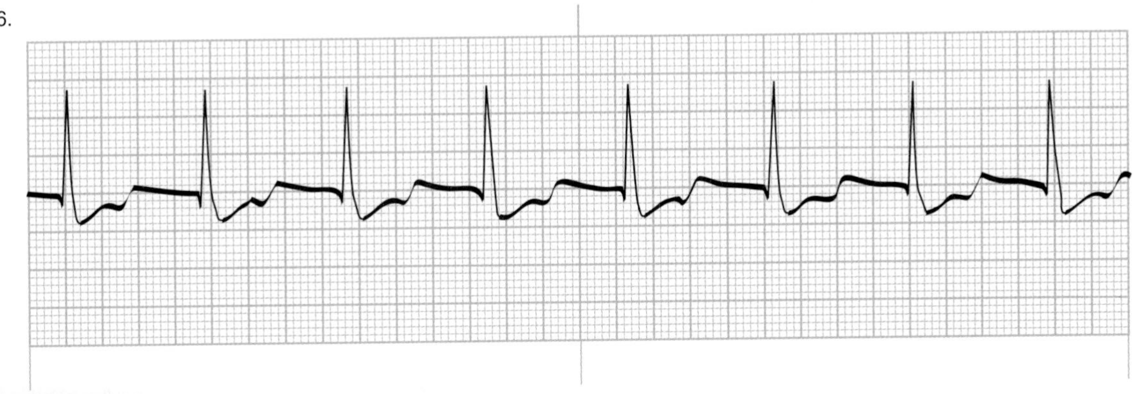

Rate ______________ Is this rhythm regular or irregular? ______________ .
What type of atrial waveform is present? ______________

7.

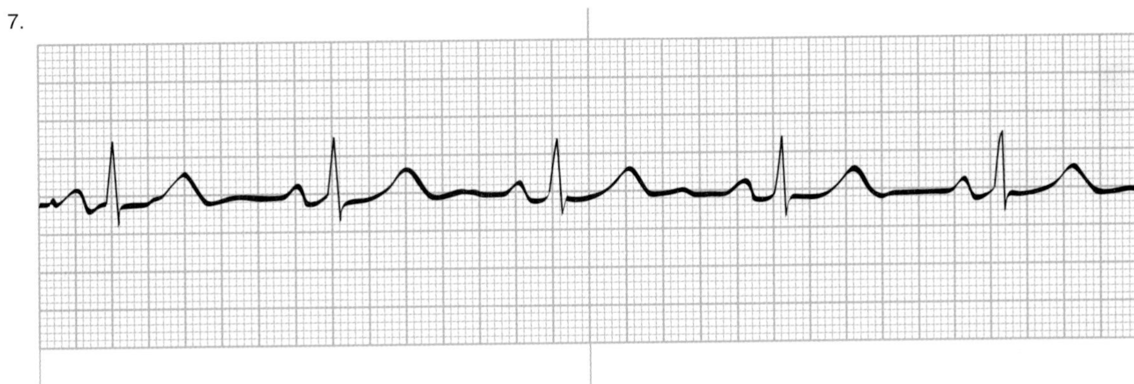

Rate ______________ Is this rhythm regular or irregular? ______________ .
What type of atrial waveform is present? ______________

8.

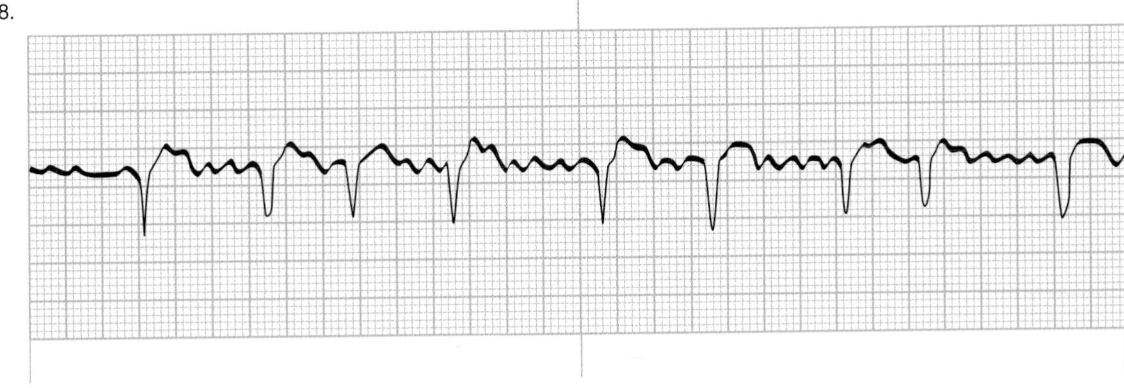

Rate ______________ Is this rhythm regular or irregular? ______________ .
What type of atrial waveform is present? ______________

PRACTICE. . . MAKES PERFECT

9.

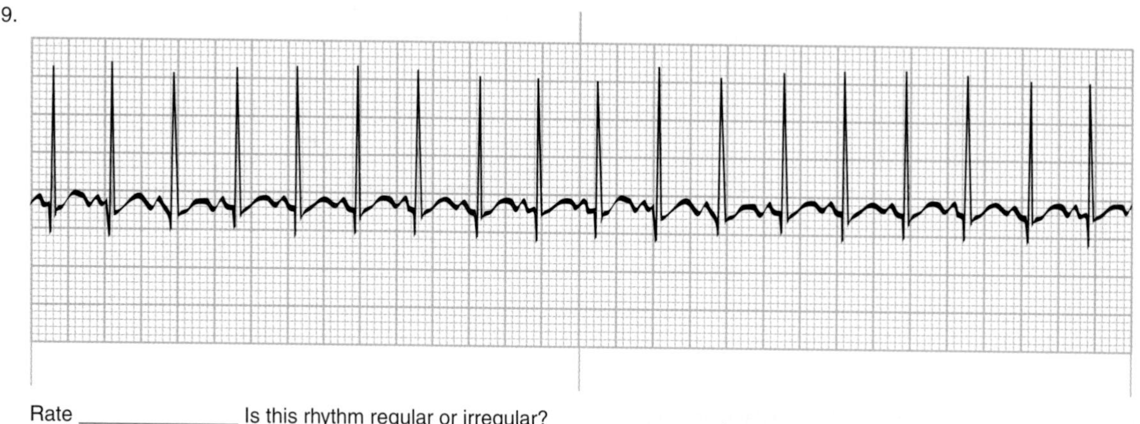

Rate ______________ Is this rhythm regular or irregular? ______________ .
What type of atrial waveform is present? ______________

10.

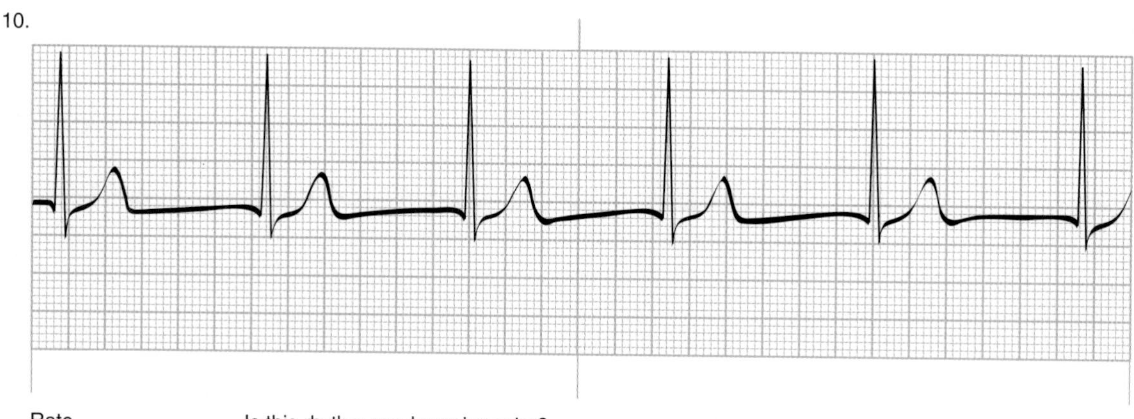

Rate ______________ Is this rhythm regular or irregular? ______________ .
What type of atrial waveform is present? ______________

11.

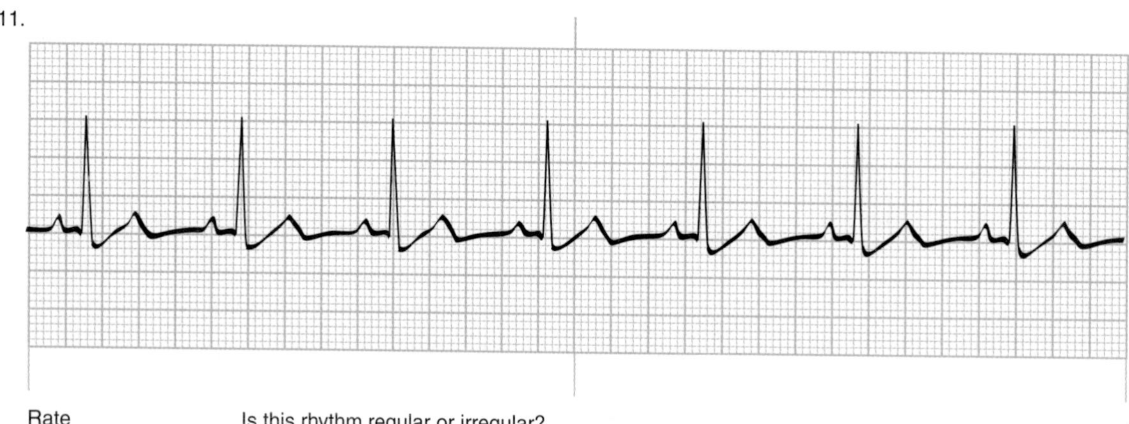

Rate ______________ Is this rhythm regular or irregular? ______________ .
What type of atrial waveform is present? ______________

PRACTICE. . . MAKES PERFECT

12.

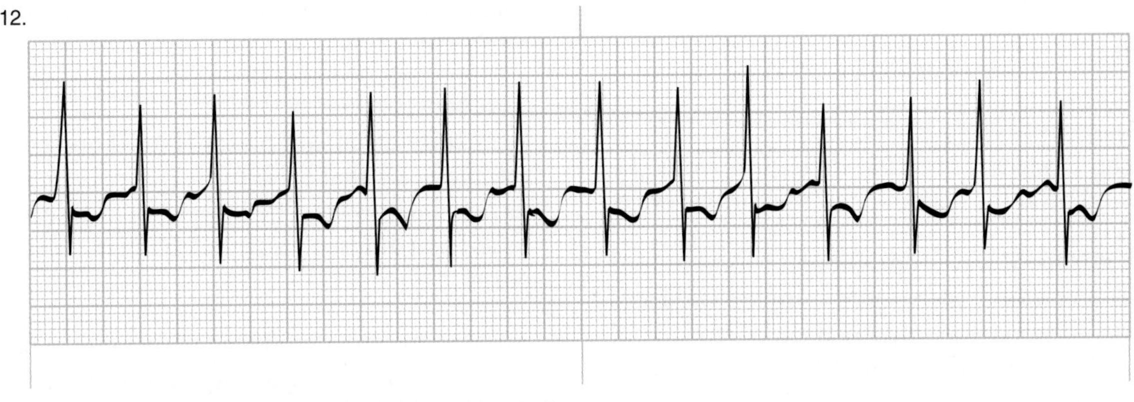

Rate ______________ Is this rhythm regular or irregular? ______________ .
What type of atrial waveform is present? ______________

13.

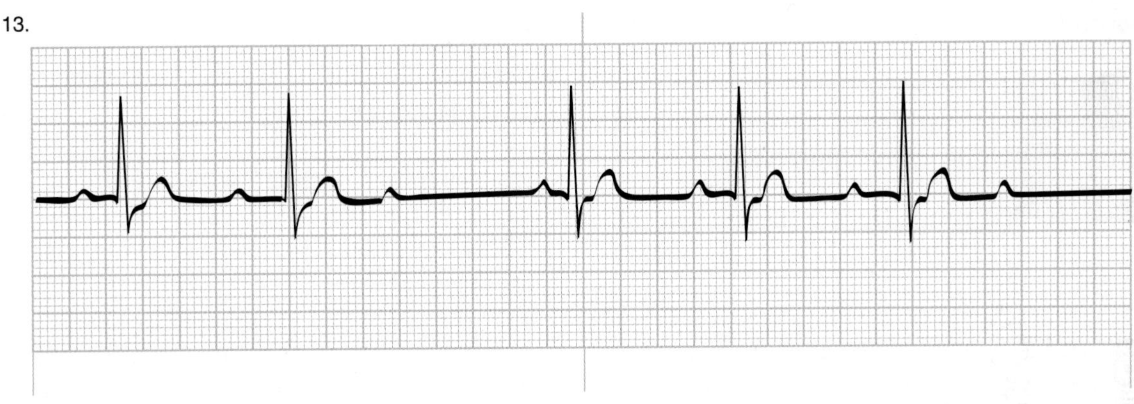

Rate ______________ Is this rhythm regular or irregular? ______________ .
What type of atrial waveform is present? ______________

14.

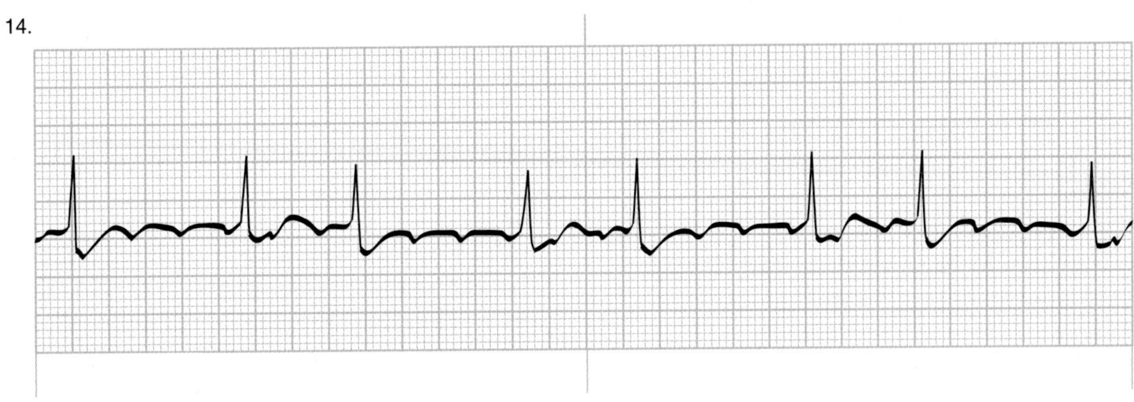

Rate ______________ Is this rhythm regular or irregular? ______________ .
What type of atrial waveform is present? ______________

Key Points

- Normally, the heart beats in a regular, rhythmic fashion producing a P wave, QRS complex, and T wave. This cycle repeats over and over.
- The third step of analyzing an ECG rhythm is examining the P waves.
- The P wave is the first deflection from the baseline at the beginning of the cardiac cycle.
- A normal P wave (upright and round in lead II) preceding each QRS complex indicates that the electrical impulse likely originated in the SA node and was carried through the atria in a normal manner.
- The amplitude of a normal P wave is 0.5 to 2.5 mm high and the duration is 0.06 to 0.10 seconds.
- P waves that originate in the SA node but conduct abnormally through altered, damaged atria will have an altered morphology.
- P waves that result from a pacemaker site outside the SA node will have an altered morphology.
- Tall and symmetrically peaked P waves may be seen with increased right atrial pressure and right atrial dilation.
- Notched or wide (enlarged) P waves may be seen in increased left atrial pressure and left atrial dilation.
- Impulses that arise from the atria produce P prime (P′) waves that look different than the sinus P waves.
- P′ waves that arise from the upper-right atrium should be upright in lead II, resembling a normal sinus P wave.
- A P′ wave that arises from the middle of the right atrium is less positive than one that originates from the upper-right atrium.
- A P′ wave that arises from the lower-right atrium near the AV node or in the left atrium results in atrial depolarization occurring in a retrograde direction. This produces an inverted P′ wave in lead II.
- Premature atrial complexes (PACs) are early ectopic beats that arise from the atria or internodal pathways. The P′ wave in these early beats has a different morphology than normal beats.
- Atrial tachycardia produces a heart rate of between 150 and 250 beats per minute. It has P′ waves, which look different than normal beats. These P′ waves are often buried in the T wave of the preceding beat.
- P waves that continuously change in their appearance indicate the presence of a wandering atrial pacemaker.
- In atrial flutter, normal P waves are absent; instead, flutter waves (F waves) are present. These are often described as having a sawtoothed pattern.
- In atrial fibrillation, there are no discernable P waves. Instead, there is a chaotic-looking baseline of f waves preceding the QRS complexes.
- Impulses that arise from the AV junction produce an inverted P′ wave that may immediately precede, or occur during or following, the QRS complex.
- Normally, there is only one P wave preceding each QRS complex.
- More P waves than QRS complexes indicate that the impulse was initiated in the SA node or atria but was blocked and did not reach the ventricles. The most common causes for this are 2nd-degree AV heart block (Type I and II), 3rd-degree AV heart block, and blocked PACs.

Assess Your Understanding

The following questions give you a chance to assess your understanding of the material discussed in this chapter. The answers can be found in Appendix A.

1. Which of the following is best evaluated by choosing the appropriate lead?
   a. Heart rate.
   b. Regularity.
   c. P waves.
   d. PR interval.
2. In lead aV_R, the P wave is normally
   a. inverted.
   b. upright.
   c. pointed.
   d. biphasic.
3. The third step in analyzing an ECG is
   a. checking the regularity.
   b. looking at the P waves.
   c. assessing the PR intervals.
   d. determining the heart rate.
4. The amplitude of the P wave normally does not exceed ____________ mm high.
   a. 1.0
   b. 2.5
   c. 3.0
   d. 0.5
5. An upright, round P wave (in lead II) that precedes each QRS complex indicates that the electrical impulse originated in the
   a. AV node and was carried through the atria in a retrograde manner.
   b. ventricles and was carried through the atria in the normal manner.
   c. SA node and was carried through the AV node in a retrograde manner.
   d. SA node and was carried through the atria in a normal manner.
6. The characteristic considered normal (in lead II) is a/an
   a. P wave that follows the QRS complex.
   b. inverted P wave.
   c. peaked or notched P wave.
   d. rounded and upright P wave.
7. Which of the following will produce P waves that look different than sinus P waves?
   a. Enlarged or damaged atria.
   b. 2nd-degree AV heart block.
   c. Sinus dysrhythmia.
   d. 3rd-degree AV heart block.
8. An impulse that arises closer to the SA node
   a. has the same appearance as a normal P wave.
   b. is inverted.
   c. looks more like a normal P wave.
   d. is biphasic or notched.
9. Premature atrial complexes
   a. arise from only the right atrium.
   b. always have an inverted P wave.
   c. may have P′ waves buried in the T wave of the preceding beat.
   d. have P waves that look the same as P waves that arise from the SA node.
10. With atrial tachycardia,
    a. the P wave is typically notched or widened.
    b. the P′ wave looks different than P waves that arise from the SA node.
    c. the P′ wave is hidden within the QRS complex.
    d. there are more P waves than QRS complexes.

11. An atrial pacemaker site that changes from location to location has
    a. P waves that continually change in appearance.
    b. one pacemaker site from which the impulses arise.
    c. inverted P′ waves.
    d. a chaotic baseline preceding each QRS complex.

12. With atrial fibrillation, the P waves
    a. are indiscernible; instead, there is a chaotic-looking baseline.
    b. appear in a saw-tooth pattern.
    c. are inverted (in lead II).
    d. are buried in the T wave of the preceding beat.

13. Junctional dysrhythmias have ________________ P′ waves.
    a. upright
    b. inverted
    c. biphasic
    d. peaked

14. With junctional dysrhythmias, the P′ waves may
    a. change in appearance.
    b. have a saw-tooth appearance.
    c. immediately precede the QRS complexes.
    d. be tall or notched.

15. Which of the following has more P waves than QRS complexes?
    a. A dysrhythmia where the pacemaker changes from site to site with each beat.
    b. Premature complexes that arise from the atria.
    c. AV heart block.
    d. Dysrhythmias that arise from the AV junction.

16. Identify the heart rate, regularity, and atrial waveform of the following ECG.

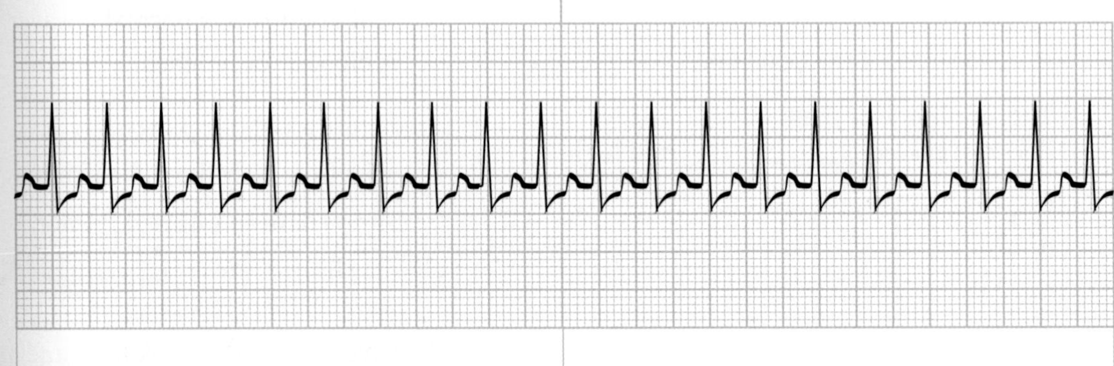

17. Identify the heart rate, regularity, and atrial waveform of the following ECG.

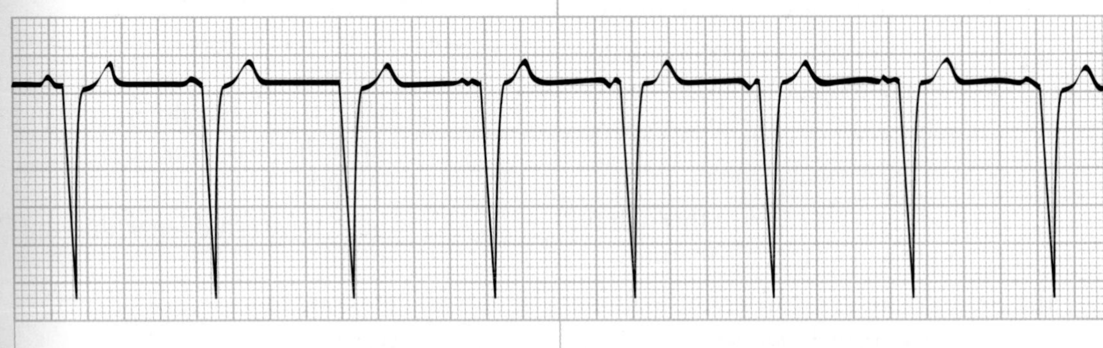

18. Identify the heart rate, regularity, and atrial waveform of the following ECG.

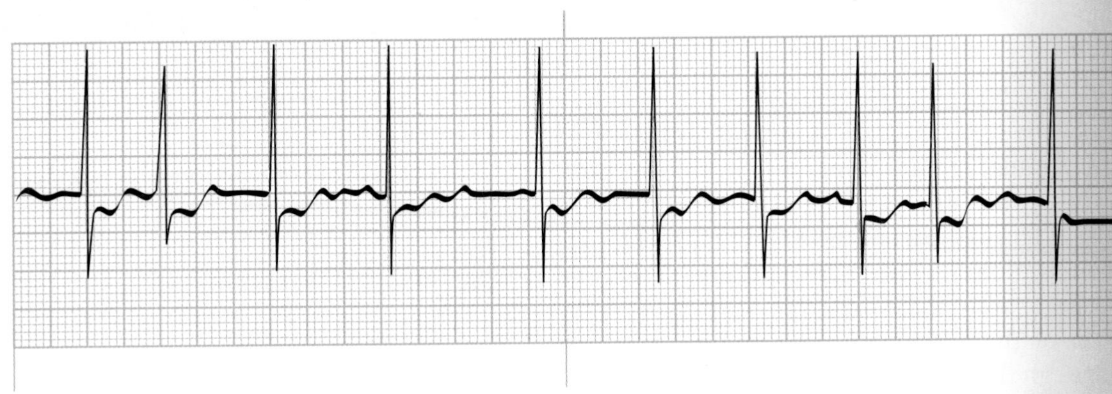

19. Identify the heart rate, regularity, and atrial waveform of the following ECG.

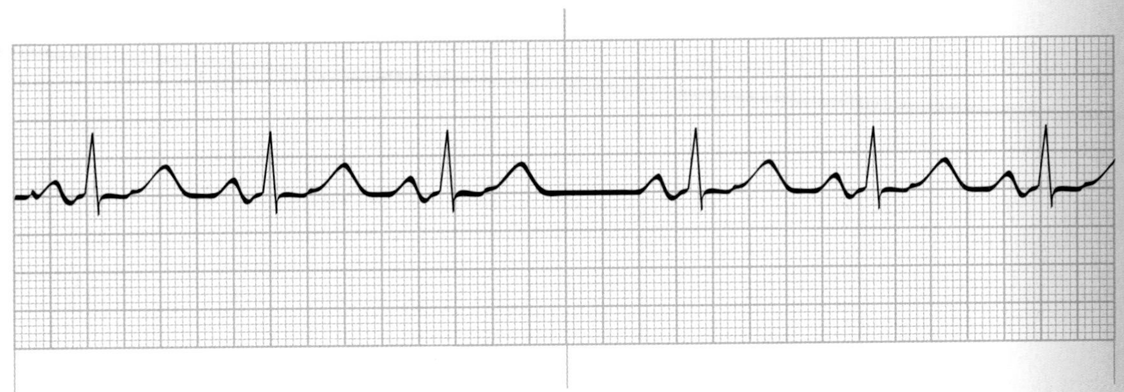

20. Identify the heart rate, regularity, and atrial waveform of the following ECG.

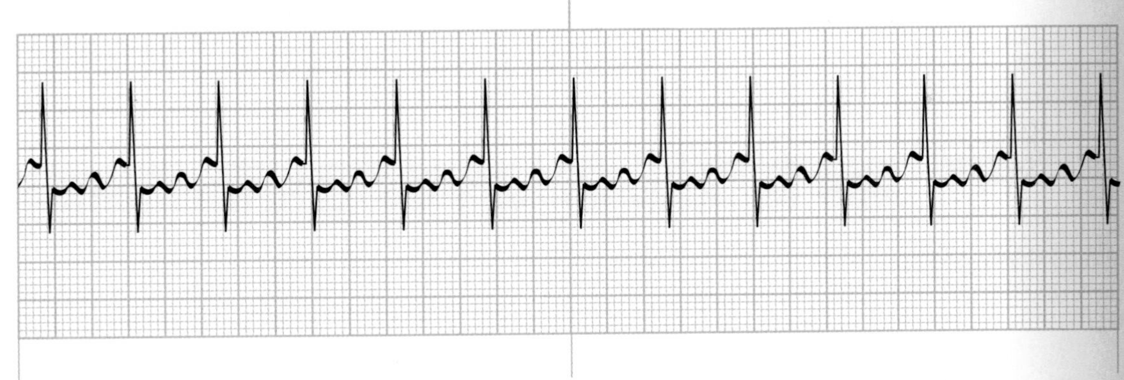

Referring to the scenario at the beginning of this chapter, answer the following questions.

21. What rhythm did the patient have?
    a. Sinus bradycardia.
    b. Junctional rhythm.
    c. Atrial fibrillation.
    d. Atrial flutter.

22. The firing rate of the F waves is ______ beats per minute.
    a. 36
    b. 72
    c. 108
    d. 144

Answers to Sidebar Questions

"What does a sinus P wave represent?"

Answer: The P wave represents initiation of the impulse in the SA node and its transmission through the atria from right to left and downward. The first part of the P wave represents depolarization of the right atrium, while the second part of the P wave represents depolarization of the left atrium. The impulse traveling through the AV node occurs during the P wave.

"Which rhythm has a characteristic heart rate of 60 to 100 beats a minute, a regular rhythm, and a P wave preceding each QRS complex?"

Answer: These features are characteristic of normal sinus rhythm.

"What type of irregularity is characteristic of wandering atrial pacemaker?"

Answer: Typically, wandering atrial pacemaker is slightly irregular.

"How fast is the atrial rate in atrial flutter?"

Answer: The atrial rate in atrial flutter ranges between 250 and 350 beats per minute.

"What type of irregularity is characteristic of atrial fibrillation?"

Answer: Atrial fibrillation produces a totally irregular rhythm, because the atria are firing so rapidly and only some of the impulses are getting through the AV node.

"What type of irregularity is characteristic of Wenckebach?"

Answer: Wenckebach (2nd-degree AV heart block, Type I) produces a patterned irregular rhythm.

"What type of ventricular heart rate is characteristic of 3rd-degree AV block?"

Answer: 3rd-degree AV block should produce a slower ventricular rate as the ventricles are stimulated to contract by an escape pacemaker that arises from somewhere below the AV node with a resultant slower heart rate.

On the DVD

- The P Wave lecture.

QRS Complexes

6

Chapter Preview

- Step 4: Examining the QRS Complexes
- The Normal QRS Complex
- Abnormal QRS Complexes

Case History

EMS is called to the home of a 39-year-old man complaining of chest pain. Upon arrival they find the patient lying on the couch. He is awake and alert. He states that he has a dull ache in his chest. His vital signs are normal, and he is quickly hooked up to the ECG monitor, which shows a normal sinus rhythm. The paramedics apply oxygen via nasal cannula to the patient and establish an intravenous line. The patient's chest pain resolves after the application of oxygen and one sublingual nitroglycerin.

En route to the hospital the paramedics notice the occurrence of extra QRS complexes without associated P waves. They are wide and bizarre in configuration and each complex appears different than the others. The patient continues to be pain free but the extra complexes appear to be coming more frequently. The paramedics contact medical control at the receiving hospital and describe the rhythm. The physician approves their request to deliver an antidysrhythmic agent and the extra complexes cease. The patient is delivered to the hospital without further incident.

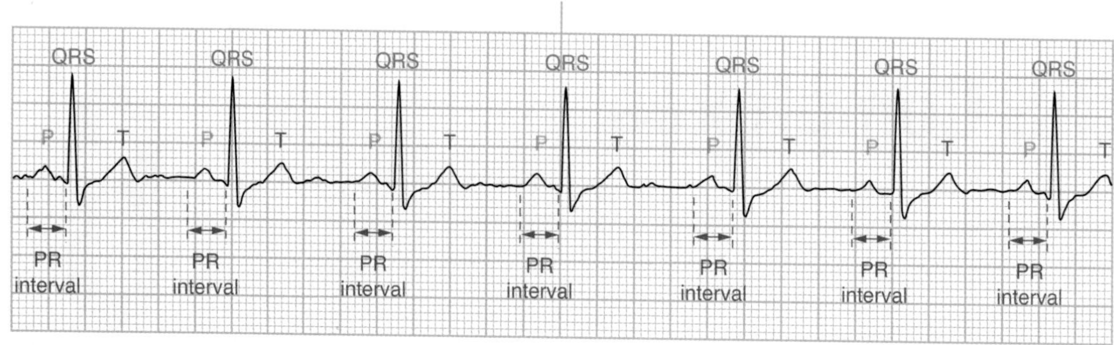

Figure 6-1
The repeating cycle of a P wave, QRS complex, and T wave.

Step 4: Examining the QRS Complexes

KEY CONCEPT
The fourth step to analyzing an ECG rhythm is to assess the QRS complexes.

As stated in earlier chapters, the heart normally beats in a regular, rhythmic fashion producing a P wave, QRS complex, and T wave with each heartbeat (Figure 6-1). This cycle repeats over and over.

After assessing the rate, regularity, and P waves of an ECG rhythm, the fourth step of ECG interpretation is to examine the QRS complexes (Figure 6-2).

INSTRUCTIONAL MOMENT
In this book we list a specific order for analyzing an ECG. This order is recommended because it gives you key information first (rate and rhythm) and then you can move into other areas to narrow the final characteristics.

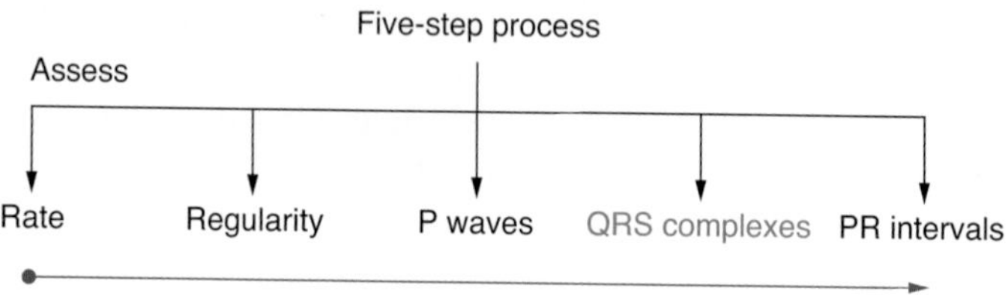

Figure 6-2
Evaluating the QRS complexes is the fourth step of analyzing an ECG tracing.

Normally the heart beats in a ______________, rhythmic fashion producing a P wave, ______________ complex, and T wave with each heartbeat. The fourth step of ECG interpretation is to examine the ______________ complexes.

[regular] [QRS] [QRS]

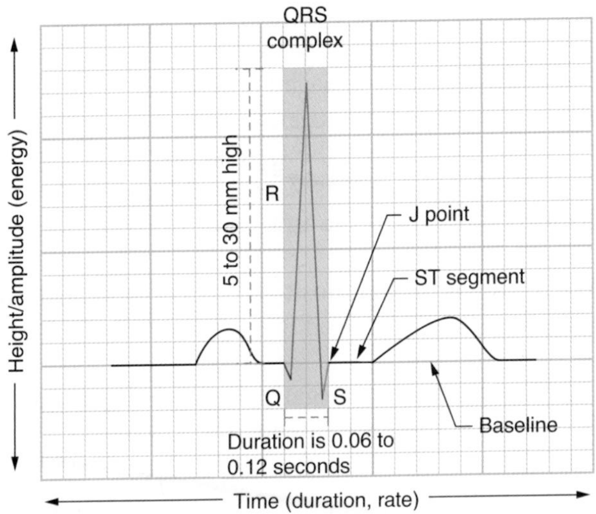

Figure 6-3
The QRS complex consists of the Q wave, R wave, and S wave. The J point is where the S wave connects to the ST segment. The ST segment is the flat line that connects the S wave with the T wave.

The Normal QRS Complex

To examine the QRS complexes we look closely at their characteristics, especially their location, configuration, and deflection (Figure 6-3). As discussed, the QRS complex is the waveform immediately following the PR interval. Its starting point is where the first wave of the complex starts to move away (sharply or gradually) from the baseline. The QRS complex ends at the point where the last wave of the complex starts to flatten (sharply or gradually) at, above, or below the baseline. The QRS complex is much bigger than the P wave because depolarization of the ventricles involves considerably larger muscle mass than depolarization of the atria. The QRS complex characteristically looks thinner than the other parts of the ECG because the ventricles depolarize so fast. This minimizes contact time between the stylus and the ECG paper.

QRS Complex Characteristics

The following are characteristics of a normal QRS complex.

- *Location.* A QRS complex follows the PR interval.
- *Amplitude.* 5 to 30 mm (but differs with each lead employed).
- *Duration.* 0.06 to 0.12 seconds. The duration is measured from the beginning of the Q wave (or the beginning of the R wave if the Q is not present) to the end of the S wave.

INSTRUCTIONAL MOMENT
In this book we use 0.12 seconds as the maximum duration of the normal QRS complex. Some references use 0.10 seconds, while others use less than 0.12 as the maximum duration. There are differing views on what is considered the maximum duration. However, any QRS duration greater than 0.12 seconds is considered wider than normal.

CLINICAL MOMENT
The Q wave represents depolarization of the interventricular septum. It is activated from left to right. The R and S waves represent simultaneous depolarization of the right and left ventricles. The QRS complex mostly represents the electrical activity occurring in the left ventricle because of its greater muscle mass.

QUESTION
"In lead II, which direction does the electrical current that produces the Q wave move in relation to the positive electrode of the electrocardiograph?" (The answer can be found on page 208.)

- *Morphology.* The QRS complex includes the Q, R, and S waves.
- ***Q wave.*** The Q wave is the first negative deflection from the baseline following the P wave. It is always negative. In some cases the Q wave is absent. The normal duration of the Q wave in the limb leads (with the exception of leads III and aV_R) is less than 0.04 seconds. The amplitude is normally less than 25% of the amplitude of the R wave in that lead.
- ***R wave.*** The R wave is the first positive, triangular deflection in the QRS complex. It follows the Q wave (if it is present).
- ***S wave.*** The S wave is the first negative deflection that *extends below* the baseline in the QRS complex following the R wave.

The point at which the QRS complex meets the ST segment is called the junction or J point.

Generally speaking, men have higher QRS complex amplitude than women and young people have higher amplitudes than the elderly. The precordial leads have higher amplitude than the limb leads because the electrodes are closer to the heart.

The QRS complex is the waveform immediately following the __________.

Normally, QRS complexes consist of up to three waveforms: the __________, __________, and __________ waves. The amplitude of the QRS complex is normally __________ high (but differs with each lead employed) and its duration is __________ seconds.

[PR interval] [Q] [R] [S] [5 to 30 mm] [0.06 to 0.12]

Variations in the QRS Configuration

The QRS complex can take various forms. While we said it consists of positive (upright) deflections called R waves and negative (inverted) deflections called Q and S waves, all three waves are not always seen. Also, the waveforms will look different depending on which lead is used. If the R wave is absent, the complex is called a QS complex (Figure 6-4). Likewise, if the Q wave is absent, the complex is called an RS complex. Waveforms of normal or greater than normal amplitude are denoted with a large case letter, whereas waveforms less than 5 mm amplitude are denoted with a small case letter (e.g., "q," "r," "s"). Later, when we discuss myocardial infarction, this will become important as it helps us determine whether a Q wave is significant.

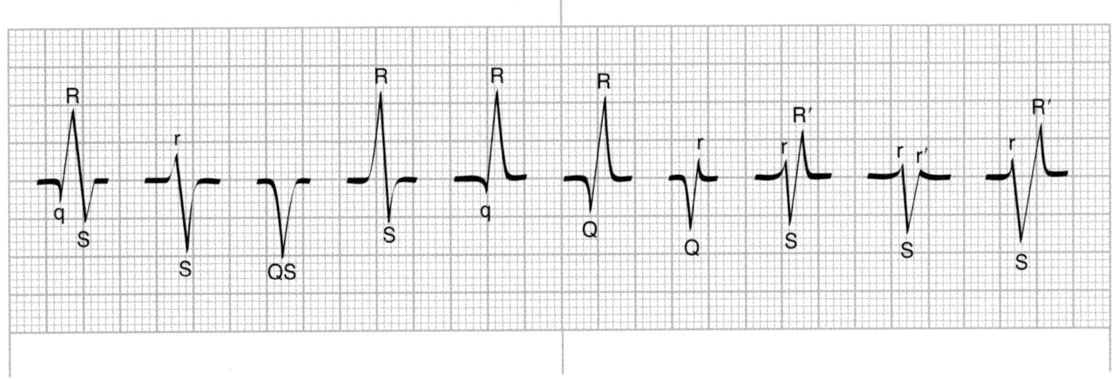

Figure 6-4
Common QRS configurations.

The positive deflection of the QRS complex is the ______________ wave. The negative deflections of the QRS complex are the ______________ wave and the ______________ wave. If the R wave is absent, the complex is called a ______________ complex. Waveforms less than ______________ mm amplitude are denoted with ______________ case letters.

[R] [Q] [S] [QS] [5] [small]

While there is only one Q wave, there can be more than one R wave and S wave in the QRS complex. A positive impulse immediately following the R wave is called R prime (R′). A double positive impulse immediately following the R wave is called double R prime (R″). A negative impulse immediately following the S wave is called S prime (S′). A double negative impulse immediately following the S wave is called double S prime (S″) (Figure 6-5). This discussion becomes more significant in Chapter 14 when we discuss bundle branch block.

______________ (R′) is the term we use to describe a positive impulse immediately following the R wave. ______________ R prime (R″) is a double positive impulse immediately following the R wave. A negative impulse immediately following the S wave is called ______________ (S′).

[R prime] [Double] [S prime]

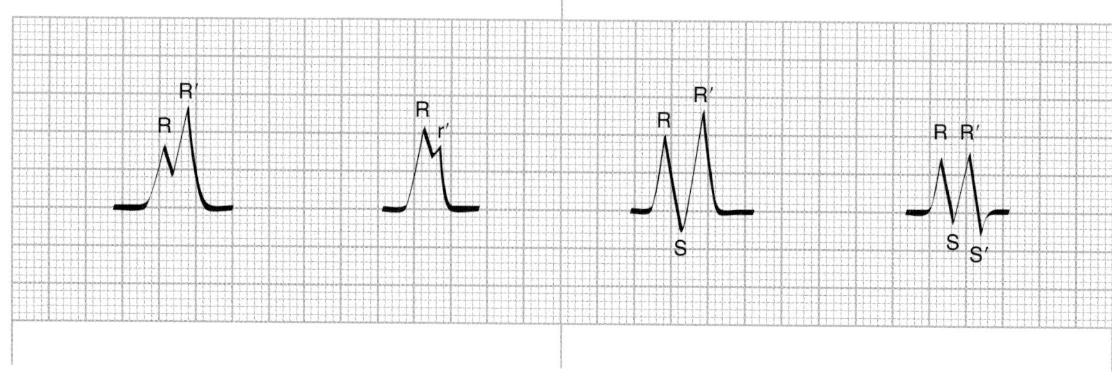

Figure 6-5
Variations in QRS configurations.

QUESTION
"Why does the QRS complex look different in the various ECG leads?" (The answer can be found on page 208.)

QRS Complexes in Different Leads

The ECG lead used affects the appearance of the QRS complexes, so you need to be familiar with how they look in the different leads (Figure 6-6). In leads I, II, III, aV_L, aV_F, and V_4 to V_6, the deflection of the QRS complex is characteristically positive or upright. In leads aV_R and V_1 to V_3, the QRS complex is usually negative or inverted. In leads III, aV_L, and V_2 to V_4 the QRS complex may also be biphasic.

When analyzing an ECG the appearance of the __________ complexes is affected by the __________ used. The QRS complex is characteristically positive or upright in leads __________, __________, __________, __________, __________ and __________ to V_6. The QRS complex is usually negative or inverted in lead __________ and V_1 to __________.

[QRS] [lead] [I] [II] [III] [aV_L] [aV_F] [V_4] [aV_R] [V_3]

INSTRUCTIONAL MOMENT
To make measuring easier, try to find a QRS complex where the waveform begins on one of the bold or thin lines. Then count the number of small squares (boxes) between the beginning and the end of the complex. If none of the Q or R waves falls squarely on a line, then you can use your calipers or paper and pencil technique. Start by placing the first point at the beginning of the complex, then place the second point at the end of the complex. This establishes the distance from the beginning to the end. Now slide the calipers or paper (with lines you have drawn) vertically across the tracing so that the first point lines up with a bold or thin line. Now count the number of squares between it and the second point.

Measuring QRS Complexes

To measure the width (duration) of a QRS complex, first identify the complex with the longest duration and the most distinct beginning and ending (Figure 6-7). Start by finding the beginning of the QRS complex. This is the point where the first wave of the complex which will either be the Q wave or the R wave begins to deviate from the baseline. Then measure to the point where the last wave of the complex transitions into the ST segment. Typically, it is where the S wave or R wave (in the absence of an S wave) begins to level out (flatten) at, above, or below the baseline. This is considered the end of the QRS complex.

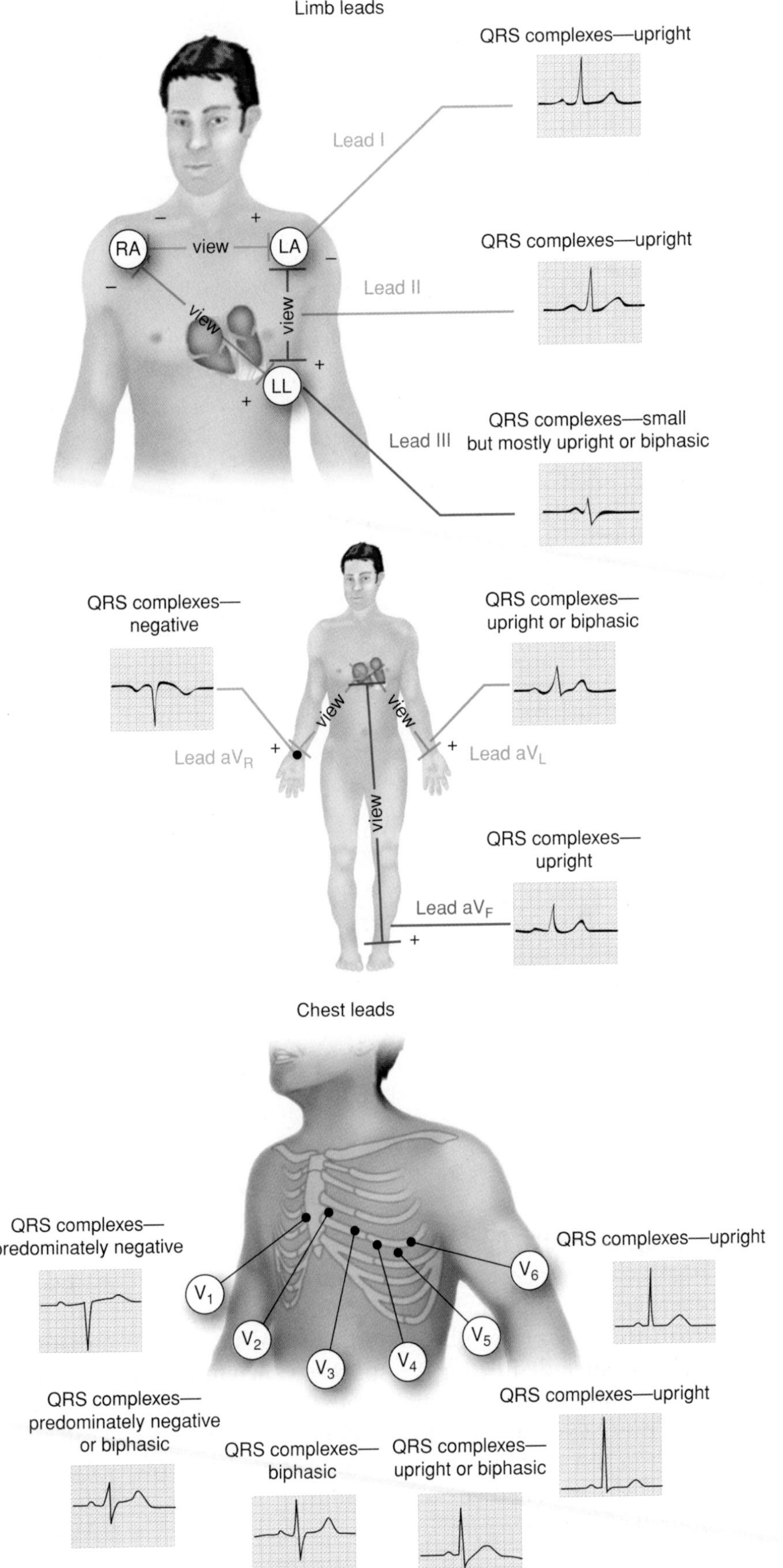

Figure 6-6
Direction of QRS waves in various leads.

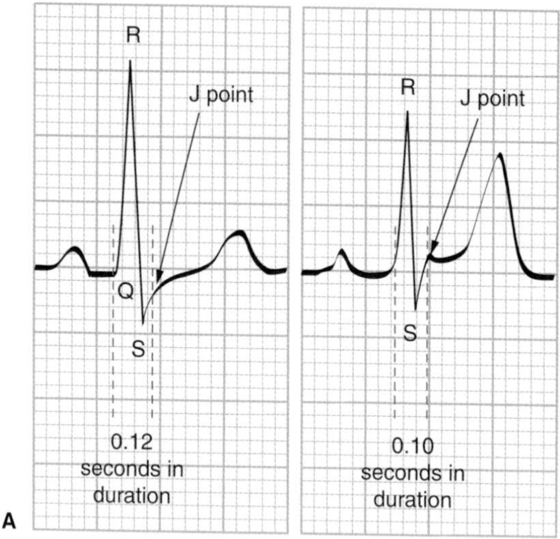

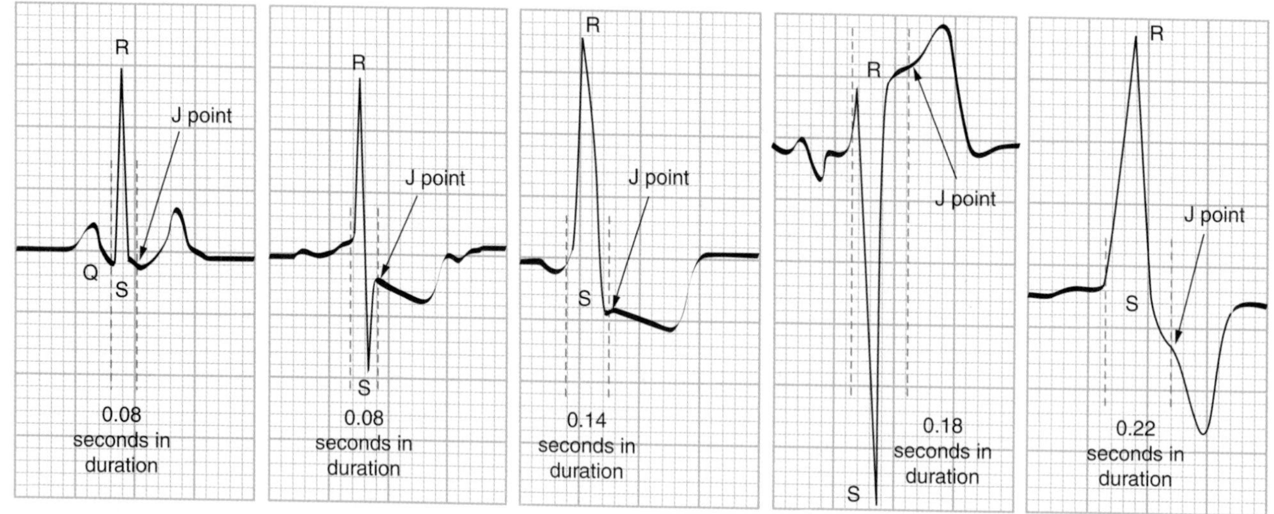

Figure 6-7

Measuring the QRS complex. (a) These two QRS complexes have easy to see J points. (b) These QRS complexes have less-defined transition making measurement of the QRS complex more challenging.

QUESTION

"What is the normal duration of the QRS complex?" (The answer can be found on page 208.)

Determining where the QRS complex ends can be difficult as you don't always see a clear transition with nice, straight lines. Instead, particularly when there is depression or elevation of the ST segment, you need to look for a small notch, slope, or other movement that suggests an alteration of electrical flow. Include in your measurement the entire S wave but don't let it overlap into the ST segment or the T wave. It is helpful to look for the end of the QRS complex in as many leads as possible as you can sometimes see it in one lead but not another. In some ECG tracings you have to use your best educated guess and common sense to conclude what is the duration of the QRS complex.

To determine the width (duration) of a QRS complex, measure from the _______________ to the _______________ of the complex. The beginning is where the first wave of the complex begins to _______________ from the _______________. The end is where the last wave of the complex transitions into the _______________ segment.

[beginning] [end] [deviate] [baseline] [ST]

INSTRUCTIONAL MOMENT
Generally, you can look at the QRS complex and get a sense of whether it is narrow or wide.

INSTRUCTIONAL MOMENT
Remember, between the S wave and the T wave is a section referred to as the ST segment.

KEY CONCEPT
If the Q wave is absent, the resulting complex is measured from the beginning of the R wave.

Where We See Normal QRS Complexes

The QRS complexes should appear normal (upright and narrow) if:

- the rhythm is initiated from a site above the ventricles—meaning in the SA node, atria, or AV junction.
- conduction has progressed normally from the bundle of His, through the right and left bundle branches, and through the Purkinje network.
- normal depolarization of the ventricles has occurred.

Unless there is a conduction delay through the ventricles, normal sinus rhythm and any dysrhythmia initiated by a pacemaker site above the ventricles can be expected to have normal QRS complexes.

Bradycardias With Narrow QRS Complexes

Let's first talk about the slow dysrhythmias. Sinus bradycardia has a rate of less than 60 beats per minute, while junctional escape has a rate of 40 to 60 beats per minute. Sinus arrest may have a slower heart rate due to the pause(s) in the heartbeat. There will be fewer QRS complexes (and P waves) with these dysrhythmias because of the slower heart rate. However, the QRS complexes should appear normal.

Normal Heart Rates With Narrow QRS Complexes

The dysrhythmias that arise above the ventricles and have a normal heart rate include sinus dysrhythmia, wandering atrial pacemaker, and accelerated junctional rhythm. For this reason we can expect to see between 60 and 100 QRS complexes per minute.

With sinus dysrhythmia, the heart rate speeds up and slows down in a rhythmic fashion, often corresponding with the respiratory cycle and

QUESTION
"What is atrial flutter or fibrillation that has a slow or fast ventricular rate called?" (The answer can be found on page 208.)

changes in intrathoracic pressure. The heart rate increases during inspiration and decreases during expiration. With wandering atrial pacemaker, the pacemaker site shifts to different locations around the atria instead of arising from the SA node. As the site changes, so does the appearance of the P waves. Accelerated junctional rhythm is an escape pacemaker that arises from the AV junction, but with a rate of between 60 and 100 beats per minute, it is faster than the usual junctional rate of 40 to 60 beats per minute. It is due to increased excitability of the AV junction.

While atrial flutter and fibrillation often have a ventricular rate that falls within normal limits, they can also have a slow or fast ventricular rate.

Again, with all these dysrhythmias, the QRS complexes should appear normal (upright and narrow).

Tachycardias With Narrow QRS Complexes

Next, let's consider the faster dysrhythmias that have normal QRS complexes. With sinus tachycardia the heart rate is 100 to 160 beats per minute, with atrial tachycardia it is 150 to 250 beats per minute, and with junctional tachycardia it is 100 to 180 beats per minute. Due to the faster heart rate, there are more QRS complexes (and P waves) per minute than normal. As we have discussed, all these dysrhythmias, because they arise from above the ventricles, should have normal looking (narrow) QRS complexes.

KEY CONCEPT
If the rhythm is initiated from the SA node, atria, or AV junction, the QRS complexes should appear normal.

Premature Beats With Narrow QRS Complexes

Atrial and junctional premature beats are early beats that fire from the atria or AV junction before the SA node has a chance to fire. The QRS complexes appear normal because the premature beats arise from sites above the ventricles.

QUESTION
"Which dysrhythmia has a characteristic heart rate of less than 60 beats a minute, a regular rhythm, and a P wave preceding each QRS complex?" (The answer can be found on page 209.)

You can practice determining the width of QRS complexes, type of atrial waveform, heart rate, and regularity with the following *Practice Makes Perfect* exercises. Answers to these exercises can be found in Appendix A.

PRACTICE. . . MAKES PERFECT

1.

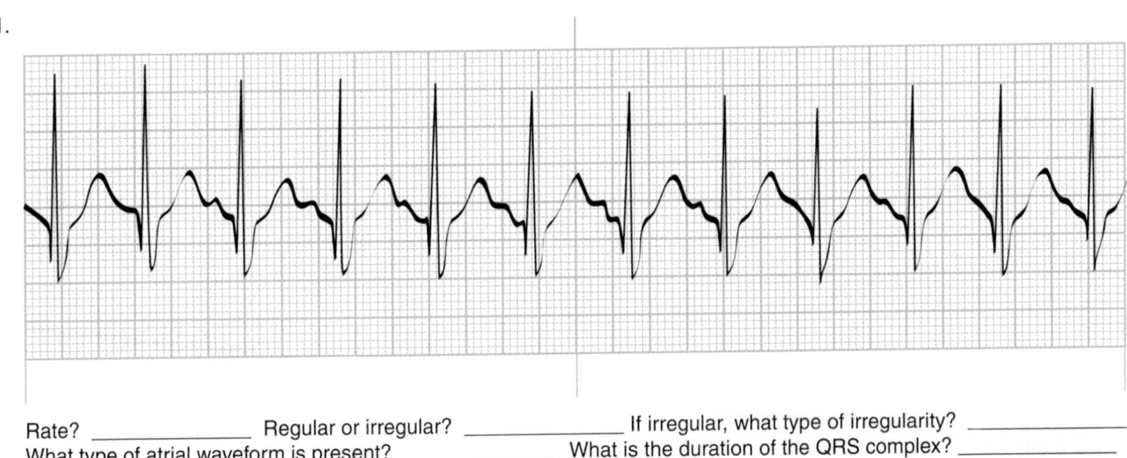

Rate? ______________ Regular or irregular? ______________ If irregular, what type of irregularity? ______________
What type of atrial waveform is present? ______________ What is the duration of the QRS complex? ______________

2.

Rate? ______________ Regular or irregular? ______________ If irregular, what type of irregularity? ______________
What type of atrial waveform is present? ______________ What is the duration of the QRS complex? ______________

3.

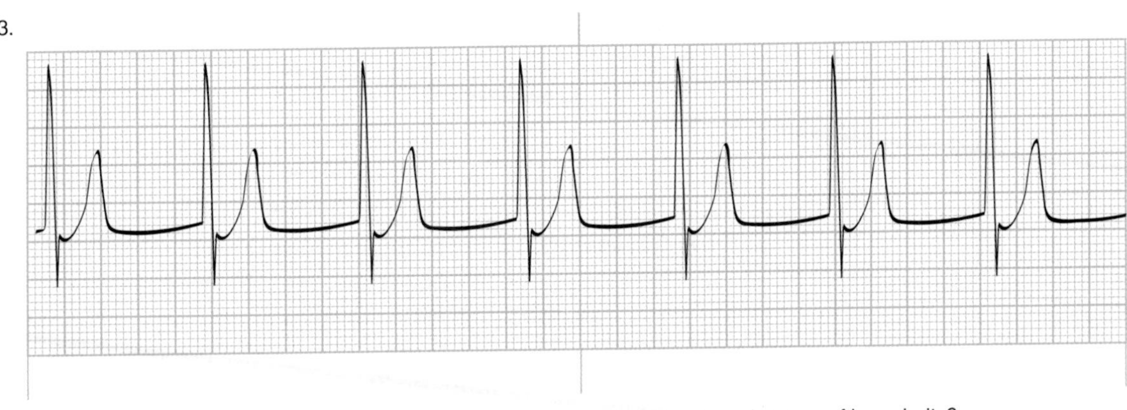

Rate? ______________ Regular or irregular? ______________ If irregular, what type of irregularity? ______________
What type of atrial waveform is present? ______________ What is the duration of the QRS complex? ______________

PRACTICE. . . MAKES PERFECT

4.

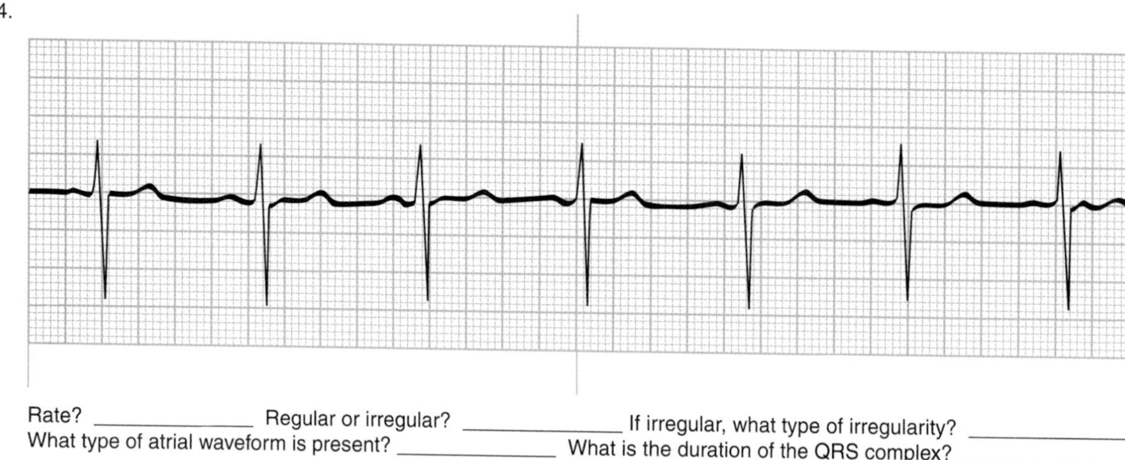

Rate? ______________ Regular or irregular? ______________ If irregular, what type of irregularity? ______________
What type of atrial waveform is present? ______________ What is the duration of the QRS complex? ______________

5.

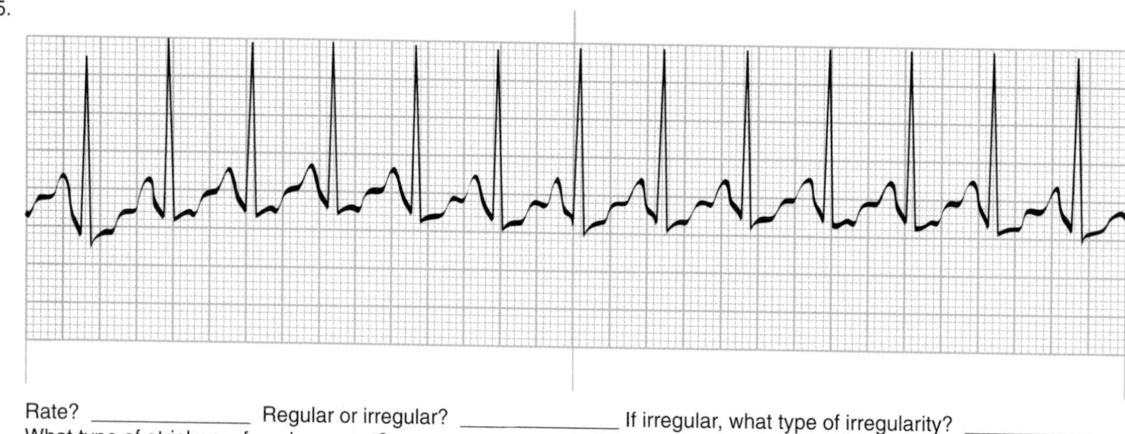

Rate? ______________ Regular or irregular? ______________ If irregular, what type of irregularity? ______________
What type of atrial waveform is present? ______________ What is the duration of the QRS complex? ______________

Abnormal QRS Complexes

Abnormal QRS complexes are produced by abnormal depolarization of the ventricles. The pacemaker site in these abnormal QRS complexes can be the SA node or an ectopic pacemaker in the atria, AV junction, bundle branches, Purkinje network, or ventricular myocardium.

The onset and end of an abnormal QRS complex are the same as those of a normal QRS complex. The direction can be mostly positive (upright), mostly negative (inverted), or biphasic. Its duration is often greater than 0.12 seconds. The amplitude of waves in the abnormal QRS complex varies from 1 to 2 mm to 20 mm or more. The morphology of the abnor-

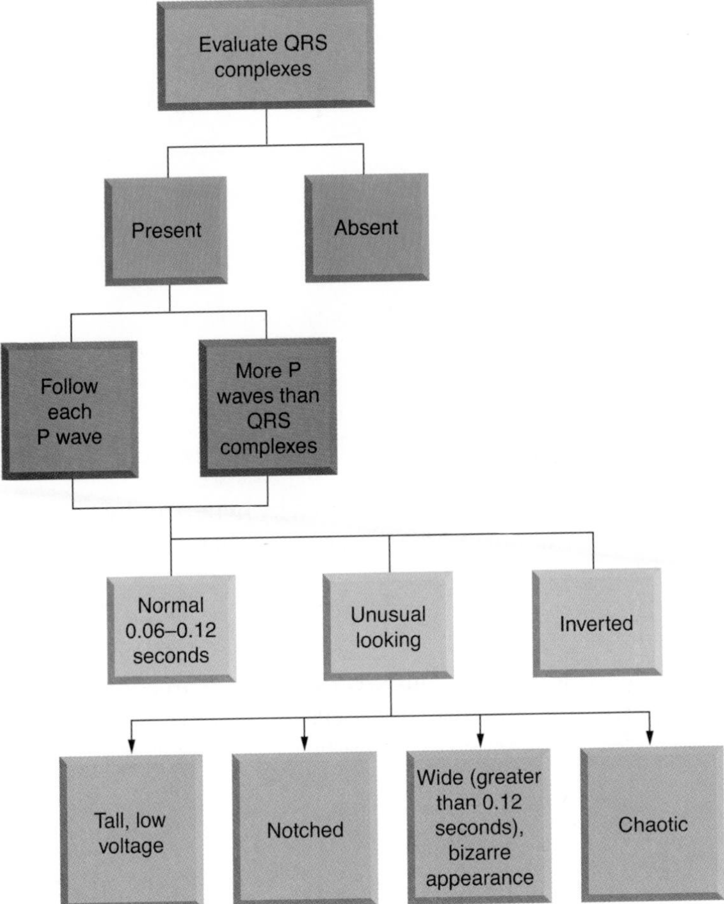

Figure 6-8
Algorithm to evaluate QRS complexes.

mal QRS complex can vary from being only slightly abnormal to extremely wide, notched, or slurred. We refer to these extremely abnormal configurations as bizarre because they deviate so far from normal (Figure 6-8).

A variety of conditions can cause abnormal QRS complexes including:

- ventricular hypertrophy
- obesity, hyperthyroidism, pleural effusion
- bundle branch block
- intraventricular conduction disturbance
- aberrant ventricular conduction
- ventricular preexcitation
- an electrical impulse originating in a ventricular ectopic or escape pacemaker
- ventricular pacing by a cardiac pacemaker

________________ depolarization of the ventricles results in abnormal ________________ complexes. These abnormal QRS complexes can arise from the ________________ node or an ________________ pacemaker in the atria, AV junction, bundle branches, ________________ network, or ________________ myocardium.

[Abnormal] [QRS] [SA] [ectopic] [Purkinje] [ventricular]

KEY CONCEPT
Tall QRS complexes suggest hypertrophy of one or both ventricles, an abnormal pacemaker, or aberrantly conducted beat.

Tall and Low Amplitude QRS Complexes

Very tall QRS complexes are usually caused by hypertrophy of one or both ventricles or by an abnormal pacemaker or aberrantly conducted beat (Figure 6-9). Hypertrophied ventricles are larger and, therefore, have more myocardial cells.

Low-voltage or abnormally small QRS complexes may be seen in obese patients, hyperthyroid patients, and pleural effusion.

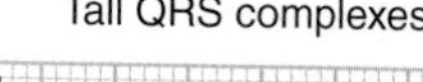

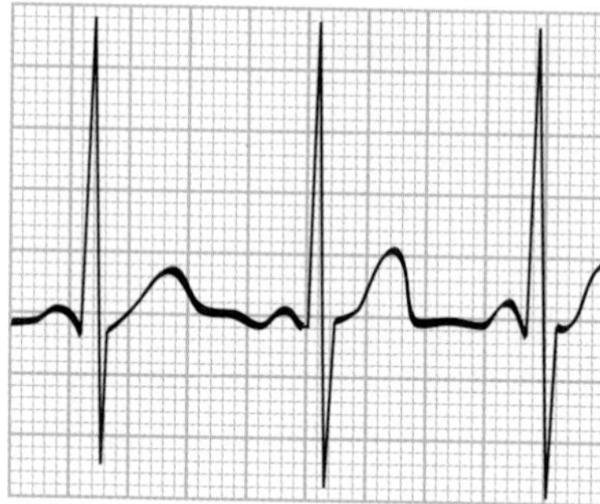

Low-voltage QRS complexes

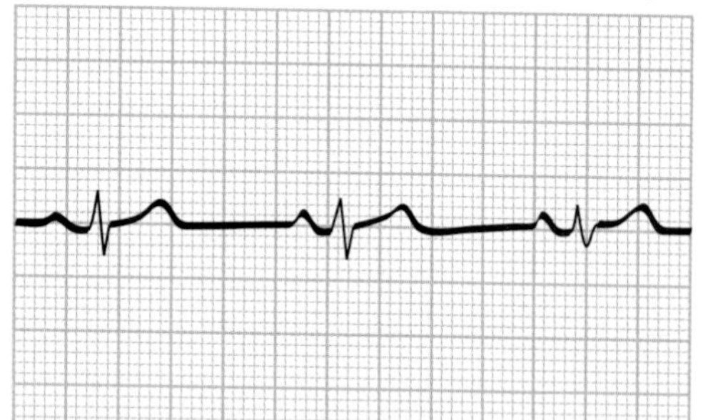

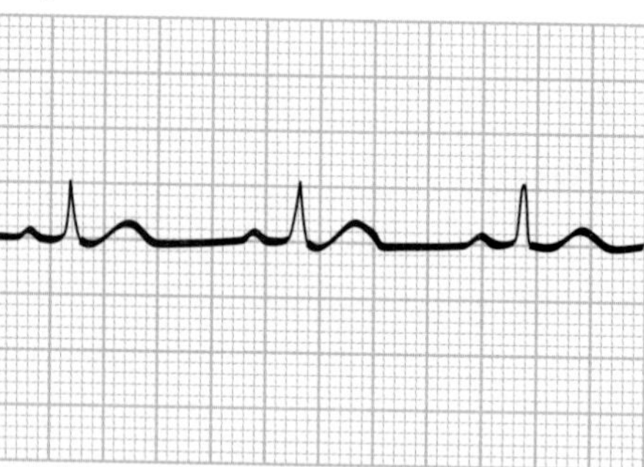

Figure 6-9
Examples of tall QRS complexes and low-voltage QRS complexes.

________________ of one or both ventricles usually produces very tall QRS complexes. They may also be caused by an ________________ pacemaker or ________________ conducted beat. Obese patients, hyperthyroid patients, and pleural effusion produce ________________ voltage or abnormally ________________ QRS complexes.

[Hypertrophy] [abnormal] [aberrantly] [low] [small]

INSTRUCTIONAL MOMENT

Waveforms that look alike from beat to beat (such as QRS complexes) are coming from the same location. Occasionally, frequently, or continuously repeating waveforms that look different are coming from a different location(s) or traveling through the conduction systems differently.

Wide QRS Complexes of Supraventricular Origin

Intraventricular Conduction Defect

Wide, bizarre QRS complexes are often the result of an intraventricular conduction defect (Figure 6-10). This is a condition where conduction through the ventricles is impaired. It usually occurs as a result of right or left bundle branch block. Bundle branch block takes place when conduction of the electrical impulse is partially or completely blocked in the right or left bundle

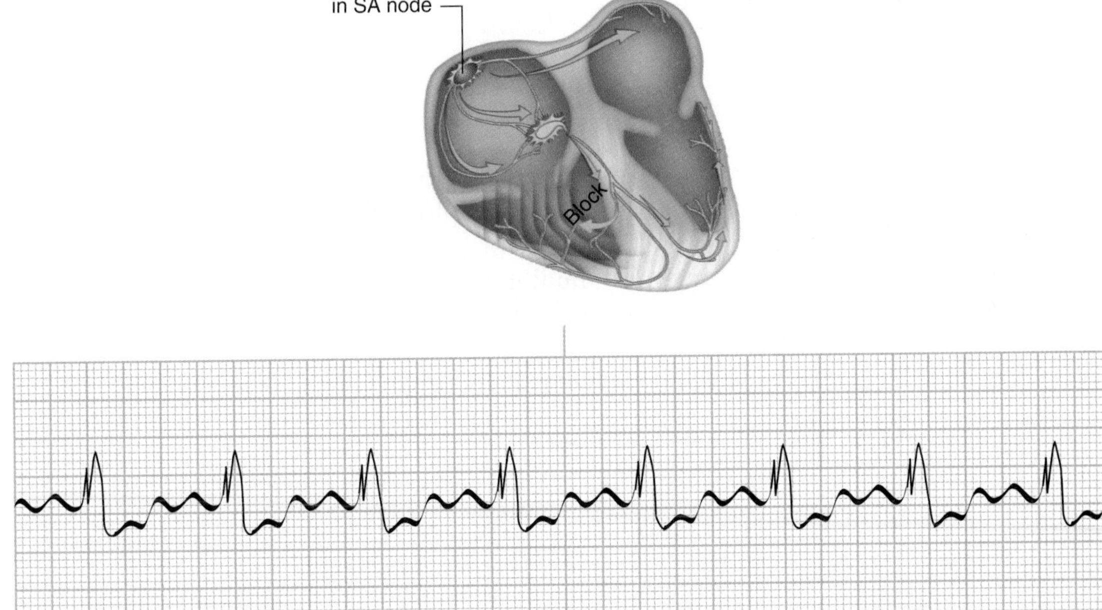

Figure 6-10
In bundle branch block, wide QRS complexes occur because conduction of the electrical impulse is partially or completely blocked in the right or left bundle branch while conduction continues uninterrupted through the unaffected bundle branch.

QUESTION
"What does the term supraventricular mean?" (The answer can be found on page 209.)

branch while conduction continues uninterrupted through the unaffected bundle branch. A block in one bundle branch causes the ventricle on that side to be depolarized later than the other. This results in an abnormal QRS complex. In bundle branch blocks the QRS complex is greater than 0.12 seconds in duration and appears bizarre (abnormal in size and shape).

Bundle branch block may be either partial or complete. As its name implies, partial, or incomplete, bundle branch block results in only part of the conduction being delayed. This results in less of a delay in ventricular depolarization than would be expected in complete bundle branch block. This causes the QRS complex to be greater than 0.10 seconds, but not greater than 0.12 seconds, in duration. However, the QRS complex has some abnormalities, such as notching, and does not appear completely normal.

Complete and partial bundle branch block may exist with normal sinus rhythm and in any supraventricular dysrhythmia. For this reason the QRS complexes are preceded by a P wave and a constant PR interval. The appearance of the P waves depends on their site of origin.

_____________ conduction defect is a condition where conduction through the ventricles is _____________. It usually occurs as a result of right or left _____________ branch block. Intraventricular conduction defect often produces _____________, _____________ QRS complexes.

[Intraventricular] [impaired] [bundle] [wide] [bizarre]

Other causes of intraventricular conduction defect include myocardial infarction; fibrosis; hypertrophy; electrolyte imbalance, such as hypokalemia and hyperkalemia; and excessive administration of such cardiac drugs such as quinidine, procainamide, and flecainide (Figure 6-11). The QRS complexes are preceded by a P wave and a constant PR interval because the pacemaker site is above the ventricles. The appearance of the P waves depends on their site of origin (Figure 6-11).

Intraventricular conduction defect can be caused by _____________ infarction, fibrosis, _____________, _____________ imbalance, and excessive administration of certain cardiac _____________. The QRS complexes are preceded by a _____________ wave and a constant _____________ interval because the pacemaker site is _____________ the ventricles.

[myocardial] [hypertrophy] [electrolyte] [drugs] [P] [PR] [above]

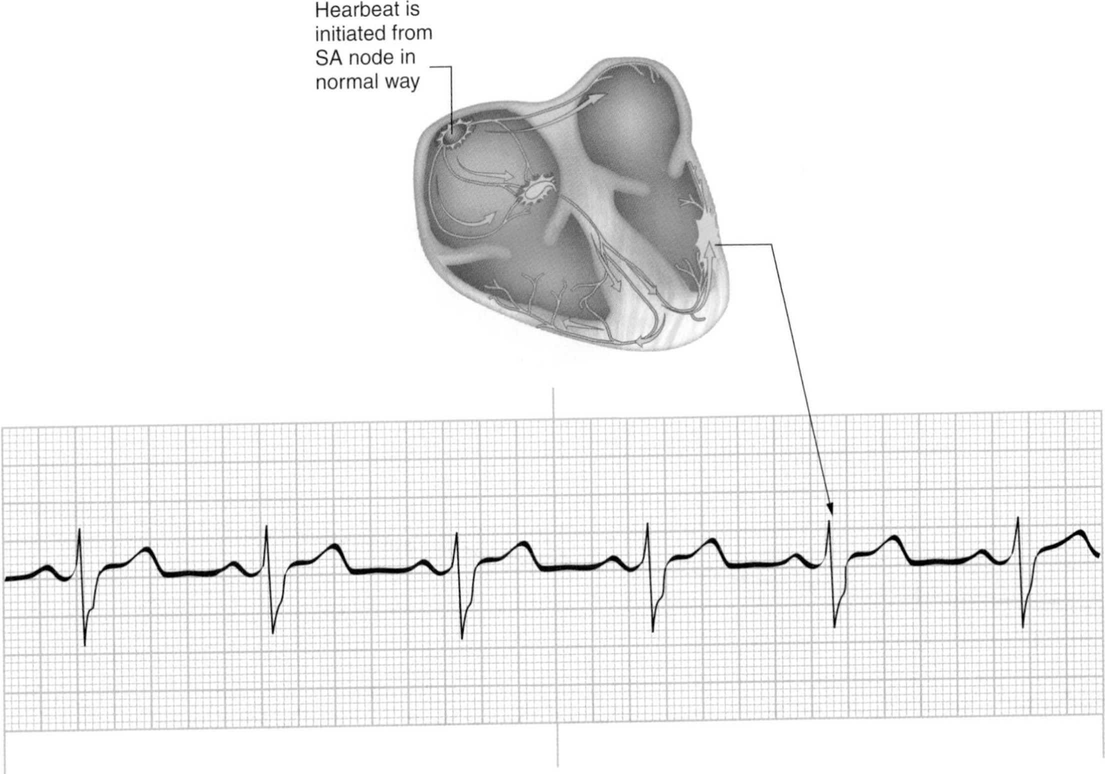

Figure 6-11
The presence of a P wave preceding each QRS complex indicates the rhythm is arising from the SA node. The wide QRS complexes result from a conduction defect through the ventricles.

Aberrant Conduction

Aberrant conduction is a brief failure of the right or left bundle branch to normally conduct an electrical impulse (Figure 6-12). It can occur when electrical impulses, such as premature contractions and tachycardias, reach the bundle branch shortly after it has just conducted an impulse. It is refractory (not able to be stimulated). One bundle branch may be less refractory than the other and will conduct the impulse. The refractory bundle branch will be stimulated following a delay. The abnormal QRS complex frequently looks like incomplete or complete bundle branch block and may mimic ventricular dysrhythmias.

Aberrant ventricular conduction can occur in many supraventricular dysrhythmias, including premature atrial and junctional complexes, atrial tachycardia, atrial flutter and fibrillation, nonparoxysmal junctional tachycardia, and paroxysmal supraventricular tachycardia.

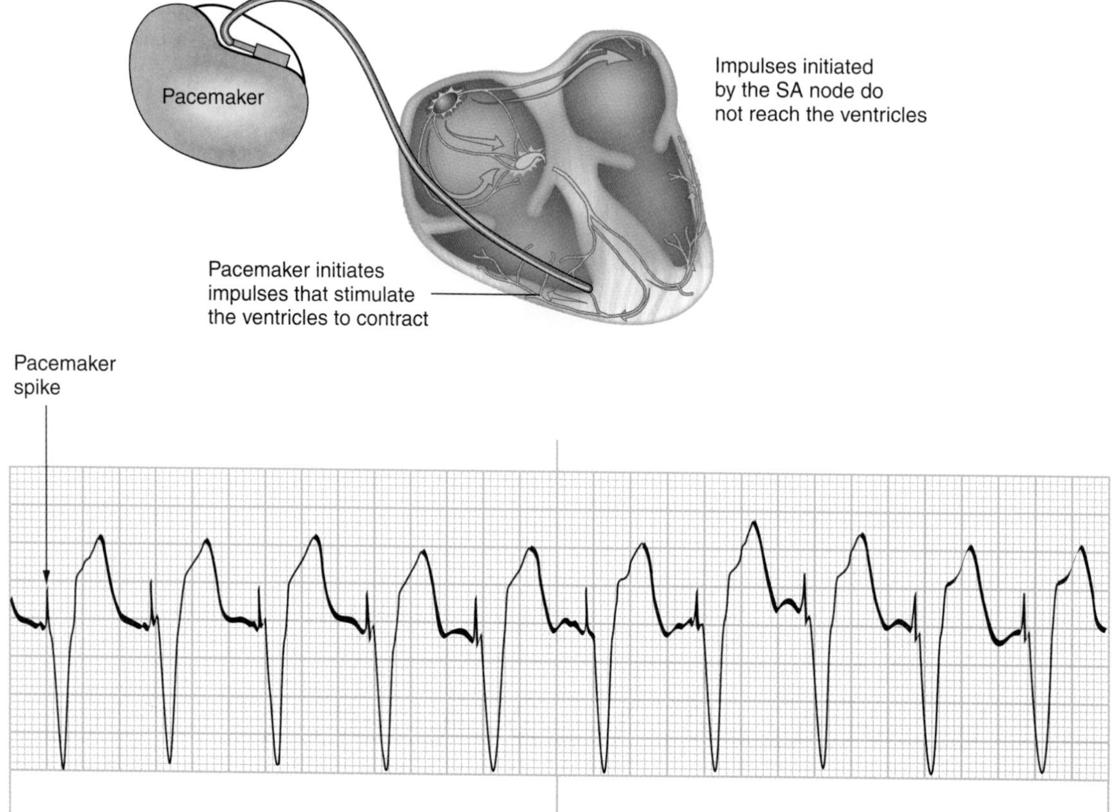

Figure 6-14
Characteristic features of cardiac pacemakers include wide QRS complexes (0.12 seconds or greater) and a narrow, often biphasic, deflection called the pacemaker spike, which precedes each pacemaker-induced QRS complex.

KEY CONCEPT
Wide QRS complexes that arise from above the ventricles are caused by intraventricular conduction defect, bundle branch block, aberrant conduction, or ventricular preexcitation.

Ventricular preexcitation is the ____________ depolarization of the ventricles that occurs when an impulse arises from a supraventricular site but travels through abnormal ____________ conduction pathways to the ____________. This causes ____________ than normal QRS complexes and characteristically abnormal ____________, and sometimes ____________, at its onset. This is called the ____________ wave.

[premature] [accessory] [ventricles] [wider] [slurring] [notching] [delta]

Pacemaker-Induced QRS Complexes

Certain conditions require the insertion of a cardiac pacemaker (Figure 6-14). Cardiac pacemaker-induced QRS complexes are generally 0.12 seconds or greater in width and appear bizarre. Preceding each pacemaker-induced QRS complex is a narrow, often biphasic, deflection called the pacemaker spike.

Another cause of wide and bizarre-looking QRS complexes is a cardiac ________________. Preceding each pacemaker-induced QRS complex is a ________________ deflection called the ________________ spike.

[pacemaker] [narrow] [pacemaker]

Wide, Bizarre QRS Complexes of Ventricular Origin

Dysrhythmias that originate from the ventricular tissue are referred to as ventricular dysrhythmias (Figure 6-15). The three dysrhythmias we will discuss are PVCs, idioventricular rhythm, and ventricular tachycardia. The key characteristic seen with ventricular dysrhythmias is wide (greater than 0.12 seconds in duration) QRS complexes. The QRS complexes are usually bizarre looking. Beats that arise from the ventricles are not preceded by a P wave (if seen, they are dissociated). The T waves of ventricular beats deflect in an opposite direction of the R waves.

KEY CONCEPT
PVCs are early ectopic beats that have a wide (greater than 0.12 seconds in duration), large QRS complex.

PVCs

Premature ventricular complexes (PVCs) are early beats that arise from the ventricles before the SA node has a chance to fire (Figure 6-16). These early beats interrupt the normal rhythm. The impulses arise from below the AV junction producing QRS complexes that look different than those that arise above or at the AV junction. As described, the QRS complexes associated with PVCs are wide, large, and bizarre looking. A pause, called a **compensatory pause,** follows the PVC. This will be discussed in more detail in Chapter 11.

KEY CONCEPT
Idioventricular rhythm is a slow (20 to 40 beats per minute) dysrhythmia that arises from the ventricles. It has wide, large, and bizarre-looking QRS complexes.

PVCs arise from the ventricles so the QRS complexes appear ________________, ________________, and ________________.

[wide] [large] [bizarre]

Idioventricular Rhythm

Idioventricular rhythm is a sustained escape rhythm that arises from the ventricles when stimuli from the SA node or AV junction fail to reach the ventricles or their rate falls to less than that of the ventricles (Figure 6-17). The key characteristics of idioventricular rhythm are a rate of 20 to 40 beats per minute and QRS complexes that are wide (greater than 0.12 seconds), large, and bizarre. As with PVCs, the T wave typically takes the opposite direction of the R wave. The rhythm arises from one site so it is usually regular. It becomes irregular as the heart dies.

CLINICAL MOMENT
Remember our discussion in Chapter 1: heart rate × stroke volume = cardiac output. Idioventricular rhythm can lead to decreased cardiac output because of the slower heart rate.

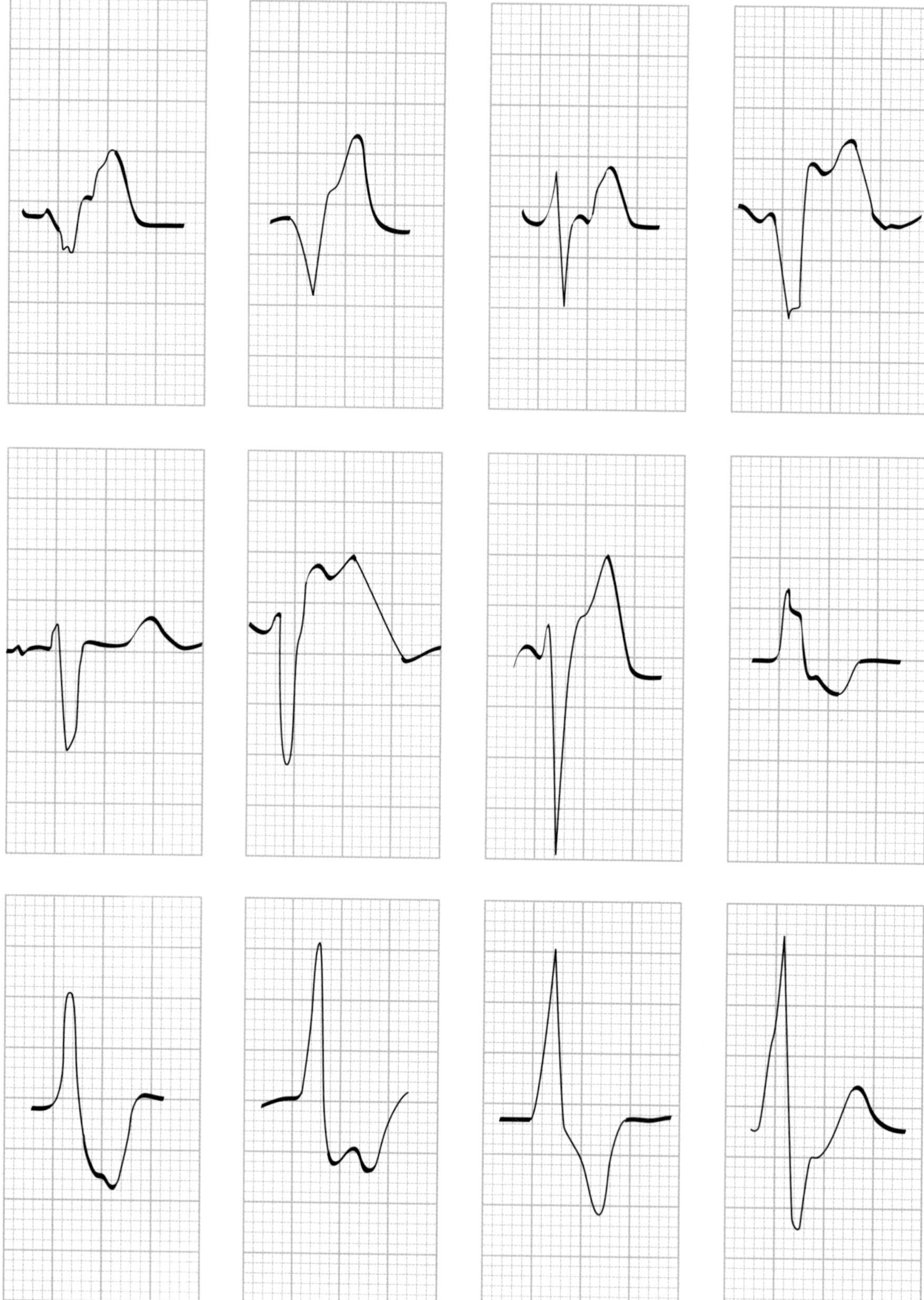

Figure 6-15
Different looking QRS complexes associated with ventricular beats and/or rhythms.

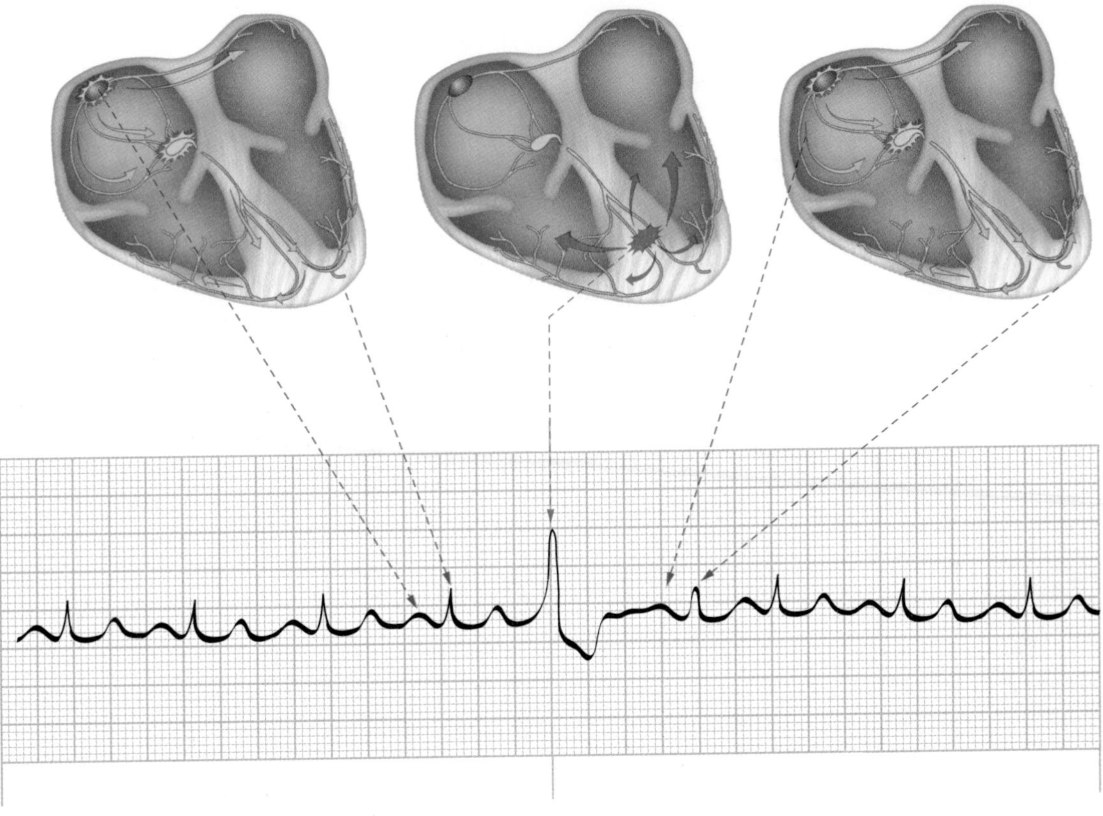

Figure 6-16
QRS complexes associated with PVCs are wide, large, and bizarre looking.

KEY CONCEPT
Ventricular tachycardia is a dysrhythmia with a heart rate of between 100 and 250 beats per minute and wide, large, and bizarre-looking QRS complexes.

Idioventricular rhythm has a rate of ______________ beats per minute and ______________, large, and bizarre ______________ complexes.

[20 to 40] [wide] [QRS]

Ventricular Tachycardia

Ventricular tachycardia results from rapid depolarization of the ventricles that overrides the SA node (Figure 6-18). It occurs when there are three or more PVCs in a row. It may occur in **bursts** of 6 to 10 complexes or be persistent. Persistence of this rhythm is called sustained ventricular tachycardia (V-Tach or VT). In sustained VT the heart rate is between 100 and 250 beats per minute. The rhythm consists of frequent, wide (greater than 0.12

CLINICAL MOMENT
Ventricular tachycardia is a very fast heart rate that causes cardiac output to decrease by lowering the stroke volume.

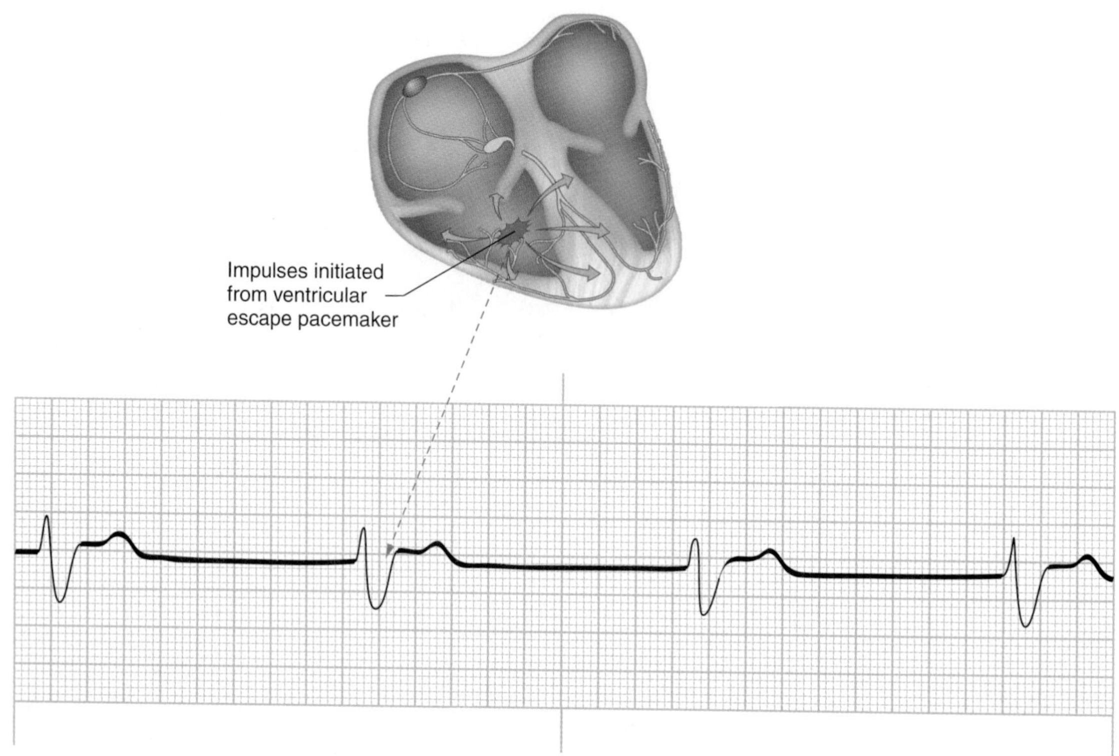

Figure 6-17
Wide, bizarre-looking QRS complexes firing at a rate of less than 40 beats per minute and an absence of P waves is seen with idioventricular rhythm.

QUESTION
"What type of regularity is characteristic of ventricular tachycardia?" (The answer can be found on page 209.)

seconds), and bizarre QRS complexes. The QRS complexes occur regularly, and there is no isoelectric line shown between the cardiac cycles. T waves may or may not be present. If seen, they are typically of the opposite direction of the R waves.

Ventricular tachycardia has a rate of ________________ beats per minute and ________________, large, and bizarre ________________ complexes.

[100 to 250] [wide] [QRS]

QUESTION
"How do the QRS complexes appear in monomorphic tachycardia?" (The answer can be found on page 209.)

Torsades de pointes Ventricular tachycardia that arises from one site is called monomorphic, whereas when it arises from more than one focus of irritability, it is called polymorphic. Torsades de pointes is a polymorphic

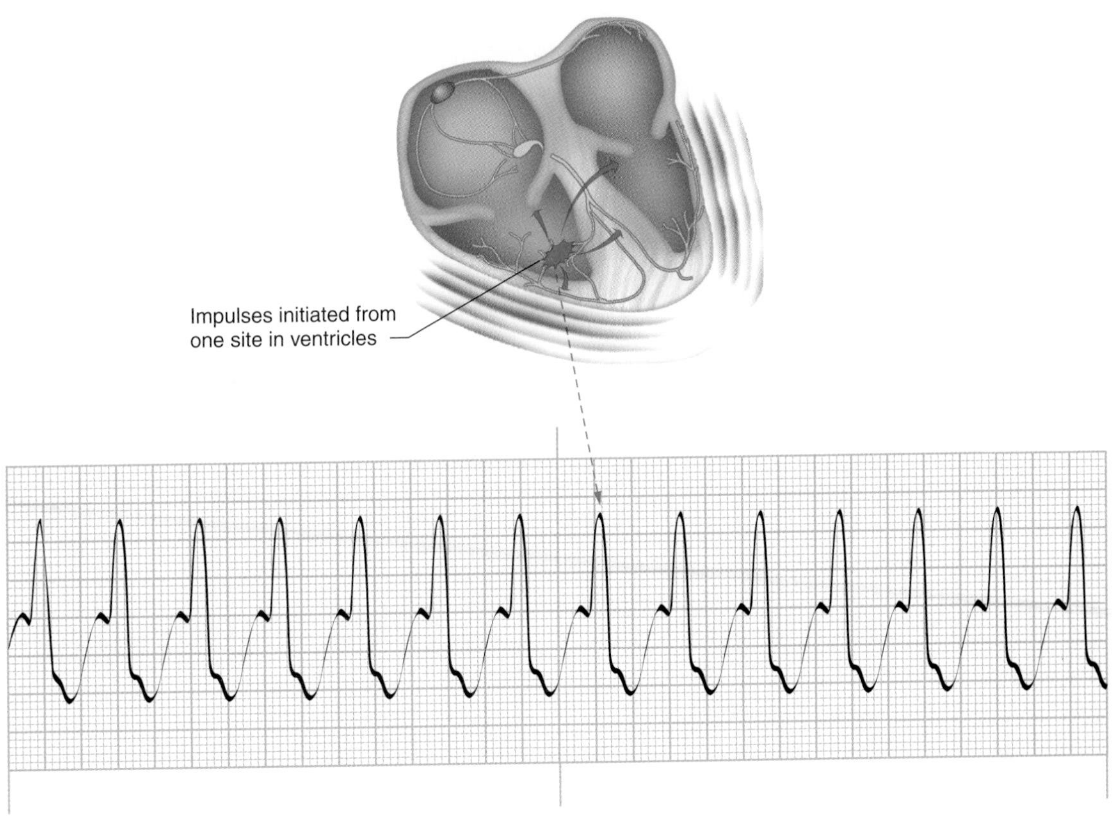

Figure 6-18
Wide, bizarre-looking QRS complexes firing at a rate of between 100 and 250 beats per minute and an absence of P waves is seen with ventricular tachycardia.

tachycardia in which the shape of the ventricular waveforms changes (Figure 6-19). It appears as a series of QRS complexes that rotate about the baseline (usually gradually) between upright deflections and downward deflections. It is described as a "spindle-shaped rhythm." The rate is 150 to 300 beats per minute (typically 200 to 250 beats per minute), the rhythm is usually irregular, the QRS complexes are wide, and the P waves are usually absent.

CLINICAL MOMENT
Torsades de pointes is French for "twisting about the points."

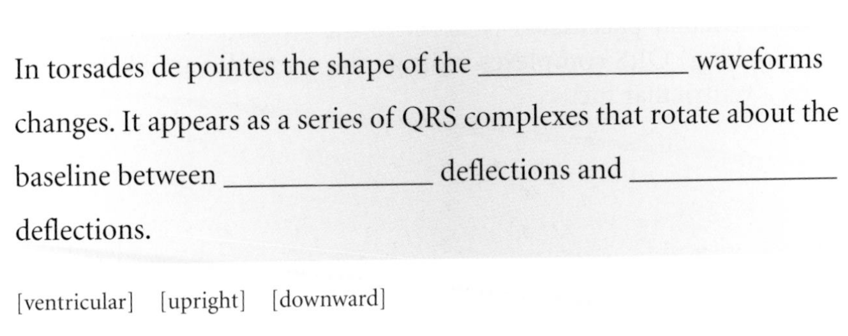

In torsades de pointes the shape of the ______________ waveforms changes. It appears as a series of QRS complexes that rotate about the baseline between ______________ deflections and ______________ deflections.

[ventricular] [upright] [downward]

KEY CONCEPT
Torsades de pointes is a polymorphic tachycardia that appears as a series of QRS complexes that rotate about the baseline between upright deflections and downward deflections.

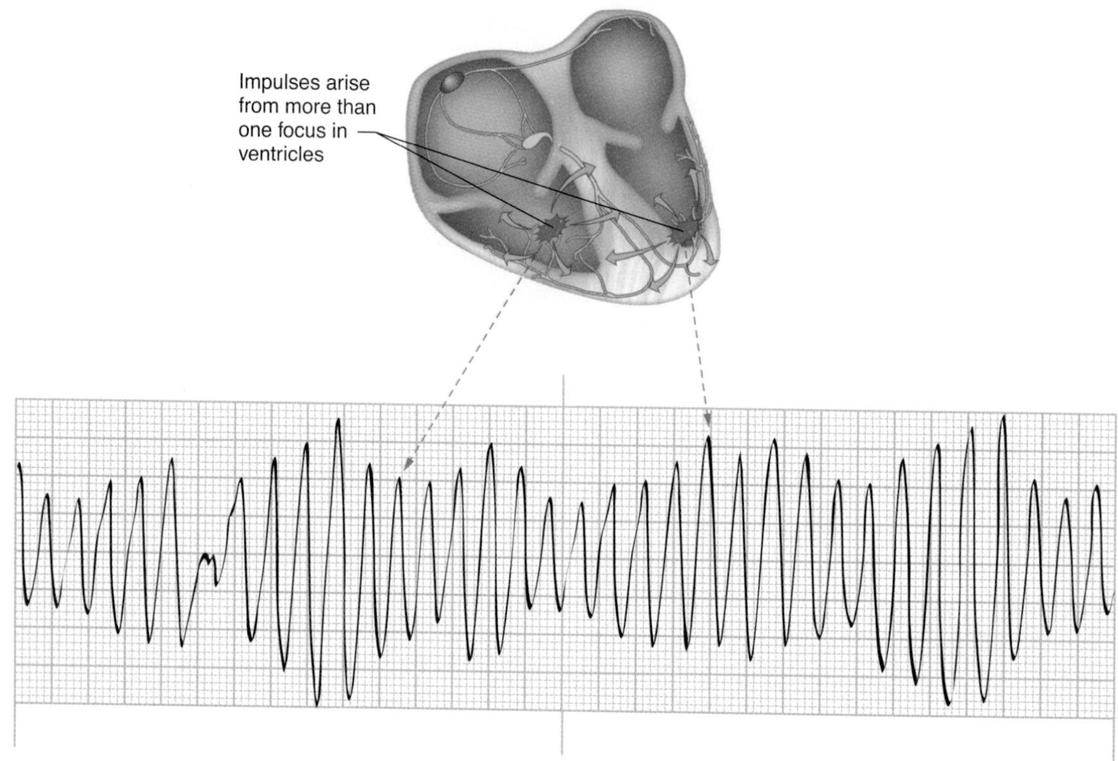

Figure 6-19
Torsades de pointes is a polymorphic tachycardia in which the shape of the ventricular waveforms change between upright and downward deflections. It appears as a spindle-shaped rhythm.

INSTRUCTIONAL MOMENT
The wide, bizarre-looking QRS complexes seen in 3rd-degree AV heart block when the ventricles are being paced by a ventricular focus are sometimes described as PVC-like.

3rd-Degree AV Heart Block

Another dysrhythmia where there may be abnormal QRS complexes is 3rd-degree AV heart block (Figure 6-20). Remember, we said that with 3rd-degree AV heart block there is complete blockage of the AV node. The atria are stimulated to contract by the impulse that originates from the SA node, while the ventricles are stimulated to contract by an escape pacemaker that arises somewhere below the AV node resulting in a slower heart rate. The location of the ventricular pacemaker site determines the appearance of the QRS complex. Normal (narrow) QRS complexes indicate the ventricular pacemaker is closer to the AV junction. Wide, large (bizarre-looking) QRS complexes indicate the ventricles are likely being paced by a ventricular focus.

CLINICAL MOMENT
Remember our discussion in Chapter 1: heart rate × stroke volume = cardiac output. AV heart blocks, which result in slower heart rates, can cause decreased cardiac output.

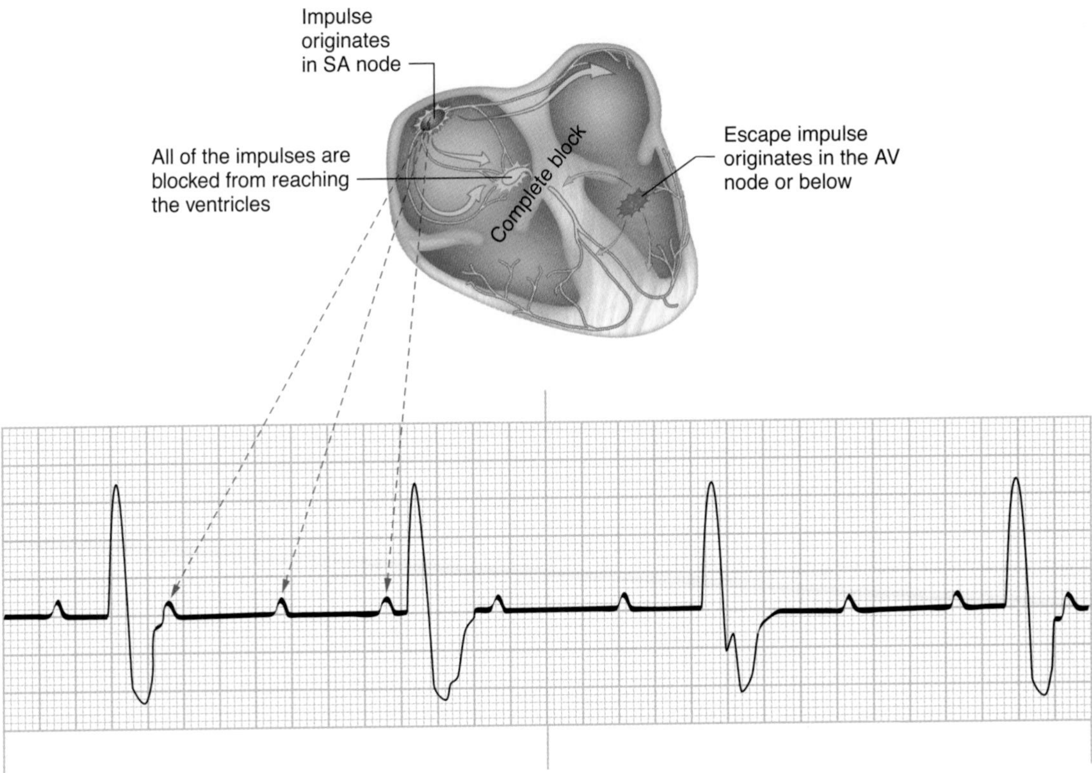

Figure 6-20
With 3rd-degree AV heart block, the ventricles are stimulated by an escape pacemaker site that arises from somewhere in the His-Purkinje system. The more distal the pacemaker site, the wider the QRS complex.

With 3rd-degree AV heart block there is ______________ blockage of the AV node resulting in the ventricles being stimulated to contract by an impulse that originates from below the ______________ junction. If the ventricles are stimulated by an impulse that arises closer to the AV node, the QRS complexes will be ______________. If the ventricles are stimulated by an impulse that arises from the ventricles, the QRS complexes will be ______________ and ______________.

[complete] [AV] [narrow] [wide] [bizarre]

KEY CONCEPT
Wide QRS complexes seen with 3rd-degree AV heart block indicate the pacemaker site is in the ventricles.

You can practice determining the type of QRS complexes, type of atrial waveform, heart rate, and regularity with the following *Practice Makes Perfect* exercises. Answers to these exercises can be found in Appendix A.

PRACTICE. . . MAKES PERFECT

6.

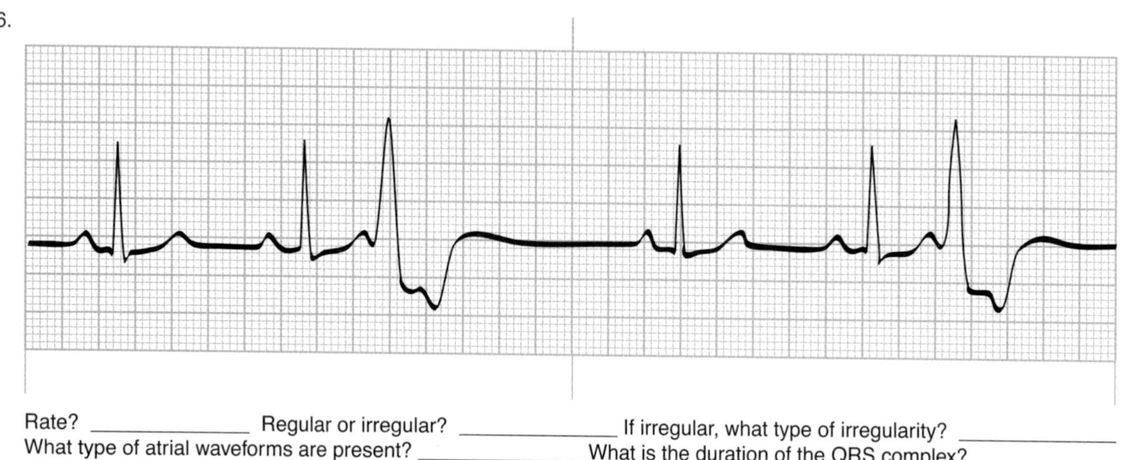

Rate? ______________ Regular or irregular? ______________ If irregular, what type of irregularity? ______________
What type of atrial waveforms are present? ______________ What is the duration of the QRS complex? ______________

7.

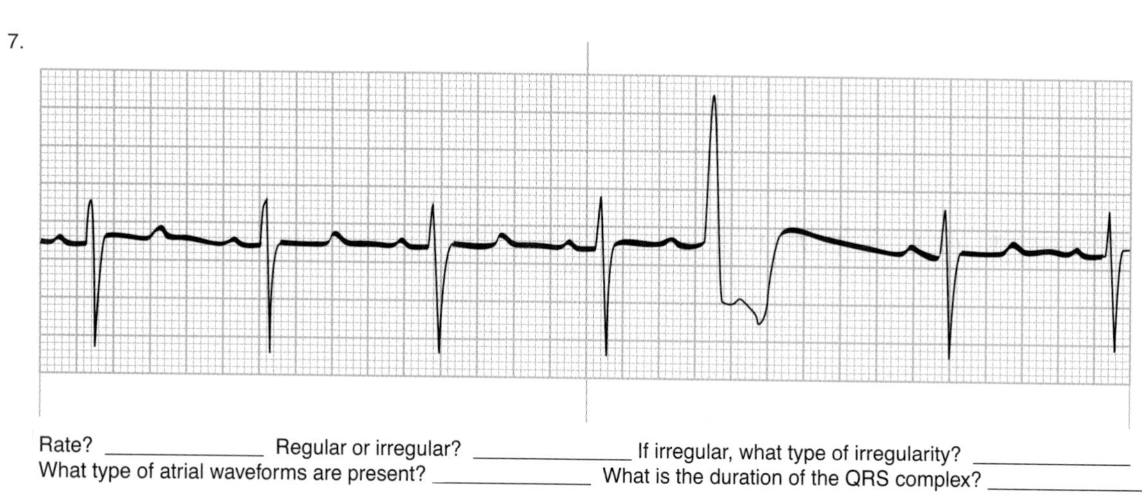

Rate? ______________ Regular or irregular? ______________ If irregular, what type of irregularity? ______________
What type of atrial waveforms are present? ______________ What is the duration of the QRS complex? ______________

8.

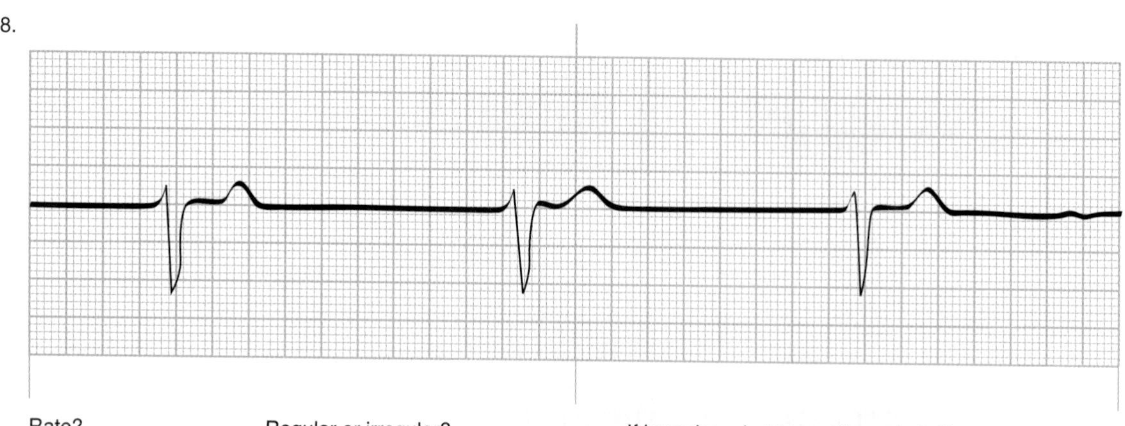

Rate? ______________ Regular or irregular? ______________ If irregular, what type of irregularity? ______________
What type of atrial waveforms are present? ______________ What is the duration of the QRS complex? ______________

PRACTICE. . . MAKES PERFECT

9.

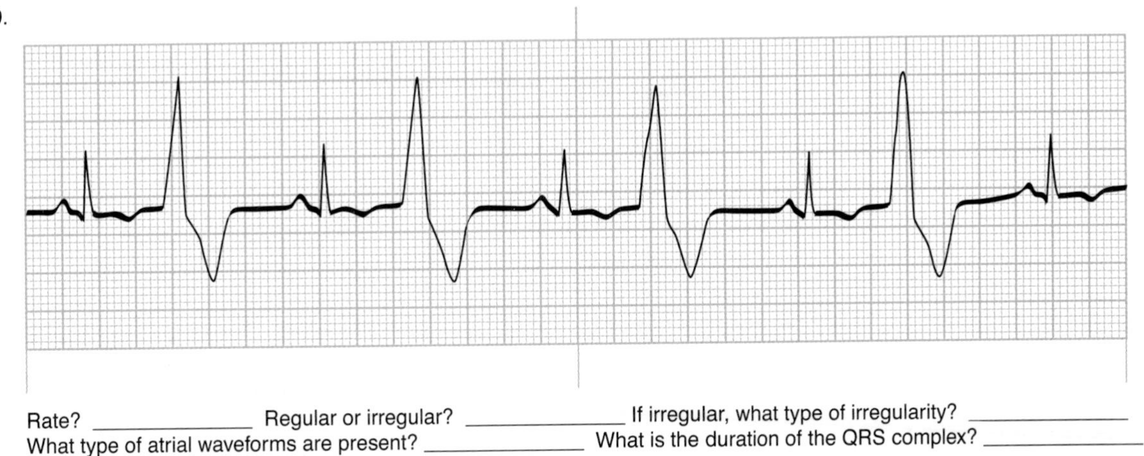

Rate? ______________ Regular or irregular? ______________ If irregular, what type of irregularity? ______________
What type of atrial waveforms are present? ______________ What is the duration of the QRS complex? ______________

10.

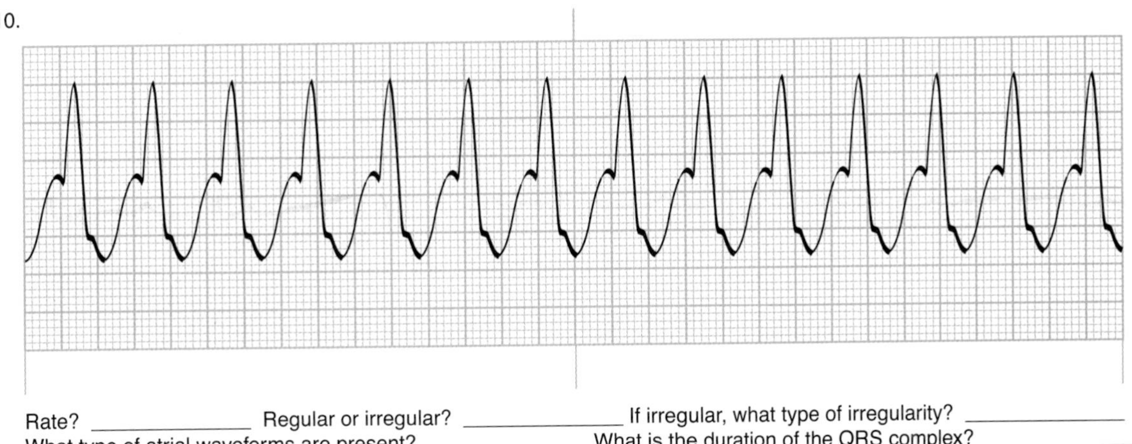

Rate? ______________ Regular or irregular? ______________ If irregular, what type of irregularity? ______________
What type of atrial waveforms are present? ______________ What is the duration of the QRS complex? ______________

Absent QRS Complexes

This section describes a number of dysrhythmias in which the QRS complexes are absent or so bizarre as to indicate that no coordinated depolarization of the ventricles is occurring and therefore the patient is pulseless.

CLINICAL MOMENT
Death occurs if ventricular fibrillation is not promptly treated. Defibrillation is considered the definitive treatment of ventricular fibrillation. VF is the most common cause of prehospital cardiac arrest in adults.

Ventricular Fibrillation

Ventricular fibrillation (VF) is the erratic firing of multiple sites in the ventricles causing the heart muscle to quiver instead of contracting as it normally does (Figure 6-21). On the ECG monitor it looks like a chaotic wavy line, rising and falling without any logic. There are no discernible

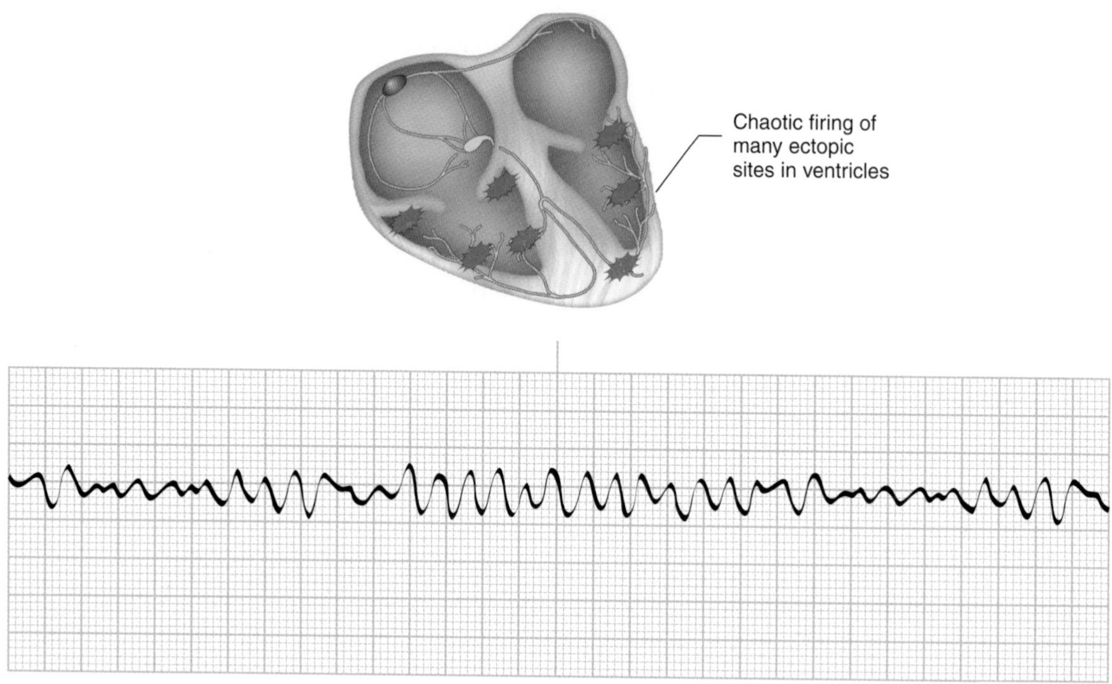

Figure 6-21
Ventricular fibrillation results in a chaotic-looking rhythm with no similarity in the waveforms or the distance between them.

waveforms. There is no coordinated contraction of the ventricles so the amount of blood pumped by the heart drops to zero. This ultimately causes all life-supporting physiological functions to cease because of a lack of circulating blood flow. Ventricular fibrillation is immediately life threatening. If the patient is not promptly treated (with CPR/defibrillation), death occurs.

KEY CONCEPT
Ventricular fibrillation has no discernible waveforms. It looks like a chaotic wavy line, rising and falling without any logic.

Ventricular fibrillation is the _______________ firing of multiple sites in the ventricles causing a _______________ wavy line, rising and falling without any logic, and an absence of _______________ waveforms on the ECG monitor.

[erratic] [chaotic] [discernible]

CLINICAL MOMENT
Asystole literally means without contraction of the heart ("a" means without and "systole" means heart contraction).

Asystole

Asystole is ventricular or cardiac standstill (Figure 6-22). It is essentially the absence of any cardiac activity in the ventricles. Asystole appears as a flat (or nearly flat) line on the ECG. It produces complete cessation of cardiac output. Like ventricular fibrillation, it is immediately life threat-

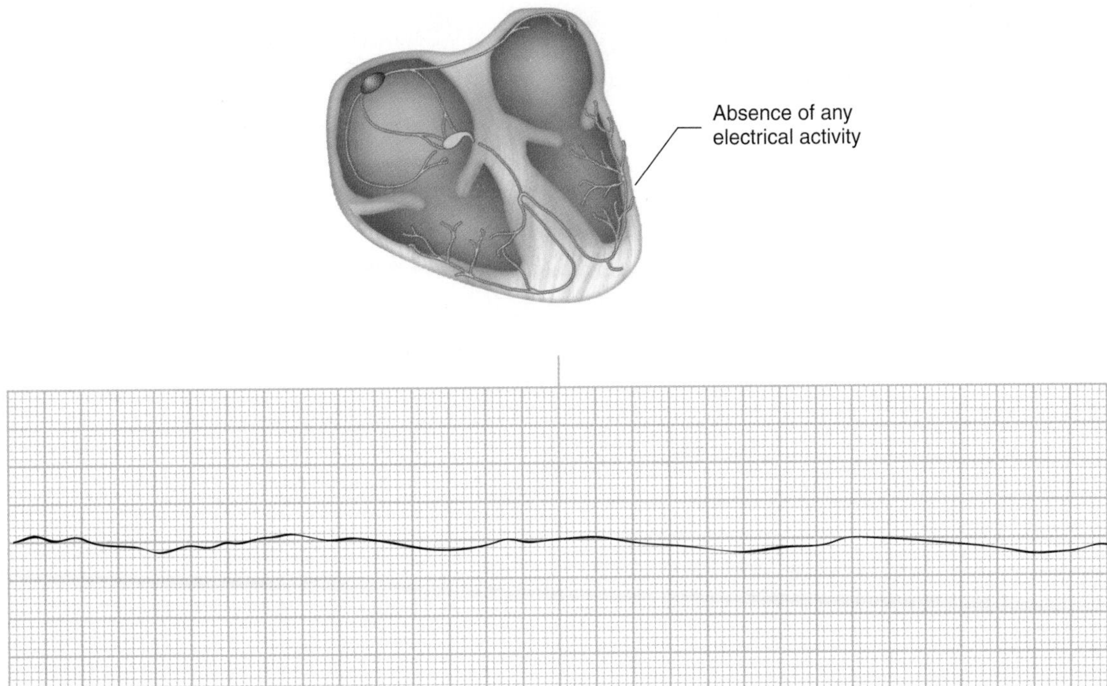

Figure 6-22
Asystole is the absence of any cardiac activity in the heart.

ening. Sometimes P waves are seen with asystole. This indicates the presence of electrical activity in the atria. They are typically only seen for a short time.

KEY CONCEPT
Asystole is the absence of any cardiac activity in the ventricles resulting in the appearance of a flat line on the ECG.

Asystole is the _______________ of any cardiac activity in the ventricles.

It appears as a _______________ line on the ECG.

[absence] [flat]

CLINICAL MOMENT
Asystole is a terminal rhythm. Once a person becomes asystolic the chances of recovery are extremely low. You must always verify the presence of asystole in two leads prior to initiating treatment. Misplacement of a lead or a loose wire can mimic asystole (or VF) on the ECG.

You can practice determining the type of QRS complexes, type of atrial waveform, heart rate, and regularity with the following *Practice Makes Perfect* exercises. Answers to these exercises can be found in Appendix A.

PRACTICE. . . MAKES PERFECT

11.

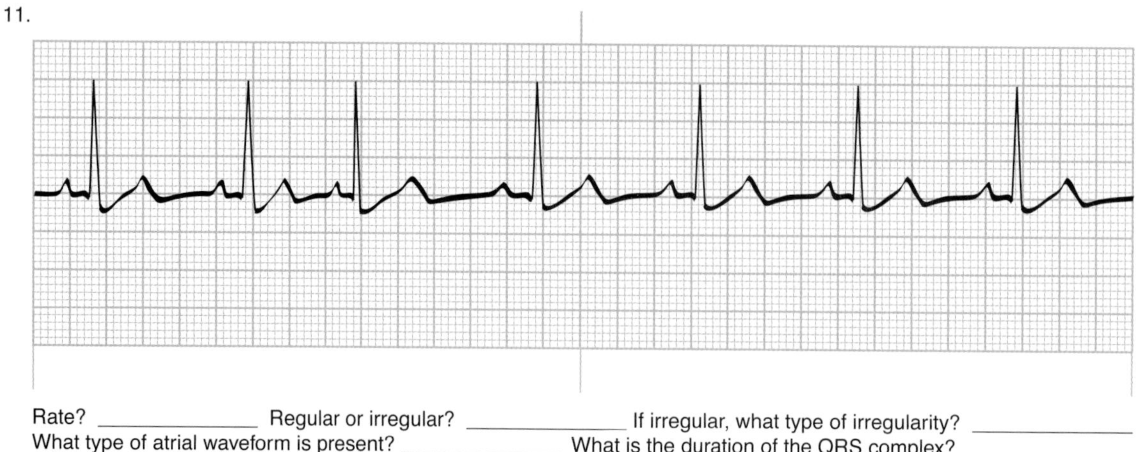

Rate? ______________ Regular or irregular? ______________ If irregular, what type of irregularity? ______________
What type of atrial waveform is present? ______________ What is the duration of the QRS complex? ______________

12.

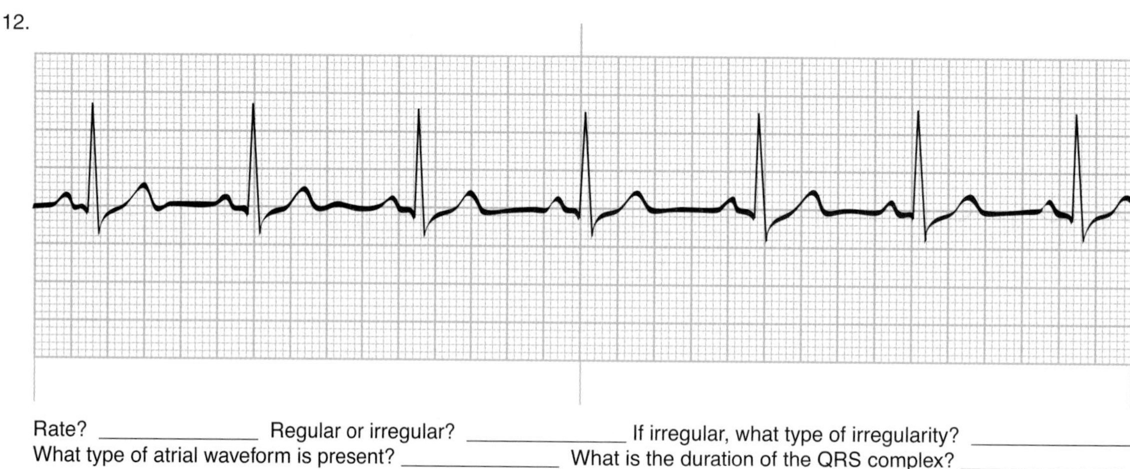

Rate? ______________ Regular or irregular? ______________ If irregular, what type of irregularity? ______________
What type of atrial waveform is present? ______________ What is the duration of the QRS complex? ______________

13.

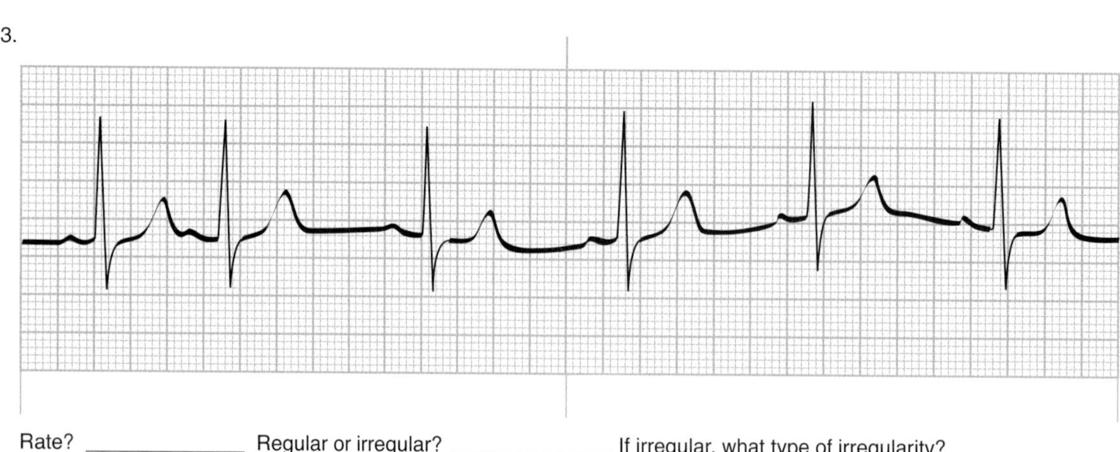

Rate? ______________ Regular or irregular? ______________ If irregular, what type of irregularity? ______________
What type of atrial waveform is present? ______________ What is the duration of the QRS complex? ______________

PRACTICE. . . MAKES PERFECT

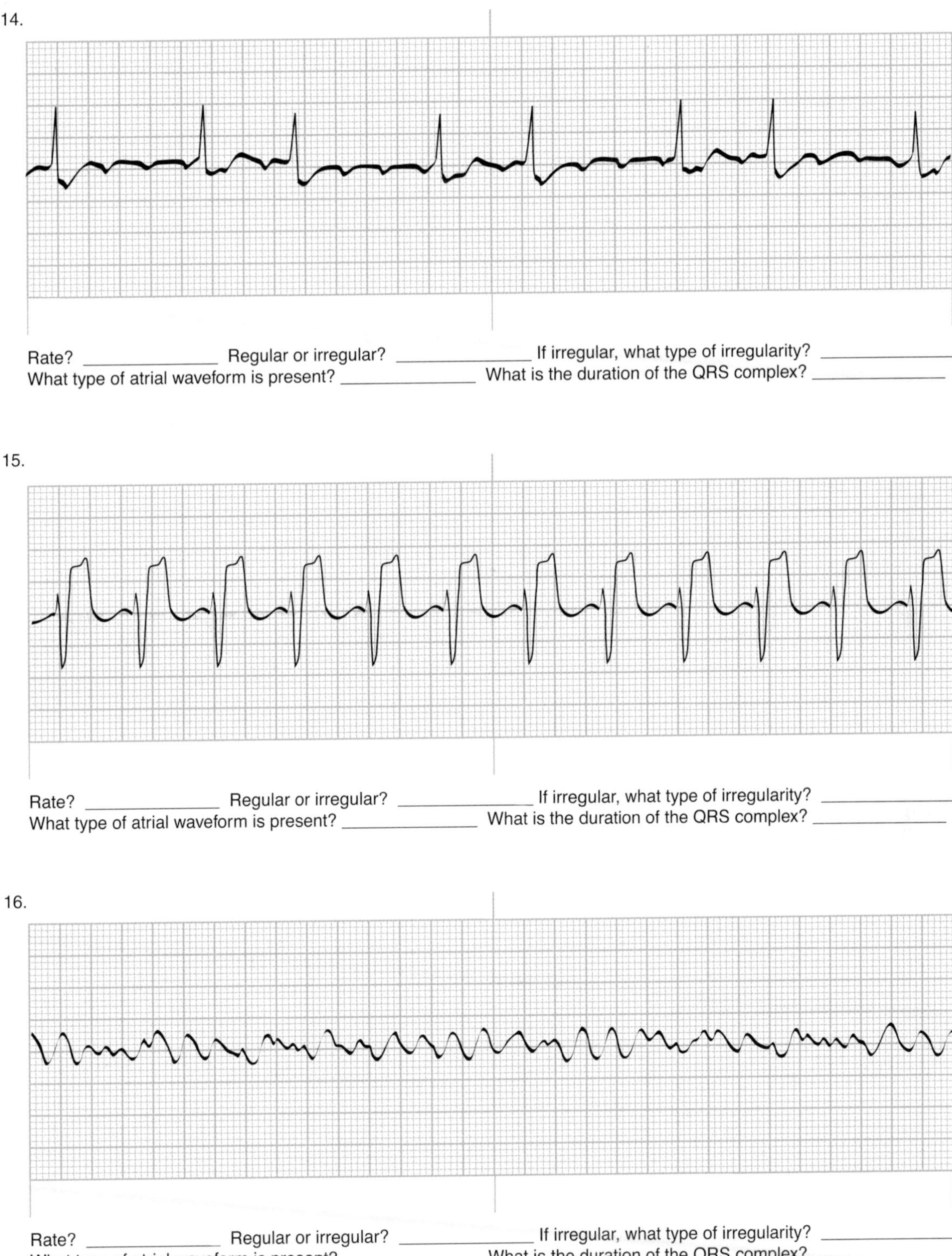

14.

Rate? ______________ Regular or irregular? ______________ If irregular, what type of irregularity? ______________
What type of atrial waveform is present? ______________ What is the duration of the QRS complex? ______________

15.

Rate? ______________ Regular or irregular? ______________ If irregular, what type of irregularity? ______________
What type of atrial waveform is present? ______________ What is the duration of the QRS complex? ______________

16.

Rate? ______________ Regular or irregular? ______________ If irregular, what type of irregularity? ______________
What type of atrial waveform is present? ______________ What is the duration of the QRS complex? ______________

PRACTICE. . . MAKES PERFECT

17.

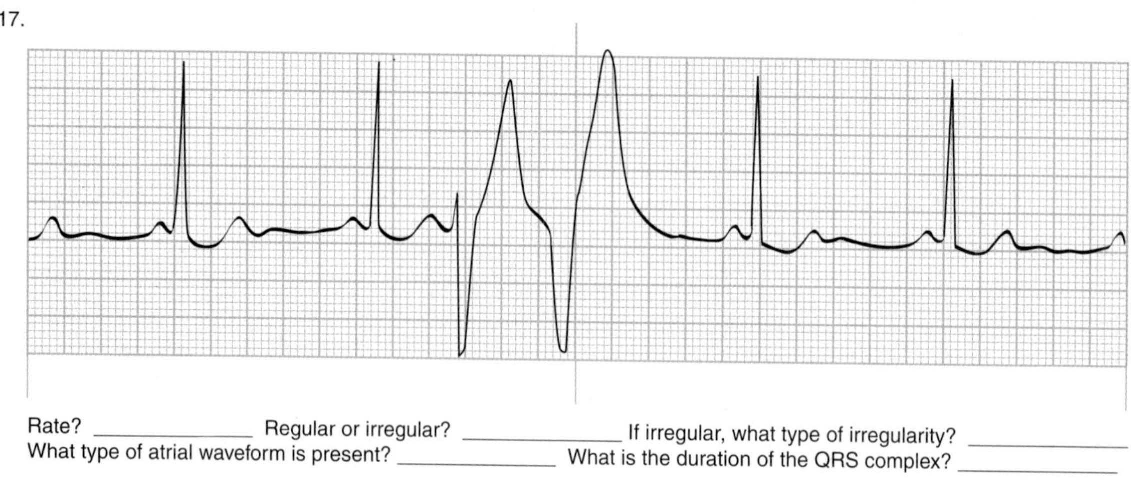

Rate? ______________ Regular or irregular? ______________ If irregular, what type of irregularity? ______________
What type of atrial waveform is present? ______________ What is the duration of the QRS complex? ______________

18.

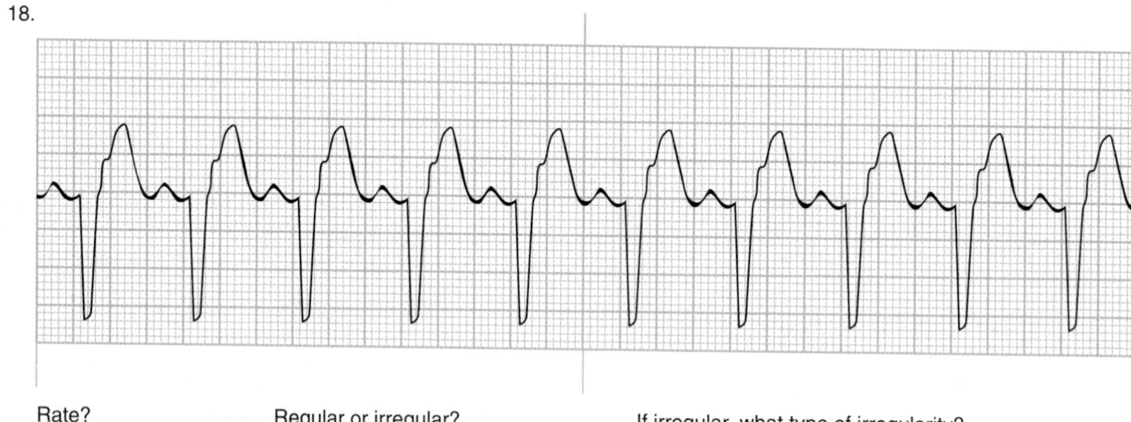

Rate? ______________ Regular or irregular? ______________ If irregular, what type of irregularity? ______________
What type of atrial waveform is present? ______________ What is the duration of the QRS complex? ______________

19.

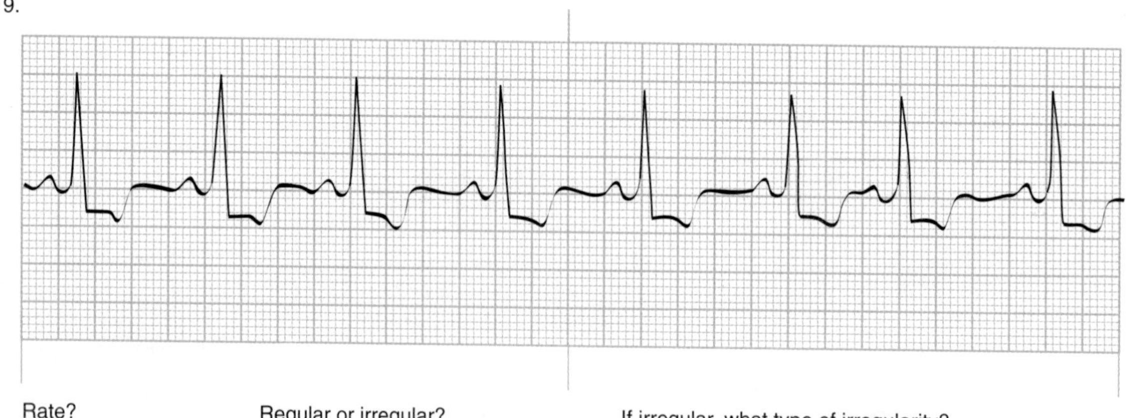

Rate? ______________ Regular or irregular? ______________ If irregular, what type of irregularity? ______________
What type of atrial waveform is present? ______________ What is the duration of the QRS complex? ______________

Key Points

- The fourth step of analyzing an ECG rhythm is examining the QRS complexes.
- The starting point of the QRS complex is where the first wave of the complex starts to move away (sharply or gradually) from the baseline. It ends at the point where the last wave of the complex transitions into the ST segment. This is where it begins to flatten (sharply or gradually) at, above, or below the baseline.
- The QRS complex is larger than the P wave because ventricular depolarization involves a considerably larger muscle mass than atrial depolarization.
- A normal QRS complex indicates the electrical impulse originated at or above the bundle of His and was carried through the ventricles in a normal manner.
- The amplitude of a normal QRS complex is 5 to 30 mm high and the duration is 0.06 to 0.12 seconds.
- The Q wave is the first negative deflection from the baseline following the P wave. The R wave is the first positive deflection following the Q wave (the P wave, if Q wave is absent). The S wave is the first negative deflection that extends below the baseline in the QRS complex following the R wave.
- The ventricles depolarize rapidly, therefore the QRS complex characteristically looks narrower than the other parts of the ECG.
- If the Q wave is absent, we measure the QRS complex from the beginning of the R wave.
- Normal sinus rhythm and dysrhythmias that arise from above the ventricles will usually (unless there is a conduction delay through the ventricles or other type of abnormality as described earlier) have normal QRS complexes.
- Abnormal QRS complexes are produced by abnormal depolarization of the ventricles.
- The pacemaker site in abnormal QRS complexes can be the SA node or an ectopic pacemaker in the atria, AV junction, bundle branches, Purkinje network, or ventricular myocardium.
- The duration of an abnormal QRS complex is greater than 0.12 seconds.
- The shape of an abnormal QRS complex varies widely from one that looks almost normal to one that is wide and bizarre and/or slurred and notched.
- Intraventricular conduction defect is a condition where conduction through the ventricles is impaired.
- Very tall QRS complexes are usually caused by hypertrophy of one or both ventricles or by an abnormal pacemaker or aberrantly conducted beat.
- Low-voltage or abnormally small QRS complexes may be seen in obese patients, hyperthyroid patients, and pleural effusion.
- Wide, bizarre QRS complexes of supraventricular origin are often the result of an intraventricular conduction defect, which usually occurs as a result of right or left bundle branch block. Bundle branch block may be either partial or complete.
- Aberrant conduction occurs when electrical impulses, such as premature complexes and tachycardias, reach the bundle branch while it is still refractory after conducting a previous electrical impulse.
- Wider than normal QRS complexes may also be due to ventricular preexcitation. This also causes an abnormal slurring, and sometimes notching, at its onset called the delta wave.

- Cardiac pacemaker-induced QRS complexes are generally 0.12 seconds or greater in width and appear bizarre. Preceding each pacemaker-induced QRS complex is a pacemaker spike.

- Ventricular dysrhythmias are those dysrhythmias that originate from the ventricular tissue.

- Wide, greater than 0.12 seconds in duration, QRS complexes are the key characteristic seen with ventricular dysrhythmias. Also, the QRS complexes are usually bizarre looking and the T waves deflect in an opposite direction to the R waves.

- Premature ventricular complexes (PVCs) are early beats that arise from the ventricles before the SA node has a chance to fire.

- Idioventricular rhythm is a sustained escape rhythm having a rate of 20 to 40 beats per minute (may be slower) that arises from the ventricles.

- Ventricular tachycardia results from rapid depolarization of the ventricles that overrides the SA node.

- Three or more PVCs in a row are considered ventricular tachycardia.

- In sustained VT, the heart rate is between 100 and 250 beats per minute.

- With torsades de pointes, the shape of the ventricular waveforms changes. It appears as a series of QRS complexes that rotate about the baseline between upright deflections and downward deflections.

- 3rd-degree AV heart block is another dysrhythmia where there may be abnormal QRS complexes. Wide, large (bizarre-looking) QRS complexes indicate the ventricles are likely being paced by a ventricular focus.

- Ventricular fibrillation is the erratic firing of multiple sites in the ventricles causing the heart muscle to quiver, instead of contracting and pumping blood throughout the body.

- Defibrillation is considered the definitive treatment of ventricular fibrillation and must be delivered promptly.

- Asystole is the lack of any cardiac activity in the ventricles. On the ECG you will see a flat (or nearly flat) line. It produces complete cessation of cardiac output.

Assess Your Understanding

The following questions give you a chance to assess your understanding of the material discussed in this chapter. The answers can be found in Appendix A.

1. The appearance of the ___________ is affected by the lead used.
   a. Heart rate
   b. QRS complexes
   c. Regularity
   d. PR interval

2. In leads I, II, III, aV_F, and V_4 to V_6 the deflection of the QRS complex is characteristically
   a. inverted.
   b. positive.
   c. pointed.
   d. biphasic.

3. The fourth step in analyzing an ECG is
   a. checking the regularity.
   b. looking at the P waves.

c. examining the QRS complexes.
d. determining the heart rate.

4. The normal duration of the QRS complex is __________ second(s).
   a. 0.06 to 0.12
   b. 0.8 to 0.12
   c. 1.0
   d. 0.06 to 0.10
5. An upright (in lead II) narrow QRS complex indicates that the electrical impulse originated
   a. in the AV node and was carried through the atria in a retrograde manner.
   b. in the ventricles and was carried through the atria in a normal manner.
   c. in the SA node and was carried through the AV node in a retrograde manner.
   d. at or above the AV node and was carried through the ventricles in a normal manner.
6. The R wave is the
   a. first positive deflection in the QRS complex.
   b. second negative deflection that extends below the baseline.
   c. first negative deflection from the baseline following the P wave.
   d. flat line that precedes the Q wave.
7. Which of the following will produce normal QRS complexes?
   a. Altered, damaged, or abnormal ventricles.
   b. Ventricular tachycardia.
   c. Premature atrial complexes.
   d. Idioventricular rhythm.
8. Which of the following is true regarding the amplitude of QRS complexes?
   a. Women have larger amplitudes than men.
   b. The elderly have higher amplitudes than young people.
   c. Precordial leads have higher amplitudes than the limb leads.
   d. Both a and c.
9. Intraventricular conduction defect
   a. is the result of accelerated conduction through the ventricles.
   b. produces tall QRS complexes.
   c. is usually due to right or left bundle branch block.
   d. is usually seen in myocardial infarction, fibrosis, and hypertrophy.
10. Low-voltage or abnormally small QRS complexes are seen in
    a. hypertrophy.
    b. obese patients.
    c. premature ventricular complexes.
    d. sinus bradycardia.
11. Which of the following is a cause of intraventricular conduction defect?
    a. Hypertrophy.
    b. Accessory pathways.
    c. Bundle branch block.
    d. A cardiac pacemaker.
12. Bundle branch blocks
    a. may be partial or complete.
    b. have a delta wave preceding the QRS complex.
    c. have a pacemaker spike.
    d. have QRS complexes not preceded by a P wave or PR interval.
13. Aberrant conduction
    a. occurs when an impulse is late arriving at the bundle branch.
    b. results in narrow, spike-shaped QRS complexes.
    c. mimics supraventricular dysrhythmias.
    d. occurs when the impulse reaches one of the bundle branches while it is still refractory.

14. Premature ventricular complexes
    a. arise from the atria.
    b. always have an inverted QRS complex.
    c. produce QRS complexes that look different than those that arise above or at the AV junction.
    d. have narrow, upright QRS complexes.

15. Idioventricular rhythm has
    a. wide, bizarre-looking QRS complexes.
    b. a P wave that precedes each QRS complex.
    c. T waves that take the same direction as the R wave.
    d. a ventricular rate of 40 to 60 beats per minute.

16. With ventricular tachycardia the
    a. pacemaker site is in the SA node.
    b. ventricular rate is 100 to 250 beats per minute.
    c. fast rate is always sustained.
    d. QRS complexes are narrow.

17. With 3rd-degree AV block, the QRS complexes
    a. are always wide and bizarre.
    b. are associated with irregular and frequent PVCs.
    c. follow each P wave but at a slower rate.
    d. are slower than the P wave rate because there is complete blockage of the AV node.

18. Torsades de pointes
    a. is monomorphic tachycardia.
    b. has an average heart rate of 100 to 250 beats per minute.
    c. has a spindle-shaped appearance.
    d. causes the ventricles to quiver instead of effectively contracting.

19. With ventricular fibrillation,
    a. there is adequate cardiac output.
    b. a chaotic wavy line is seen on the ECG.
    c. there is erratic firing from one site in the ventricles.
    d. there is a flat line on the ECG.

20. Asystole
    a. is the erratic firing of multiple sites in the ventricles.
    b. produces an effective electrical rhythm but no contraction of the heart muscle.
    c. usually produces P waves.
    d. is seen as a flat line on the ECG.

21. Identify the heart rate and regularity of the following ECG. What type of QRS complexes are present? What type of atrial waveforms are present?

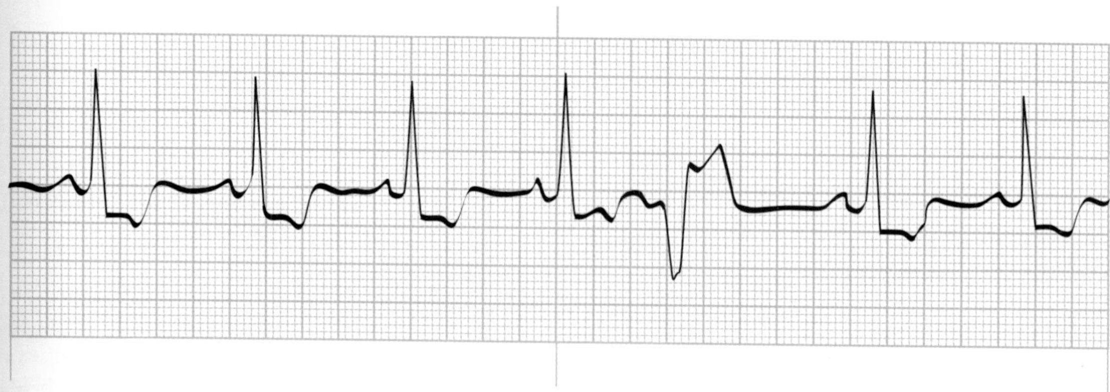

22. Identify the heart rate and regularity of the following ECG. What type of QRS complexes are present? What type of atrial waveforms are present?

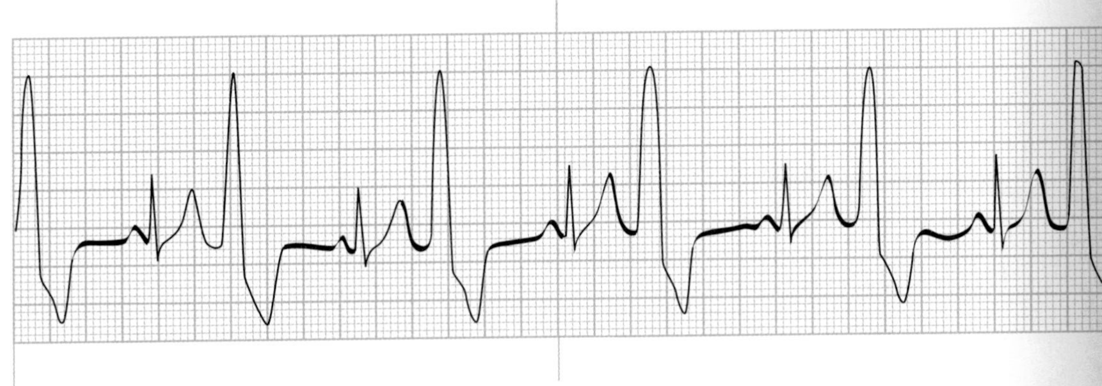

23. Identify the heart rate and regularity of the following ECG. What type of QRS complexes are present? What type of atrial waveforms are present?

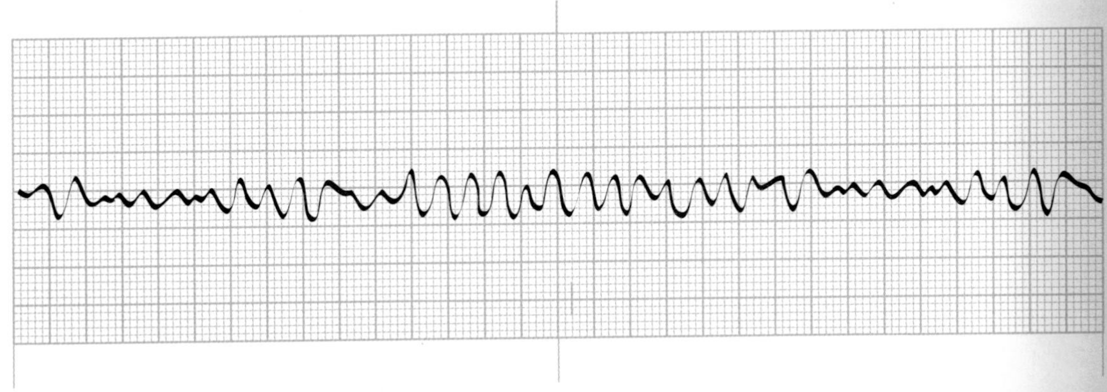

24. Identify the heart rate and regularity of the following ECG. What type of QRS complexes are present? What type of atrial waveforms are present?

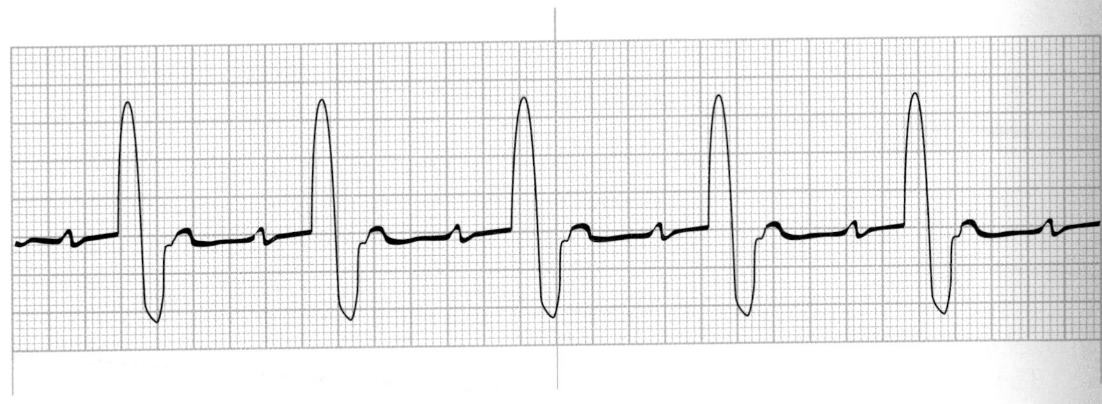

25. Identify the heart rate and regularity of the following ECG. What type of QRS complexes are present? What type of atrial waveforms are present?

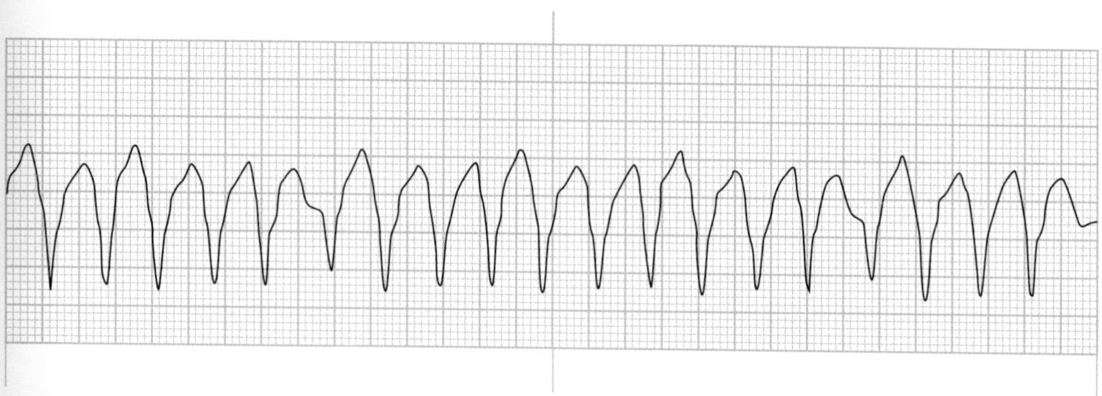

Referring to the scenario at the front of this chapter answer the following questions.

26. What is the name of the extra QRS complexes the patient had?
    a. Premature atrial complexes.
    b. Multifocal atrial tachycardia.
    c. PVCs.
    d. PJCs.

27. The most likely cause of the patient's extra beats is
    a. anxiety.
    b. pain.
    c. ischemia.
    d. infarction.

Answers to Sidebar Questions

"In lead II, which direction does the electrical current that produces the Q wave move in relation to the positive electrode of the electrocardiograph?"

Answer: More of the current is moving away from the positive electrode than moving toward it.

"Why does the QRS complex look different in the various ECG leads?"

Answer: The direction the electrical current takes, toward a positive or negative electrode, determines the direction a waveform points on an ECG. The waveforms seen in each lead look different because they reveal another view of the heart.

"What is the normal duration of the QRS complex?"

Answer: The normal duration of the QRS complex is 0.06 to 0.12 seconds.

"What is atrial flutter or fibrillation that has a slow or fast ventricular rate called?"

Answer: Atrial flutter or fibrillation that has a slow or fast ventricular rate is referred to as "atrial flutter or fibrillation with a slow or rapid ventricular response." With a fast ventricular response, these rhythms are also called "uncontrolled atrial flutter or fibrillation."

"Which dysrhythmia has a characteristic heart rate of less than 60 beats a minute, a regular rhythm, and a P wave preceding each QRS complex?"

Answer: These features are characteristic of sinus bradycardia.

"What does the term supraventricular mean?"

Answer: Supraventricular means above the ventricles—this could be the SA node, atria, or AV junction.

"What type of regularity is characteristic of ventricular tachycardia?"

Answer: Ventricular tachycardia is regular because the dysrhythmia arises from one pacemaker site.

"How do the QRS complexes appear in monomorphic tachycardia?"

Answer: The QRS complexes should appear the same in monomorphic tachycardia as it arises from one site.

On the DVD

- The QRS Complex lecture.
- Compensatory vs. Noncompensatory Pause lecture.
- Physiologic Consequences of Abnormal QRS Complexes lecture.
- Demonstration of Measuring the QRS Complex.

Notes

PR Intervals

7

Case History

A 77-year-old woman who had a heart attack three days ago is transferred from the ICU to the medical floor for continued observation. Her heart rhythm is continuously monitored by the telemetry unit. During the patient's morning walk the nurses receive a call from the telemetry unit informing them that the patient's rhythm has become irregular. After locating the woman, the nurses return her to her bed and obtain the rhythm strips from the telemetry unit. Her attending physician is summoned and her vital signs obtained and found to be normal except for a regularly irregular pulse.

The patient's physician arrives and examines the rhythm strip with the nurse. He notes that the PR interval increases in length following each P wave until after every third one when the QRS complex is missing entirely. They discuss that this is a common complication after a myocardial infarction. The patient is moved back to the ICU for close observation because of the possibility for further deterioration.

Chapter Preview

- Step 5: Examining the PR Intervals
- PR Intervals That Are Different

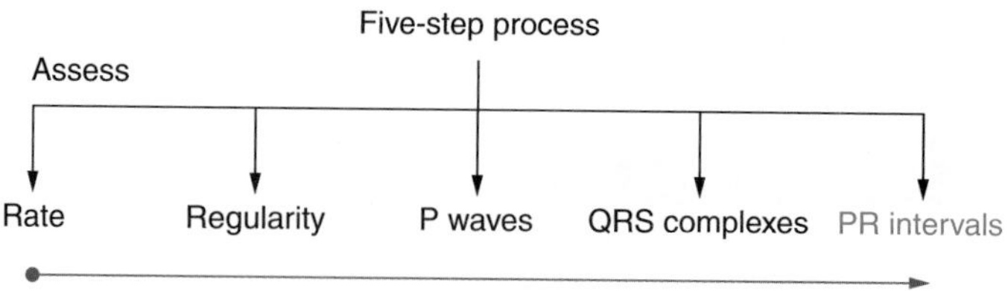

Figure 7-1
Evaluating the PR intervals is the fifth step of analyzing an ECG tracing.

Step 5: Examining the PR Intervals

KEY CONCEPT
The fifth step of analyzing an ECG rhythm is assessing the PR intervals.

The fifth step of analyzing an ECG rhythm is examining the PR intervals (Figure 7-1). As discussed previously, the PR interval is the distance from the beginning of the P wave to the beginning of the Q wave (or R wave if the Q wave is absent). The PR interval denotes depolarization of the heart from the SA node through the atria, AV node, and His-Purkinje system. A normal PR interval indicates the impulse originated from the SA node (or close to it) and traveled through the atria and AV node in a regular and unobstructed course (Figure 7-2).

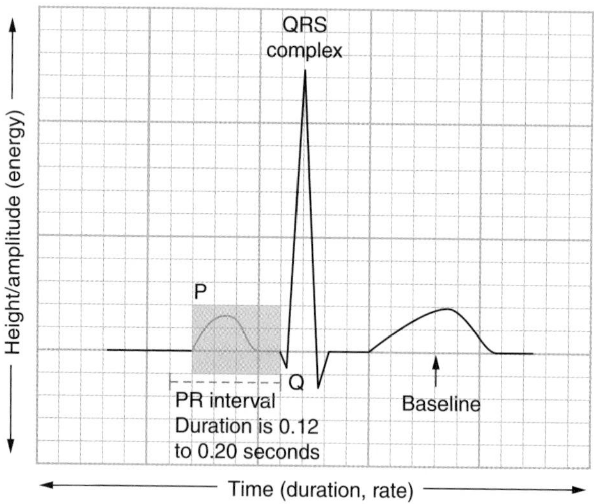

Figure 7-2
The PR interval.

The following are characteristic features of normal PR intervals.

- *Location.* Starts at the beginning of the P wave and ends at the beginning of the Q wave (or R wave if the Q wave is absent).
- *Duration.* 0.12 to 0.20 seconds.
- *Morphology.* P wave and a flat line.

QUESTION
"How many squares is the normal PR interval?" (The answer can be found on page 239.)

Step 5 of analyzing an ECG rhythm is to examine the ______________. The PR interval starts at the beginning of the ______________ wave and ends at the beginning of the ______________ wave. Its duration is normally ______________ seconds.

[PR intervals] [P] [Q] [0.12 to 0.20]

INSTRUCTIONAL MOMENT
To make measuring the PR interval easier, find a P wave that begins on a vertical line, then measure to where the Q or R wave begins.

If a P wave precedes each QRS complex and the duration of the PR interval is normal and constant, you can assume that this electrical impulse originated in the SA node and was carried through the atria, AV junction, and His-Purkinje system in a normal manner. As such, we can say that the PR interval is usually normal with normal sinus rhythm, sinus bradycardia, sinus tachycardia, sinus dysrhythmia, and sinus arrest. A PR interval within 0.12 to 0.20 seconds can also be present with some dysrhythmias that arise from the atria, provided the ectopic site is located in the upper-atrial wall. As an example, premature atrial complexes or atrial tachycardia can have a normal PR interval if the ectopic site from which they arise is high enough in the atria.

QUESTION
"What type of QRS complex is normally seen with dysrhythmias that arise from the SA node, atria, and AV junction?" (The answer can be found on page 239.)

A P wave preceding each ______________ complex that has a PR interval within ______________ to ______________ seconds and is constant, suggests the electrical impulse originated in the SA node and was carried through the atria and AV junction in a ______________ manner.

[QRS] [0.12] [0.20] [normal]

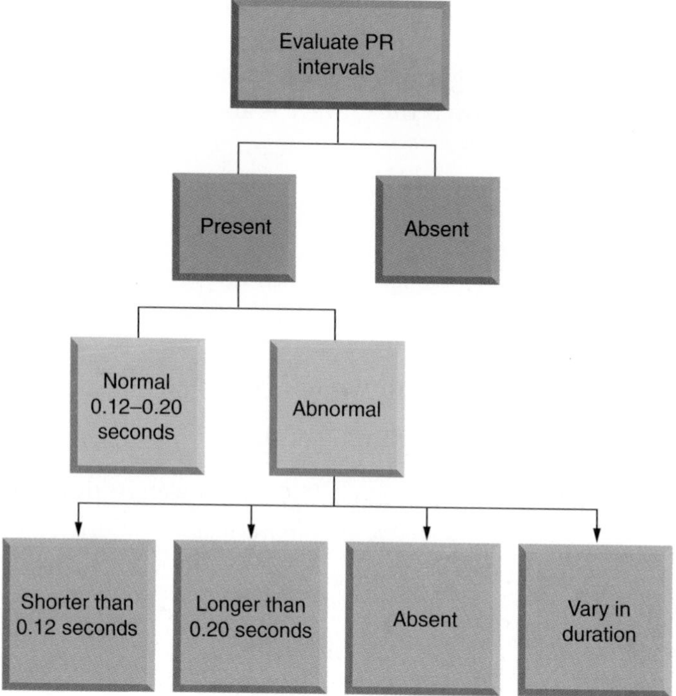

Figure 7-3
Algorithm for normal and abnormal PR intervals.

PR Intervals That Are Different

PR intervals are considered abnormal if they are shorter than 0.12 seconds, longer than 0.20 seconds, absent, or vary in duration (Figure 7-3). A variety of conditions can cause abnormal PR intervals.

Shorter PR Intervals

A shorter than normal PR interval is less than 0.12 seconds in duration. Shorter PR intervals occur when the impulse originates in the atria close to or in the AV junction. The shorter the distance the impulse has to travel, the shorter the duration of the PR interval. A variety of conditions can cause the PR interval to be shorter than normal. If we suspect the P wave is not originating in the SA node, we refer to this shortened PR interval as a P′R (P prime R) interval.

QUESTION
"What does P′ mean?" (The answer can be found on page 239.)

A shorter than normal PR interval is ______________ than 0.12 seconds in duration. Shorter P′R intervals occur when the impulse originates in the ______________ close to the AV junction or in the ______________.

[less] [atria] [AV junction]

Short P'R Intervals Seen With Impulses Arising From the Atria

Premature Atrial Complexes Premature (early) beats that arise from the atria or internodal pathways before the SA node has a chance to fire can produce P′R intervals that differ from the underlying rhythm. If the PAC arises from a site in the lower-right atrium or in the upper part of the AV junction, the P′R interval should be less than 0.12 seconds in duration (Figure 7-4). If the PAC is initiated in the upper- or middle-right atrium, the P′R interval is generally normal (0.12 to 0.20 seconds in duration). If the ectopic impulse arises from a site high in the left atrium, the PR interval may be prolonged. The P′ waves may be buried in the T wave of the preceding beat (due to the short P′-P interval) so it may be hard to determine the P′R interval.

QUESTION
"Why would a PAC have a PR interval longer in duration?" (The answer can be found on page 239.)

Atrial Tachycardia Atrial tachycardia is a rapid heart rate of between 150 and 250 beats per minute that overrides the SA node (Figure 7-5). As with PACs, the P′ wave in atrial tachycardia has a different morphology than normal beats. The P′ wave is likely to be buried in the T wave of the preceding beat (due to the short P′-P interval). For this reason it can be hard or even impossible to accurately measure the P′R interval. Remember our discussion from before—when the impulse arises close to or in the AV junction, depolarization of the atria occurs in a retrograde fashion.

KEY CONCEPT
PACs that arise in the lower-right atrium or in the upper part of the AV junction have a PR interval less than 0.12 seconds in duration.

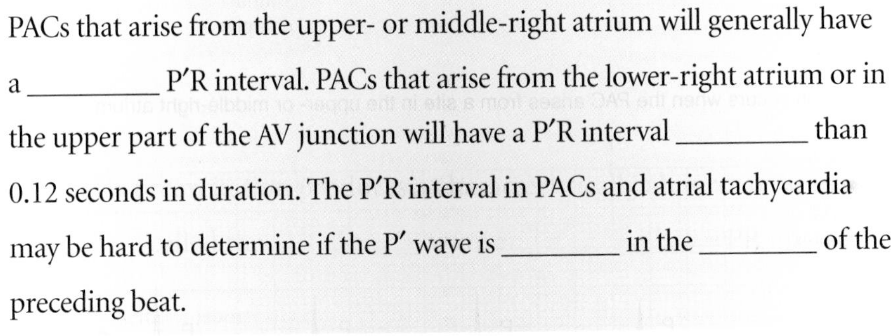

PACs that arise from the upper- or middle-right atrium will generally have a ________ P′R interval. PACs that arise from the lower-right atrium or in the upper part of the AV junction will have a P′R interval ________ than 0.12 seconds in duration. The P′R interval in PACs and atrial tachycardia may be hard to determine if the P′ wave is ________ in the ________ of the preceding beat.

[normal] [less] [buried] [T wave]

QUESTION
"What does the term retrograde mean?" (The answer can be found on page 239.)

Shorter PR Intervals Due to Ventricular Preexcitation

Preexcitation is the premature depolarization of the ventricles that occurs when an impulse arises from a site above the ventricles but travels through abnormal accessory conduction pathways to the ventricles. These abnormal conduction tracts bypass the AV junction or bundle of His, allowing the electrical impulses to initiate depolarization of the ventricles early. It has characteristically abnormal slurring at its onset, called the delta wave, and a short PR interval (Figure 7-6).

CLINICAL MOMENT
Remember our discussion in Chapter 1—heart rate × stroke volume = cardiac output. Atrial tachycardia is a very fast heart rate that can cause cardiac output to decrease by lowering the stroke volume (as the ventricles don't have a chance to fill).

PRACTICE. . . MAKES PERFECT

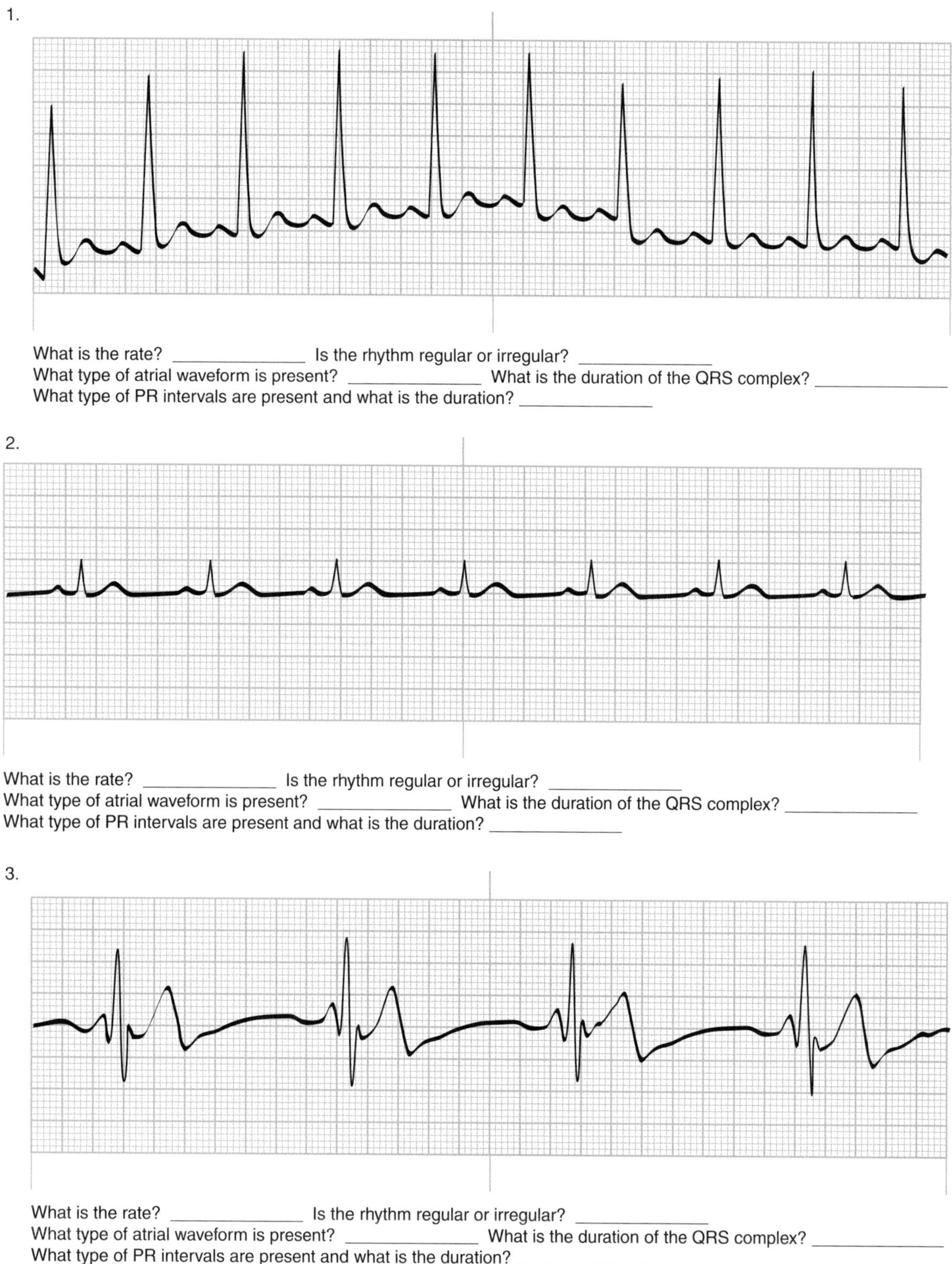

1.

What is the rate? ______________ Is the rhythm regular or irregular? ______________
What type of atrial waveform is present? ______________ What is the duration of the QRS complex? ______________
What type of PR intervals are present and what is the duration? ______________

2.

What is the rate? ______________ Is the rhythm regular or irregular? ______________
What type of atrial waveform is present? ______________ What is the duration of the QRS complex? ______________
What type of PR intervals are present and what is the duration? ______________

3.

What is the rate? ______________ Is the rhythm regular or irregular? ______________
What type of atrial waveform is present? ______________ What is the duration of the QRS complex? ______________
What type of PR intervals are present and what is the duration? ______________

PRACTICE. . . MAKES PERFECT

4.

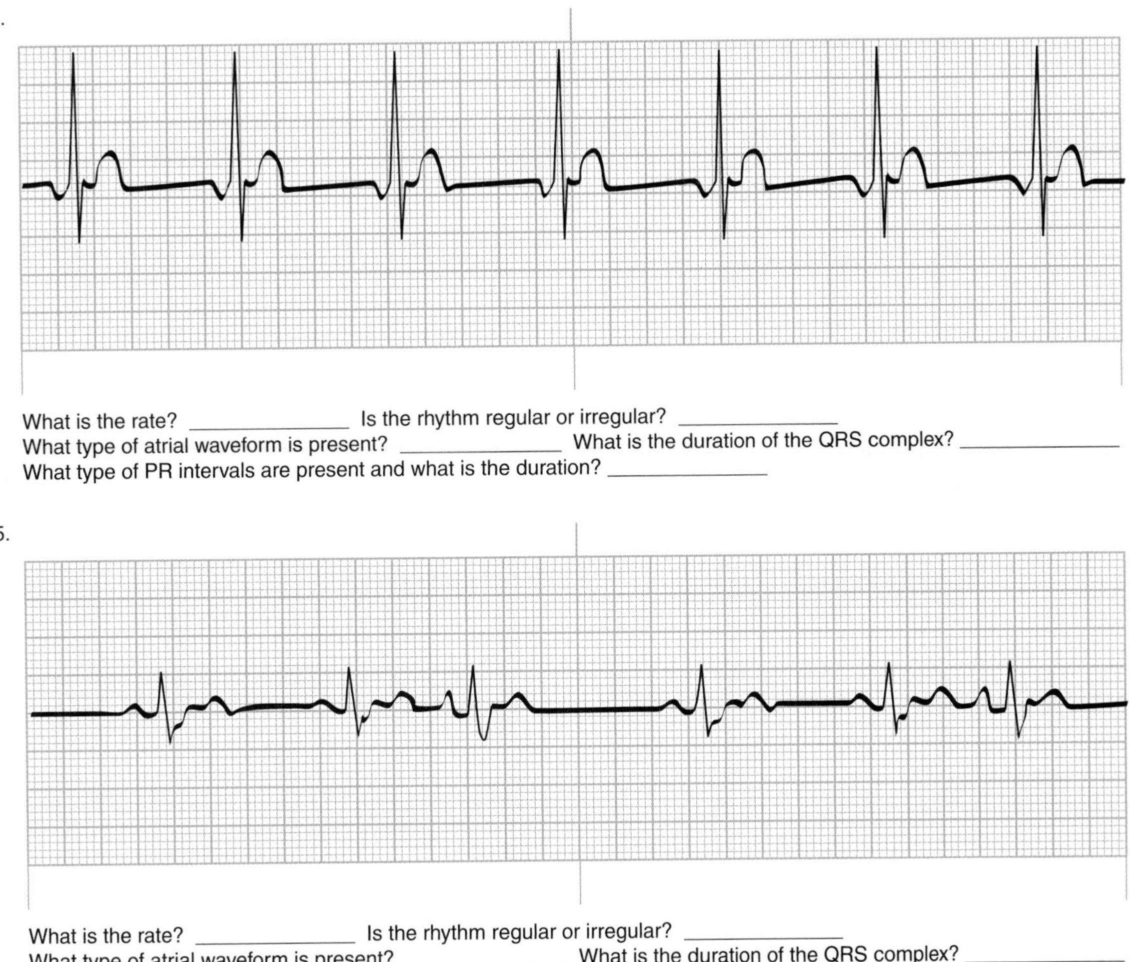

What is the rate? ______________ Is the rhythm regular or irregular? ______________
What type of atrial waveform is present? ______________ What is the duration of the QRS complex? ______________
What type of PR intervals are present and what is the duration? ______________

5.

What is the rate? ______________ Is the rhythm regular or irregular? ______________
What type of atrial waveform is present? ______________ What is the duration of the QRS complex? ______________
What type of PR intervals are present and what is the duration? ______________

Longer PR Intervals

A longer than normal PR interval is greater than 0.20 seconds in duration. Greater PR intervals occur when the impulse is delayed beyond normal as it passes through the AV junction. The longer it takes the impulse to travel through the AV node, the longer the duration of the PR interval. A variety of conditions can cause the PR interval to be longer than normal.

1st-Degree AV Heart Block

The most common cause of longer than normal PR intervals is 1st-degree AV heart block (Figure 7-8). With this type of block there is a delay in impulse conduction through the AV junction. While there is a delay, the impulse is still able to reach the bundle of His, bundle branches, and the

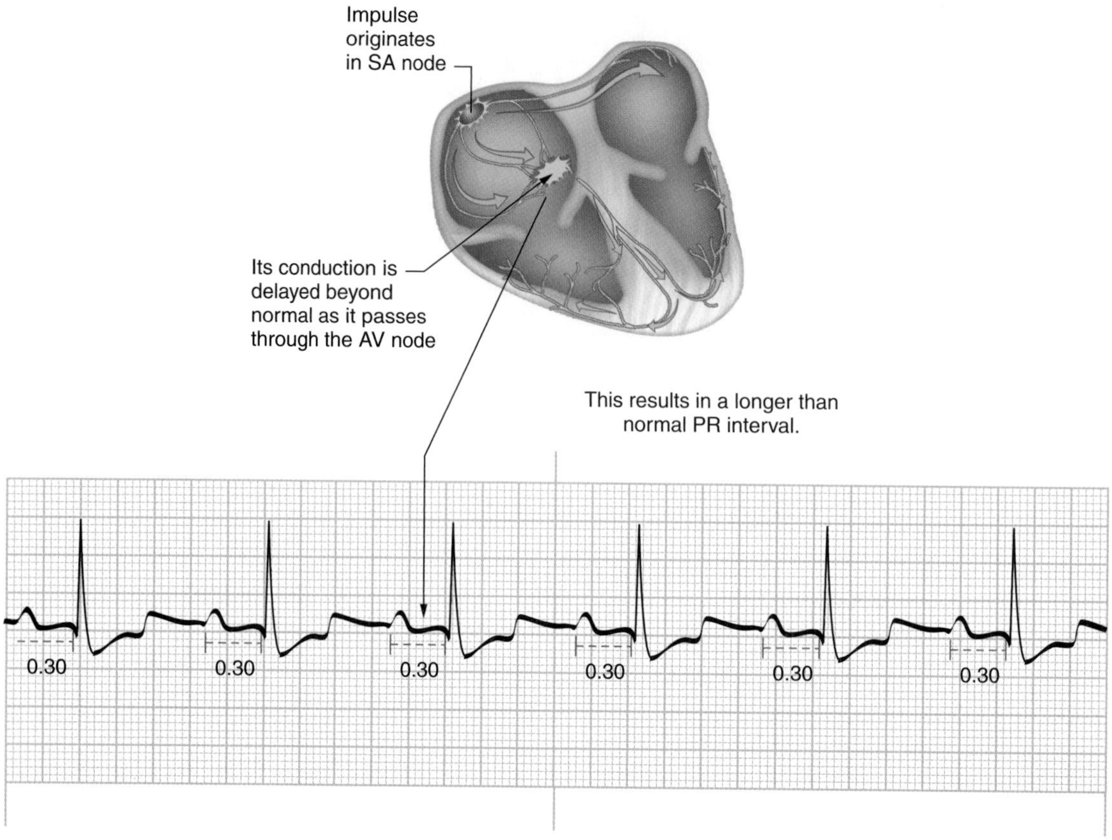

Impulse originates in SA node

Its conduction is delayed beyond normal as it passes through the AV node

This results in a longer than normal PR interval.

0.30 0.30 0.30 0.30 0.30 0.30

Figure 7-8
Due to an abnormal delay in conduction through the AV node, the PR interval is greater than 0.20 seconds in duration in 1st-degree AV heart block.

ventricles. The key characteristic of this condition is a PR interval greater than 0.20 seconds that is constant in duration with each beat. 1st-degree AV heart block can occur with any rhythm originating in the SA node, such as sinus rhythm, bradycardia, or tachycardia.

CLINICAL MOMENT
1st-degree AV heart block differs from the other types of heart block previously discussed (2nd and 3rd degree) because all the P waves are conducted through the AV node to the ventricles. The reason it is called a "block" is because there is an abnormal conduction delay in the AV node/junction.

A delay in conducting the impulse through the ________________ junction will cause the PR intervals to look different. With 1st-degree AV heart block, the PR intervals are ________________ than 0.20 seconds, and the interval is the ________________ from complex to complex.

[AV] [longer] [same]

Varying PR Intervals

The PR interval varies or changes in two dysrhythmias, wandering atrial pacemaker and in Type I, 2nd-degree AV heart block.

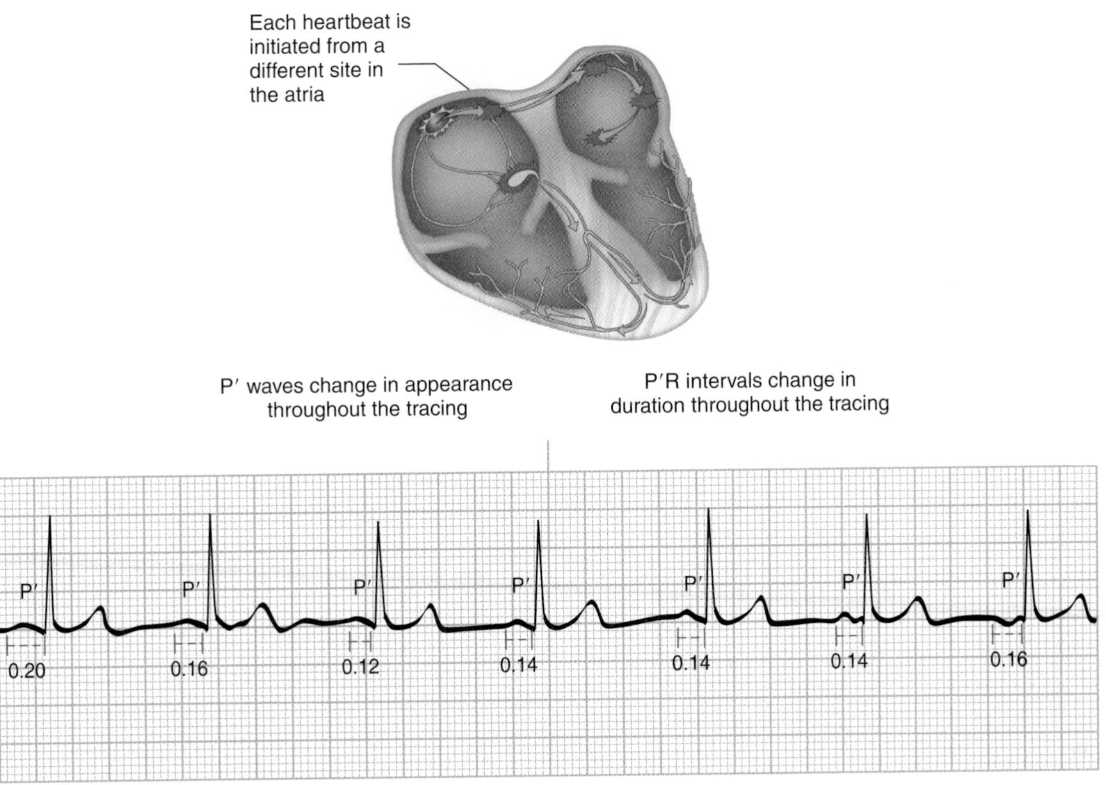

Figure 7-9
With wandering atrial pacemaker, the duration of the P'R interval varies.

Wandering Atrial Pacemaker

In wandering atrial pacemaker, the pacemaker site moves from beat to beat from the sinus node to other latent pacemaker sites in the atria and AV junction (Figure 7-9). The P′ waves appear different and the P′R intervals may vary from beat to beat because of the changing pacemaker site.

KEY CONCEPT
In wandering atrial pacemaker, the P'R interval varies from beat to beat.

In wandering atrial pacemaker, the P'R interval may _________.

[vary]

Type I, 2nd-Degree AV Heart Block

Another dysrhythmia where the PR interval varies is Type I, 2nd-degree AV heart block. In Chapter 4 we described how in this dysrhythmia the weakened AV node fatigues more and more with each conducted impulse until finally it is so tired that it fails to conduct an impulse through to the ventricles. This results in a changing PR interval—one that becomes increasingly longer until there is a dropped QRS complex (Figure 7-10). With the dropped ventricular beat the AV node has a chance to rest. The next impulse conducting through the AV node is carried through faster but each subsequent impulse is delayed until another ventricular beat is dropped.

QUESTION
"What type of QRS complex is seen with wandering atrial pacemaker?" (The answer can be found on page 239.)

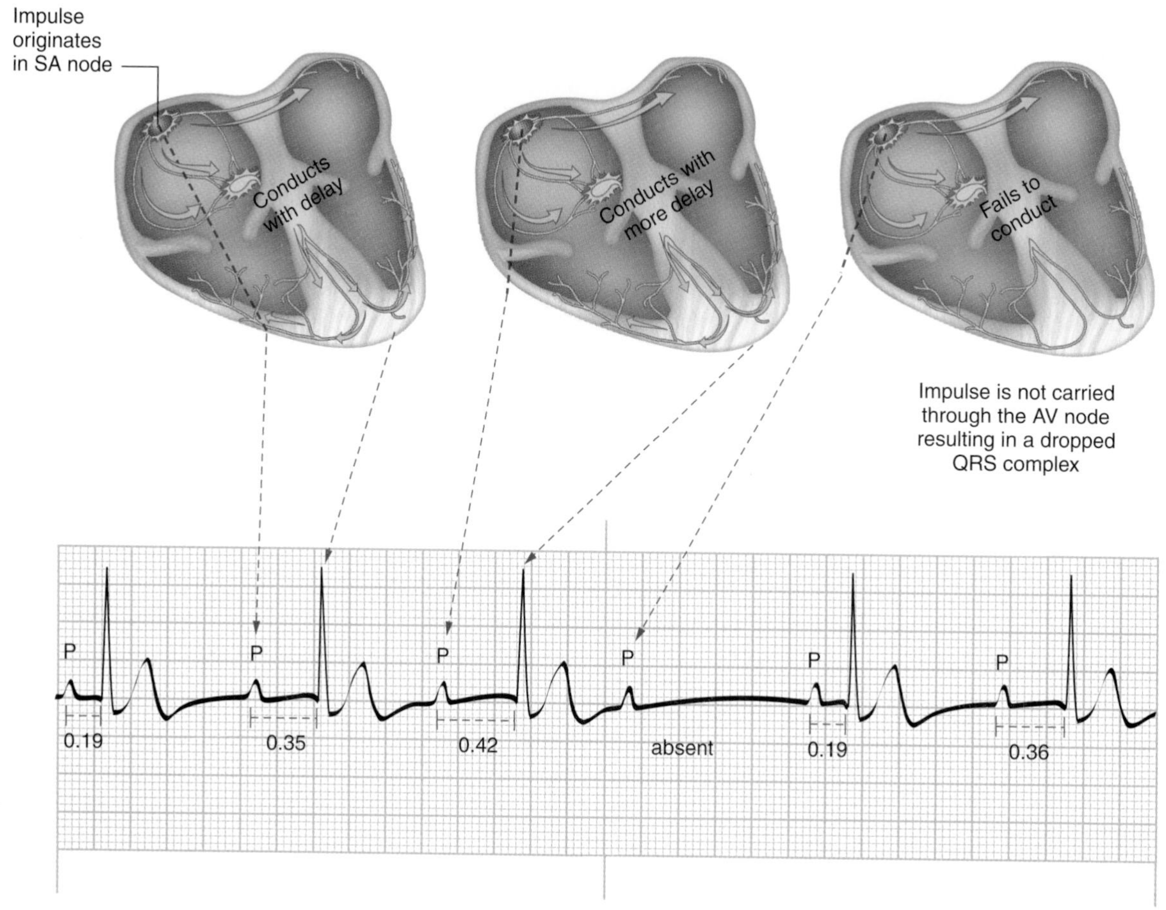

Impulse originates in SA node

Conducts with delay

Conducts with more delay

Fails to conduct

Impulse is not carried through the AV node resulting in a dropped QRS complex

P P P P P P

0.19 0.35 0.42 absent 0.19 0.36

Figure 7-10

In Type I, 2nd-degree AV heart block, the PR interval becomes increasingly longer until finally a QRS complex is dropped. The cycle then starts all over.

QUESTION
"What should the P waves associated with Type I, 2nd-degree AV heart block look like?" (The answer can be found on page 239.)

With Type I, 2nd-degree AV heart block there is a cycle of progressively ______________ PR intervals and a dropped ______________ complex that repeats over and over.

[longer] [QRS]

Absent or Not Measurable PR Intervals

The PR interval will be absent or not measurable in atrial flutter and atrial fibrillation or if the impulse originates in the ventricles.

Atrial Flutter

In atrial flutter the atria fire at a rate of between 250 and 350 beats per minute (Figure 7-11). Normal P waves are absent. Instead, we see flutter waves (F waves). The PR intervals are not measurable.

KEY CONCEPT
In atrial flutter, the PR intervals are not measurable.

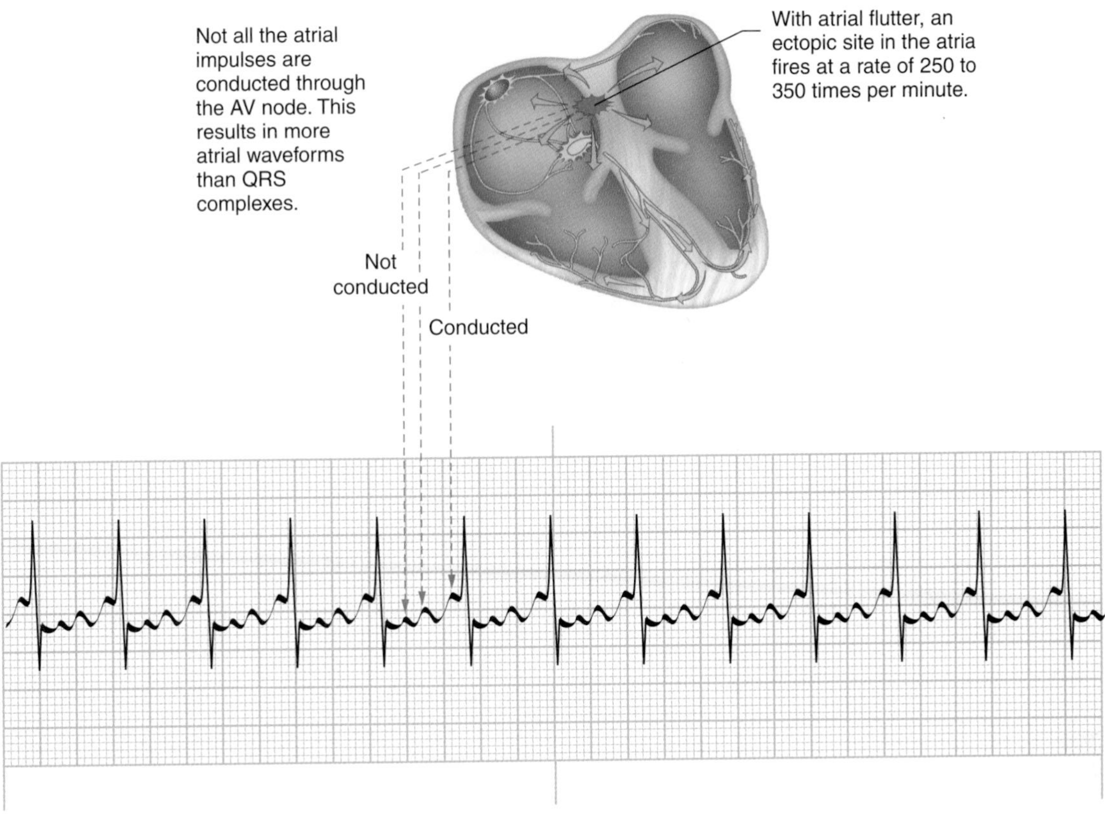

Figure 7-11
With atrial flutter, the PR intervals cannot be determined.

With atrial flutter there are ______________ waves and PR intervals that are ______________.

[flutter] [not measurable]

QUESTION
"What characteristic appearance do the atrial waveforms seen with atrial flutter produce?" (The answer can be found on page 239.)

Atrial Fibrillation

In atrial fibrillation the atria fire faster than 350 beats per minute (Figure 7-12). This produces a chaotic-looking baseline with no discernable P waves (in other words, an absence of P waves). Instead of P waves, we see an uneven baseline of f waves. There are no PR intervals.

In atrial fibrillation there is a ______________-looking baseline and ______________ of uniform P waves and ______________ intervals.

[chaotic] [absence] [PR]

QUESTION
"What type of QRS complexes do we see with atrial fibrillation?" (The answer can be found on page 239.)

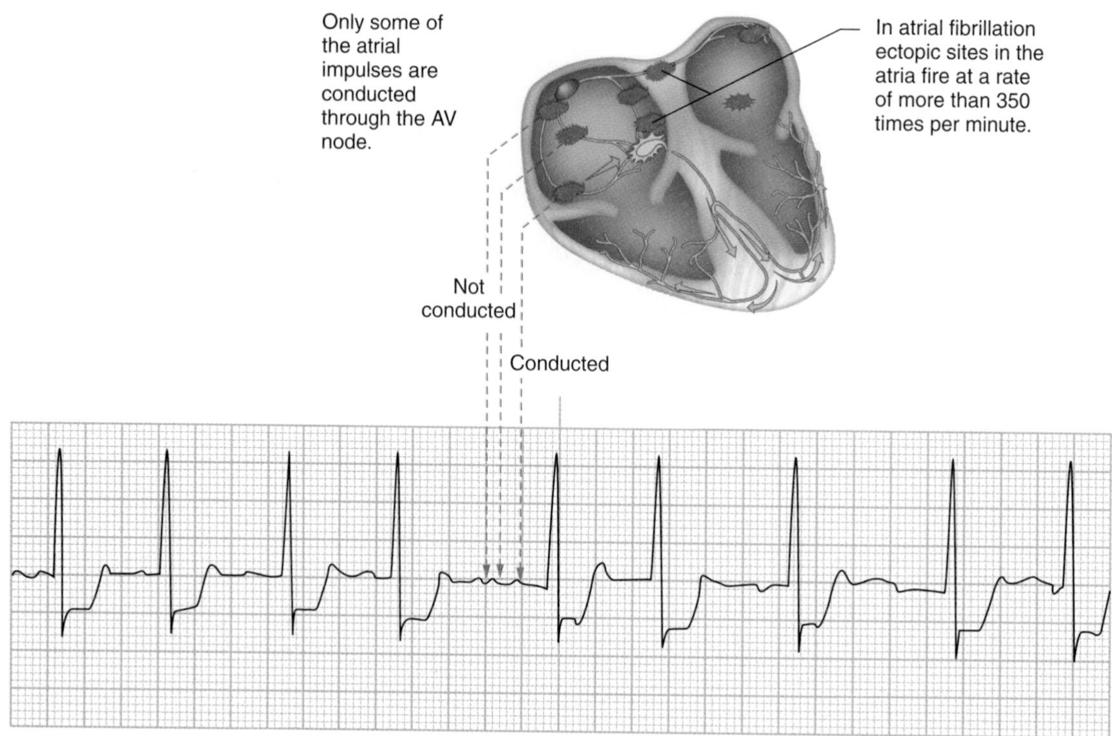

Figure 7-12
With atrial fibrillation, the PR intervals cannot be determined as there are no discernable P waves.

KEY CONCEPT
Ectopy that arises from the ventricles lacks measurable PR intervals.

Ventricular Dysrhythmias

Dysrhythmias that originate in the ventricular tissue are referred to as ventricular dysrhythmias (Figure 7-13). The key characteristic seen with ventricular dysrhythmias are wide, bizarre-looking QRS complexes. Beats that arise from the ventricles are not preceded by a P wave (if seen, the P waves are dissociated) and the PR intervals are not measurable.

KEY CONCEPT
In 3rd-degree AV heart block, the PR interval is not measurable due to the atria and ventricles being depolarized from different pacemaker sites.

3rd-Degree AV Heart Block

With 3rd-degree AV heart block there is complete blockage of the AV node (Figure 7-14). The atria are stimulated to contract by the impulse that originates from the SA node. For this reason the atrial rate should be within a normal range. The ventricles are stimulated to contract by an escape pacemaker that arises from somewhere below the AV node resulting in a slower rate. The pacemaker sites (SA node and ventricles) are firing independently of each other, so the P-P interval and the R-R interval will not appear to be associated with one another. For this reason, the PR intervals are not measurable. The P waves will march through the QRS complexes.

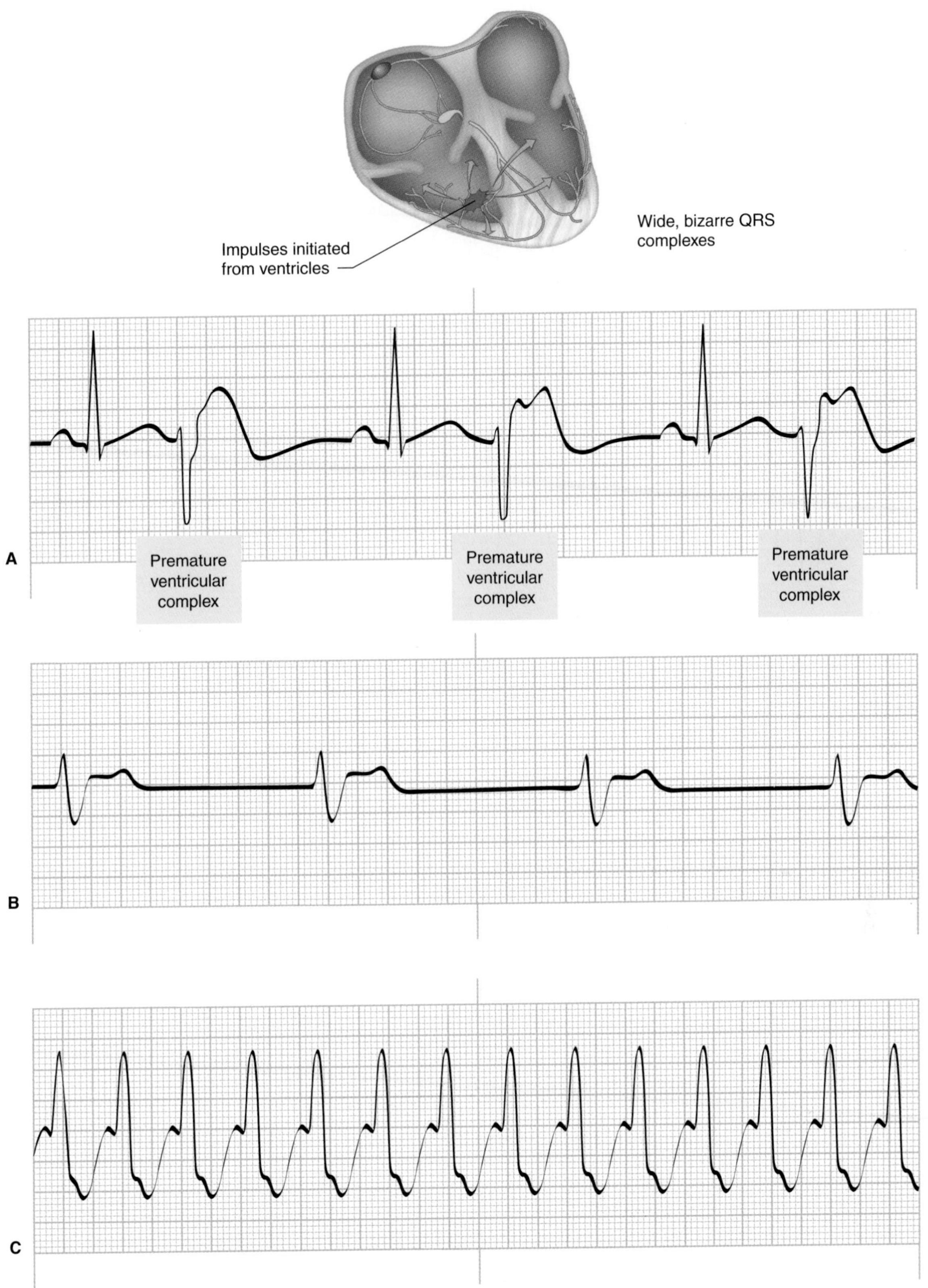

Figure 7-13
With ventricular dysrhythmias, there is an absence of P waves and no PR intervals. (a) Premature ventricular complexes. (b) Idioventricular rhythm. (c) Ventricular tachycardia.

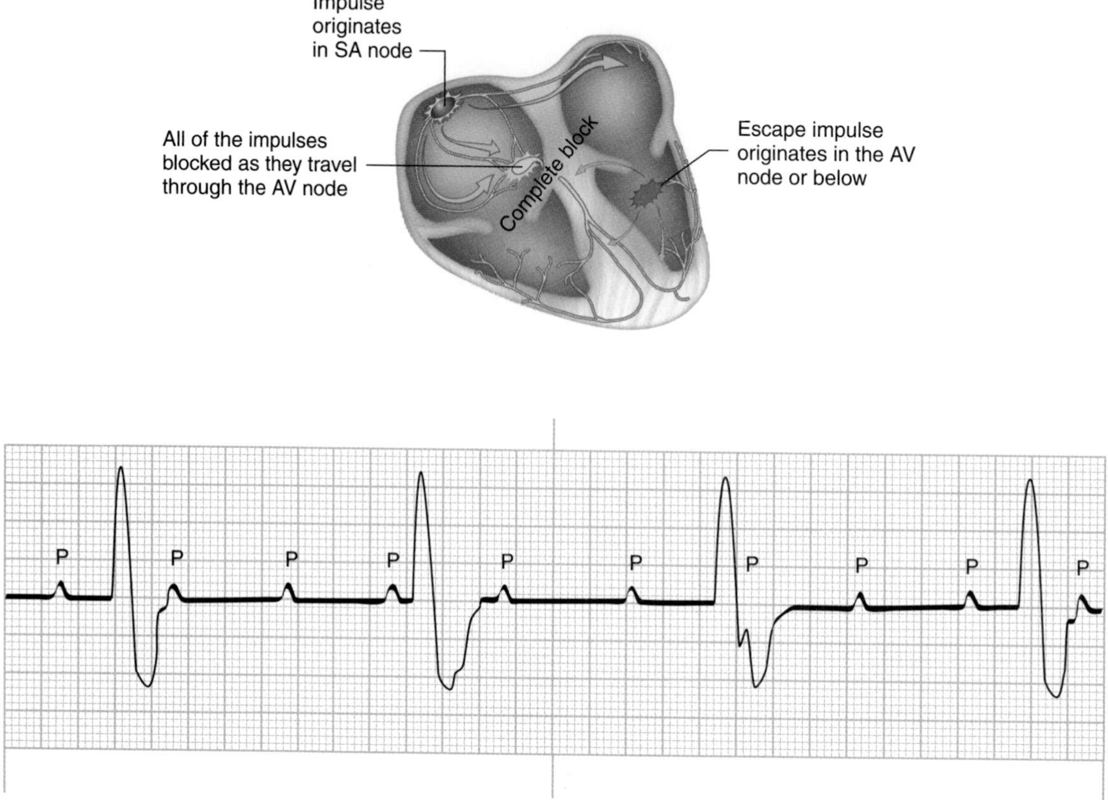

Figure 7-14
With 3rd-degree AV heart block, there are no PR intervals as the P waves appear to march through the QRS complexes.

With 3rd-degree AV heart block there is ______________ blockage of the AV node resulting in the atria being stimulated to contract by the impulse that originates from the ______________ node and the ventricles being stimulated to contract by an escape pacemaker that arises from somewhere below the ______________ node. For this reason, the PR interval is ____________.

[complete] [SA] [AV] [not measurable]

You can practice determining the PR interval, type of QRS complexes, type of atrial waveform, heart rate, and regularity with the following *Practice Makes Perfect* exercises. Answers to these exercises can be found in Appendix A.

PRACTICE. . . MAKES PERFECT

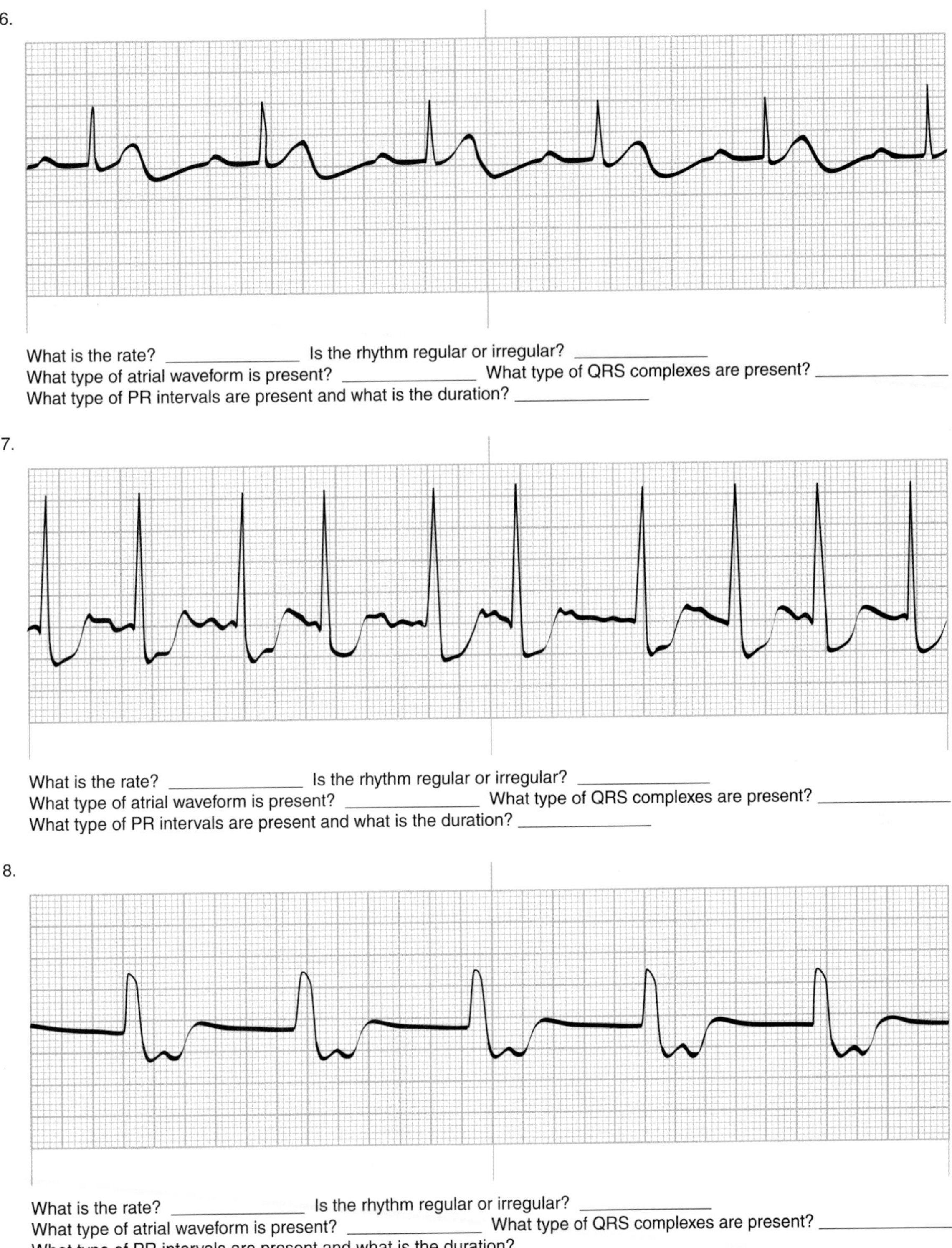

6.

What is the rate? ______________ Is the rhythm regular or irregular? ______________
What type of atrial waveform is present? ______________ What type of QRS complexes are present? ______________
What type of PR intervals are present and what is the duration? ______________

7.

What is the rate? ______________ Is the rhythm regular or irregular? ______________
What type of atrial waveform is present? ______________ What type of QRS complexes are present? ______________
What type of PR intervals are present and what is the duration? ______________

8.

What is the rate? ______________ Is the rhythm regular or irregular? ______________
What type of atrial waveform is present? ______________ What type of QRS complexes are present? ______________
What type of PR intervals are present and what is the duration? ______________

PRACTICE. . . MAKES PERFECT

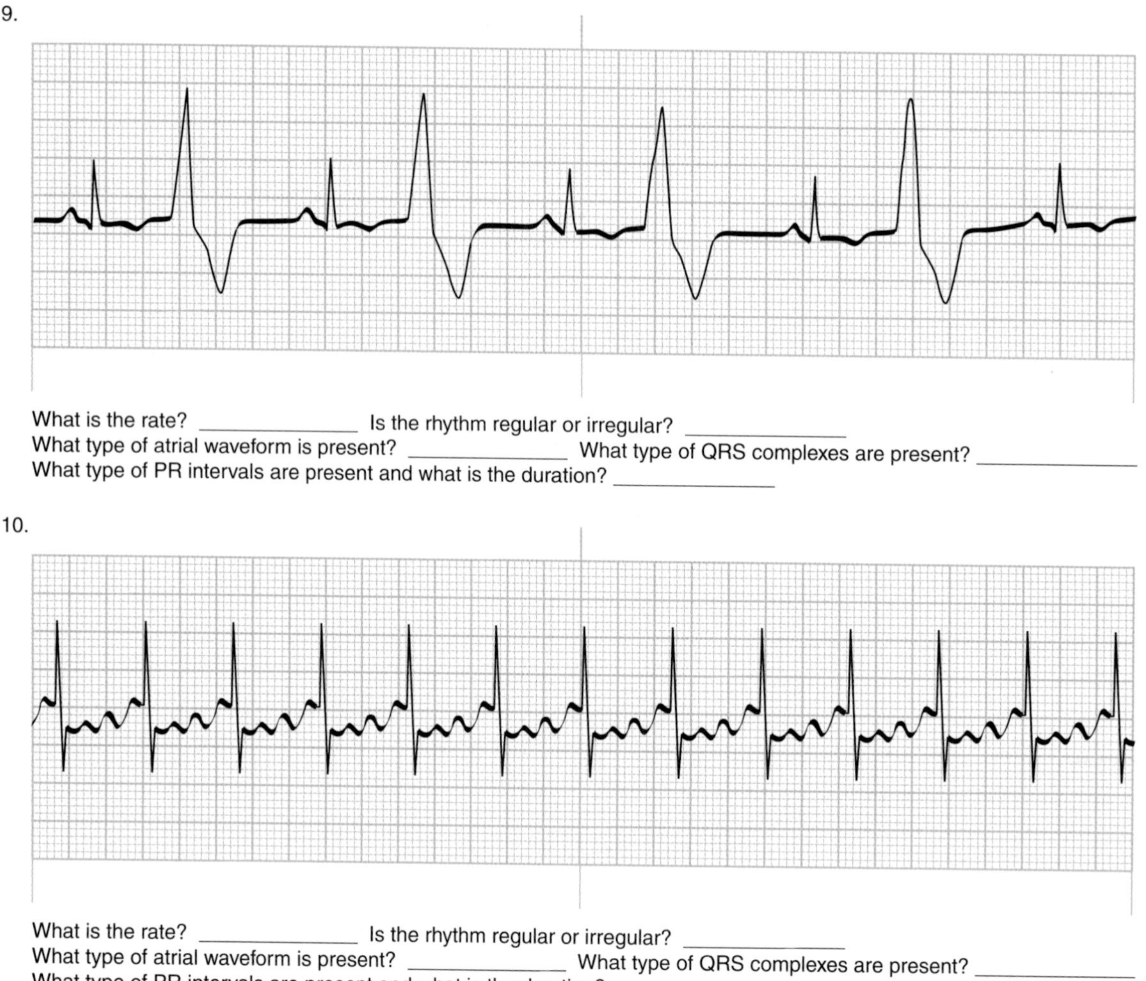

9.

What is the rate? ______________ Is the rhythm regular or irregular? ______________
What type of atrial waveform is present? ______________ What type of QRS complexes are present? ______________
What type of PR intervals are present and what is the duration? ______________

10.

What is the rate? ______________ Is the rhythm regular or irregular? ______________
What type of atrial waveform is present? ______________ What type of QRS complexes are present? ______________
What type of PR intervals are present and what is the duration? ______________

Constant PR Intervals

Type II, 2nd-Degree AV Heart Block

With Type II, 2nd-degree AV heart block, some of the sinus beats are blocked in the AV node and do not reach the ventricles (Figure 7-15). This leads to more P waves than QRS complexes. The atrial-to-ventricular conduction ratio is usually 2:1, 3:1, or 4:1. The PR intervals associated with the P waves followed by a QRS complex are constant. The PR interval can be normal in duration or prolonged.

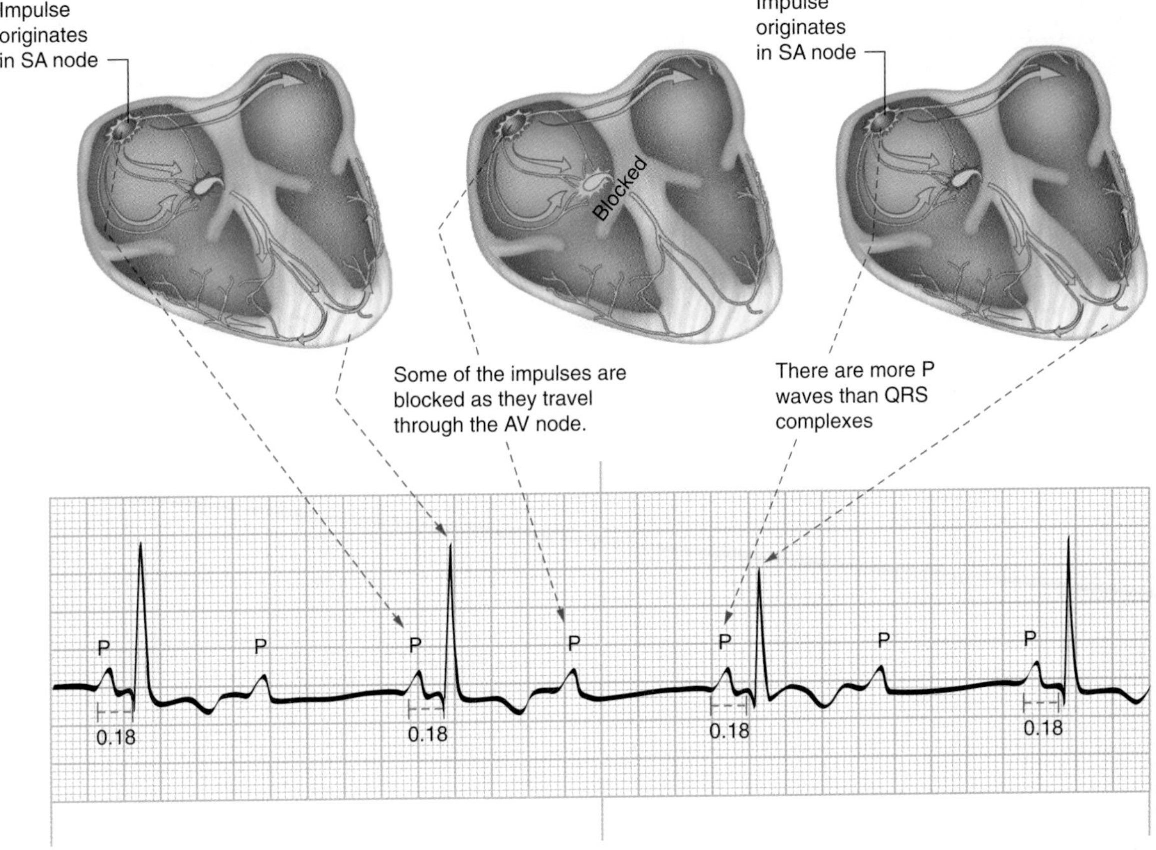

Figure 7-15
With Type II, 2nd-degree AV heart block, the PR intervals of the conducted beats are constant.

With Type II, 2nd-degree AV heart block the PR intervals associated with the P waves that are followed by a QRS complex are ________________.

[constant]

You can practice determining the PR interval, type of QRS complexes, type of atrial waveform, heart rate, and regularity with the following *Practice Makes Perfect* exercises. Answers to these exercises can be found in Appendix A.

PRACTICE. . . MAKES PERFECT

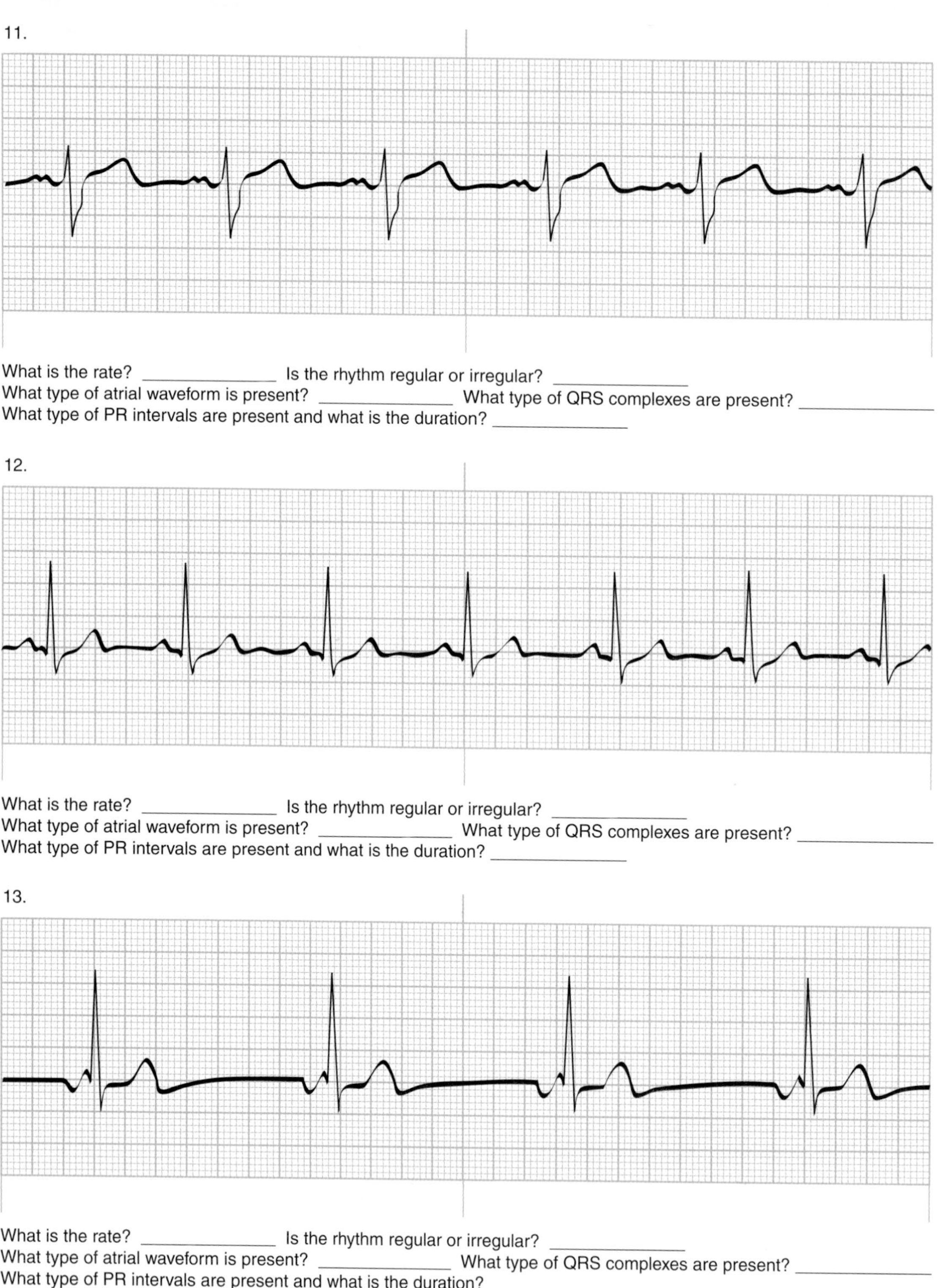

11.

What is the rate? ______________ Is the rhythm regular or irregular? ______________
What type of atrial waveform is present? ______________ What type of QRS complexes are present? ______________
What type of PR intervals are present and what is the duration? ______________

12.

What is the rate? ______________ Is the rhythm regular or irregular? ______________
What type of atrial waveform is present? ______________ What type of QRS complexes are present? ______________
What type of PR intervals are present and what is the duration? ______________

13.

What is the rate? ______________ Is the rhythm regular or irregular? ______________
What type of atrial waveform is present? ______________ What type of QRS complexes are present? ______________
What type of PR intervals are present and what is the duration? ______________

PRACTICE. . . MAKES PERFECT

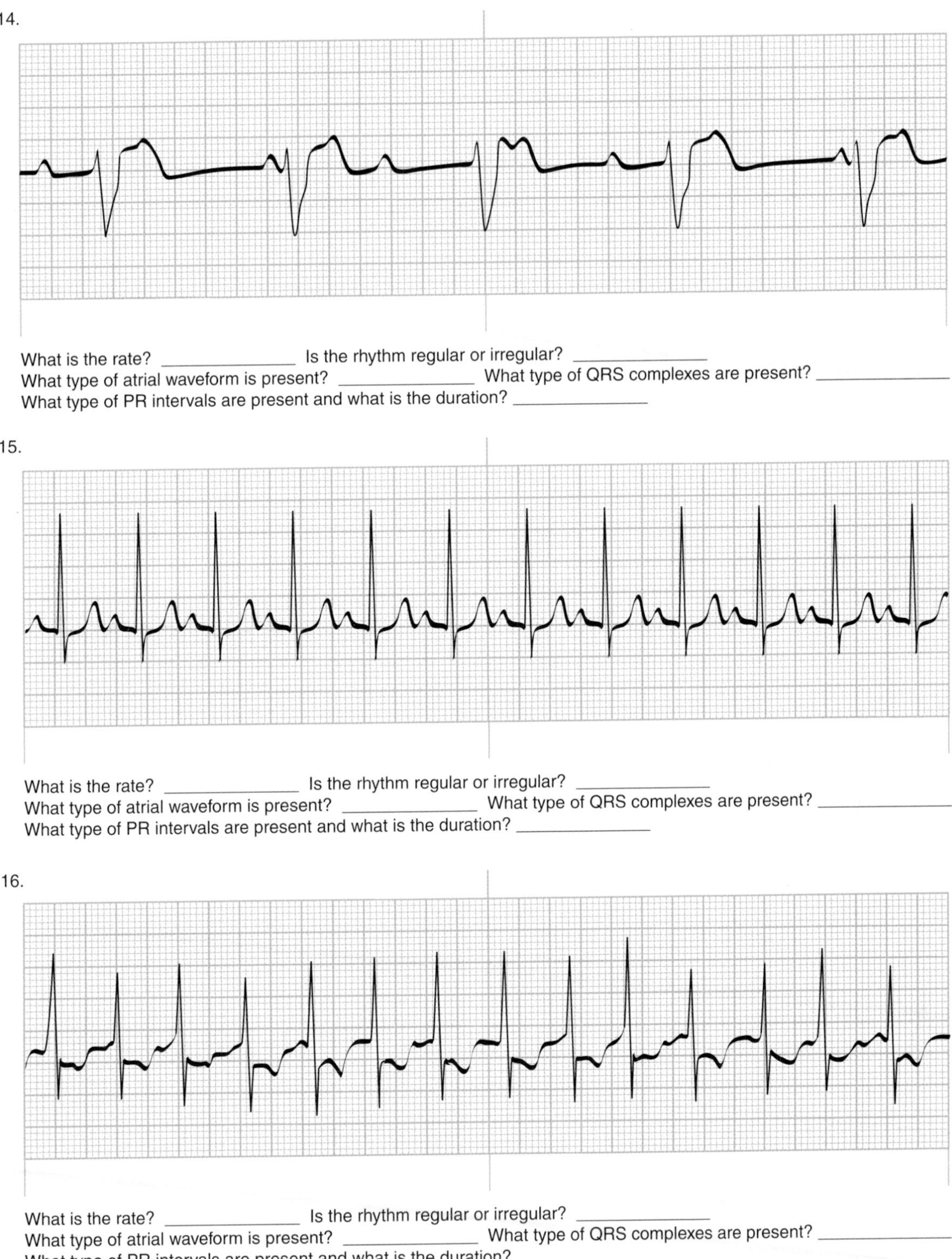

14.

What is the rate? ______________ Is the rhythm regular or irregular? ______________
What type of atrial waveform is present? ______________ What type of QRS complexes are present? ______________
What type of PR intervals are present and what is the duration? ______________

15.

What is the rate? ______________ Is the rhythm regular or irregular? ______________
What type of atrial waveform is present? ______________ What type of QRS complexes are present? ______________
What type of PR intervals are present and what is the duration? ______________

16.

What is the rate? ______________ Is the rhythm regular or irregular? ______________
What type of atrial waveform is present? ______________ What type of QRS complexes are present? ______________
What type of PR intervals are present and what is the duration? ______________

PRACTICE. . . MAKES PERFECT

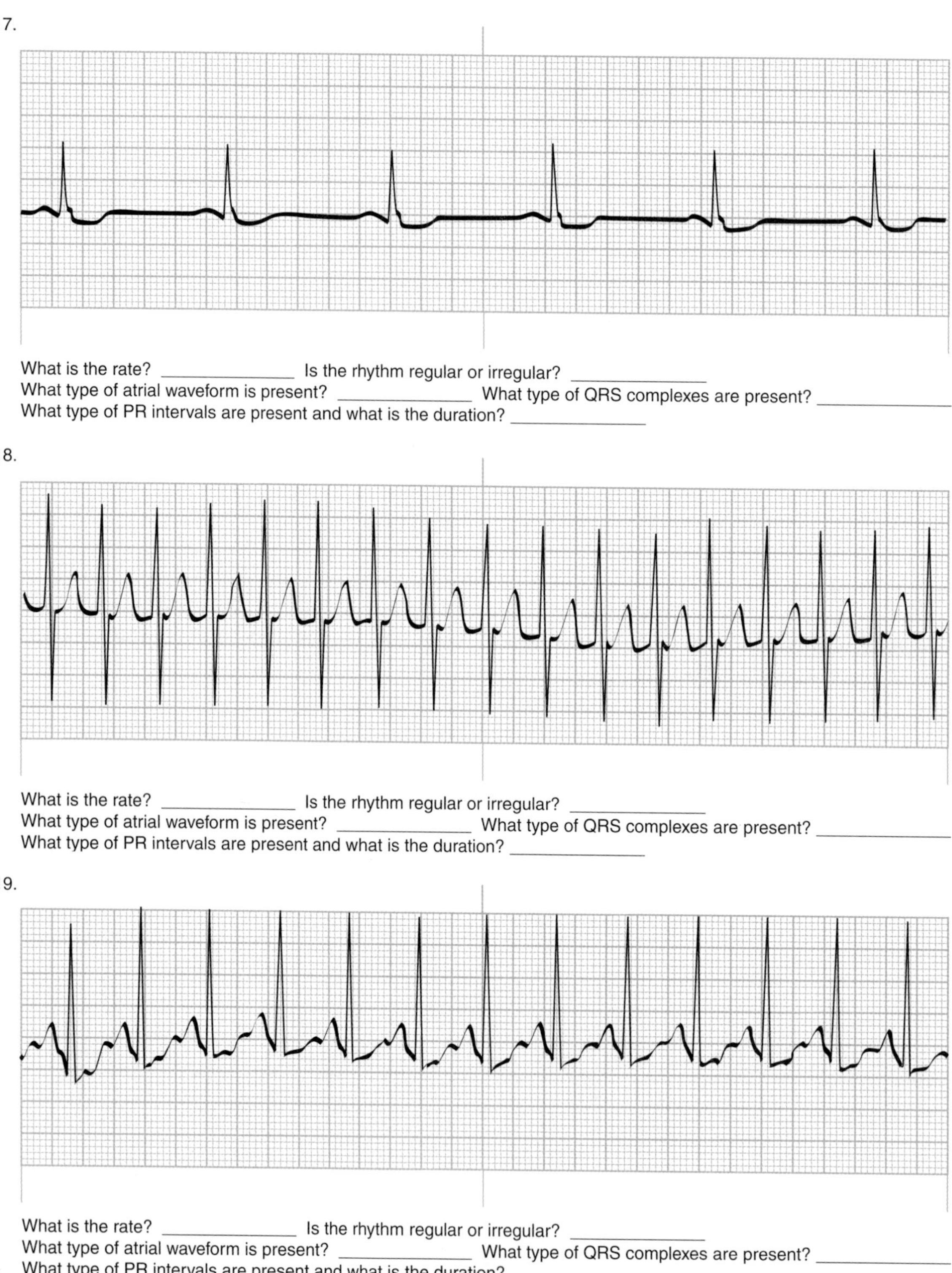

17.

What is the rate? ______________ Is the rhythm regular or irregular? ______________
What type of atrial waveform is present? ______________ What type of QRS complexes are present? ______________
What type of PR intervals are present and what is the duration? ______________

18.

What is the rate? ______________ Is the rhythm regular or irregular? ______________
What type of atrial waveform is present? ______________ What type of QRS complexes are present? ______________
What type of PR intervals are present and what is the duration? ______________

19.

What is the rate? ______________ Is the rhythm regular or irregular? ______________
What type of atrial waveform is present? ______________ What type of QRS complexes are present? ______________
What type of PR intervals are present and what is the duration? ______________

Key Points

- The fifth step of analyzing an ECG rhythm is examining the PR intervals.
- The PR interval is the distance from the beginning of the P wave to the beginning of the Q wave (or R wave if the Q wave is absent).
- The PR interval denotes depolarization of the heart from the SA node through the atria and AV node.
- A normal PR interval indicates the impulse originated in the SA node (or close to it) and traveled through the atria and AV node in a regular and unobstructed course.
- The duration of the PR interval is normally 0.12 to 0.20 seconds.
- PR intervals are considered abnormal if they are shorter or longer than normal, absent, or vary in duration.
- Shorter P′R intervals occur when the impulse originates in the atria close to the AV junction or in the AV junction.
- 1st-degree AV heart block is the most common cause of longer than normal PR intervals.
- In wandering atrial pacemaker, the pacemaker site moves from beat to beat causing the P′ waves to appear different and the P′R intervals to vary.
- With Type I, 2nd-degree AV heart block, PR intervals are progressively longer until a QRS complex is dropped and then the cycle starts over.
- There will be an absence of PR intervals in atrial flutter and fibrillation and in ventricular dysrhythmias.
- In 3rd-degree AV heart block, the PR interval is not measurable.
- In Type II, 2nd-degree AV heart block, some of the sinus beats are blocked in the AV node and do not reach the ventricles. This leads to more P waves than QRS complexes. The PR intervals associated with the P waves conducted through to the ventricles are constant.

Assess Your Understanding

The following questions give you a chance to assess your understanding of the material discussed in this chapter. The answers can be found in Appendix A.

1. The fifth step in analyzing an ECG is
   a. checking the regularity.
   b. looking at the P waves.
   c. assessing the PR intervals.
   d. determining the heart rate.
2. PR interval is the distance from the
   a. end of the P wave to the beginning of the Q wave.
   b. beginning of the P wave to the beginning of the Q wave.
   c. beginning of the Q wave to the end of the S wave.
   d. end of the Q wave to the beginning of the R wave.

3. The PR interval denotes depolarization of the heart from the
   a. bundle of His through the ventricles.
   b. SA node through the atria, AV node, and His-Purkinje system.
   c. AV node through the bundle of His.
   d. SA node through the atria and AV node.

4. The normal duration of the PR interval is ___________ second(s).
   a. 0.06 to 0.10
   b. 0.8 to 0.12
   c. 1.0
   d. 0.12 to 0.20

5. A shorter than normal PR interval is less than ___________ second(s) in duration.
   a. 0.12
   b. 0.08
   c. 0.10
   d. 0.20

6. Which of the following characteristics is considered normal in lead II?
   a. P wave that follows the QRS complex.
   b. Inverted P wave.
   c. Peaked or notched P wave.
   d. Rounded and upright P wave.

7. Which of the following is characteristic of 1st-degree AV heart block?
   a. Varying PR intervals.
   b. PR intervals of less than 0.12 seconds.
   c. More P waves than QRS complexes.
   d. Constant PR intervals of greater than 0.20 seconds.

8. With wandering atrial pacemaker, the P'R intervals
   a. are constant.
   b. vary.
   c. are longer in duration than 0.20 seconds.
   d. become progressively longer.

9. With Type I, 2nd-degree AV heart block, the PR intervals
   a. are constant.
   b. are absent.
   c. are shorter in duration than 0.12 seconds.
   d. become progressively longer.

10. There will be an absence of PR intervals in
    a. premature atrial complexes.
    b. 1st-degree AV heart block.
    c. 3rd-degree AV heart block.
    d. wandering atrial pacemaker.

11. Type II, 2nd-degree AV heart block has PR intervals that
    a. continually change in duration.
    b. are constant.
    c. have no relationship.
    d. are less than 0.12 seconds in duration.

12. Identify the heart rate, regularity, atrial waveform, QRS complex, and PR intervals of the following ECG.

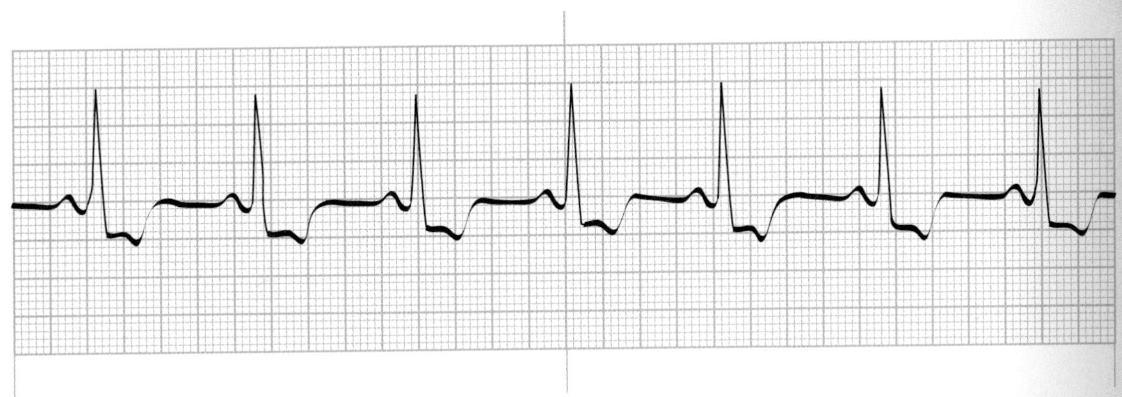

13. Identify the heart rate, regularity, atrial waveform, QRS complex, and PR intervals of the following ECG.

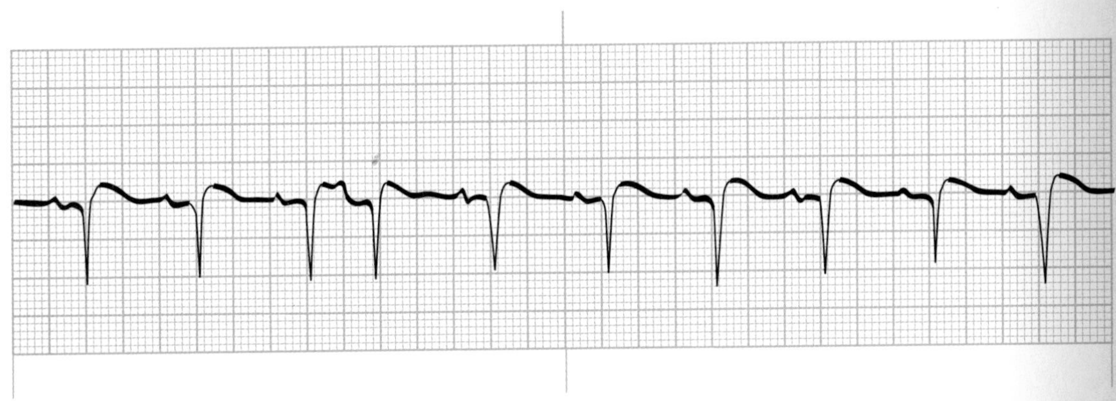

14. Identify the heart rate, regularity, atrial waveform, QRS complex, and PR intervals of the following ECG.

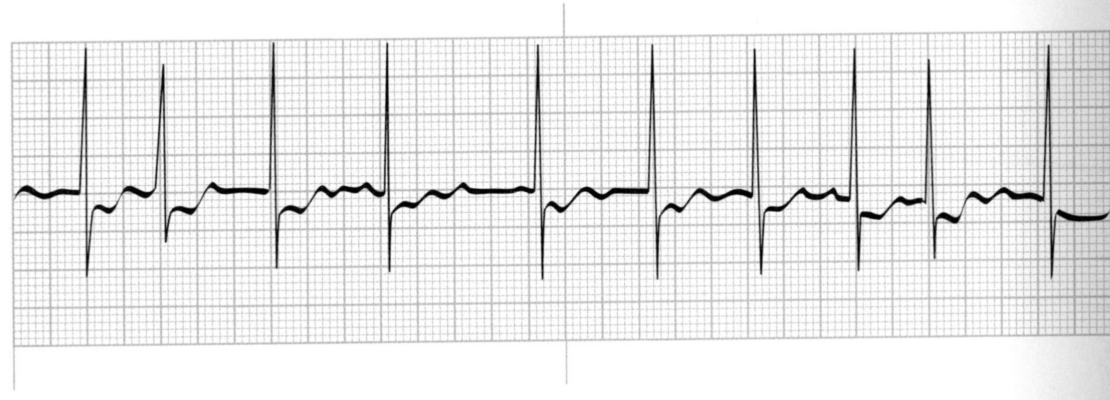

15. Identify the heart rate, regularity, atrial waveform, QRS complex, and PR intervals of the following ECG.

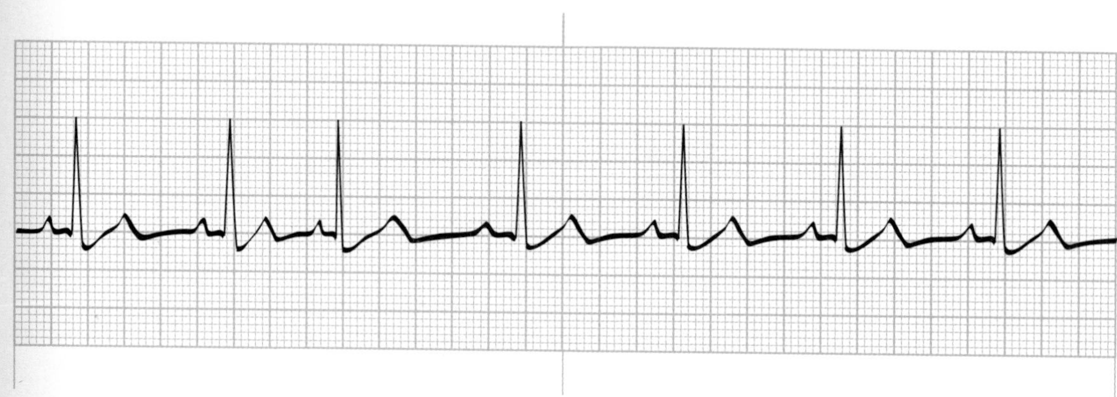

16. Identify the heart rate, regularity, atrial waveform, QRS complex, and PR intervals of the following ECG.

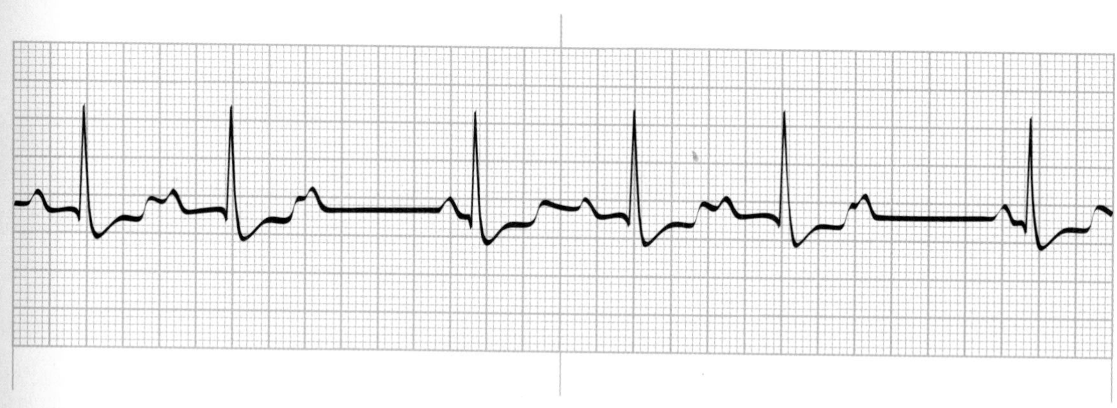

Referring to the scenario at the beginning of this chapter, answer the following questions.

17. What rhythm is the patient most likely in?
    a. Atrial fibrillation.
    b. 3rd-degree AV heart block.
    c. Type I, 2nd-degree AV heart block.
    d. 1st-degree AV heart block.

18. What rhythm could result if the condition deteriorated?
    a. 3rd-degree AV heart block.
    b. Atrial flutter.
    c. Junctional rhythm.
    d. Ventricular fibrillation.

Answers to Sidebar Questions

"How many squares is the normal PR interval?"

Answer: The PR interval extends across 3 to 5 small squares.

"What type of QRS complex is normally seen with dysrhythmias that arise from the SA node, atria, and AV junction?"

Answer: The QRS complexes can be expected to be upright (in lead II) and narrow.

"What does P′ mean?"

Answer: P′ means that the P wave arises from an ectopic site.

"Why would a PAC have a PR interval longer in duration?"

Answer: In a PAC the PR interval can be normal or longer in duration if the PAC arises nearer to the SA node or in the upper-left atrium.

"What does the term retrograde mean?"

Answer: The term retrograde means that the impulse conducts backward (upward) through the heart instead of through the normal pathway.

"What is the difference between junctional escape, accelerated junctional rhythm, and junctional tachycardia?"

Answer: The difference among the junctional rhythms is the rate. Junctional escape has a rate of 40 to 60 beats per minute, accelerated junctional rhythm has a rate of 60 to 100 beats per minute, and junctional tachycardia has a rate of 100 to 180 beats per minute.

"What type of QRS complex is seen with wandering atrial pacemaker?"

Answer: The QRS complex seen with wandering atrial pacemaker is typically upright (in lead II) and narrow.

"What should the P waves associated with Type I, 2nd-degree AV heart block look like?"

Answer: The P waves associated with Type I, 2nd-degree AV heart block look normal as they are initiated from the SA node. They just aren't all followed by a QRS complex.

"What characteristic appearance do the atrial waveforms seen with atrial flutter produce?"

Answer: The atrial waveforms seen with atrial flutter produce a saw-toothed pattern.

"What type of QRS complexes do we see with atrial fibrillation?"

Answer: With atrial fibrillation we should see normal QRS complexes unless there is aberrant conduction.

On the DVD

- The PR Interval lecture.
- Demonstration of Measuring the PR Interval.

Notes

Origin and Clinical Aspects of Sinus Node Dysrhythmias

8

Case History

A 26-year-old woman is visiting her dying grandmother in the nursing home when she begins to cry and hyperventilate. She faints and collapses to the floor. The nursing staff brings the code cart to the woman's side while 911 is summoned. The nursing supervisor feels for a pulse and comments that the woman's heart is beating slowly. The cardiac monitor is applied while vital signs are obtained revealing a blood pressure of 60/30, pulse of 44, and respiratory rate of 16 and unlabored.

The cardiac monitor shows a slow narrow QRS complex rhythm with a normal P wave before every QRS complex and a QRS complex after every P wave and a normal PR interval. The nurses elevate the woman's legs and place a cool cloth on her forehead.

By the time EMS arrives the patient is awake and alert. Her pulse is now 68 and her blood pressure normal. She refuses transport to the hospital after disclosing that she has not eaten in 24 hours, which she is certain contributed to her fainting episode.

Chapter Preview

- Dysrhythmia Interpretation
- Rhythms Originating from the Sinus Node
- Normal Sinus Rhythm
- Sinus Bradycardia
- Sinus Tachycardia
- Sinus Dysrhythmia
- Sinus Arrest

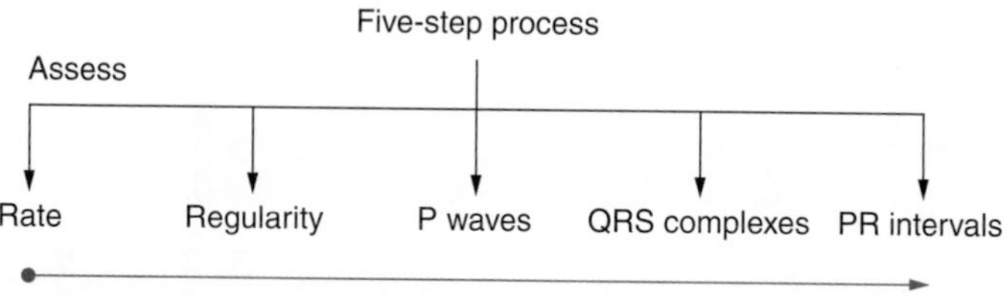

Figure 8-1
Use the five-step process to analyze the ECG tracing.

Dysrhythmia Interpretation

In the previous chapters we talked about the anatomy and physiology of the heart and the machines and leads used to obtain an ECG tracing. We also discussed the five-step process used to examine the ECG. We will continue to use this process to evaluate the ECGs through the rest of this book. One of the things we look for when we examine the ECG is the presence of dysrhythmias. This chapter focuses on dysrhythmias—the characteristics associated with them (which allow us to identify them), how they occur, and their significance. First, let's define what we mean by the term dysrhythmia. A dysrhythmia is an ECG rhythm that differs from normal sinus rhythm. Dysrhythmias were referred to as arrhythmias but that name was changed because "a"rrhythmia suggests there is an absence of a rhythm instead of "dys"rrhythmia, which suggests there is a problem with the rhythm.

When we assess the ECG rhythm on the ECG monitor or we examine the ECG tracing, it is important that we do it in a systematic, organized way (Figure 8-1). For this reason we encourage you to use the five-step method:

1. Determine the heart rate (atrial and ventricular)
2. Determine the regularity
3. Assess the P waves
4. Assess the QRS complexes
5. Assess the PR intervals

The ECG tracing should be examined in a _______________ and _______________ way. One method that can be used to do this examination is called the _______________ -step method.

[systematic] [organized] [five]

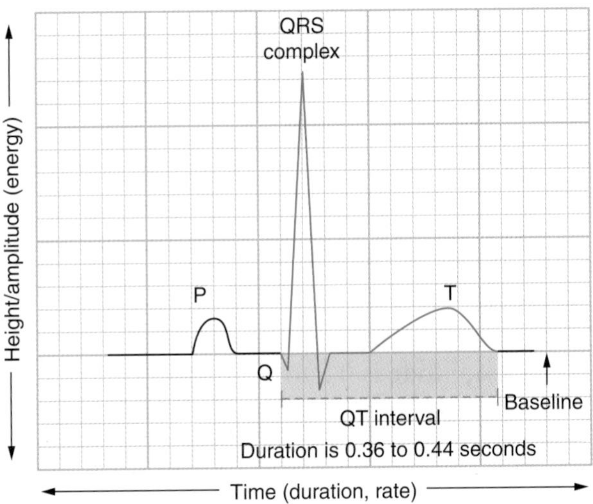

Figure 8-2
The QT interval.

QT Interval

In addition to the five steps, it is also important to assess the QT intervals (Figure 8-2). The QT interval represents the time needed for ventricular depolarization and repolarization. An abnormal duration can indicate a myocardial irregularity. The QT extends from the beginning of the QRS complex to the end of the T wave. The duration varies according to age, sex, and heart rate but it is usually between 0.36 and 0.44 seconds.

INSTRUCTIONAL MOMENT
A good rule to follow is that the QT interval should not be greater than half the distance between consecutive R waves when the rhythm is regular.

A prolonged QT interval indicates prolonged ventricular repolarization, which means the relative refractory period is longer. In certain conditions such as myocardial ischemia or infarction, a prolonged QT interval can predispose the patient to life-threatening ventricular dysrhythmias such as torsades de pointes. A shortened QT interval can be caused by hypercalcemia or digoxin toxicity.

The QT interval represents the time needed for ventricular _______________ and _______________. The QT extends from the beginning of the _______________ to the end of the _____________.
The duration is usually between _____________ and _____________ seconds.

[depolarization] [repolarization] [QRS complex] [T wave] [0.36] [0.44]

Additional Steps for Analyzing the ECG

Additional steps to analyze an ECG, which we will discuss later, include the examination of the T waves, PR segments, and ST segments. However, for the purpose of interpreting the majority of dysrhythmias all you need to focus on are the first five steps (as well as assessing the QT interval).

When we refer to the P waves as being normal, we mean they appear as an upright and round waveform. There is one P wave preceding each QRS complex. Its amplitude is 0.5 to 2.5 mm in height and its duration is 0.06 to 0.10 seconds. In leads I, II, aV_F, and V_2 through V_6, the deflection of the P wave is characteristically upright or positive. In leads III, aV_L, and V_1, the P wave is usually upright but may be negative or biphasic (both positive and negative). In lead aV_R, the P wave is negative or inverted (Figure 8-3).

When we refer to QRS complexes as being normal we are saying they are narrow (0.06 to 0.12 seconds in duration) and normal looking. In leads I, II, III, aV_L, aV_F, and V_4 to V_6, the deflection of the QRS complex is characteristically positive or upright. In leads aV_R and V_1 to V_3 the QRS complex is usually negative or inverted. Leads III, aV_L, and V_2 to V_4 may also be biphasic (see Figure 8-3).

Rhythms Originating From the Sinus Node

QUESTION
"What is the rate of the heart's three primary pacemaker sites—the SA node, AV junction, and ventricles?" (The answer can be found on page 266.)

Rhythms originating from the SA node are called sinus rhythms (Figure 8-4). These include:

- Normal sinus rhythm
- Sinus bradycardia
- Sinus tachycardia
- Sinus dysrhythmia
- Sinus arrest

The key characteristics for these rhythms include a normal P wave preceding each normal QRS complex and PR intervals within normal duration of 0.12 to 0.20 seconds and constant.

KEY CONCEPT
Sinus rhythms originate from the SA node and produce a normal P wave that precedes each QRS complex.

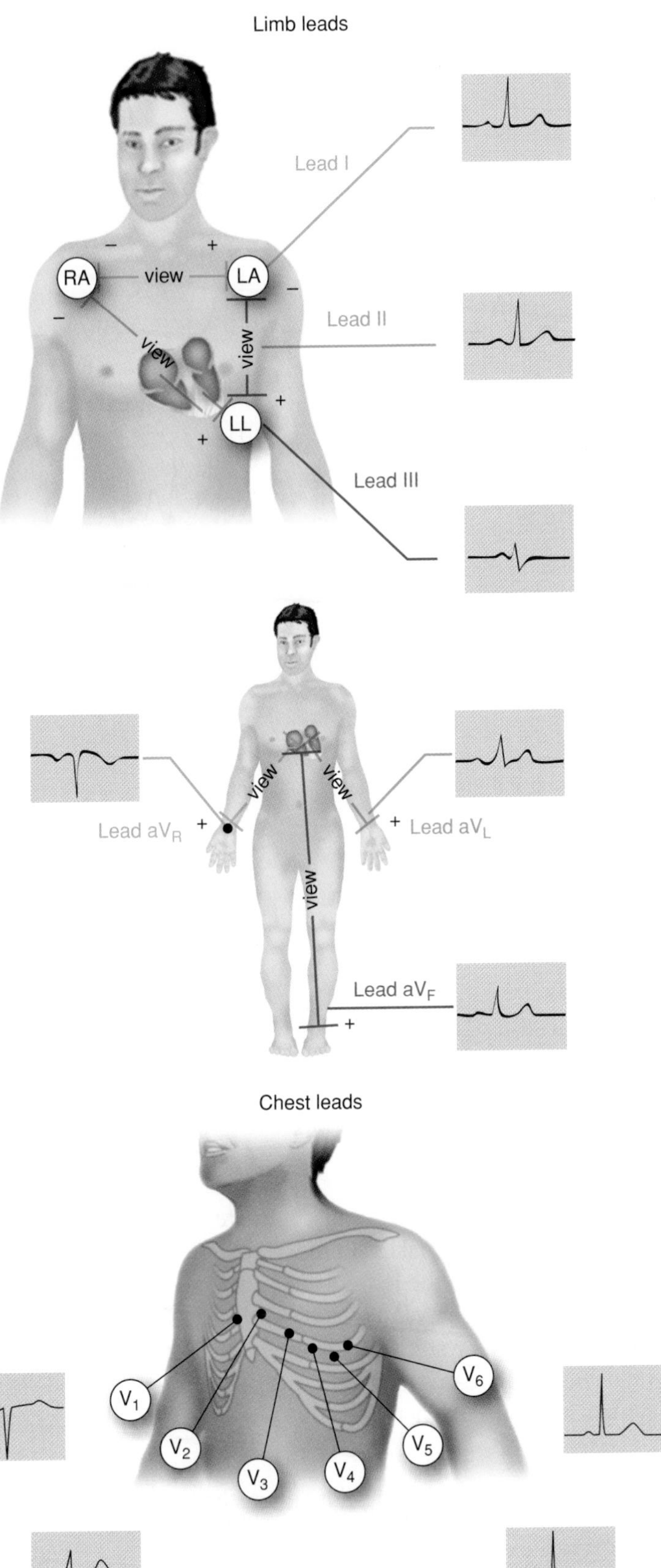

Figure 8-3
Deflections of the waveforms in the various ECG leads.

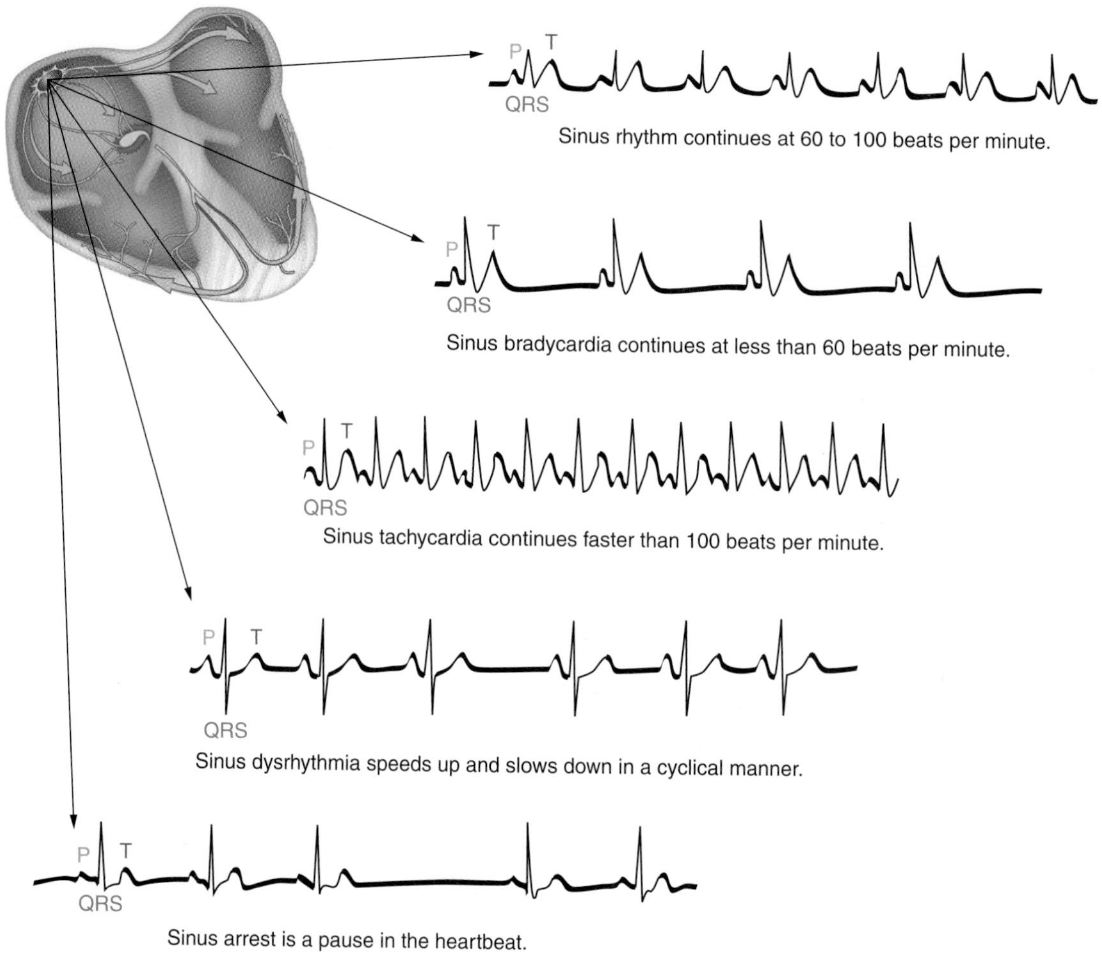

Sinus rhythm continues at 60 to 100 beats per minute.

Sinus bradycardia continues at less than 60 beats per minute.

Sinus tachycardia continues faster than 100 beats per minute.

Sinus dysrhythmia speeds up and slows down in a cyclical manner.

Sinus arrest is a pause in the heartbeat.

Figure 8-4
Sinus dysrhythmias originate from the SA node.

INSTRUCTIONAL MOMENT
In any dysrhythmia where P waves or QRS complexes should be normal, such as with sinus bradycardia, they can instead appear different but yet not change what the dysrhythmia is called. For example, the P waves might be notched or wider than normal due to atrial enlargement or the QRS complexes might be wide or unusual looking if there is intraventricular conduction defect. This does not change what we categorize the dysrhythmia; instead, we might refer to it as sinus bradycardia with wide QRS complexes (although it would also be correct to call it sinus bradycardia).

During normal heart activity, the SA (sinoatrial) node acts as the primary pacemaker. It assumes this role because the rate it fires automatically is faster than that of the other pacemakers in the heart. The right coronary artery and the circumflex branch of the left coronary artery supply the SA node with oxygen and nutrients. The vagus nerve, and several sympathetic nerves (of the autonomic nervous system) richly innervate the sinus node. Stimulation of the vagus nerve decreases the firing rate of the SA node while stimulation of the sympathetic system increases it.

______________ rhythms originate from the SA node. With these rhythms you can expect to see a normal ______________ wave preceding each normal ______________ complex.

[Sinus] [P] [QRS]

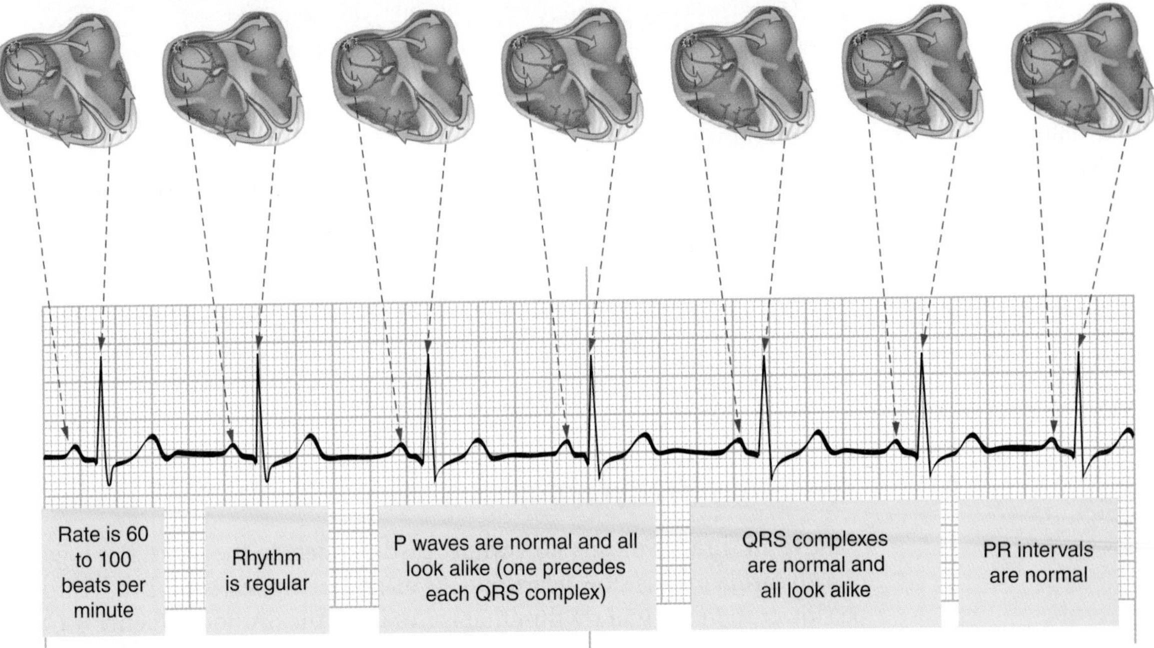

Figure 8-5
Normal sinus rhythm.

Normal Sinus Rhythm

Normal sinus rhythm (NSR) (also referred to as regular sinus rhythm) is considered the normal electrical activity of the heart. Normal sinus rhythm is the rhythm to which we compare all other rhythms. Normal sinus rhythm has a heart rate of 60 to 100 beats per minute (in the average adult). It is a regular rhythm with a normal P wave preceding each normal QRS complex. The PR intervals are within the range of 0.12 to 0.20 seconds in duration and are constant (each PR interval is the same). Each QRS complex is followed by a normal T wave (Figure 8-5).

INSTRUCTIONAL MOMENT
Remember, we can use the term "supraventricular" dysrhythmias to describe dysrhythmias that arise from above the ventricles. This includes dysrhythmias whose origins are the SA node, atria, and AV junction.

In the average adult the heart rate in NSR is ______________ beats per minute and the rhythm is ______________.

[60 to 100] [regular]

INSTRUCTIONAL MOMENT

In some rhythms, called normal sinus rhythm, there may be some slight variances such as a slightly irregular rhythm or an elevated ST segment. You may see it described as a regular sinus rhythm because it doesn't fit the textbook description of NSR.

Review of key characteristics associated with normal sinus rhythm

Rate:	60 to 100 beats per minute
Regularity:	It is regular
P waves:	Present and normal; all the P waves are followed by a QRS complex
QRS complexes:	Normal
PR interval:	Within normal range (0.12 to 0.20 seconds)
QT interval:	Within normal range (0.36 to 0.44 seconds)

Sinus Bradycardia

The term "brady" means slow while "cardia" refers to the heart. Put together bradycardia means slow heart rate. As its name implies, sinus bradycardia is a slower than normal rhythm that arises from the SA node (Figure 8-6). Sinus bradycardia has all the characteristics of normal sinus rhythm but the heart rate is less than 60 beats per minute (BPM). It looks like a slow NSR. It results from a slowing of the rate at which the pacemaker, the SA node, fires.

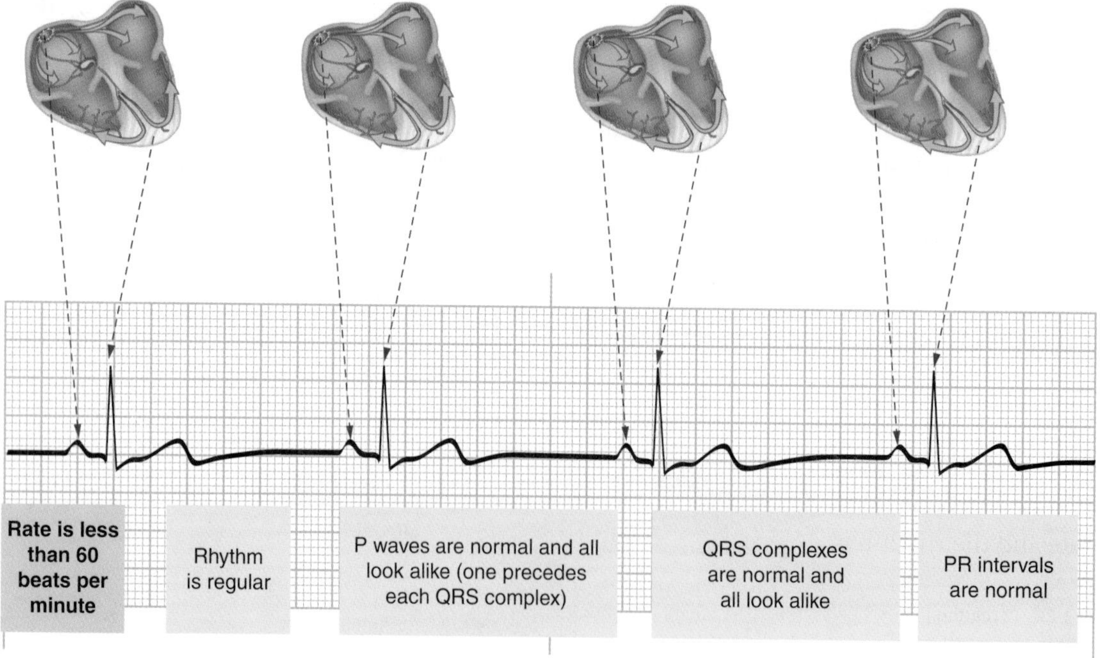

Figure 8-6
Sinus bradycardia.

Sinus bradycardia very often occurs naturally, as the body's way to conserve energy during times of reduced demand for blood flow. In which case, vagal stimulation increases and sympathetic stimulation decreases, resulting in decreased SA node stimulation and the heart rate slowing.

CLINICAL MOMENT

You may remember from our discussion in Chapter 1 that the autonomic nervous system has a branch, the parasympathetic division, responsible for the vegetative functions and a branch, the sympathetic division, responsible for helping the body address its needs during times of excitement, work, and stress. The parasympathetic division, supplied by the vagus nerve, slows the heart rate and decreases the AV conduction. Both branches exert their effects via neurotransmitters that bind specific receptors.

This occurs normally during sleep as a result of circadian variations in the heart rate. Sinus bradycardia is considered normal in aerobically conditioned persons or in athletes, whose hearts are well-conditioned and can maintain a normal stroke volume with less-than-normal effort. They often have slower heart rates of 40 to 50 beats per minute.

Sinus bradycardia is a ______________ than normal rhythm that arises from the SA node. The heart rate characteristic of sinus bradycardia is less than ____________ beats per minute. Sinus bradycardia often occurs ______________.

[slower] [60] [naturally]

Sinus bradycardia can also occur as a result of various conditions, such as anterior wall myocardial infarction that involves the right coronary artery, which supplies blood to the SA node. It may also result from a host of other conditions, including noncardiac disorders, conditions involving excessive parasympathetic stimulation or decreased sympathetic stimulation, cardiac diseases, and the use of certain drugs (Table 8-1).

KEY CONCEPT

Sinus bradycardia often occurs naturally as a means of conserving energy during times of rest or sleep.

Sinus bradycardia can also serve as a protective mechanism in the patient experiencing acute myocardial infarction by reducing myocardial oxygen consumption—providing that the patient is well perfused.

Often sinus bradycardia is insignificant and the patient is asymptomatic. Typically, most adults are able to tolerate a heart rate of 45 to 59 beats per

Table 8.1 Causes of Sinus Bradycardia

Cause	Examples
Cardiac diseases	Intrinsic sinoatrial node disease, cardiomyopathy, myocarditis, myocardial ischemia and/or infarction, and heart block
Use of certain drugs	Digoxin, beta-adrenergic blockers, calcium channel blockers, lithium, amiodarone, propafenone, and quinidine
Excessive vagal tone or decreased sympathetic stimulation	Carotid sinus massage, vomiting, Valsalva's maneuver, deep relaxation, sleep
Noncardiac disorders	Hypothermia, hypoxia, hyperkalemia, increased intracranial pressure, hypothyroidism, sleep, and glaucoma

minute. They are less tolerant of rates less than 45 beats per minute, particularly if they have underlying heart disease that prevents them from compensating for the slow heart rate with an increase in stroke volume.

In some patients the slower rate associated with sinus bradycardia can compromise cardiac output, resulting in hypotension; angina pectoris; and central nervous system symptoms such as lightheadedness, vertigo, and syncope. Recall the bradycardic patient in the case history at the beginning of this chapter. She experienced a syncopal episode (she fainted) due to her bradycardia. If a patient is symptomatic (e.g., short of breath, chest pain, dizziness), you should consider the presence of sinus bradycardia to be abnormal and potentially significant. Bradycardia is considered a diagnostic indicator of the seriously ill child because it denotes significant hypoxia and inadequate perfusion.

CLINICAL MOMENT
Bradycardia can predispose some patients to more serious dysrhythmias such as ventricular tachycardia and ventricular fibrillation.

The first thing you will note with sinus bradycardia is the slower than normal heart rate. This causes longer R-R intervals and P-P intervals (making it appear as if there are large spaces between the groups of complexes). The reason for the longer R-R intervals and P-P intervals is because there are fewer R waves and P waves making the distance between each much greater. Other than that, all the features are essentially the same as what we would expect to see with normal sinus rhythm (Figure 8-7).

Review of key characteristics associated with sinus bradycardia

Rate:	Less than 60 beats per minute
Regularity:	It is regular
P waves:	Present and normal; all the P waves are followed by a QRS complex
QRS complexes:	Normal
PR interval:	Within normal range (0.12 to 0.20 seconds)
QT interval:	Within normal range (0.36 to 0.44 seconds) but may be prolonged

KEY CONCEPT
Sinus bradycardia originates from the SA node and has the same characteristics as normal sinus rhythm except that the rate is slower (less than 60 beats per minute).

Causes of bradycardia include excessive _____________ stimulation. Cardiac output can be _____________ in some patients with sinus bradycardia resulting in _____________. Particularly in seriously ill _____________ bradycardia can indicate the presence of significant hypoxia and inadequate perfusion.

[parasympathetic] [compromised] [hypotension] [children]

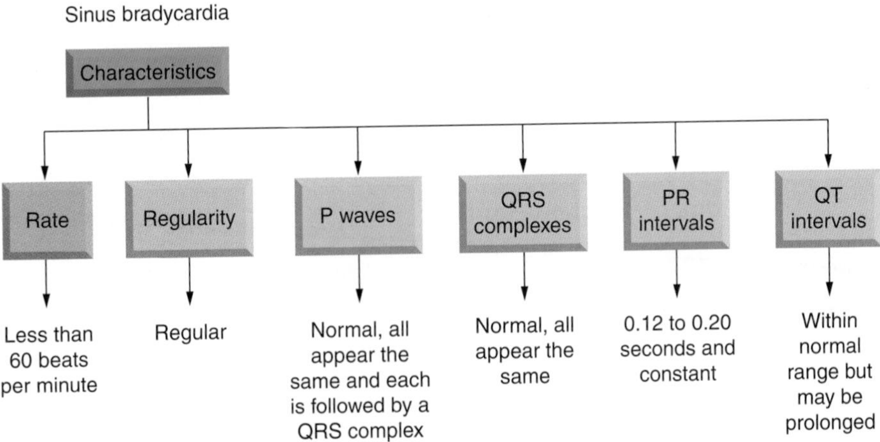

Figure 8-7
Algorithm for sinus bradycardia.

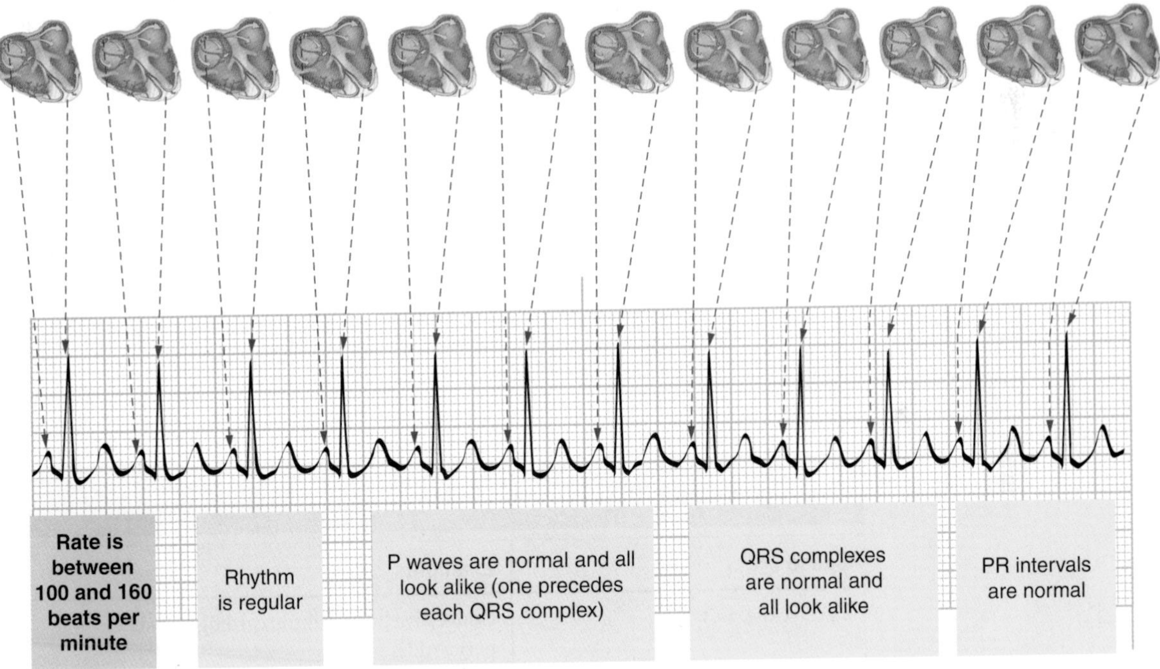

Figure 8-8
Sinus tachycardia.

Sinus Tachycardia

The opposite of bradycardia is tachycardia. "Tachy" means fast. With "cardia" to form the term tachycardia, it means a fast heart rate. As its name implies, sinus tachycardia is a faster than normal rhythm that results from an increase in the rate of sinus node discharge (Figure 8-8). It has the same

QUESTION
"Sinus tachycardia is produced by stimulation of which branch of the autonomic nervous system?" (The answer can be found on page 266.)

characteristics as normal sinus rhythm but has a rate greater than 100 beats per minute.

Sinus tachycardia is _______________ than normal. It results from a quicker discharge of the _______________ node. With sinus tachycardia the rate is _______________ than _______________ beats per minute.

[faster] [SA] [greater] [100]

KEY CONCEPT
Sinus tachycardia often occurs naturally as a means of increasing delivery of oxygen and nutrients and removing waste products during times of exertion, exercise, or stress.

Sinus tachycardia may be of no clinical significance. We often see it with physical labor, exercise, pain, fear, excitement, or anxiety where increased sympathetic stimulation occurs in response to the need for more oxygen and nutrients at the cellular level.

We also see sinus tachycardia with the ingestion of caffeine or alcohol; smoking; fever; or where there is some type of underlying illness, such as hypovolemia, respiratory distress, hyperthyroidism, or anemia. When the stimulus for the tachycardia is removed, the dysrhythmia spontaneously resolves (Table 8-2).

Sinus tachycardia is brought about by increased _______________ stimulation. The tachycardia spontaneously _______________ once the stimulus causing it is _______________.

[sympathetic] [resolves] [removed]

Table 8.2 Causes of Sinus Tachycardia

Cause	Examples
Cardiac diseases	Congestive heart failure, cardiogenic shock, and pericarditis
Use of certain drugs	Sympathomimetic drugs such as epinephrine; isoproterenol; dopamine; dobutamine; vagolytic drugs such as atropine; or other drugs such as alcohol, caffeine, nicotine, and amphetamines
Increased sympathetic stimulation	Exercise; pain; stress; fever; fear; anxiety; or as a compensatory mechanism in shock, respiratory distress, hypoxia, pulmonary embolism, anemia, sepsis, and hyperthyroidism

The most significant problem associated with sinus tachycardia is that it increases myocardial oxygen consumption, which can aggravate ischemia (bringing on chest pain), and infarction. It can predispose the patient to more serious rhythm disturbances, particularly in persons with coronary artery disease or obstructive types of heart conditions such as aortic stenosis and hypertrophic cardiomyopathy.

The most significant problem associated with sinus tachycardia is that it increases myocardial _______________ consumption, which can aggravate _______________.

[oxygen] [ischemia]

Review of key characteristics associated with sinus tachycardia

Rate:	100 to 160 beats per minute
Regularity:	It is regular
P waves:	Present and normal; all the P waves are followed by a QRS complex
QRS complexes:	Normal
PR interval:	Within normal range (0.12 to 0.20 seconds)
QT interval:	May be within normal range (0.36 to 0.44 seconds) but commonly shortened

The most obvious characteristic you will see with sinus tachycardia is the faster than normal rate. This causes shorter R-R intervals and P-P intervals (making it appear as if there are smaller spaces between the groups of complexes). With the faster rates, the P wave may be superimposed on the T wave of the preceding beat making it harder to identify and the QT interval is normally shorter than with normal sinus rhythm (Figure 8-9).

KEY CONCEPT
Sinus tachycardia arises from the SA node and has basically the same characteristics as normal sinus rhythm except that the rate is faster (greater than 100 beats per minute).

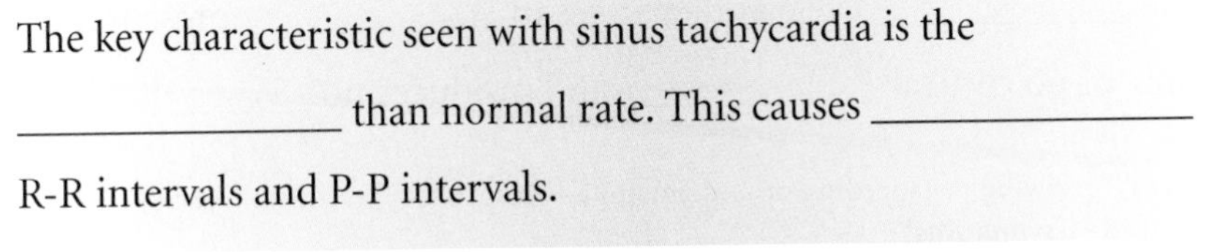

The key characteristic seen with sinus tachycardia is the _______________ than normal rate. This causes _______________ R-R intervals and P-P intervals.

[faster] [shorter]

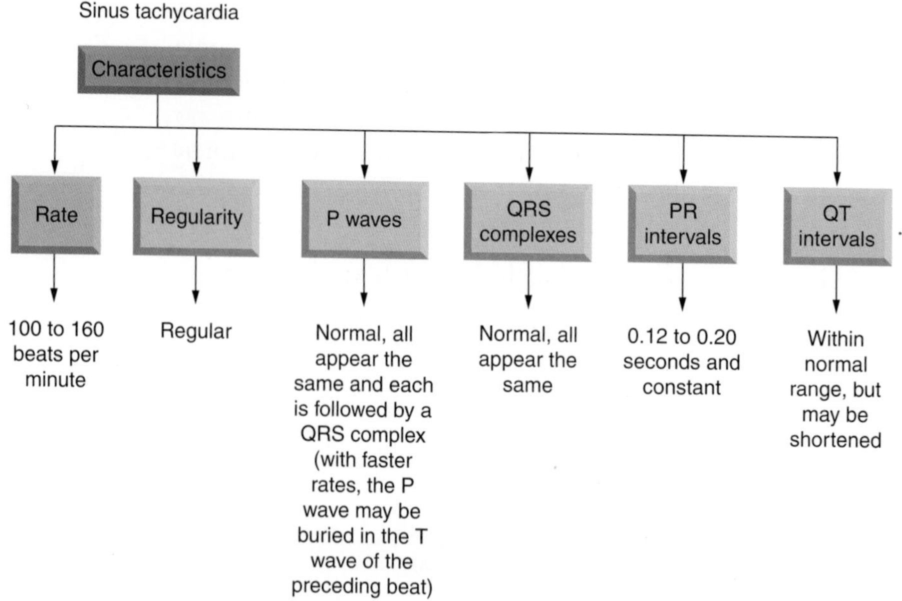

Figure 8-9
Algorithm for sinus tachycardia.

Sinus Dysrhythmia

With the exception of a patterned irregularity, sinus dysrhythmia is characteristically the same as sinus rhythm (normal P waves, QRS complexes, and T waves) (Figure 8-10). It can be described as a repeating cycle of "slowing, then speeding up, then slowing again." The beat-to-beat variation produced by the irregular firing of the pacemaker cells of the SA node corresponds with the respiratory cycle and changes in intrathoracic pressure. The heart rate increases during inspiration and decreases during expiration.

The difference between sinus rhythm and sinus dysrhythmia is a ____________ irregularity to the rhythm. The irregularity can be described as "____________, then ____________, then ____________ again." The irregular firing of the SA node corresponds with the ____________ cycle and changes in ____________ pressure. It is usually of no clinical ____________ and produces no ____________.

[patterned] [slowing] [speeding up] [slowing] [respiratory] [intrathoracic] [significance] [symptoms]

Sinus dysrhythmia can occur naturally in athletes, children, and older adults, but is uncommon in infants. It can also occur in patients with heart disease or inferior wall myocardial infarction, advanced age, in those

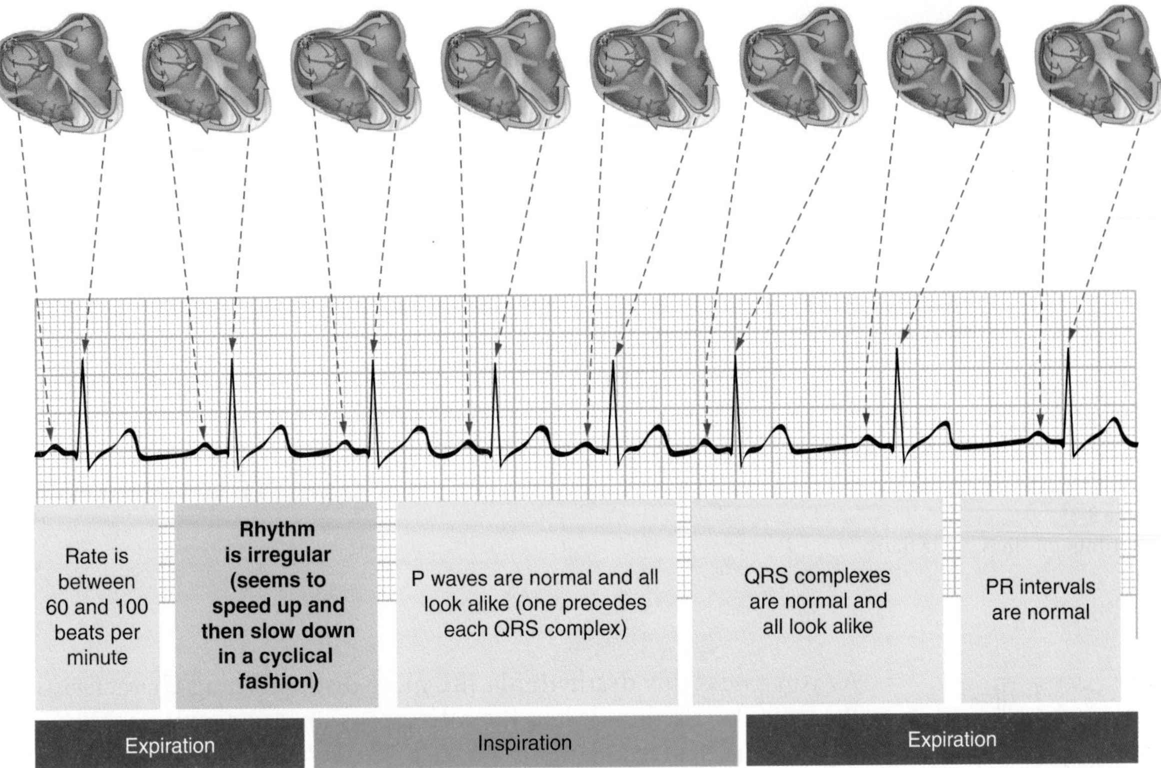

Figure 8-10
Sinus dysrhythmia.

receiving certain drugs such as digitalis and morphine, and in conditions where there is increased intracranial pressure. It is usually of no clinical significance and produces no symptoms. However, in some patients and conditions it may be associated with palpitations, dizziness, and syncope.

CLINICAL MOMENT
Sinus dysrhythmia is frequently present in highly toned athletes. These individuals' circulatory systems work so efficiently that their heart rate speeds up and slows down dependant upon the availability of oxygen in the respiratory system. At the peak of inspiration the greatest amount of oxygen is present in the alveolar/capillary membrane so the heart rate speeds up to maximize the perfusion to this area. During exhalation, the heart rate drops. This describes "vagal tone."

Review of key characteristics associated with sinus dysrhythmia

Rate:	Typically 60 to 100 beats per minute
Regularity:	It is regularly irregular (patterned irregularity); seems to speed up, slow down, and speed up in a cyclical fashion
P waves:	Present and normal; all the P waves are followed by a QRS complex
QRS complexes:	Normal
PR interval:	Within normal range (0.12 to 0.20 seconds)
QT interval:	May vary slightly but usually within normal range (0.36 to 0.44 seconds)

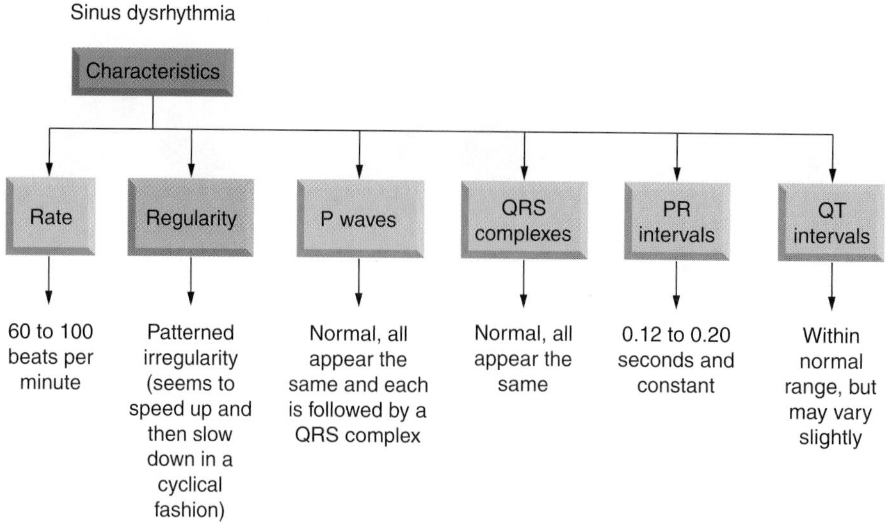

Figure 8-11
Algorithm for sinus dysrhythmia.

QUESTION
"What method of calculating the heart rate should be used in sinus dysrhythmia?" (The answer can be found on page 266.)

KEY CONCEPT
Sinus dysrhythmia arises from the SA node and has the same characteristics as normal sinus rhythm except that it has a patterned irregularity.

As you assess this dysrhythmia the most distinguishing characteristic is the irregular rhythm. When the rate speeds up, the complexes are closer together; this shortens the P-P and R-R intervals. When the rate slows down, the complexes are farther away, lengthening the P-P and R-R intervals. The other features are essentially the same as normal sinus rhythm, particularly the round normal P wave preceding each QRS complex. The QRS complexes should be normal. The QT interval may vary slightly (Figure 8-11).

The key characteristic of sinus dysrhythmia is a ________________ irregularity to the rhythm. When the rate speeds up, the complexes are ________________ together, thereby ________________ the P-P and R-R intervals. When the rate slows down, the P-P and R-R intervals are ________________.

[patterned] [closer] [shortening] [lengthened]

Sinus Arrest

Sinus arrest occurs when the SA node transiently stops firing (Figure 8-12). It results from a marked depression in SA node automaticity. Failure of the sinus node causes short periods of cardiac standstill until a lower-level pacemaker discharges (creating an escape beat) or the sinus node resumes its normal function. The usual result of sinus arrest is a brief pause in all

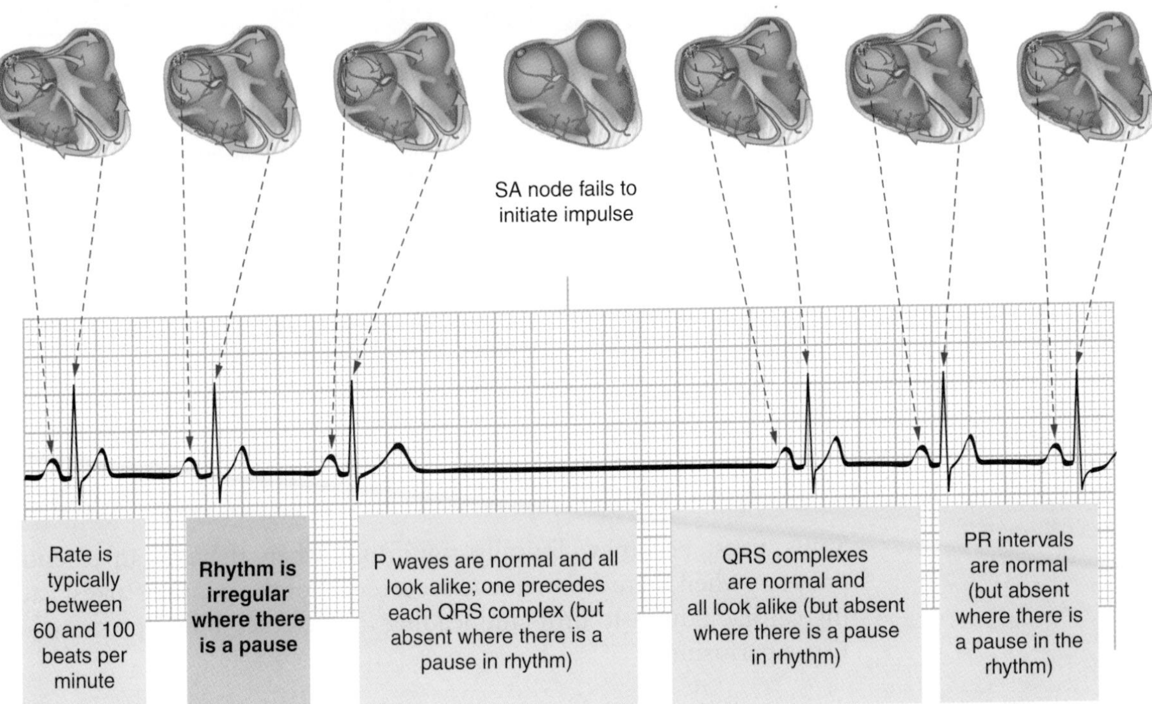

Figure 8-12
Sinus arrest.

electrical activity. The ECG rhythm looks like normal sinus rhythm except there is a pause in the rhythm or an absence of the P, QRS, and T waveforms until a pacemaker site reinitiates the rhythm.

Sinus arrest results when the ________________ node transiently ________________ firing. The usual result of sinus arrest is a brief ________________ in all ________________ activity. The dysrhythmia looks like ________________ except there is an ________________ of the P, QRS, and T waveforms until a ________________ site reinitiates the rhythm.

[SA] [stops] [pause] [electrical] [NSR] [absence] [pacemaker]

CLINICAL MOMENT
This dysrhythmia is referred to as sinus pause when one or two beats are not formed and sinus arrest when three or more beats are not formed.

Causes of sinus arrest include an increase in parasympathetic tone on the SA node, hypoxia or ischemia, excessive administration of digitalis or propranolol (Inderal), hyperkalemia, and damage to the SA node (such as acute myocardial infarction [AMI] or degenerative fibrotic disease) (Table 8-3).

Table 8-3 Causes of Sinus Arrest

Cause	Examples
Sinus node disease	Fibrosis, idiopathetic degeneration
Cardiac disorders	Chronic coronary artery disease, myocardial ischemia or infarction, acute myocarditis, cardiomyopathy, hypertensive heart disease
Use of certain drugs	Digoxin, procainamide, quinidine, salicylates (particularly in toxic doses), excessive doses of beta-adrenergic blockers such as propranolol and metapronol, or calcium channel blockers
Increased vagal tone	Valsalva's maneuver, carotid sinus massage, vomiting
Others	Hyperkalemia, hypoxia

Sinus arrest becomes clinically significant when there is an extended pause or when there are frequent occurrences of the pause or arrest causing cardiac output to drop and leading to decreased blood pressure and tissue perfusion.

Review of key characteristics associated with sinus arrest

Rate:	Typically 60 to 100 beats per minute
Regularity:	It is irregular where there is pause in the rhythm (the SA node fails to initiate a beat)
P waves:	Present and normal; all the P waves are followed by a QRS complex
QRS complexes:	Normal
PR interval:	Within normal range (0.12 to 0.20 seconds)
QT interval:	Within normal range (0.36 to 0.44 seconds); unmeasurable during a pause

CLINICAL MOMENT
Palpitation is a sensation of pounding or racing of the heart. Syncope is a transient, usually sudden, loss of consciousness due to inadequate perfusion of the brain. These symptoms may occur together or individually. Palpitations and syncope result from cardiac dysrhythmias, other types of heart disease, nervous system disorders, anxiety, and thyroid disease.

The most prominent characteristic of this dysrhythmia is a pause in the ECG rhythm. This produces an irregularity in the rhythm. The rhythm typically resumes its normal appearance after this transient pause in the rhythm unless an escape pacemaker resumes the rhythm (Figure 8-13).

Depending on how frequently it occurs and how long the sinus arrest lasts, the rate may be normal to slow (less than 60 beats per minute).

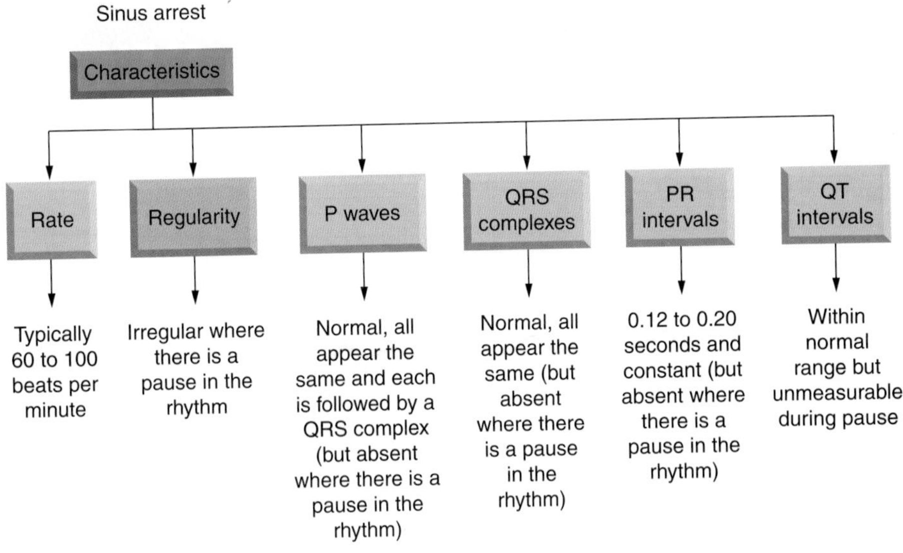

Figure 8-13
Algorithm for sinus arrest.

Again, because the rhythm arises from the SA node, the P waves are normal and each is followed by a QRS complex.

Frequent or protracted episodes of sinus arrest can compromise cardiac output by decreasing heart rate and eliminating the atrial contribution to ventricular filling. There is also a danger that SA node activity will completely cease and an escape pacemaker may not take over pacing (resulting in asystole).

KEY CONCEPT
Sinus arrest arises from the SA node. It occurs when the SA node transiently stops firing. The SA node then begins to fire again after a brief pause or a pacemaker lower in the conduction system fires to reinitiate the heartbeat.

Normally, sinus arrest has ______________ clinical significance.
However, frequent or protracted episodes of sinus arrest can ______________ cardiac output by ______________ the heart rate.

[no] [compromise] [decreasing]

You can practice interpreting sinus node dysrhythmias with the following *Practice Makes Perfect* exercises. Answers to these exercises can be found in Appendix A.

4.

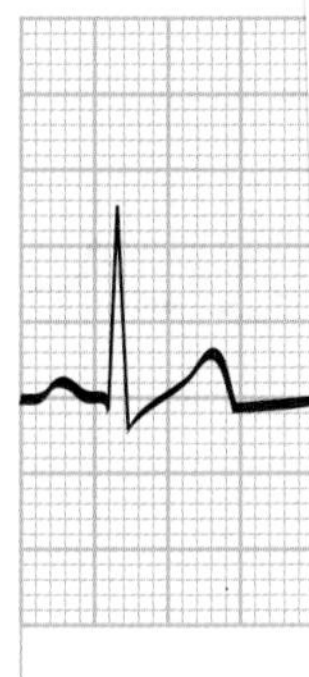

Rate: ________
P waves: ______
QT intervals: ___

5.

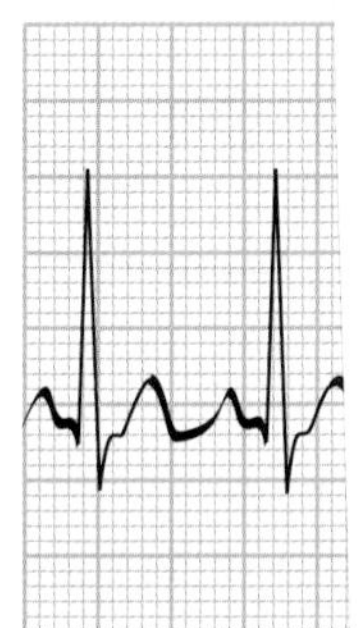

Rate: __________
P waves: _______
QT intervals: _____

6.

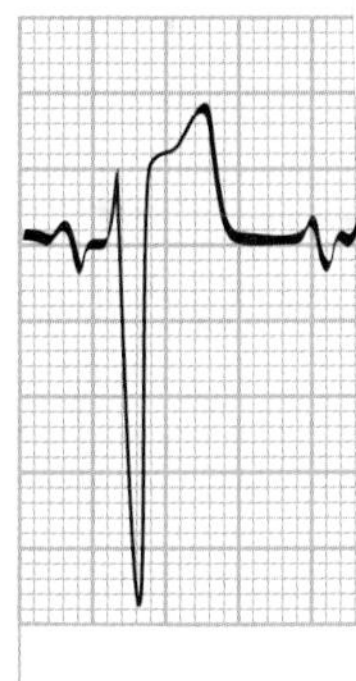

Rate: __________
P waves: _______
QT intervals: _____

PRA

1.

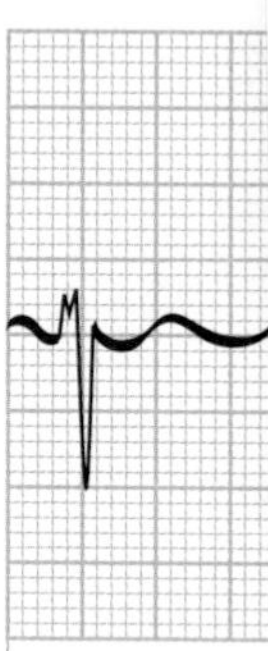

Rate: ________
P waves: ______
QT intervals: __

2.

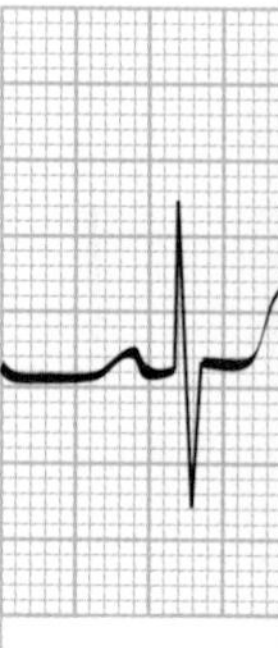

Rate: ________
P waves: ______
QT intervals: __

3.

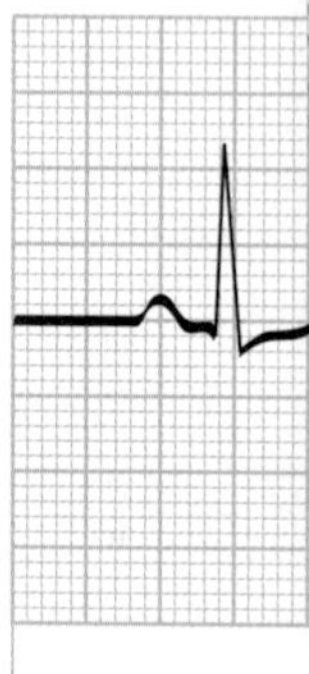

Rate: ________
P waves: ______
QT intervals: __

Answers to Sidebar Questions

"What is the rate of the heart's three primary pacemaker sites—the SA node, AV junction, and ventricles?"

Answer: The SA node has an inherent rate of 60 to 100 beats per minute while the AV junction has an inherent rate of 40 to 60 beats per minute. The ventricles have an inherent rate of 20 to 40 beats per minute.

"Sinus tachycardia is produced by stimulation of which branch of the autonomic nervous system?"

Answer: Stimulation of the sympathetic branch of the autonomic nervous system produces sinus tachycardia.

"What method of checking the heart rate should be used in sinus dysrhythmia?"

Answer: The 6-second interval × 10 method should be used because of the irregularity of the rhythm.

On the DVD

- Approach to Sinus Rhythms Lecture.

Origin and Clinical Aspects of Atrial Dysrhythmias

9

Case History

EMS is called to evaluate an elderly man who passed out in church. The man has a history of chronic obstructive pulmonary disease (COPD) and hypertension. Upon their arrival, the EMS team is met by a physician attending services with the patient. He tells you that the gentleman was sitting in the pew when he arose for prayer and then slumped back down and fell over on his side. The doctor then rushed to the man's side and checked for a pulse, which he says was fast and regular but barely palpable. He says the patient never stopped breathing or became cyanotic and that once he lay flat he returned to his normal self.

The paramedics introduce themselves and begin their assessment. Oxygen is applied and vital signs are taken showing a blood pressure of 100/90, pulse 150, respirations of 16 per minute, and oxygen saturation of 92% on room air. They apply the cardiac monitor to the patient and see a fast, regular heart rate with narrow QRS complexes. One of the paramedics comments that the rhythm looks like sinus tachycardia. But the physician says, "No, look closely. See the saw-tooth pattern?"

The paramedics nod in agreement after confirming that indeed, there are no normal P waves and that the QRS complexes are preceded by F waves.

Chapter Preview

- Rhythms Originating in the Atria
- Wandering Atrial Pacemaker
- Premature Atrial Complex (PACs)
- Atrial Tachycardia
- Multifocal Atrial Tachycardia (MAT)
- Supraventricular Tachycardia (SVT)
- Atrial Flutter
- Atrial Fibrillation

Rhythms Originating in the Atria

Dysrhythmias that originate outside the SA node in the atrial tissue or in the internodal pathways are called atrial dysrhythmias. These dysrhythmias can affect ventricular filling time and diminish the strength of the atrial "kick," the atrial contraction that normally supplies the ventricles with about 30% of their blood. This can lead to decreased cardiac output and ultimately decreased tissue perfusion.

CLINICAL MOMENT
Decreased tissue perfusion can have dire consequences. First, there is not enough oxygen and nutrients for the body to satisfy its energy needs. Second, if the waste products of metabolism are not removed, they accumulate in the tissues and create a toxic environment. If not corrected, both factors can lead to shock and, ultimately, death of the patient.

_______________ dysrhythmias originate in the atrial tissue or in the internodal pathways. These dysrhythmias can affect _______________ filling time and diminish the strength of the _______________ kick.

[Atrial] [ventricular] [atrial]

The three mechanisms believed to be responsible for atrial dysrhythmias are: increased automaticity, triggered activity (after depolarization), and reentry. Increased automaticity and triggered activity are disorders of impulse formation. Reentry is a problem with impulse conduction.

In increased automaticity, the atrial cells spontaneously depolarize and initiate impulses before the SA node has a chance to generate a normal impulse. The most common causes include ischemia; hypoxia; and atrial stretching or dilation usually due to congestive heart failure (CHF), mitral valve disease, increased pulmonary artery pressures, or a combination of these conditions.

Injured cells sometimes only partially repolarize. Partial repolarization can lead to repetitive ectopic firing called triggered activity. The depolarization produced by triggered activity is known as afterdepolarization and can bring about atrial or ventricular tachycardia. Afterdepolarization can occur with cell injury, digoxin toxicity, and other conditions.

Reentry occurs when an impulse is delayed along a slow conduction pathway and the impulse is able to remain active long enough to produce another impulse during myocardial repolarization. Reentry can occur with coronary artery disease, cardiomyopathy, or myocardial infarction.

CLINICAL MOMENT
Atrial dysrhythmias are the most common type of cardiac rhythm disturbance.

The three mechanisms thought responsible for atrial dysrhythmias are increased _______________, _______________ activity, and _______________.

[automaticity] [triggered] [reentry]

Atrial dysrhythmias include the following:

- Wandering atrial pacemaker
- Premature atrial complex (PAC)
- Atrial tachycardia
- Multifocal atrial tachycardia (MAT)
- Supraventricular tachycardia (SVT)
- Atrial flutter
- Atrial fibrillation

INSTRUCTIONAL MOMENT
Dysrhythmias that originate from above the ventricles are called supraventricular dysrhythmias.

The key characteristics of atrial dysrhythmias include P′ waves (if present) that differ in appearance from normal sinus P waves and abnormal, shortened, or prolonged P′R intervals. As with all dysrhythmias that arise from above the ventricles (sinus, atrial, and junctional dysrhythmias) the QRS complexes appear narrow and normal (unless there is an intraventricular conduction defect or aberrancy).

KEY CONCEPT
The P waves associated with dysrhythmias that arise from the atria appear different than the P waves that arise from the SA node.

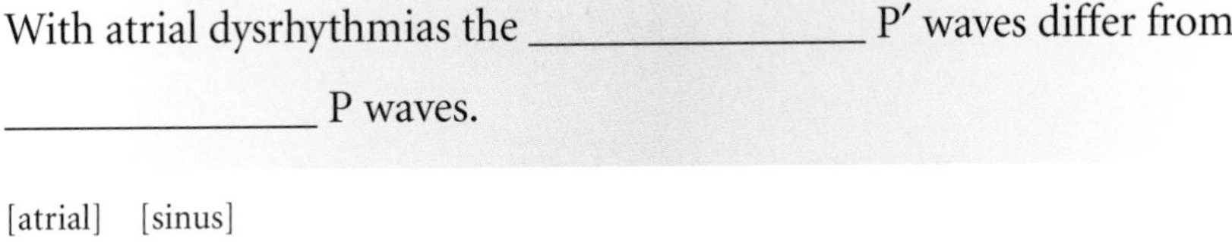

With atrial dysrhythmias the ______________ P′ waves differ from ______________ P waves.

[atrial] [sinus]

KEY CONCEPT
As with sinus dysrhythmias the QRS complexes in atrial dysrhythmias appear normal (unless there is an intraventricular conduction defect or aberrancy).

When we refer to the P waves as being normal, we mean they appear as an upright and round waveform. There is one P wave preceding each QRS complex. Its amplitude is 0.5 to 2.5 mm in height and its duration is 0.06 to 0.10 seconds. In leads I, II, aV_F, and V_2 through V_6, the deflection of the P wave is characteristically upright or positive. In leads III, aV_L, and V_1, the P wave is usually upright but may be negative or biphasic (both positive and negative). In lead aV_R, the P wave is negative or inverted.

When we refer to QRS complexes as being normal, we are saying they are narrow (0.06 to 0.12 seconds in duration) and normal looking. In leads I, II, III, aV_L, aV_F, and V_4 to V_6, the deflection of the QRS complex is characteristically positive or upright. In leads aV_R and V_1 to V_3, the QRS complex is usually negative or inverted. Leads III, aV_L, and V_2 to V_4 may also be biphasic. Further, in any dysrhythmia where the QRS complexes should be normal, they can instead be wide or unusual looking if there is intraventricular conduction defect, aberrancy, or ventricular preexcitation.

QUESTION
"What would you expect the appearance of the P waves to be if they originate from one site?" (The answer can be found on page 297.)

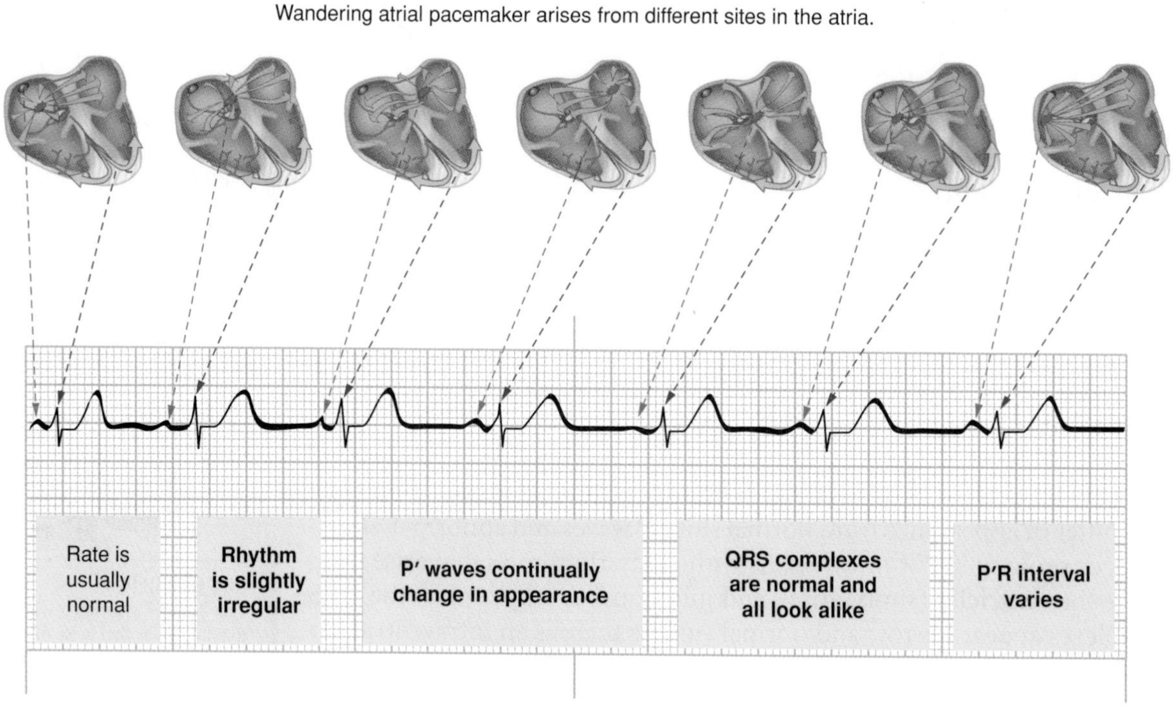

Wandering atrial pacemaker arises from different sites in the atria.

Rate is usually normal

Rhythm is slightly irregular

P′ waves continually change in appearance

QRS complexes are normal and all look alike

P′R interval varies

Figure 9-1
Wandering atrial pacemaker.

Wandering Atrial Pacemaker

Wandering atrial pacemaker is a rhythm in which the pacemaker site shifts between the SA node, atria, and/or AV junction (Figure 9-1). This produces its most characteristic feature—P′ waves that change in appearance, sometimes as often as from beat to beat. At least three different P wave configurations (seen in the same lead) are needed to diagnose a dysrhythmia as wandering atrial pacemaker.

With wandering atrial pacemaker, the pacemaker site shifts between the __________ node, __________, and/or __________ junction producing its most characteristic feature—P′ waves that __________ in appearance, sometimes as often as from __________ to __________.

[SA] [atria] [AV] [change] [beat] [beat]

Wandering atrial pacemaker is generally caused by the inhibitory vagal effect of respiration on the SA node and AV junction. It is a normal finding in children, older adults, and well-conditioned athletes and is not usually of any clinical significance. However, it may also be related to some types of organic heart disease and drug toxicity, particularly digitalis.

Wandering Atrial Pacemaker

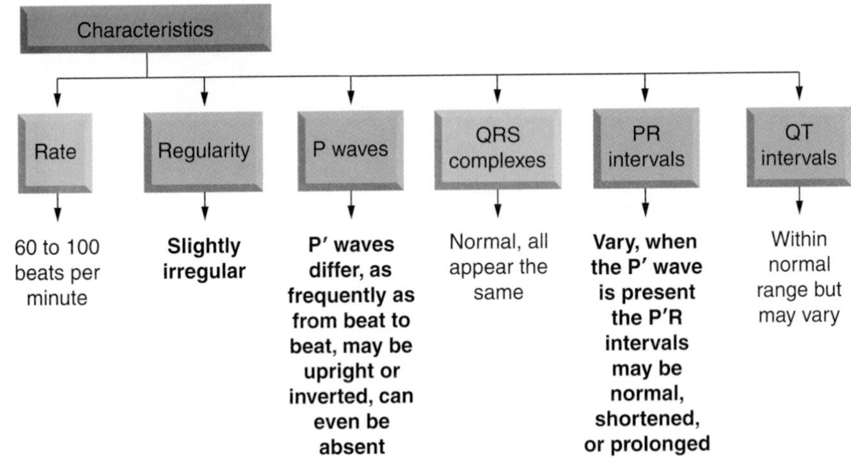

Figure 9-2
Algorithm for wandering atrial pacemaker.

Review of key characteristics associated with wandering atrial pacemaker

Rate:	Usually within normal limits
Regularity:	Slightly irregular
P waves:	Continuously change in appearance
QRS complexes:	Normal
PR interval:	Varies
QT interval:	Usually within normal limits but may vary

Again, the most distinguishing characteristic of this dysrhythmia is P′ waves of varying size, shape, and direction in any one lead (as often as from beat to beat) (Figure 9-2). Due to the changing pacemaker site, the P′R interval and the regularity of the rhythm often varies. The QRS complexes are normal because the impulse arises above the ventricles.

KEY CONCEPT
Wandering atrial pacemaker is a rhythm in which the pacemaker site shifts from site to site between the SA node and locations throughout the atria. This produces P′ waves that change in appearance and a rhythm that varies slightly.

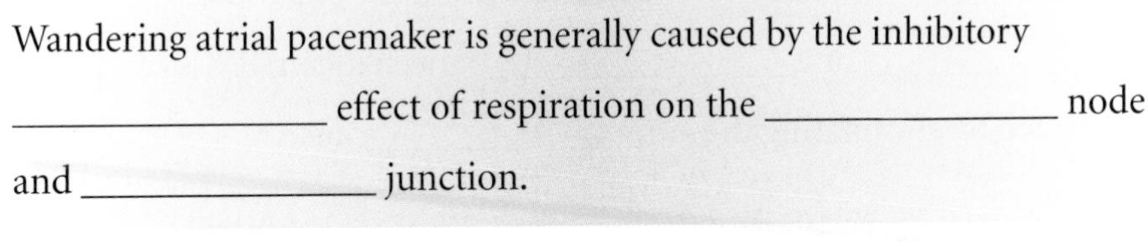
Wandering atrial pacemaker is generally caused by the inhibitory _______________ effect of respiration on the _______________ node and _______________ junction.

[vagal] [SA] [AV]

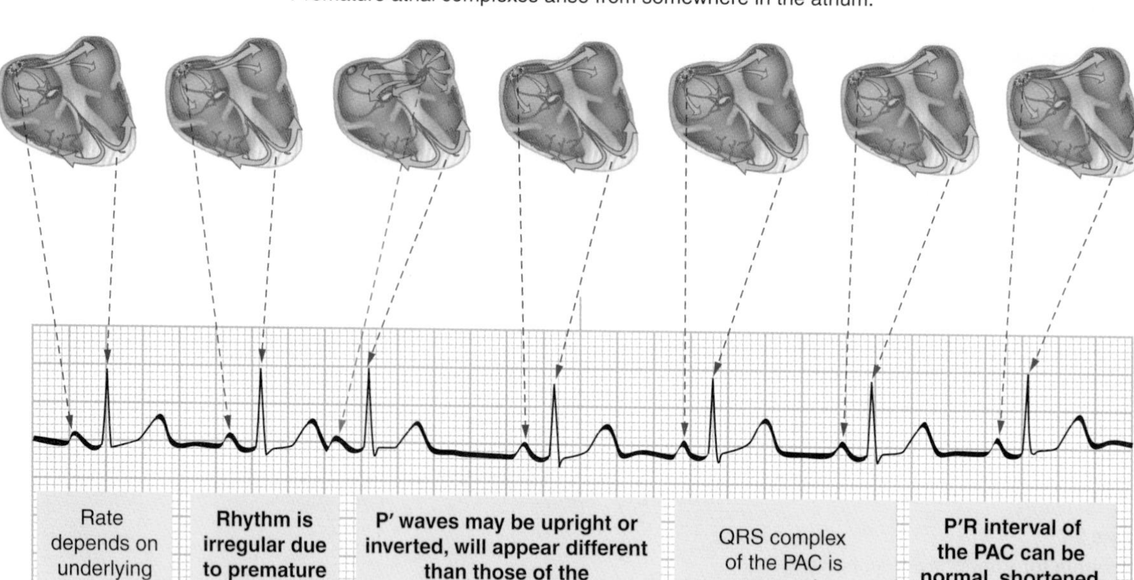

Figure 9-3
Premature atrial complex (PAC).

Premature Atrial Complexes (PACs)

Premature atrial complexes (PACs) are early ectopic beats that originate outside the SA node (Figure 9-3). The SA node fires an impulse, but then an irritable focus jumps in, firing its own impulse before the SA node can fire again. PACs can originate from a single ectopic site or from multiple sites in the atria. They can be brought about by enhanced automaticity or a reentry mechanism. Patients with healthy hearts can experience PACs with the use of caffeine, tobacco, or alcohol, or with anxiety, fatigue, or fever. In this case, the PACs can be controlled by eliminating the underlying cause.

INSTRUCTIONAL MOMENT
With premature beats (atrial, junctional, or ventricular) the term *complex* or *contraction* may be used. For example, we can call an early ectopic atrial beat a "premature atrial complex" or a "premature atrial contraction." The term contraction is the appropriate term if the premature beat produces a pulse. The term complex may be more fitting though, because not all premature beats produce a pulse.

Premature atrial complexes (PACs) are early ________________ beats.

PACs can originate from a single ectopic site or from multiple sites in the ________________. They can be brought about by enhanced ________________ or a ________________ mechanism. PACs can be controlled by eliminating the ________________ cause.

[ectopic] [atria] [automaticity] [reentry] [underlying]

Table 9-1 Premature Atrial Complexes

Causes of premature atrial complexes (PACs)	Examples
Cardiac disorders	Coronary or valvular heart disease, pulmonary disease
Use of certain drugs	Digitalis toxicity
Others	Acute respiratory failure, hypoxia, certain electrolyte imbalances, fever, alcohol, cigarettes, anxiety, fatigue, infectious diseases

Other common causes of PACs include increased catecholamines and sympathetic tone, electrolyte imbalance, and hypoxia (Table 9-1).

INSTRUCTIONAL MOMENT
Ectopic means occurring in an unusual location, or off the normal conduction pathway. It could also mean arising from any of the pacing sites other than the SA node, like the AV junction or His-Purkinje system.

In some cases there is no apparent cause. Isolated PACs seen in patients with healthy hearts are considered insignificant. They commonly cause no symptoms and can go unrecognized for years. Asymptomatic patients usually only require observation. The patient may perceive PACs as "palpitations" or skipped beats.

However, in patients with heart disease, frequent PACs may predispose the patient to serious atrial dysrhythmias such as atrial tachycardia, atrial flutter, or atrial fibrillation. In a patient experiencing an acute myocardial infarction, PACs can serve as an early indicator of an electrolyte imbalance or congestive heart failure. PACs with aberrant ventricular conduction may cause wide QRS complexes and be confused with premature ventricular complexes.

INSTRUCTIONAL MOMENT
Remember, in PACs with aberrant ventricular conduction, the QRS complexes are preceded by a P′ wave and a constant P′R interval because the pacemaker site is above the ventricles. This is one of the characteristics we can use to differentiate between PACs with aberrancy and premature ventricular complexes.

Review of key characteristics associated with PACs

Rate:	Depends on the underlying rhythm
Regularity:	May be occasionally irregular or frequently irregular (depends on the number of PACs present)
P waves:	May be upright or inverted, will appear different than those of the underlying rhythm
QRS complexes:	Normal
PR interval:	Will be normal duration if ectopic beat arises from the upper- or middle-right atrium. It is shorter than 0.12 seconds in duration if the ectopic impulse arises from the lower right atrium or in the upper part of the AV junction. In some cases it can also be prolonged
QT interval:	Usually within normal limits but may vary

When PACs are present, the first thing you see as you look across the ECG tracing is an irregular rhythm. As you look at it closer you can see that wherever there is irregularity the P′-P and R′-R intervals are shorter than the P-P and R-R intervals of the underlying rhythm. In other words, if you look across the ECG tracing at P-P intervals and R-R intervals of three consecutive normal beats, the distance should be relatively the same. Where there is an ectopic beat the P′-P and R′-R interval is shorter. This tells you that the beat(s) producing the irregularity occurred early. Now that we know there are early beats, it is a matter of identifying from where they are arising. We can determine this by looking at the P waves and QRS complexes associated with the early beats. There should be an upright P′ wave (in lead II) preceding the QRS complex but it will have a different morphology (appearance) than the P waves in the underlying rhythm. The QRS complexes are normal. Another characteristic that allows us to conclude that early beats are PACs is that they are followed by a noncompensatory pause.

QUESTION
"Why is it important to check for a pulse when there are premature beats in the rhythm?" (The answer can be found on page 297.)

Key characteristics of PACs are an ______________ heart rhythm and ______________ waves that differ from P waves in the underlying rhythm. Where there is an ectopic beat, the P′-P and R′-R intervals are ______________. The PAC is usually followed by a ______________ pause.

[irregular] [P′] [shorter] [noncompensatory]

INSTRUCTIONAL MOMENT
A compensatory pause occurs when there are two full R-R intervals between the R wave of the normal beat that precedes the PAC and the R wave of the first normal beat that follows it. A compensatory pause is characteristically seen with premature beats that arise from the ventricles. These are referred to as premature ventricular complexes.

The pause that follows a premature beat is called a **noncompensatory pause** if the beat following the premature complex is normal and occurs before it was expected. In other words, the space between the complex before and after the premature beat is less than the sum of two R-R intervals. To determine the presence of a noncompensatory pause we measure the R-R interval preceding the early beat. We then measure to the R wave of the first normal beat that follows it. If the distance is less than the sum of two R-R intervals, the pause is considered a noncompensatory pause (Figure 9-4).

INSTRUCTIONAL MOMENT
Nonconducted PACs or blocked PACs occur when an atrial impulse arrives too early, before the AV node has a chance to repolarize. As a result, the P′ wave fails to conduct to the ventricles. You will know this has occurred when you see a premature P′ wave not followed by a QRS complex.

The pause that follows a premature beat is called a ______________ pause if there are less than two full R-R intervals between the R wave of the normal beat that ______________ the PAC and the R wave of the first normal beat that ______________ it.

[noncompensatory] [precedes] [follows]

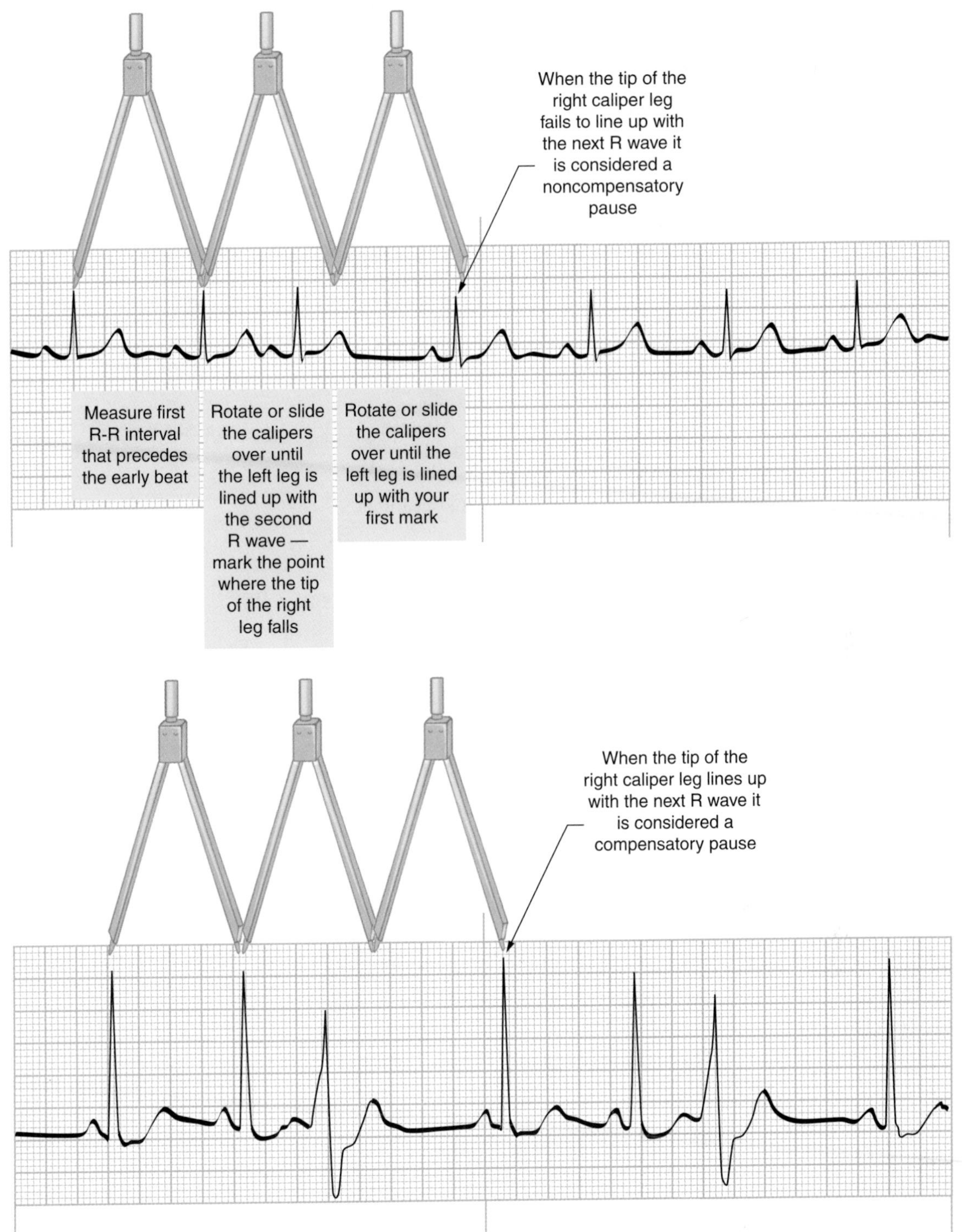

Figure 9-4
Noncompensatory pause and compensatory pause.

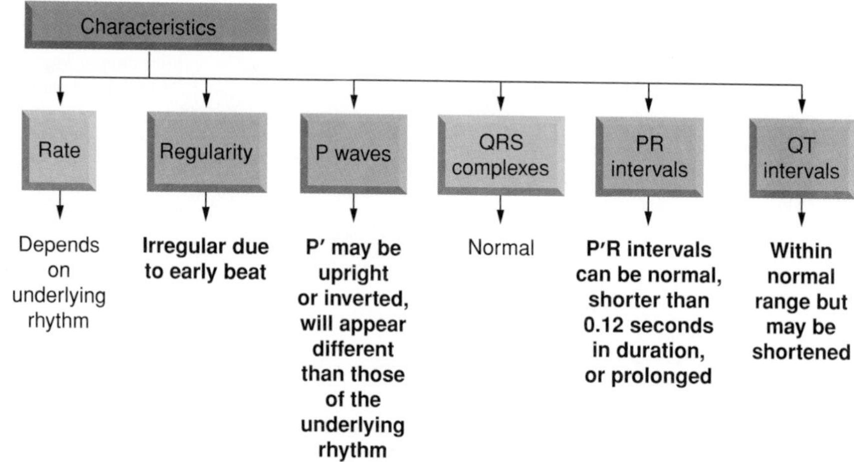

Figure 9-5
Premature atrial complexes (PACs) algorithm.

INSTRUCTIONAL MOMENT
Remember, bi = 2, tri = 3, and quad = 4.

Figure 9-5 illustrates the characteristics of a PAC.

Another way to describe PACs is how they are intermingled among the normal beats. When every other beat is a PAC, it is called bigeminal PACs or atrial bigeminy. If every third beat is a PAC, it is called trigeminal PACs or atrial trigeminy. Likewise, if a PAC occurs every fourth beat, it is called quadrigeminal PACs or atrial quadrigeminy. Regular PACs at greater intervals than every fourth beat have no special name (Figure 9-6).

KEY CONCEPT
Premature atrial complexes are early ectopic beats that arise from the atria.

_______________ PACs are present when every other beat is a PAC.

_______________ PACs are present when every third beat is a PAC. A PAC occurring every fourth beat is called a _______________ PAC.

[Bigeminal] [Trigeminal] [quadrigeminal]

QUESTION
"What is the heart rate associated with sinus tachycardia?" (The answer can be found on page 297.)

 Atrial Tachycardia

Atrial tachycardia is a rapid dysrhythmia (having a rate of 150 to 250 beats per minute) that arises from the atria (Figure 9-7). It is so fast that it overrides the SA node. When the onset of the tachycardia is sudden (and typically witnessed) it is called paroxysmal. Atrial tachycardia may occur in short bursts or it may be sustained. Short bursts of the tachycardia are well tolerated in otherwise normally healthy people. With sustained rapid ventricular rates, ventricular filling may be decreased during diastole.

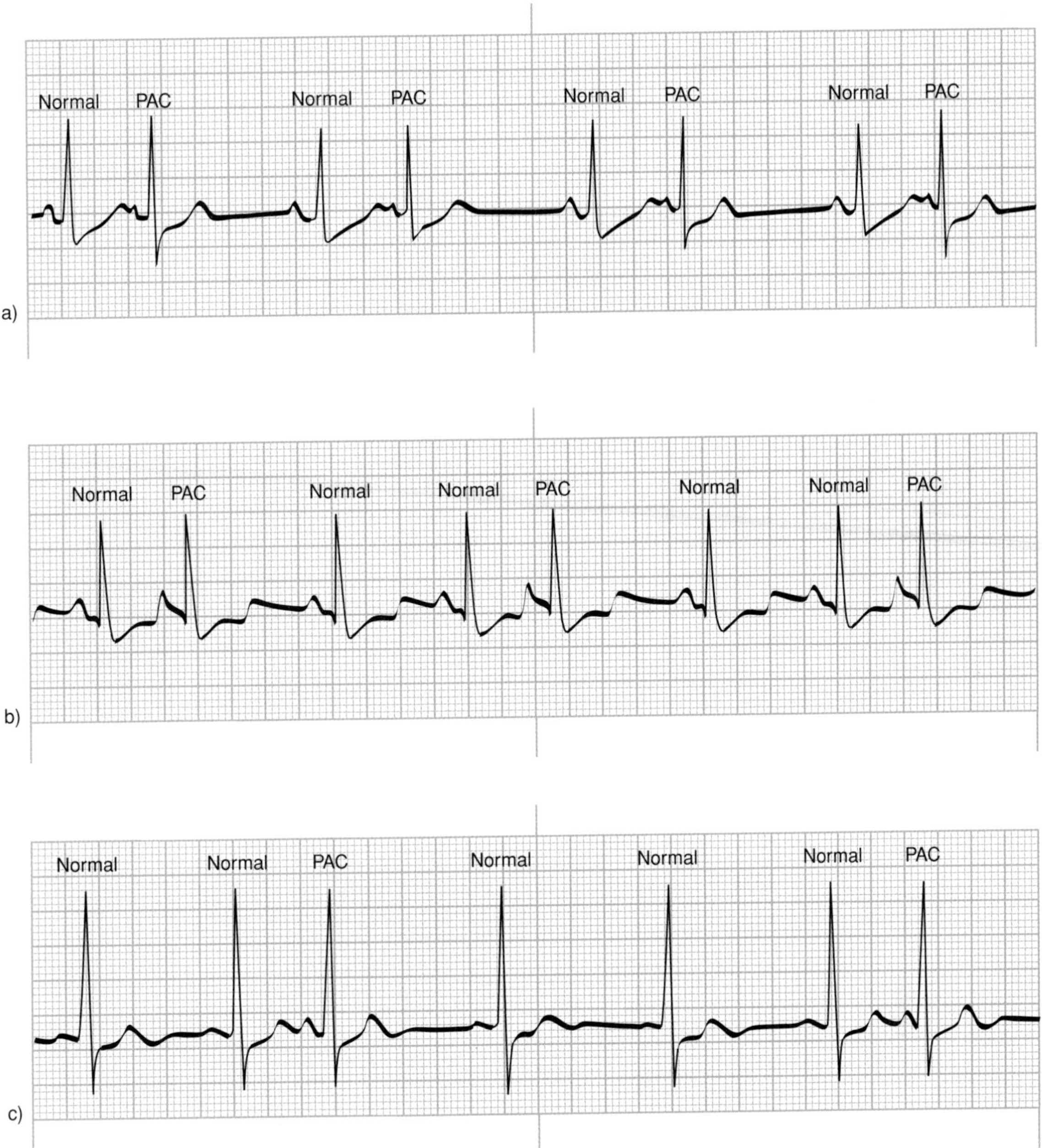

Figure 9-6
Premature atrial complexes occurring in a a) bigeminal, b) trigeminal, and c) quadrigeminal pattern.

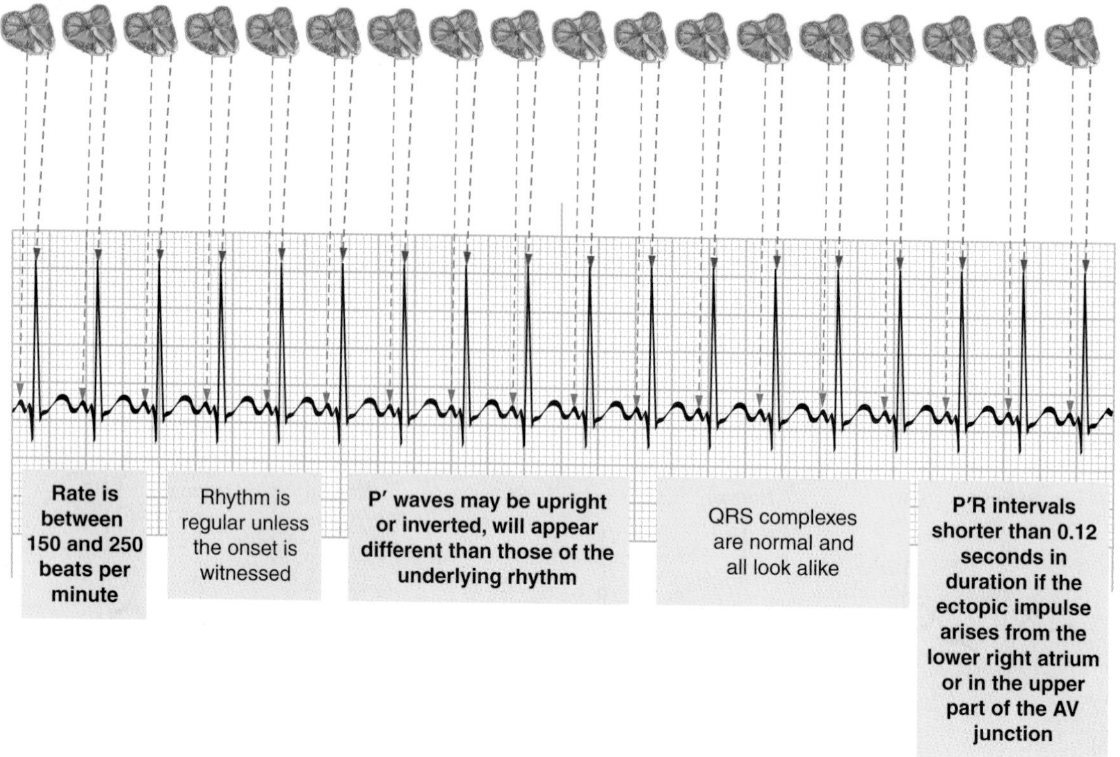

Figure 9-7
Atrial tachycardia.

Atrial tachycardia is a rapid dysrhythmia with a rate of ______________ beats per minute. When the onset of the tachycardia is sudden (and typically witnessed) it is called ______________. Atrial tachycardia may occur in short ______________ or it may be ______________. With sustained rapid ventricular rates, ventricular ______________ may be ______________ during diastole.

[150 to 250] [paroxysmal] [bursts] [sustained] [filling] [decreased]

Atrial tachycardia can occur at any age. Palpitations, nervousness, and anxiety frequently accompany it. Patients with healthy hearts can experience PACs, which can precipitate atrial tachycardia, due to the excessive use of caffeine or other stimulants, marijuana use, electrolyte imbalances, hypoxia, and physical or psychological stress. Sudden onset atrial tachycardia is also common in patients who have Wolff-Parkinson-White syndrome (Table 9-2).

Table 9-2 Atrial Tachycardia

Causes of atrial tachycardia	Examples
Sinus node disease	Sick sinus syndrome
Cardiac disorders	Myocardial infarction, cardiomyopathy, congenital anomalies, Wolff-Parkinson-White syndrome, valvular heart disease, systemic hypertensive, cor pulmonale
Use of certain drugs	Digitalis toxicity (the most common cause)
Others	Hyperthyroidism

Atrial tachycardia can significantly compromise cardiac output in patients with underlying heart disease, leading to vertigo (dizziness), lightheadedness, syncope, hypotension, and congestive heart failure. Further, the fast heart rate increases cardiac oxygen requirements that may increase myocardial ischemia and the frequency and severity of the patient's chest pain and potentially lead to myocardial infarction. Digitalis toxicity is the most common cause of atrial tachycardia.

INSTRUCTIONAL MOMENT

Paroxysmal tachycardia may originate in the atria (paroxysmal atrial tachycardia [PAT]) or AV junction (paroxysmal junctional tachycardia [PJT]). It is characterized by repeated episodes (paroxysms) of supraventricular tachycardia, which often have a sudden onset (lasting minutes to hours) and an abrupt termination. It looks like an extremely fast rate with narrow QRS complexes.

In patients with underlying ______________ disease atrial tachycardia can significantly ______________ cardiac output.

[heart] [compromise]

Review of key characteristics associated with atrial tachycardia

Rate:	150 to 250 beats per minute
Regularity:	Regular unless the onset is witnessed (thereby producing paroxysmal irregularity)
P waves:	May be upright or inverted, will appear different than those of the underlying rhythm
QRS complexes:	Normal
PR interval:	Will be normal duration if ectopic beat arises from the upper- or middle-right atrium. It is shorter than 0.12 seconds in duration if the ectopic impulse arises from the lower-right atrium or in the upper part of the AV junction
QT interval	Usually within normal limits but may be shorter due to the rapid rate

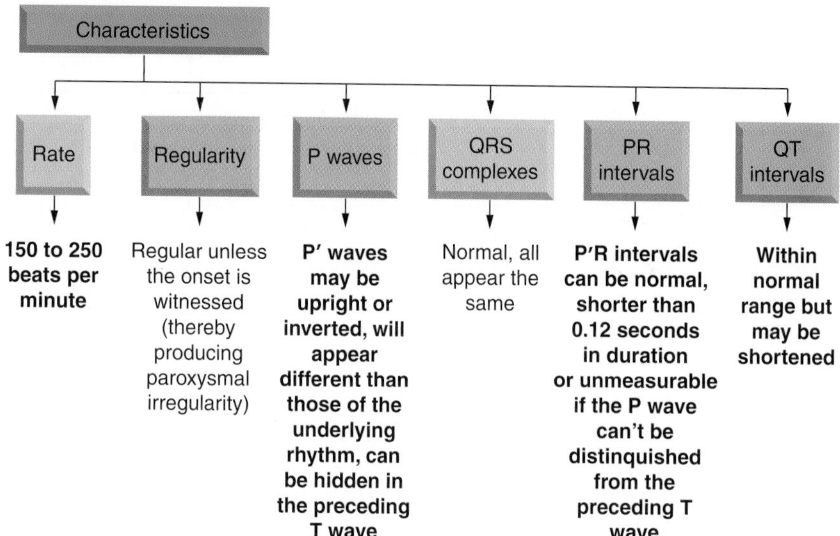

Figure 9-8
Algorithm for atrial tachycardia.

KEY CONCEPT
Atrial tachycardia is a rapid tachycardia that arises from the atria.

The most striking feature of atrial tachycardia is its rapid rate of 150 to 250 beats per minute. For this reason you should be able to see it almost immediately. It arises from one site, so the rhythm should be regular unless you see the onset or termination as with paroxysmal atrial tachycardia. While there is one P′ wave preceding each QRS complex, it is typically buried in the T wave of the preceding beat. If present, the P′ waves may be flattened or notched. The P′R intervals are typically indeterminable because the P′ waves tend to be buried. If visible, the P′R interval is often shortened but it may also be normal. The dysrhythmia arises above the ventricles, so the QRS complexes are normal (Figure 9-8) unless there is aberrant conduction.

The most striking feature of atrial tachycardia is its rapid rate of ______________ beats per minute. While there is one P′ wave preceding each QRS complex, it is typically ______________ in the T wave of the ______________ beat.

[150 to 250] [buried] [preceding]

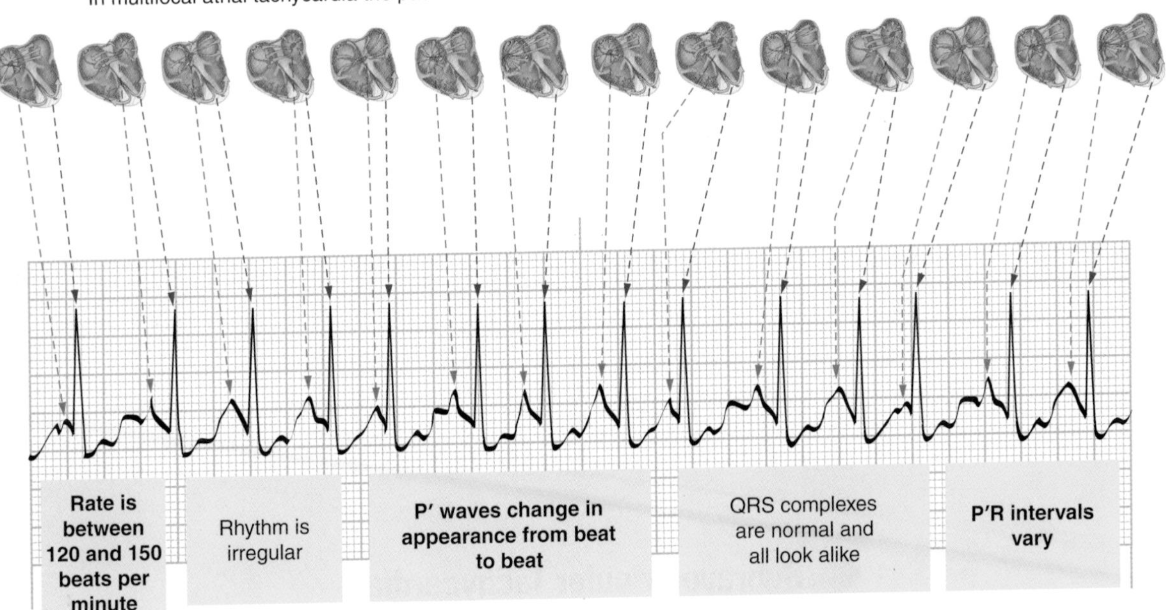

Figure 9-9
Multifocal atrial tachycardia.

Multifocal Atrial Tachycardia (MAT)

Multifocal atrial tachycardia (MAT) is a pathological condition that presents with the same characteristics as wandering atrial pacemaker but has heart rates in the 120 to 150 beats per minute range (Figure 9-9). MAT may be precipitated by acute exacerbation of emphysema, CHF, or acute mitral valve regurgitation. MAT is often misdiagnosed as atrial fibrillation with rapid ventricular response but can be distinguished by closely looking for the clearly visible but changing P′ waves seen with MAT. In lead II the P′ waves change in morphology (appearance) from beat to beat. P waves may be upright, rounded, notched, inverted, biphasic, or buried in the QRS complex.

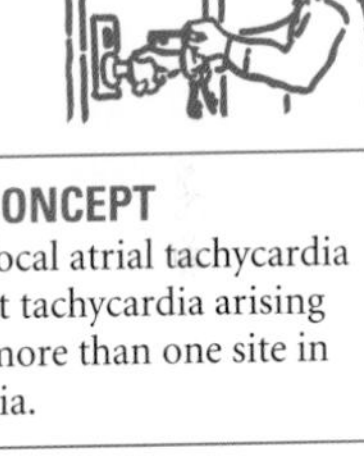

KEY CONCEPT
Multifocal atrial tachycardia is a fast tachycardia arising from more than one site in the atria.

Multifocal ______________ tachycardia (MAT) presents with the same characteristics as ______________ atrial pacemaker but has heart rates in the ______________ beats per minute range. MAT is often misdiagnosed as ______________ fibrillation with rapid ______________ response.

[atrial] [wandering] [120 to 150] [atrial] [ventricular]

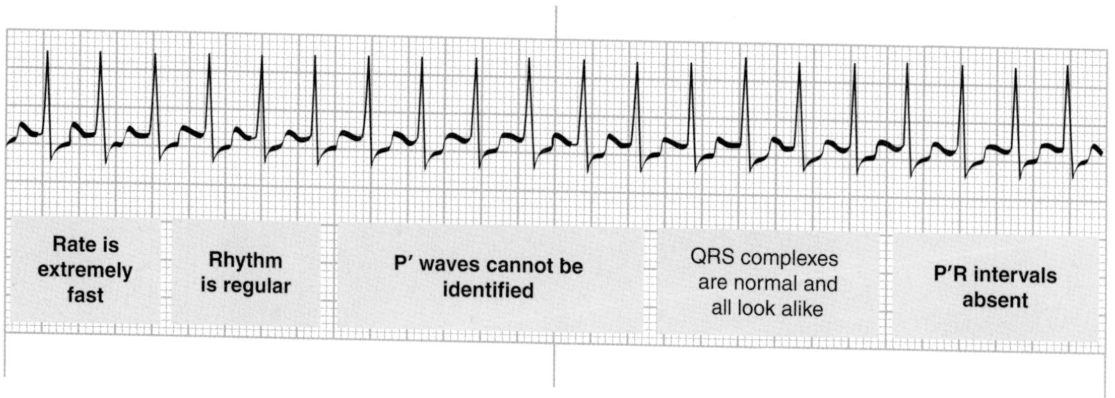

Figure 9-10
The term supraventricular tachycardia is used when the rate is so fast you cannot determine whether or not P′ waves are present.

Supraventricular Tachycardia

INSTRUCTIONAL MOMENT
Sometimes with supraventricular tachycardia we see QRS complexes that appear wide. This is due to an intraventricular conduction defect or other condition such as aberrant conduction. This makes the assessment of supraventricular tachycardia difficult as it appears to be ventricular tachycardia. This is called wide complex tachycardia of unknown origin.

In very fast rates with narrow QRS complexes, it may be difficult to determine whether the tachycardia arises from the atria or AV junction (Figure 9-10) because the P′ waves are often buried in the T wave of the preceding beat. We describe these as **supraventricular** tachycardia (SVT) meaning that it is arising from above the ventricles. This group of tachycardias includes paroxysmal supraventricular tachycardia (PSVT), nonparoxysmal atrial tachycardia, multifocal atrial tachycardia, and junctional tachycardia. Distinguishing among these tachycardias is often difficult as the ventricular rate is so fast it is hard to tell if there are P′ waves or P′R intervals.

Determining whether a rapid dysrhythmia with narrow QRS complex tachycardia is arising from the ______________ or ______________ may be difficult because the P′ waves are often buried in the ______________ wave of the preceding beat. In these cases we refer to them as ______________ tachycardia.

[atria] [AV junction] [T] [supraventricular]

KEY CONCEPT
Supraventricular is a term used to describe a tachycardia that arises from above the ventricles but is so fast that you cannot determine if the site of origin is in the atria or AV junction.

Atrial Flutter

Atrial flutter is a rapid depolarization of a single focus in the atria at a rate of 250 to 350 beats per minute (Figure 9-11). It results from circus reentry, a condition during which the impulse from the SA node circles back through the intranodal pathways and restimulates the AV node over and over. Another cause is increased automaticity. On the ECG, the P

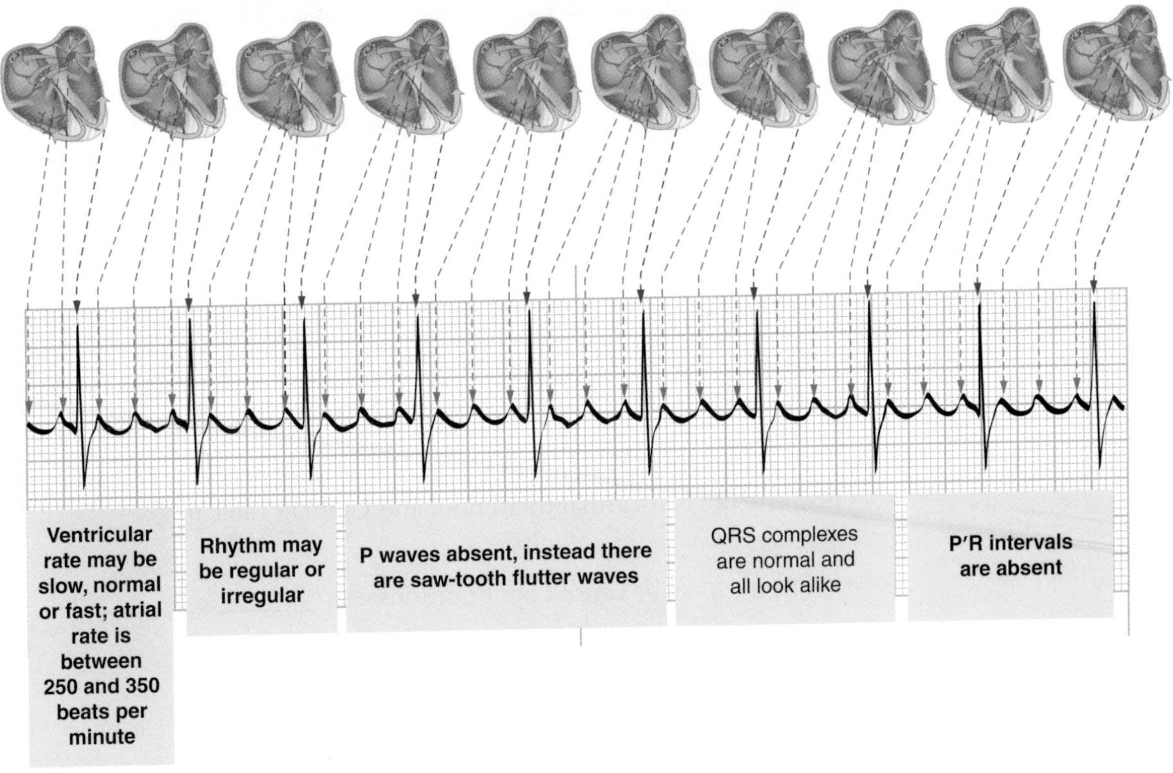

Figure 9-11
Atrial flutter.

waves lose their distinction due to the rapid atrial rate. The waves blend together in a saw-tooth or picket fence pattern. They are called **flutter** waves, or F waves.

Atrial flutter is the result of the ________________ depolarization of a single focus in the atria at a rate of ________________ beats per minute. It originates from ________________ reentry and possibly increased ________________. The atrial waveforms called ________________ waves, or F waves, associated with atrial flutter blend together in a ________________ pattern.

[rapid] [250 to 350] [circus] [automaticity] [flutter] [saw-tooth]

While atrial flutter occasionally occurs in patients with healthy hearts, it is usually caused by conditions that enlarge the atria and elevate atrial pressures. It is commonly seen in patients with severe mitral valve disease, hyperthyroid disease, pericardial disease, and primary myocardial disease.

Table 9-3 Atrial Flutter

Causes of atrial flutter	Examples
Cardiac disorders	Conditions that enlarge atrial tissue and elevate atrial pressures, following cardiac surgery, severe mitral valve disease, cardiomyopathy, pericarditis, myocarditis, hypertrophy, CHF, acute infarction
Others	COPD, hypoxia, digitalis toxicity, hyperthyroidism, infection, catecholamine release during exercise; may also occur in healthy people who use coffee, alcohol, or cigarettes to an excess or who are fatigued and under stress

It is sometimes encountered in patients after surgery or in patients with hypoxia, acute myocardial infarction, and COPD (Table 9-3).

Atrial flutter may be caused by conditions that _______________ the atria and _______________ atrial pressures.

[enlarge] [elevate]

Atrial flutter is often well tolerated. However, the number of impulses conducted through the AV node, as expressed as the conduction ratio, determines the ventricular rate. Slower ventricular rates (fewer than 40 beats per minute) or faster ventricular rates (greater than 150 beats per minute) can seriously compromise cardiac output. For example, a conduction ratio of 2:1 (atrial to ventricular beats) produces a rapid ventricular rate. This may result in loss of atrial kick, decreased ventricular filling time, and decreased coronary artery perfusion leading to angina, heart failure, pulmonary edema, hypotension, and syncope.

Review of key characteristics associated with atrial flutter

Rate:	Ventricular rate may be slow, normal, or fast; atrial rate is between 250 and 350 beats per minute
Regularity:	May be regular or irregular (depending on whether the conduction ratio stays the same or varies)
P waves:	Absent, instead there are flutter waves; the ratio of atrial waveforms to QRS complexes may be 2:1, 3:1, or 4:1. An atrial to ventricular conduction ratio of 1:1 is rare
QRS complexes:	Normal
PR interval	Not measurable
QT interval	Not measurable

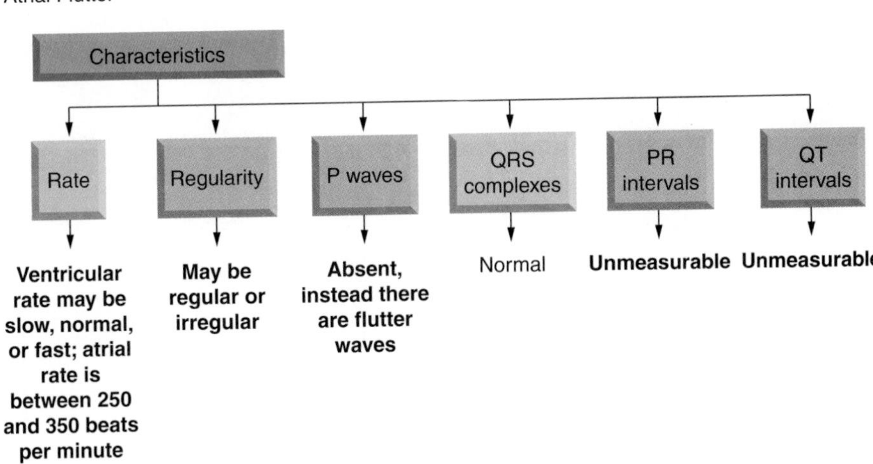

Figure 9-12
Algorithm for atrial flutter.

The key feature of atrial flutter is the presence of saw-tooth flutter waves. These flutter waves correspond to the rapid atrial rate of 250 to 350 beats per minute. The atrial rhythm is regular, and depending on conduction ratio, the ventricular rhythm may be regular or irregular. The ventricular rate depends on ventricular response; it may be normal, slow, or fast. A 1:1 atrial-ventricular conduction is rare; it is usually 2:1, 3:1, or 4:1. The PR interval is not measurable. QRS complexes are usually normal (Figure 9-12).

KEY CONCEPT
Atrial flutter arises from a single focus in the atria at a rate of 250 to 350 beats per minute.

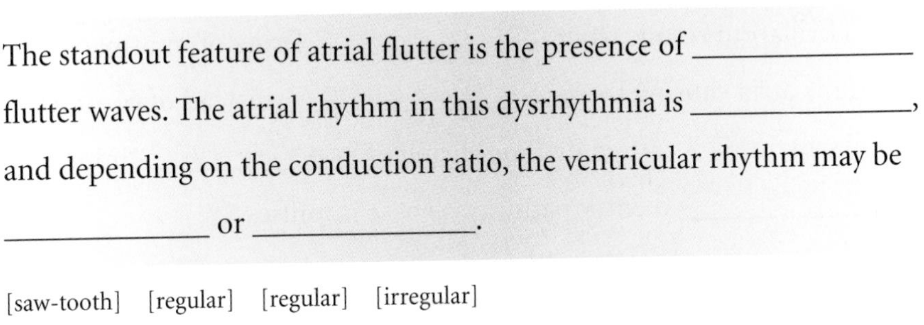

The standout feature of atrial flutter is the presence of ____________ flutter waves. The atrial rhythm in this dysrhythmia is ____________, and depending on the conduction ratio, the ventricular rhythm may be ____________ or ____________.

[saw-tooth] [regular] [regular] [irregular]

 Atrial Fibrillation

Atrial fibrillation occurs when there is chaotic, asynchronous firing of multiple areas within the atria (Figure 9-13). This completely suppresses normal SA node output and causes the atria to quiver instead of contract. Atrial fibrillation stems from the rapid firing of ectopic impulses (greater than 350 beats per minute) in circus reentry pathways. These impulses bombard the AV node but are only conducted to the ventricles in an irregular and sporadic fashion.

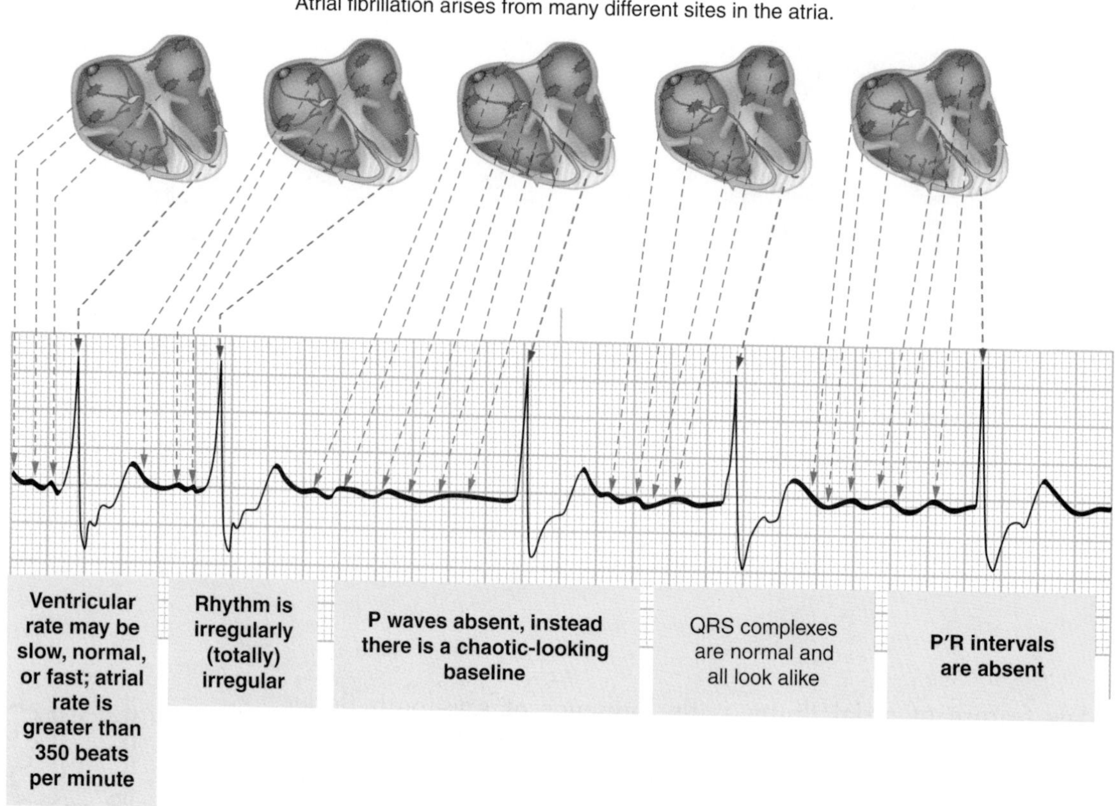

Figure 9-13
Atrial fibrillation.

Atrial fibrillation results from ______________ firing of multiple areas within the atria causing them to ______________ instead of contract. This dysrhythmia is caused by rapid firing of ______________ impulses in ______________ reentry pathways. These impulses ______________ the AV node but are only conducted to the ventricles in an ______________ and ______________ fashion.

[chaotic] [quiver] [ectopic] [circus] [bombard] [irregular] [sporadic]

As with atrial flutter, atrial fibrillation leads to a loss of the atrial kick. This decreases ventricular filling by up to 30%. Patients experiencing atrial fibrillation may develop intra atrial emboli as the atria are not contracting and blood stagnates in the atrial chambers forming a

Table 9-4 Atrial Fibrillation

Causes of atrial fibrillation	Examples
Cardiac disorders	Following cardiac surgery, mitral regurgitation, mitral stenosis, chronic coronary artery disease, myocardial infarction, pericarditis, atrial septal defects, pulmonary embolism
Use of certain drugs	Digitalis toxicity, aminophylline
Increased vagal tone	Valsalva's maneuver, carotid sinus massage, vomiting
Others	Hypoxia, hyperthyroidism, infection, catecholamine release during exercise; may also occur in healthy people who use coffee, alcohol, or cigarettes to excess or who are fatigued and under stress

thrombus (clot). This predisposes the patient to systemic emboli—particularly stroke. A ventricular response within the normal rate (60 to 100 beats per minute) is often well-tolerated, whereas a fast ventricular response can result in decreased cardiac output that leads to heart failure, angina, or syncope. Patients who have preexisting heart disease, such as hypertrophic obstructive cardiomyopathy, mitral stenosis, rheumatic heart disease, and mitral prosthetic valves, are less tolerant of atrial fibrillation and may experience shock and severe heart failure.

Atrial fibrillation is more common than atrial tachycardia or atrial flutter. It can occur in healthy persons after excessive caffeine, alcohol, or tobacco ingestion or because of fatigue and acute stress. It can also be caused by the catecholamines released during exercise. Atrial fibrillation may also be seen with other conditions including rheumatic heart disease, CHF (atrial dilation), and atherosclerotic heart disease. Less commonly, atrial fibrillation may occur with cardiomyopathy, acute myocarditis and pericarditis, and chest trauma. It is rarely caused by digitalis toxicity, but a very slow, regular ventricular response with atrial fibrillation should raise suspicion of digitalis toxicity (Table 9-4).

INSTRUCTIONAL MOMENT
An irregularly irregular supraventricular rhythm is atrial fibrillation until proven otherwise.

Patients experiencing atrial fibrillation may develop an intraatrial ______________ as the atria are not contracting and blood ______________ in the atrial chambers. Atrial fibrillation is more common than atrial ______________ or atrial ______________.

[thrombus] [stagnates] [tachycardia] [flutter]

Review of key characteristics associated with atrial fibrillation

Rate:	Ventricular rate may be slow, normal, or fast; atrial rate is greater than 350 beats per minute
Regularity:	Totally (chaotically) irregular
P waves:	Absent, instead there is a chaotic-looking baseline
QRS complexes:	Normal
PR interval:	Absent
QT interval:	Unmeasurable

KEY CONCEPT
Atrial fibrillation occurs when there is rapid, chaotic firing of ectopic impulses (greater than 350 beats per minute) in the atria.

The standout feature in atrial fibrillation is a totally (grossly) irregular rhythm (also referred to as irregularly irregular). Another key characteristic is there are no discernible P waves. Instead, a chaotic baseline of **fibrillatory** waves, or f waves, represents the atrial activity. The absence of discernable P waves occurs because the atria are firing so rapidly (greater than 350 beats per minute). The ventricular rate depends on how many impulses bombarding the AV node are conducted through to the ventricles. It may be normal, slow, or fast. There are no PR intervals present because of the absence of P waves. The QRS complexes are usually normal (Figure 9-14).

QUESTION
"Why is the appearance of the atrial waveforms in atrial flutter constant in atrial flutter and not in atrial fibrillation?" (The answer can be found on page 297.)

The key characteristics in atrial fibrillation are a ________________ irregular rhythm and a ________________ baseline of ________________ waves that represents the atrial activity.

[totally] [chaotic] [fibrillatory]

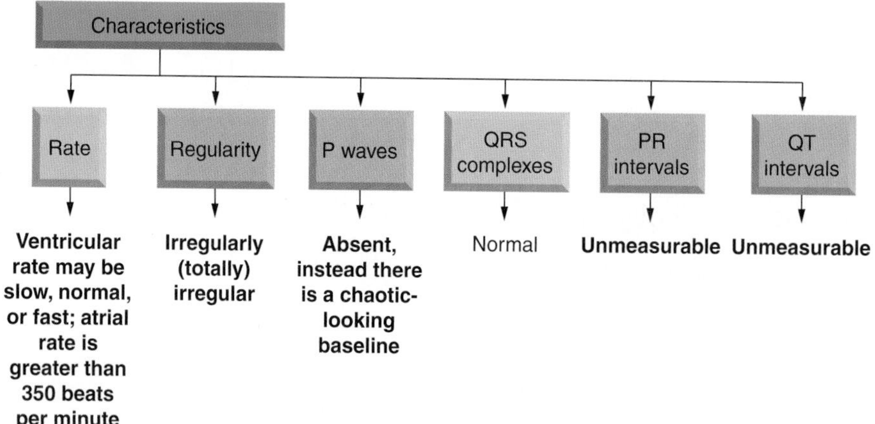

Figure 9-14
Algorithm for atrial fibrillation.

You can practice interpreting atrial dysrhythmias with the following *Practice Makes Perfect* exercises. Answers to these exercises can be found in Appendix A.

PRACTICE. . . MAKES PERFECT

1.

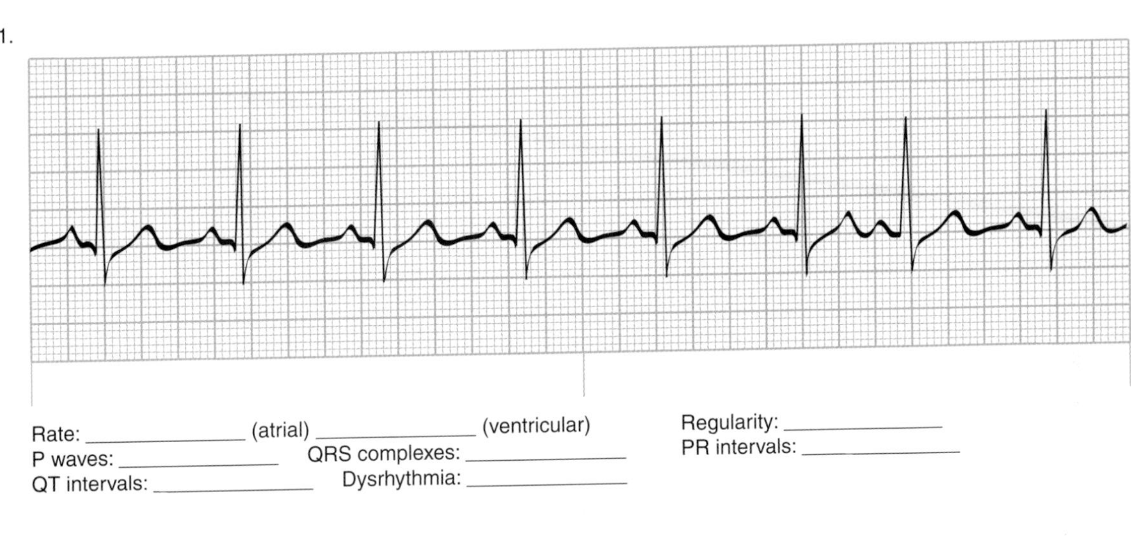

Rate: ______________ (atrial) ______________ (ventricular)
Regularity: ______________
P waves: ______________
QRS complexes: ______________
PR intervals: ______________
QT intervals: ______________
Dysrhythmia: ______________

2.

Rate: ______________ (atrial) ______________ (ventricular)
Regularity: ______________
P waves: ______________
QRS complexes: ______________
PR intervals: ______________
QT intervals: ______________
Dysrhythmia: ______________

PRACTICE. . . MAKES PERFECT

3.

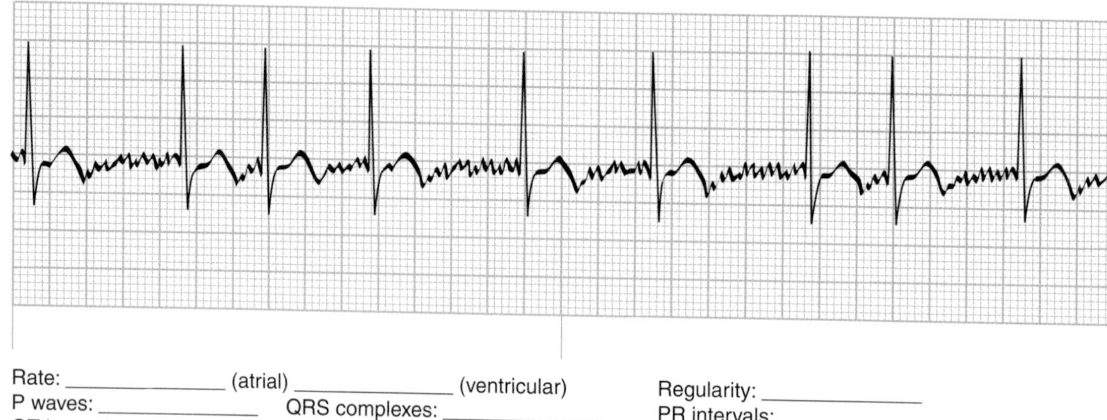

Rate: ______________ (atrial) ______________ (ventricular)
P waves: ______________
QRS complexes: ______________
QT intervals: ______________
Dysrhythmia: ______________
Regularity: ______________
PR intervals: ______________

4.

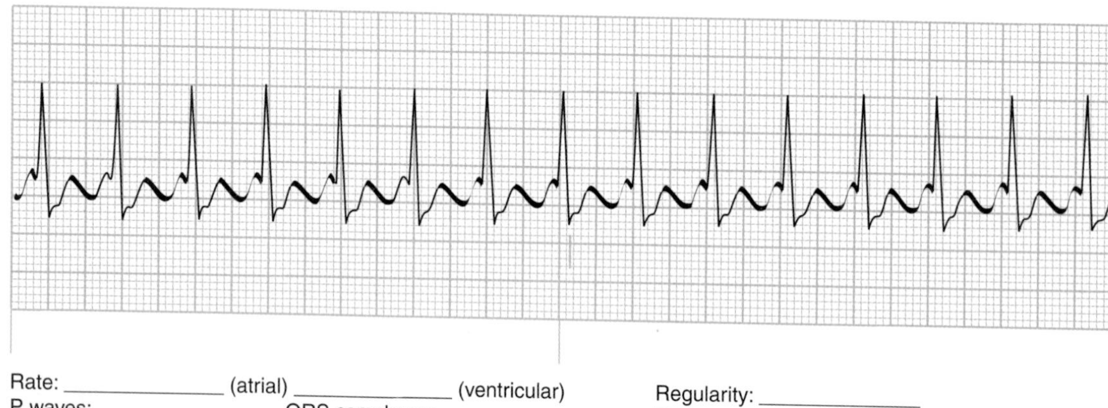

Rate: ______________ (atrial) ______________ (ventricular)
P waves: ______________
QRS complexes: ______________
QT intervals: ______________
Dysrhythmia: ______________
Regularity: ______________
PR intervals: ______________

5.

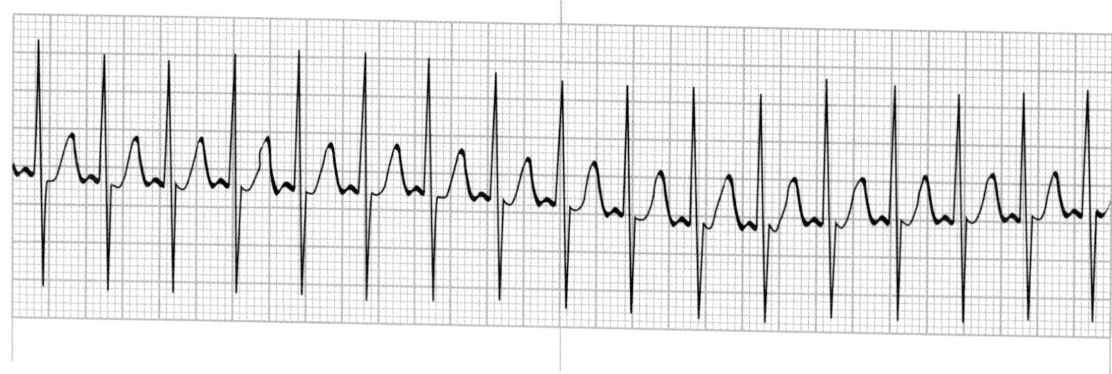

Rate: ______________ (atrial) ______________ (ventricular)
P waves: ______________
QRS complexes: ______________
QT intervals: ______________
Dysrhythmia: ______________
Regularity: ______________
PR intervals: ______________

PRACTICE. . . MAKES PERFECT

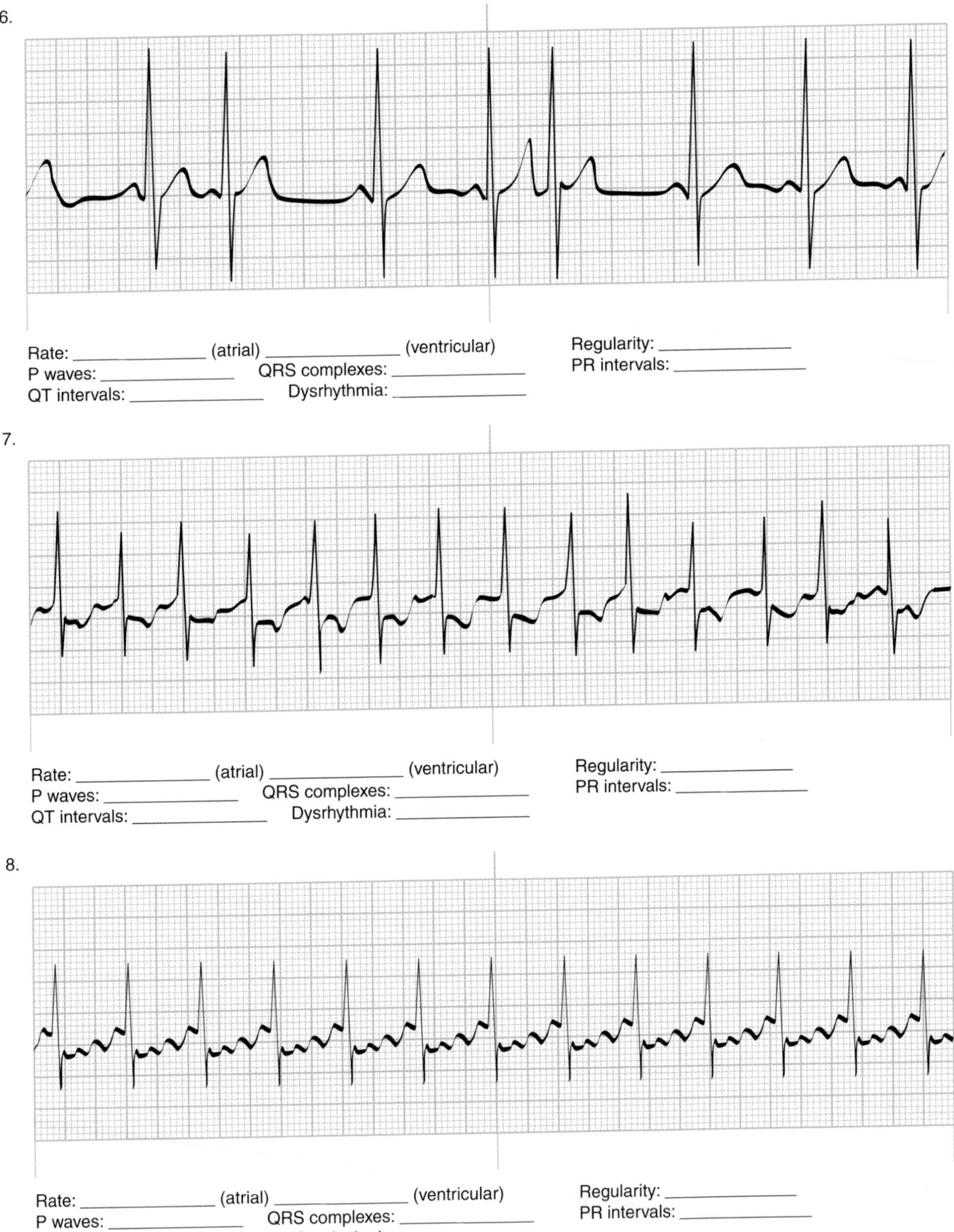

6.

Rate: ______________ (atrial) ______________ (ventricular)
Regularity: ______________
P waves: ______________
QRS complexes: ______________
PR intervals: ______________
QT intervals: ______________
Dysrhythmia: ______________

7.

Rate: ______________ (atrial) ______________ (ventricular)
Regularity: ______________
P waves: ______________
QRS complexes: ______________
PR intervals: ______________
QT intervals: ______________
Dysrhythmia: ______________

8.

Rate: ______________ (atrial) ______________ (ventricular)
Regularity: ______________
P waves: ______________
QRS complexes: ______________
PR intervals: ______________
QT intervals: ______________
Dysrhythmia: ______________

PRACTICE. . . MAKES PERFECT

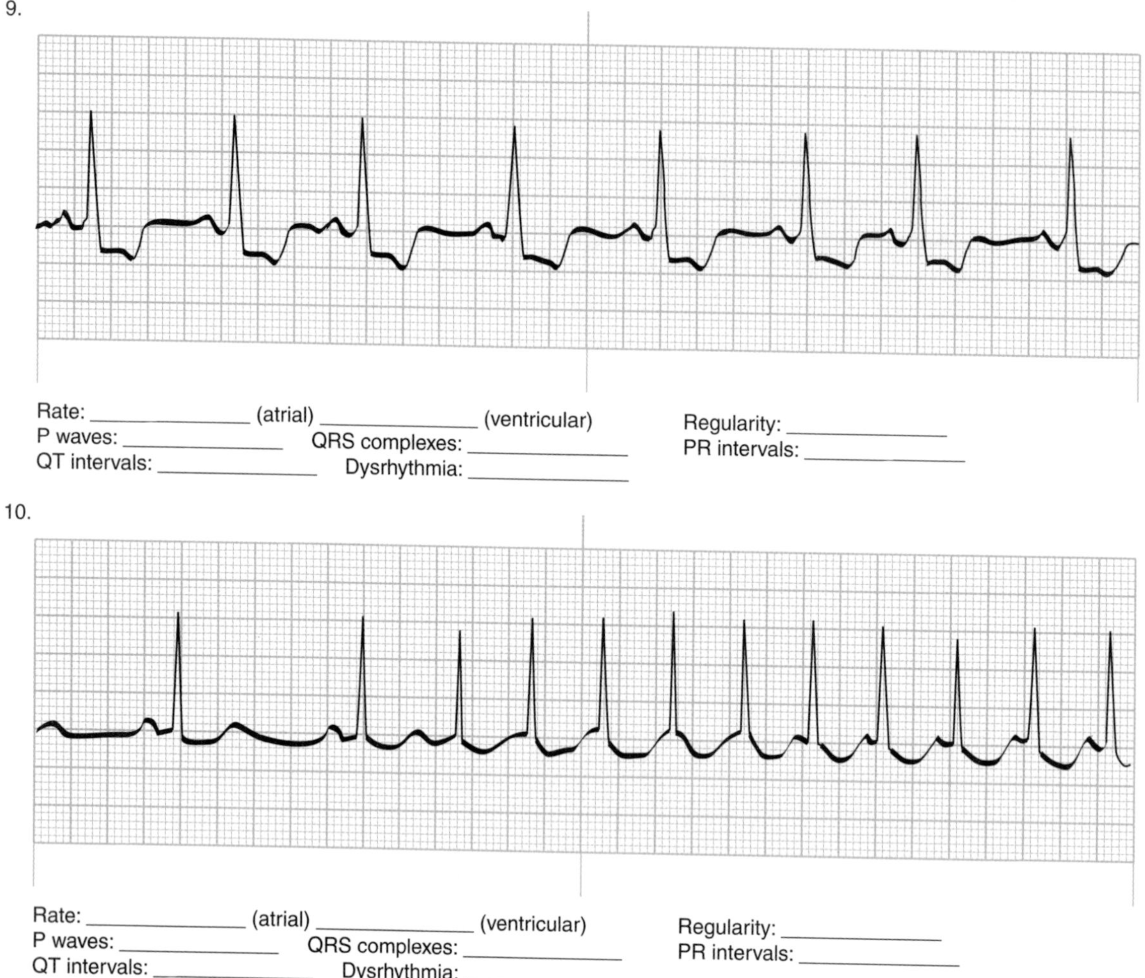

You can practice interpreting sinus node dysrhythmias (as discussed in Chapter 8) with the following *Practice Makes Perfect* exercises. Answers to these exercises can be found in Appendix A.

PRACTICE. . . MAKES PERFECT

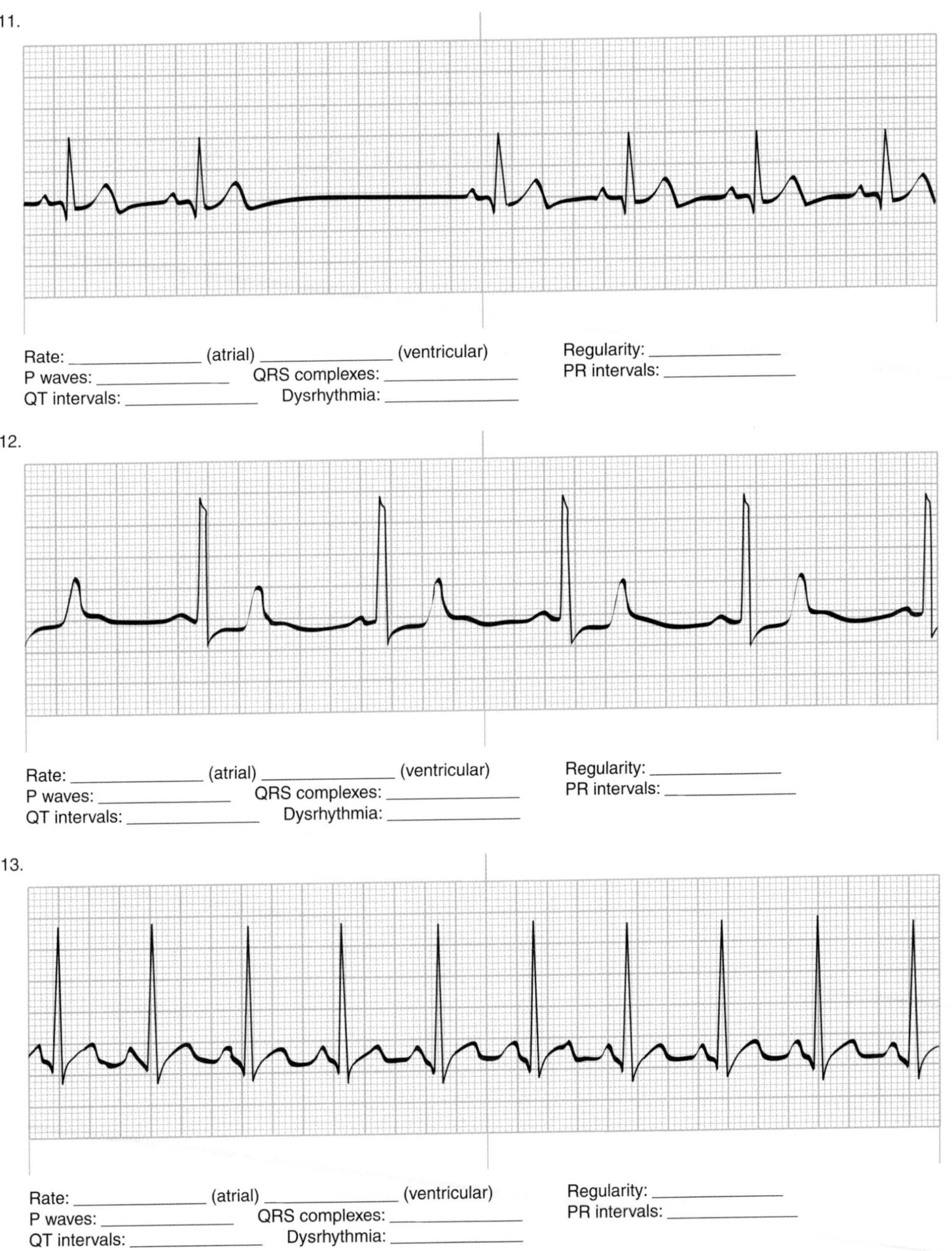

11.

Rate: ______________ (atrial) ______________ (ventricular) Regularity: ______________
P waves: ______________ QRS complexes: ______________ PR intervals: ______________
QT intervals: ______________ Dysrhythmia: ______________

12.

Rate: ______________ (atrial) ______________ (ventricular) Regularity: ______________
P waves: ______________ QRS complexes: ______________ PR intervals: ______________
QT intervals: ______________ Dysrhythmia: ______________

13.

Rate: ______________ (atrial) ______________ (ventricular) Regularity: ______________
P waves: ______________ QRS complexes: ______________ PR intervals: ______________
QT intervals: ______________ Dysrhythmia: ______________

PRACTICE. . . MAKES PERFECT

14.

Rate: _______________ (atrial) _______________ (ventricular) Regularity: _______________
P waves: _______________ QRS complexes: _______________ PR intervals: _______________
QT intervals: _______________ Dysrhythmia: _______________

15.

Rate: _______________ (atrial) _______________ (ventricular) Regularity: _______________
P waves: _______________ QRS complexes: _______________ PR intervals: _______________
QT intervals: _______________ Dysrhythmia: _______________

Key Points

- Dysrhythmias originating outside the SA node in the atrial tissue or in the internodal pathways are called atrial dysrhythmias.
- Three mechanisms responsible for atrial dysrhythmias are increased automaticity, triggered activity, and reentry.
- Key characteristics for atrial dysrhythmias are P′ waves (if present) that differ in appearance from normal sinus P waves; abnormal, shortened, or prolonged P′R intervals; and QRS complexes that appear narrow and normal (unless there is an intraventricular conduction defect, aberrancy, or preexcitation).
- Wandering atrial pacemaker is a rhythm in which the pacemaker site shifts between the SA node, atria, and/or AV junction producing its most characteristic features, P′ waves that change in appearance and a rhythm that varies slightly.
- Premature atrial complexes (PACs) are early ectopic beats that originate outside the SA node.
- PACs produce an irregularity in the rhythm where the P′-P and R′-R intervals are shorter than the P-P and R-R intervals of the underlying rhythm. The P′ waves should be an upright (in lead II) preceding the QRS complex but will have a different morphology (appearance) than the P waves in the underlying rhythm.
- Atrial tachycardia is a rapid dysrhythmia (having a rate of 150 to 250 beats per minute) that arises from the atria. It is so fast that it overrides the SA node.
- When the onset of the atrial tachycardia is sudden (and typically witnessed), it is called paroxysmal.
- Atrial tachycardia is regular unless you see the onset or termination, as with paroxysmal atrial tachycardia, and there is one P′ wave preceding each QRS complex, although it is typically buried in the T wave of the preceding beat.
- Multifocal atrial tachycardia (MAT) is a pathological condition that presents with the same characteristics as wandering atrial pacemaker but has heart rates in the 120 to 150 beats per minute range.
- Supraventricular tachycardia arises from above the ventricles but cannot be definitively identified as atrial or junctional because the P′ waves cannot be seen with any real degree of certainty.
- Supraventricular tachycardias include paroxysmal supraventricular tachycardia, (PSVT), nonparoxysmal atrial tachycardia, and multifocal atrial tachycardia (MAT).
- Atrial flutter is a rapid depolarization of a single focus in the atria at a rate of 250 to 350 beats per minute.
- Atrial flutter produces atrial waveforms that have a characteristic saw-tooth or picket fence appearance. They are called flutter waves, or F waves.
- Atrial fibrillation occurs when there is chaotic, asynchronous firing of multiple areas within the atria. It stems from the rapid firing of ectopic impulses (greater than 350 beats per minute) in circus reentry pathways.
- Atrial fibrillation is a totally (grossly) irregular rhythm in which there are no discernible P waves. Instead, a chaotic baseline of fibrillatory waves or f waves represents the atrial activity.

Assess Your Understanding

The following questions give you a chance to assess your understanding of the material discussed in this chapter. The answers can be found in Appendix A.

1. With atrial dysrhythmias, the
   a. atrial waveforms differ in appearance from normal sinus P waves.
   b. P′R intervals are almost always prolonged.
   c. QRS complexes are wider than normal.
   d. site of origin is in the bundle of His.
2. In wandering atrial pacemaker, the pacemaker site shifts between the SA node, atria, and/or
   a. Purkinje fibers.
   b. ventricles.
   c. AV junction.
   d. bundle of His.
3. Your patient is a 67-year-old female with a history of cardiac problems. After attaching her to the monitor, you see a slightly irregular rhythm with normal QRS complexes, but each P′ wave is different. This rhythm is
   a. frequent PACs.
   b. sinus arrest.
   c. sinus dysrhythmia.
   d. wandering atrial pacemaker.
4. Premature atrial complexes
   a. are typically preceded by an inverted P′ wave.
   b. are followed by a compensatory pause.
   c. have a wide and bizarre QRS complex.
   d. may have normal P′R intervals.
5. A PAC arises earlier in the cardiac cycle and will interrupt the regularity of the underlying rhythm.
   a. True
   b. False
6. The heart rate characteristic of atrial tachycardia is ________ beats per minute.
   a. 60 to 100
   b. 100 to 150
   c. 150 to 250
   d. 300 to 350
7. The QRS complexes seen with atrial tachycardia are normally ________ seconds in duration.
   a. 0.06 to 0.12
   b. 0.10 to 0.20
   c. 0.12 to 0.20
   d. 0.20 to 0.24
8. With multifocal atrial tachycardia, the
   a. P′ waves have the same morphology from beat to beat.
   b. heart rate is 120 to 150 beats per minute.
   c. QRS complexes are usually greater than 0.12 seconds.
   d. Both b and c.
9. Which of the following rhythms has a characteristic saw-tooth pattern?
   a. Sinus dysrhythmia.
   b. Ventricular flutter.
   c. Atrial flutter.
   d. Atrial tachycardia.
10. Atrial flutter has an atrial rate of ________ beats per minute.
    a. between 40 and 60
    b. between 100 and 150
    c. between 250 and 350
    d. greater than 350
11. Atrial fibrillation has
    a. a regular rhythm.
    b. an atrial rate of between 250 and 350 beats per minute.
    c. normal QRS complexes.
    d. a PR intervals of greater than 0.20 seconds.

12. The atrial waveforms associated with atrial fibrillation are ______________ and the PR intervals are ______________.
    a. referred to as saw toothed; variable
    b. indiscernible; nonexistent
    c. inverted; less than 0.12 seconds
    d. dissociated; between 0.12 and 0.20 seconds

13. Which of the following dysrhythmias is totally irregular?
    a. Sinus bradycardia.
    b. 3rd-degree AV heart block.
    c. Ventricular tachycardia.
    d. Atrial fibrillation.

14. Atrial fibrillation has an atrial rate of ______ beats per minute.
    a. between 40 and 60
    b. between 100 and 150
    c. between 250 and 350
    d. greater than 350

Referring to the scenario at the beginning of this chapter answer the following questions.

15. What rhythm is the patient in?
    a. Accelerated junctional.
    b. Atrial fibrillation.
    c. Atrial flutter.
    d. Ventricular tachycardia.

16. The patient passed out because of a decrease in his
    a. diastolic blood pressure.
    b. cardiac output.
    c. epinephrine levels.
    d. heart rate.

17. The formula for cardiac output is
    a. heart rate × systolic blood pressure.
    b. systolic blood pressure − diastolic blood pressure.
    c. stroke volume × heart rate.
    d. heart rate × respiratory rate.

Answers to Sidebar Questions

"What would you expect the appearance of the P waves to be if they originate from one site?"

Answer: They appear the same from beat to beat.

"Why is it important to check for a pulse when there are premature beats in the rhythm?"

Answer: We check for a pulse in rhythms that have premature beats to determine if they are perfusing beats. Typically, PACs produce a pulse but premature beats that arise from the ventricles may not. You can detect this by watching the ECG in the dynamic mode while simultaneously feeling for a pulse.

"What is the heart rate associated with sinus tachycardia?"

Answer: The heart rate associated with sinus tachycardia is 100 to 160 beats per minute.

"Why is the appearance of the atrial waveforms in atrial flutter constant in atrial flutter and not in atrial fibrillation?"

Answer: The origin of the atrial impulse with atrial flutter is constant, thus the consistent appearance of the F waves. Remember that with atrial fibrillation the site of the atrial impulse is not consistent resulting in irregularly shaped f waves and a chaotic baseline.

On the DVD

- Approach to Atrial Dysrhythmias.

Origin and Clinical Aspects of Junctional Dysrhythmias

10

Case History

A 48-year-old woman presents to the urgent care center complaining of a rapid heart rate. She tells the triage nurse that she has had this before and the condition is called paroxysmal supraventricular tachycardia (PSVT). The patient is quickly taken back to the exam room and the physician is summoned. Her vital signs are normal except for a pulse rate of 180 beats per minute. When the physician enters the exam room the woman states that she has had this before but usually it goes away if she performs vagal maneuvers such as bearing down and holding her breath. But that today it is not working. The physician orders a 12-lead ECG, which he then examines while the nurse establishes an IV. The physician notes that the patient's heart rate is fast and the rhythm is regular with narrow QRS complexes. He is unable to distinguish discernable P waves because of the fast rate. The nurse administers a medication to slow the heart rate. Within seconds the patient's rhythm converts to normal sinus rhythm.

After further questioning, the physician determines that the woman has not been compliant with her medications and she continues to smoke and drink a lot of caffeinated beverages, all of which have contributed to the return of her dysrhythmia. He schedules her an appointment with her family physician and refills her medication of beta-blockers. He encourages her to remove nicotine and caffeine from her life.

Chapter Preview

- Dysrhythmias Originating in the AV Junction
- Premature Junctional Complex (PJC)
- Junctional Escape Rhythm
- Accelerated Junctional Rhythm
- Junctional Tachycardia

Dysrhythmias Originating in the AV Junction

QUESTION
"What would you expect the appearance of the P′ waves to be if they originate from the AV junction?" (The answer can be found on page 323.)

CLINICAL MOMENT
Retrograde depolarization is the backward conveyance of an electrical impulse originating in the AV junction or ventricles. It travels backward to the atria causing atrial depolarization. This is abnormal conduction.

KEY CONCEPT
As with sinus dysrhythmias and atrial dysrhythmias, the QRS complexes in junctional dysrhythmias appear normal (unless there is intraventricular conduction defect or aberrancy).

KEY CONCEPT
Junctional rhythms originate in the AV junction, the area around the AV node and the bundle of His.

Rhythms that originate in the AV junction, the area around the AV node and the bundle of His, are referred to as junctional rhythms. These usually result when the SA node is suppressed and fails to generate electrical impulses or there is a block in conduction. The most common causes are hypoxia, ischemia, myocardial infarction, and drug toxicity (such as digitalis preparations). In these cases, the next lower pacemaker (the AV junction) takes over.

The AV junction is located in the middle of the heart, therefore the impulse travels upward and causes backward or retrograde depolarization of the atria (Figure 10-1). This results in an inverted P′ wave (when they would otherwise be upright) with a short P′R interval (less than 0.12 seconds in duration). At the same time, the impulse travels down to the ventricles and depolarizes them. Alternatively, the P′ wave may be absent (if it is buried in the QRS complex), or it may follow the QRS complex. If the P′ wave is buried in the QRS complex it can change the morphology of the QRS complex.

In junctional rhythms, the atria are depolarized in an abnormal way while the ventricles depolarize normally. Electrical impulses travel in a normal pathway from the AV junction through the bundle of His and bundle branches to the Purkinje fibers, ending in the ventricular muscle. This results in the QRS complexes usually being within normal limits of 0.06 to 0.12 seconds.

Junctional rhythms originate in the __________ junctional area and the bundle of __________. Dysrhythmias arising from this area of the heart travel upward and cause __________ depolarization of the __________. This leads to __________ P′ waves with a __________ P′R interval, absent P′ waves, or P′ waves that follow the QRS complex. If present, the P′R intervals are usually __________ than 0.12 seconds in duration. The QRS complexes are usually within normal limits of __________ seconds.

[AV] [His] [retrograde] [atria] [inverted] [short] [less] [0.06 to 0.12]

When we refer to the P waves as being normal, we mean they appear as an upright and round waveform. There is one P wave preceding each QRS complex. Its amplitude is 0.5 to 2.5 mm in height and its duration is 0.06 to 0.10 seconds. In leads I, II, aV_F, and V_2 through V_6, the deflection of the P wave is characteristically upright or positive. In leads III, aV_L, and V_1, the P wave is usually upright but may be negative or biphasic (both positive and negative). In lead aV_R, the P wave is negative or inverted.

When we refer to QRS complexes as being normal we are saying they are narrow (0.06 to 0.12 seconds in duration) and normal looking. In leads I, II, III,

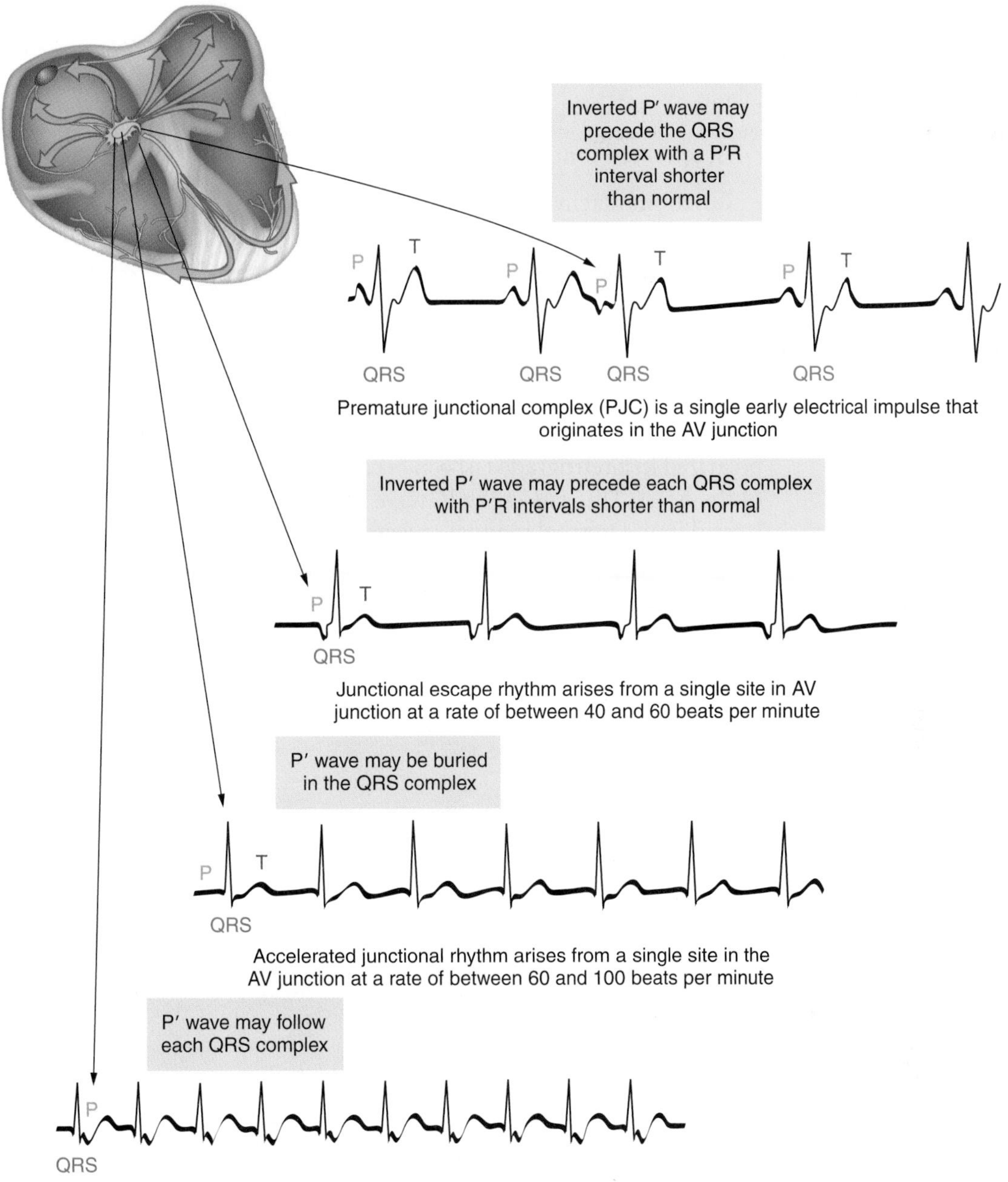

Figure 10-1
Junctional dysrhythmias originate from the AV junction and may have inverted P waves which precede, occur during, or follow the QRS complexes.

aV_L, aV_F, and V_4 to V_6, the deflection of the QRS complex is characteristically positive or upright. In leads aV_R and V_1 to V_3, the QRS complex is usually negative or inverted. Leads III, aV_L, and V_2 to V_4 may also be biphasic. Further, in any dysrhythmia where the QRS complexes should be normal they can instead be wide or unusual looking if there is intraventricular conduction defect, aberrancy, or ventricular preexcitation.

CLINICAL MOMENT
Like atrial dysrhythmias, aberrant conduction may also occur with dysrhythmias that originate from the AV junction.

CLINICAL MOMENT
All dysrhythmias arising from the AV junction or atria can also be collectively called supraventricular dysrhythmias.

Junctional dysrhythmias include:

- Premature junctional complex (PJC)
- Junctional escape complexes or rhythms
- Accelerated junctional rhythm
- Junctional tachycardia

Premature Junctional Complex (PJC)

A premature junctional complex (PJC) is a single early electrical impulse that originates in the AV junction (Figure 10-2). It occurs before the next expected sinus impulse, causing an irregularity in the rhythm. PJCs are thought to result from enhanced automaticity or a reentry mechanism. The atria are depolarized in a retrograde fashion because the impulse arises from the middle of the heart. This causes the P′ wave to be inverted. The ventricles are depolarized in the normal manner (measuring 0.06 to 0.12 seconds in duration).

A premature junctional complex (PJC) is an early electrical impulse that originates in the ___________ junction. ___________ automaticity or a ___________ mechanism is the likely cause of PJCs.

[AV] [Enhanced] [reentry]

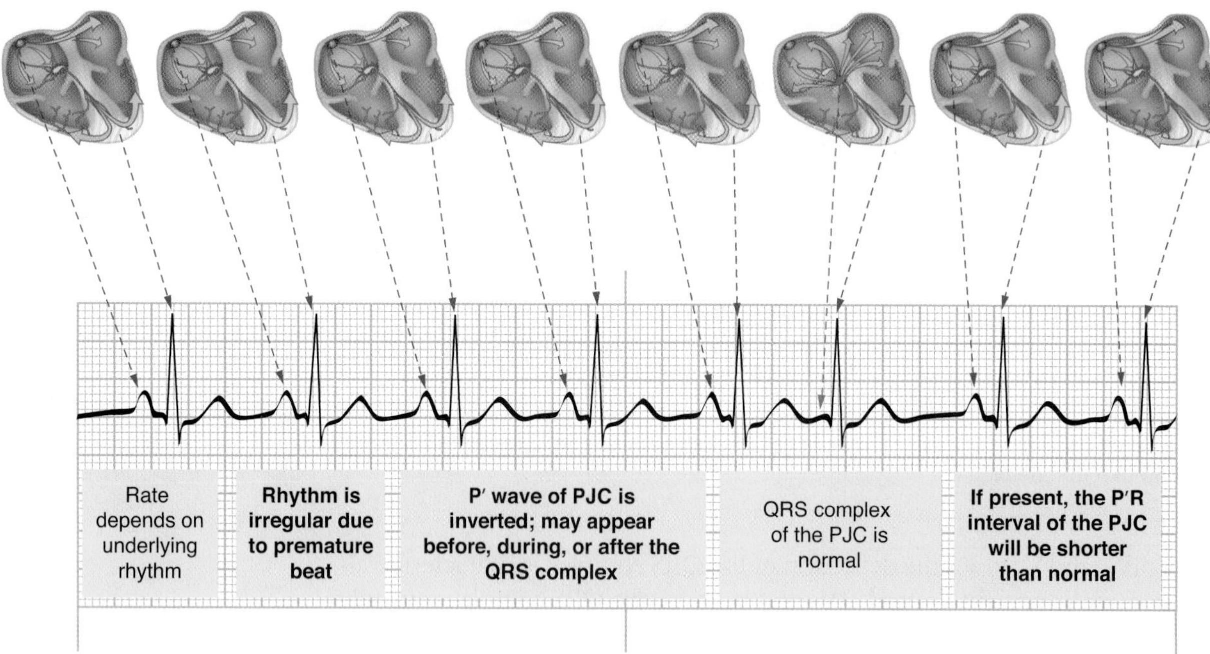

Figure 10-2
Premature junctional complex (PJC).

Causes of PJC include toxic levels of digoxin, excessive caffeine intake, inferior wall myocardial infarction, rheumatic heart disease, or swelling of the AV junction after heart surgery (Table 10-1).

In the healthy heart, isolated PJCs are of little clinical significance. However, frequent PJCs (more than 4 to 6 per minute) warn of more serious conditions.

The patient may be asymptomatic or may experience palpitations. Your assessment will likely reveal the presence of an irregular pulse. Frequent PJCs may cause the patient to experience hypotension due to a transient decrease in cardiac output.

QUESTION

"Can impulses arise from the AV node?" (The answer can be found on page 323.)

INSTRUCTIONAL MOMENT

Be sure to check for a pulse in rhythms that have premature beats to determine if they are perfusing beats. Typically, PJCs produce a pulse but premature beats that arise from the ventricles may not. You can detect this by watching the ECG in the dynamic mode while feeling for a pulse.

Review of key characteristics associated with PJCs

Rate:	Depends on the underlying rhythm
Regularity:	May be occasionally irregular or frequently irregular (depends on the number of PJCs present)
P waves:	Inverted—may immediately precede, occur during (absent), or follow the QRS complex
QRS complexes:	Normal
PR interval:	Will be shorter than normal if the P′ wave precedes the QRS complex, absent if the P′ wave is buried in the QRS, and it is referred to as the RP′ interval if the P′ wave follows the QRS complex
QT interval:	Usually within normal limits

When looking at the ECG rhythm, PJCs appear as "early beats." This causes the R-R interval to be shorter between the preceding beat and the early beat (as compared to the underlying rhythm).

Table 10-1 Premature Junctional Complexes

Causes of PJCs	Examples
Cardiac disorders	Ischemia, acute myocardial infarction, damage to the AV junction, congestive heart failure, valvular disease, rheumatic heart disease, swelling of the AV junction after heart surgery
Use of certain drugs	Digitalis toxicity, other cardiac medications (quinidine, procainamide), sympathomimetic drugs (cocaine, methamphetamine)
Other	Excessive caffeine, tobacco, or alcohol intake; increased vagal tone on the SA node; hypoxia; electrolyte imbalance (particularly magnesium and potassium); exercise

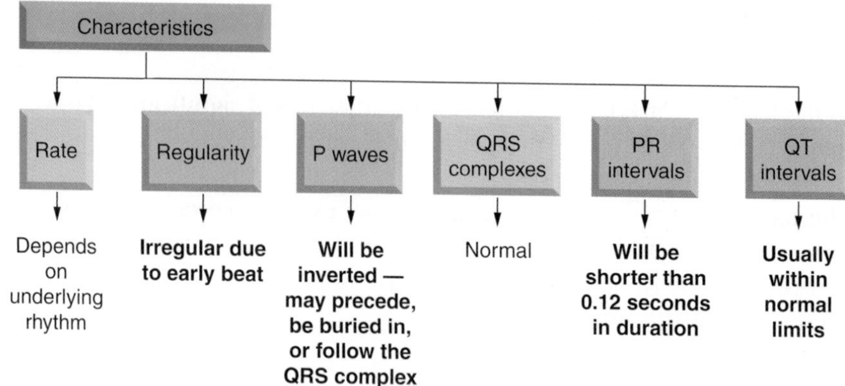

Figure 10-3
Algorithm for premature junctional complexes.

QUESTION
"What is the difference between noncompensatory and compensatory pauses when discussing premature beats?" (The answer can be found on page 323.)

As with any premature beats, you first see an irregular rhythm as the underlying rhythm is disrupted by the presence of early beats. When you look at the area(s) of irregularity you see a shorter R-R wave between the beat of the underlying rhythm and the premature beat. P waves may or may not be seen with the PJCs. If P′ waves are present with the premature beats, they will differ from the P waves of the underlying rhythm and are usually inverted. PR intervals, if present with the premature junctional beats, will be less than 0.12 seconds. The impulse arises above the ventricles, therefore the QRS complexes of PJCs are normal and look the same as QRS complexes of the underlying rhythm. T waves of the premature beats deflect in the same direction as the R waves. PJCs are followed by a noncompensatory pause (Figure 10-3).

PJCs disrupt the ____________ rhythm causing it to be ____________. If P′ waves are present with PJCs, they ____________ from the P waves of the underlying rhythm and are usually ____________. The P′R intervals, if present with the PJCs, will be less than ____________ seconds. The impulse arises ____________ the ventricles, therefore the QRS complexes seen with PJCs are ____________ and appear the same as QRS complexes of the ____________ rhythm. PJCs are usually followed by a ____________ pause.

[underlying] [irregular] [differ] [inverted] [0.12] [above] [narrow] [underlying] [noncompensatory]

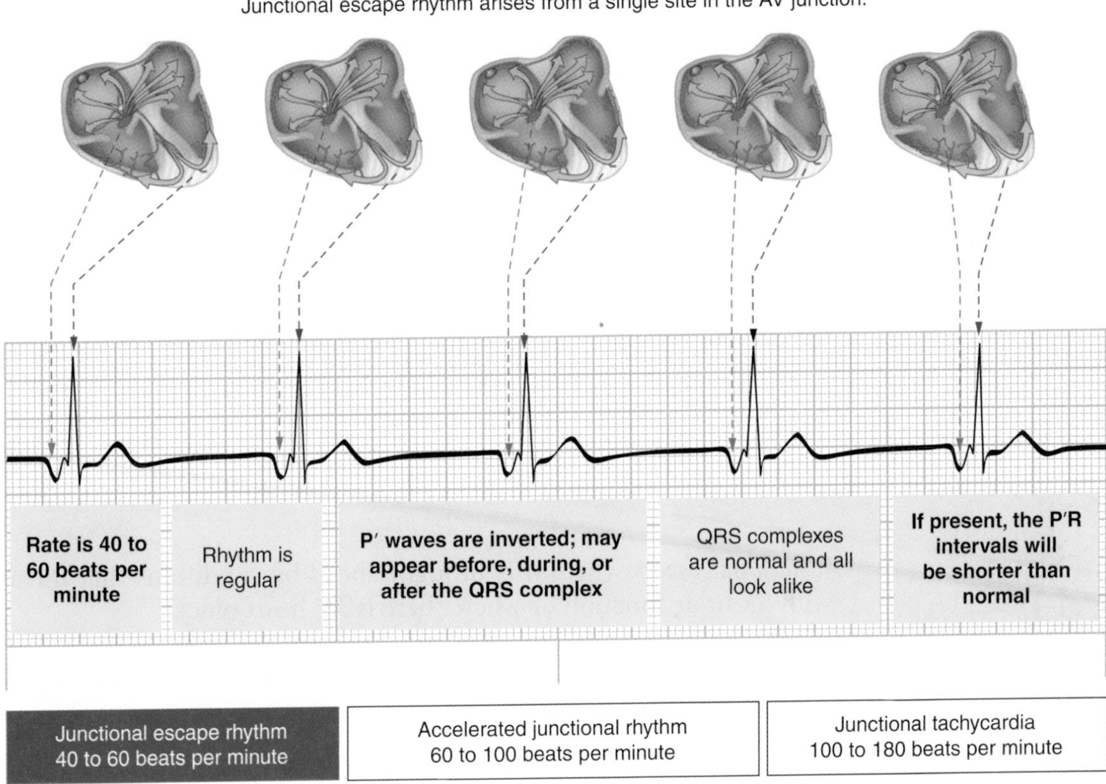

Figure 10-4
Junctional escape rhythm.

PJCs intermingled between normal beats are named depending on how frequent they occur. When every other beat is a PJC, it is called bigeminal PJCs, or junctional bigeminy. If every third beat is a PJC, it is called trigeminal PJCs, or junctional trigeminy. Likewise, if a PJC occurs every fourth beat, it is called quadrigeminal PJCs, or junctional quadrigeminy. Regular PJCs at greater intervals than every fourth beat have no special name.

INSTRUCTIONAL MOMENT
Remember, bi = 2, tri = 3, and quad = 4.

PJCs that arise every other beat are called ______________ PJCs. If every third beat is a PJC, it is called ______________ PJCs. If PJCs occur every fourth beat, it is called ______________ PJCs.

[bigeminal] [trigeminal] [quadrigeminal]

KEY CONCEPT
A premature junctional complex (PJC) is a single, early electrical impulse that arises from the AV junction.

 Junctional Escape Rhythm

Junctional escape rhythm is a series of impulses that typically occurs when the rate of the primary pacemaker (SA node) falls below that of the AV junctional area (Figure 10-4). Remember, if the pacemaker site in the

SA node fails to fire or slows down, the AV junction (or ventricles) in their role as backup pacemakers, should jump in to initiate the heartbeat. It serves as a safety mechanism to prevent cardiac standstill.

INSTRUCTIONAL MOMENT
Remember this helpful hint—except for the heart rate, the characteristics are essentially the same in junctional escape rhythm, accelerated junctional rhythm, and junctional tachycardia.

Junctional ______________ rhythm typically occurs when the rate of the ______________ falls below that of the AV junctional area. This rhythm serves as a ______________ mechanism to prevent cardiac ______________.

[escape] [SA node] [safety] [standstill]

CLINICAL MOMENT
In junctional escape rhythm, the rhythm is regular as it originates from one area.

Junctional escape rhythm is brought about by conditions that interfere with SA node function or where there is AV heart block.

Causes of this dysrhythmia include increased vagal tone on the SA node, sick sinus syndrome, digitalis toxicity, inferior wall myocardial infarction, and rheumatic heart disease (Table 10-2).

QUESTION
"What is the inherent rate of the ventricles?" (The answer can be found on page 323.)

The normal firing rate of the AV junction is 40 to 60 beats per minute. Rates of greater than 50 beats per minute are usually well tolerated. Slower rates can cause decreased cardiac output and may lead to symptoms (chest pain or pressure, syncope, altered level of consciousness, hypotension). Remember, from our earlier discussion decreased cardiac output leads to decreased tissue perfusion.

CLINICAL MOMENT
Decreased tissue perfusion can have dire consequences. First, there is not enough oxygen and nutrients for the body to satisfy its energy needs. Second, if the waste products of metabolism are not removed, they accumulate in the tissues and create a toxic environment. If not corrected, both factors can lead to shock and ultimately, death of the patient.

Review of key characteristics associated with junctional escape rhythm

What we have learned so far:

Rate:	40 to 60 beats per minute
Regularity:	Regular
P waves:	Inverted—may immediately precede, occur during (absent), or follow the QRS complex
QRS complexes:	Normal
PR interval:	Will be shorter than normal if the P′ wave precedes the QRS complex, absent if the P′ wave is buried in the QRS, and it is referred to as the RP′ interval if the P′ wave follows the QRS complex
QT interval:	Usually within normal limits

Table 10-2 Junctional Escape Rhythm

Causes of junctional escape rhythm	Examples
Cardiac disorders	Increased vagal tone on the SA node, disease of the SA node (sick sinus syndrome), inferior wall myocardial infarction, rheumatic heart disease, valvular disease
Use of certain drugs	Digitalis, quinidine, beta-blockers, calcium channel blockers
Other	Postcardiac surgery, hypoxia

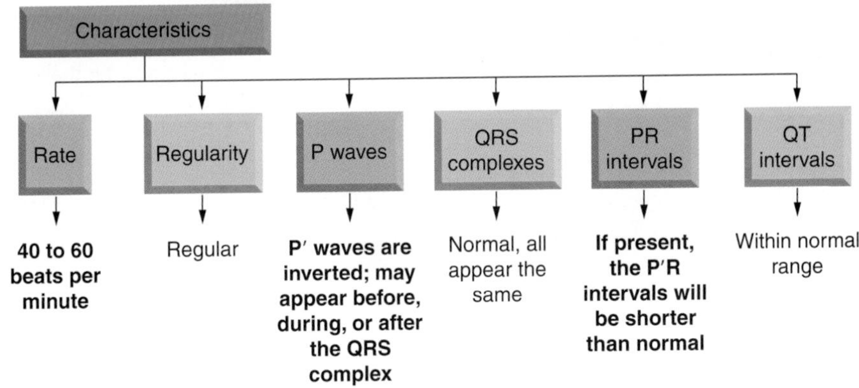

Figure 10-5
Algorithm for junctional escape rhythm.

The key features of this dysrhythmia are a slow heart rate of between 40 and 60 beats per minute; inverted P′ waves that precede, are lost in (absent), or follow the QRS complexes; and if present, a P′R interval less than 0.12 seconds in duration. The rhythm is regular if it is an escape rhythm but irregular if it is an isolated escape beat. The QRS complexes are normal (Figure 10-5).

INSTRUCTIONAL MOMENT
Junctional escape may also be seen as an isolated junctional complex (escape complex) that occurs when the SA node fails to initiate an impulse.

The rate associated with junctional escape rhythm is __________ beats per minute. If present, the P′ waves will be __________ or __________ the QRS complexes. P′R intervals, if present, are __________ than 0.12 seconds in duration. The rhythm is __________ if it is an escape rhythm but irregular if it is an isolated escape beat. The QRS complexes should be within __________ limits of __________ to __________ seconds.

[40 to 60] [inverted] [follow] [less] [regular] [normal] [0.06] [0.12]

KEY CONCEPT
Junctional escape rhythm arises from the AV junction at a rate of 40 to 60 beats per minute.

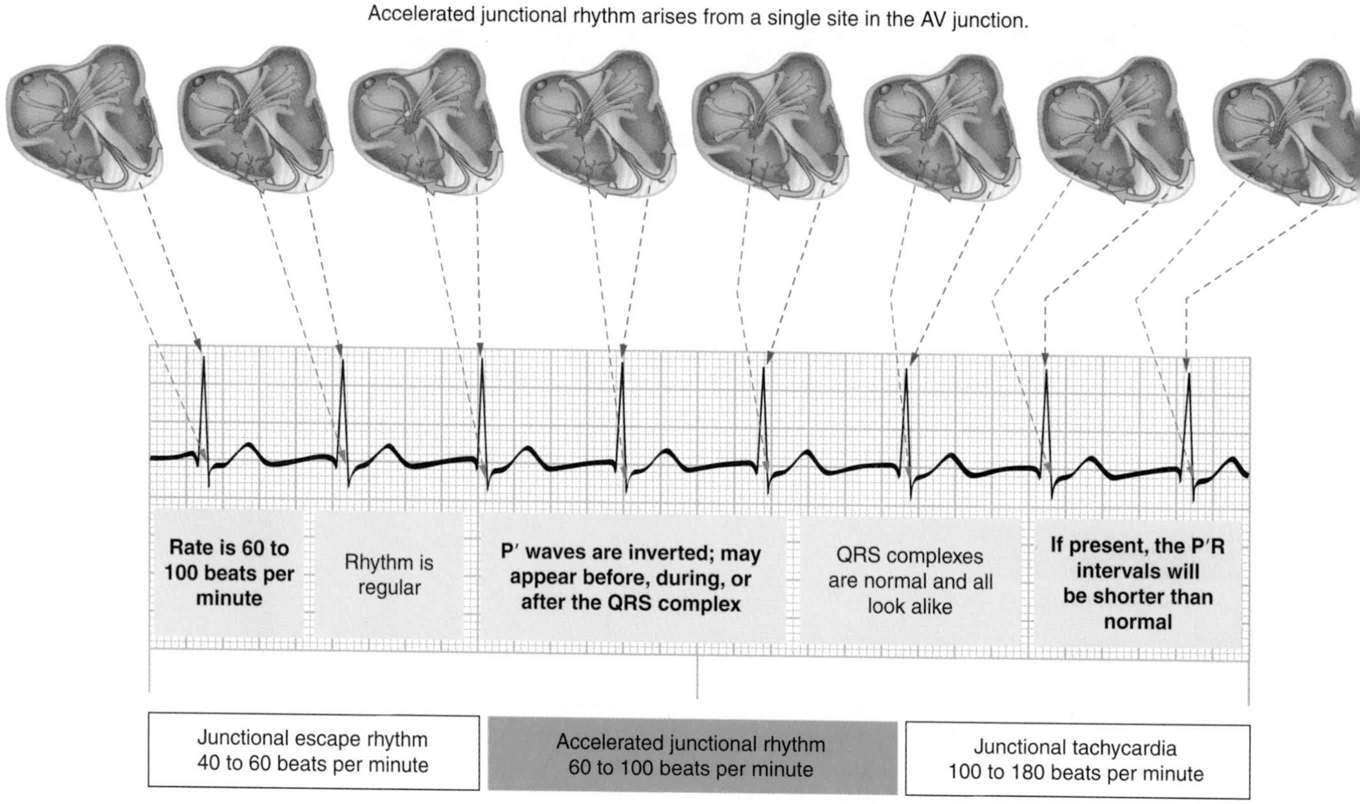

Figure 10-6
Accelerated junctional rhythm.

If the junctional escape rhythm has a rate of less than 40 beats per minute it is described as slow or bradycardic junctional escape rhythm or junctional escape rhythm with bradycardia.

INSTRUCTIONAL MOMENT
Remember that the term tachycardia is applied to heart rates above 100 beats per minute. The inherent rate of the AV node/junction is 40 to 60 beats per minute. A heart rate above 60 beats per minute cannot correctly be classified as "tachycardia" until it reaches a rate of 100 beats per minute, so we use the term accelerated to describe this dysrhythmia. The word accelerated emphasizes that it is faster than the inherent rate.

Accelerated Junctional Rhythm

Accelerated junctional rhythm is a dysrhythmia that arises from the AV junction (Figure 10-6). At a rate of 60 to 100 beats per minute it speeds up to take over as the heart's pacemaker. Accelerated junctional rhythm is due to increased automaticity or irritability of the AV junction. Table 10-3 lists the causes of accelerated junctional rhythm.

A dysrhythmia that arises from the AV junction at a rate of 60 to 100 beats per minute is called ____________ junctional rhythm. It is due to increased ____________ or irritability of the AV junction.

[accelerated] [automaticity]

Table 10-3 Accelerated Junctional Rhythm

Causes of Accelerated Junctional Rhythm	Examples
Cardiac disorders	Inferior or posterior wall myocardial infarction, rheumatic fever, post open-heart surgery
Use of certain drugs	Digoxin toxicity
Other	Hypokalemia, COPD

Accelerated junctional rhythm has the same rate as normal sinus rhythm, so it is usually well tolerated. However, it may predispose patients with myocardial ischemia to more serious dysrhythmias. Also, because the atria are depolarized by way of retrograde conduction and may actually follow ventricular depolarization, blood ejection from the atria into the ventricles (atrial kick) may be prevented. This may cause decreased cardiac output. If cardiac output is low, the patient may exhibit signs of decreased tissue perfusion.

Accelerated junctional rhythm is often the result of ____________ toxicity. It is usually well tolerated as it has the same ____________ as normal sinus rhythm.

[digitalis] [rate]

Review of key characteristics associated with accelerated junctional rhythm

Rate:	60 to 100 beats per minute
Regularity:	Regular
P waves:	Inverted—may immediately precede, occur during (absent), or follow the QRS complex
QRS complexes:	Normal
PR interval:	Will be shorter than normal if the P′ wave precedes the QRS complex, absent if the P′ wave is buried in the QRS, and it is referred to as the RP′ interval if the P′ wave follows the QRS complex
QT interval:	Usually within normal limits

The key characteristic of accelerated junctional rhythm is a regular rhythm with P′ waves that precede, are lost in (absent), or follow the QRS complex. When present, the P′ waves are inverted. The P′R intervals, if

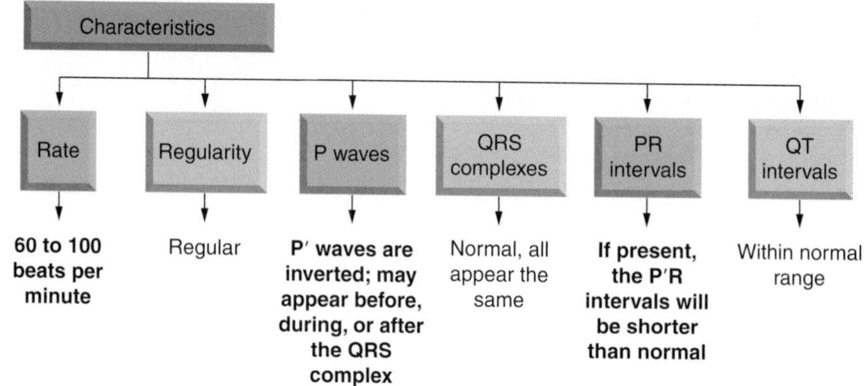

Figure 10-7
Algorithm for accelerated junctional rhythm.

CLINICAL MOMENT
In accelerated junctional rhythm, the rhythm is regular as it originates from one site.

KEY CONCEPT
Accelerated junctional rhythm arises from the AV junction at a rate of 60 to 100 beats per minute.

present, are less than 0.12 seconds. The rate is 60 to 100 beats per minute. Accelerated junctional rhythm arises from above the ventricles, so the QRS complexes are normal (Figure 10-7).

Accelerated junctional rhythm is a ____________ rhythm with P′ waves that ____________, are ____________, or ____________ the QRS complex. When present, the P′ waves are ____________. The P′R intervals, if present, are less than ____________ seconds while the QRS complexes are within ____________ limits.

[regular] [precede] [lost in] [follow] [inverted] [0.12] [normal]

Junctional Tachycardia

Junctional tachycardia is a fast ectopic rhythm that originates from an irritable focus in the bundle of His and overrides the SA node (Figure 10-8). It is said to be present when there are three or more premature junctional complexes in a row or there is a junctional rhythm occurring at a rate of between 100 and 180 beats per minute. As with other junctional rhythms, the atria are depolarized by retrograde conduction while conduction through the ventricles occurs in the normal manner. When the rate in junctional tachycardia exceeds 150 beats per minute, the rhythm becomes hard to distinguish from atrial tachycardia and is often referred to as supraventricular tachycardia.

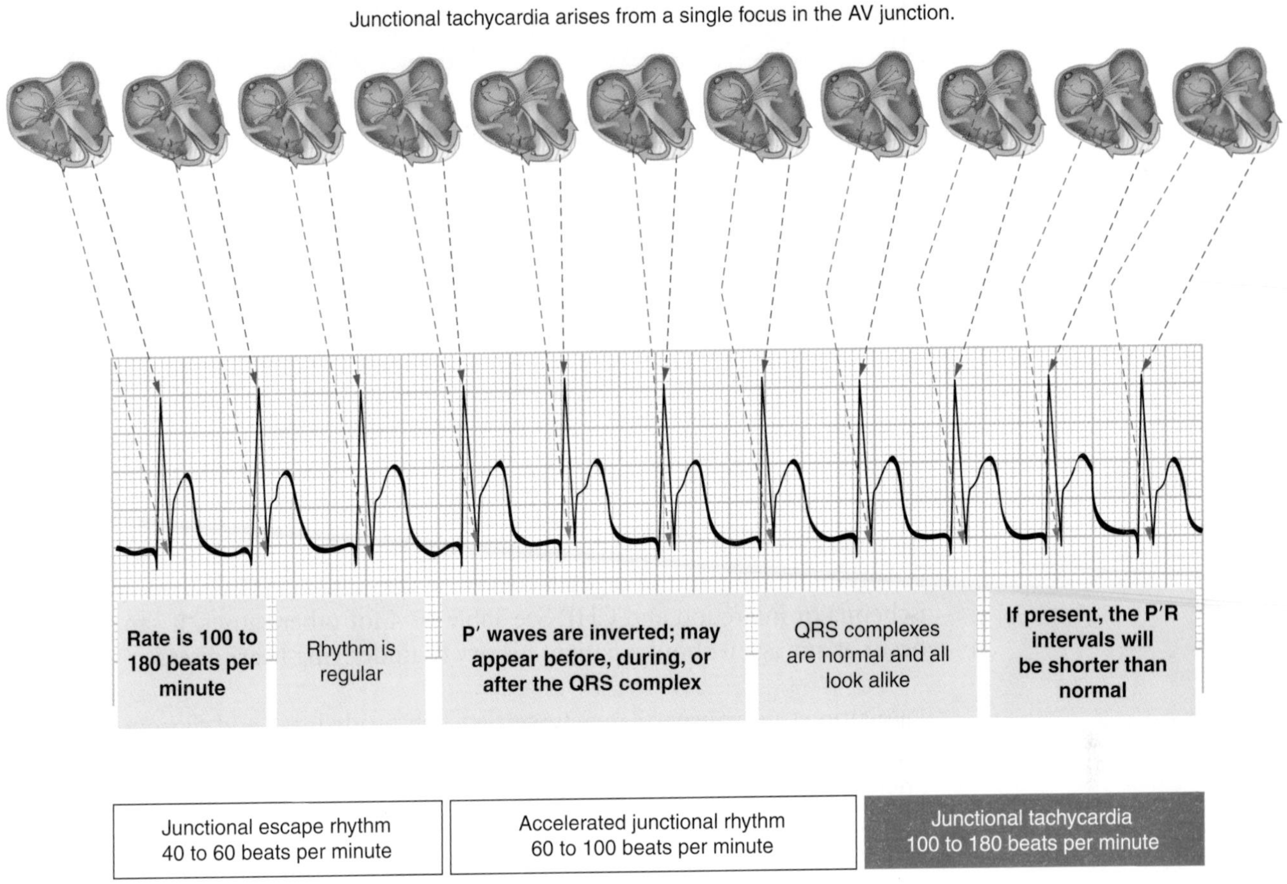

Junctional tachycardia arises from a single focus in the AV junction.

Rate is 100 to 180 beats per minute

Rhythm is regular

P′ waves are inverted; may appear before, during, or after the QRS complex

QRS complexes are normal and all look alike

If present, the P′R intervals will be shorter than normal

Junctional escape rhythm 40 to 60 beats per minute	Accelerated junctional rhythm 60 to 100 beats per minute	Junctional tachycardia 100 to 180 beats per minute

Figure 10-8
Junctional tachycardia.

____________ tachycardia is considered to be present when there are ____________ or more PJCs in a row or there is a junctional rhythm occurring at a rate of ____________ beats per minute. With junctional tachycardia the ____________ are depolarized by retrograde conduction while ____________ depolarization occurs in the normal manner. Junctional tachycardia that exceeds ____________ beats per minute is often referred to as ____________ tachycardia as it is hard to distinguish from the other tachycardias that arise from above the ____________.

[Junctional] [three] [100 to180] [atria] [ventricular] [150] [supraventricular] [ventricles]

INSTRUCTIONAL MOMENT

The term paroxysmal is added to describe junctional tachycardia that starts and ends suddenly. It is frequently precipitated by a premature junctional complex.

Table 10-4 Junctional Tachycardia

Causes of junctional tachycardia	Examples
Cardiac disorders	Inferior or posterior wall myocardial infarction, swelling of the AV junction after heart surgery, damage to AV junction from inferior wall MI or rheumatic fever, post open-heart surgery
Use of certain drugs	Digoxin toxicity, particularly in the presence of hypokalemia
Other	Excessive catecholamine administration, anxiety, hypoxia, electrolyte imbalance (particularly hypokalemia)

Junctional tachycardia is believed to be caused by enhanced automaticity and is commonly the result of digitalis toxicity. Other causes include myocardial ischemia or infarction and CHF. See Table 10-4 for other causes. It can also occur at any age without a patient history of underlying heart disease.

Palpitations, nervousness, anxiety, vertigo, lightheadedness, and syncope frequently accompany this dysrhythmia. Short bursts of junctional tachycardia are well tolerated in otherwise healthy people. With sustained rapid ventricular rates and retrograde depolarization of the atria, ventricular filling is not as complete during diastole, leading to compromised cardiac output in patients with underlying heart disease. The loss of the atrial kick may cause up to a 30% reduction in cardiac output. Increases in cardiac oxygen requirements may increase myocardial ischemia and the frequency and severity of the patient's chest pain. It can extend the size of myocardial infarction; cause congestive heart failure, hypotension, and cardiogenic shock; and possibly predispose the patient to ventricular dysrhythmias.

Review of key characteristics associated with junctional tachycardia

Rate:	100 to 180 beats per minute
Regularity:	Regular
P waves:	Inverted—may immediately precede, occur during (absent), or follow the QRS complex
QRS complexes:	Normal
PR interval:	Will be shorter than normal if the P′ wave precedes the QRS complex, absent if the P′ wave is buried in the QRS, and it is referred to as the RP′ interval if the P′ wave follows the QRS complex
QT interval:	Usually within normal limits

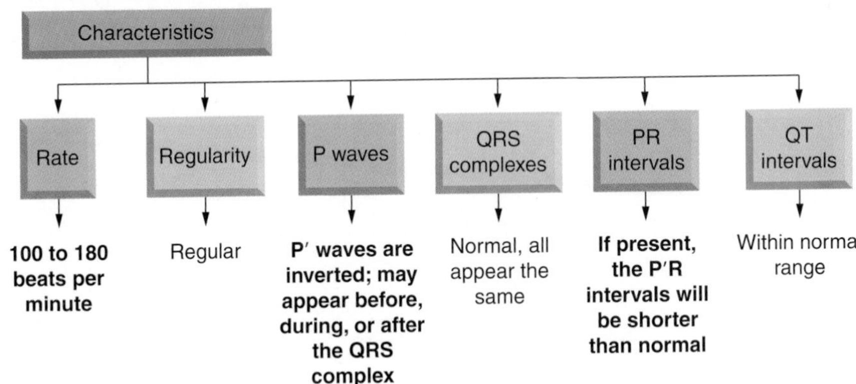

Figure 10-9
Algorithm for junctional tachycardia.

The most evident feature of junctional tachycardia is a rapid heart rate with narrow QRS complexes. The rate is 100 to 180 beats per minute. P waves may precede, be lost in (absent), or follow the QRS complexes. When present, the P waves will be inverted. The PR intervals, if present, will be less than 0.12 seconds. It is coming from one site, so the rhythm is regular (except if there is an onset or termination as seen with PSVT). The QRS complexes are normal (Figure 10-9).

KEY CONCEPT
Junctional tachycardia is a fast, ectopic rhythm that arises from the bundle of His at a rate of between 100 and 180 beats per minute.

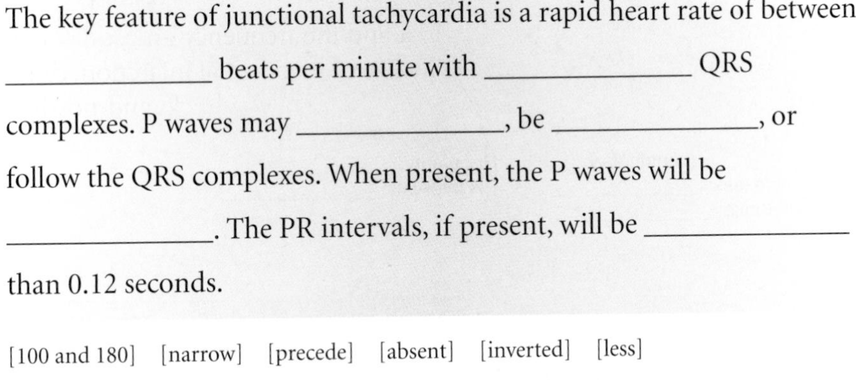

The key feature of junctional tachycardia is a rapid heart rate of between ______________ beats per minute with ______________ QRS complexes. P waves may ______________, be ______________, or follow the QRS complexes. When present, the P waves will be ______________. The PR intervals, if present, will be ______________ than 0.12 seconds.

[100 and 180] [narrow] [precede] [absent] [inverted] [less]

You can practice interpreting junctional dysrhythmias with the following *Practice Makes Perfect* exercises. Answers to these exercises can be found in Appendix A.

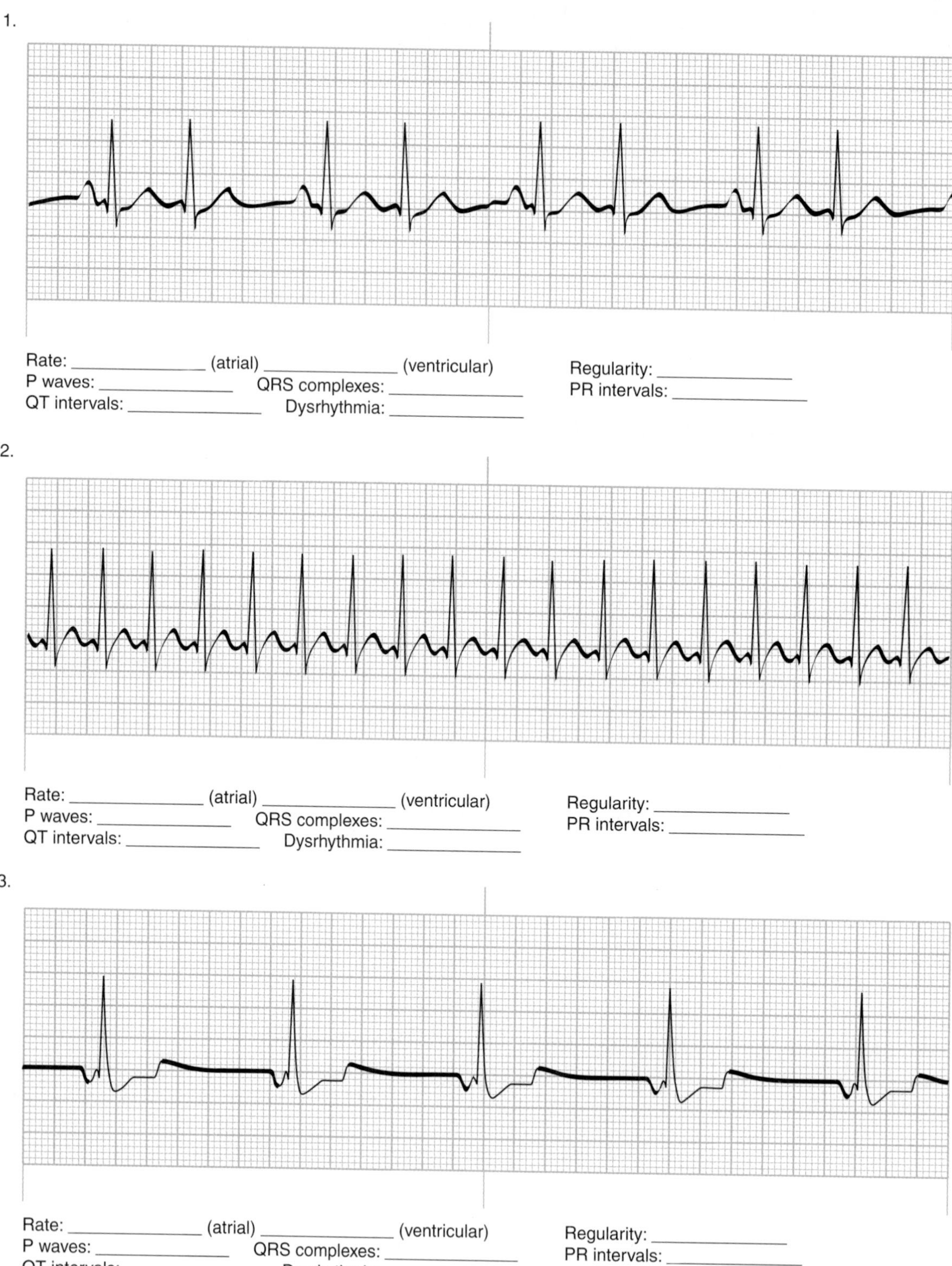
PRACTICE. . . MAKES PERFECT
1.
Rate: ______ (atrial) ______ (ventricular)
Regularity: ______
P waves: ______
QRS complexes: ______
PR intervals: ______
QT intervals: ______
Dysrhythmia: ______
2.
Rate: ______ (atrial) ______ (ventricular)
Regularity: ______
P waves: ______
QRS complexes: ______
PR intervals: ______
QT intervals: ______
Dysrhythmia: ______
3.
Rate: ______ (atrial) ______ (ventricular)
Regularity: ______
P waves: ______
QRS complexes: ______
PR intervals: ______
QT intervals: ______
Dysrhythmia: ______

PRACTICE. . . MAKES PERFECT

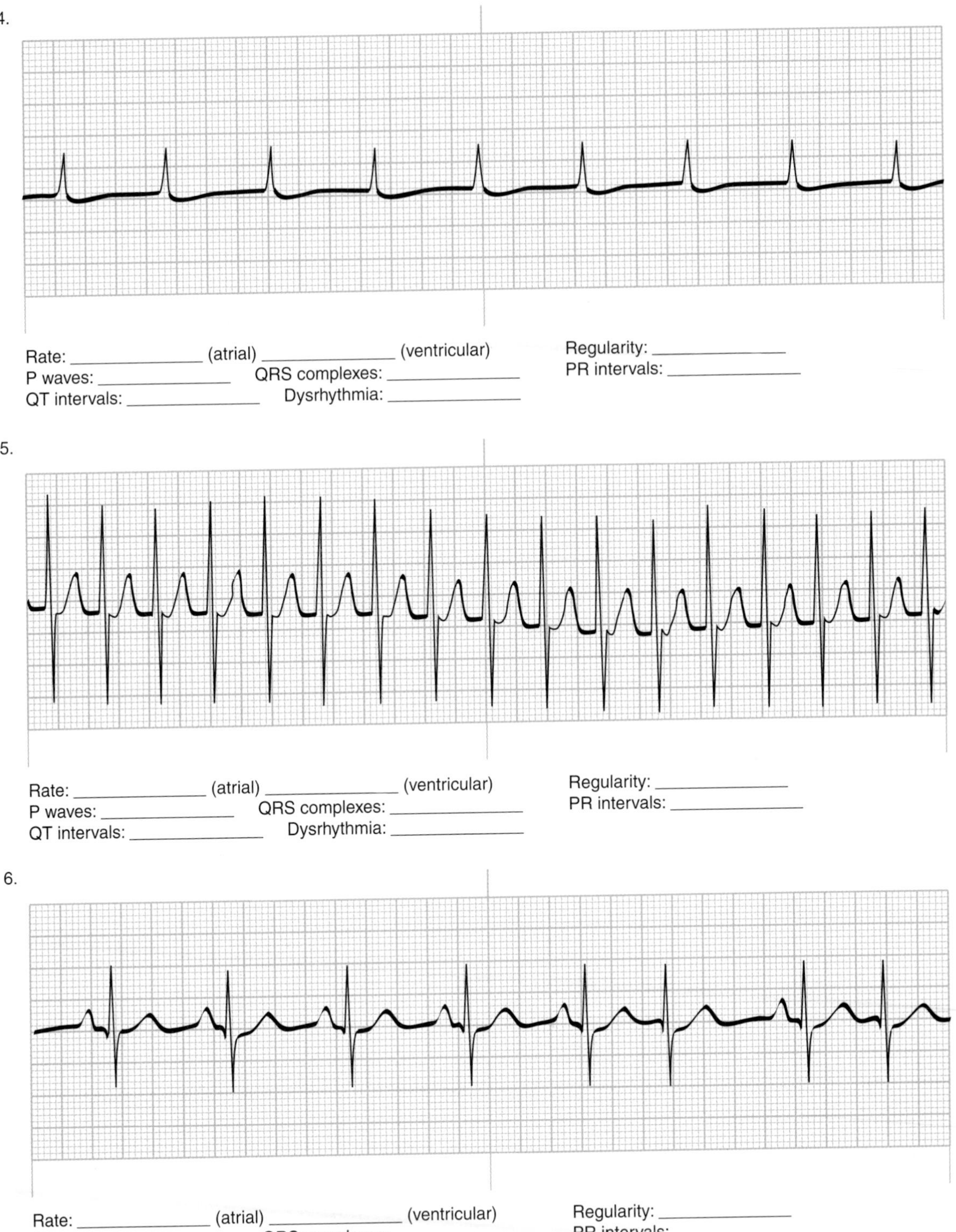

4.

Rate: _______________ (atrial) _______________ (ventricular) Regularity: _______________
P waves: _______________ QRS complexes: _______________ PR intervals: _______________
QT intervals: _______________ Dysrhythmia: _______________

5.

Rate: _______________ (atrial) _______________ (ventricular) Regularity: _______________
P waves: _______________ QRS complexes: _______________ PR intervals: _______________
QT intervals: _______________ Dysrhythmia: _______________

6.

Rate: _______________ (atrial) _______________ (ventricular) Regularity: _______________
P waves: _______________ QRS complexes: _______________ PR intervals: _______________
QT intervals: _______________ Dysrhythmia: _______________

PRACTICE. . . MAKES PERFECT

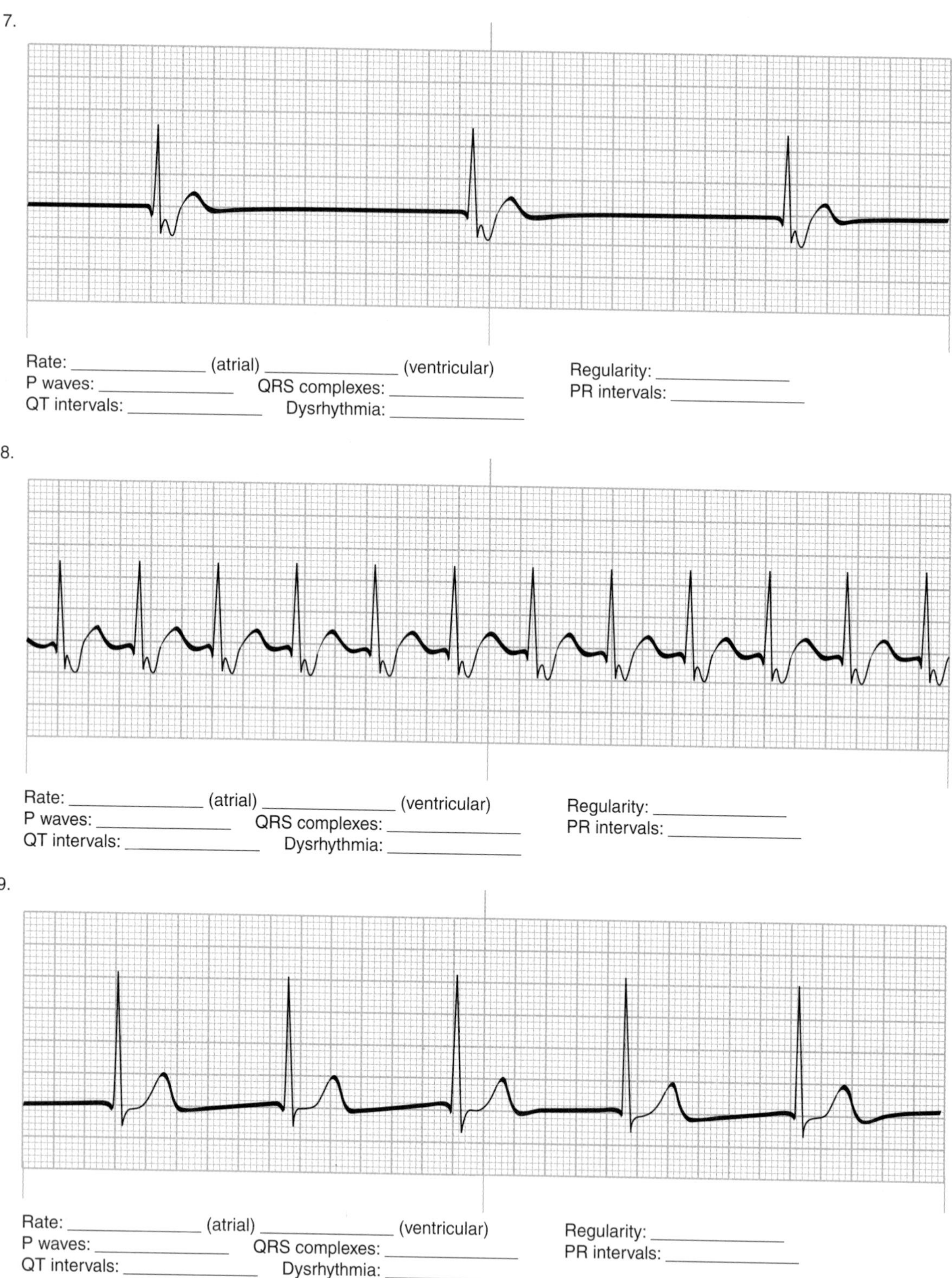

7.

Rate: ______________ (atrial) ______________ (ventricular) Regularity: ______________
P waves: ______________ QRS complexes: ______________ PR intervals: ______________
QT intervals: ______________ Dysrhythmia: ______________

8.

Rate: ______________ (atrial) ______________ (ventricular) Regularity: ______________
P waves: ______________ QRS complexes: ______________ PR intervals: ______________
QT intervals: ______________ Dysrhythmia: ______________

9.

Rate: ______________ (atrial) ______________ (ventricular) Regularity: ______________
P waves: ______________ QRS complexes: ______________ PR intervals: ______________
QT intervals: ______________ Dysrhythmia: ______________

PRACTICE. . . MAKES PERFECT

10.

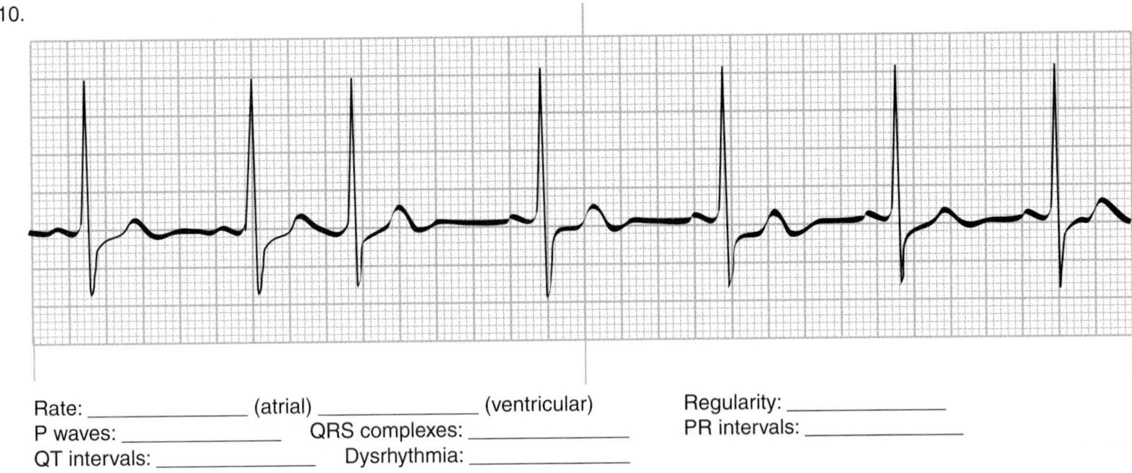

Rate: _______________ (atrial) _______________ (ventricular)
Regularity: _______________
P waves: _______________
QRS complexes: _______________
PR intervals: _______________
QT intervals: _______________
Dysrhythmia: _______________

You can practice interpreting sinus and atrial dysrhythmias (as discussed in Chapters 8 and 9) with the following *Practice Makes Perfect* exercises. Answers to these exercises can be found in Appendix A.

PRACTICE. . . MAKES PERFECT

11.

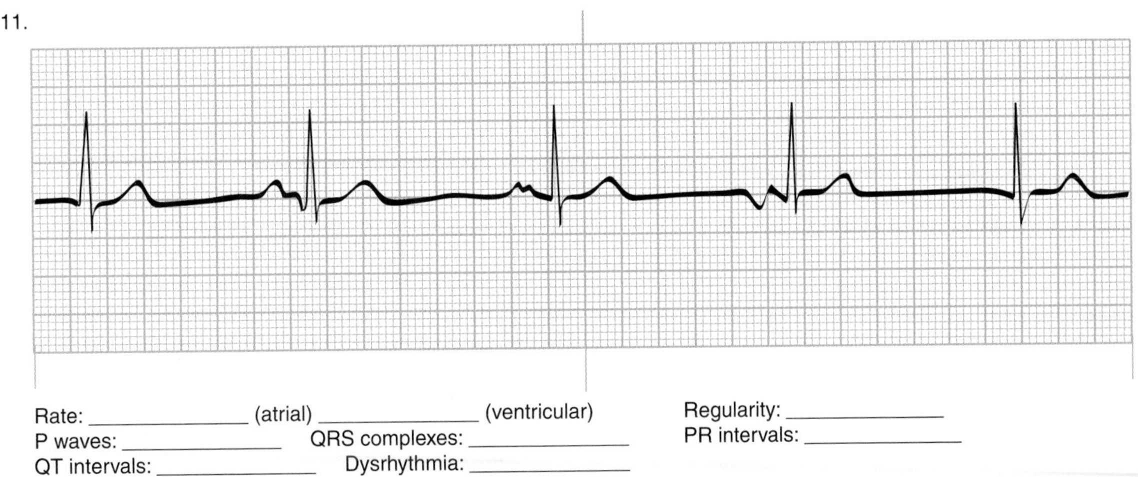

Rate: _______________ (atrial) _______________ (ventricular)
Regularity: _______________
P waves: _______________
QRS complexes: _______________
PR intervals: _______________
QT intervals: _______________
Dysrhythmia: _______________

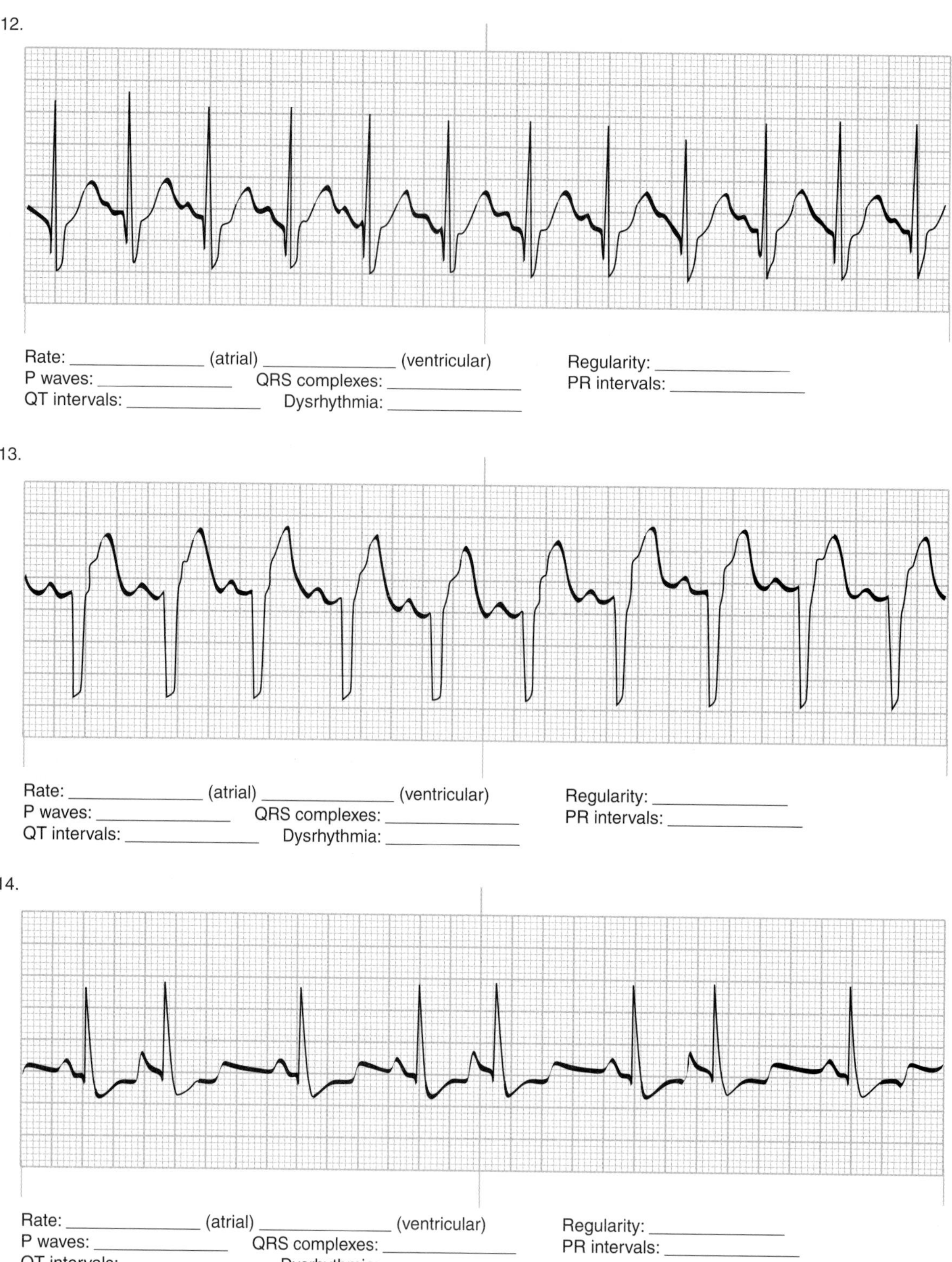
PRACTICE. . . MAKES PERFECT
12.
Rate: ______ (atrial) ______ (ventricular)
Regularity: ______
P waves: ______
QRS complexes: ______
PR intervals: ______
QT intervals: ______
Dysrhythmia: ______
13.
Rate: ______ (atrial) ______ (ventricular)
Regularity: ______
P waves: ______
QRS complexes: ______
PR intervals: ______
QT intervals: ______
Dysrhythmia: ______
14.
Rate: ______ (atrial) ______ (ventricular)
Regularity: ______
P waves: ______
QRS complexes: ______
PR intervals: ______
QT intervals: ______
Dysrhythmia: ______

PRACTICE. . . MAKES PERFECT

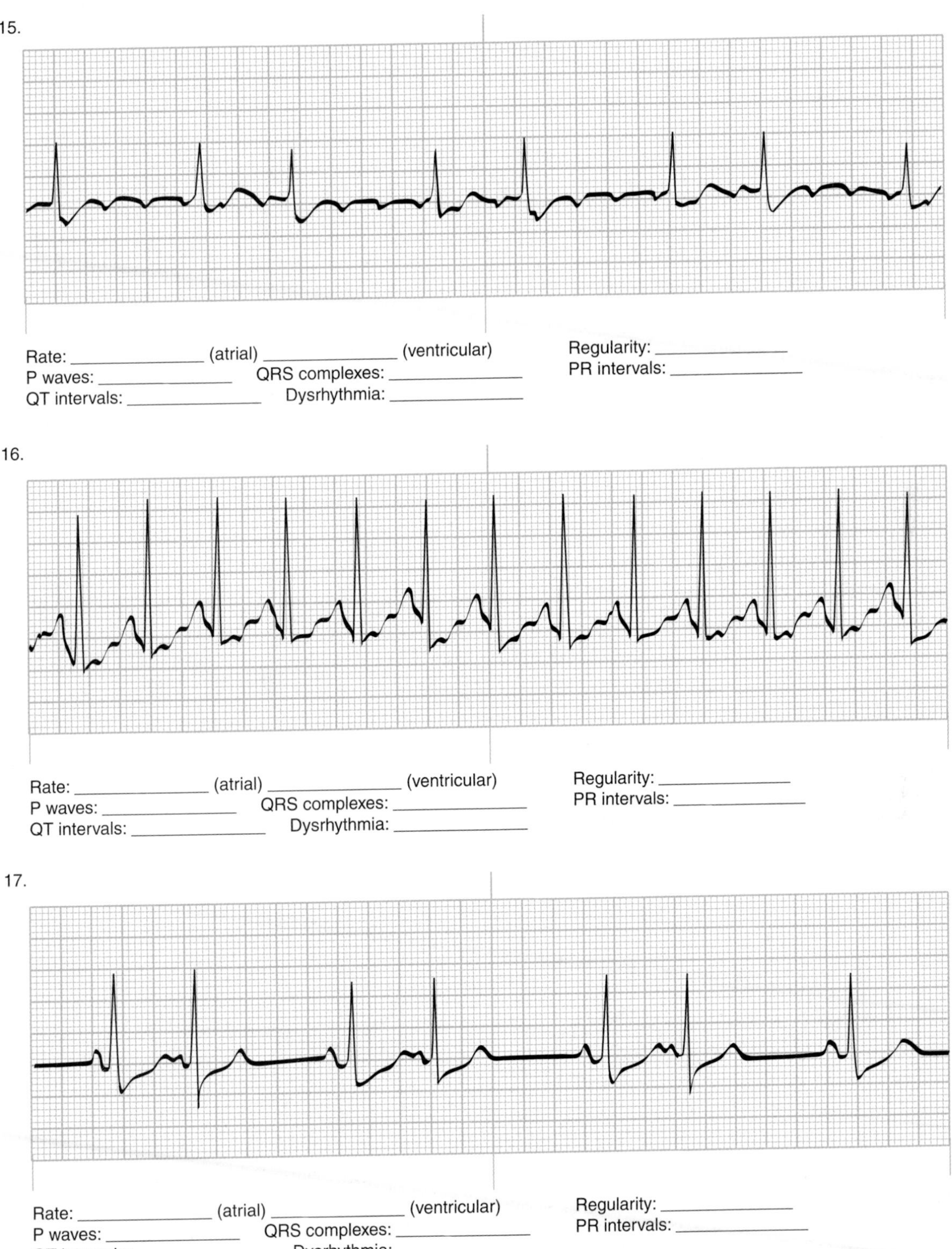

15.

Rate: ______________ (atrial) ______________ (ventricular)
Regularity: ______________
P waves: ______________
QRS complexes: ______________
PR intervals: ______________
QT intervals: ______________
Dysrhythmia: ______________

16.

Rate: ______________ (atrial) ______________ (ventricular)
Regularity: ______________
P waves: ______________
QRS complexes: ______________
PR intervals: ______________
QT intervals: ______________
Dysrhythmia: ______________

17.

Rate: ______________ (atrial) ______________ (ventricular)
Regularity: ______________
P waves: ______________
QRS complexes: ______________
PR intervals: ______________
QT intervals: ______________
Dysrhythmia: ______________

PRACTICE. . . MAKES PERFECT

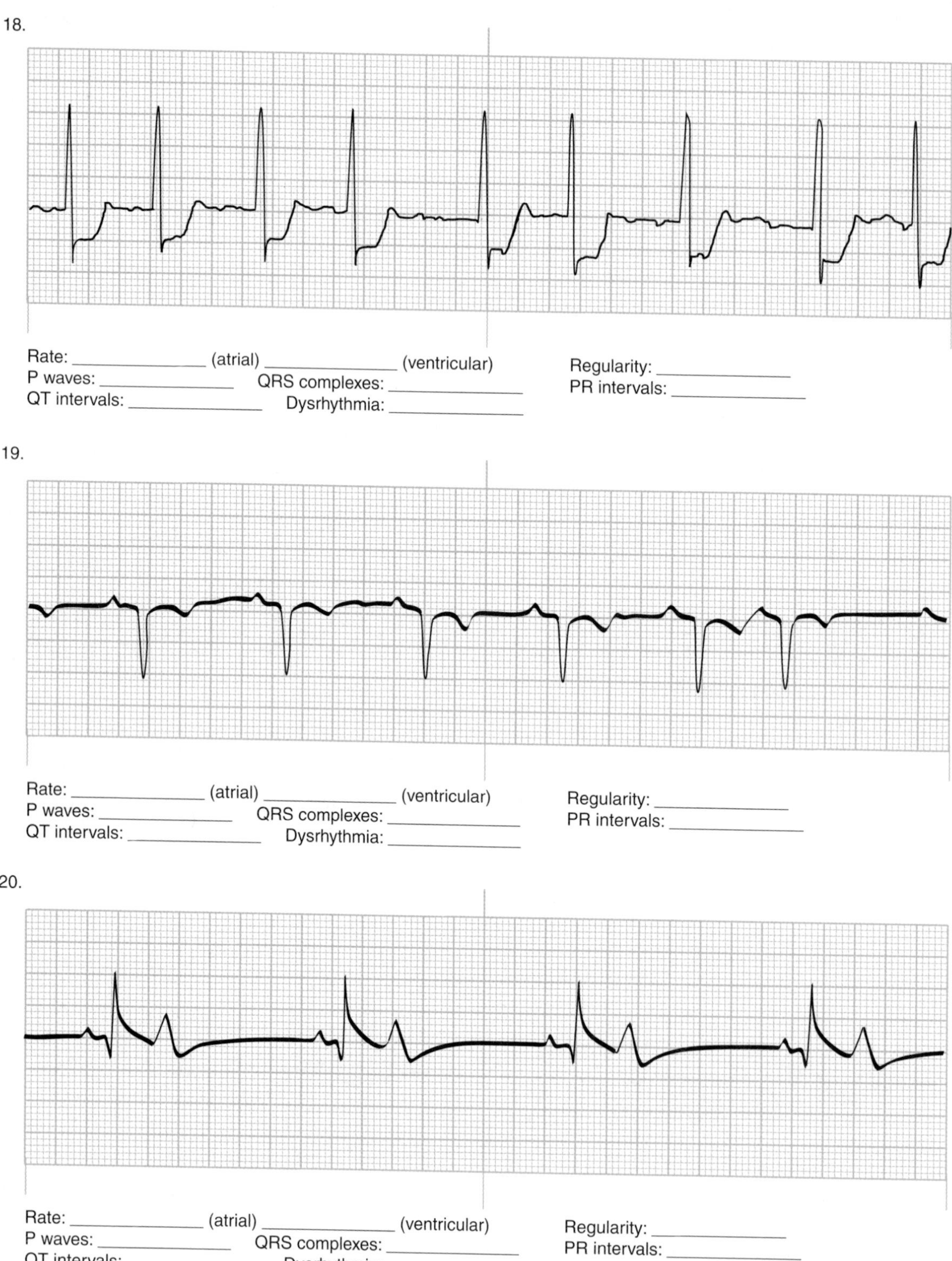

18.

Rate: ______________ (atrial) ______________ (ventricular)
P waves: ______________
QRS complexes: ______________
QT intervals: ______________
Dysrhythmia: ______________
Regularity: ______________
PR intervals: ______________

19.

Rate: ______________ (atrial) ______________ (ventricular)
P waves: ______________
QRS complexes: ______________
QT intervals: ______________
Dysrhythmia: ______________
Regularity: ______________
PR intervals: ______________

20.

Rate: ______________ (atrial) ______________ (ventricular)
P waves: ______________
QRS complexes: ______________
QT intervals: ______________
Dysrhythmia: ______________
Regularity: ______________
PR intervals: ______________

Key Points

- Rhythms that originate in the AV junction, the area around the AV node and the bundle of His, are referred to as junctional rhythms.
- Impulses originating in the AV junction travel upward and cause backward or retrograde depolarization of the atria resulting in inverted P′ waves in lead II with a short P′R interval, absent P′ waves (as they are buried by the QRS complex), or retrograde P′ waves.
- With junctional dysrhythmias the QRS complexes are usually normal (unless there is an intraventricular conduction defect, aberrancy, or preexcitation).
- A premature junctional complex (PJC) is a single early electrical impulse that arises from the AV junction.
- Junctional escape rhythm arises from the AV junction at a rate of 40 to 60 beats per minute.
- Accelerated junctional rhythm arises from the AV junction at a rate of 60 to 100 beats per minute.
- Junctional tachycardia is a fast, ectopic rhythm that arises from the bundle of His at a rate of between 100 and 180 beats per minute.

Assess Your Understanding

The following questions give you a chance to assess your understanding of the material discussed in this chapter. The answers can be found in Appendix A.

1. The normal PR interval is ______ seconds.
   a. 0.06 to 0.12
   b. 0.10 to 0.20
   c. 0.12 to 0.20
   d. 0.20 to 0.24
2. PR intervals of less than 0.12 seconds in duration are indicative of a(n)
   a. intermittent blocking of the impulse as it passes through the AV node.
   b. delay in conduction of the impulse between the SA node and the ventricles.
   c. increased rate of impulse discharge from the SA node.
   d. pacemaker site, either in or close to the AV junction.
3. Your patient shows normal sinus rhythm with occasional ectopic beats on the ECG. The ectopic beats appear with absent P waves along with a normal QRS complex. The ectopic beats are premature ______ complexes.
   a. atrial
   b. bundle
   c. junctional
   d. ventricular
4. Which of the following originates from the AV junction?
   a. Atrial tachycardia.
   b. Junctional escape rhythm.
   c. Premature atrial complex.
   d. Sinus bradycardia.

Match the following junctional rhythms with the appropriate heart rate.

Beats per minute		*Dysrhythmias*
5. Junctional tachycardia	____	a. 20 to 30
6. Junctional escape rhythm	____	b. 40 to 60
7. Accelerated junctional rhythm	____	c. 100 to 180
		d. 60 to 100

8. P′R intervals seen with junctional rhythms will appear
   a. longer than 0.20 seconds in duration.
   b. shorter than 0.12 seconds in duration.
   c. within normal ranges.
   d. varied.

9. Which of the following rhythms may be preceded by an inverted P′ wave?
   a. Atrial flutter.
   b. Junctional escape rhythm.
   c. Atrial tachycardia.
   d. Idioventricular rhythm.

Match the following types of PJCs with the correct description.

Types of PJCs		*Descriptions*
10. Bigeminal	____	a. PJCs that occur every third beat
11. Quadrigeminal	____	b. PJCs that occur every other beat
12. Trigeminal	____	c. three or more PJCs in a row
		d. PJCs that occur every fourth beat

13. In junctional escape rhythm, the pacemaker site is in the
    a. SA node.
    b. atrial and internodal conduction pathways.
    c. AV junction.
    d. bundle of His.

14. Accelerated junctional rhythm
    a. is regularly irregular.
    b. has upright P′ waves in all leads.
    c. has normal P′R intervals.
    d. has normal QRS complexes.

Referring to the scenario at the beginning of this chapter answer the following questions.

15. PSVT stands for
    a. premature ventricular tachycardia.
    b. premature atrial tachycardia.
    c. paroxysmal supraventricular tachycardia.
    d. paradoxical supraventricular tachycardia.

16. The P waves are not discernable because
    a. they are not there.
    b. they are hidden in the T wave.
    c. f waves are present instead.
    d. F waves are present instead.

17. This rhythm is caused by an electrical impulse circulating in what part of the heart?
    a. Atria.
    b. AV node.
    c. Bundle of His.
    d. Purkinje fibers.

Answers to Sidebar Questions

"What would you expect the appearance of the P′ waves to be if they originate from the AV junction?"

Answer: The P′ waves are inverted if they originate from the AV junction.

"Can impulses arise from the AV node?"

Answer: Electrophysiological studies have demonstrated that the AV node does not contain pacemaker cells. The cells nearest the bundle of His in the AV junction are responsible for secondary pacing function.

"What is the difference between noncompensatory and compensatory pauses when discussing premature beats?"

Answer: The pause that follows a premature beat is called a noncompensatory pause if the beat following the premature complex is normal and occurs before it was expected. In other words, the space between the complex before and after the premature beat is less than two normal R-R intervals. To determine if there is a noncompensatory, we measure from the R wave of the normal beat that precedes the PAC or PJC to the R wave of the first normal beat that follows it. If there are less than two full R-R intervals between those R waves (with the PAC or PJC in between), it is considered a noncompensatory pause. If, on the other hand, there are two full R-R intervals between those R waves, it is considered a compensatory pause.

"What is the inherent rate of the ventricles?"

Answer: The inherent rate of the ventricles is 20 to 40 beats per minute.

On the DVD

- Approach to Junctional Rhythms.

Notes

Origin and Clinical Aspects of Ventricular Dysrhythmias

11

Chapter Preview

- Dysrhythmias Originating in the Ventricles
- Premature Ventricular Complexes (PVCs)
- Idioventricular Rhythm
- Accelerated Idioventricular Rhythm
- Ventricular Tachycardaia
- Ventricular Fibrillation
- Asystole
- Pulseless Electrical Activity

Case History

It's two o'clock A.M. in the hospital when pagers go off alerting the code team to the presence of a cardiac arrest on the medical floor.

Upon arrival you find the patient in the hospital bed. CPR is in progress and you feel a carotid pulse with compressions. The patient is being ventilated with a bag-valve-mask (BVM) and 100% oxygen. While preparing the defibrillator, you ask that CPR be stopped while you check again for a pulse. Finding none, you order CPR to be continued.

After the defibrillator has been turned on and the pads applied to the patient's chest you again hold CPR and examine the monitor. You see a chaotic and random waveform with no discernable P waves or QRS complexes. "It's ventricular fibrillation," you say to your team, "Let's charge up and shock." You set the power to 200 joules and push the charge button. The machine makes a characteristic whine as the capacitors prepare the energy for delivery. "I'm clear. You're clear. Everyone is clear," you say while visually confirming that no one is touching the patient. You then push the shock button and the energy is delivered. You watch the monitor as it initially shows a flat line for about 6 seconds then see ventricular fibrillation return. You repeat the series of charge and shock twice more while increasing the energy level with each successive shock. Unfortunately you obtain the same results.

With the patient remaining in ventricular fibrillation you request CPR be continued and have a team member intubate the patient. An IV is established and you administer epinephrine per protocol, defibrillate the patient again, after which the rhythm appears to be a flat line. CPR is continued as you administer epinephrine and atropine per protocol. Despite your efforts the patient is pronounced dead after 30 minutes of resuscitative efforts.

Dysrhythmias Originating in the Ventricles

Ventricular dysrhythmias originate in the ventricles below the bundle of His (Figure 11-1). Although ventricular dysrhythmias may be benign, many ventricular dysrhythmias are potentially life threatening because the ventricles are ultimately responsible for cardiac output. Ventricular dysrhythmias typically result when the atria, AV junction, or both are unable to initiate an electrical impulse or when there is enhanced automaticity of

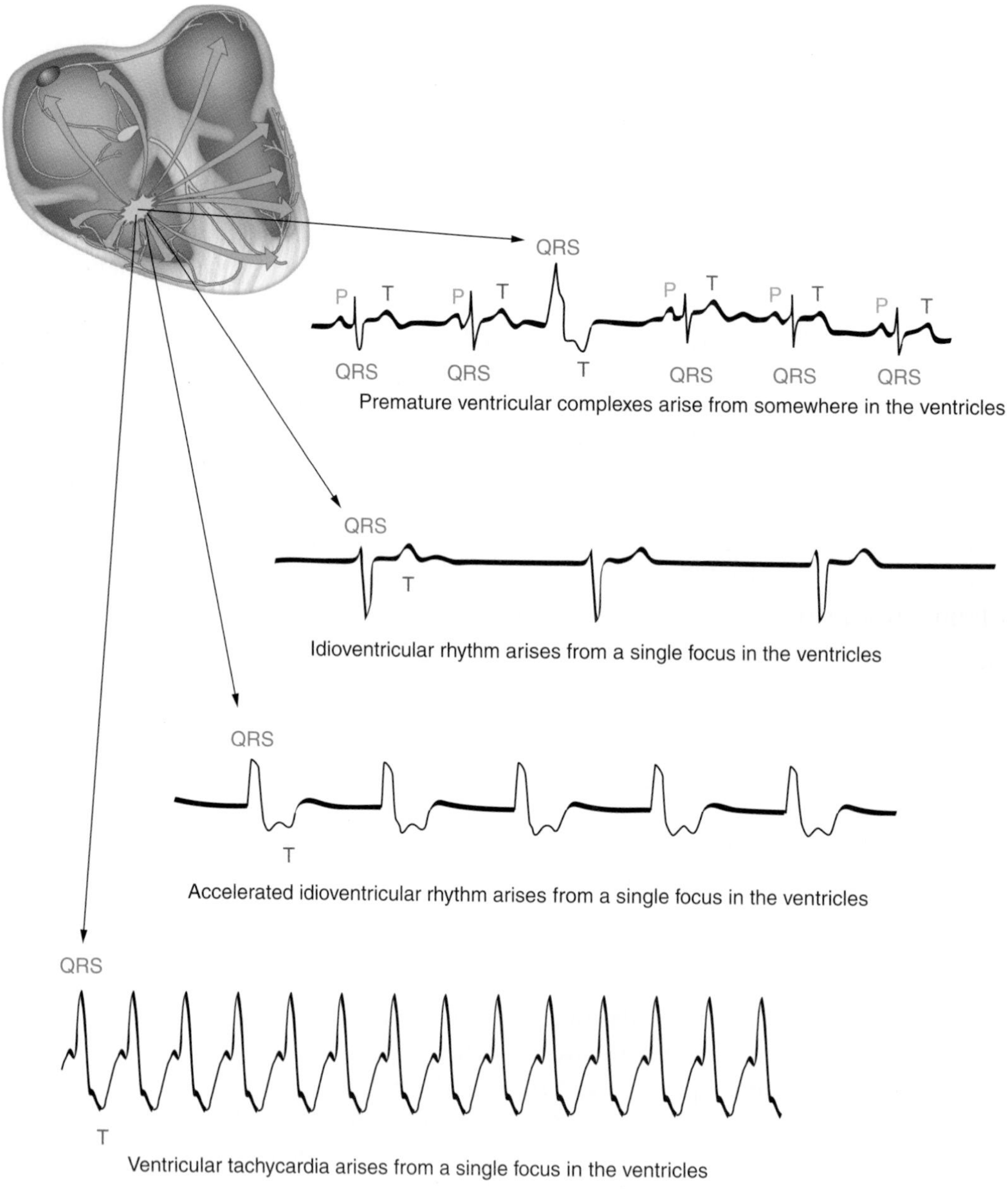

Premature ventricular complexes arise from somewhere in the ventricles

Idioventricular rhythm arises from a single focus in the ventricles

Accelerated idioventricular rhythm arises from a single focus in the ventricles

Ventricular tachycardia arises from a single focus in the ventricles

Figure 11-1
Ventricular dysrhythmias originate from the ventricles.

the ventricular myocardium. Myocardial ischemia is the most common cause of enhanced automaticity. Features common to most ventricular dysrhythmias are bizarre-looking, wide QRS complexes (greater than 0.12 seconds in duration), and T waves in the opposite direction of the R wave. P waves are not visible as they are hidden in the QRS complexes.

KEY CONCEPT
Ventricular dysrhythmias occur when the atria, AV junction, or both are unable to initiate an electrical impulse or when there is enhanced excitability of the ventricular myocardium.

Ventricular dysrhythmias include:

- Premature ventricular complex (PVC)
- Idioventricular rhythm
- Accelerated idioventricular rhythm
- Ventricular tachycardia
- Ventricular fibrillation
- Asystole

KEY CONCEPT
A stand-out feature of ventricular dysrhythmias are wide (greater than 0.12 seconds in duration), bizarre QRS complexes that have T waves in the opposite direction of the R wave. P waves are not visible as they are hidden in the QRS complexes.

Ventricular dysrhythmias originate in the ventricles below the _______________. Many ventricular dysrhythmias are potentially _______________. Ventricular dysrhythmias may occur when the pacemaker sites above the _______________ fail to initiate an electrical impulse or when there is enhanced _______________ of the ventricular myocardium. Myocardial _______________ is the most common cause of enhanced automaticity. Key characteristics of most ventricular dysrhythmias are _______________, _______________ QRS complexes that have T waves in the _______________ direction of the R wave.

[bundle of His] [life threatening] [ventricles] [automaticity] [ischemia] [wide] [bizarre] [opposite]

 Premature Ventricular Complexes (PVCs)

Premature ventricular complexes (PVCs) are early ectopic beats that interrupt the normal rhythm and originate from an irritable focus in the ventricular conduction system or muscle tissue (Figure 11-2). These beats occur earlier than the next expected sinus beat. PVCs may be caused by enhanced automaticity or reentry, brought about by disruption of the normal electrolyte shifts during cell depolarization and repolarization.

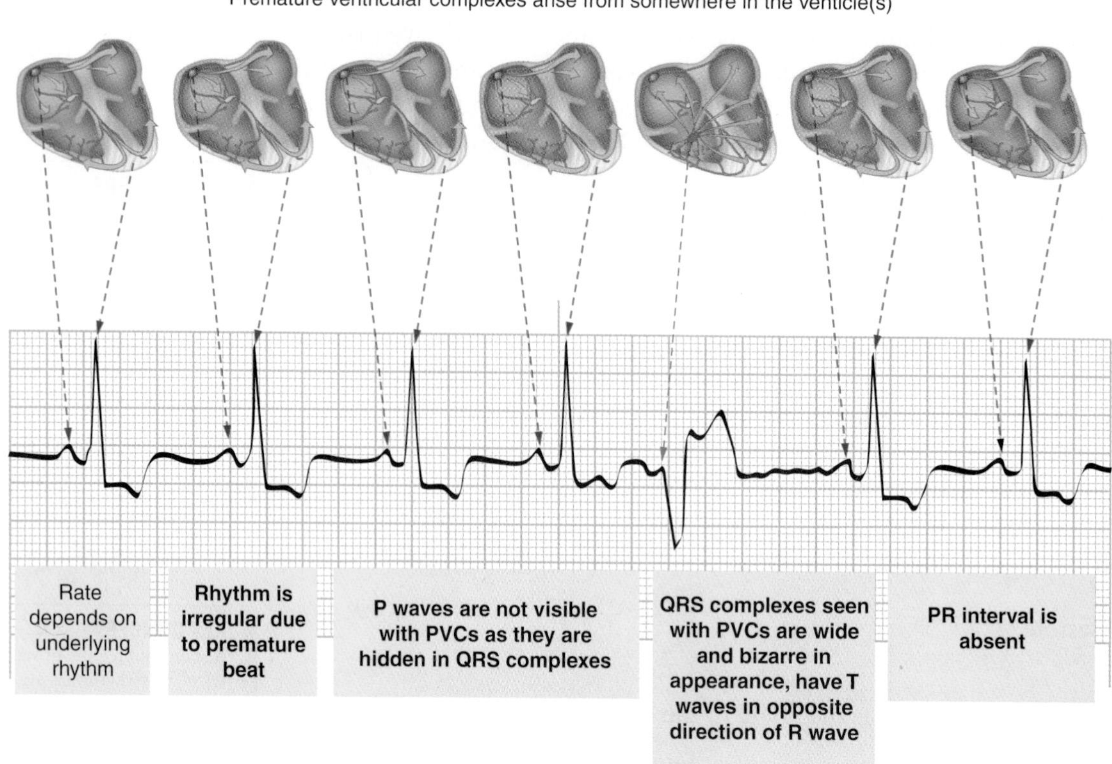

Figure 11-2
Premature ventricular complex (PVC).

KEY CONCEPT
Premature ventricular complexes (PVCs) are early ectopic beats originating from the ventricular conduction system or muscle tissue.

Premature ventricular complexes are ______________ ectopic beats that interrupt the normal rhythm and originate from an irritable focus in the ventricular ______________ system or ______________ tissue.

[early] [conduction] [muscle]

PVCs can occur for no apparent reason in individuals who have healthy hearts. They are usually of no significance. The incidence of PVCs increases with age and can occur during exercise or at rest.

PVCs may also result from conditions such as myocardial ischemia, hypoxia, acid-base and electrolyte imbalance, hypokalemia, increased catecholamine and sympathetic tone (as in emotional stress), ingestion of stimulants (alcohol, caffeine, tobacco), drug toxicity, and sympathomimetic drugs (Table 11-1).

PVCs may be significant for two reasons. First, they can precipitate more serious dysrhythmias such as ventricular tachycardia or fibrillation. The danger is greater in patients experiencing myocardial ischemia and/or infarction. Second, PVCs can result in decreased cardiac output due to

Table 11-1 Premature Ventricular Complex

Causes of PVCs	Examples
Cardiac disorders	Myocardial ischemia and infarction, enlargement of the ventricular chambers, congestive heart failure, myocarditis
Use of certain drugs	Drug intoxication, particularly cocaine, amphetamines, tricyclic antidepressants; use of stimulants, such as alcohol, caffeine, tobacco; sympathomimetic drugs, such as phencyclidine (PCP), cocaine, epinephrine, isoproterenol
Other	Hypoxia, electrolyte imbalance, such as hypokalemia, hyperkalemia, hypomagnesemia, and hypocalcemia; metabolic acidosis, increased sympathetic stimulation

reduced diastolic filling time and a loss of atrial kick. This leads to a diminished or nonpalpable pulse. When no pulse is felt during a PVC it is called a nonperfusing PVC. Patients frequently experience the sensation of "skipped beats." Whether PVCs result in decreased cardiac output hinges on how long the abnormal rhythm lasts. Given our previous discussion, be sure to count and document how many PVCs are seen each minute.

CLINICAL MOMENT
With PVCs, it is important to check for a pulse to determine if they are perfusing PVCs. The absence of a pulse may require treatment if the underlying heart rate is slow or there are many PVCs. As an example, a rhythm in which there are bigeminal PVCs and the heart rate is 60 beats per minute, cardiac output will likely be adequate if the PVCs are producing a pulse. Conversely, cardiac output will likely be inadequate if the PVCs are not producing a pulse and the actual heart rate is 30 beats per minute.

PVCs can precipitate ventricular _____________ or _____________, particularly in patients experiencing myocardial ischemia and/or infarction. PVCs can lead to _____________ cardiac output and may result in a _____________ pulse. When the pulse is absent with a PVC, it is called a _____________ PVC.

[tachycardia] [fibrillation] [decreased] [nonpalpable] [nonperfusing]

You should pay special attention to these rhythm disturbances in persons with acute myocardial ischemia. PVCs that occur with myocardial ischemia may indicate the presence of enhanced automaticity, a reentry mechanism, or both, and may trigger lethal ventricular dysrhythmias. If the PVCs are frequent enough and occur early enough in the cardiac cycle, cardiac output is compromised. PVCs that serve as warning signs of the potential development of serious ventricular dysrhythmias in patients with myocardial ischemia include the following:

- Frequent PVCs
- Presence of multifocal PVCs
- Early PVCs (R-on-T)
- Patterns of grouped PVCs

QUESTION
"What type of irregularity does an occasional PVC produce?" (The answer can be found on page 361.)

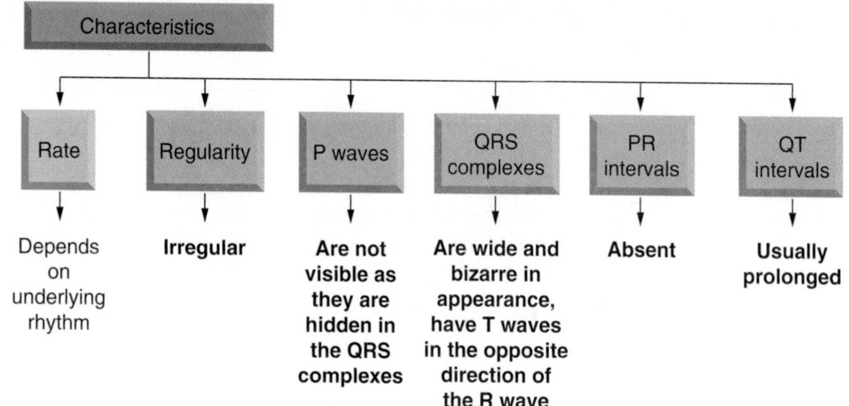

Figure 11-3
Algorithm for premature ventricular complexes (PVCs).

Review of key characteristics associated with PVCs

Rate:	Depends on the underlying rhythm
Regularity:	May be occasionally irregular or frequently irregular (depends on the number of PVCs present)
P waves:	Not preceded by a P wave (if seen, they are dissociated)
QRS complexes:	Wide, large, and bizarre looking
PR interval:	Not measurable
QT interval:	Usually prolonged with the PVC

Like other early ectopic beats the first thing you see with PVCs is an irregular rhythm. When you look at the area(s) of irregularity, the PVCs appear earlier in the cycle than the normal set of complexes would be expected to occur (Figure 11-3). Another characteristic that stands out is a wide (greater than 0.12 seconds), bizarre-looking QRS complex with a T wave that takes an opposite direction to the R wave of the PVC.

QUESTION
"In which type of premature beats will there be a noncompensatory pause?" (The answer can be found on page 361.)

The QRS complexes of the PVCs differ from QRS complexes of the underlying rhythm. P waves and PR intervals are typically present with the underlying rhythm but not the premature beats. A pause, called a compensatory pause, typically follows the PVC.

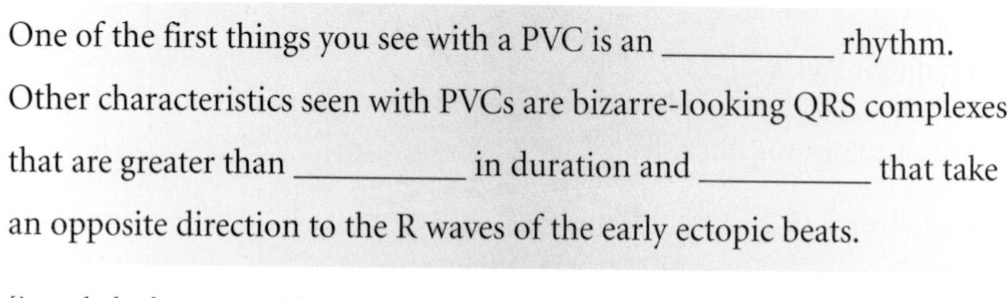

One of the first things you see with a PVC is an __________ rhythm.

Other characteristics seen with PVCs are bizarre-looking QRS complexes that are greater than __________ in duration and __________ that take an opposite direction to the R waves of the early ectopic beats.

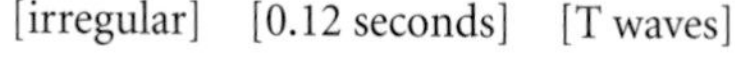

[irregular] [0.12 seconds] [T waves]

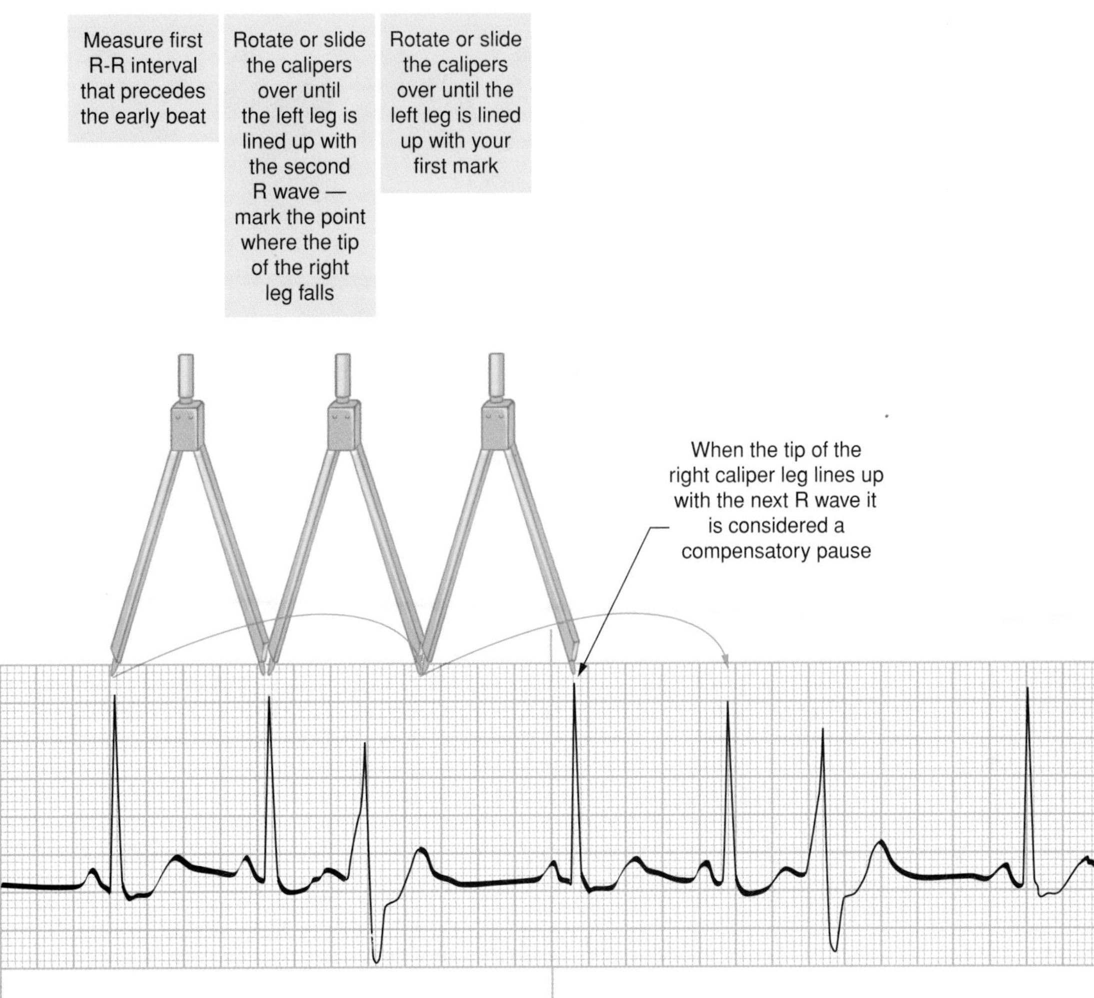

Figure 11-4
A compensatory pause is seen with premature ventricular complexes.

As discussed in previous chapters, the pause that follows a premature beat is called a compensatory pause if the normal beat following the premature complex occurs when it was expected (Figure 11-4). In other words, the period between the complex before and after the premature beat is the same as two normal R-R intervals. The pause occurs because the ventricle is refractory and cannot respond to the next regularly scheduled P wave from the sinus node. To determine if there is a compensatory pause we measure from the R wave of the beat that precedes the PVC to the R wave of the first beat that follows it. If there are two full R-R intervals between those R waves (with the PVC between), it is considered a compensatory pause.

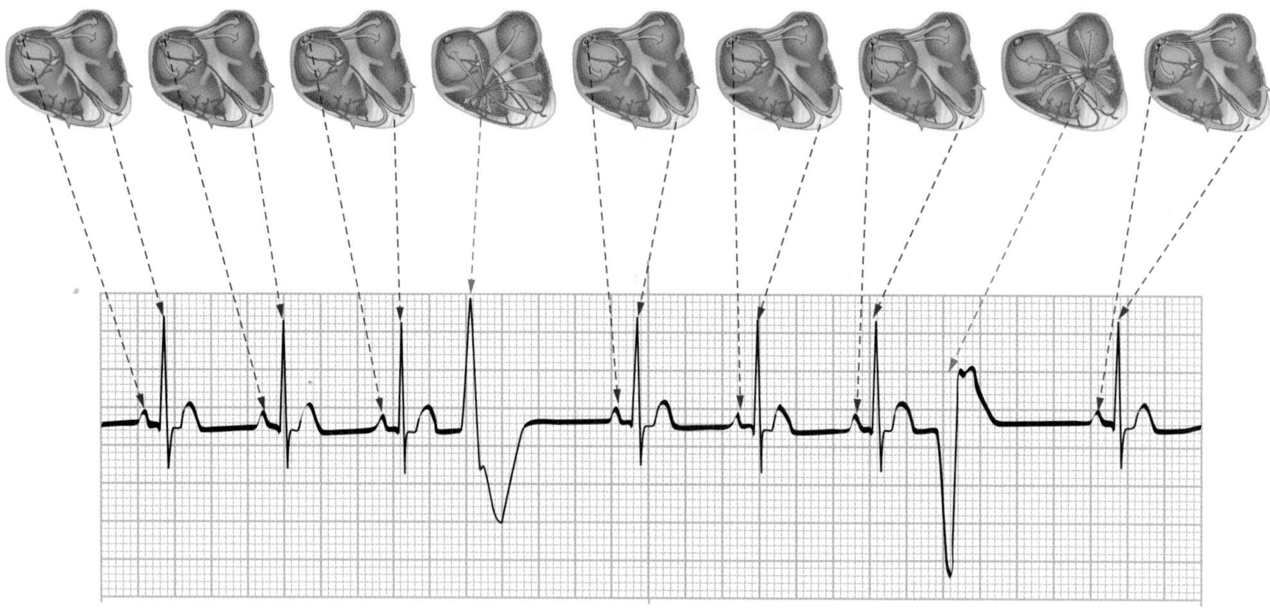

Figure 11-5
Multifocal PVCs arise from different sites within the ventricles and look different from each other.

A _______________ pause usually follows the PVC. In other words, the period between the complex before and after the premature beat is equal to _______________ R-R intervals.

[compensatory] [two]

PVCs may occur as a single beat, in clusters of two or more, or in repeating patterns. Sometimes, PVCs originate from only one location in the ventricle. These beats look the same and are called uniform (also referred to as unifocal) PVCs. Other times, PVCs arise from different sites in the ventricles. These beats tend to look different from each other and are called multiformed (multifocal) PVCs. Multiform PVCs indicate an irritable myocardium and should prompt you to take corrective action (Figure 11-5).

PVCs that look the same are called _______________, while PVCs that look different from each other are called _______________ and indicate an _______________ myocardium.

[uniform] [multiform] [irritable]

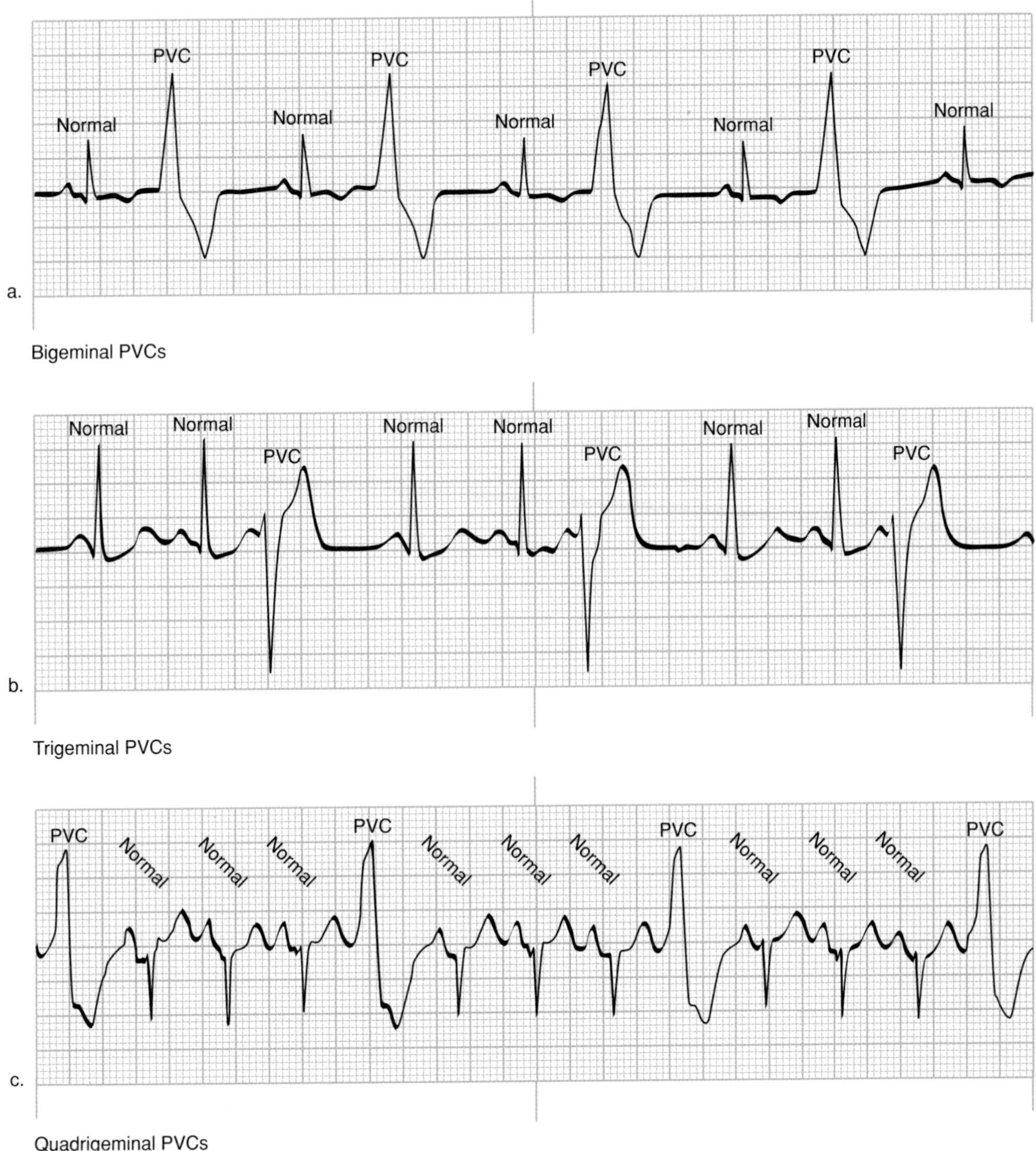

Figure 11-6
Premature ventricular complexes occurring in a) a bigeminal, b) trigeminal, and c) quadrigeminal pattern.

PVCs may occur as a single, early beat or more frequently (Figure 11-6). PVCs intermingled between normal beats are named depending on their frequency. Bigeminal PVCs are said to be present when every other beat is a PVC, regardless if unifocal or multifocal. If every third beat is a PVC, the condition is called trigeminal PVCs, or ventricular trigeminy. Similarly, a PVC every fourth beat is called ventricular quadrigeminy.

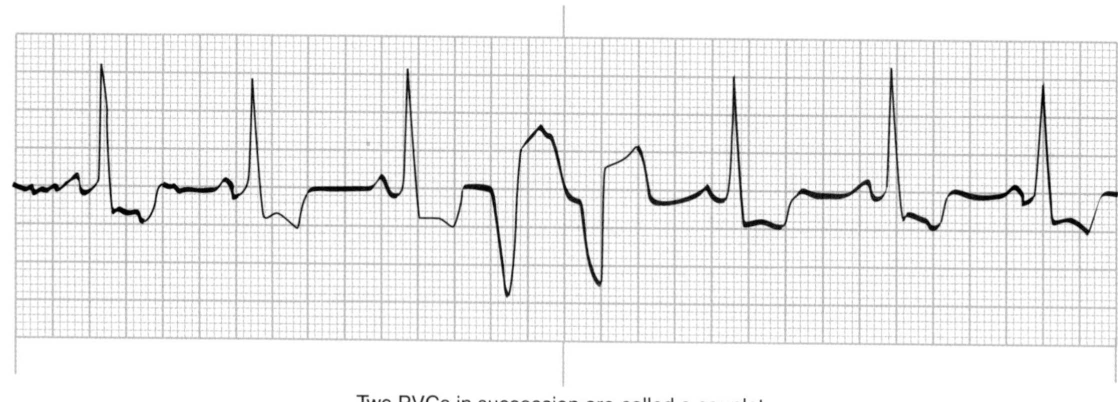

Two PVCs in succession are called a couplet

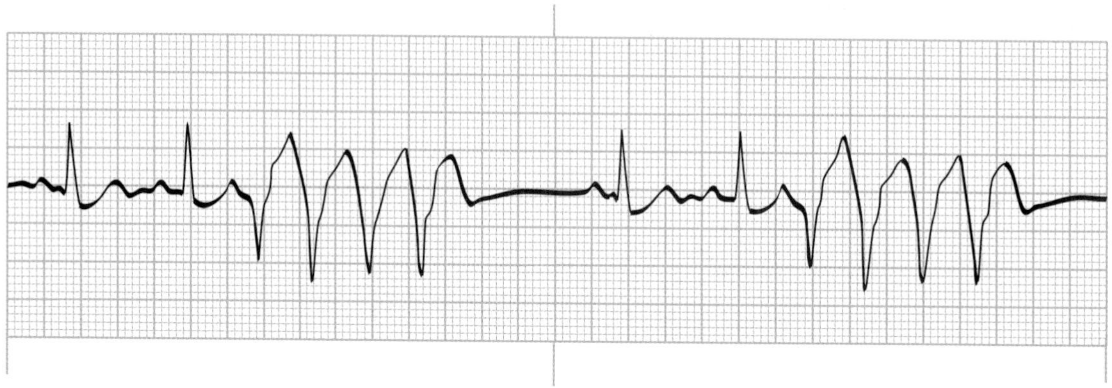

Three or more PVCs in a row are called a run of ventricular tachycardia or a run of PVCs

Figure 11-7
Couplet of PVCs and run of ventricular tachycardia.

QUESTION
"What type of irregularity do bigeminal, trigeminal, or quadrigeminal PVCs produce?" (The answer can be found on page 361.)

Regular PVCs at greater intervals than every fourth beat have no special name and are referred to as frequent PVCs.

PVCs seen every other beat are called ______________ PVCs. PVCs seen every third beat are called ______________ PVCs. PVCs seen every fourth beat are called ______________ PVCs.

[bigeminal] [trigeminal] [quadrigeminal]

PVCs may also occur one after the other. Two PVCs in a row are called a couplet, or pair. A couplet indicates the ventricles are extremely irritable. Three or more PVCs in a row at a ventricular rate of at least 100 beats per minute constitute an abnormal rhythm known as ventricular tachycardia. It may be called a **salvo, run,** or **burst** of ventricular tachycardia (Figure 11-7).

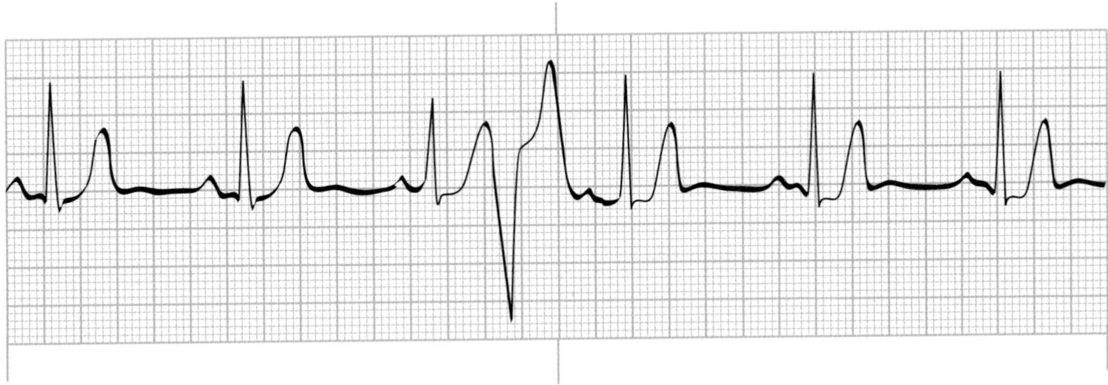

Figure 11-8
An interpolated PVC.

Two PVCs in a row are called a _______________. Three or more PVCs in a row are referred to as ventricular _______________. It may be called a _______________, _______________, or _______________ of ventricular tachycardia.

[couplet] [tachycardia] [salvo] [run] [burst]

Another type of PVC is called an **interpolated** PVC (Figure 11-8). It occurs when a PVC does not disrupt the normal cardiac cycle. It appears as a PVC squeezed between two regular complexes. Another feature is the PR interval of the cardiac cycle that follows the PVC may be longer than normal.

A PVC that occurs but does not disrupt the normal cardiac cycle is called an _______________ PVC.

[interpolated]

Frequent PVCs, especially if bigeminal, trigeminal, or couplets or runs of ventricular tachycardia, may foretell the deterioration of the rhythm into ventricular fibrillation. PVCs occurring on or near the previous T wave (R-on-T PVCs) also are likely to progress to more life-threatening ventricular dysrhythmias (such as ventricular fibrillation) because a portion of the T wave is vulnerable to electrical stimulation during the relative refractory period (Figure 11-9). A PVC occurring during this period of the cardiac cycle may precipitate ventricular tachycardia or fibrillation.

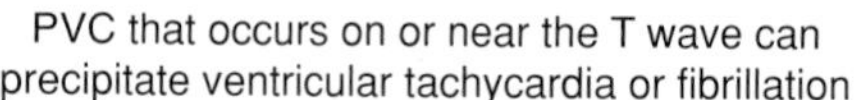

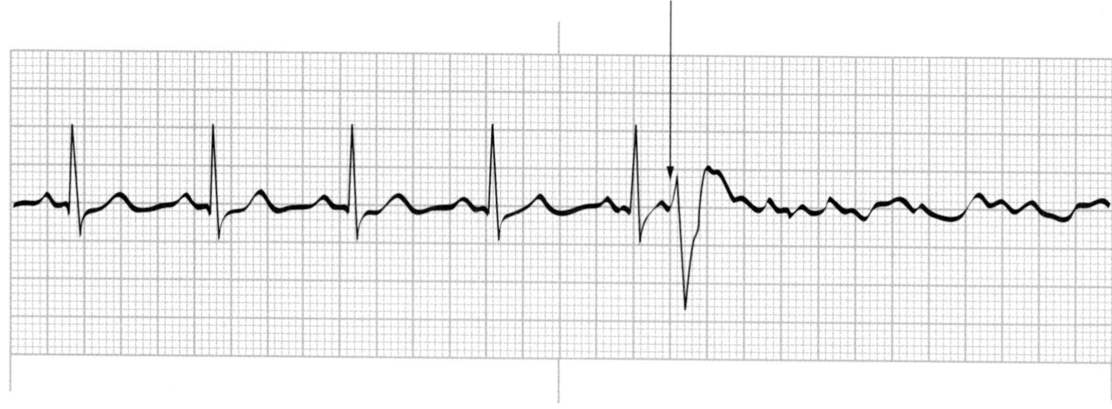

Figure 11-9
R-on-T PVC.

PVCs occurring on or near the previous T wave are called ____________ and are more likely to precipitate ventricular fibrillation.

[R-on-T]

A PVC is not an entire rhythm—it is a single beat. To describe it, refer to the underlying rhythm along with the ectopic beat(s), such as "sinus rhythm at a rate of 48 beats per minute with frequent PVCs."

CLINICAL MOMENT
Remember what has been emphasized throughout this text: heart rate × stroke volume = cardiac output. Slow dysrhythmias, because of the slower heart rate, cause decreased cardiac output.

 Idioventricular Rhythm

Idioventricular rhythm is a dysrhythmia that occurs when stimuli from higher pacemakers, such as the SA node or AV junction, fail to reach the ventricles or their rate falls to less than that of the ventricles (Figure 11-10). It may also occur due to a block in the heart's conduction system. The cells of the His-Purkinje system take over and act as the heart's pacemaker to generate electrical impulses. It normally fires at the inherent rate of the ventricles, 20 to 40 beats per minute. When it occurs as an escape complex or rhythm, it is considered a safety mechanism to prevent cardiac standstill. Idioventricular rhythm is often the first organized rhythm following defibrillation.

CLINICAL MOMENT
Sometimes idioventricular rhythm is also called "agonal rhythm." The term agonal rhythm usually indicates that the heart rate is less than 10 beats per minute. Patients in the final dying stage from a terminal disease often exhibit this rhythm prior to dying. Agonal rhythm has no cardiac output.

Idioventricular rhythm can be caused by myocardial ischemia or infarction, digoxin toxicity, pacemaker failure, and metabolic imbalances.

The decreased cardiac output associated with this dysrhythmia will likely cause the patient to be symptomatic (showing signs of such things as hypotension and/or syncope). Further, patient assessment is essential because the escape rhythm may be perfusing or nonperfusing. Idioventricular dysrhythmias are also common during cardiac arrest as they represent the final escape rhythm to be generated in an attempt to perfuse the body.

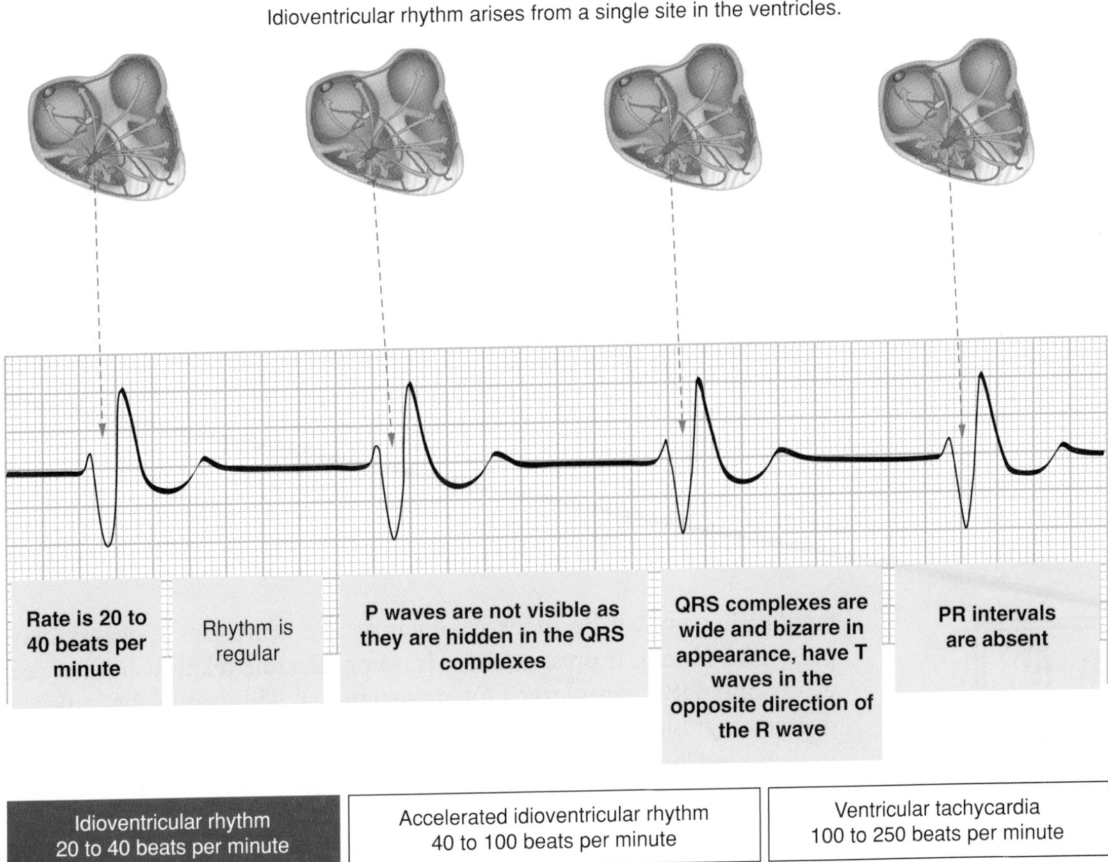

Figure 11-10
Idioventricular rhythm.

Review of key characteristics associated with idioventricular rhythm

Rate:	20 to 40 beats per minute (may be slower)
Regularity:	Regular
P waves:	Not preceded by a P wave (if seen, they are dissociated and would therefore be a 3rd-degree heart block with an idioventricular escape)
QRS complexes:	Wide, large, and bizarre looking
PR interval:	Not measurable
QT interval:	Usually prolonged

The most obvious characteristics of this dysrhythmia are a slow heart rate (usually 20 to 40 beats per minute although it may be slower) and wide (greater than 0.12 seconds) QRS complexes (Figure 11-11). Also, the T wave typically takes the opposite direction of the R wave. The rhythm is usually

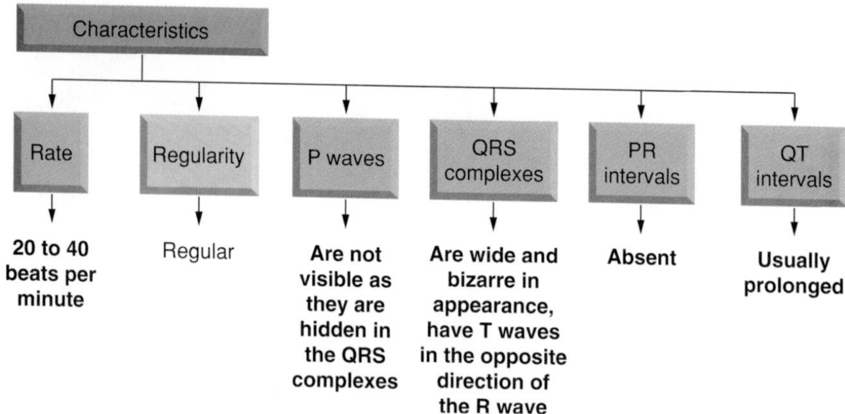

Figure 11-11
Algorithm for idioventricular rhythm.

regular; however, it becomes irregular as the heart dies. P waves may be present or absent. If present, there is no predictable relationship between P waves and QRS complexes (AV dissociation). This would be called 3rd-degree heart block with an idioventricular escape. Heart blocks are covered in detail in Chapter 12.

INSTRUCTIONAL MOMENT
Wide QRS complexes in a slow regular rhythm are key features of idioventricular rhythm.

Idioventricular rhythm occurs when the cells of the ____________ system take over and act as the heart's ____________ to generate electrical impulses. It normally fires at a rate of ____________ beats per minute and is often the first organized rhythm seen following ____________.

[His-Purkinje] [pacemaker] [20 to 40] [defibrillation]

KEY CONCEPT
Idioventricular rhythm arises from the ventricles at a rate of 20 to 40 beats per minute.

Accelerated Idioventricular Rhythm

When the rate of the idioventricular rhythm exceeds the inherent rate of the ventricles and is between 40 and 100 beats per minute, it is called accelerated idioventricular rhythm (Figure 11-12). Because it is a rhythm that originates from the ventricles it has the same characteristics as idioventricular rhythm except that it is faster.

This dysrhythmia can be caused by the same conditions that cause PVCs. It also occurs following acute myocardial infarction and may be seen after the administration of thrombolytic medications. It usually results in no ill effect because the heart rate is close to normal.

As Figure 11-13 shows, the key difference that separates this dysrhythmia from idioventricular rhythm and ventricular tachycardia is the heart rate.

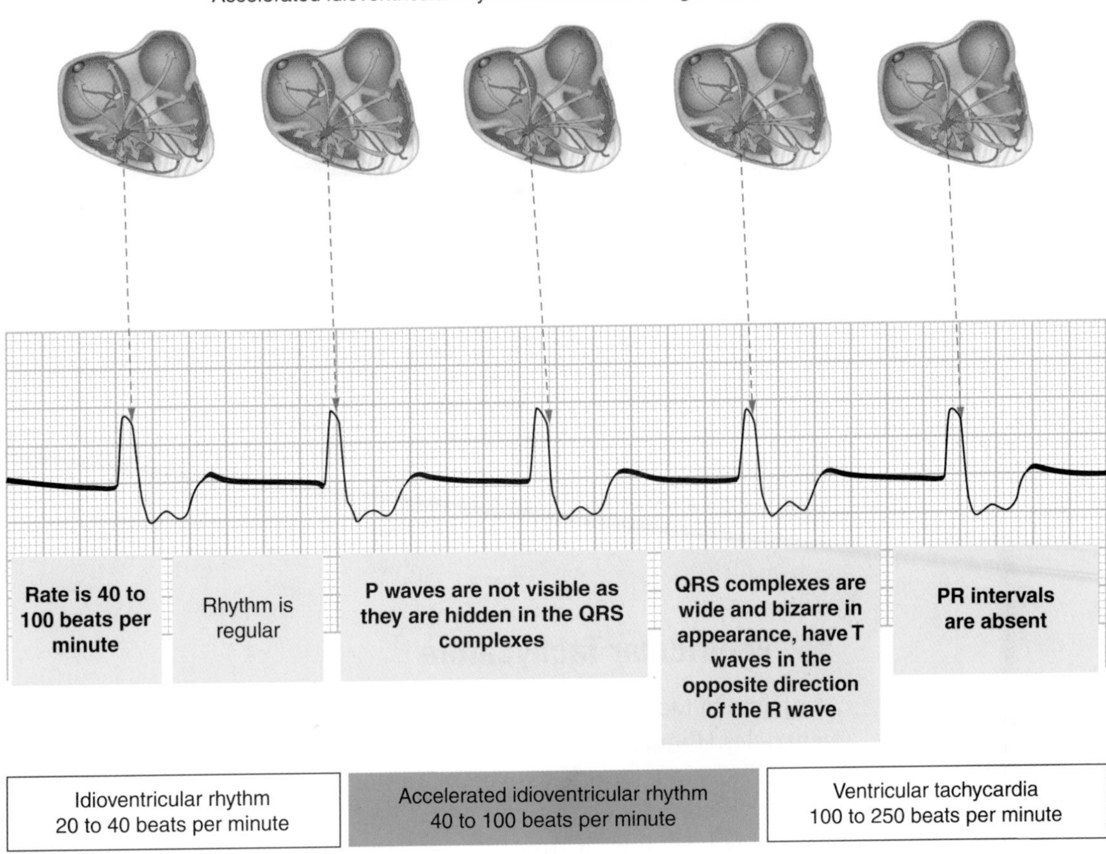

Figure 11-12
Accelerated idioventricular rhythm.

The heart rate associated with accelerated idioventricular rhythm is between ______________ and ______________ beats per minute.

[40] [100]

Review of key characteristics associated with accelerated idioventricular rhythm

Rate:	40 to 100 beats per minute
Regularity:	Regular
P waves:	Not preceded by a P wave
QRS complexes:	Wide, large, and bizarre looking
PR interval:	Not measurable
QT interval:	Usually prolonged

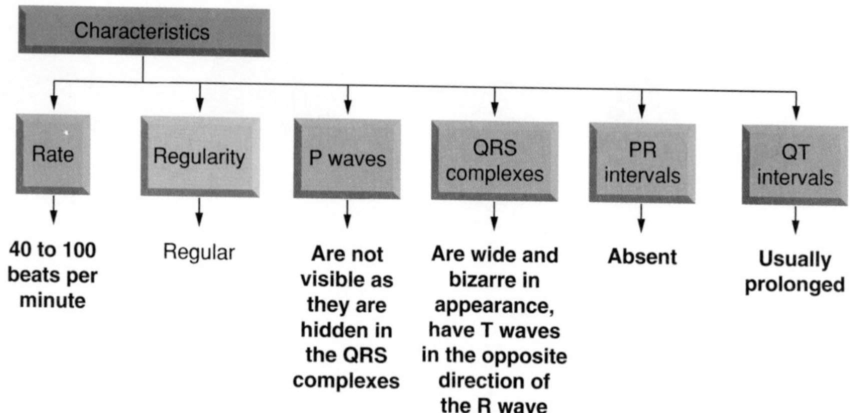

Figure 11-13
Algorithm for accelerated idioventricular rhythm.

Ventricular Tachycardia

Ventricular tachycardia (VT) is a fast dysrhythmia that arises from the ventricles (Figure 11-14). It is said to be present when there are three or more PVCs in a row. It may come in bursts of 6 to 10 complexes or may persist (sustained VT). It can occur with or without pulses, and the patient may be stable or unstable with this rhythm. Usually this dysrhythmia occurs in the presence of myocardial ischemia or significant cardiac disease. Ventricular tachycardia often precedes ventricular fibrillation and sudden death. It is one of the most common rhythms encounterd in out-of-hospital cardiac arrest.

INSTRUCTIONAL MOMENT
Ventricular tachycardia is commonly called VT or V-Tach.

Ventricular tachycardia arises from the ______________ and is said to be present when there are ______________ or more PVCs in a row. It may come in bursts of ______________ to ______________ complexes or may be ______________

[ventricles] [three] [6] [10] [sustained]

KEY CONCEPT
Ventricular tachycardia is a fast dysrhythmia that arises from the ventricles.

Causes of ventricular tachycardia include acid-base and electrolyte imbalance, hypoxia, congestive heart failure, elevated catecholamine levels, ingestion of stimulants, and drug toxicity (Table 11-2).

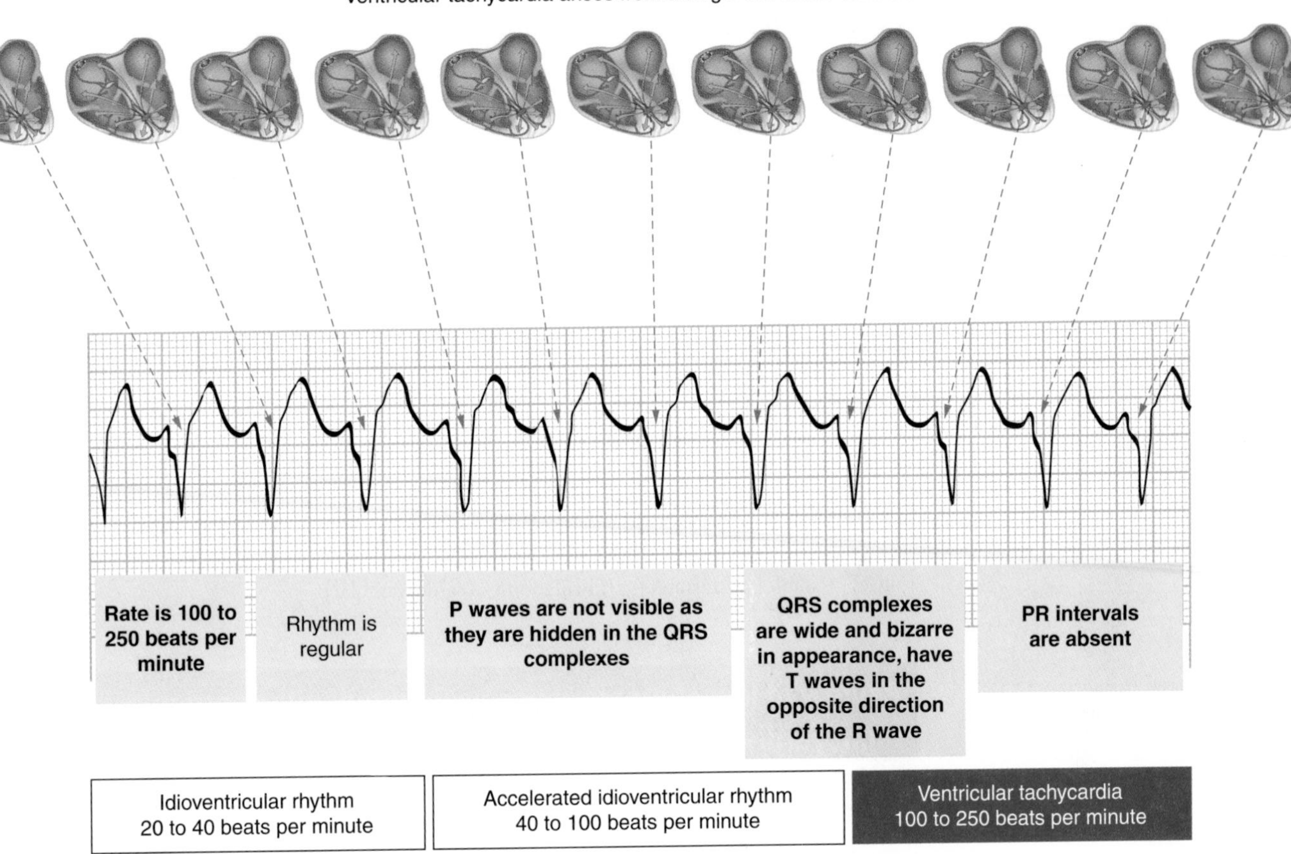

Figure 11-14
Ventricular tachycardia.

Table 11-2 Ventricular Tachycardia

Causes of ventricular tachycardia	Examples
Cardiac disorders	Myocardial ischemia and infarction, coronary artery disease, valvular heart disease, congestive heart failure, cardiomyopathy
Use of certain drugs	Drug intoxication from digitalis, tricyclic antidepressants, cocaine, amphetamines
Other	Electrolyte imbalance, such as hypokalemia; acid-base imbalance; trauma; ingestion of stimulants (alcohol, caffeine, tobacco)

CLINICAL MOMENT
Remember what has been emphasized throughout this text: heart rate × stroke volume = cardiac output. Fast dysrhythmias, because of the decreased stroke volume associated with the fast heart rate, cause decreased cardiac output.

Clinically, ventricular tachycardia is always significant. Even if the rhythm results in a pulse, it should be considered as potentially unstable, as patients are likely to develop more life-threatening rhythms and cardiac arrest. Usually VT indicates significant underlying cardiovascular disease. The rapid rate and concurrent loss of atrial kick associated with VT results in compromised cardiac output and decreased coronary artery and cerebral perfusion. The severity of symptoms varies with the rate of the VT and the presence and degree of underlying myocardial dysfunction. VT may be perfusing or nonperfusing. It may initiate or deteriorate into ventricular fibrillation.

Ventricular tachycardia can occur with or without a ____________, and the patient may be ____________ or ____________. Ventricular tachycardia often precedes ventricular ____________. The presence of VT usually indicates significant underlying ____________ disease.

[pulse] [stable] [unstable] [fibrillation] [cardiovascular]

Review of key characteristics associated with ventricular tachcyardia

Rate:	100 to 250 beats per minute
Regularity:	Regular
P waves:	Not preceded by a P wave (if seen, they are dissociated)
QRS complexes:	Wide, large, and bizarre looking
PR interval:	Not measurable
QT interval:	Not measurable

The most visible characteristics of VT are a rapid rate of between 100 and 250 beats per minute and wide (greater than 0.12 seconds), bizarre QRS complexes. The T waves may or may not be present and typically are of the opposite direction of the R waves. If the rate is between 100 and 150 beats per minute it is referred to as slow VT. Rarely, the rate may be greater than 250 and is then referred to as ventricular flutter. Typically, P waves are not discernable (if seen, they are dissociated). The rhythm is typically regular (Figure 11-15).

The key characteristics of VT are a _________ rate of between _________ beats per minute and _________, bizarre QRS complexes. If present, the T waves are typically in the _________ direction of the R waves.

[rapid] [100 and 250] [wide] [opposite]

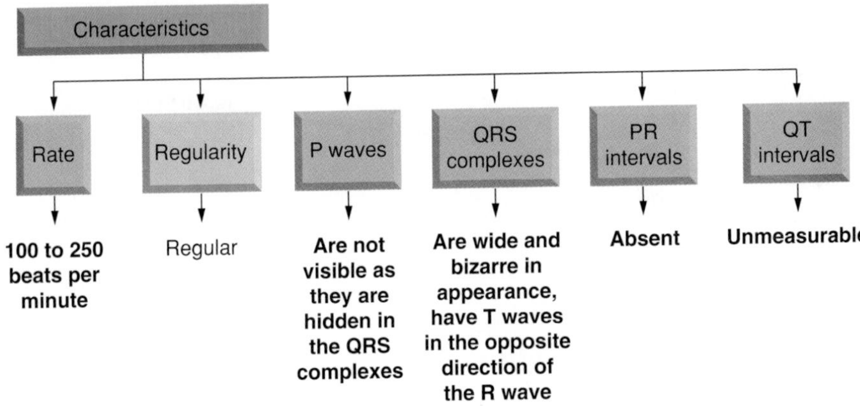

Figure 11-15
Algorithm for ventricular tachycardia.

Polymorphic VT

VT may be monomorphic, where the appearance of each QRS complex is similar, or polymorphic, where the appearance varies considerably from complex to complex. Either is potentially life threatening (Figure 11-16).

A unique variant of polymorphic ventricular tachycardia is called **torsades de pointes,** which means "twisting about the points." It is characterized by QRS complexes that alternate (usually gradually) between upright deflections and downward deflections. Unless the patient is in cardiac arrest, torsades often responds to infusion of magnesium sulfate. Standard antidysrhythmic drugs (such as procainamide) can worsen the condition, leading to cardiac arrest. If the patient is in cardiac arrest, the treatment of choice is prompt defibrillation.

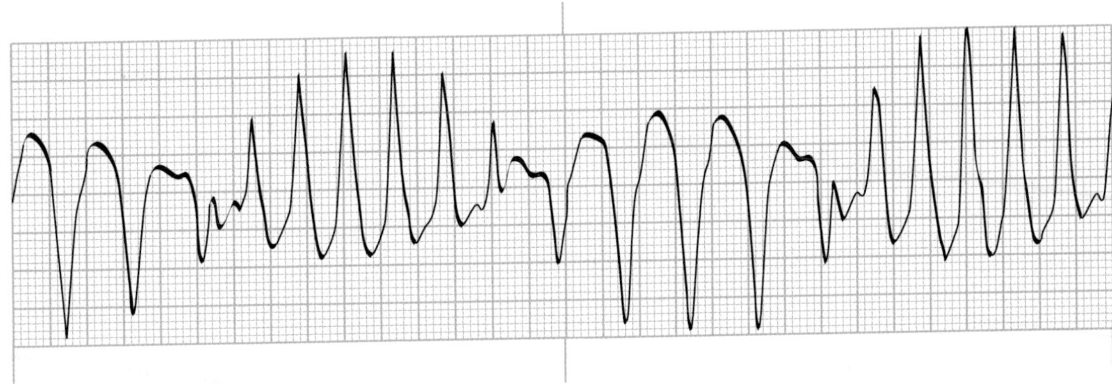

Figure 11-16
Polymorphic ventricular tachycardia. Torsades de pointes is characterized by QRS complexes that alternate between upright deflections and downward deflections.

_______________ ventricular tachycardia is where the appearance of each QRS complex is similar. _______________ ventricular tachycardia is where the appearance varies considerably from complex to complex. _______________ is a polymorphic ventricular tachycardia that means "twisting about the points."

[Monomorphic] [Polymorphic] [Torsades de pointes]

Ventricular Fibrillation

Ventricular fibrillation (VF) results from chaotic firing of multiple sites in the ventricles (Figure 11-17). This causes the heart muscle to quiver, much like a handful of worms, rather than contracting efficiently. It produces no effective muscular contraction and no cardiac output. Within 10 seconds, the amount of blood pumped by the heart diminishes to zero causing all life-supporting physiological functions to cease because of lack of circu-

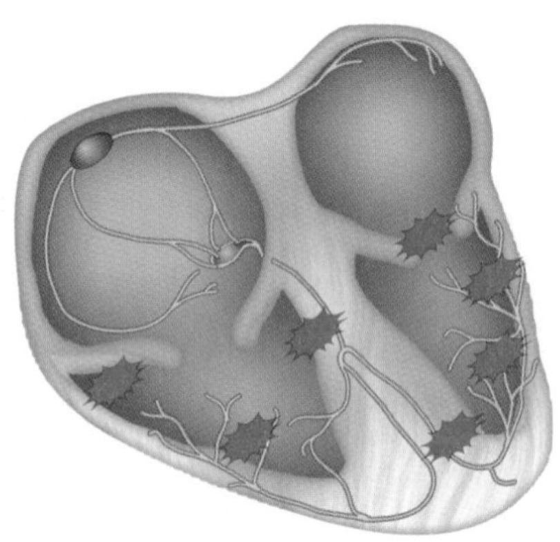

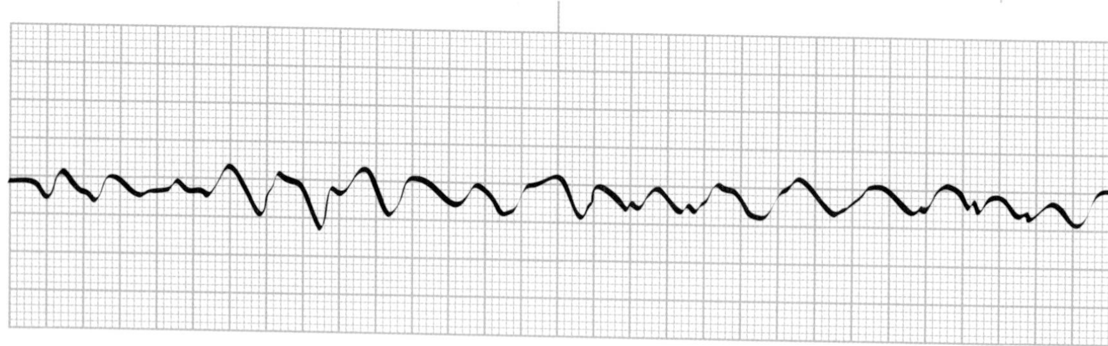

Figure 11-17
Ventricular fibrillation results from chaotic firing of multiple sites in the ventricles.

lating blood flow. Death occurs if the patient is not promptly treated (with defibrillation). VF is the most common cause of prehospital cardiac arrest in adults.

CLINICAL MOMENT
Defibrillation is considered the true definitive treatment of ventricular fibrillation.

VF is most commonly associated with significant cardiovascular system disease. It may be precipitated by PVCs, R-on-T phenomenon, or sustained VT. Other causes include myocardial ischemia or infarction, 3rd-degree AV heart block with a slow ventricular escape rhythm, cardiomyopathy, digitalis toxicity, hypoxia, acidosis, electrolyte imbalance (hypokalemia, hyperkalemia, near-drowning), electrical injury, and drug overdose or toxicity (cocaine, tricyclic) (Table 11-3).

KEY CONCEPT
Ventricular fibrillation is a chaotic firing of multiple sites in the ventricles. This causes the heart muscle to quiver instead of contract.

Ventricular fibrillation is generally easy to recognize on the cardiac monitor; it appears like a wavy line, totally chaotic, without any logic. There are no coordinated ventricular complexes present. The unsynchronized ventricular impulses occur at rates from 300 to 500 beats per minute. There are no discernible P waves, QRS complexes, or PR intervals (Figure 11-18).

Table 11-3 Ventricular Fibrillation

Causes of ventricular fibrillation	Examples
Cardiac disorders	Myocardial ischemia/infarction, untreated ventricular tachycardia, underlying heart disease
Other	Acid-base imbalance; electric shock; severe hypothermia; electrolyte imbalances, such as hypokalemia, hyperkalemia, hypercalcemia

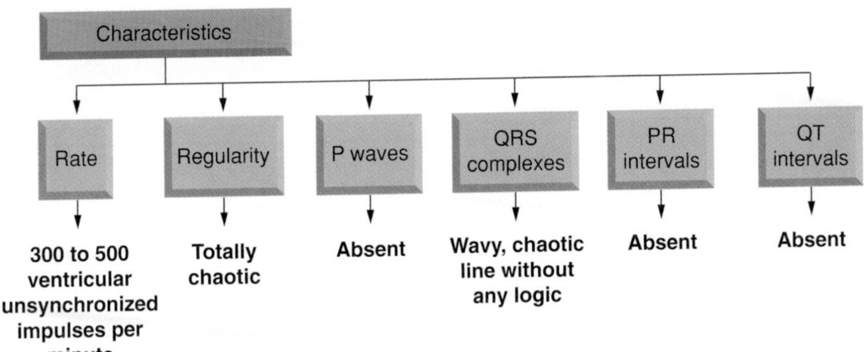

Figure 11-18
Algorithm for ventricular fibrillation.

In ventricular fibrillation (VF) the heart muscle ______________ rather than contracting efficiently. This occurs because there is ______________ firing of ______________ sites in the ventricles. VF results in an absence of effective ______________ contraction and cardiac output. The patient experiencing VF will die if he or she is not promptly ______________. On the cardiac monitor, ventricular fibrillation appears as a wavy line, totally ______________, without any logic. There are no discernible P waves, ______________, or PR intervals.

[quivers] [chaotic] [multiple] [muscular] [treated] [chaotic] [QRS complexes]

Asystole

CLINICAL MOMENT
Asystole means "without contraction of the heart"; "a" means without and "systole" means contraction of the heart.

Asystole is the absence of any cardiac activity. It appears as a flat (or nearly flat) line on the monitor screen (Figure 11-19). It may be the primary event in cardiac arrest or it may occur in complete heart block when there is no functional escape pacemaker. It is usually associated with global myocardial ischemia or necrosis and often follows VT, VF, PEA, or an agonal escape rhythm in the dying heart. Asystole produces complete cessation of cardiac output. It is a terminal rhythm, and once a person has become asystolic, the chances of recovery are extremely low. Some use the term **ventricular standstill** to define a condition where the atria continue to beat but the ventricles have stopped. A rhythm strip of ventricular standstill will only have P waves present without QRS complexes. An ominous dysrhythmia, asystole often represents a predictor of death, as the likelihood or resuscitation from asystole is dismal. Table 11-4 lists some conditions that cause asystole.

Table 11-4 Asystole

Causes of asystole	Examples
Cardiac disorders	Myocardial infarction, underlying heart disease
Other	Severe uncorrected acid-base imbalance; electric shock; electrolyte imbalances, such as hyperkalemia; massive pulmonary embolism; prolonged hypoxemia; drug intoxication (such as cocaine overdose)

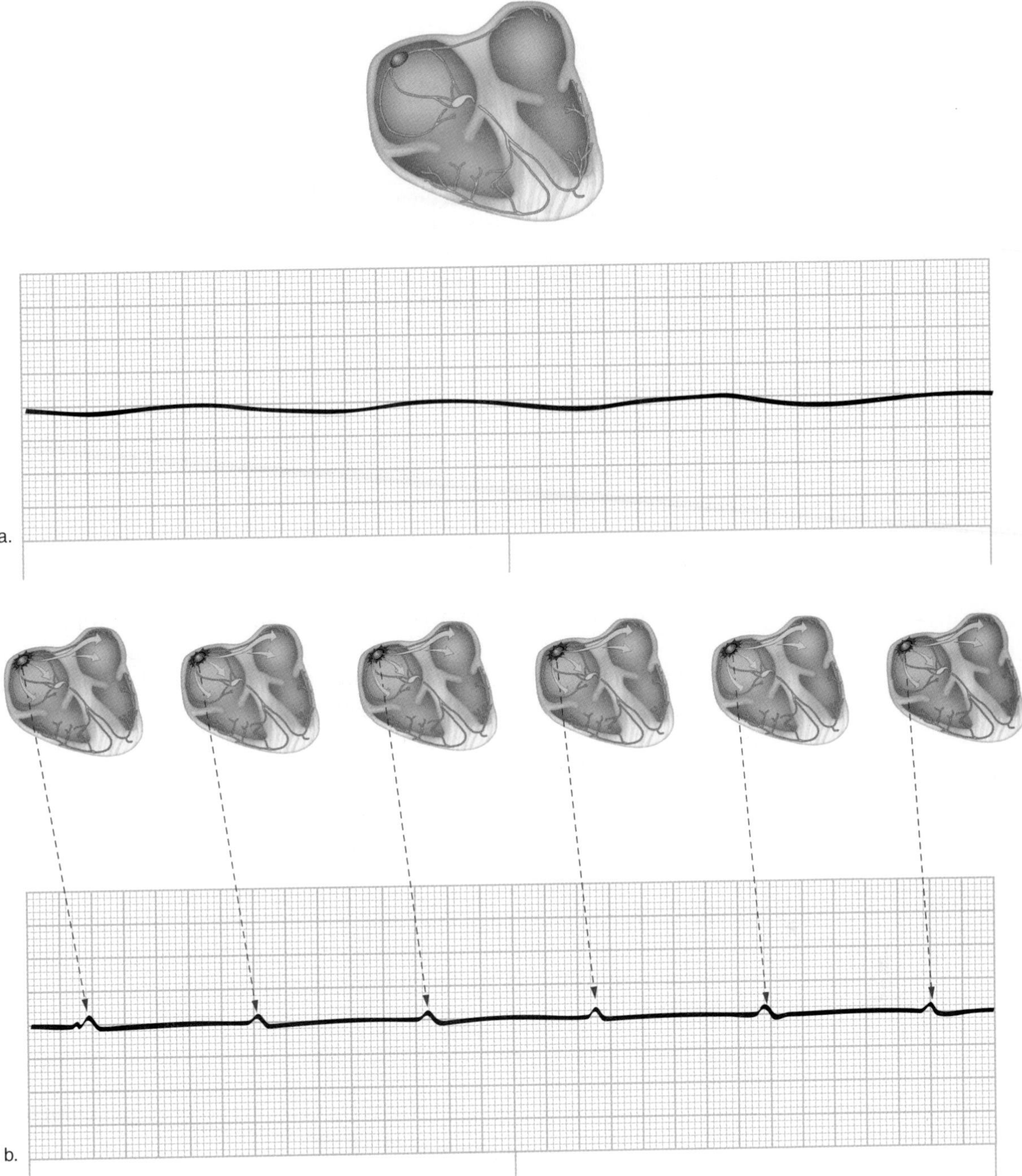

Figure 11-19
Asystole and ventricular standstill. (a) Asystole is a complete absence of cardiac activity. (b) Ventricular standstill occurs when there is electrical activity from the atria but none from the ventricles.

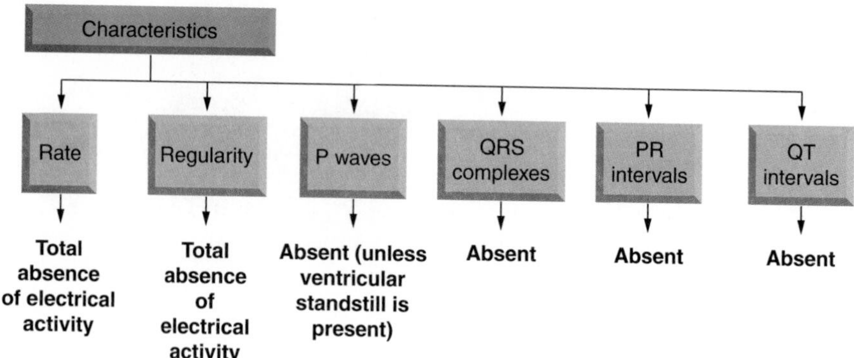

Figure 11-20
Algorithm for asystole.

There is no electrical activity with asystole, only a flat line (Figure 11-20).

KEY CONCEPT
Asystole is the absence of electrical activity in the heart.

Always verify the presence of asystole in two leads prior to initiating treatment. Misplacement of an ECG lead or a loose wire, can mimic asystole (or VF) on the monitor. If a patient is in cardiac arrest and appears to be in asystole, be sure to check the following:

- The leads are attached in the proper places to both the machine and the patient.
- The correct lead (eg., I, II, III) is selected on the monitor.
- The rhythm in more than one lead.
- The monitor batteries are functioning appropriately.

The absence of any cardiac activity is called ______________. It appears as a ______________ line on the monitor screen and produces complete ______________ of cardiac output. Once a person is in asystole, the likelihood of recovery is extremely ______________. Asystole must be verified because ______________ of a lead or a ______________ wire can mimic this condition on the cardiac monitor.

[asystole] [flat] [cessation] [low] [misplacement] [loose]

Pulseless Electrical Activity

Pulseless electrical activity (PEA) is a condition rather than a dysrhythmia. We cover it here for the sake of completeness in our discussion of the various causes of cardiac arrest. With PEA we see an organized electrical rhythm on the ECG monitor that should result in contraction of the heart muscle but there is no corresponding pulse. This results in the patient being pulseless and apneic. In other words, there is organized electrical activity in the heart that fails to generate effective cardiac contraction. The electrical activity seen with PEA may be sinus rhythm, sinus tachycardia, idioventricular rhythm, or any rhythm that is generally expected to generate a pulse.

KEY CONCEPT
The primary characteristic associated with PEA is the presence of an organized electrical rhythm without a corresponding pulse.

This condition is often associated with severe underlying heart disease but you should always consider reversible causes of PEA, which include hypovolemia (most common); tension pneumothorax; hypoxia; acidosis; pericardial tamponade; hypothermia; hyperkalemia; massive myocardial infarction; and an overdose of drugs, such as tricyclic antidepressants.

With PEA there is ________________ activity in the heart that fails to generate effective cardiac ________________. The electrical activity seen with PEA may be sinus ________________, sinus ________________, ________________ rhythm, or any rhythm that is expected to generate a ________________.

[electrical] [contraction] [rhythm] [tachycardia] [idioventricular] [pulse]

You can practice interpreting ventricular dysrhythmias with the following *Practice Makes Perfect* exercises. Answers to these exercises can be found in Appendix A.

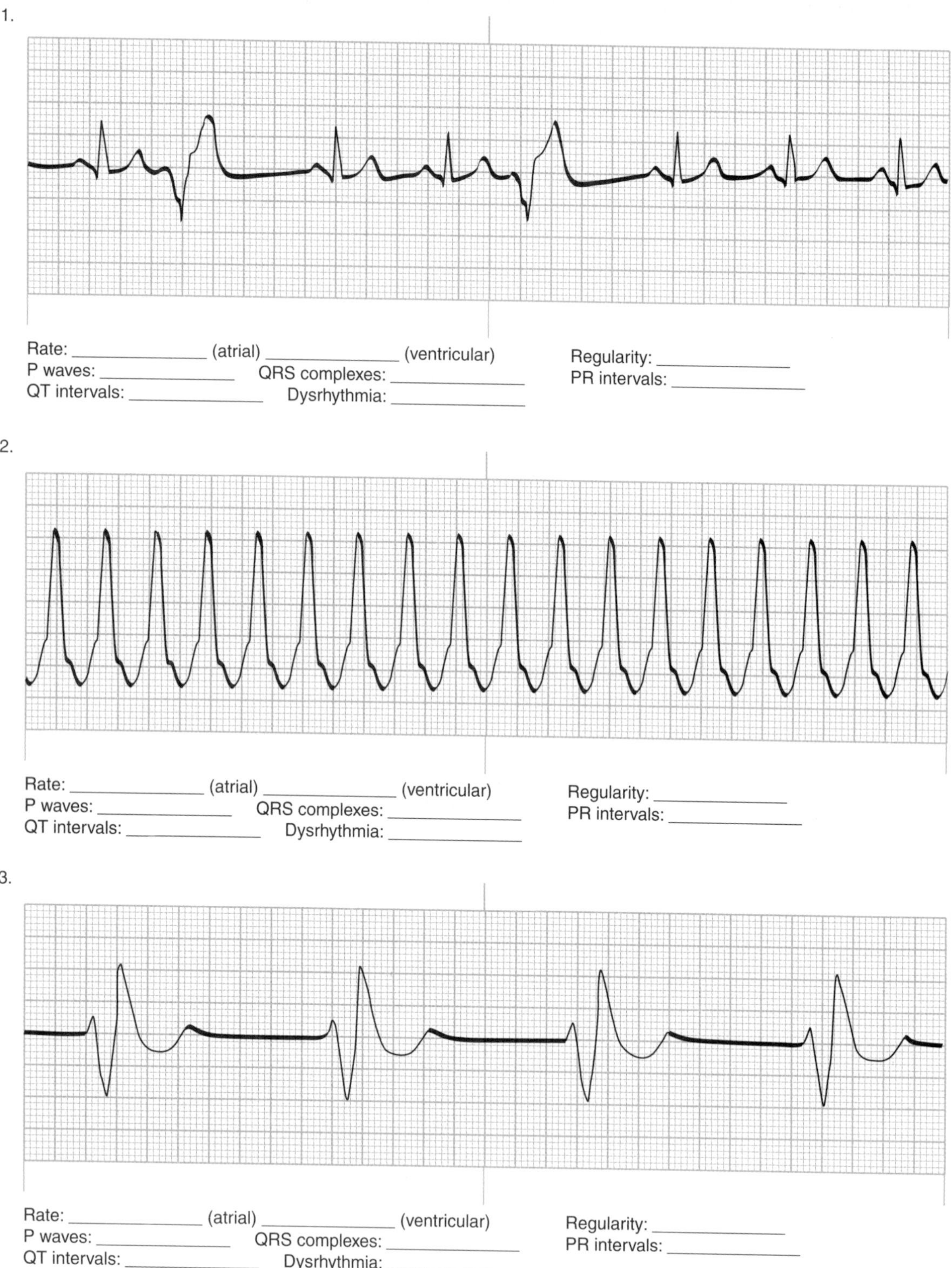

1.

Rate: ______________ (atrial) ______________ (ventricular)
P waves: ______________ QRS complexes: ______________
QT intervals: ______________ Dysrhythmia: ______________
Regularity: ______________
PR intervals: ______________

2.

Rate: ______________ (atrial) ______________ (ventricular)
P waves: ______________ QRS complexes: ______________
QT intervals: ______________ Dysrhythmia: ______________
Regularity: ______________
PR intervals: ______________

3.

Rate: ______________ (atrial) ______________ (ventricular)
P waves: ______________ QRS complexes: ______________
QT intervals: ______________ Dysrhythmia: ______________
Regularity: ______________
PR intervals: ______________

PRACTICE. . . MAKES PERFECT

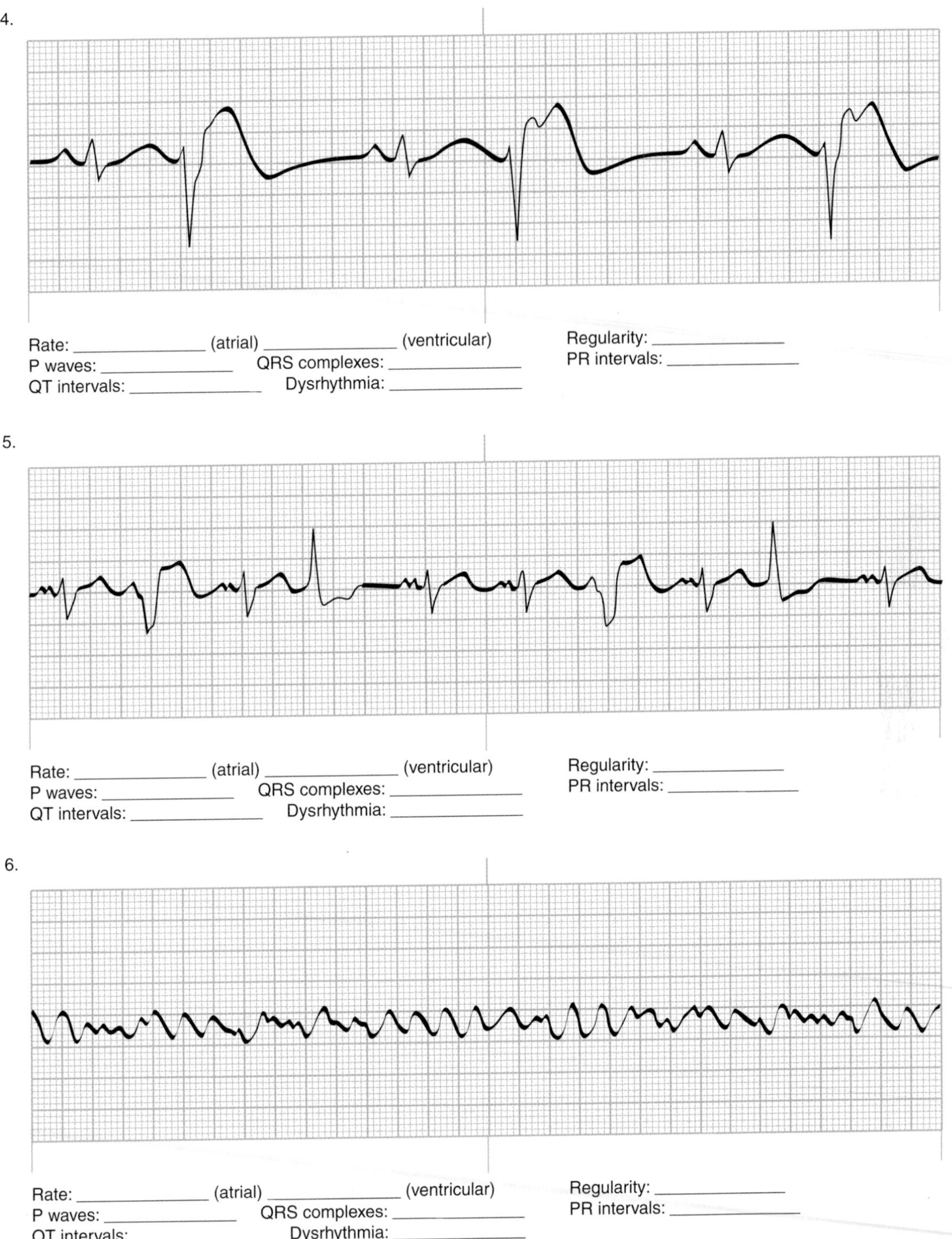

4.

Rate: ______________ (atrial) ______________ (ventricular)
Regularity: ______________
P waves: ______________
QRS complexes: ______________
PR intervals: ______________
QT intervals: ______________
Dysrhythmia: ______________

5.

Rate: ______________ (atrial) ______________ (ventricular)
Regularity: ______________
P waves: ______________
QRS complexes: ______________
PR intervals: ______________
QT intervals: ______________
Dysrhythmia: ______________

6.

Rate: ______________ (atrial) ______________ (ventricular)
Regularity: ______________
P waves: ______________
QRS complexes: ______________
PR intervals: ______________
QT intervals: ______________
Dysrhythmia: ______________

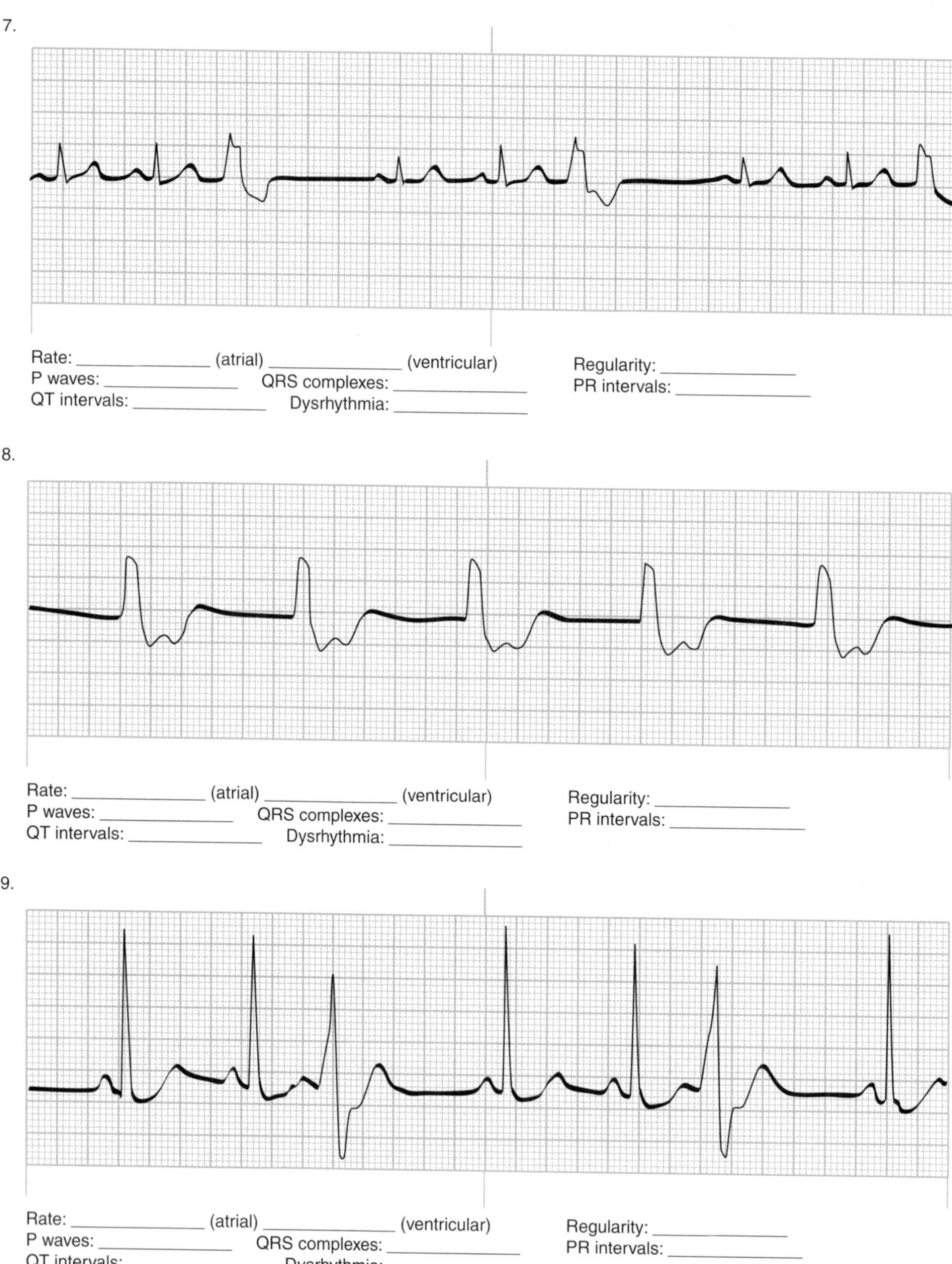
PRACTICE. . . MAKES PERFECT
7.
Rate: ______ (atrial) ______ (ventricular)
Regularity: ______
P waves: ______
QRS complexes: ______
PR intervals: ______
QT intervals: ______
Dysrhythmia: ______
8.
Rate: ______ (atrial) ______ (ventricular)
Regularity: ______
P waves: ______
QRS complexes: ______
PR intervals: ______
QT intervals: ______
Dysrhythmia: ______
9.
Rate: ______ (atrial) ______ (ventricular)
Regularity: ______
P waves: ______
QRS complexes: ______
PR intervals: ______
QT intervals: ______
Dysrhythmia: ______

PRACTICE. . . MAKES PERFECT

10.

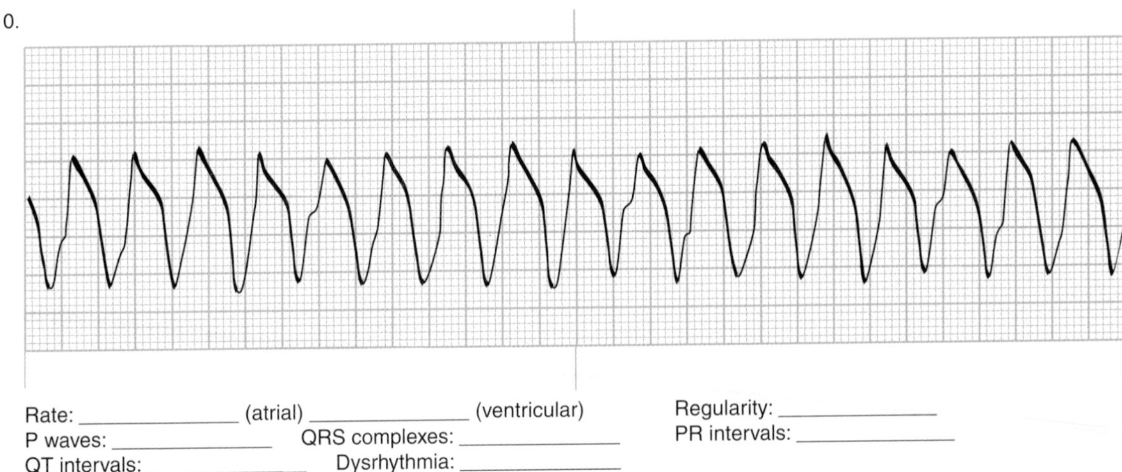

Rate: ______________ (atrial) ______________ (ventricular)
Regularity: ______________
P waves: ______________
QRS complexes: ______________
PR intervals: ______________
QT intervals: ______________
Dysrhythmia: ______________

You can practice interpreting sinus, atrial and junctional dysrhythmias (as discussed in chapters 8, 9, and 10) with the following *Practice Makes Perfect* exercises. Answers to these exercises can be found in Appendix A.

PRACTICE. . . MAKES PERFECT

11.

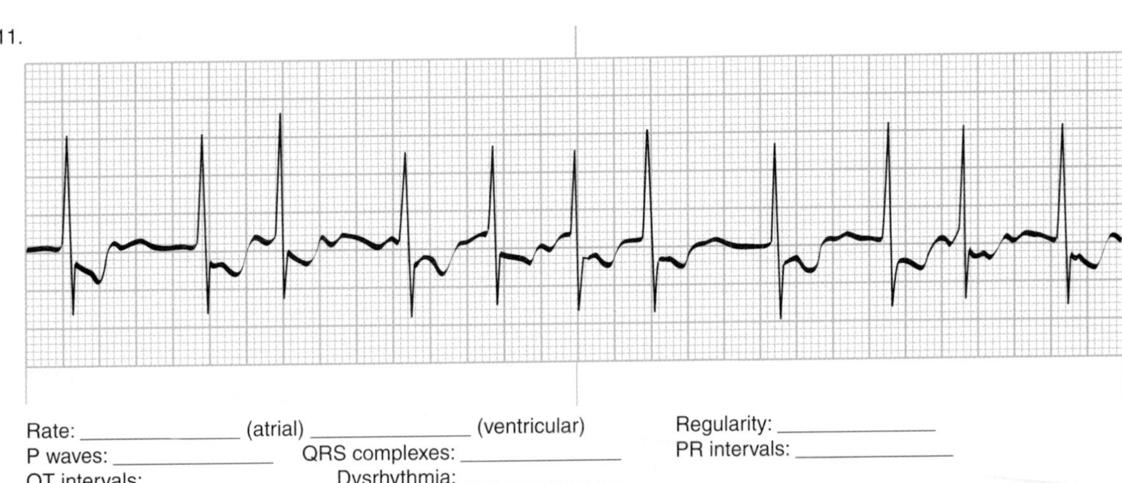

Rate: ______________ (atrial) ______________ (ventricular)
Regularity: ______________
P waves: ______________
QRS complexes: ______________
PR intervals: ______________
QT intervals: ______________
Dysrhythmia: ______________

PRACTICE. . . MAKES PERFECT

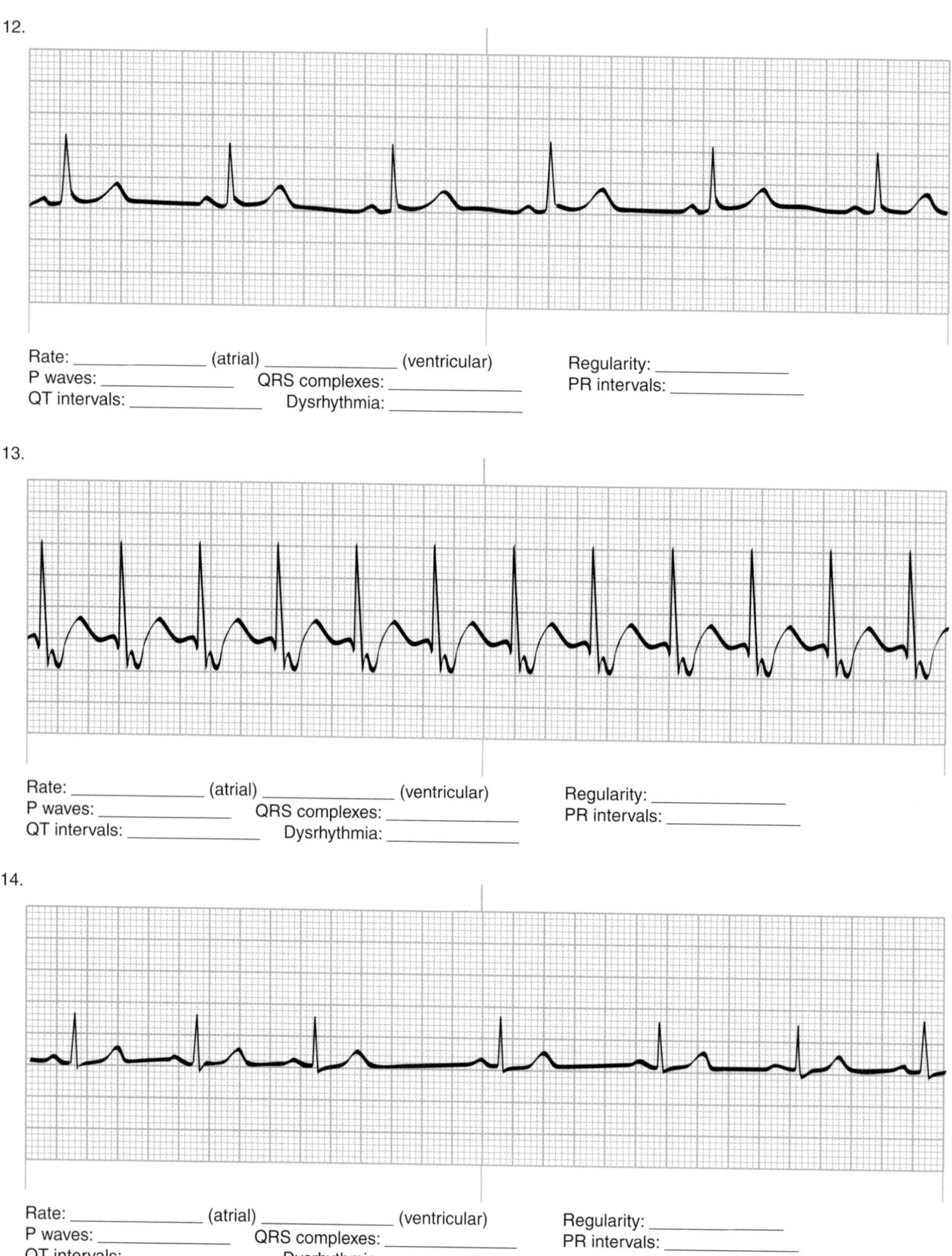

PRACTICE. . . MAKES PERFECT

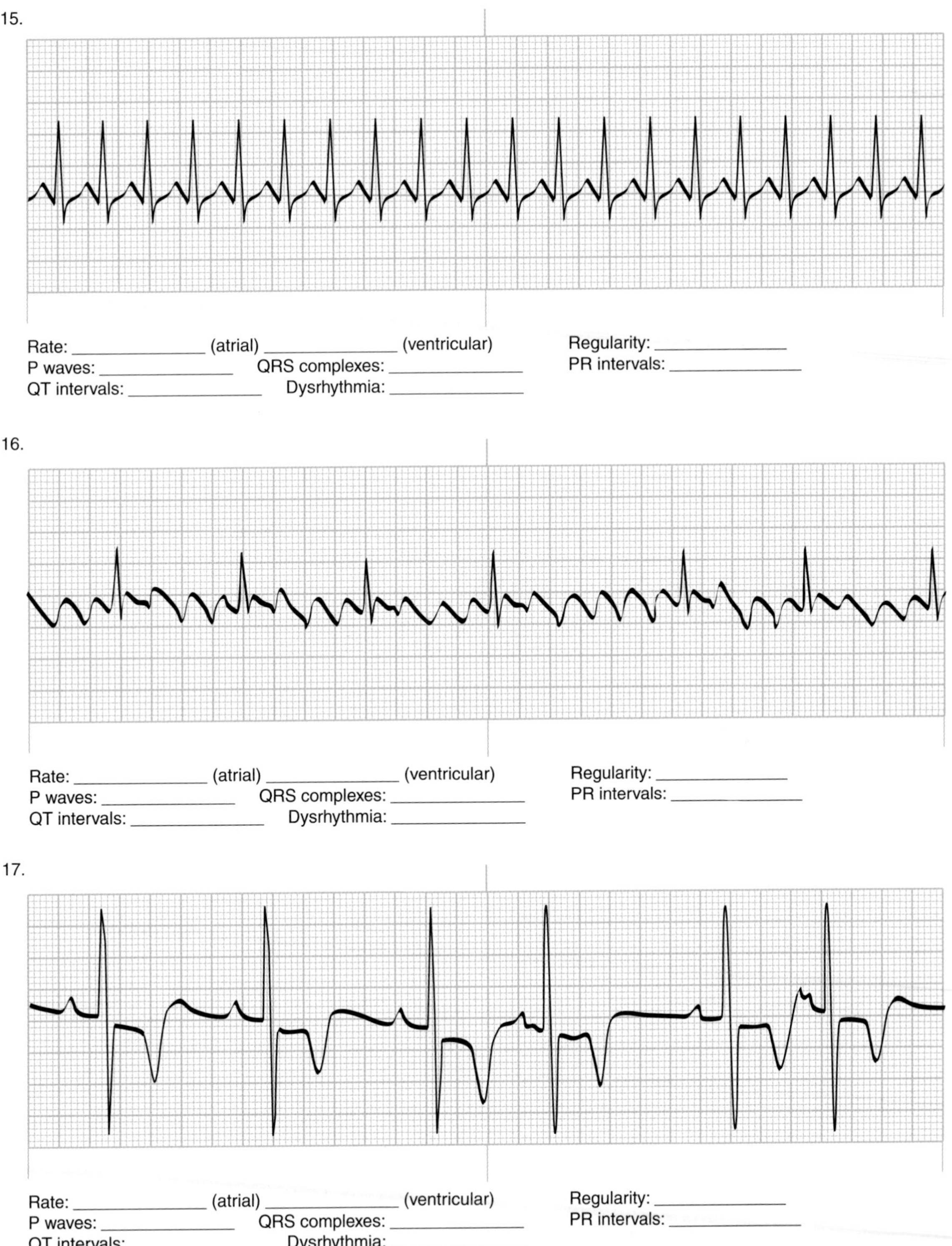

15.

Rate: ______________ (atrial) ______________ (ventricular) Regularity: ______________
P waves: ______________ QRS complexes: ______________ PR intervals: ______________
QT intervals: ______________ Dysrhythmia: ______________

16.

Rate: ______________ (atrial) ______________ (ventricular) Regularity: ______________
P waves: ______________ QRS complexes: ______________ PR intervals: ______________
QT intervals: ______________ Dysrhythmia: ______________

17.

Rate: ______________ (atrial) ______________ (ventricular) Regularity: ______________
P waves: ______________ QRS complexes: ______________ PR intervals: ______________
QT intervals: ______________ Dysrhythmia: ______________

PRACTICE. . . MAKES PERFECT

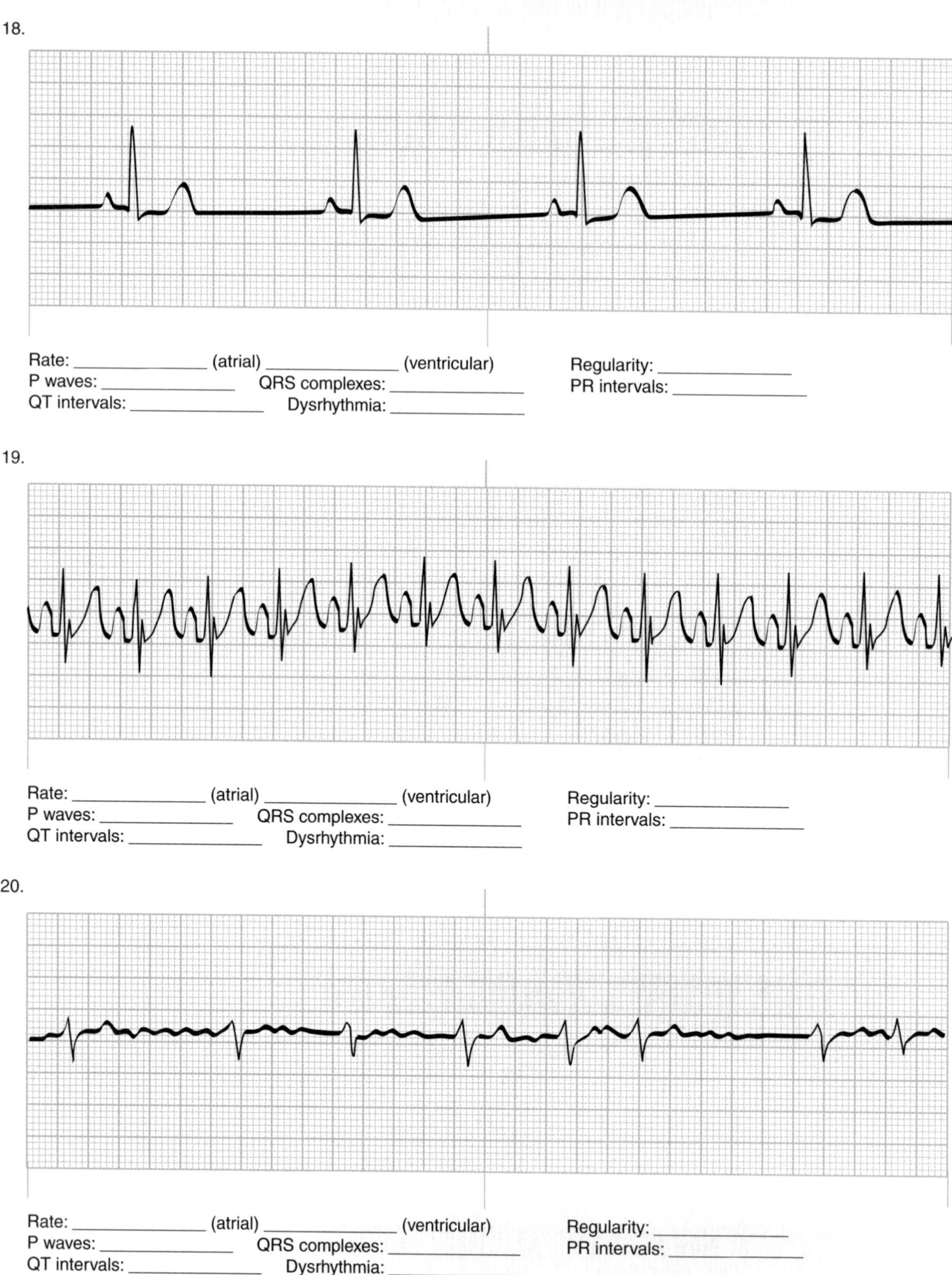

18.

Rate: ______________ (atrial) ______________ (ventricular) Regularity: ______________
P waves: ______________ QRS complexes: ______________ PR intervals: ______________
QT intervals: ______________ Dysrhythmia: ______________

19.

Rate: ______________ (atrial) ______________ (ventricular) Regularity: ______________
P waves: ______________ QRS complexes: ______________ PR intervals: ______________
QT intervals: ______________ Dysrhythmia: ______________

20.

Rate: ______________ (atrial) ______________ (ventricular) Regularity: ______________
P waves: ______________ QRS complexes: ______________ PR intervals: ______________
QT intervals: ______________ Dysrhythmia: ______________

PRACTICE. . . MAKES PERFECT

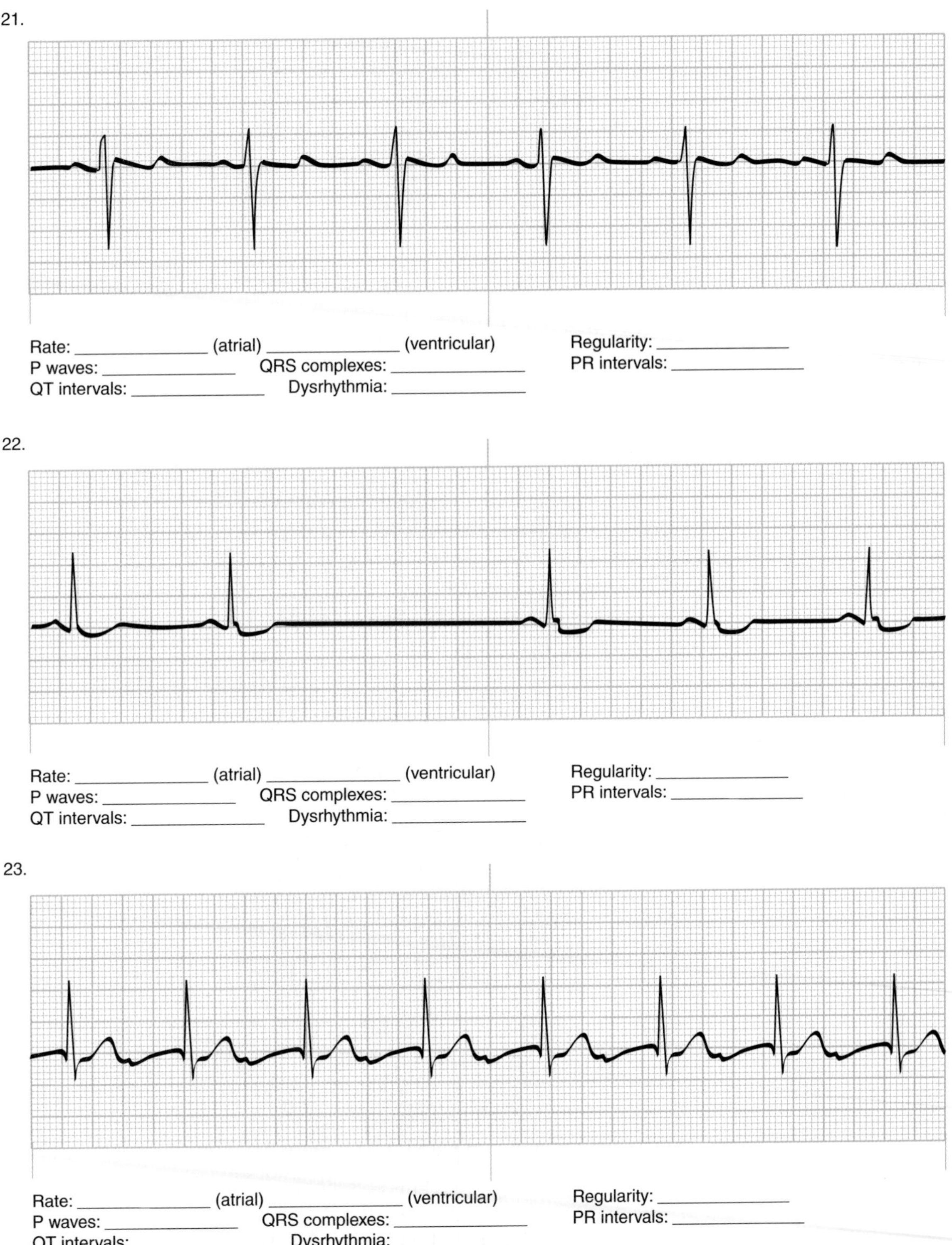

21.

Rate: _______________ (atrial) _______________ (ventricular) Regularity: _______________
P waves: _______________ QRS complexes: _______________ PR intervals: _______________
QT intervals: _______________ Dysrhythmia: _______________

22.

Rate: _______________ (atrial) _______________ (ventricular) Regularity: _______________
P waves: _______________ QRS complexes: _______________ PR intervals: _______________
QT intervals: _______________ Dysrhythmia: _______________

23.

Rate: _______________ (atrial) _______________ (ventricular) Regularity: _______________
P waves: _______________ QRS complexes: _______________ PR intervals: _______________
QT intervals: _______________ Dysrhythmia: _______________

PRACTICE. . . MAKES PERFECT

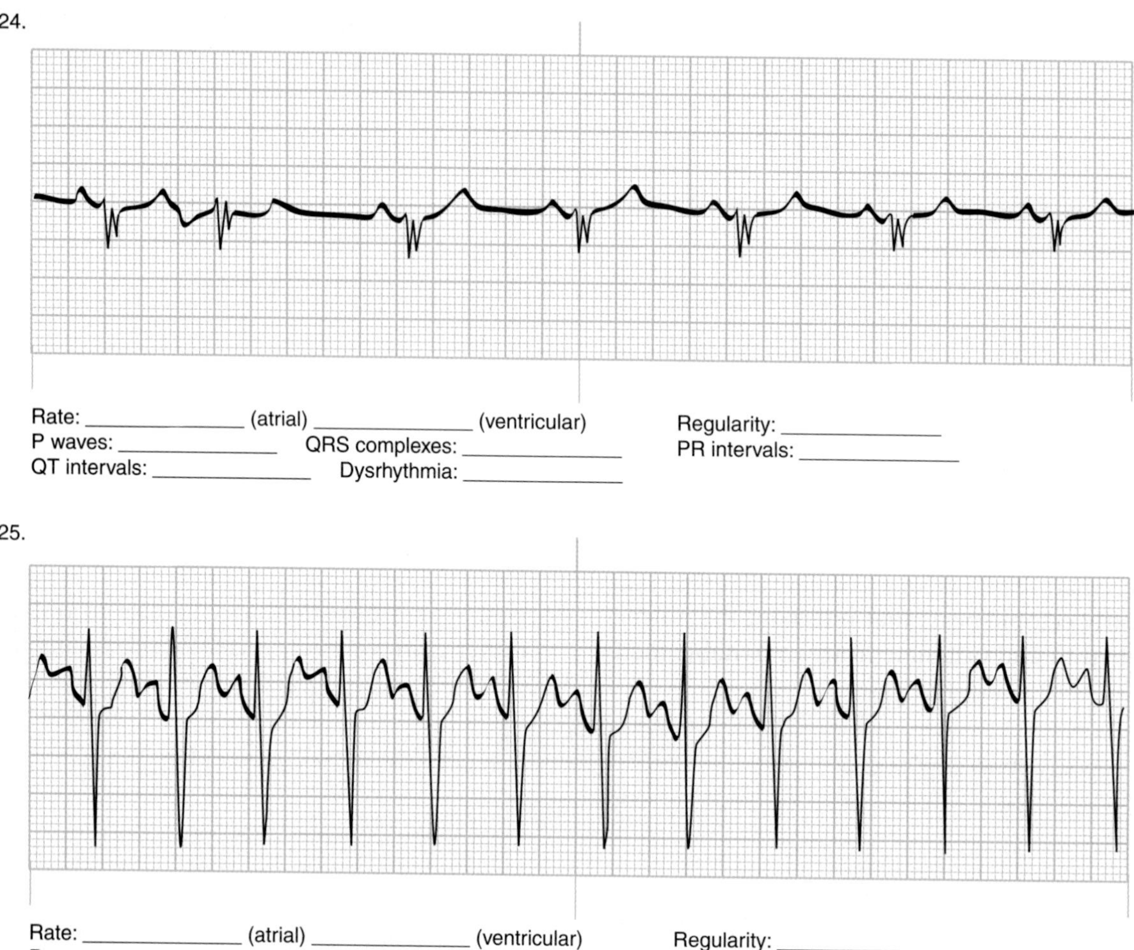

24.

Rate: _______________ (atrial) _______________ (ventricular)
P waves: _______________
QRS complexes: _______________
QT intervals: _______________
Dysrhythmia: _______________
Regularity: _______________
PR intervals: _______________

25.

Rate: _______________ (atrial) _______________ (ventricular)
P waves: _______________
QRS complexes: _______________
QT intervals: _______________
Dysrhythmia: _______________
Regularity: _______________
PR intervals: _______________

Key Points

- Ventricular dysrhythmias occur when the atria, AV junction, or both, are unable to initiate an electrical impulse or when there is enhanced automaticity of the ventricular myocardium.

- A key feature of ventricular dysrhythmias are wide (greater than 0.12 seconds in duration), bizarre QRS complexes that have T waves in the opposite direction of the R wave and an absence of P waves.

- Ventricular dysrhythmias include: premature ventricular contraction (PVC), ventricular escape complexes or rhythm, ventricular tachycardia, ventricular fibrillation, and asystole.

- Premature ventricular complexes (PVCs) are early ectopic beats that interrupt the normal rhythm and originate from an irritable focus in the ventricular conduction system or muscle tissue.

- PVCs that look the same are called uniform (unifocal), while PVCs that look different from each other are called multiform (multifocal).

- PVCs occurring every other beat are called bigeminal PVCs, while PVCs occurring every third beat are called trigeminal PVCs and a PVC seen every fourth beat is called ventricular quadrigeminy.

- Two PVCs in a row are called a couplet and indicate extremely irritable ventricles.

- An interpolated PVC occurs during a PVC but does not disrupt the normal cardiac cycle. It appears as a PVC squeezed between two regular complexes.

- Idioventricular rhythm is a slow dysrhythmia with wide QRS complexes that arise from the ventricles at a rate of 20 to 40 beats per minute.

- Ventricular tachycardia is a fast dysrhythmia, between 100 and 250 beats per minute that arises from the ventricles. It is said to be present when there are three or more PVCs in a row. It may come in bursts of 6 to 10 complexes or may persist (sustained VT).

- Ventricular tachycardia can occur with or without pulses, and the patient may be stable or unstable with this rhythm.

- VT may be monomorphic, where the appearance of each QRS complex is similar, or polymorphic, where the appearance varies considerably from complex to complex.

- Ventricular fibrillation (VF) results from chaotic firing of multiple sites in the ventricles. This causes the heart muscle to quiver rather than contract efficiently, producing no effective muscular contraction and no cardiac output.

- On the cardiac monitor, ventricular fibrillation appears like a wavy line, totally chaotic, without any logic.

- Asystole is the absence of any cardiac activity. It appears as a flat (or nearly flat) line on the monitor screen and produces a complete cessation of cardiac output.

- The presence of asystole should always be verified in two leads prior to initiating treatment.

- PEA is a condition in which there is an organized electrical rhythm on the ECG monitor (which should produce a pulse) but the patient is pulseless and apneic. Sinus rhythm, sinus tachycardia, idioventricular rhythm, or any rhythm that is generally expected to generate a pulse may be the electrical activity seen with PEA.

Assess Your Understanding

The following questions give you a chance to assess your understanding of the material discussed in this chapter. The answers can be found in Appendix A.

1. Ventricular dysrhythmias
   a. originate above the bundle of His.
   b. are seldom life threatening.
   c. have QRS complexes greater than 0.12 seconds in duration.
   d. have notched P waves that precede each QRS complex.

2. The presence of PVCs is an indication of which of the following?
   a. Irritability of the myocardium.
   b. Possible hypoxia.
   c. Drug toxicity.
   d. All of the above.

3. Premature ventricular complexes (PVCs)
   a. arise from the AV node.
   b. have a QRS complex that appears narrow and normal in configuration.
   c. have T waves in the same direction as the R waves of complexes.
   d. are followed by a compensatory pause.

Match the following types of PVCs with the correct description.

Descriptions		*Types of PVCs*
4. PVCs that occur every other beat.	___	a. R-on-T phenomenon
5. PVCs that appear different from one another.	___	b. multiformed
6. Occurs when the PVC wave falls on the T wave.	___	c. bigeminal
		d. quadrigeminal

7. Two PVCs in a row are called
   a. a run of PVCs.
   b. polymorphic.
   c. a couplet.
   d. interpolated.

8. Three PVCs in succession are referred to as a ________________ of ventricular tachycardia.
   a. couplet
   b. run
   c. trigeminy
   d. succession

9. Idioventricular rhythm has a rate of ________________ beats per minute.
   a. 20 to 40
   b. 30 to 60
   c. 50 to 75
   d. 100 to 150

10. Idioventricular rhythm
    a. is regularly irregular.
    b. has wide, bizarre-looking QRS complexes.
    c. has upright P waves preceding each QRS complex.
    d. arises from the AV junction.

11. Ventricular tachycardia has
    a. inverted T waves.
    b. a rate of between 60 and 100 beats per minute.
    c. an irregular rhythm.
    d. QRS complexes greater than 0.12 seconds in duration.

12. Polymorphic ventricular tachycardia
    a. arises from one location in the ventricles.
    b. has narrow QRS complexes.
    c. has an appearance that varies considerably from complex to complex.
    d. results from chaotic firing of multiple sites in the ventricles.

13. Ventricular fibrillation appears on the ECG monitor as having
    a. an overall pattern that appears irregularly shaped, chaotic, and lacks any regular repeating features.
    b. narrow QRS complexes.
    c. electrical signals that are the same height.
    d. P waves interspersed between bizarre-looking QRS complexes.

14. With asystole
    a. the heart quivers.
    b. there is a flat line on the ECG monitor.
    c. there are QRS complexes but no P waves.
    d. there is an organized rhythm but no corresponding mechanical contraction of the heart.

Referring to the scenario at the beginning of this chapter answer the following questions.

15. There is no pulse with ventricular fibrillation because the
    a. heart is contracting too fast.
    b. heart is contracting too slow.
    c. heart is not contracting at all.
    d. stroke volume is too high.

16. The flat line rhythm that occurred after defibrillation is called
    a. asystole.
    b. sinus arrest.
    c. ventricular arrest.
    d. agonal.

17. The goal of defibrillation is to create ________ and hope that a pacemaker will awaken and stimulate ventricular contraction.
    a. sinus rhythm
    b. sinus tachycardia
    c. asystole
    d. ventricular tachycardia

Answers to Sidebar Questions

"What type of irregularity does an occasional PVC produce?"

Answer: PVCs produce occasional irregularity unless there are many PVCs.

"In which type of premature beats will there be a noncompensatory pause?"

Answer: Noncompensatory pauses are seen with premature atrial complexes and premature junctional complexes.

"What type of irregularity do bigeminal, trigeminal, or quadrigeminal PVCs produce?"

Answer: Bigeminal, trigeminal, or quadrigeminal PVCs produce regularly or patterned irregularity. This is where the irregularity repeats over and over in a cycle.

On the DVD

- Approach to Ventricular Dysrhythmias lecture.

Origin and Clinical Aspects of AV Heart Blocks

12

Case History

A 65-year-old man presents to the emergency department complaining of palpitations. He denies chest pain, shortness of breath, or light headedness. He had a heart attack five years ago and has hypertension controlled by medication.

After obtaining his vital signs, normal except for regular irregularity to his pulse, the charge nurse attaches the ECG leads and turns on the monitor. The emergency room physician enters the room and examines the tracing while the nurse starts an IV. The physician calls the paramedic student into the exam room and hands her the ECG strip and asks her to interpret it. The student indicates that the rate is normal, and the rhythm has patterned irregularity with a QRS complex missing after every third P wave. She also notices that the PR interval is normal and that there are more P waves than QRS complexes.

Chapter Preview

- Block of the AV Node
- 1st-Degree AV Heart Block
- 2nd-Degree AV Heart Block, Type I
- 2nd-Degree AV Heart Block, Type II
- 3rd-Degree AV Heart Block
- Atrioventricular Dissociation

INSTRUCTIONAL MOMENT

When we refer to the P waves as being normal, we mean they appear as an upright and round waveform. There is one P wave preceding each QRS complex. Its amplitude is 0.5 to 2.5 mm in height and its duration is 0.06 to 0.10 seconds. In leads I, II, aV_F, and V_2 through V_6 the deflection of the P wave is characteristically upright or positive. In leads III, aV_L, and V_1 the P wave is usually upright but may be negative or biphasic (both positive and negative). In lead aV_R, the P wave is negative or inverted.

When we refer to QRS complexes as being normal we are saying they are narrow (0.06 to 0.12 seconds in duration) and normal looking. In leads I, II, III, aV_L, aV_F, and V_4 to V_6 the deflection of the QRS complex is characteristically positive or upright. In leads aV_R and V_1 to V_3 the QRS complex is usually negative or inverted. Leads III and V_2 to V_4 may also be biphasic. Further, in any dysrhythmia where the QRS complexes should be normal they can instead be wide or unusual looking if there is intraventricular conduction defect, aberrancy, or ventricular preexcitation.

QUESTION

"Describe how the impulse that brings about the heartbeat is conducted from the SA node to the AV node." (The answer can be found on page 391.)

Block of the AV Node

Heart blocks are partial delays or complete interruptions in the cardiac conduction pathway between the atria and ventricles (Figure 12-1). The block can occur at the AV node, the bundle of His, or the bundle branches.

The most common causes of heart block are ischemia, myocardial infarction, degenerative disease of the conduction system, congenital anomalies, and medications (especially digitalis preparations). Dysrhythmias resulting from AV heart blocks include the following:

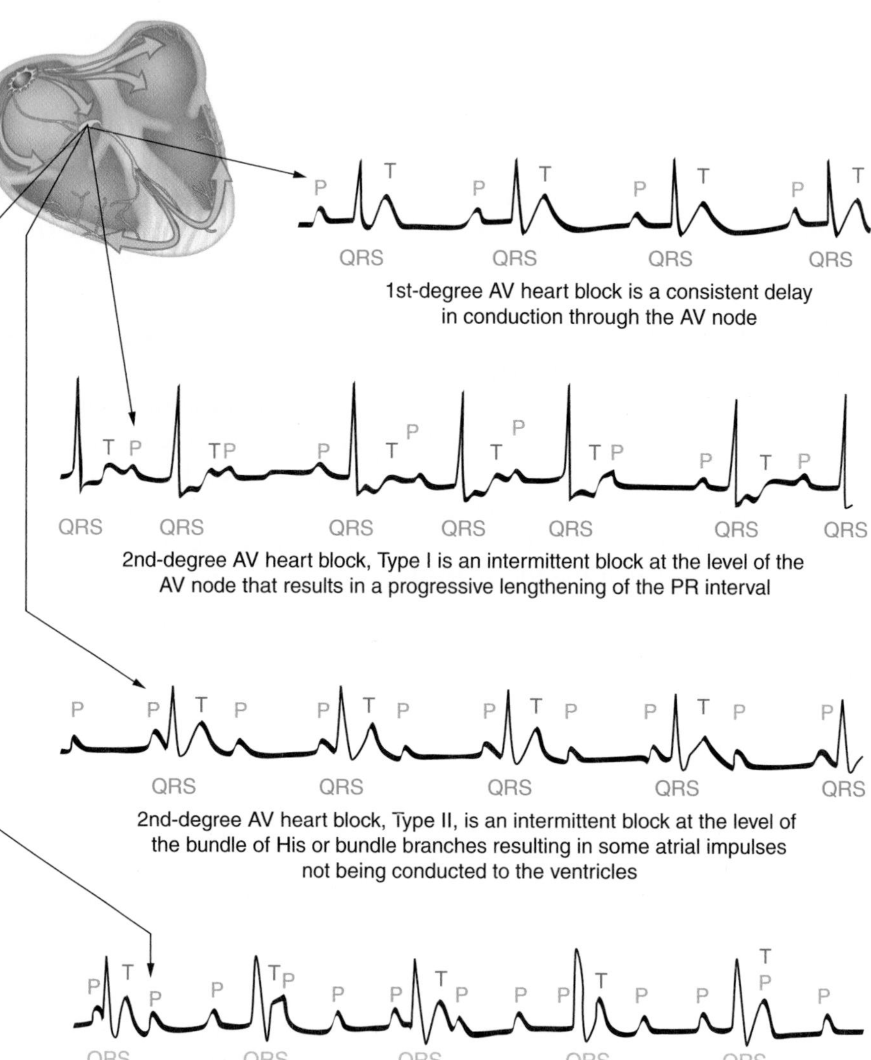

Figure 12-1
AV heart blocks.

- 1st-degree AV heart block
- 2nd-degree AV heart block, Type I (Wenckebach)
- 2nd-degree AV heart block, Type II
- 3rd-degree AV heart block

QUESTION
"In which of the AV heart blocks are there more P waves than QRS complexes?" (The answer can be found on page 391.)

Heart blocks are partial ______________ or complete ______________ at the ______________, the bundle of His, or the bundle branches.

[delays] [interruptions] [AV node]

1st-Degree AV Heart Block

1st-degree AV heart block is not a true block as all impulses are conducted from the atria to the ventricles, but rather a consistent delay of conduction at the level of the AV node (Figure 12-2). It results in prolongation of the PR interval that remains the same duration from beat to beat.

KEY CONCEPT
Heart blocks are partial delays or complete interruptions in the cardiac conduction pathway between the atria and ventricles.

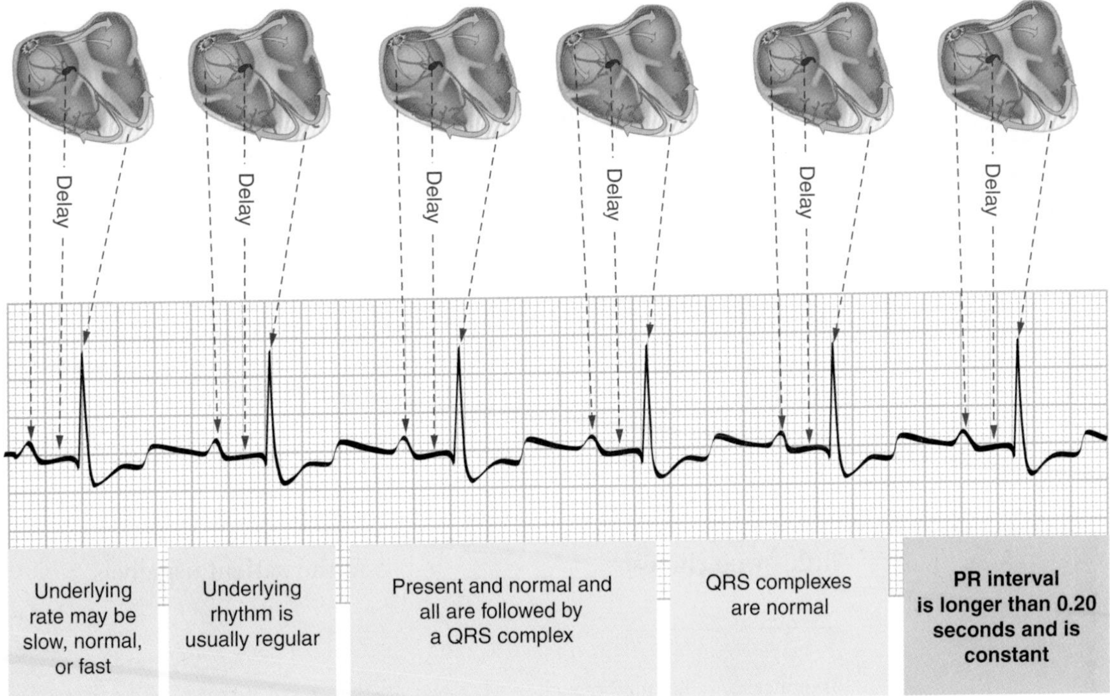

Figure 12-2
1st-degree AV heart block.

Table 12-1 1st-Degree AV Heart Block

Causes of 1st-degree AV heart block	Examples
Cardiac disorders	Myocardial ischemia or infarction (often inferior wall MI), injury or ischemia to the AV node or junction, myocarditis, degenerative changes in the heart
Use of certain drugs	Digoxin, calcium channel blockers, beta-adrenergic blockers, quinidine, procainamide, amiodarone
Other	Increased vagal tone, hyperkalemia

CLINICAL MOMENT
Those types of heart block that result in dropped QRS complexes or a slower ventricular rate can lead to a decrease in cardiac output (↓ heart rate × stroke volume = ↓ cardiac output).

1st-degree AV heart block is a consistent ______________ of conduction from beat to beat at the level of the ______________. With this type of heart block ______________ the impulses are conducted from the ______________ to the ventricles.

[delay] [AV node] [all] [atria]

While 1st-degree AV heart block may occur in healthy persons, particularly athletes, for no apparent reason, it is sometimes associated with other conditions such as myocardial ischemia, acute myocardial infarction, increased vagal (parasympathetic) tone, and digitalis toxicity (Table 12-1).

QUESTION
"What is the normal duration for the PR interval?" (The answer can be found on page 391.)

1st-degree AV heart block is of little or no clinical significance because all impulses are conducted to the ventricles. The patient experiencing this condition is usually asymptomatic. 1st-degree AV heart block may be temporary, particularly if it stems from ischemia early in the course of myocardial infarction or certain medications. Conversely, it may also progress to higher degree block, especially in the presence of inferior wall myocardial infarction.

No ventricular beats are dropped with this type of AV block so it is of little or no clinical ______________ and the patient usually is ______________.

[significance] [asymptomatic]

Review of key characteristics associated with 1st-degree AV heart block

Rate:	Underlying rate may be slow, normal, or fast
Regularity:	Underlying rhythm is usually regular
P waves:	Present and normal and all are followed by a QRS complex
QRS complexes:	Should be normal
PR interval:	Longer than 0.20 seconds and is constant (the same each time)
QT interval:	Usually within normal limits

The most obvious characteristic of 1st-degree AV heart block are PR intervals greater than 0.20 seconds in duration and constant. The underlying rhythm is usually regular while the rate is that of the underlying rhythm. It can occur in bradycardic, normal rate, and tachycardic rhythms. The P waves are normal; one precedes each QRS complex and the QRS complexes are within normal limits (Figure 12-3).

KEY CONCEPT
With 1st-degree AV heart block the PR interval is greater than 0.20 seconds in duration.

The key feature of 1st-degree AV block is PR intervals ______________ than 0.20 seconds in duration and ______________.

[greater] [constant]

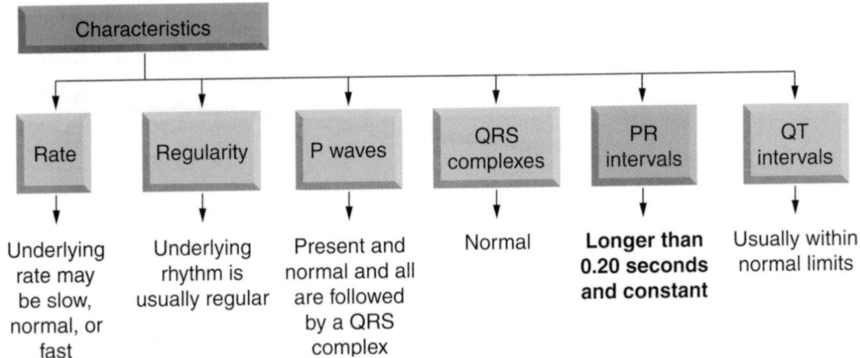

Figure 12-3
Algorithm for 1st-degree AV heart block.

2nd-Degree AV Heart Block, Type I

CLINICAL MOMENT
The dropped beat can occur after a different number of complexes with different patients. For example, one patient may have a dropped beat after every third beat and another patient may drop the QRS complex after every fifth complex.

2nd-degree AV heart block, Type I (also called Wenckebach), is an intermittent block at the level of the AV node (Figure 12-4). The PR interval (representing AV conduction time) increases until a QRS complex is dropped. By then, AV conduction recovers and the sequence repeats. Some describe the pathophysiology of this dysrhythmia as a weakened AV junction that grows more tired with each heartbeat (thus producing a progressively longer PR interval following each P wave). Finally, the AV junction is too tired to carry the impulse and a QRS complex is dropped (only a P wave appears). The lack of conduction through the AV junction allows it to rest, thus the next PR interval is shorter. Then as each subsequent impulse is generated and transmitted through the AV junction, there is a progressively longer PR interval until again, a QRS complex is dropped. This cycle repeats.

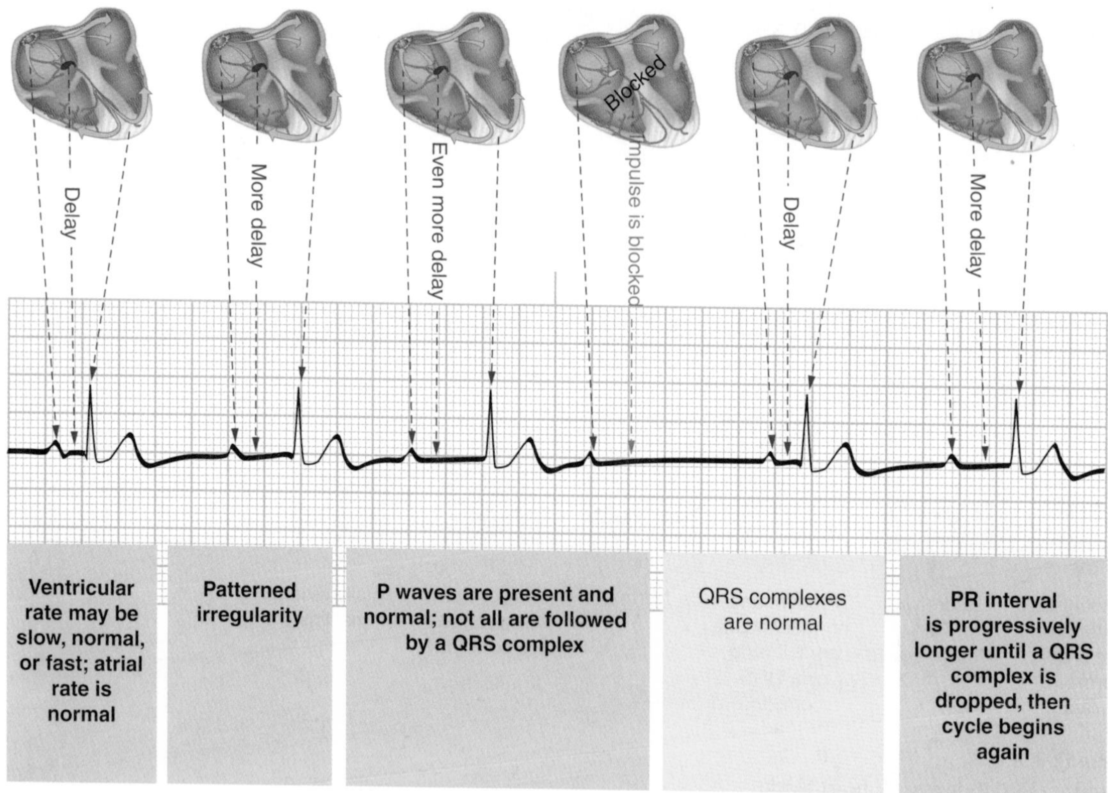

Figure 12-4
2nd-degree AV heart block, Type I (Wenckebach).

2nd-degree AV heart block, Type I is an ________________ block at the level of the ________________ resulting in a PR interval that ________________ until a QRS complex is ________________.

[intermittent] [AV node] [increases] [dropped]

2nd-degreee AV heart block, Type I often occurs in acute myocardial infarction or acute myocarditis. Other causes include increased vagal tone, ischemia, acute cardiac disease, drug toxicity (digitalis, propranolol, verapamil), head injury, and electrolyte imbalance (Table 12-2).

2nd-degree AV heart block, Type I, may occur in otherwise healthy persons. By itself, it is usually transient and reversible, resolving when the underlying condition is corrected. However, particularly if it occurs early in myocardial infarction, it may progress to more serious blocks. If dropped beats occur frequently, the patient may show signs and symptoms of decreased cardiac output.

QUESTION
"What type of irregularity does 2nd-degree AV heart block, Type I, produce?" (The answer can be found on page 391.)

Review of key characteristics associated with 2nd-degree AV heart block, Type I

Rate:	Ventricular rate may be slow, normal, or fast; atrial rate is within normal range
Regularity:	Patterned irregularity
P waves:	Present and normal; not all the P waves are followed by a QRS complex
QRS complexes:	Should be normal
PR interval:	Progressively longer until a QRS complex is dropped, the cycle then begins again
QT interval:	Usually within normal limits

Table 12-2 2nd-Degree AV Heart Block

Causes of 2nd-degree AV heart block, Type I	Examples
Cardiac disorders	AV nodal ischemia secondary to right coronary artery occlusion, myocardial ischemia or infarction (inferior wall MI), myocarditis, rheumatic fever
Use of certain drugs	Digitalis, calcium channel blockers, beta-adrenergic blockers, verapamil
Other	Increased vagal tone, hyperkalemia

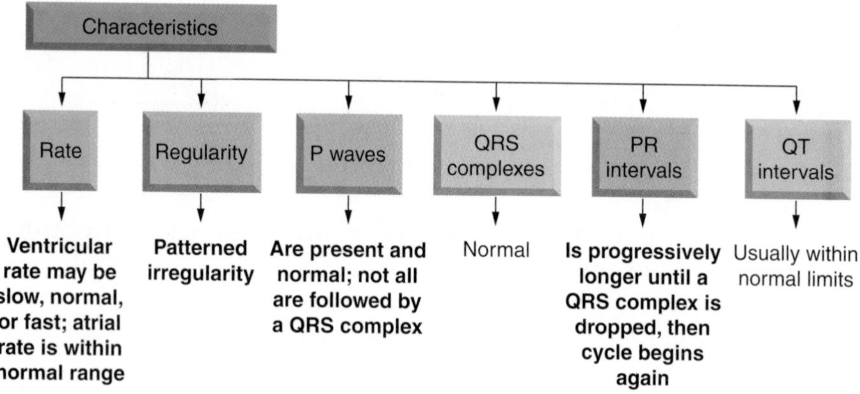

Figure 12-5
Algorithm for 2nd-degree AV heart block, Type I.

KEY CONCEPT
With 2nd-degree AV heart block, Type I, the key feature that helps identify it are PR intervals that become progressively longer until a QRS complex is dropped. There are also more P waves than QRS complexes and the QRS complexes are normal.

The characteristics that stand out in 2nd-degree AV heart block, Type I are a patterned, irregular rhythm; cycles of progressively longer PR intervals; and more P waves than QRS complexes. The irregularity appears as a pattern (the cycle seems to occur over and over); it is often described as "grouped beating." The PR intervals become progressively longer until a P wave fails to conduct, resulting in a "dropped" QRS complex. After the blocked beat, the cycle starts again. The P waves are upright and uniform but there are more P waves than QRS complexes as some of the QRS complexes are blocked (Figure 12-5).

The atrial rate is that of the underlying rhythm while the ventricular rate is slightly less than the atrial rate (slower than normal). The QRS complexes are within normal limits. The P-P interval is constant while the R-R interval increases until a QRS complex is dropped.

2nd-degree AV heart block, Type I, results in a patterned, ____________ rhythm with cycles of ____________ longer PR intervals and ____________ P waves than QRS complexes. The P-P intervals are ____________. The impulse originates from the SA node so the P waves are ____________ and ____________ (in lead II) and the QRS complexes are ____________.

[irregular] [progressively] [more] [constant] [upright] [round] [normal]

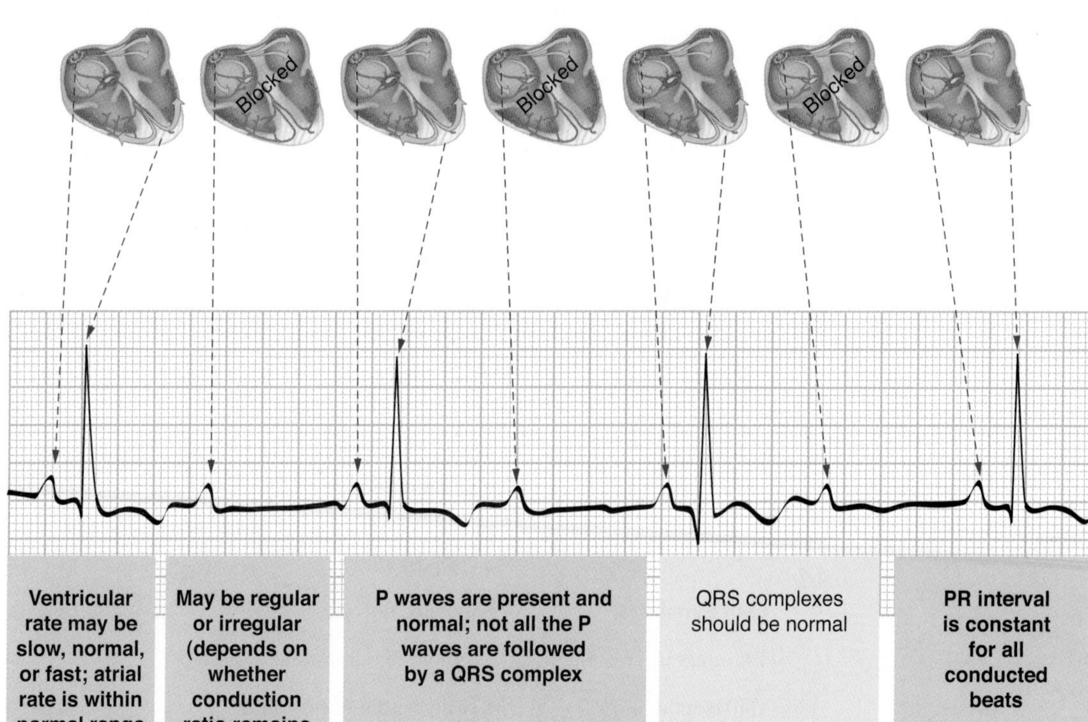

Figure 12-6
2nd-degree AV heart block, Type II.

2nd-Degree AV Heart Block, Type II

2nd-degree AV heart block, Type II is an intermittent block at the level of the bundle of His or bundle branches resulting in atrial impulses that are not conducted to the ventricles (Figure 12-6). It is less common than Type I but it is more serious as it may progress to complete AV heart block. It differs from Type I in that the PR interval is *constant* prior to a beat being "dropped."

Type II is an ____________ block at the level of the ____________ or ____________ resulting in some atrial impulses being ____________.

[intermittent] [bundle of His] [bundle branches] [blocked]

Type II block is usually associated with left coronary artery disease, anterior-wall myocardial infarction, degenerative changes in the conduction system, or severe coronary artery disease.

Type II is a serious dysrhythmia, usually considered malignant in the emergency setting when it is symptomatic. Slow ventricular rates result in decreased cardiac output and may produce signs and symptoms of hypoperfusion (low blood pressure, shortness of breath, congestive heart failure, pulmonary congestion, and decreased level of consciousness). It may progress to a more severe heart block and even to ventricular asystole.

Review of key characteristics associated with 2nd-degree AV heart block, Type II

Rate:	Ventricular rate may be slow, normal, or fast; atrial rate is within normal range
Regularity:	May be regular or irregular (depends on whether conduction ratio remains the same)
P waves:	Present and normal; not all the P waves are followed by a QRS complex
QRS complexes:	Should be normal
PR interval:	Constant for all conducted beats
QT interval:	Usually within normal limits

KEY CONCEPT
With 2nd-degree AV heart block, Type II, the key feature that helps identify it are more P waves than QRS complexes and constant PR intervals for the conducted beats.

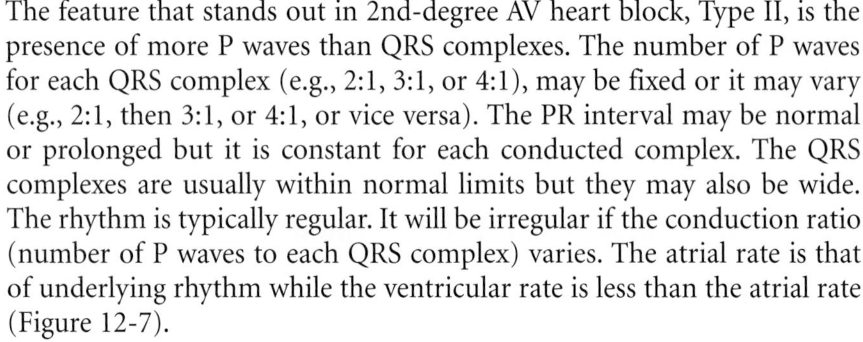

The feature that stands out in 2nd-degree AV heart block, Type II, is the presence of more P waves than QRS complexes. The number of P waves for each QRS complex (e.g., 2:1, 3:1, or 4:1), may be fixed or it may vary (e.g., 2:1, then 3:1, or 4:1, or vice versa). The PR interval may be normal or prolonged but it is constant for each conducted complex. The QRS complexes are usually within normal limits but they may also be wide. The rhythm is typically regular. It will be irregular if the conduction ratio (number of P waves to each QRS complex) varies. The atrial rate is that of underlying rhythm while the ventricular rate is less than the atrial rate (Figure 12-7).

INSTRUCTIONAL MOMENT
The key characteristic that helps you differentiate between the types of 2nd-degree AV block is whether the PR interval changes or remains constant.

With 2nd-degree AV heart block, Type II, there are ____________ P waves than QRS complexes. The P-P intervals are ____________, while the R-R intervals are ____________. The impulse originates from the SA node so the P waves are ____________ and ____________ (in lead II), and because the QRS complexes arise from above the ventricles, they are within ____________ duration.

[more] [constant] [irregular] [upright] [round] [normal]

2nd-Degree AV Heart Block, Type II

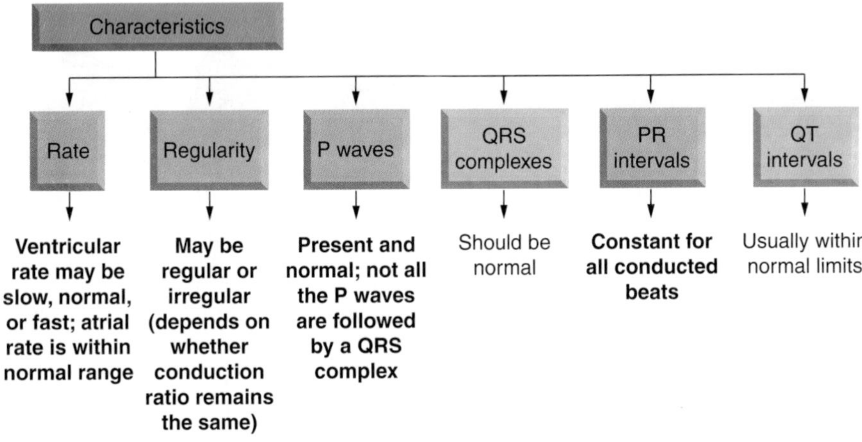

Figure 12-7
Algorithm for 2nd-degree AV heart block, Type II.

3rd-Degree AV Heart Block

3rd-degree AV heart block is a complete block of the conduction at or below the AV node, and impulses from the atria cannot reach the ventricles (Figure 12-8). The SA node serves as the pacemaker for the atria, typically maintaining a regular rate of 60 to 100 beats per minute. The pacemaker for the ventricles arises as an escape rhythm from the AV junction at a rate of 40 to 60 beats per minute or from the ventricles at a rate of 20 to 40 beats per minute. P waves and QRS complexes occur rhythmically but the rhythms are unrelated to each other.

QUESTION
"How can you distinguish between a nonconducted PAC and 2nd-degree AV heart block?" (The answer can be found on page 391.)

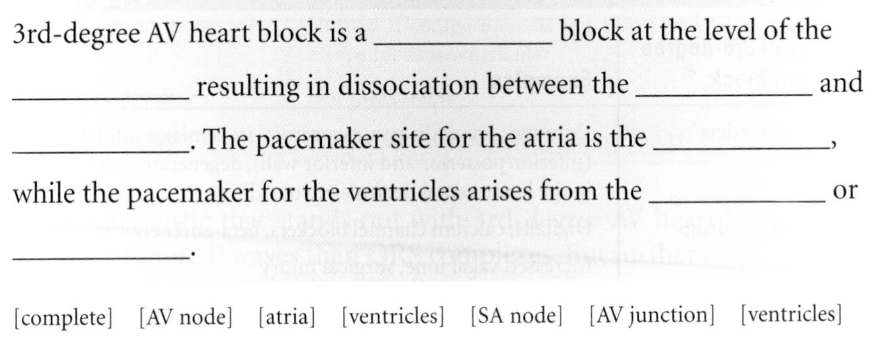

3rd-degree AV heart block is a ____________ block at the level of the ____________ resulting in dissociation between the ____________ and ____________. The pacemaker site for the atria is the ____________, while the pacemaker for the ventricles arises from the ____________ or ____________.

QUESTION
"What is the inherent rate of the AV junction and the ventricles?" (The answer can be found on page 391.)

[complete] [AV node] [atria] [ventricles] [SA node] [AV junction] [ventricles]

3rd-degree AV heart block occurring at the AV node is most commonly caused by a congenital condition. Other causes include increased vagal tone (which may produce a transient AV dissociation), septal infarction, acute myocarditis, digitalis, beta-blocker, or calcium channel blocker toxicity and electrolyte imbalance. It may also occur in older adults because of chronic degenerative changes in the conduction system (Table 12-3).

INSTRUCTIONAL MOMENT
3rd-degree AV heart block is also referred to as complete AV heart block.

PRACTICE. . . MAKES PERFECT

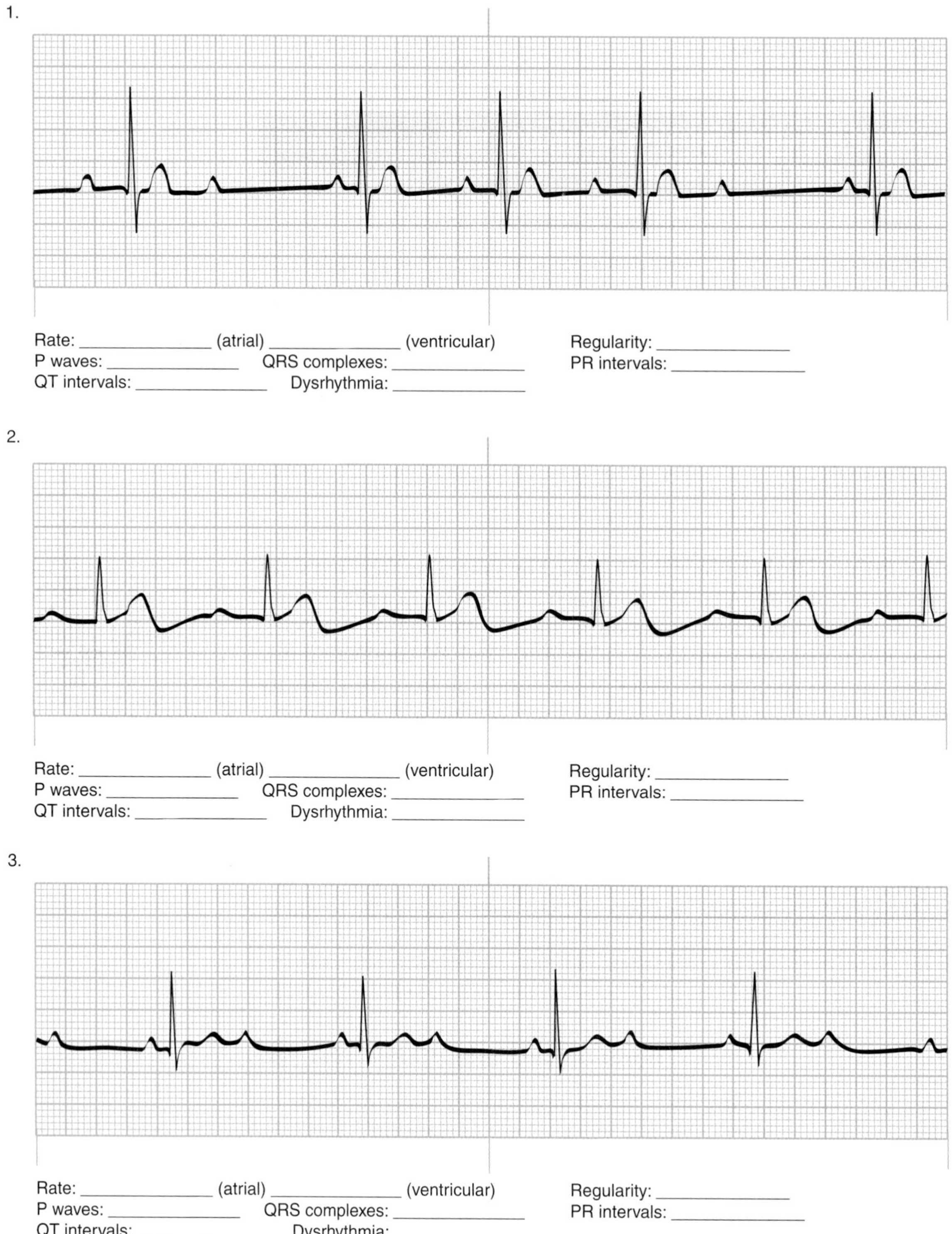

1.

Rate: ______________ (atrial) ______________ (ventricular)
P waves: ______________ QRS complexes: ______________
QT intervals: ______________ Dysrhythmia: ______________
Regularity: ______________
PR intervals: ______________

2.

Rate: ______________ (atrial) ______________ (ventricular)
P waves: ______________ QRS complexes: ______________
QT intervals: ______________ Dysrhythmia: ______________
Regularity: ______________
PR intervals: ______________

3.

Rate: ______________ (atrial) ______________ (ventricular)
P waves: ______________ QRS complexes: ______________
QT intervals: ______________ Dysrhythmia: ______________
Regularity: ______________
PR intervals: ______________

PRACTICE. . . MAKES PERFECT

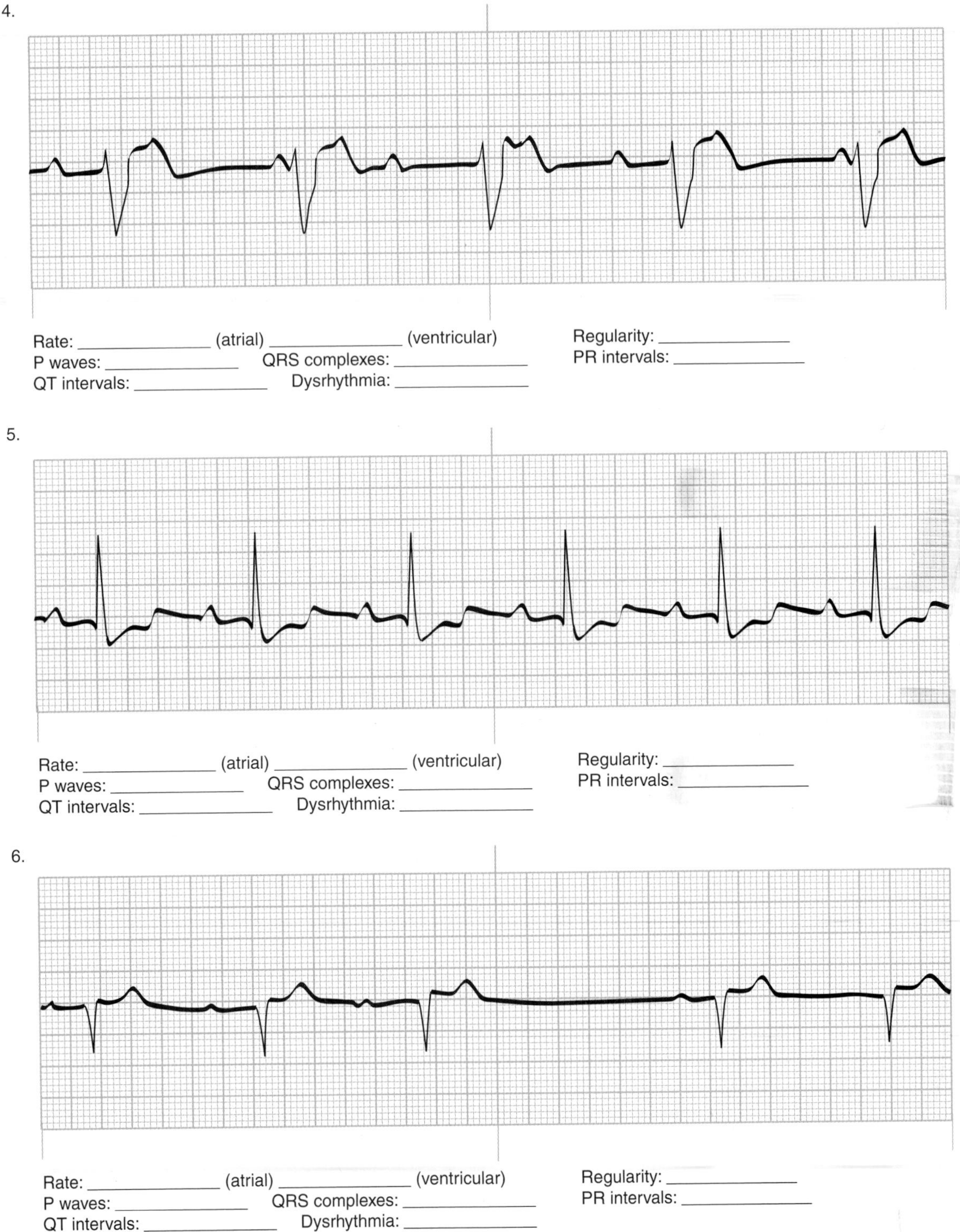

4.

Rate: ______________ (atrial) ______________ (ventricular) Regularity: ______________

P waves: ______________ QRS complexes: ______________ PR intervals: ______________

QT intervals: ______________ Dysrhythmia: ______________

5.

Rate: ______________ (atrial) ______________ (ventricular) Regularity: ______________

P waves: ______________ QRS complexes: ______________ PR intervals: ______________

QT intervals: ______________ Dysrhythmia: ______________

6.

Rate: ______________ (atrial) ______________ (ventricular) Regularity: ______________

P waves: ______________ QRS complexes: ______________ PR intervals: ______________

QT intervals: ______________ Dysrhythmia: ______________

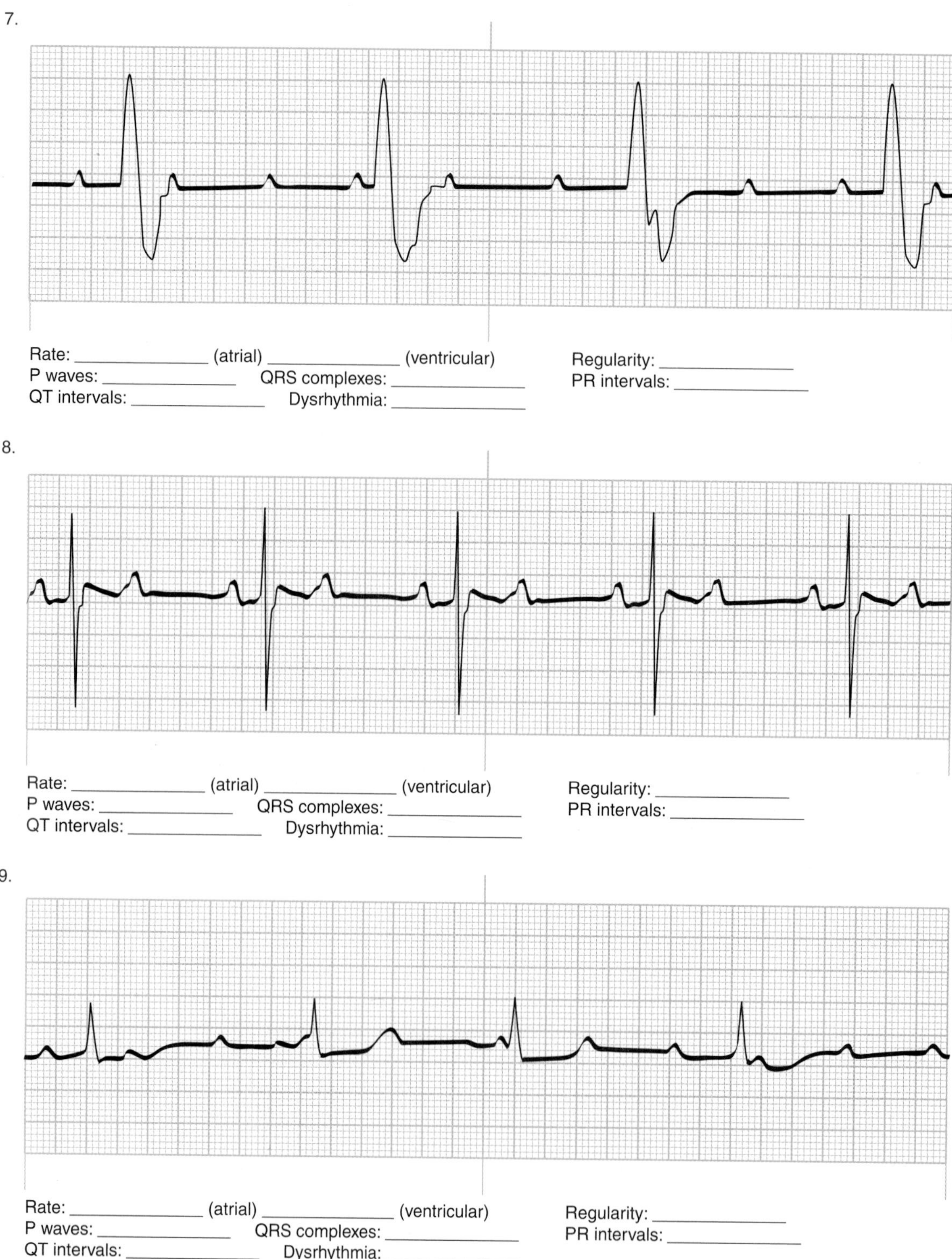
PRACTICE. . . MAKES PERFECT
7.
Rate: ______ (atrial) ______ (ventricular)
Regularity: ______
P waves: ______
QRS complexes: ______
PR intervals: ______
QT intervals: ______
Dysrhythmia: ______
8.
Rate: ______ (atrial) ______ (ventricular)
Regularity: ______
P waves: ______
QRS complexes: ______
PR intervals: ______
QT intervals: ______
Dysrhythmia: ______
9.
Rate: ______ (atrial) ______ (ventricular)
Regularity: ______
P waves: ______
QRS complexes: ______
PR intervals: ______
QT intervals: ______
Dysrhythmia: ______

PRACTICE. . . MAKES PERFECT

10.

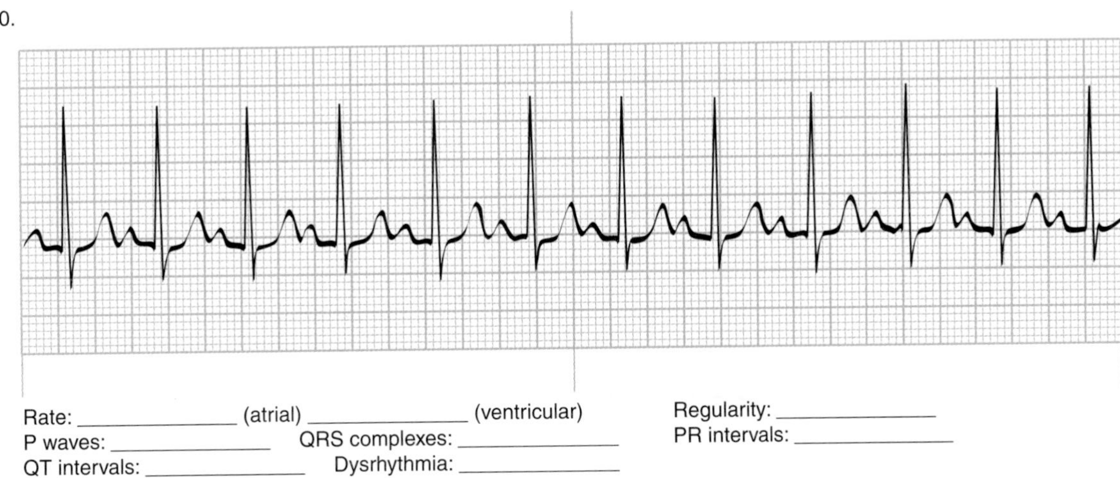

Rate: ______________ (atrial) ______________ (ventricular)
P waves: ______________ QRS complexes: ______________
QT intervals: ______________ Dysrhythmia: ______________
Regularity: ______________
PR intervals: ______________

You can practice interpreting sinus, atrial, junctional, and dysrhythmias (as discussed in chapters 8, 9, 10, and 11) and AV heart blocks with the following *Practice Makes Perfect* exercises. Answers to these exercises can be found in Appendix A.

PRACTICE. . . MAKES PERFECT

11.

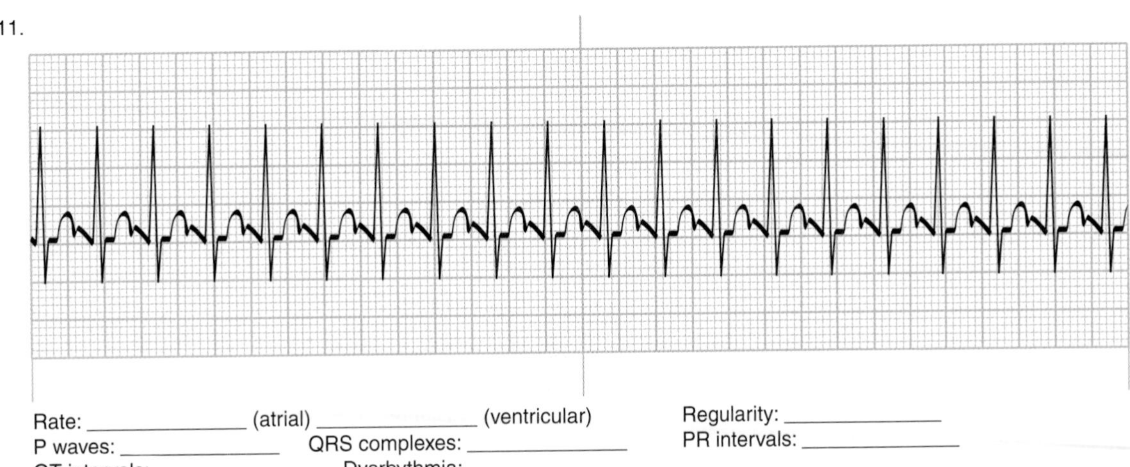

Rate: ______________ (atrial) ______________ (ventricular)
P waves: ______________ QRS complexes: ______________
QT intervals: ______________ Dysrhythmia: ______________
Regularity: ______________
PR intervals: ______________

PRACTICE. . . MAKES PERFECT

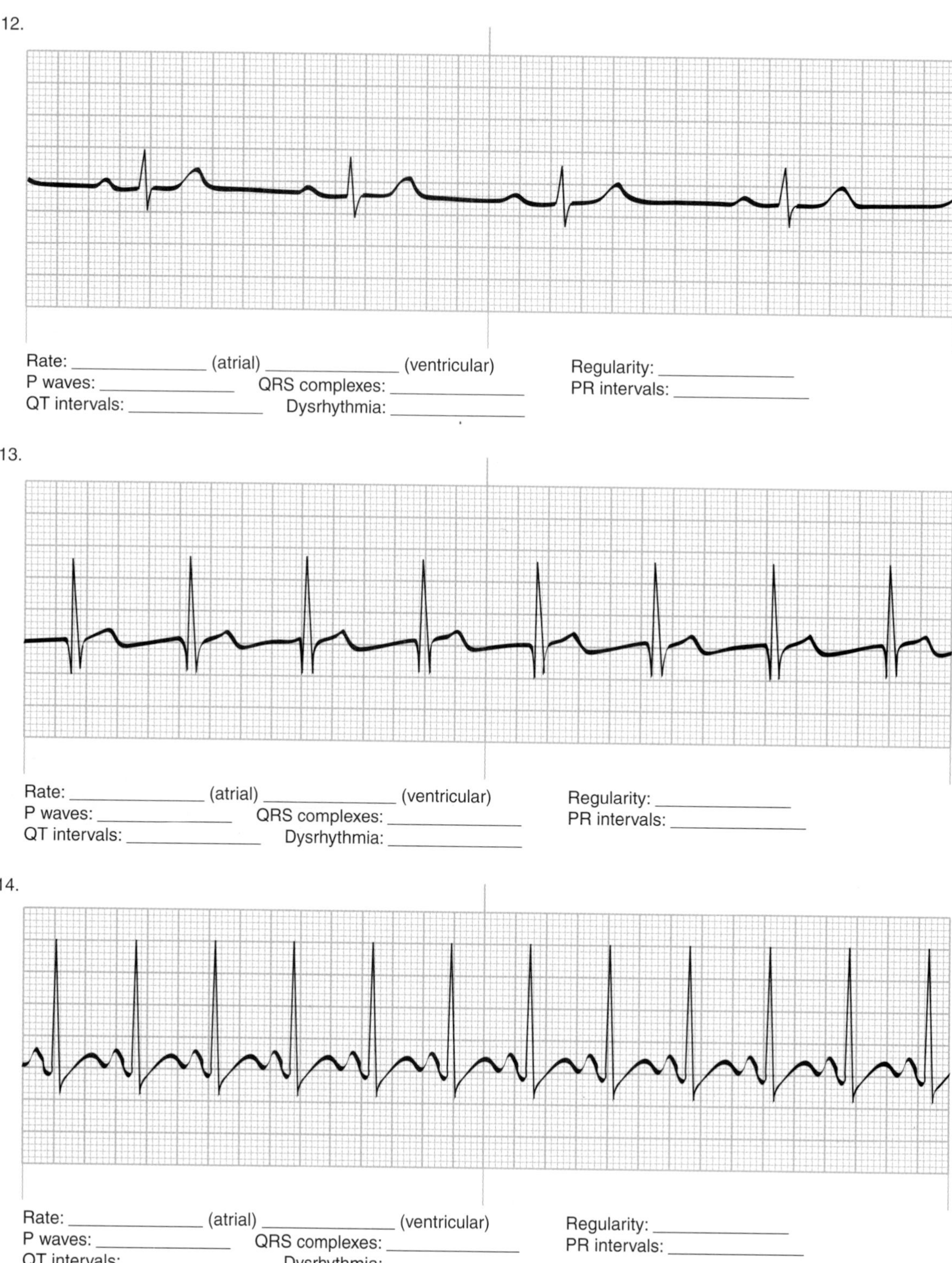

12.

Rate: ______________ (atrial) ______________ (ventricular)
P waves: ______________ QRS complexes: ______________
QT intervals: ______________ Dysrhythmia: ______________
Regularity: ______________
PR intervals: ______________

13.

Rate: ______________ (atrial) ______________ (ventricular)
P waves: ______________ QRS complexes: ______________
QT intervals: ______________ Dysrhythmia: ______________
Regularity: ______________
PR intervals: ______________

14.

Rate: ______________ (atrial) ______________ (ventricular)
P waves: ______________ QRS complexes: ______________
QT intervals: ______________ Dysrhythmia: ______________
Regularity: ______________
PR intervals: ______________

PRACTICE. . . MAKES PERFECT

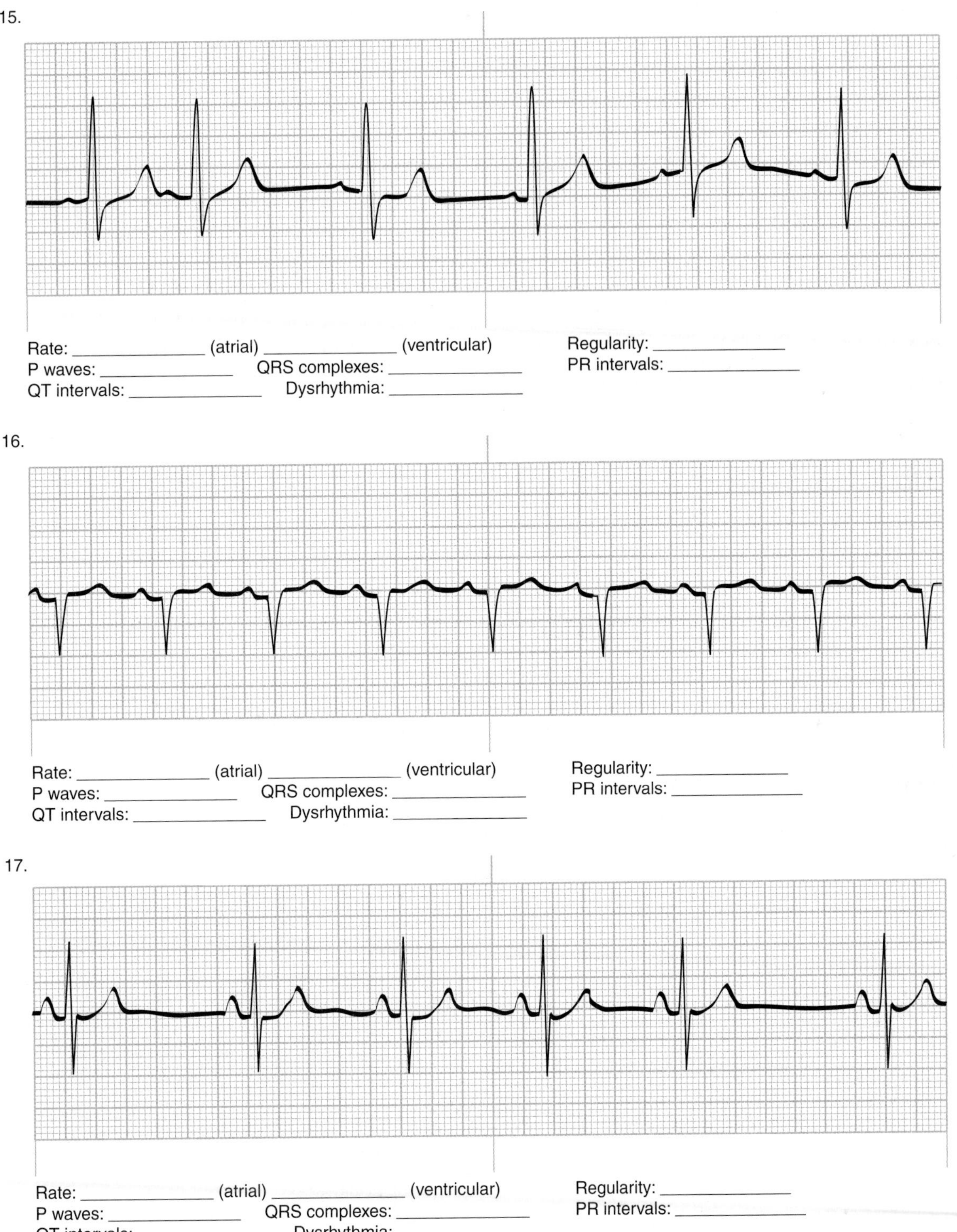

15.

Rate: ______________ (atrial) ______________ (ventricular) Regularity: ______________
P waves: ______________ QRS complexes: ______________ PR intervals: ______________
QT intervals: ______________ Dysrhythmia: ______________

16.

Rate: ______________ (atrial) ______________ (ventricular) Regularity: ______________
P waves: ______________ QRS complexes: ______________ PR intervals: ______________
QT intervals: ______________ Dysrhythmia: ______________

17.

Rate: ______________ (atrial) ______________ (ventricular) Regularity: ______________
P waves: ______________ QRS complexes: ______________ PR intervals: ______________
QT intervals: ______________ Dysrhythmia: ______________

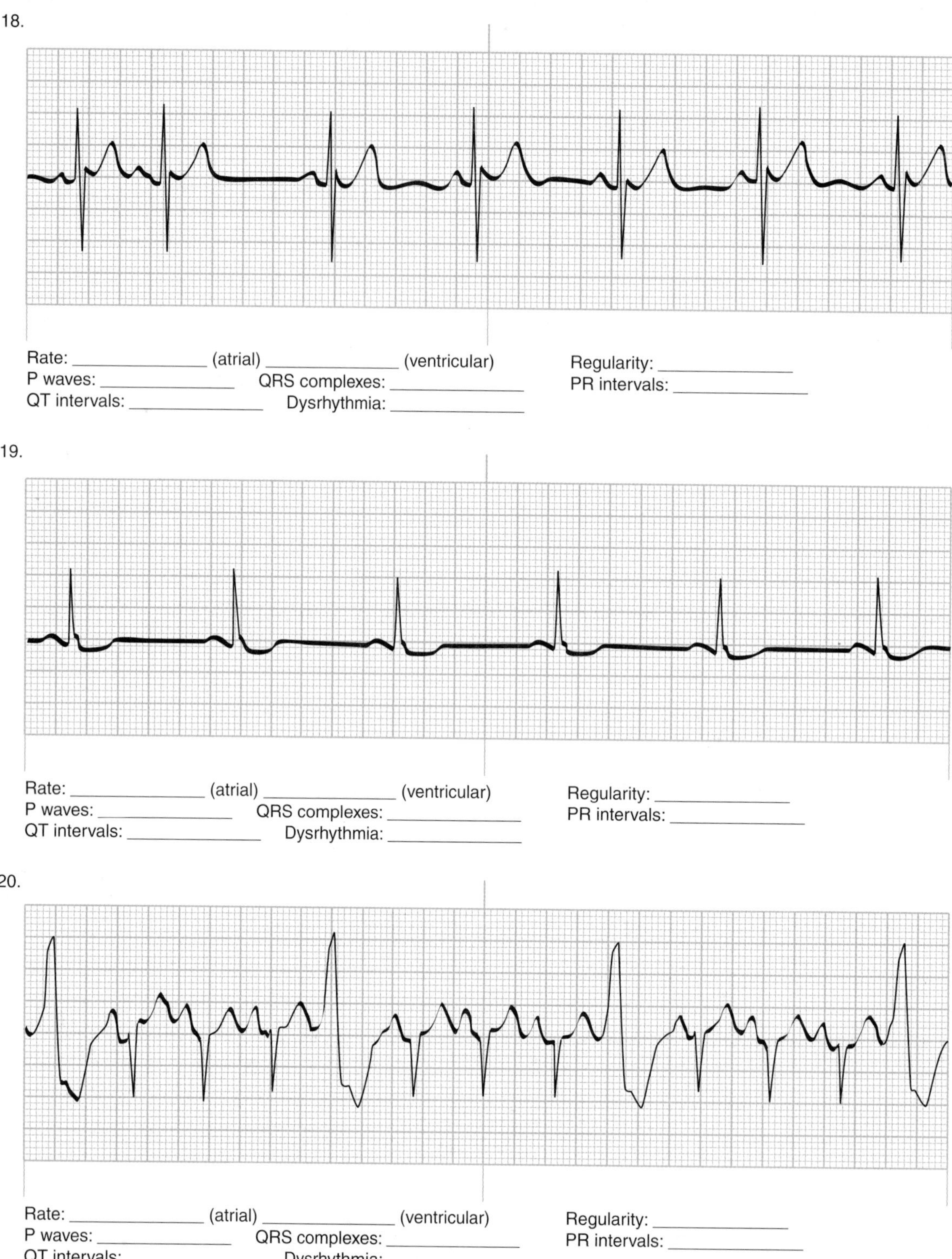

PRACTICE... MAKES PERFECT

18.

Rate: ______________ (atrial) ______________ (ventricular) Regularity: ______________
P waves: ______________ QRS complexes: ______________ PR intervals: ______________
QT intervals: ______________ Dysrhythmia: ______________

19.

Rate: ______________ (atrial) ______________ (ventricular) Regularity: ______________
P waves: ______________ QRS complexes: ______________ PR intervals: ______________
QT intervals: ______________ Dysrhythmia: ______________

20.

Rate: ______________ (atrial) ______________ (ventricular) Regularity: ______________
P waves: ______________ QRS complexes: ______________ PR intervals: ______________
QT intervals: ______________ Dysrhythmia: ______________

PRACTICE. . . MAKES PERFECT

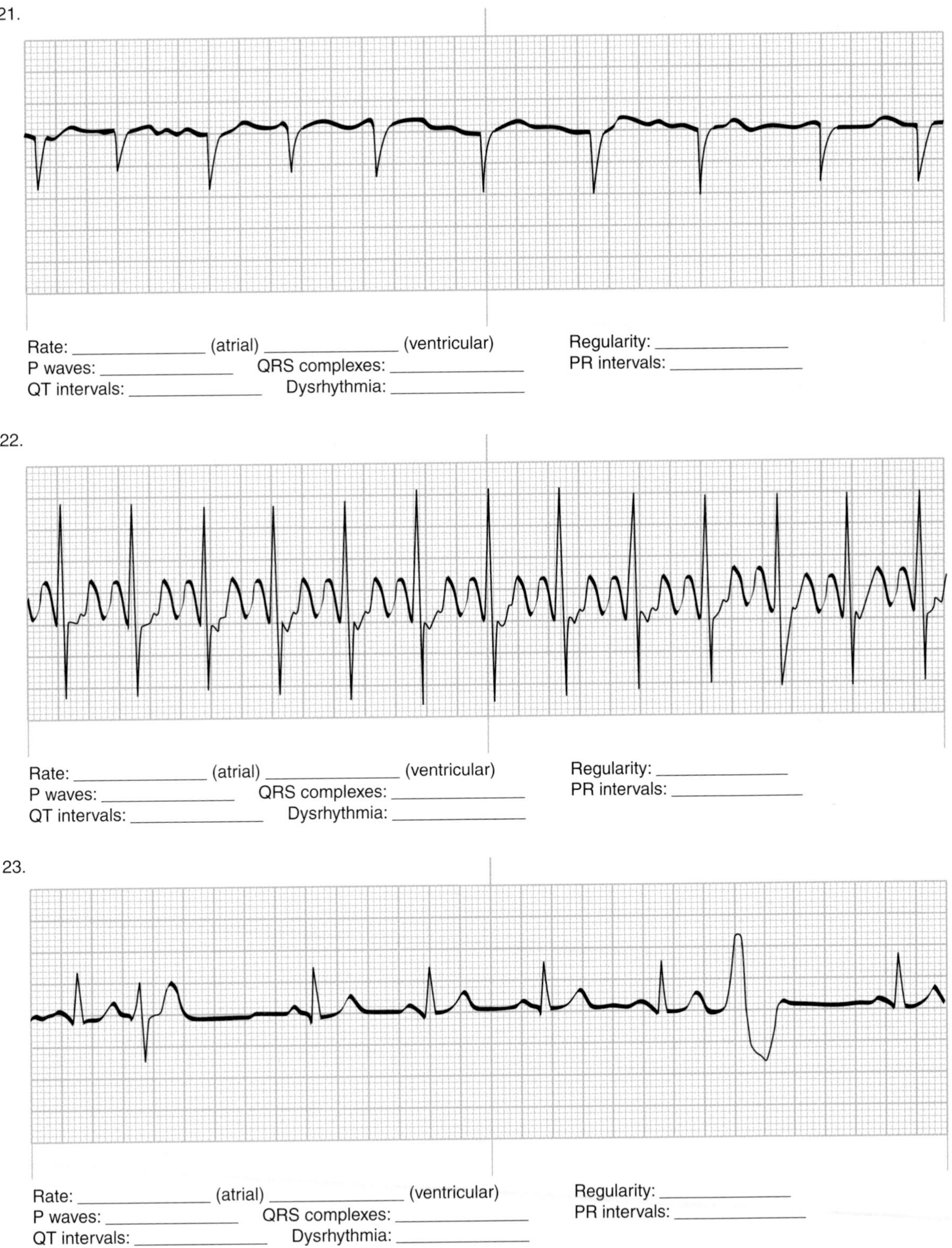

21.

Rate: ______________ (atrial) ______________ (ventricular)
P waves: ______________
QT intervals: ______________
QRS complexes: ______________
Dysrhythmia: ______________
Regularity: ______________
PR intervals: ______________

22.

Rate: ______________ (atrial) ______________ (ventricular)
P waves: ______________
QT intervals: ______________
QRS complexes: ______________
Dysrhythmia: ______________
Regularity: ______________
PR intervals: ______________

23.

Rate: ______________ (atrial) ______________ (ventricular)
P waves: ______________
QT intervals: ______________
QRS complexes: ______________
Dysrhythmia: ______________
Regularity: ______________
PR intervals: ______________

PRACTICE. . . MAKES PERFECT

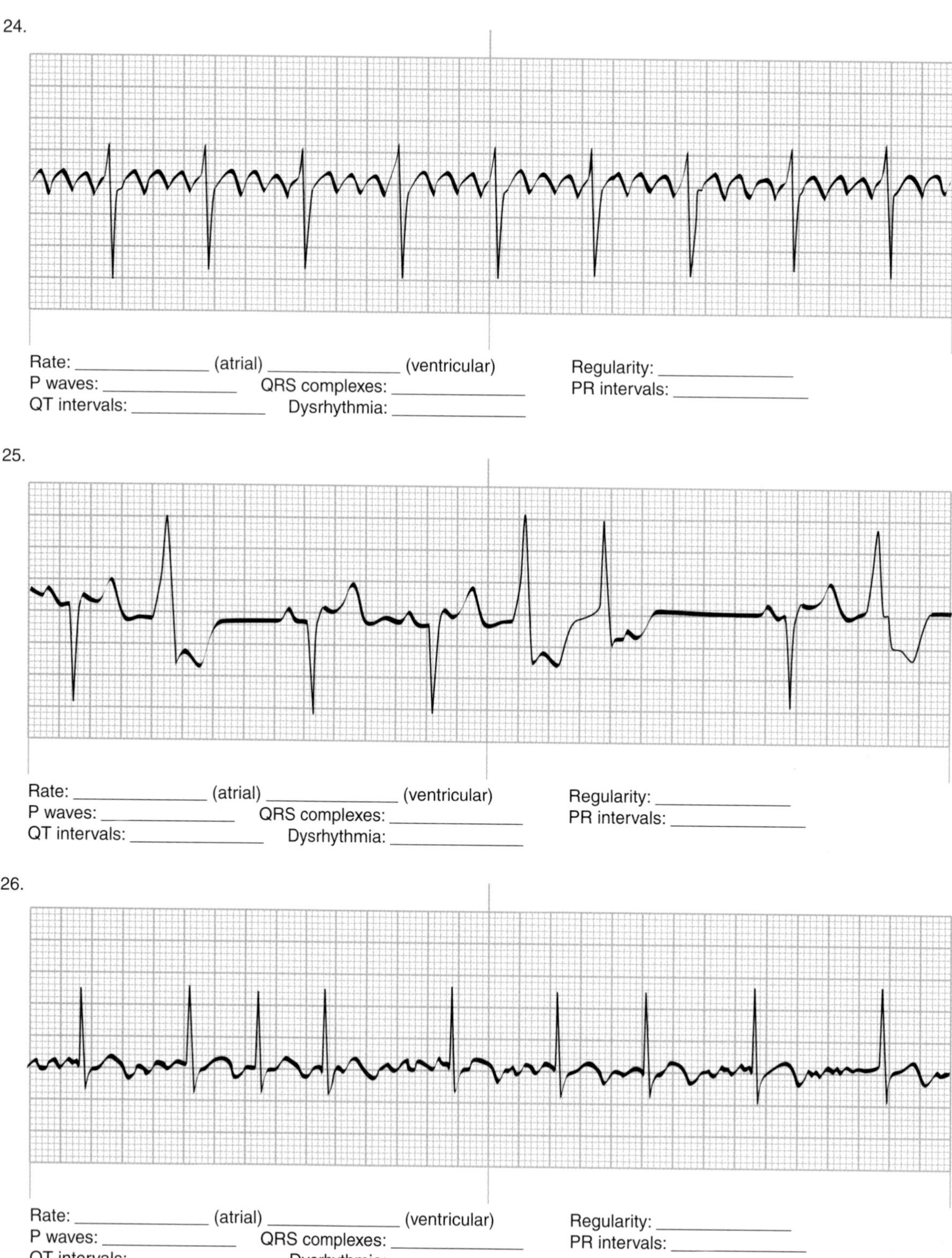

24.

Rate: ______________ (atrial) ______________ (ventricular) Regularity: ______________
P waves: ______________ QRS complexes: ______________ PR intervals: ______________
QT intervals: ______________ Dysrhythmia: ______________

25.

Rate: ______________ (atrial) ______________ (ventricular) Regularity: ______________
P waves: ______________ QRS complexes: ______________ PR intervals: ______________
QT intervals: ______________ Dysrhythmia: ______________

26.

Rate: ______________ (atrial) ______________ (ventricular) Regularity: ______________
P waves: ______________ QRS complexes: ______________ PR intervals: ______________
QT intervals: ______________ Dysrhythmia: ______________

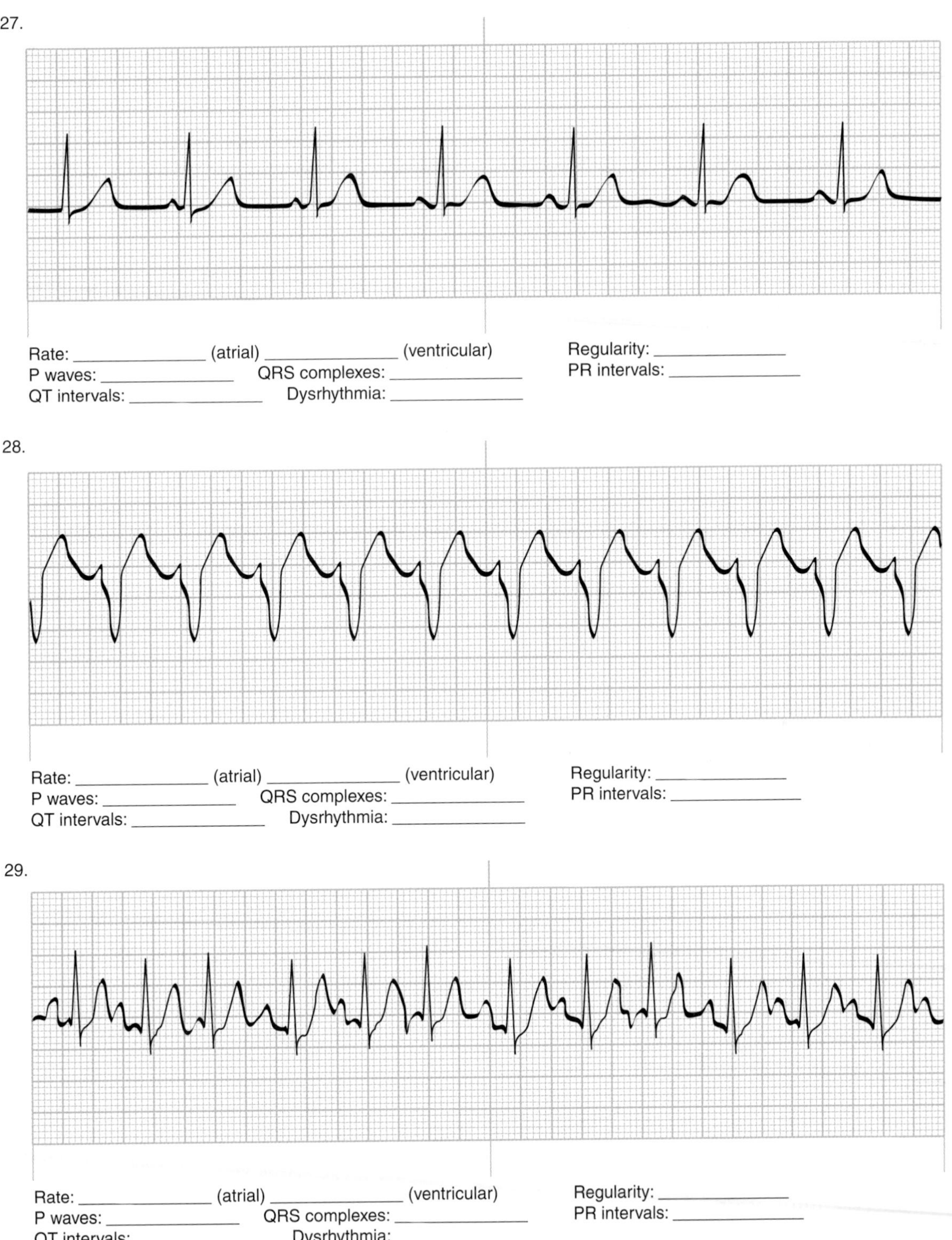

PRACTICE. . . MAKES PERFECT

27.

Rate: _______________ (atrial) _______________ (ventricular)
P waves: _______________
QRS complexes: _______________
QT intervals: _______________
Dysrhythmia: _______________
Regularity: _______________
PR intervals: _______________

28.

Rate: _______________ (atrial) _______________ (ventricular)
P waves: _______________
QRS complexes: _______________
QT intervals: _______________
Dysrhythmia: _______________
Regularity: _______________
PR intervals: _______________

29.

Rate: _______________ (atrial) _______________ (ventricular)
P waves: _______________
QRS complexes: _______________
QT intervals: _______________
Dysrhythmia: _______________
Regularity: _______________
PR intervals: _______________

PRACTICE. . . MAKES PERFECT

30.

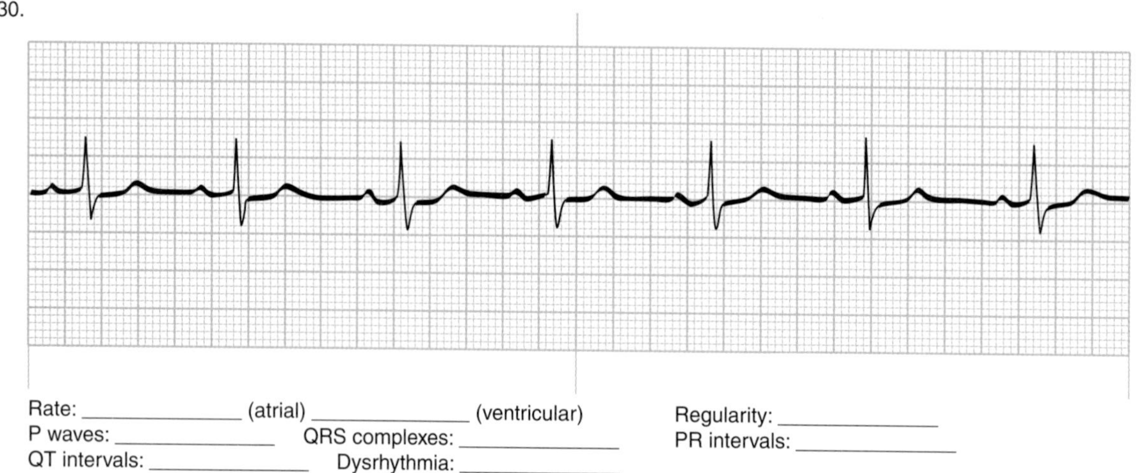

Key Points

- Heart blocks are partial delays or complete interruptions in the cardiac conduction pathway between the atria and ventricles. It can occur at the AV node, the bundle of His, or the bundle branches.
- 1st-degree AV heart block is not a true block. Instead, it is a consistent delay of conduction at the level of the AV node that results in a PR interval greater than 0.20 seconds in duration.
- 2nd-degree AV heart block, Type I, is also referred to as Wenckebach. It is an intermittent block at the level of the AV junction.
- With 2nd-degree AV heart block, Type I, the PR interval increases until a QRS complex is dropped. After the dropped beat, the next PR interval is shorter. Then, as each subsequent impulse is generated and transmitted through the AV junction, there is a progressively longer PR interval until again, a QRS complex is dropped. This cycle can repeat over and over.
- With 2nd-degree AV heart block, Type I, there are more P waves than QRS complexes and the rhythm is regularly irregular. This is also called a patterned irregularity.
- 2nd-degree AV heart block, Type II, is an intermittent block at the level of the bundle of His or bundle branches resulting in atrial impulses that are not conducted to the ventricles.
- With 2nd-degree AV heart block, Type II, there are more P waves than QRS complexes, and the duration of PR interval of the conducted beats remains the same (are constant).
- 3rd-degree AV heart block is a complete block of the conduction at or below the AV junction, and impulses from the atria cannot reach the ventricles.
- In 3rd-degree AV heart block, the pacemaker for the atria arises from the SA node while the pacemaker for the ventricles arises as an escape rhythm from the AV junction at a rate

of 40 to 60 beats per minute or from the ventricles at a rate of 20 to 40 beats per minute.

- With 3rd-degree AV heart block, the upright and round P waves seem to march right through the QRS complexes. This reveals that there is no relationship between the P waves and QRS complexes.
- 2nd- and 3rd-degree AV heart block can lead to decreased cardiac output.
- In atrioventricular dissociation, the SA node loses control of the ventricular rate leading to the atria and ventricles beating independently of each other, usually at about the same rate.

Assess Your Understanding

The following questions give you a chance to assess your understanding of the material discussed in this chapter. The answers can be found in Appendix A.

1. Heart blocks are
   a. partial delays or complete interruptions in the cardiac conduction pathway between the atria and ventricles.
   b. early ectopic beats that originate outside the SA node.
   c. a shifting of the pacemaker site between the SA node, atria, and/or AV junction.
   d. the result of accessory conduction pathways between the atria and ventricles.
2. With 1st-degree AV heart block
   a. the PR intervals are greater than 0.20 seconds in duration.
   b. not all the P waves are followed by QRS complexes.
   c. the P waves are inverted.
   d. the underlying rhythm is slow.
3. 1st-degree AV heart block is considered a/an
   a. intermittent block.
   b. complete block.
   c. consistent delay in conduction.
   d. partial block.
4. With 2nd-degree AV heart block, Type I
   a. the PR intervals get progressively shorter.
   b. not all the P waves are followed by a QRS complex.
   c. the P waves are inverted.
   d. the rhythm appears to be irregularly irregular.
5. With 2nd-degree AV heart block, Type II
   a. the P waves are all the same.
   b. a QRS complex follows each P wave.
   c. the pacemaker site is in the AV junction.
   d. the ventricular rate is less than 40 beats per minute.
6. Which of the following rhythms has a constant PR interval for all conducted beats?
   a. 2nd-degree AV heart block, Type I.
   b. 3rd-degree AV heart block.
   c. 2nd-degree AV heart block, Type II.
   d. All of the above.
7. The difference between 2nd-degree AV heart block, Type I and Type II is that
   a. with Type II, the PR intervals are constant.
   b. the ventricular rate with Type II is usually greater than 60 beats per minute.
   c. with Type II, the P waves appear to march right through the QRS complexes.
   d. with Type II, there appears to be a pattern to the irregularity.

8. An ECG rhythm that has no correlation between P waves and QRS complexes is known as
   a. 1st-degree AV heart block.
   b. 2nd-degree AV heart block, Type II.
   c. 2nd-degree AV heart block, Type I.
   d. 3rd-degree AV heart block.
9. Which of the following dysrhythmias has P waves that seem to march through the QRS complexes?
   a. 2nd-degree AV heart block, Type I.
   b. 2nd-degree AV heart block, Type II.
   c. 3rd-degree AV heart block.
   d. 1st-degree AV heart block.
10. Which of the following heart blocks is irregular?
    a. 1st-degree AV heart block.
    b. 2nd-degree AV heart block, Type I.
    c. 3rd-degree AV heart block.
    d. All of the above.

Match the following heart blocks with the correct characteristics.

Heart Blocks		*Characteristics*
11. 1st-degree AV heart block	___	a. PR interval gets progressively longer until a P wave fails to conduct, resulting in a dropped QRS complex. After the blocked beat, the cycle starts again.
12. 2nd-degree AV heart block, Type I	___	b. There is a complete block at or below the AV node; there is no relationship between the P waves and QRS complexes.
13. 2nd-degree AV heart block, Type II	___	c. Some beats are conducted while others are blocked.
14. 3rd-degree AV heart block	___	d. Not a true block; there is a delay at the AV node; each impulse is eventually conducted.

Referring to the scenario at the beginning of this chapter answer the following questions.

15. What rhythm is the patient in?
    a. 1st-degree AV heart block.
    b. 2nd-degree AV heart block, Type I.
    c. 2nd-degree AV heart block, Type II.
    d. 3rd-degree AV heart block.
16. The most common cause of this condition is
    a. medication.
    b. myocardial infarction.
    c. atherosclerotic heart disease.
    d. malfunctioning artificial pacemaker.
17. The treatment of this condition usually requires which of the following?
    a. An artificial pacemaker.
    b. An implanted defibrillator.
    c. A heart transplant.
    d. Cardiac stimulant medication.

Answers to Sidebar Questions

"Describe how the impulse that brings about the heartbeat is conducted from the SA node to the AV node."

Answer: The initial electrical impulse begins high in the right atrium, in the SA node. It travels through the atria via intraatrial and internodal pathways to the atrioventricular (AV) node.

"In which of the AV heart blocks are there more P waves than QRS complexes?"

Answer: There are more P waves than QRS complexes in both types of 2nd-degree AV heart block and in 3rd-degree AV heart block.

"What is the normal duration for the PR interval?"

Answer: The normal PR interval is 0.12 to 0.20 seconds in duration.

"What type of irregularity does 2nd-degree AV heart block, Type I, produce?

Answer: 2nd-degree AV heart block, Type I, produces regularly or patterned irregularity. This is where the irregularity repeats over and over in a cyclic fashion.

"How can you distinguish between a nonconducted PAC and 2nd-degree AV heart block?"

Answer: With nonconducted PACs (or blocked PACs) the P-P interval, including the extra P wave, isn't constant, whereas with 2nd-degree AV heart block, the P-P interval, including the extra P wave, is constant.

"What is the inherent rate of the AV junction and the ventricles?"

Answer: The inherent rate of the AV junction is 40 to 60 beats per minute, while the inherent rate of the ventricles is 20 to 40 beats per minute.

On the DVD

- Introduction to Heart Blocks lecture.

Notes

Electrical Axis

13

Case History

Paramedics are called to the home of an 83-year-old man complaining of shortness of breath. After obtaining a set of vital signs that reveal the patient to be hypertensive, one of the paramedics auscultates the lungs and discovers rales throughout both lung fields. They place the patient on high concentration oxygen, give him some furosemide, and take a 12-lead ECG. The 12-lead ECG indicates that the patient has an enlarged heart but does not show evidence of a heart attack.

Chapter Preview

- Vectors
- Electrical Axis
- Waveform Direction
- Ventricular Depolarization and Mean QRS Axis
- Calculating the Electrical Axis
- Normal QRS Axis
- Altered QRS Axis

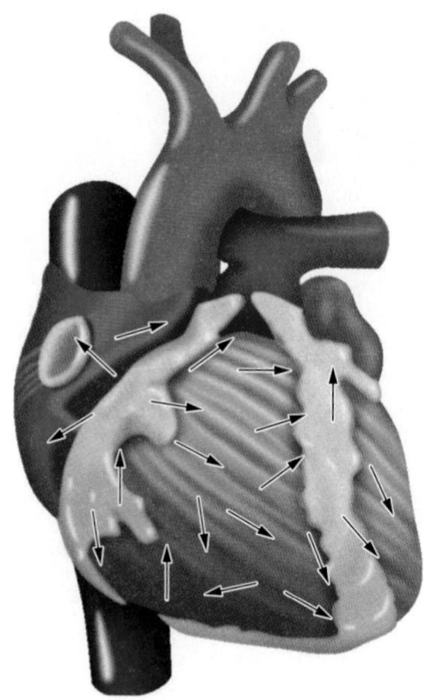

Figure 13-1
Depolarization and repolarization of the heart produces many small electrical currents or impulses.

As discussed in earlier chapters, the 12-lead ECG records twelve different views of the heart's electrical activity. Changes in the size or condition of the heart muscle and/or conduction system will affect how electrical impulses are conducted through the tissue and subsequently the appearance of the ECG waveforms. If an area of the heart is enlarged or damaged specific ECG leads will provide a view of that portion of the heart. What we discuss next will help you to understand why given waveforms change in direction, duration, or appearance.

QUESTION
"A 12-lead ECG includes what two general types of leads?" (The answer can be found on page 419.)

Vectors

The wave of depolarization and repolarization of the cardiac cells produces many small electrical currents or impulses called instantaneous vectors. If you think about the millions of cells in the ventricles alone, that is a lot of electrical currents. These currents vary in intensity and direction and can be visually represented by arrows (Figure 13-1). While these tiny swirls of current are moving simultaneously in many different directions, the ECG only records the sum or average of the current flow or instantaneous vectors at any given moment. The sum of these vectors is called the mean instantaneous vector.

CLINICAL MOMENT
Remember, depolarization is the advancing wave of sodium ions.

The currents produced by depolarization and repolarization are called instantaneous ________________. Each can be visually represented by an ________________.

[vectors] [arrow]

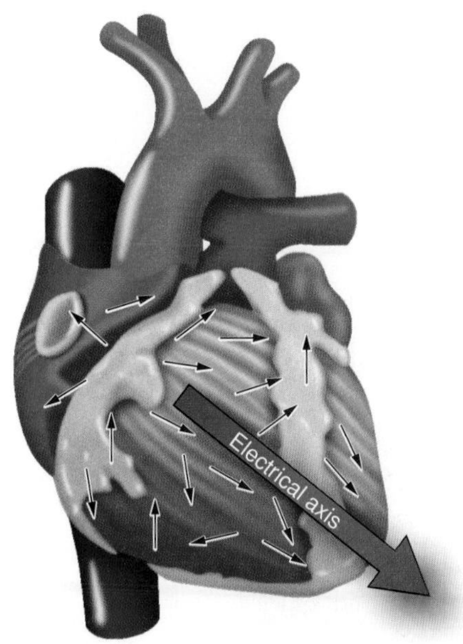

Figure 13-2
The overall direction and force of the current flow through the heart is called the heart's electrical axis.

Electrical Axis

While the sum of the small vectors is called the mean instantaneous vector, its direction and magnitude as it travels through the heart is called the heart's **electrical axis.** The axis is depicted as a single large arrow. The angle of orientation represents the direction of current flow, while its length represents its voltage (amperage). Axis is defined in the frontal plane only. The mean instantaneous vector generated during the depolarization of the atria and its direction and amplitude is called the P axis. It is rarely determined. The mean instantaneous vector generated during the depolarization of the ventricles and its direction and amplitude is referred to as the mean QRS axis. The mean QRS axis is the most clinically important and therefore the axis we measure (Figure 13-2). Normally, the QRS axis points to the left and downward, reflecting the dominance of the left ventricle over the right ventricle.

The wave of electrical ______________ moves through the myocardium in a specific ______________. The mean vector is the ______________ of all the ________ vectors that the ECG detects. The direction of the mean vector is called the electrical ______________. It is depicted as a single, large ______________.

[depolarization] [direction] [sum] [instantaneous] [axis] [arrow]

INSTRUCTIONAL MOMENT
The instantaneous vectors are represented by each part of the QRS complex. The mean vector or electrical axis is derived by looking at the QRS complex as a whole and deciding whether it is more positive or negative. This is what clinically determines the axis.

CLINICAL MOMENT
The heart's electrical axis reveals important information about the movement of electrical impulses through the heart.

KEY CONCEPT
The mean vector is the average of all the instantaneous vectors that the ECG detects. Its direction is called the electrical axis and is depicted as a single, large arrow.

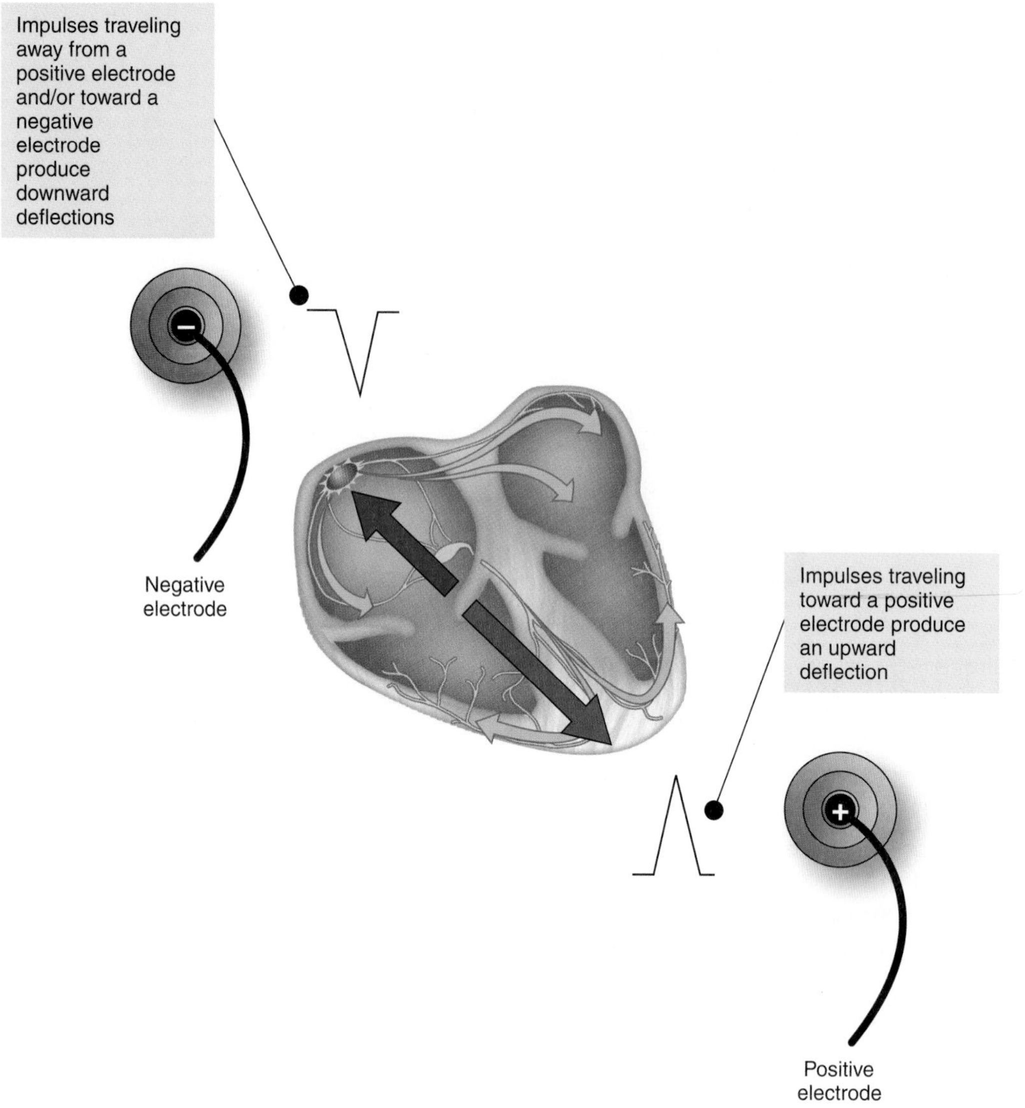

Impulses traveling away from a positive electrode and/or toward a negative electrode produce downward deflections

Negative electrode

Impulses traveling toward a positive electrode produce an upward deflection

Positive electrode

Figure 13-3
Direction of ECG waveforms when the electrical current is traveling toward a positive ECG electrode or away from it.

QUESTION
"What direction will the ECG waveform deflection take when depolarization is moving toward a positive electrode?" (The answer can be found on page 419.)

Waveform Direction

Remember from our earlier discussion that when the electrical current traveling through the heart is moving toward a positive electrode, the ECG machine records it as a positive or upright waveform. When the impulse is traveling away from a positive electrode and toward a negative electrode the ECG machine records it as a negative or downward deflection (Figure 13-3).

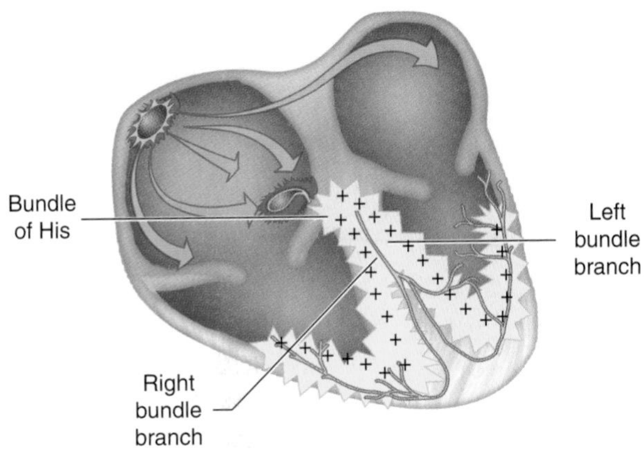

Figure 13-4
The ventricular conduction system quickly conducts the impulse to the ventricles.

Ventricular Depolarization and Mean QRS Axis

In a healthy heart, waves of depolarization originate in the SA node and travel through the atria, the AV node, and on to the ventricles. The ventricular conduction system quickly conducts the stimulus to the ventricles (Figure 13-4). The Purkinje fibers carry the impulse from the endocardial lining of the right and left ventricles in the apical region of the heart near the septum through the full thickness of the ventricular wall toward the outside surface (or epicardium). The impulse continues through the ventricles in all areas at once and ends in the lateral and posterior aspect of the left ventricle near its base.

KEY CONCEPT
The ECG machine records current traveling through the heart and moving toward a positive ECG electrode as a positive or upright waveform.

Even though the impulse arrives at the subendocardial lining of both ventricles at about the same time, completion of right ventricle depolarization occurs first. This is because the thinner wall of the right ventricle transmits the impulse in a fraction of the time that it takes the impulse to travel through the thick lateral wall of the left ventricle.

As identified earlier, the QRS complex represents the simultaneous depolarization of both ventricles (Figure 13-5).

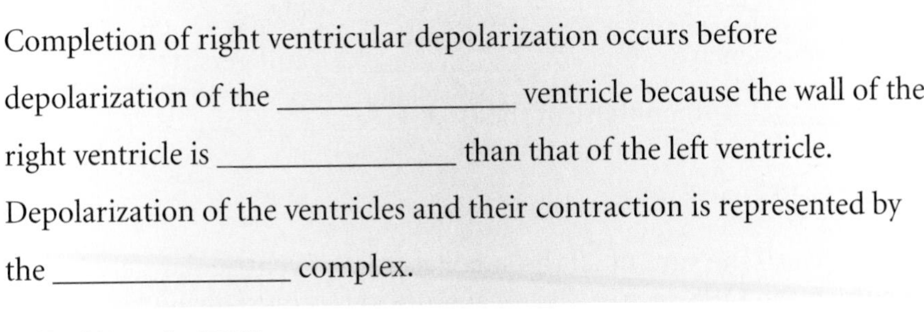

Completion of right ventricular depolarization occurs before depolarization of the ______________ ventricle because the wall of the right ventricle is ______________ than that of the left ventricle.

Depolarization of the ventricles and their contraction is represented by the ______________ complex.

[left] [thinner] [QRS]

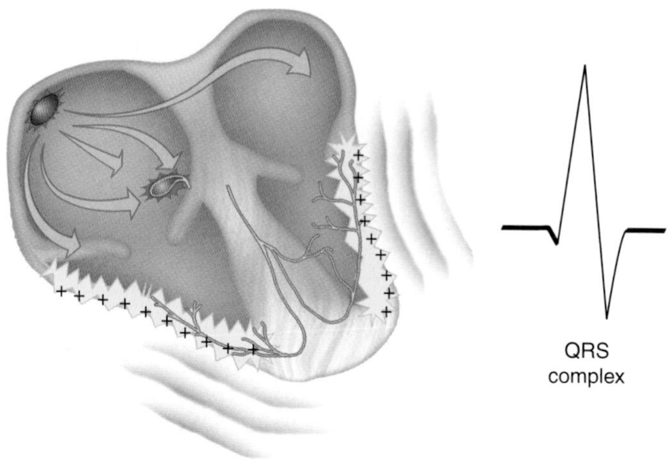

Figure 13-5
Ventricular depolarization and the QRS complex.

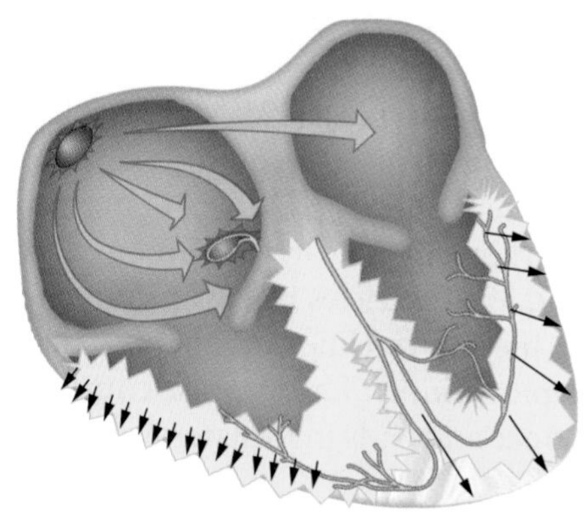

Figure 13-6
The vectors of the left ventricle are larger and persist longer than those of the right ventricle.

The vectors arising in the right ventricle are directed mostly to the right when viewed in the frontal plane; those in the left ventricle are directed mostly to the left (Figure 13-6). The left ventricular vectors are larger and persist longer than those of the smaller right ventricle, primarily because of the greater thickness of the left ventricular wall.

KEY CONCEPT
The vectors of the left ventricle are larger and persist longer because the muscular wall of the left ventricle is thicker than the right ventricle.

The left ventricular vectors are ______________ and persist ______________ than those of the ______________.

[larger] [longer] [right]

Again, we call the sum of all the small vectors of ventricular depolarization the mean QRS vector. The mean QRS axis represents both its direction and magnitude. The small depolarization vectors of the thicker left

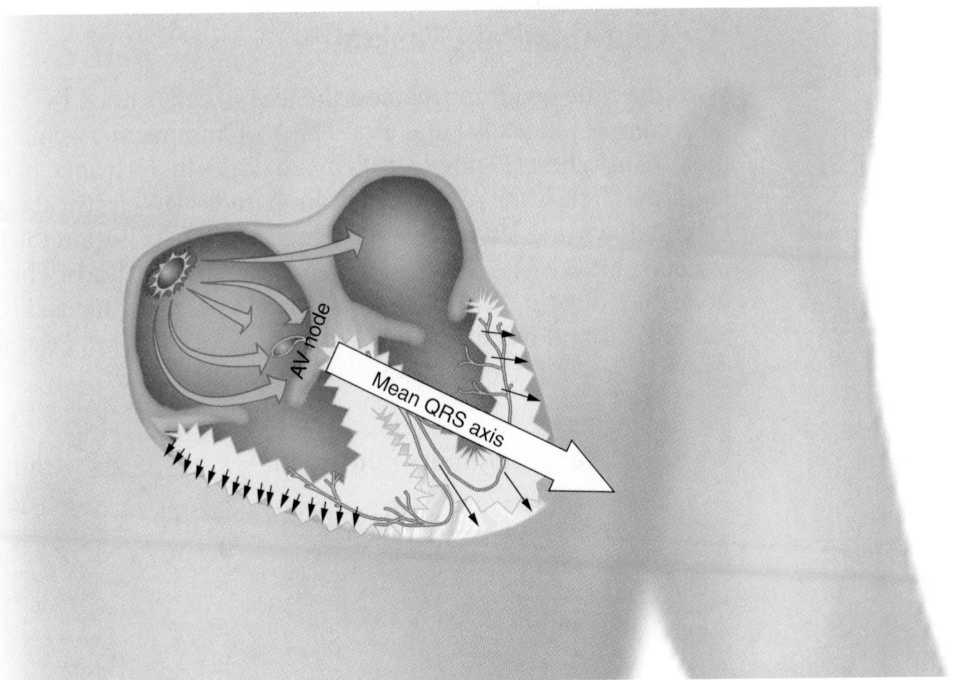

Figure 13-7
The mean QRS axis points downward and toward the patient's left side.

ventricle are larger resulting in greater magnitude, so the mean QRS axis points more to the left (Figure 13-7). The ventricles are in the left side of the chest and angle downward to the left. For this reason the mean QRS axis points downward and toward the patient's left side.

The mean QRS vector normally points ________ and to the ________.

[downward] [left]

Calculating the Electrical Axis

There are several methods you can use to determine the direction of the patient's electrical axis. These include the triaxial reference system, which calculates the axis using the three standard limb leads (I, II, and III), and the hexaxial reference system, which uses the three standard limb leads and the three augmented limb leads (aV_R, aV_L, and aV_F). Both of these reference systems, however, are difficult to use. An easier way to determine the heart's axis is to use the four-quadrant method.

KEY CONCEPT
The mean QRS magnitude normally points downward and to the patient's left, because this is the general direction of ventricular depolarization.

QUESTION
"Can you list the six limb leads and identify which are augmented?" (The answer can be found on page 418.)

Four-Quadrant Method

With the four-quadrant method the axis is determined by examining the QRS complex in leads I and aV_F. Think of an imaginary circle drawn over the patient's chest (Figure 13-8). This circle lies in the frontal plane. The center of the circle is the AV node. The limb leads view electrical forces moving up and down and left and right through this circle. Within the circle are six bisecting lines, each representing one of the six limb leads. The intersection of all lines divides the circle into equal, 30-degree segments. Lead I starts at +0 degrees and is located at the three o'clock position. Lead aV_F starts at +90 degrees and is located at the six o'clock position.

We can locate the position of the mean ____________ within a large ____________ drawn over the patient's chest. The ____________ is at the center of the circle.

[QRS vector] [circle] [AV node]

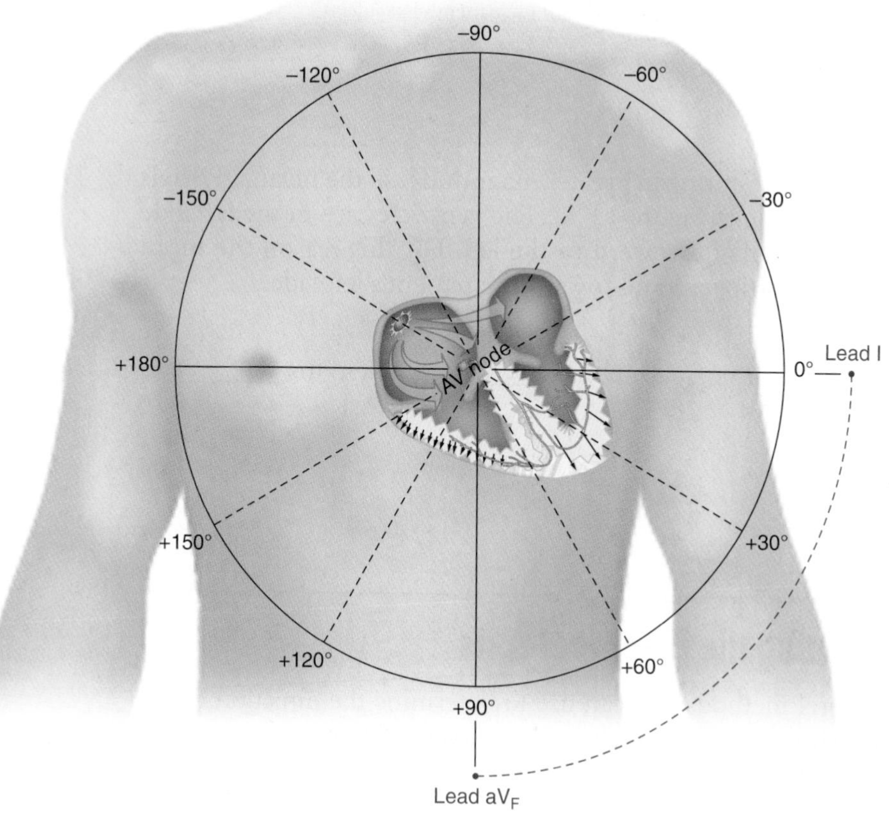

Figure 13-8
The imaginary circle used to determine the heart's axis is divided into equal 30-degree segments with lead I at the three o'clock position and lead aV_F located at the six o'clock position.

Normal QRS Axis

The mean QRS axis normally points downward and to the patient's left, between 0 and +90 degrees (Figure 13-9). As long as it remains within this range, it is considered normal. If it is outside this range, it is considered abnormal.

Any lead records a positive deflection if the wave of depolarization is moving toward it. Lead I is oriented at 0°. If the mean QRS axis is directed anywhere between −90° and +90°, the right half of the circle, you can expect lead I to record a positive QRS complex (Figure 13-10).

INSTRUCTIONAL MOMENT
Lead I is created by making the left arm positive and the right arm negative. For this reason the left half of the circle is positive while the right half is negative.

Lead I will record a ______________ QRS complex if the mean QRS axis is directed anywhere between −90° and ______________.

[positive] [+90°]

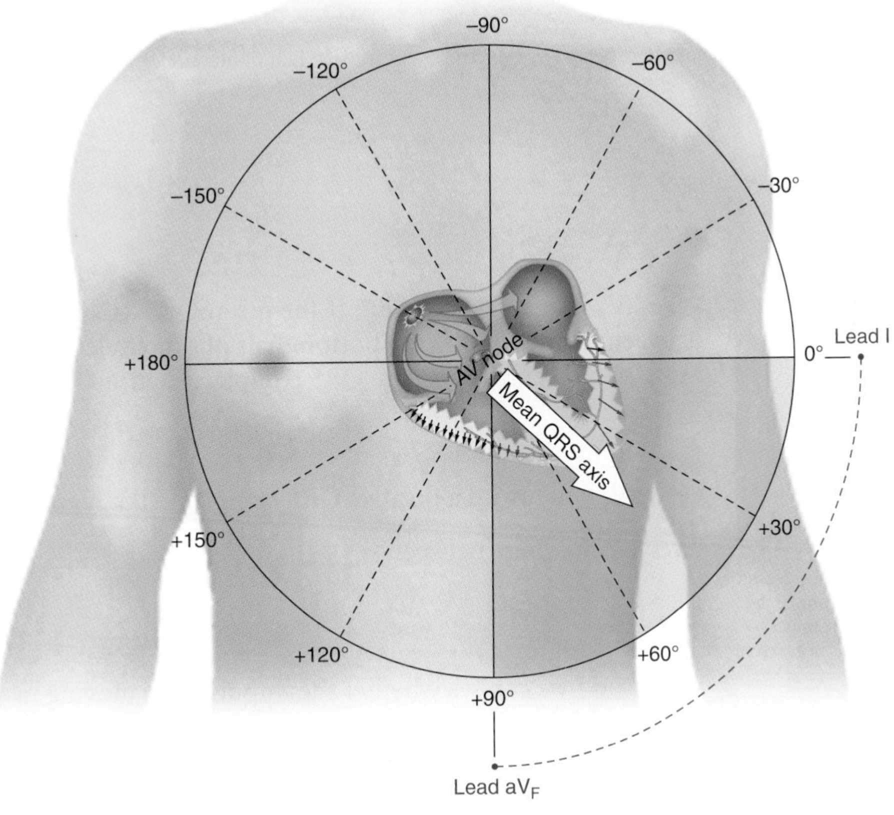

Figure 13-9
The mean QRS axis normally points downward and to the patient's left between 0 and +90 degrees.

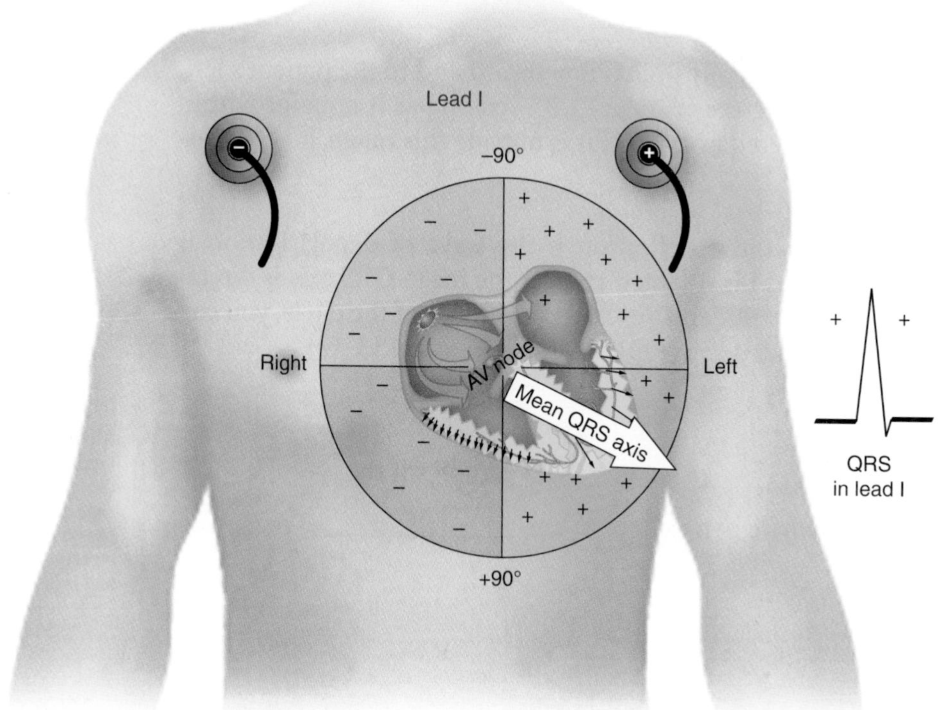

Figure 13-10
If the mean QRS axis is directed anywhere between −90° and +90° (the left half of our circle), a positive QRS complex is seen in lead I.

Lead aV_F is oriented at +90°. If the mean QRS axis is directed anywhere between 0° and +180°, the bottom half of our circle, you can expect lead aV_F lead to record a positive QRS complex (Figure 13-11).

INSTRUCTIONAL MOMENT
Lead aV_F is created by making the legs positive and the other limbs negative. For this reason the bottom half of our circle is positive while the upper half of our circle is negative.

Lead aV_F will record a positive QRS complex if the mean QRS axis is directed anywhere between ______________ and ______________.

[0°] [+180°]

With lead I we can see whether the impulses are moving to the right or to the left while lead aV_F tells us whether they're moving up or down.

If the main deflection of the QRS complex points up (positive) in lead I, then the electrical impulses are moving from right to left in a nor-

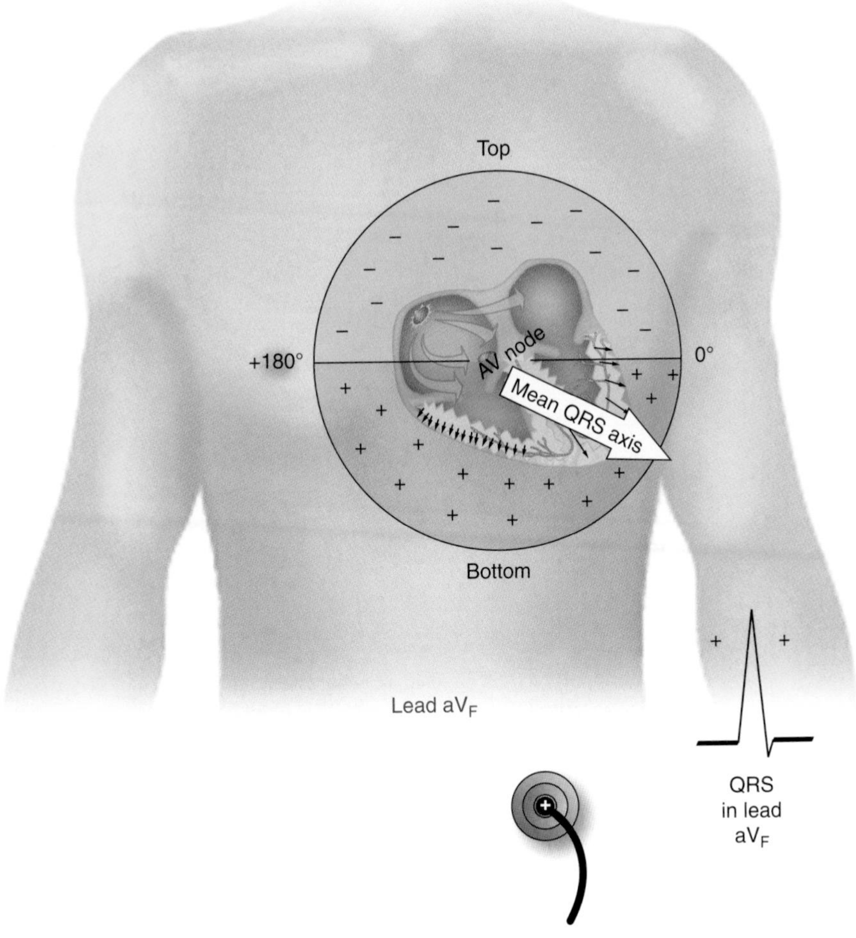

Figure 13-11
If the mean QRS axis is directed anywhere between 0 and +180 degrees (the bottom half of our circle), a positive QRS complex is seen in lead aV_F.

mal manner. Conversely, if the deflection points down (negative), then the impulses are moving abnormally from left to right (Figure 13-12).

If the deflection of the QRS complex is positive in lead aV_F, the electrical impulses are traveling downward in a normal manner. If the deflection is negative, the impulses are traveling upward; this would be considered abnormal (Figure 13-13).

A ________________ QRS complex in leads I and aV_F indicates the QRS axis is normal.

[positive]

INSTRUCTIONAL MOMENT

An easy way to remember the direction of the deflection of the QRS complexes in leads I and aV_F is to think of your thumbs pointing up or down. Two thumbs up indicates normal axis; anything else is considered abnormal. See the lecture on the companion DVD for further explanation.

KEY CONCEPT
By assessing leads I and aV_F you can quickly determine whether the mean QRS axis on any ECG is normal. If the QRS complex is positive in leads I and aV_F, the QRS axis is normal.

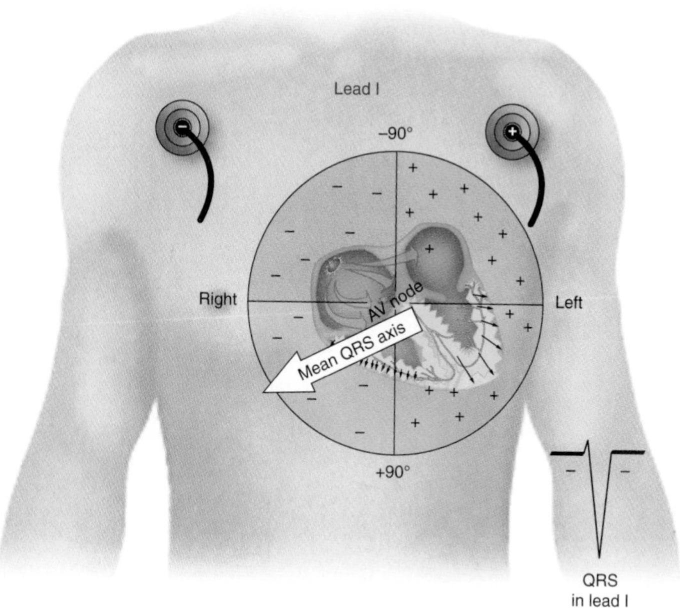

Figure 13-12
If the mean QRS axis is directed anywhere between −90° and +90° (the right half of our circle), a negative QRS complex is seen in lead I.

CLINICAL MOMENT
To determine whether the QRS complex is positive or negative you examine it and decide whether the average deflection is positive or negative. Often, this is easy to estimate by merely looking at the QRS complex and deciding what the overall complex looks like. More accuracy can be obtained by measuring the number of boxes of negative and positive deflection. If there are more boxes on the negative side, the QRS complex is referred to as negative. If there are more boxes on the positive side, the QRS complex is referred to as positive.

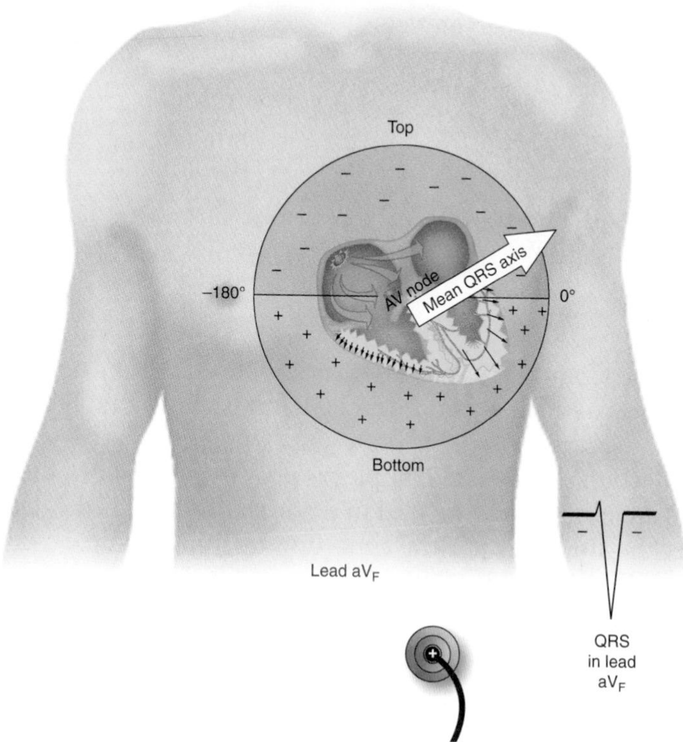

Figure 13-13
If the mean QRS axis is directed anywhere between 0 and −180 degrees (the top half of our circle), a negative QRS complex is seen in lead aV_F.

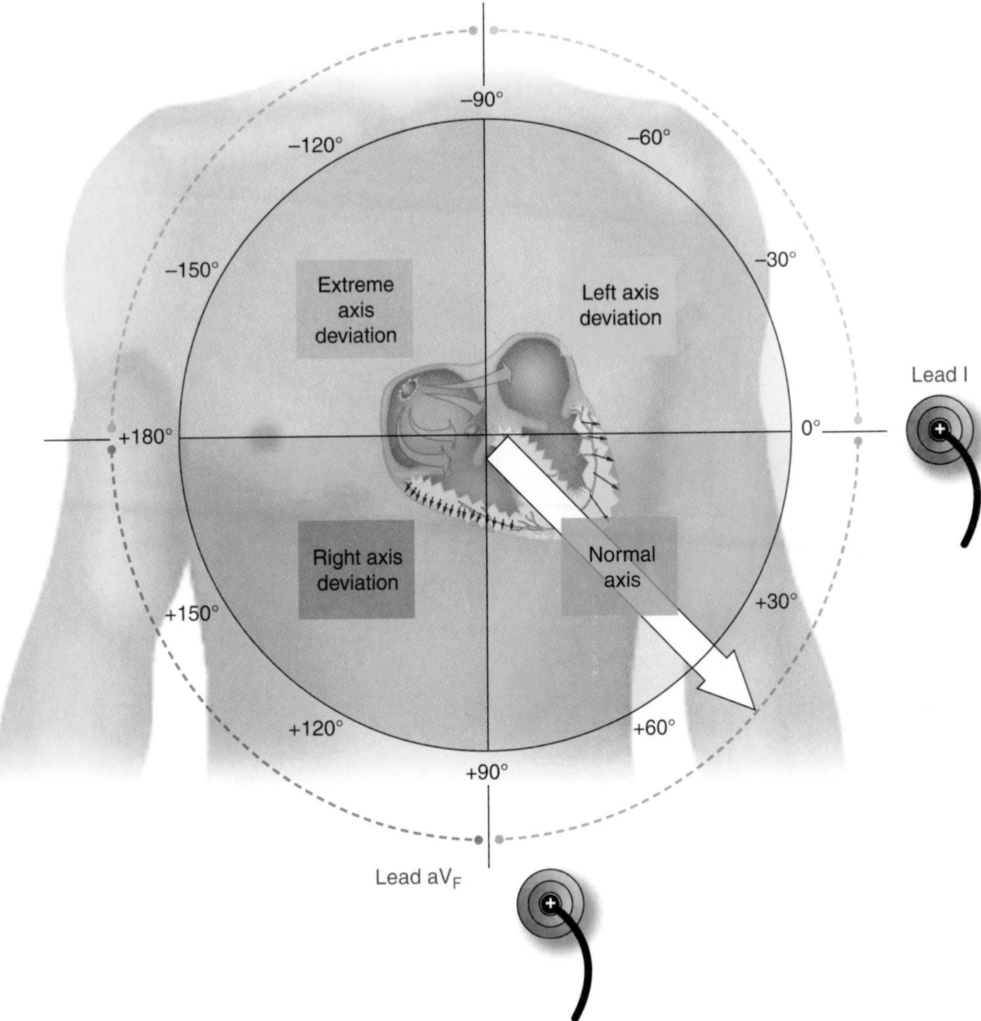

Figure 13-14
Normal axis, right axis deviation, extreme axis deviation, and left axis deviation.

Altered QRS Axis

As was mentioned earlier, the mean QRS axis normally points downward and to the patient's left, between 0 and +90 degrees. An axis between +90 and +180 degrees indicates right axis deviation, and one between 0 and −90 degrees indicates left axis deviation. An axis deviation between −180 and −90 degrees indicates extreme axis deviation and is called an indeterminate axis (Figure 13-14).

The mean QRS axis normally points downward and to the patient's

________________, between ________________ degrees.

[left] [0 and +90]

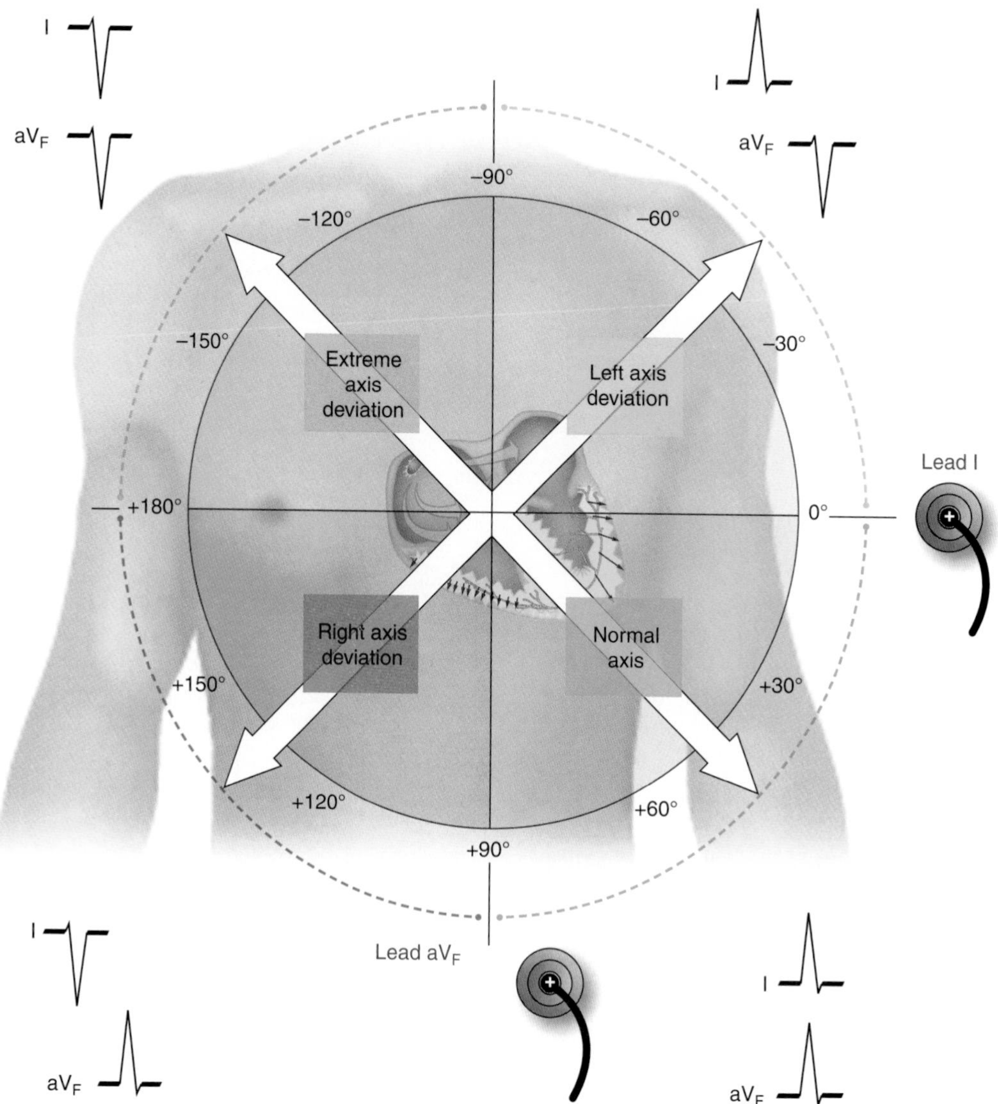

Figure 13-15

Positive QRS complexes in leads I and aV_F indicate a normal QRS axis. A negative QRS complex in lead I and an upright QRS complex in lead aV_F indicate right axis deviation. Negative QRS complexes in both lead I and lead aV_F indicate extreme axis deviation, and an upright QRS complex in lead I and a negative QRS complex in lead aV_F indicate left axis deviation.

Again, if the QRS complex deflection is positive in both leads I and aV_F, the electrical axis is normal. If the QRS complex in lead I is upright and the QRS complex in lead aV_F has a negative deflection, then left axis deviation exists. If the QRS complex in lead I is negative and lead aV_F has a QRS complex with a positive deflection, then right axis deviation exists. If the QRS complex is negative in both leads, extreme axis deviation exists (Figure 13-15).

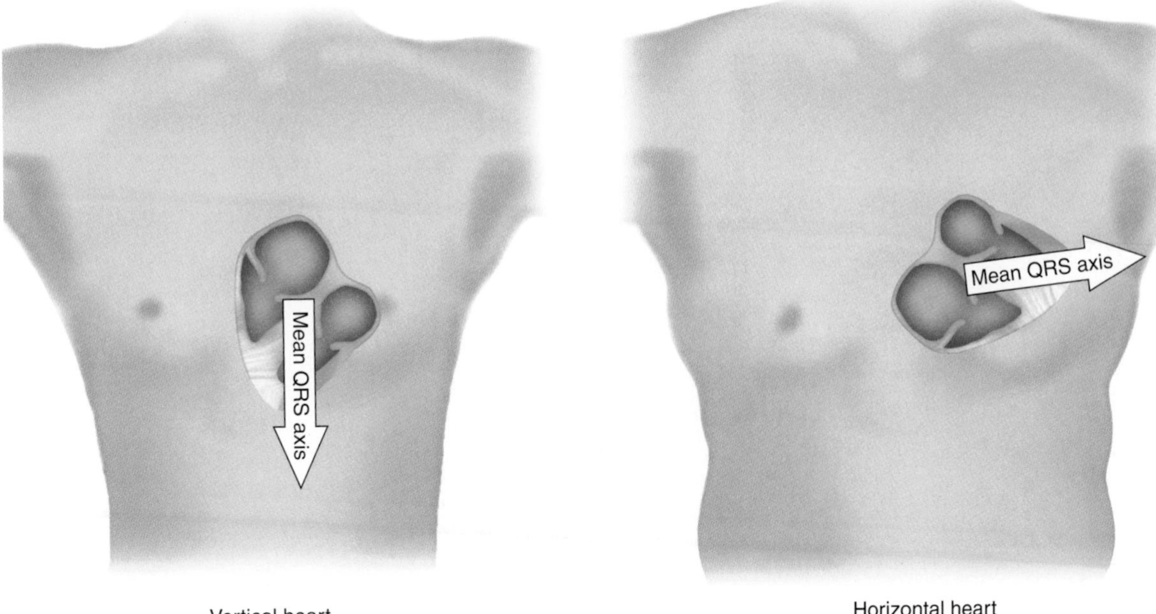

Figure 13-16
In thin individuals, the apex of the heart can be directed vertically, whereas with very obese individuals and in pregnancy the apex can be directed horizontally. As the apex of the heart shifts, so does the mean QRS axis.

_______________ QRS complex deflection in both leads I and aV_F indicates normal electrical axis. _______________ QRS complex deflection in lead I and _______________ deflection in lead aV_F indicate left axis deviation. _______________ QRS complex deflection in lead I and _______________ deflection in lead aV_F indicate right axis deviation. _______________ QRS complex deflection in both leads I and aV_F indicates extreme axis deviation.

[Positive] [Upright] [negative] [Negative] [upright] [Negative]

Causes of Altered Electrical Axis

If the heart is displaced, the mean QRS axis is also displaced in the same direction. As an example, in tall, slender individuals the heart may be rotated toward the patient's right side. This is referred to as a vertical heart. This causes the mean QRS axis to shift toward the right. With obesity and in pregnancy, the diaphragm (and the heart) is pushed up by the increased abdominal pressure so that the mean QRS axis will likely point directly to the patient's left. This may be called a horizontal heart (Figure 13-16).

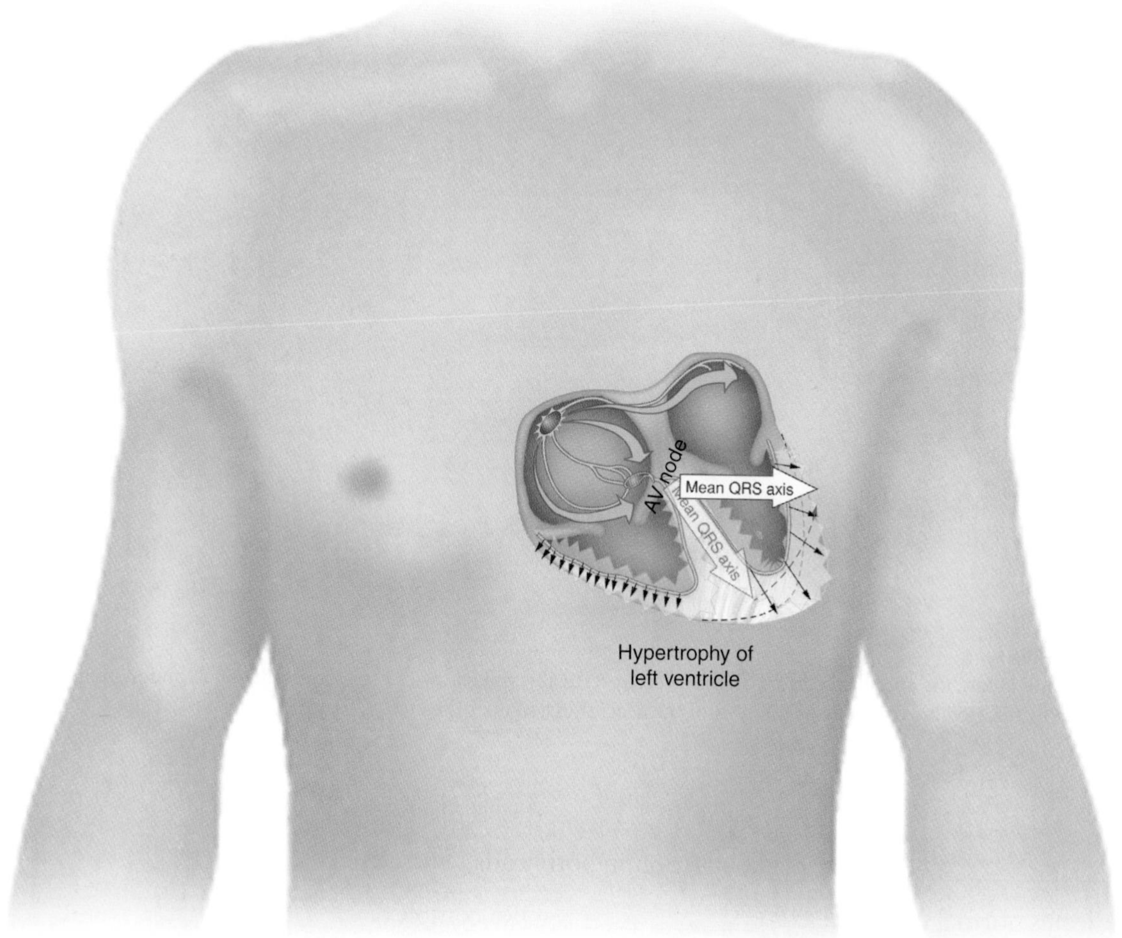

Figure 13-17
With enlargement or hypertrophy of one or both of the heart's chambers, the mean QRS axis shifts toward the enlarged or hypertrophied side.

Tall, slender individuals may have hearts rotated toward the patient's _______________ side. With obesity and in pregnancy, the heart may be pushed _______________ by the increased abdominal pressure. This causes a change in the _______________ axis.

[right] [up] [QRS]

Another condition that causes the axis to shift is enlargement or **hypertrophy** of one or both of the heart's chambers (Figure 13-17). The resultant greater depolarization activity displaces the mean P or QRS axis toward the enlarged or hypertrophied region. This is because an enlarged or hypertrophied chamber has more (and larger) vectors, which draws the mean P or QRS axis in that direction.

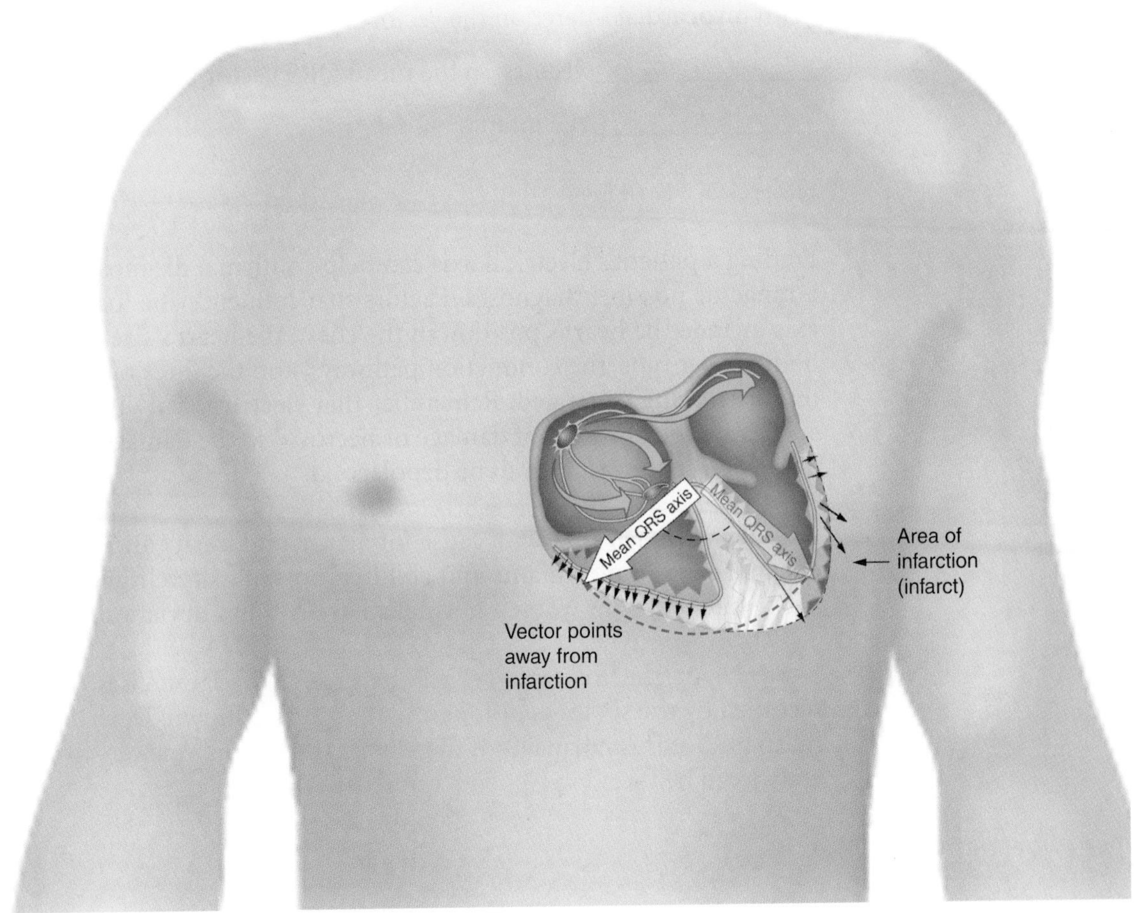

Figure 13-18
The infarcted tissue seen with myocardial infarction cannot depolarize and therefore has no vectors. The vectors from the other side are unopposed vectors because of this, so the mean QRS vector tends to point away from the infarct.

There is increased depolarization in an ______________ or ______________ chamber. So, the mean P or QRS axis deviates ______________ the enlarged or hypertrophied chamber.

[enlarged] [hypertrophied] [toward]

Myocardial infarction is another condition that causes the mean QRS axis to point in a different direction than normal (Figure 13-18). With myocardial infarction, a branch of the coronary arteries supplying an area of the heart with blood becomes occluded and the tissue becomes necrotic. This infarcted tissue cannot depolarize and therefore has no vectors. The vectors from the other side are unopposed vectors because of this, so the mean QRS vector tends to point away from the infarct.

With myocardial infarction the vectors from the other side are

_______________ vectors, so the mean QRS vector tends to point

_______________ the infarct.

[unopposed] [away from]

Finding a patient's electrical axis can help confirm a diagnosis or narrow a range of possible diagnoses. Factors that influence the location of the axis include the heart's position in the chest, the heart's size, the patient's body size or type, the conduction pathways, and the force of the electrical impulses being generated. Remember that electrical activity in the heart swings away from areas of damage or necrosis, so the damaged part of the heart will be the last area to be depolarized.

Axis deviation isn't always a cause for alarm, and it isn't always cardiac in origin. For example, infants and children normally have right axis deviation while pregnant women normally have left axis deviation.

For each of the following *Practice Makes Perfect* exercises, the waves recorded by the six leads of the frontal plane are shown. Determine if the mean QRS axis is normal or if there is axis deviation. Answers to these exercises can be found in Appendix A.

PRACTICE. . . MAKES PERFECT

Determine if the mean QRS is normal or if there is axis deviation.

1.

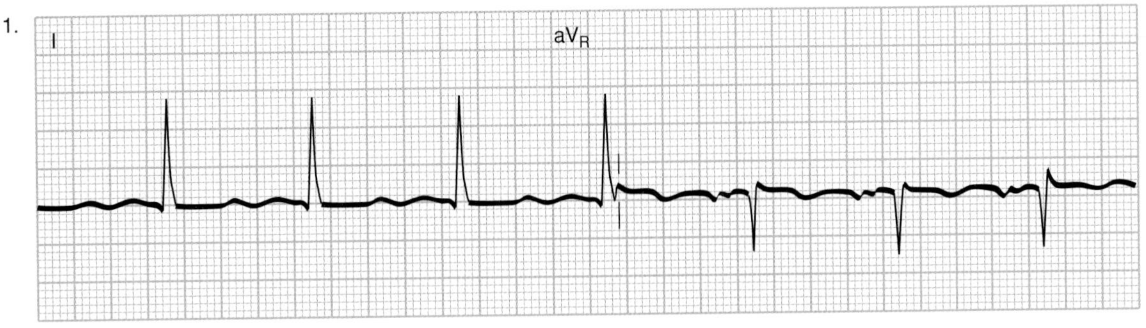

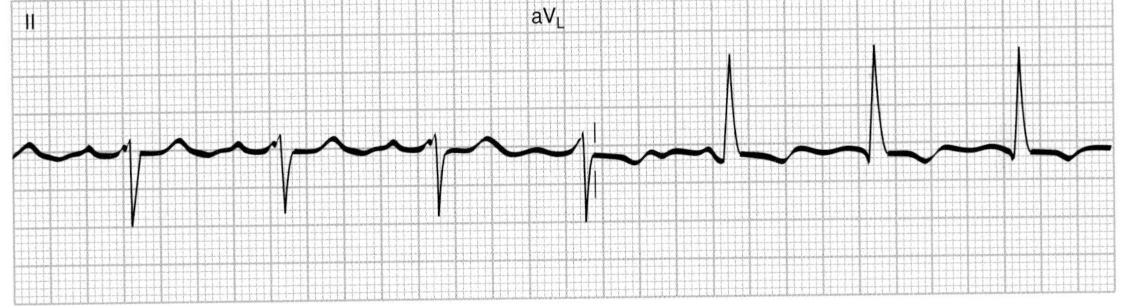

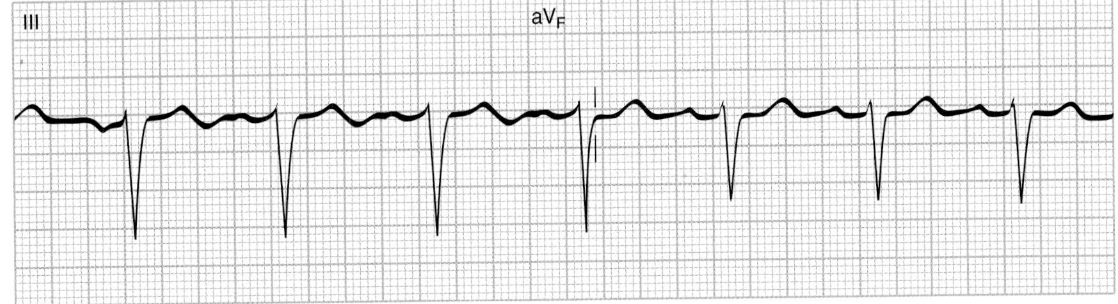

PRACTICE. . . MAKES PERFECT

Determine if the mean QRS is normal or if there is axis deviation.

2.

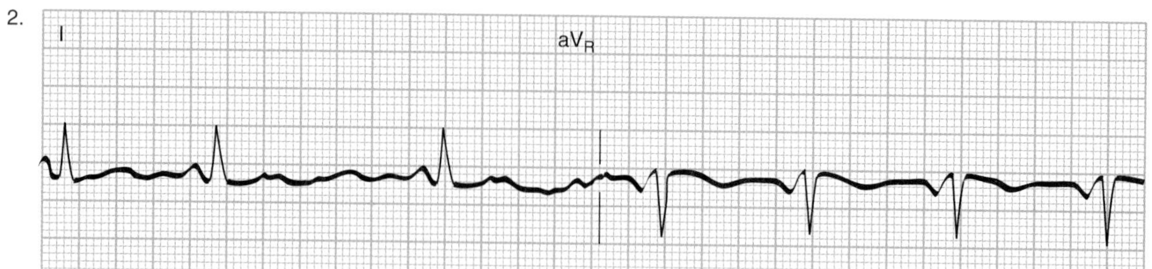

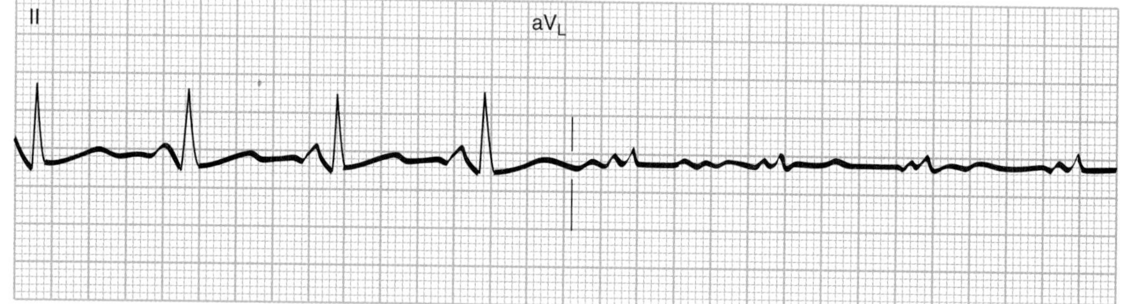

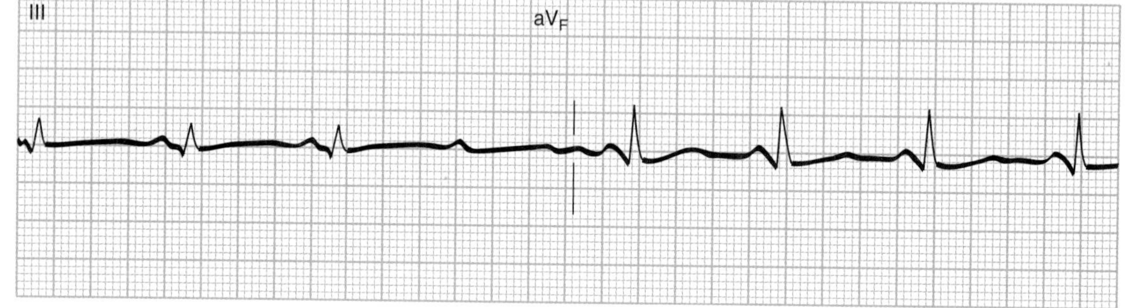

PRACTICE. . . MAKES PERFECT

Determine if the mean QRS is normal or if there is axis deviation.

3.

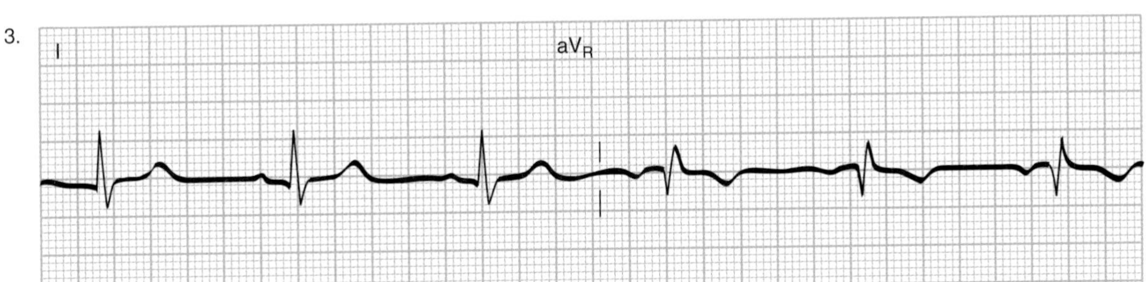

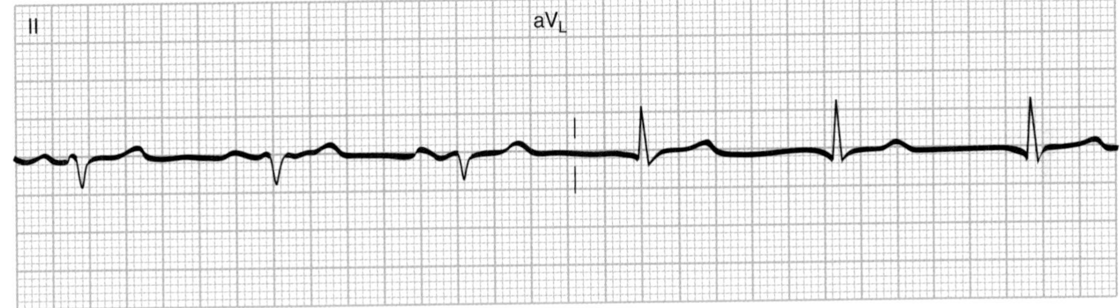

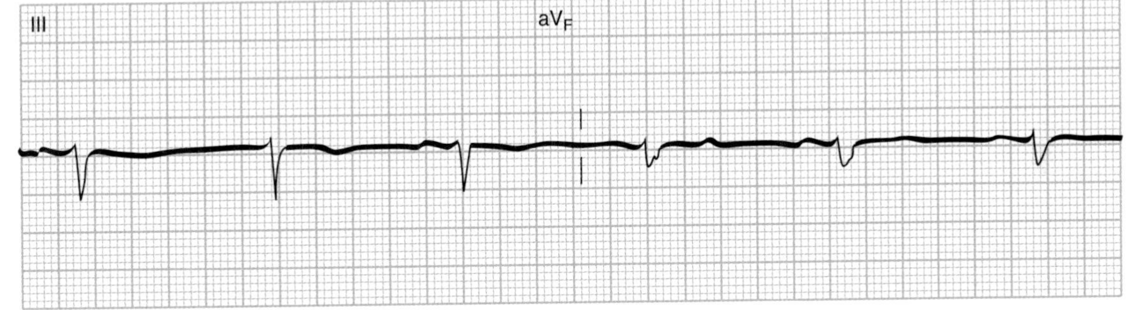

PRACTICE. . . MAKES PERFECT

Determine if the mean QRS is normal or if there is axis deviation.

4.

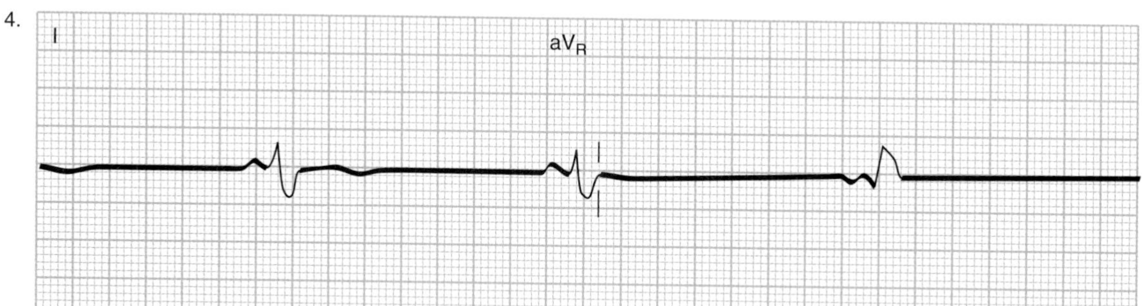

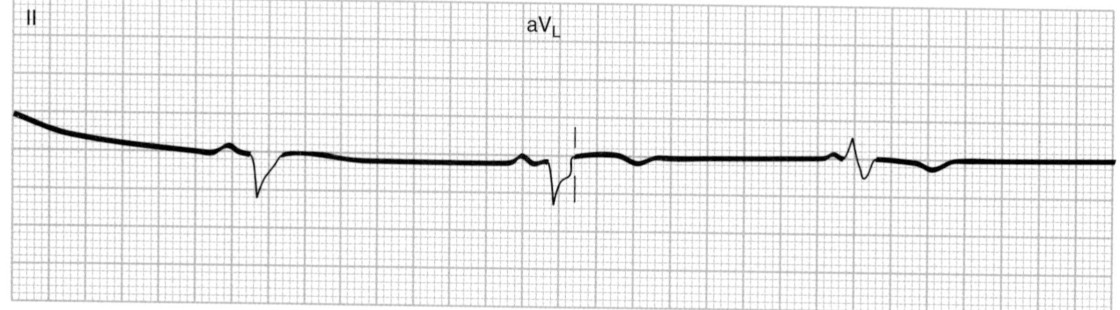

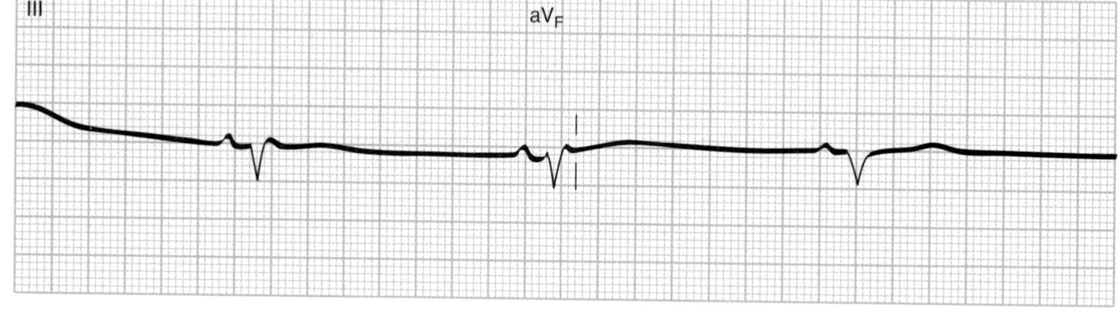

Key Points

- Depolarization and repolarization of the cardiac cells produce many small electrical currents or impulses that vary in intensity and direction. These currents are called instantaneous vectors.
- The mean or average of all the instantaneous vectors the ECG detects is called the mean vector. The direction of the mean vector is called the electrical axis.
- When the electrical current traveling through the heart is moving toward a positive electrode the ECG machine records it as a positive or upright waveform.
- When the impulse is traveling away from a positive electrode and toward a negative electrode, the ECG machine records it as a negative or downward deflection.
- The mean of all vectors that result from ventricular depolarization is called the QRS axis. It is the most important and also the most frequently determined axis.
- A sequence of vectors is produced as the Purkinje fibers carry the impulse from the endocardial lining of the right and left ventricles through the full thickness of the ventricular wall toward the epicardium.
- Completion of right ventricular depolarization occurs first because the thinner wall of the right ventricle transmits the impulse in a fraction of the time it takes the impulse to travel through the thick lateral wall of the left ventricle.
- The sum of all the small vectors of ventricular depolarization is called the mean QRS vector. The mean QRS axis points more to the left because the instantaneous vectors of the thicker left ventricle are larger.
- The limb leads provide information about the frontal plane and are used to determine the position of the mean QRS axis, described in degrees within an imaginary circle drawn over the patient's chest. The center of the circle is the AV node.
- Leads I and aV_F can be used to quickly determine whether the mean QRS axis on any ECG is normal.
- The intersection of all lines divides the circle into equal, 30-degree segments. Lead I starts at +0 degrees and is located at the three o'clock position. The mean QRS axis normally points downward and to the patient's left, between 0 and +90 degrees.
- An axis between +90 and +180 degrees indicates right axis deviation, and one between 0 and −90 degrees indicates left axis deviation. An axis deviation between −180 and −90 degrees indicates extreme axis deviation and is called an indeterminate axis.
- If the QRS complex is positive in leads I and aV_F, the QRS axis is normal.
- If the QRS complex is upright in lead I and negative in lead aV_F, then left axis deviation exists. If the QRS complex is negative in lead I and positive in lead aV_F, then right axis deviation exists. If the QRS complex is negative in both leads, extreme right axis deviation exists.
- Factors that influence the location of the axis include the heart's position in the chest, the heart's size, the patient's body size or type, the conduction pathways, and the force of the electrical impulses being generated.

Assess Your Understanding

The following questions give you a chance to assess your understanding of the material discussed in this chapter. The answers can be found in Appendix A.

1. The currents produced by depolarization and repolarization of the cardiac cells are called
   a. mean vectors.
   b. instantaneous vectors.
   c. the mean electrical axis.
   d. positive deflections.

2. The electrical axis is depicted as a
   a. large circle.
   b. negative deflection.
   c. positive deflection.
   d. single large arrow.

3. Axis is defined
   a. in the frontal plane only.
   b. immediately upon attaching the ECG leads.
   c. as a waveform that has a negative deflection.
   d. as the amperage of a waveform.

4. The QRS axis
   a. is rarely determined.
   b. is the mean of all vectors generated during the depolarization of the atria.
   c. is the most important and also the most frequently determined axis.
   d. normally points up and to the right.

5. Completion of right ventricular depolarization occurs __________ completion of left ventricular depolarization.
   a. before
   b. after
   c. during
   d. Both a and b.

6. The right ventricular vectors are larger and persist longer than those of the left ventricle.
   a. True
   b. False

7. The sum of all the small vectors of ventricular depolarization is called the mean
   a. P wave vector.
   b. QRS axis.
   c. T axis.
   d. ST axis.

8. The center of the circle used to determine the axis of the mean QRS vector is (are) the
   a. AV node.
   b. SA node.
   c. Purkinje fibers.
   d. apical region of the ventricle.

9. The circle used to determine the axis of the mean QRS vector is divided into equal, __________ -degree segments.
   a. 10
   b. 15
   c. 30
   d. 60

10. On the circle used to determine the axis of the mean QRS vector, lead I starts at __________ degrees and is located at the __________ o'clock position.
    a. +90°, six
    b. +180°, nine
    c. – 120°, 11
    d. +0°, three

11. The mean QRS axis normally points __________ and to the patient's __________, between __________ degrees.
    a. downward, right, +90 and +180
    b. upward, left, 0 and –90
    c. downward, left, 0 and +90
    d. upward, right, +180 and –90

12. Match the following axis deviations with the correct degrees.

Deviation		*Degrees*
Right axis deviation	___	a. 0 and +90 degrees
Left axis deviation	___	b. 0 and −90 degrees
Extreme axis deviation	___	c. −180 and −90 degrees
		d. +90 and +180 degrees

13. Fill in the following table of QRS deflections

Direction of QRS in lead I	Direction of QRS in lead aV_F	Electrical axis
Positive	Positive	
Positive	Negative	
Negative	Positive	
Negative	Negative	

14. What direction will the ECG waveform take (negative, positive, or biphasic) in this example?

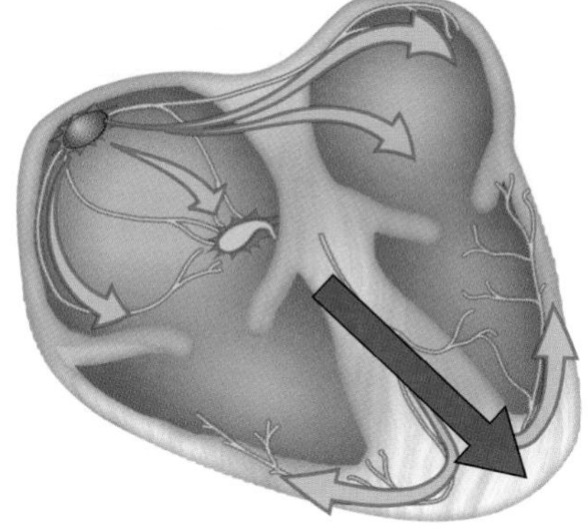

Positive electrode

15. In this illustration showing lead I, identify with + or – signs which half of the circle will be positive and which half will be negative.

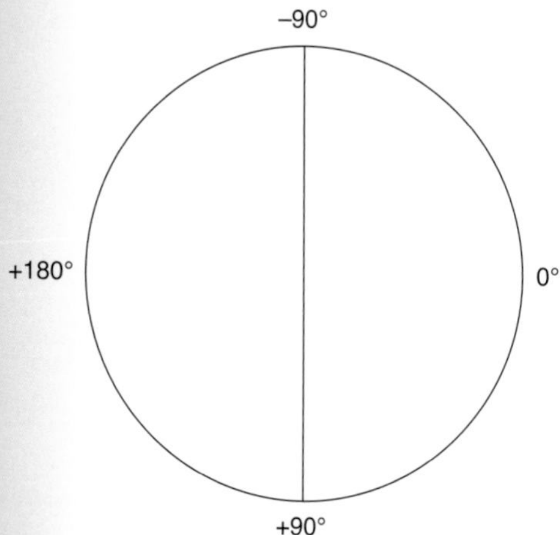

16. In this illustration showing lead aV_F, identify with + or – signs which half of the circle will be positive and which half will be negative.

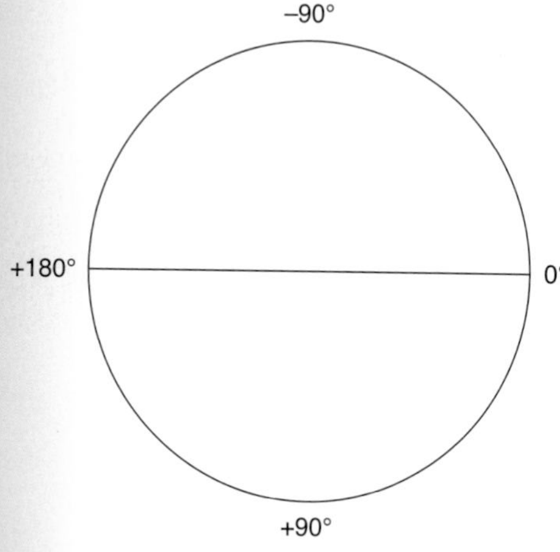

Referring to the scenario at the beginning of this chapter answer the following questions.

17. When the left ventricle is enlarged, the axis of the heart moves
    a. leftward.
    b. rightward.
    c. upward.
    d. lower.

18. The axis shifts because the sum of the electrical impulses in the enlarged ventricle is
    a. equal on both sides of the heart.
    b. greater on the left than the right.
    c. lesser on the left than the right.
    d. greater on the bottom than the top.

19. Long-standing hypertension causes
    a. both ventricles to enlarge simultaneously.
    b. the right ventricle to enlarge first.
    c. both atria to enlarge.
    d. the left ventricle to enlarge more than the right.

Answers to Sidebar Questions

"A 12-lead ECG includes what two general types of leads?"

Answer: A 12-lead ECG includes extremity leads, called limb leads, and chest, or precordial, leads.

"What direction will the ECG waveform deflection take when depolarization is moving toward a positive electrode?"

Answer: Depolarization moving toward a positive electrode produces a positive or upright deflection on the ECG machine.

"Can you list the six limb leads and identify which are augmented?"

Answer: The six limb leads are I, II, III, aV_R, aV_L, and aV_F. Leads aV_R, aV_L, and aV_F are considered augmented leads.

On the DVD

- Electrical Axis lecture.

Notes

Hypertrophy, Bundle Branch Block, and Preexcitation

14

Case History

You are a member of the EMS squad who responds to the local high school for a 16-year-old boy complaining of chest pain. You enter the nurse's station where the school nurse is kneeling over a thin, pale young man lying on a cot. He is awake and alert but is holding his chest. After introducing yourself you ask him how he feels. The patient indicates that he gets chest pain when he overexerts himself in physical education class. The nurse hands you a card with the patient's medical history. It indicates that he has an enlarged heart as a result of a viral infection that attacked his heart resulting in cardiomyopathy.

You apply oxygen to the patient and establish an intravenous line. After obtaining a 12-lead ECG, you hand it to your partner who comments on the pattern of the QRS complex in V_1. You note that it looks like rabbit ears. The QRS complex is also much longer than normal indicating that the patient's heart has a conduction defect in addition to being enlarged.

Chapter Preview

- Hypertrophy and Enlargement
- Ventricular Conduction Disturbances
- Preexcitation Syndromes

Hypertrophy and Enlargement

Hypertrophy is a condition in which the muscular wall of the ventricle(s) becomes thicker than normal (Figure 14-1). It results from the ventricle having to pump against increased resistance within the cardiovascular system. Conditions that cause hypertrophy include systemic hypertension and aortic stenosis.

QUESTION
"What do the heart's ventricles do?" (The answer can be found on page 456.)

The muscular wall of a hypertrophied ventricle is ________________ than normal. It results from the ventricle having to pump against increased ________________ within the ________________ system.

[thicker] [resistance] [cardiovascular]

CLINICAL MOMENT
Hypertrophy means an increase in muscle mass.

Another condition we discuss is **dilation** or **enlargement** of a chamber (Figure 14-2). An enlarged chamber occurs as the result of volume overload—the chamber dilates to accommodate the increased blood

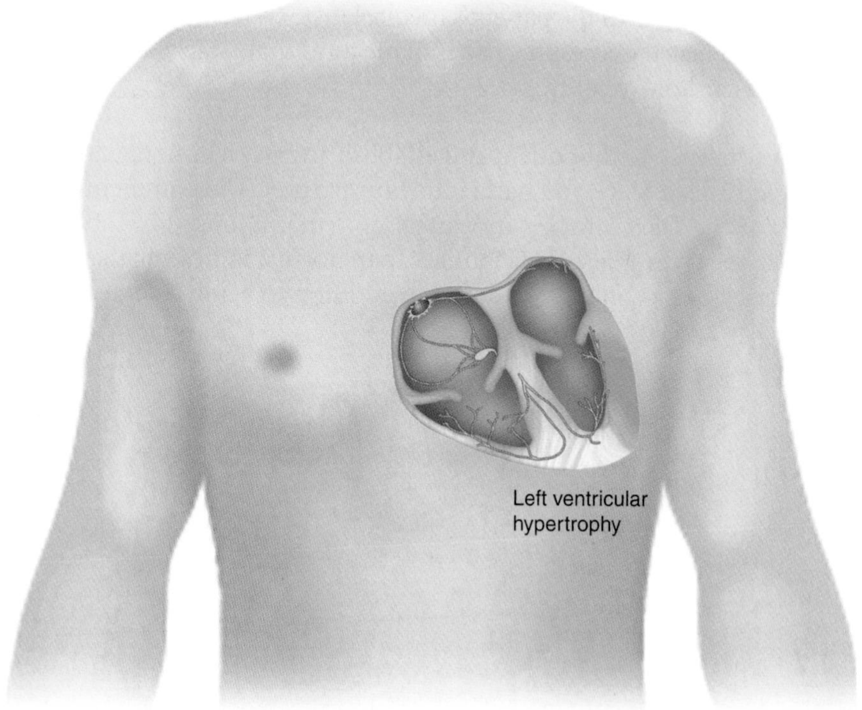

Figure 14-1
Hypertrophy is a condition in which the muscular wall of the ventricle becomes thicker.

volume. It is therefore bigger and can hold more blood than normal. Unlike hypertrophy, the muscular wall of the dilated chamber typically does not become thicker. Enlargement is most often seen with certain types of valvular disease. For example, left atrial enlargement can result from mitral valve insufficiency.

An enlarged chamber results from volume ________________ as the chamber ________________ to accommodate ________________ blood volume. In contrast to ________________, the muscular wall of an enlarged chamber does not become ________________.

[overload] [dilates] [increased] [hypertrophy] [thicker]

Enlargement and hypertrophy often exist together as both are ways in which the heart tries to increase its cardiac output.

KEY CONCEPT
A hypertrophied ventricle has a thick muscular wall. An enlarged chamber is bigger and can hold more blood than normal but does not necessarily have a thicker muscular wall.

It is common to associate enlargement with the atria (as they dilate more than they hypertrophy) and hypertrophy with the ventricles. We look at

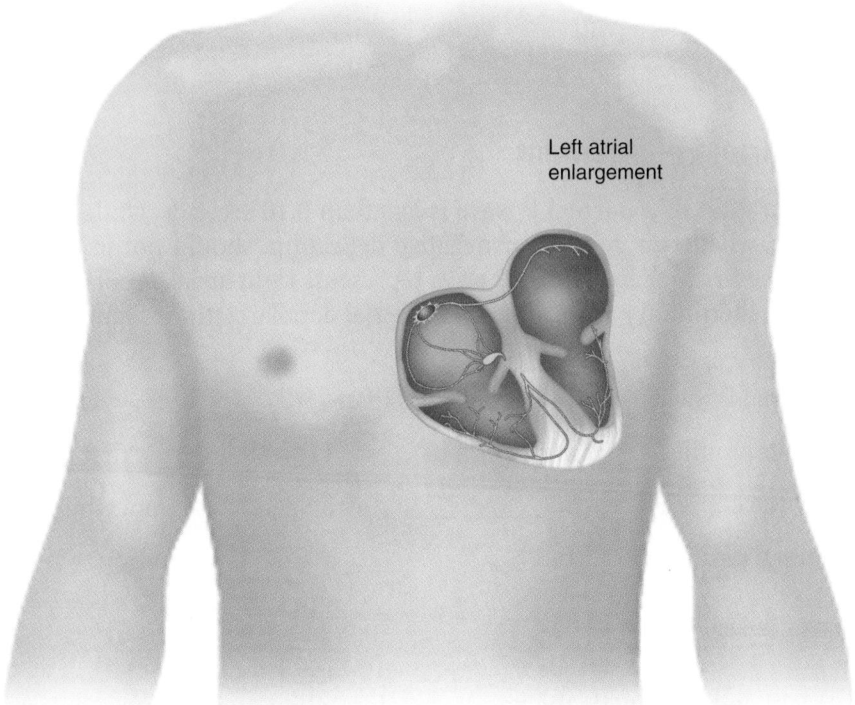

Figure 14-2
Enlargement of a heart chamber occurs to accommodate increased blood volume.

CLINICAL MOMENT
The ECG is not all that effective at identifying hypertrophy. In about 50% of cases where hypertrophy exists, the ECG will be normal. Other diagnostic tools, such as x-ray and echocardiography, are much more effective at finding hypertrophy. However, when the electrocardiographic indicators are present, it is (about 90%) accurate.

KEY CONCEPT
Chamber enlargement is associated with the atria, while hypertrophy is associated with the ventricles.

QUESTION
"Which of the heart's atria depolarizes first?" (The answer can be found on page 456.)

QUESTION
"How many small squares on the ECG paper represent 0.10 seconds in duration? How many represent an amplitude of 2.5 mm?" (The answer can be found on page 457.)

the P wave to assess for atrial enlargement because the P wave represents atrial depolarization. Similarly, we examine the QRS complex to help us identify ventricular hypertrophy.

We use the _______________ to assess for atrial enlargement and the _______________ to assess for ventricular hypertrophy.

[P wave] [QRS complex]

Changes that we see in the ECG that indicate the presence of enlargement or hypertrophy include:

- An increase in duration of the waveform
- An increase in the amplitude of the waveform
- Axis deviation

An ___________ in the duration of the waveform, an ___________ in the amplitude of the waveform, and ___________ deviation are indicators of the presence of enlargement or hypertrophy.

[increase] [increase] [axis]

Atrial Enlargement

The duration of a normal P wave is less than 0.10 seconds, while its amplitude, whether a positive or negative deflection, should not exceed 2.5 mm. The first portion of the P wave represents right atrial depolarization while the terminal part represents left atrial depolarization (Figure 14-3).

A normal P wave has a duration of less than _______________ seconds, while its amplitude is a maximum of _______________. The first part of the P wave represents _______________ atrial depolarization, while the terminal part represents _______________ atrial depolarization.

[0.10] [2.5 mm] [right] [left]

Leads II and V_1 provide the necessary information to assess atrial enlargement. Lead II is nearly parallel to the flow of current through the atria (the mean P wave vector). For this reason it records the largest deflections and is more likely to reveal abnormalities in atrial depolarization. Lead V_1 is placed just to the right of the sternum in the fourth intercostal space. This

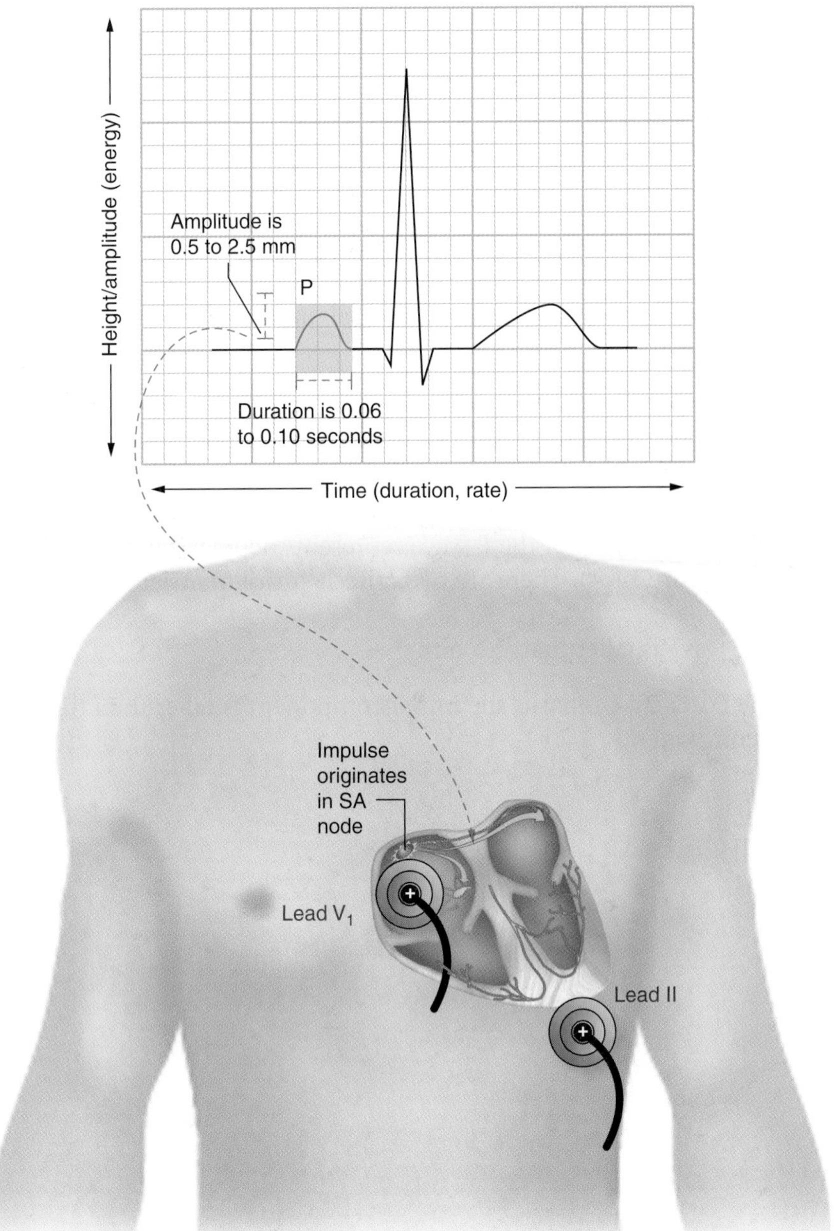

Figure 14-3
Atrial conduction and the normal P wave. Leads II and V_1 provide the best information regarding atrial conduction.

positions it directly over the atria and gives the most accurate information about atrial enlargement. This allows easy separation of the right and left atrial components of the P wave. A P wave that has both positive and negative deflections is termed biphasic. A biphasic P wave indicates that either or both of the atria are enlarged. A biphasic P wave will have two components, the initial component from the right atrium and the terminal component from the left atrium.

INSTRUCTIONAL MOMENT
A biphasic P wave has deflections above and below the baseline.

The best leads for assessing for atrial enlargement are leads ____________ and ____________. Lead II records the largest ____________ deflections and can reveal ____________ in atrial depolarization. Lead V_1 provides the most ____________ view of the P wave to detect atrial enlargement. Atrial enlargement is present if the P wave is ____________ in V_1.

[II] [V_1] [positive] [abnormalities] [effective] [biphasic]

KEY CONCEPT
We use leads II and V_1 to diagnose atrial enlargement.

Right Atrial Enlargement

Right atrial enlargement results in the right atrium being electrically dominate over the left atrium. The diagnosis of right atrial enlargement is made when you see an increase in the amplitude of the first part of the P wave (remember, the first part of the P wave represents depolarization of the right atrium) (Figure 14-4). There are two criteria for right atrial enlargement:

- The P wave is taller than 2.5 mm
- If the P wave is biphasic, the initial component is taller than the terminal component

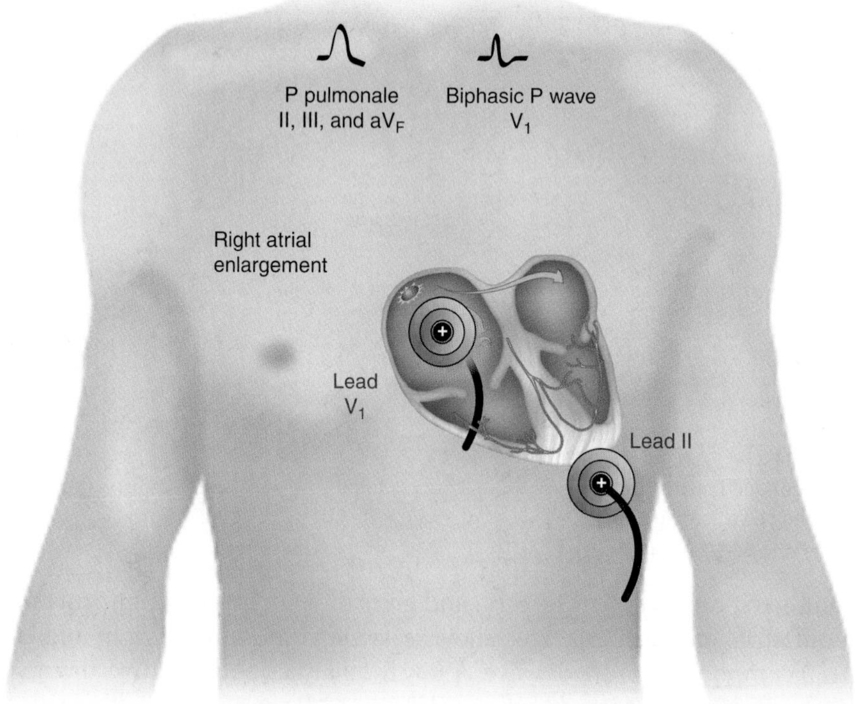

Figure 14-4
Right atrial enlargement leads to an increase in the amplitude of the first part of the P wave.

The width of the P wave, however, stays within normal limits because its terminal part originates from the left atrium, which depolarizes normally if left atrial enlargement is absent.

Characteristics of right atrial enlargement are that the first part of the _______________ in lead _______________ will be _______________ than normal. In leads II, III, and aV_F, the P waves exceed _______________ in amplitude. The _______________ of the P wave, however, stays within normal limits.

[P wave] [V_1] [taller] [2.5 mm] [width]

KEY CONCEPT
Right atrial enlargement is diagnosed by the first part of the biphasic P wave being taller than normal in lead V_1 and the P waves exceeding 2.5 mm in amplitude in the inferior leads II, III, and aV_F.

Left Atrial Enlargement

With left atrial enlargement, the amplitude of the terminal portion of the P wave may increase in V_1 (Figure 14-5). Diagnostically we say left atrial enlargement is present when the terminal (left atrial) portion of the P wave drops at least 1 mm below the isoelectric line (in lead V_1).

INSTRUCTIONAL MOMENT
Key characteristics of right atrial enlargement include:

- The first part of the P wave will be taller than normal in lead V_1
- P waves have an amplitude that exceeds 2.5 mm in the inferior leads
- There is no change in the duration of the P wave

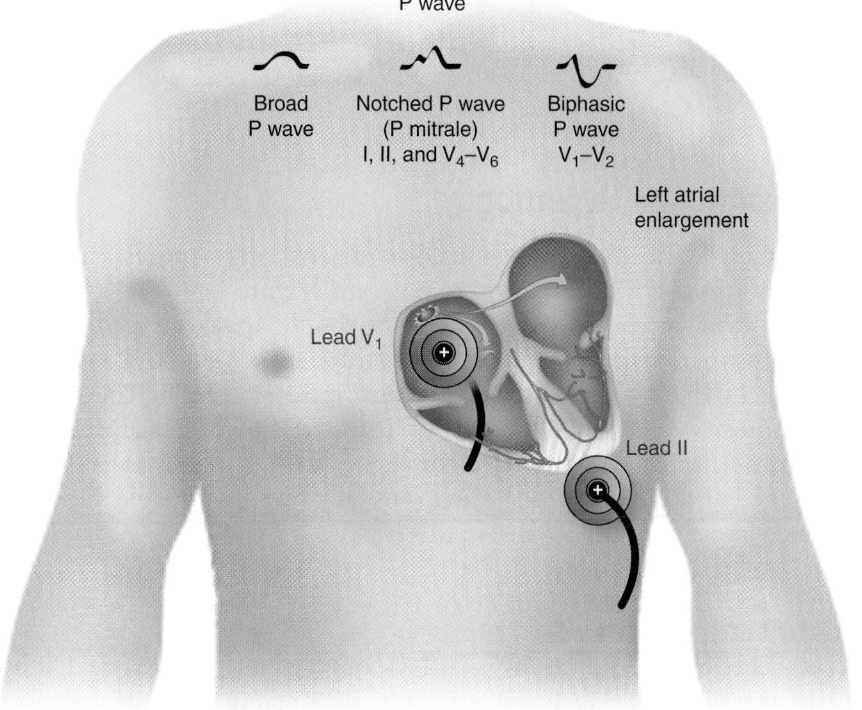

Figure 14-5
Left atrial enlargement leads to an increase in the amplitude and width of the terminal portion of the P wave.

CLINICAL MOMENT
Right atrial enlargement is often secondary to pulmonary hypertension related to emphysema. Therefore, the P wave changes in right atrial enlargement are termed P pulmonale.

CLINICAL MOMENT
The duration of the P wave does not appear longer in right atrial enlargement because it is hidden by the portion of the P wave that represents left atrial depolarization.

However, a more telling indicator of left atrial enlargement is an increase in the duration or width of the terminal portion of the P wave. This occurs because depolarization of the left atrium is the latter part of atrial depolarization. The diagnosis of left atrial enlargement requires that the terminal portion of the P wave be at least one small square (0.04 seconds) in width.

Often the presence of ECG evidence of left atrial enlargement only reflects a nonspecific conduction irregularity. However, it may also be the result of mitral valve stenosis causing the left atrium to enlarge to force blood across the stenotic (tight) mitral valve. For this reason you must carefully weigh the interpretation of atrial enlargement on the ECG with the patient's clinical presentation.

KEY CONCEPT
Left atrial enlargement is diagnosed by the terminal (left atrial) portion of the P wave dropping at least 1 mm below the isoelectric line in V_1 and an increase in the duration of the P wave.

Left atrial enlargement is diagnosed when the amplitude of the terminal portion of the P wave ______________, dropping at least ______________ below the isoelectric line in V_1. A more telling indicator of left atrial enlargement is an increase in the ______________ of the P wave. The appearance of the P wave on the ECG in left atrial enlargement is also called ______________.

[increases] [1 mm] [duration] [P mitrale]

CLINICAL MOMENT
The presence of left atrial enlargement from mitral stenosis is termed P mitrale.

Ventricular Hypertrophy

Using the ECG to diagnose ventricular hypertrophy requires careful assessment of the QRS complex in many leads (Figure 14-6). Let's begin by quickly reviewing how the QRS complex should appear in lead V_1. Ventricular depolarization will move downward to the left side and posteriorly because the thicker left ventricle is located mostly posterior. The V_1 electrode is positive; therefore, the wave of depolarization moving through the left ventricle will be moving away from it producing a mainly negative QRS complex. For this reason, the R wave is usually very short, while the S wave is much larger than the R wave in this lead.

INSTRUCTIONAL MOMENT
Key characteristics of left atrial enlargement include the:

- Amplitude of the terminal (negative) portion of the P wave increases, descending at least 1 mm below the isoelectric line in lead V_1
- Duration of the P wave is increased, and the terminal (negative) portion of the P wave must be at least 1 small square (0.04 seconds) in width

Right Ventricular Hypertrophy

Right ventricular hypertrophy is far less common than left ventricular hypertrophy (Figure 14-7). It is often the result of severe pulmonary stenosis or primary pulmonary hypertension.

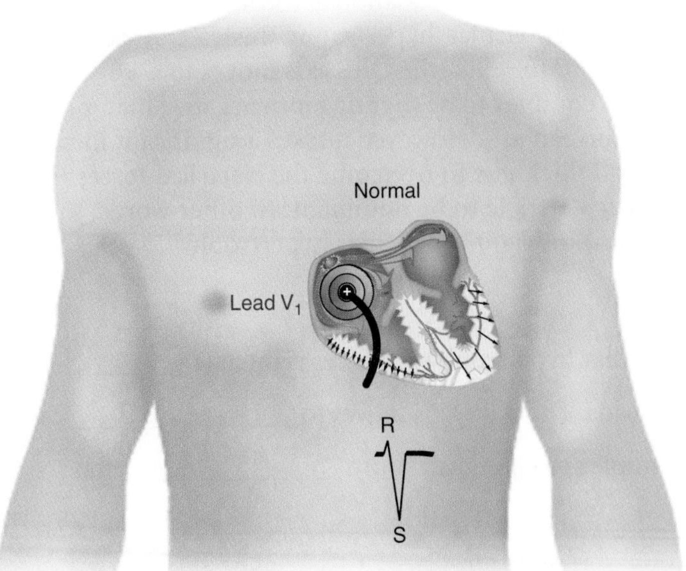

Figure 14-6
In lead V_1 the QRS complex normally has a short R wave and a larger S wave.

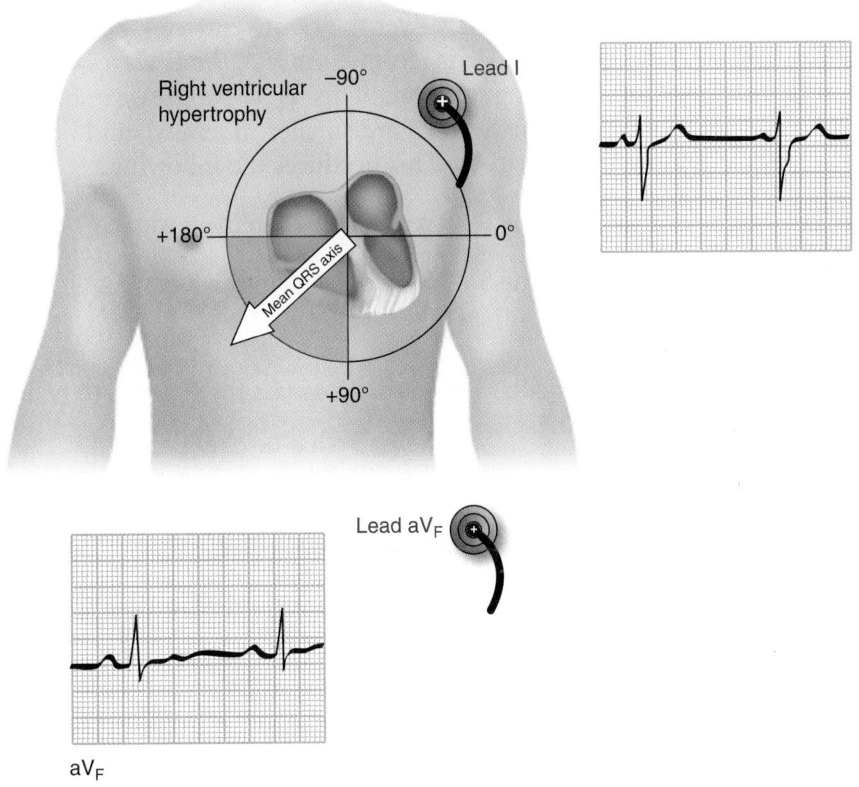

Figure 14-7
In right ventricular hypertrophy the QRS axis moves to between +90 and 180 degrees. The QRS complexes in right ventricular hypertrophy are slightly more negative in lead I and positive in lead aV_F.

QUESTION
"The QRS axis in the normal heart lies between ___ and ___ degrees?" (The answer can be found on page 457.)

In the limb leads, right axis deviation is the most common characteristic seen with right ventricular hypertrophy. Instead of falling within the normal range of 0° to +90°, the QRS axis moves to +90° to −180°. This causes the QRS complex to be slightly more negative than positive in lead I and positive in lead aV_F. However, it takes a significant increase in right ventricular wall thickness to overcome the electrical forces that naturally allow the left ventricle to be dominant. In other words, to see it, there has to be significant right ventricular hypertrophy.

KEY CONCEPT
The most common attribute seen with right ventricular hypertrophy is right axis deviation in the limb leads. The QRS axis moves to +90° to −180° resulting in the QRS complex being slightly more negative than positive in lead I and positive in lead aV_F.

Right ventricular hypertrophy produces right axis ______________ in the limb leads. The QRS axis moves to ______________ causing the QRS complex to be slightly more ______________ than ______________ in lead I and ______________ in lead aV_F.

[deviation] [+90° to −180°] [negative] [positive] [positive]

The precordial leads are also used to identify right ventricular hypertrophy (Figure 14-8). The thick wall of the enlarged right ventricle causes the R waves to be more positive in the leads that lie closer to lead V_1 (the electrode located directly over the right ventricle). So moving from the right to the left chest leads (from V_1 to V_6), the R waves should go from being larger to being smaller. This is a progressive but gradual change. Conversely, the S waves are smaller in lead V_1 and become larger as you move from V_1 to V_6. This produces the following:

- Lead V_1—the R wave is larger than the S wave
- Lead V_6—the S wave is larger than the R wave

CLINICAL MOMENT
Remember, normally the R waves are more positive in the leads closer to the left ventricle.

Right ventricular hypertrophy causes the R waves to be more ______________ in the leads that lie closer to lead V_1. So moving from V_1 to V_6, the R waves should go from being ______________ to being ______________. Conversely, the S waves are ______________ in lead V_1 and become ______________ as you move to V_6.

[positive] [larger] [smaller] [smaller] [larger]

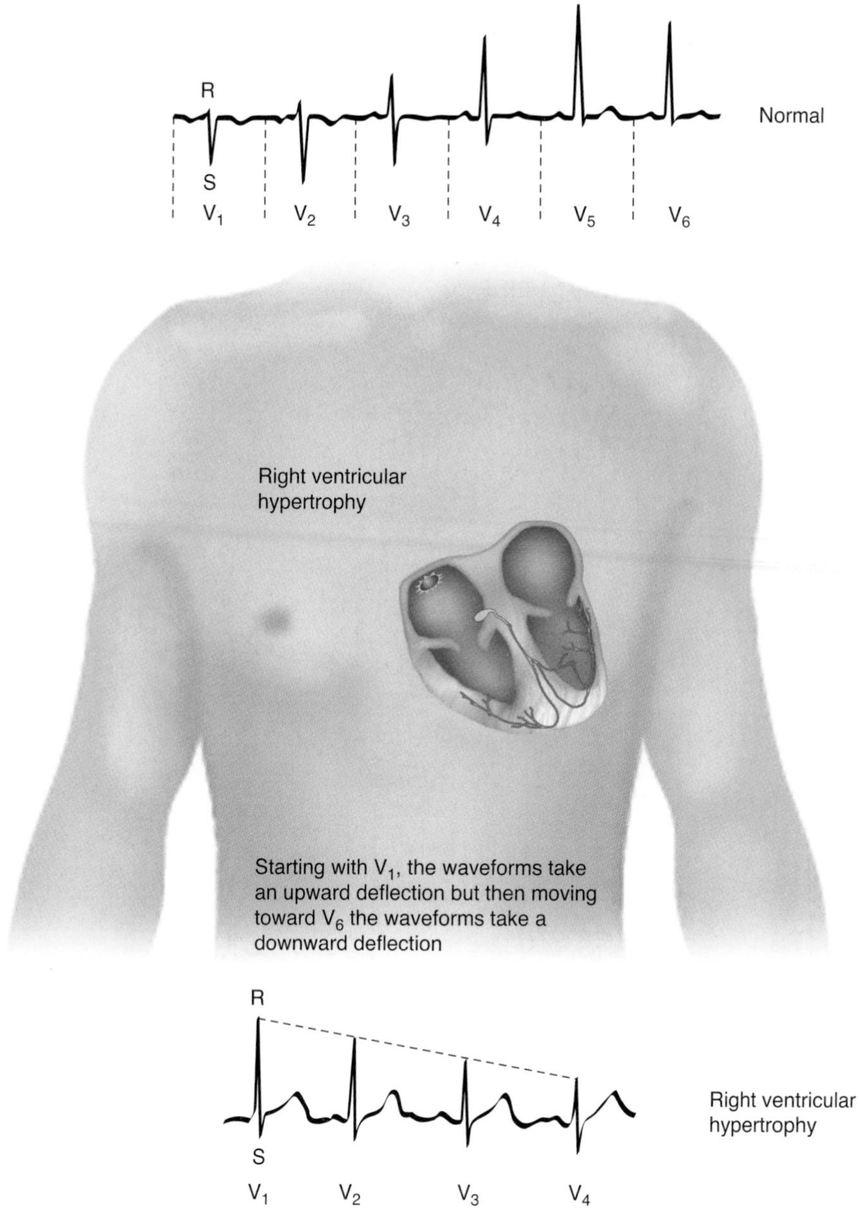

R S V_1 V_2 V_3 V_4 V_5 V_6 Normal

Right ventricular hypertrophy

Starting with V_1, the waveforms take an upward deflection but then moving toward V_6 the waveforms take a downward deflection

R S V_1 V_2 V_3 V_4 Right ventricular hypertrophy

Figure 14-8
The thick wall of the enlarged right ventricle causes the R waves to be more positive in the leads that lie closer to lead V_1.

Left Ventricular Hypertrophy

Frequent causes of left ventricular hypertrophy are systemic hypertension and valvular heart disease.

Diagnosing left ventricular hypertrophy is more complicated than diagnosing right ventricular hypertrophy (Figure 14-9). An axis deviation of −15 is often seen but is not a very helpful diagnostic tool.

KEY CONCEPT
Key indicators of right ventricular hypertrophy include the presence of right axis deviation (with the QRS axis exceeding +100°) and the R wave larger than the S wave in lead V_1, whereas the S wave is larger than the R wave in lead V_6.

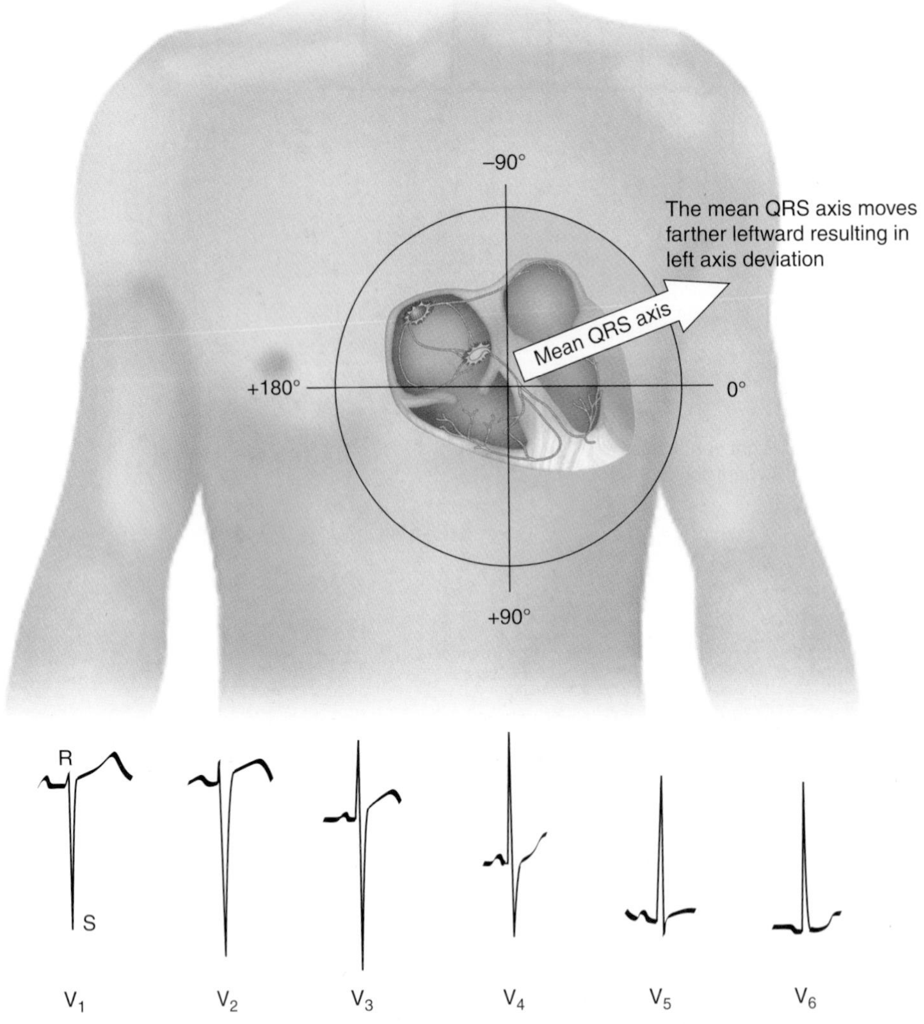

Figure 14-9
The thick wall of the enlarged left ventricle causes the R waves to be more positive in the leads that lie closer to lead V_6, and the S waves to be larger in the leads that are closer to V_1.

The precordial leads are more sensitive than the limb leads in the diagnosis of left ventricular hypertrophy. Therefore, increased R wave amplitude in those leads overlying the left ventricle forms the basis for the ECG diagnosis of left ventricular hypertrophy. Also, the S waves are smaller in the leads overlying the left ventricle (lead V_6) but larger in the leads overlying the right ventricle (lead V_1) .

The most useful criteria for identifying left ventricular hypertrophy in the precordial leads are the:

- Amplitude of R wave in lead V_5 or V_6 plus the amplitude of the S wave in V_1 or V_2 exceeds 35 mm
- R wave amplitude in lead V_5 exceeds 26 mm
- R wave amplitude in lead V_6 exceeds the R wave amplitude in lead V_5

The more criteria present, the more likely the patient has left ventricular hypertrophy.

INSTRUCTIONAL MOMENT
The criteria listed are of little value in persons younger than 35 years of age as they frequently have increased voltage due to a relatively thin chest wall.

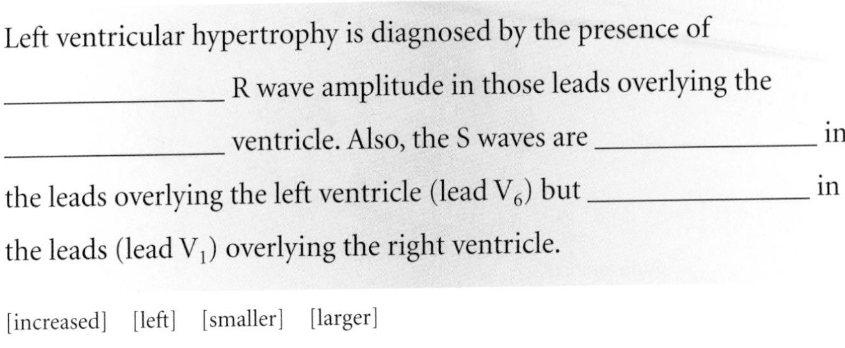

Left ventricular hypertrophy is diagnosed by the presence of ______________ R wave amplitude in those leads overlying the ______________ ventricle. Also, the S waves are ______________ in the leads overlying the left ventricle (lead V_6) but ______________ in the leads (lead V_1) overlying the right ventricle.

[increased] [left] [smaller] [larger]

The limb leads can also provide evidence of left ventricular hypertrophy. The limb lead criteria for left ventricular hypertrophy include the R wave amplitude in:

- lead aV_L exceeds 13 mm
- lead aV_F exceeds 21 mm
- lead I exceeds 14 mm
- lead I plus the S wave amplitude in lead III exceeds 25 mm

It is possible for both the right and left ventricles to both be hypertrophied. This produces a combination of features such as left ventricular hypertrophy in the precordial leads and right axis deviation in the limb leads. However, most often the indicators of left ventricular hypertrophy hide those of right ventricular hypertrophy.

KEY CONCEPT
Key ECG indicators of left ventricular hypertrophy include increased R wave amplitude over those leads overlying the left ventricle. Also, the S waves are smaller in the leads overlying the left ventricle (lead V_6) but larger in the leads (lead V_1) overlying the right ventricle.

QUESTION
"Describe how the impulse that brings about the heartbeat is conducted from the SA node to the AV node."
(The answer can be found on page 457.)

Ventricular Conduction Disturbances

Ventricular conduction disturbances involve delays in electrical conduction through either the AV node, the bundle branches (right or left), the fascicles (anterior, posterior), or a combination of these. Each of these conduction delays is referred to as a heart block.

1. Electrical impulses originate in the SA node and travel across the wall of the atrium (*arrows*) from the SA node to the AV node
2. Electrical impulses pass through the AV node and along the bundle of His, which extends from the AV node, through the fibrous skeleton, into the interventricular septum
3. The bundle of His divides into right and left bundle branches and electrical impulses descend to the apex of each ventricle along the bundle branches
4. Electrical impulses are carried by the Purkinje fibers from the bundle branches to the ventricular walls

Sinoatrial (SA) node
Left atrium
Atrioventricular (AV) node
Left ventricle
Atrioventricular (AV) node
Left and right bundle branches
Purkinje fibers
Apex

Enlarged section of the His-Purkinje system

AV node
Bundle of His
Left bundle branch
Right bundle branch
Septal fascicle
Left anterior fascicle
Left posterior fascicle
Purkinje fibers

Figure 14-10
The heart's conduction system with enlarged section showing the His-Purkinje system and the three divisions of the left bundle branch.

The Bundle Branches

The normal wave of depolarization moves rapidly out of the AV node and into the bundle of His. Here the conduction system divides to form the right and left **bundle branches** (Figure 14-10). The right bundle branch continues in the direction of the apex, spreading throughout the right ventricle. The left bundle branch divides further into three divisions—the septal fascicle, the anterior fascicle, and the posterior fascicle. The septal fascicle carries the impulse to the interventricular septum in a right-to-left direction. The anterior fascicle carries the impulse to the anterior (superior) portions of the left ventricle. The posterior fascicle carries the impulse to the posterior (inferior) portions of the left ventricle. The very small Purkinje fibers take the current from the bundle branches to the individual myocardial cells.

QUESTION
"Which side of the interventricular septum is the first to be depolarized?" (The answer can be found on page 457.)

The bundle of His divides to form the ______________ and ______________ bundle branches. The left bundle branch separates to form the septal, ______________, and ______________ fascicles.

[right] [left] [anterior] [posterior]

The right and left ventricles are quickly and simultaneously stimulated so that the QRS complex, which represents ventricular depolarization from beginning to end, is narrow (Figure 14-11). Although depolarization of both ventricles is simultaneous, the electrical forces of the left ventricle dominate those of the right because the mass of the left ventricle is so much larger than that of the right. This results in the electrical axis being drawn leftward, lying between 0° and +90°. Thus, with normal ventricular depolarization, the QRS complex is narrow and the electrical axis is between 0° and +90°. Bundle branch block changes this.

KEY CONCEPT
With normal ventricular depolarization the QRS complex is narrow—0.12 seconds or less in duration—and the electrical axis lies between 0° and +90°

The QRS complex is ______________—______________ seconds or less in duration.

[narrow] [0.12]

Block of the Bundle Branch

A bundle branch block leads to one or both of the bundle branches failing to conduct impulses (Figure 4-12). This produces a delay in the depolarization of the ventricle it supplies, as the impulse must travel through the surrounding muscle (which conducts more slowly than the specialized tissue of the bundle branch) to stimulate the bundle branch below the block. Once the impulse is below the block, the impulse conducts rapidly again. Depolarization of the individual ventricles is still of normal duration; however, the unblocked ventricle will depolarize out of synch with the blocked ventricle.

KEY CONCEPT
Bundle branch block is a disorder that leads to one or both of the bundle branches failing to conduct impulses. This produces a delay in the depolarization of the ventricle it supplies.

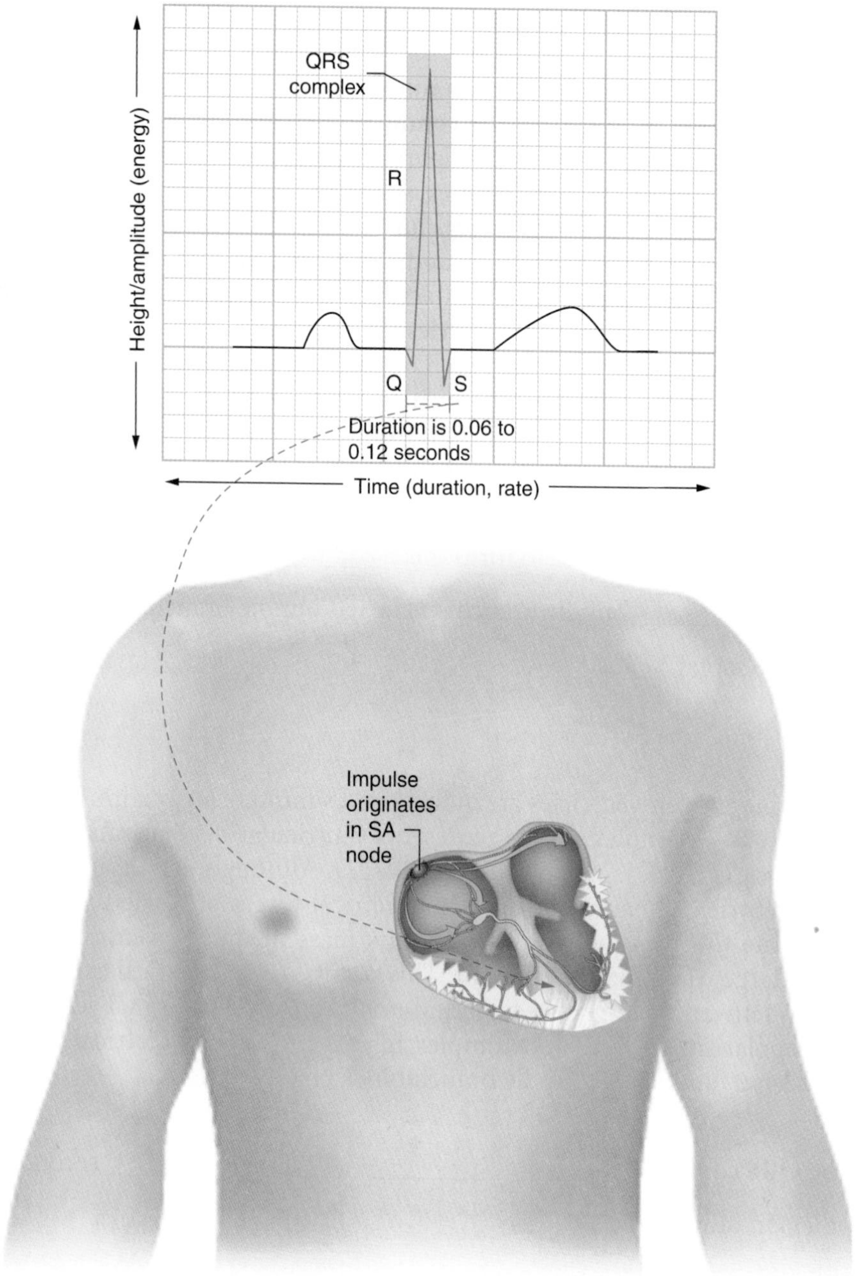

Figure 14-11
The QRS complex represents ventricular depolarization from beginning to end and is narrow—0.12 seconds or less in duration.

QUESTION
"What is the normal duration of the QRS complex?" (The answer can be found on page 457.)

This causes what looks like two joined QRS complexes to appear on the ECG (Figure 14-13). The two QRS complexes appear superimposed on one another and the ECG records this combined electrical activity as a widened QRS complex with two peaks. As such, bundle branch block is diagnosed by analyzing the width and morphology of the QRS complexes.

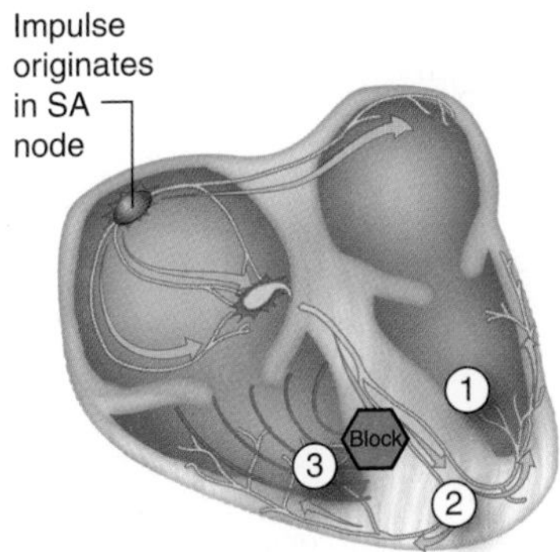

Figure 14-12
In bundle branch block, conduction of the electrical impulse is partially or completely blocked in one of the bundle branches while conduction (1) continues uninterrupted through the unaffected bundle branch. Then the impulse activates the intraventricular septum (2). Finally the impulse activates the other ventricle (3).

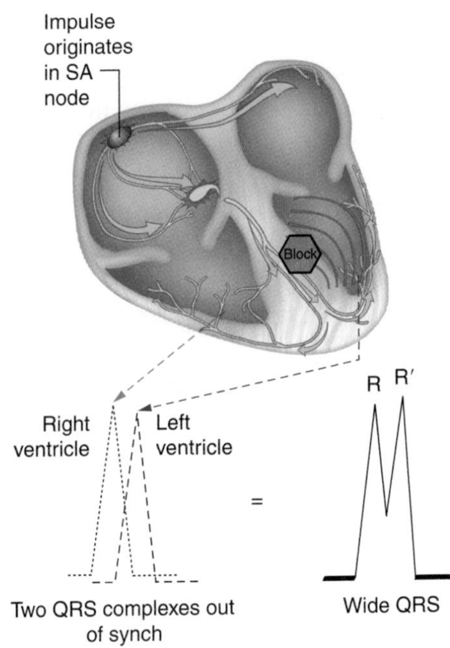

Figure 14-13
QRS complex changes in bundle branch block are due to depolarization of the ventricles being out of sync with each other.

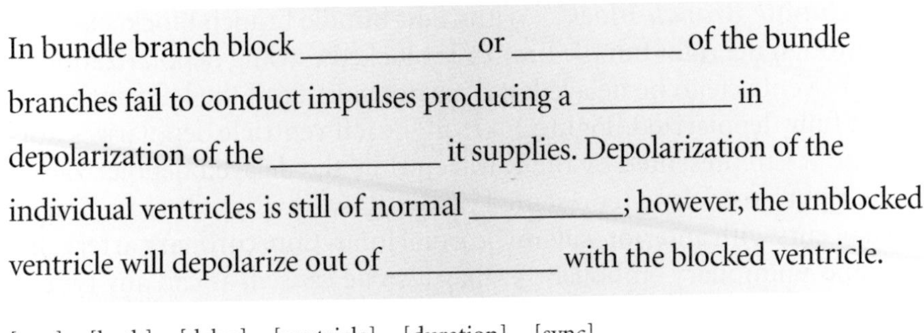

In bundle branch block ____________ or ____________ of the bundle branches fail to conduct impulses producing a ___________ in depolarization of the ____________ it supplies. Depolarization of the individual ventricles is still of normal ___________; however, the unblocked ventricle will depolarize out of ____________ with the blocked ventricle.

[one] [both] [delay] [ventricle] [duration] [sync]

CLINICAL MOMENT
Some patients with bundle branch block require treatment with a temporary pacemaker. Others can be monitored to determine if they progress to a more complete block.

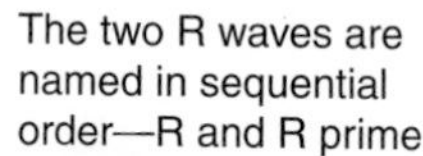

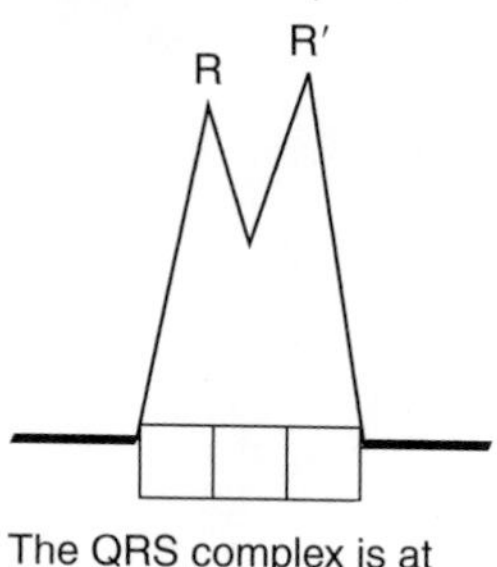

Figure 14-14
QRS complexes seen with bundle branch block are wider than normal and appear as two complexes joined together.

KEY CONCEPT
With bundle branch block, because the two QRS complexes are not in sync they appear superimposed on one another and the ECG records this combined electrical activity as a widened QRS complex with two peaks.

In bundle branch block, the QRS complex is at least 0.12 seconds (three small squares) or greater. Also, because of the nonsimultaneous depolarization of the ventricles (one normally depolarizes while the other is delayed), we should see two R waves named in sequential order, R and R′. The R′ is referred to as R prime and represents delayed depolarization of the blocked ventricle (Figure 14-14).

Possible sites of block within the ventricular conduction system include:

- The right bundle branch—right bundle branch block (RBBB)
- The left bundle branch—left bundle branch block (LBBB)
- The left anterior fascicle—left anterior fascicular block (LAFB), also called left anterior hemiblock (LAHB)
- The left posterior fascicle—left posterior fascicular block (LPFB), also called left posterior hemiblock (LPHB)
- Any combination of these

CLINICAL MOMENT
If only a portion of one of the bundle branches is blocked, this is called a fascicular block.

Right Bundle Branch Block With right bundle branch block, conduction through the right bundle branch is blocked causing depolarization of the right ventricle to be delayed; it does not start until the left ventricle is almost fully depolarized (Figure 14-15). The left ventricle depolarizes normally so it is represented by the R wave, while the delayed depolarization of the right ventricle is represented by the R′ wave. Right bundle branch block occurs with anterior wall myocardial infarction, coronary artery disease, and pulmonary embolism. It may also be caused, as can any type of heart block, by drug toxicity.

KEY CONCEPT
In bundle branch block you will see a widened QRS complex and the R, R′ configuration in the chest leads.

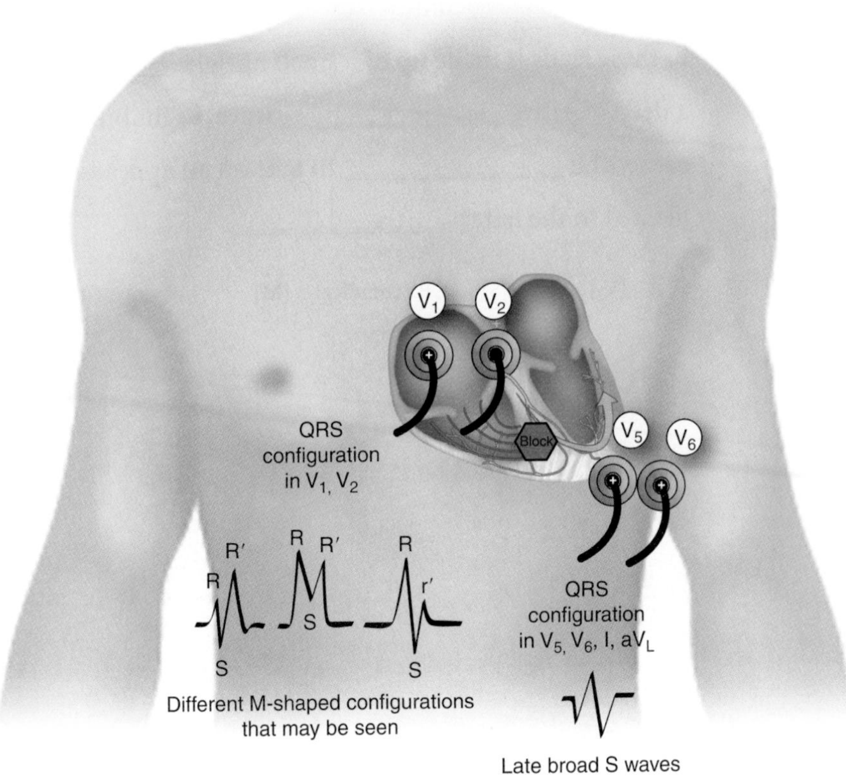

Figure 14-15
In right bundle branch block, conduction through the right bundle is blocked causing depolarization of the right ventricle to be delayed; it does not start until the left ventricle is almost fully depolarized.

The best leads for identifying right bundle branch are V_1 and V_2. Normally, the QRS complex in these leads is made up of a small upright R wave and a deep negative S wave. This represents the electrical dominance of the left ventricle.

Right bundle branch block causes the QRS complex to have a unique shape. Its appearance has been likened to rabbit ears or the letter "M." As the left ventricle depolarizes, it produces the initial R and S waves, but as the right ventricle begins its delayed depolarization, it produces a tall R wave (called the R′). Meanwhile, in the left lateral leads overlying the left ventricle (I, aV_L, V_5, and V_6), late right ventricular depolarization causes reciprocal late broad S waves to be generated.

QUESTION
"Which leads are best for assessing the electrical activity in the right ventricle?" (The answer can be found on page 457.)

KEY CONCEPT
To diagnose right bundle branch block, check for an R, R′ wave in leads V_1 or V_2. The appearance of right bundle block has been likened to the letter M.

The best leads for identifying right bundle branch block are _______________ and _______________. Normally, the QRS complex in these leads is made up of a small upright _______________ wave and a deep negative _______________ wave. Right bundle branch block causes the _______________ to take on an appearance that has been likened to the letter _______________.

[V_1] [V_2] [R] [S] [QRS complex] [M]

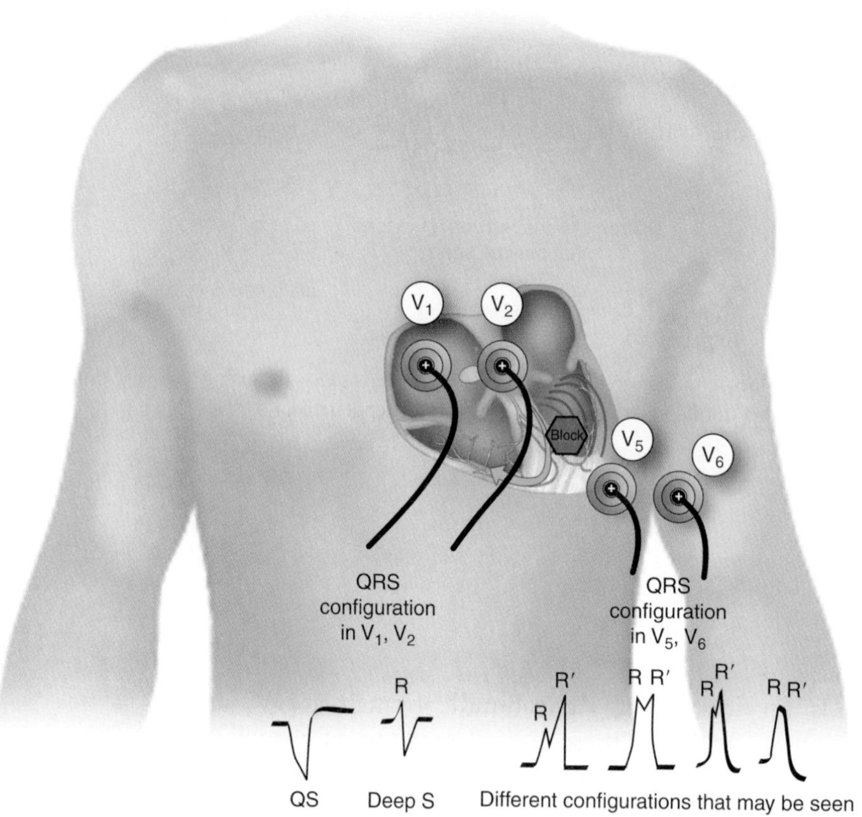

Figure 14-16
In left bundle branch block, conduction through the left bundle is blocked causing depolarization of the left ventricle to be delayed; it does not start until the right ventricle is almost fully depolarized.

Left Bundle Branch Block In left bundle branch block, left ventricular depolarization is delayed (Figure 14-16). The right ventricle depolarizes on time so it is represented by the R wave, while the delayed depolarization of the left ventricle is represented by an R′ wave. Left bundle branch block can be caused by anterior wall myocardial infarction, hypertensive heart disease, aortic stenosis, or degenerative changes of the conduction system.

KEY CONCEPT
To diagnose left bundle branch block, check for an R, R′ wave in leads V_5 or V_6.

Leads V_5 and V_6 are best for identifying left bundle branch block. The QRS complexes in these leads normally have tall R waves. Delayed left ventricular depolarization leads to a marked prolongation in the rise of those tall R waves, which will either be flattened on top or notched (with two tiny points). True rabbit ears are less likely to be seen than in right bundle branch block. Those leads overlying the right ventricle will show reciprocal, broad, deep S waves.

CLINICAL MOMENT
Sometimes an R, R′ wave is seen in a QRS complex of normal duration. This is called incomplete bundle branch block.

The best leads for identifying left bundle branch block are ________________, and ________________. In these leads the QRS complexes of left bundle branch block have ________________ R waves and a marked ________________ in the rise of those tall R waves. These QRS complexes are either ________________ on top or are ________________.

[V_5] [V_6] [tall] [prolongation] [flattened] [notched]

INSTRUCTIONAL MOMENT
The right bundle branch does not divide into separate fascicles (or at least they have not yet been identified anatomically).

Hemiblock

As previously described, the left bundle branch consists of three separate branches or fascicles. A block in conduction through one of the fascicles is called **hemiblock.** There are many fascicles in the heart's conduction system, but the anterior and posterior fascicles of the left bundle branch are the most clinically significant. While the ECG appearance of anterior and posterior hemiblocks differ from that of bundle branch blocks, the mechanism is essentially the same—the normal conduction pathway is blocked and the affected myocardium receives its electrical stimulation via cell-to-cell depolarization and retrograde conduction from the remaining intact parts of the conduction system. Smaller areas are involved, so the width of the QRS complex is usually not affected but the morphology of the QRS complex does change.

KEY CONCEPT
Hemiblocks cause axis deviation.

Axis deviation is the key ECG characteristic of hemiblocks. It occurs because when one fascicle is blocked, the electrical current travels down the other to stimulate the heart. This causes the axis to shift accordingly.

The anterior fascicle is longer and thinner and has a more fragile blood supply than the posterior fascicle, so left anterior hemiblock is far more common than left posterior hemiblock. While left anterior hemiblock can be seen in both normal and diseased hearts, left posterior hemiblock almost always is associated with heart disease.

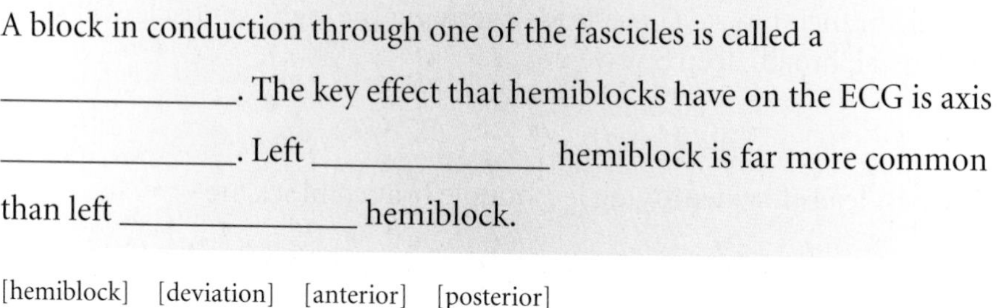

A block in conduction through one of the fascicles is called a _____________. The key effect that hemiblocks have on the ECG is axis _____________. Left _____________ hemiblock is far more common than left _____________ hemiblock.

[hemiblock] [deviation] [anterior] [posterior]

QUESTION
"What ECG changes tell us left axis deviation is present?" (The answer can be found on page 457.)

Left Anterior Hemiblock (LAHB) With left anterior hemiblock, conduction down the left anterior fascicle is blocked (Figure 14-17). For this reason, the electrical impulse rushes down the left posterior fascicle to the inferior surface of the heart. Depolarization of the left ventricle occurs, progressing in an inferior-to-superior and right-to-left direction. The axis of ventricular depolarization is therefore redirected upward and slightly to the left, producing tall positive R waves in the left lateral leads and deep S waves inferiorly. This results in left axis deviation.

KEY CONCEPT
Left anterior hemiblock results in left axis deviation.

Left Posterior Hemiblock (LAHB) In left posterior hemiblock, the electrical impulse rushes down the left anterior fascicle resulting in ventricular myocardial depolarization occurring in a superior-to-inferior and left-to-right direction (Figure 14-18). Therefore, the main electrical axis is directed downward and to the right, producing tall R waves inferiorly and deep S waves in the left lateral leads. This results in right axis deviation.

In contrast to complete left and right bundle branch block, the QRS complex in hemiblock S is not prolonged.

INSTRUCTIONAL MOMENT
There is some very minimal prolongation with hemiblock, but not enough to widen the QRS complex to any appreciable degree.

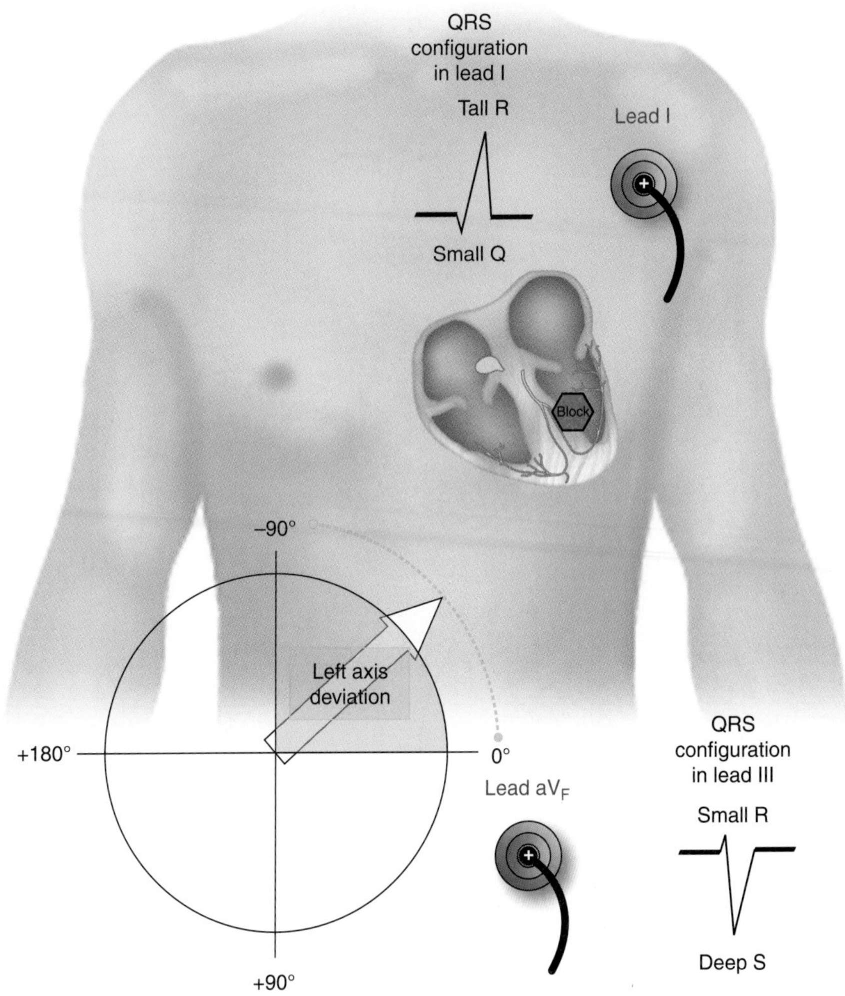

Figure 14-17
With left anterior hemiblock, conduction down the left anterior fascicle is blocked resulting in all the current rushing down the left posterior fascicle to the inferior surface of the heart. There are tall positive R waves in the left lateral leads (lead I), deep S waves inferiorly (lead aV_F) and left axis deviation.

Patients with any type of ventricular conduction block and especially those with a combination of blocks are at high risk of developing complete heart block.

CLINICAL MOMENT
When diagnosing hemiblock, be sure to rule out other causes of axis deviation, such as ventricular hypertrophy and patients with severe chronic lung disease.

Left ________________ hemiblock results in left axis deviation while left ________________ hemiblock results in right axis deviation.

[anterior] [posterior]

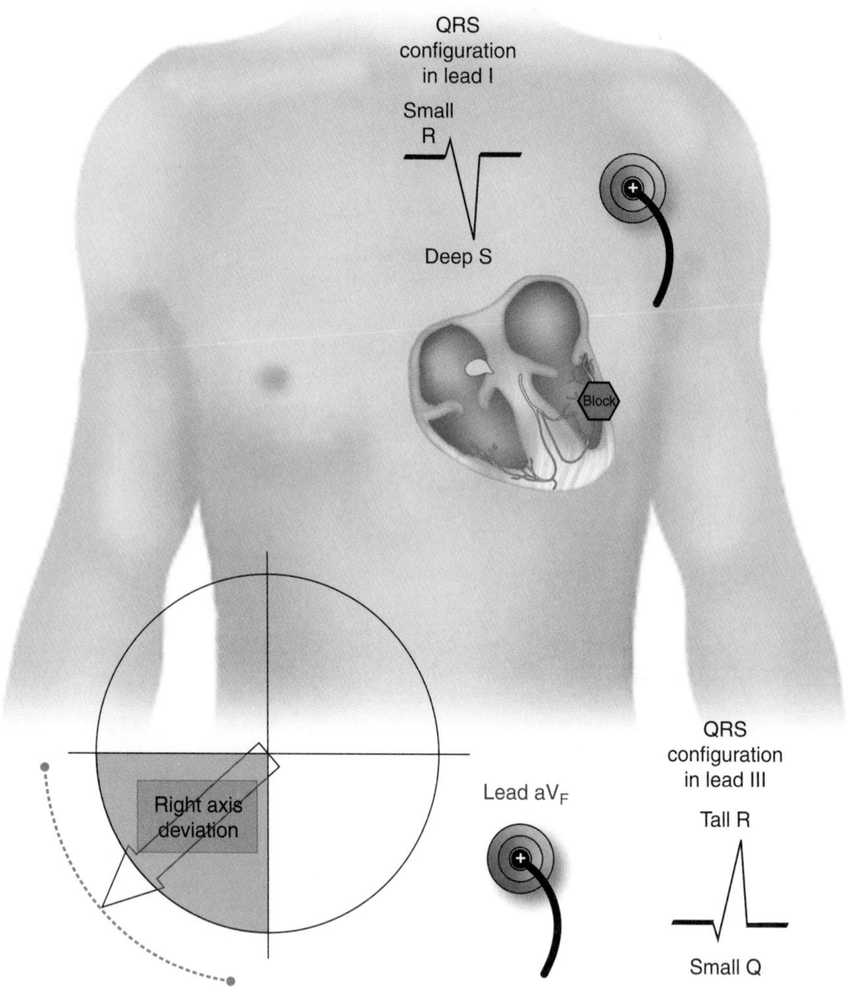

Figure 14-18
With left posterior hemiblock, conduction down the left posterior fascicle is blocked resulting in ventricular myocardial depolarization occurring in a superior-to-inferior and left-to-right direction. There are deep S waves in the left lateral leads (lead I), tall positive R waves inferiorly (lead aV_F), and right axis deviation.

Preexcitation Syndromes

Normally, conduction of the impulse from the atria to the ventricles is delayed in the AV node for about 0.1 seconds. This is long enough for the atria to contract and empty their contents into the ventricles. Preexcitation syndromes are the result of accessory conduction pathways between the atria and ventricles. These pathways bypass the AV node and bundle of His, allowing atrial impulses to depolarize the ventricles earlier than usual.

KEY CONCEPT
Left posterior hemiblock results in right axis deviation.

Accessory pathways sometimes occur in normal healthy hearts as an isolated finding, or they may be in conjunction with mitral valve prolapse, hypertrophic cardiomyopathy, as well as various congenital disorders.

KEY CONCEPT
Preexcitation syndromes occur in some persons because accessory conduction pathways exist between the atria and ventricles that bypass the AV node and bundle of His and allow the atria to depolarize the ventricles earlier than usual.

The most common preexcitation syndromes are Wolff-Parkinson-White (WPW) syndrome and Lown-Ganong-Levine (LGL) syndrome. Both of these disorders can be diagnosed by the ECG and can present as supraventricular tachycardia.

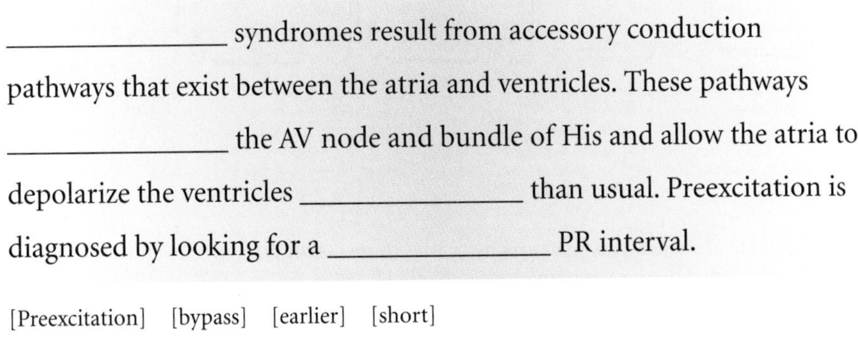

______________ syndromes result from accessory conduction pathways that exist between the atria and ventricles. These pathways ______________ the AV node and bundle of His and allow the atria to depolarize the ventricles ______________ than usual. Preexcitation is diagnosed by looking for a ______________ PR interval.

[Preexcitation] [bypass] [earlier] [short]

KEY CONCEPT
Preexcitation is diagnosed by looking for a short PR interval.

Wolff-Parkinson-White (WPW) Syndrome

In WPW, the bundle of Kent, an accessory pathway, connects the atria to the ventricles, bypassing the AV node (Figure 14-19). It can be left sided (connecting the left atrium and left ventricle) or right sided (connecting the right atrium and right ventricle). ECG features include:

- Rate is normal
- Rhythm is regular
- P waves are normal
- QRS complexes are widened with slurring of the initial portion (delta wave)
- PR interval is usually shortened (less than 0.12 seconds)

INSTRUCTIONAL MOMENT
Be sure to scan the entire ECG as a true delta wave may be seen in only a few leads.

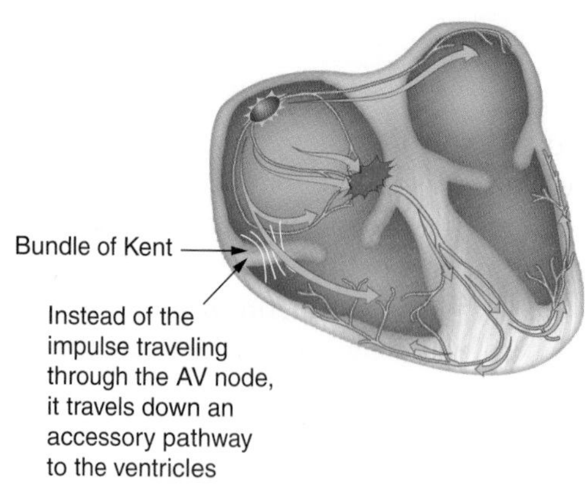

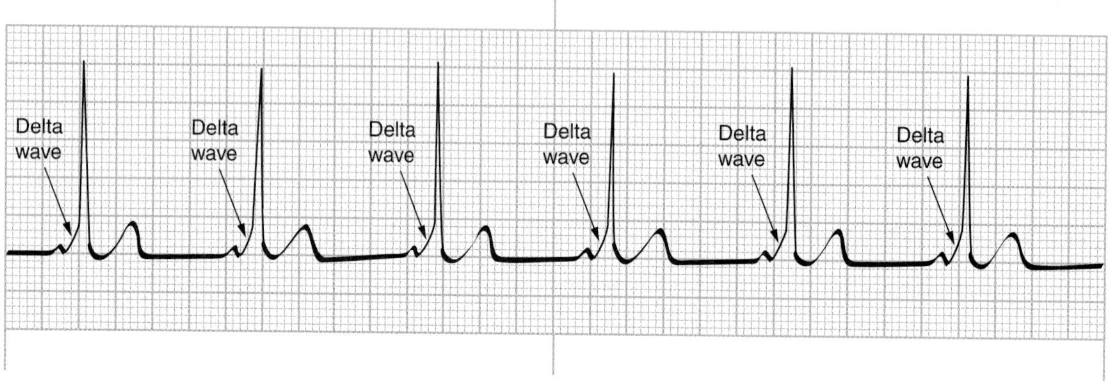

Figure 14-19
In WPW, the impulse travels through the bundle of Kent, an accessory pathway that connects the atria to the ventricles, bypassing the AV node. The QRS complex is widened because of premature activation.

In contrast to bundle branch block, where the QRS complex is widened due to delayed ventricular activation, in WPW it is widened because of premature activation. The QRS complex associated with WPW is a fusion beat. While most of the ventricular myocardium is stimulated through the normal conduction pathways, a small area is depolarized early via the bundle of Kent. This produces a characteristic slurred initial upstroke, called the delta wave, in the QRS complex.

Patients with WPW are vulnerable to paroxysmal supraventricular tachycardia (PSVT).

KEY CONCEPT
Criteria for WPW include a PR interval less than 0.12 seconds, wide QRS complexes, and a delta wave seen in some leads. Patients with WPW are vulnerable to PSVT with rapid ventricular response.

In WPW, the bundle of ________________ connects the atria to the ventricles and bypasses the AV node. Criteria for WPW include a PR interval less than ________________ seconds, ________________ QRS complexes, and a ________________ wave seen in some leads.

[Kent] [0.12] [wide] [delta]

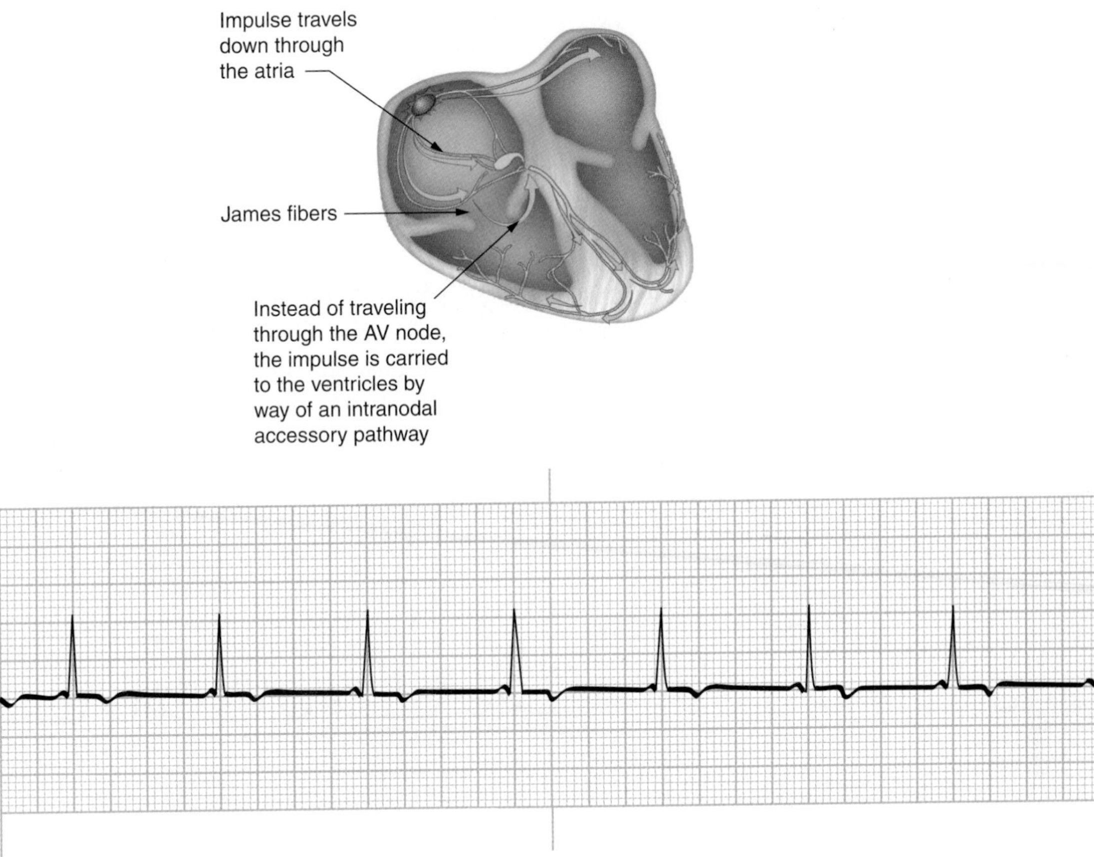

Figure 14-20
In LGL, the impulse travels through an intranodal accessory pathway, referred to as the James fibers, bypassing the normal delay within the AV node. This produces a shortening of the PR interval but no widening of the QRS complex.

Lown-Ganong-Levine (LGL) Syndrome

In LGL the accessory pathway, referred to as the James fibers, is within the AV node (Figure 14-20). This accessory pathway bypasses the normal delay within the AV node but unlike WPW, there is no small region of ventricular myocardium depolarized independently of the rest of the ventricles. Instead, all ventricular conduction occurs through the usual ventricular conduction pathways. For this reason, there is no delta wave and the QRS complex is not widened. The only indication of LGL on the ECG is shortening of the PR interval as a result of the accessory pathway bypassing the delay within the AV node.

ECG criteria for LGL include:

- The PR interval is less than 0.12 seconds
- The QRS complex is not widened
- There is no delta wave

KEY CONCEPT
In LGL there is an intranodal accessory pathway that bypasses the normal delay within the AV node. Criteria for LGL include a PR interval less than 0.12 seconds and a normal QRS complex.

Unless tachycardia is present, WPW and LGL are usually of no clinical significance. However, preexcitation (specifically WPW) can predispose the patient to various tachydysrhythmias, the most common of which is PSVT. It is paroxysmal because it occurs abruptly and supraventricular because the origin of the rhythm is above the AV node. The QRS complex is usually narrow unless a bundle branch block is also present. When the QRS complex is wide the rhythm may be easily confused with ventricular tachycardia.

The accessory pathway in LGL is within the _______________. LGL has a PR interval _______________ than 0.12 seconds and a _______________ QRS complex.

[AV node] [less] [normal]

For each of the following *Practice Makes Perfect* exercises determine if any of the following are present: right or left atrial enlargement; right or left ventricular hypertrophy; right or left bundle branch block; left anterior or posterior hemiblock and/or WPW or LGL syndrome. Answers to these exercises can be found in Appendix A.

PRACTICE. . . MAKES PERFECT

1. For the following 12-lead ECG, identify if any of the following is present: right and/or left atrial enlargement, right and/or left ventricular hypertrophy, right or left bundle branch block, left anterior hemiblock, left posterior hemiblock, and/or Wolff-Parkinson-White (WPW) syndrome or Lown-Ganong-Levine (LGL) syndrome.

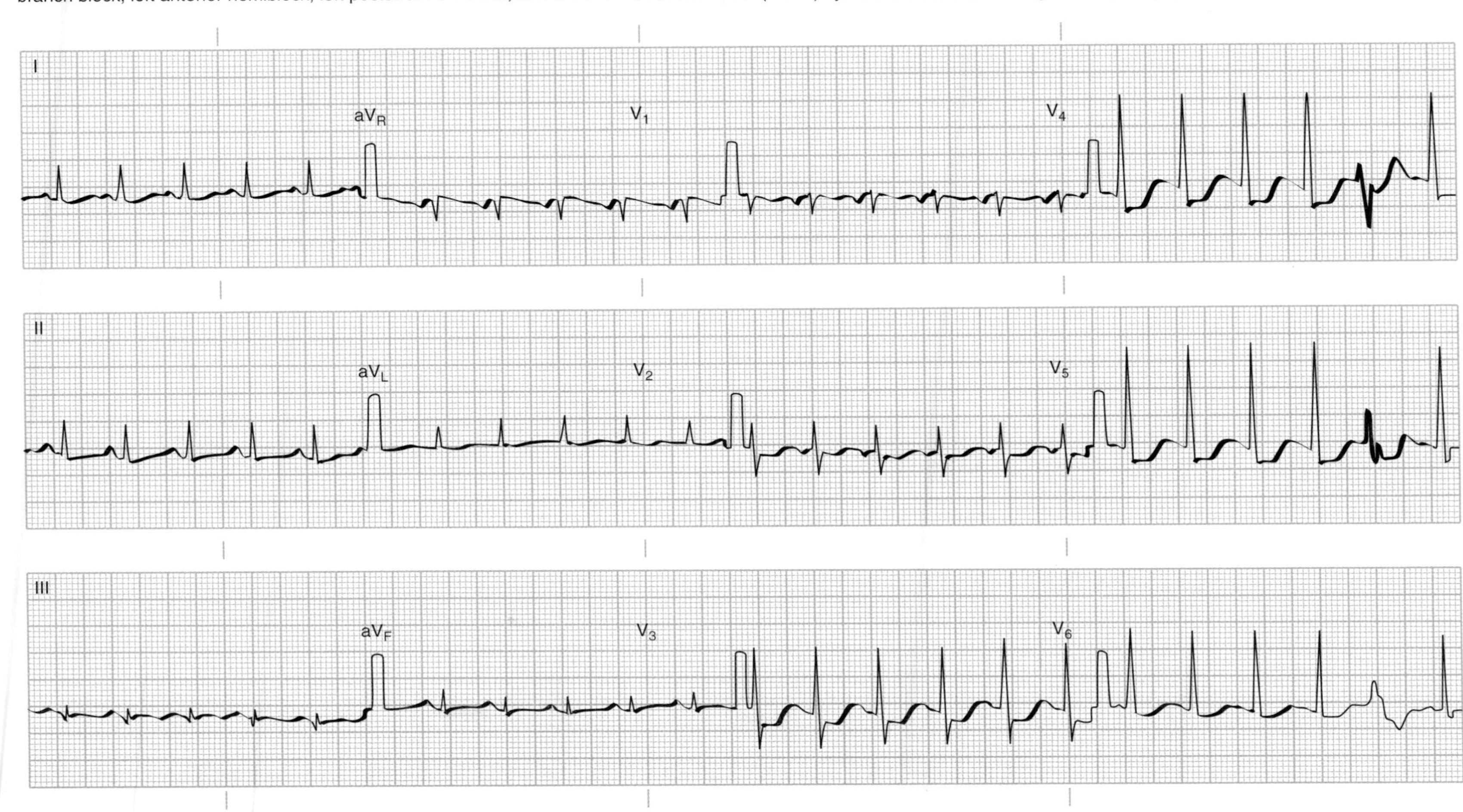

* *Note that the heart rate calculator will not be accurate with these 12-lead ECG strips.*

PRACTICE. . . MAKES PERFECT

2. For the following 12-lead ECG, identify if any of the following is present: right and/or left atrial enlargement, right and/or left ventricular hypertrophy, right or left bundle branch block, left anterior hemiblock, left posterior hemiblock, and/or Wolff-Parkinson-White (WPW) syndrome or Lown-Ganong-Levine (LGL) syndrome.

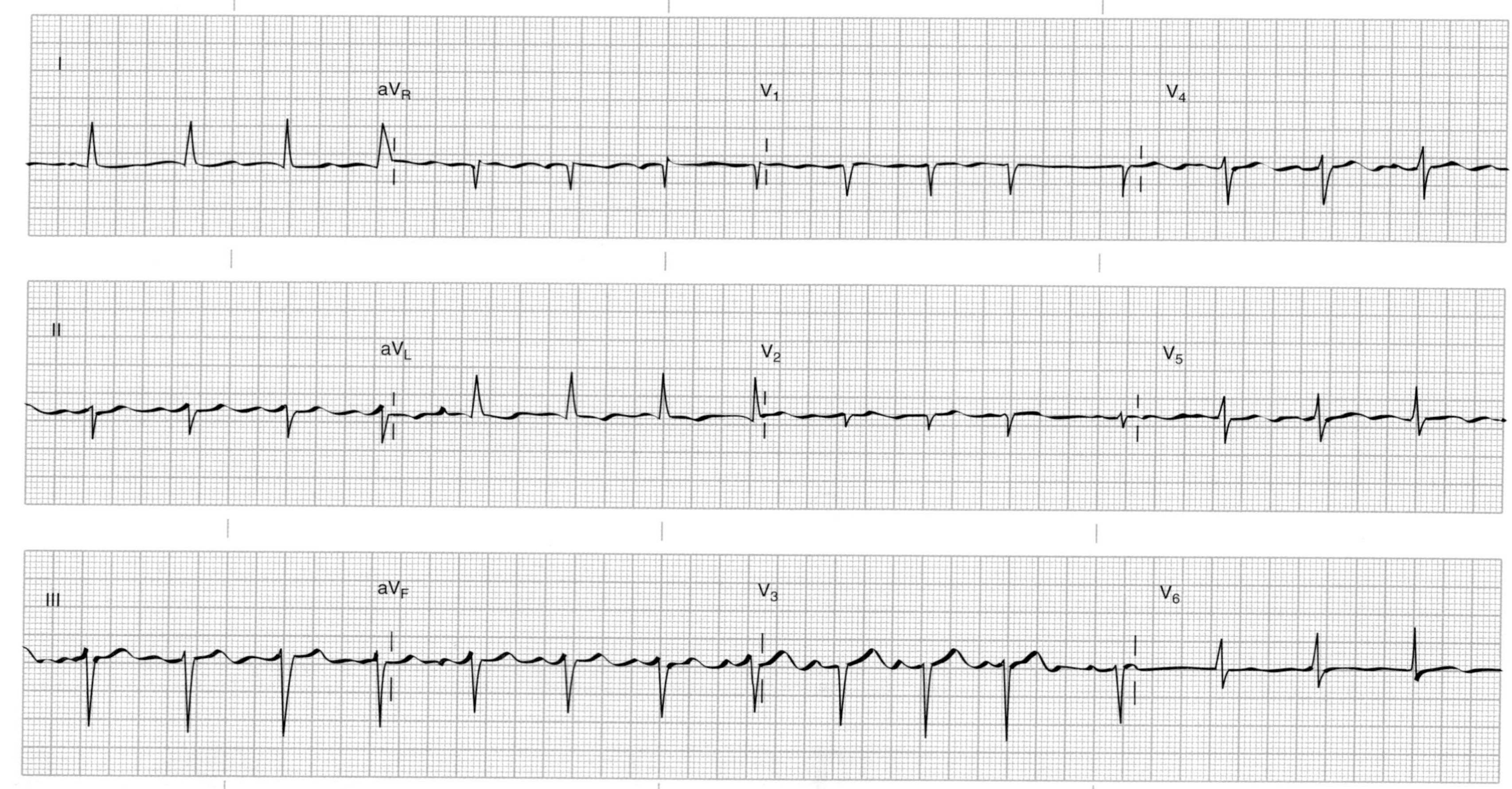

* *Note that the heart rate calculator will not be accurate with these 12-lead ECG strips.*

PRACTICE. . . MAKES PERFECT

3. For the following 12-lead ECG, identify if any of the following is present: right and/or left atrial enlargement, right and/or left ventricular hypertrophy, right or left bundle branch block, left anterior hemiblock, left posterior hemiblock, and/or Wolff-Parkinson-White (WPW) syndrome or Lown-Ganong-Levine (LGL) syndrome.

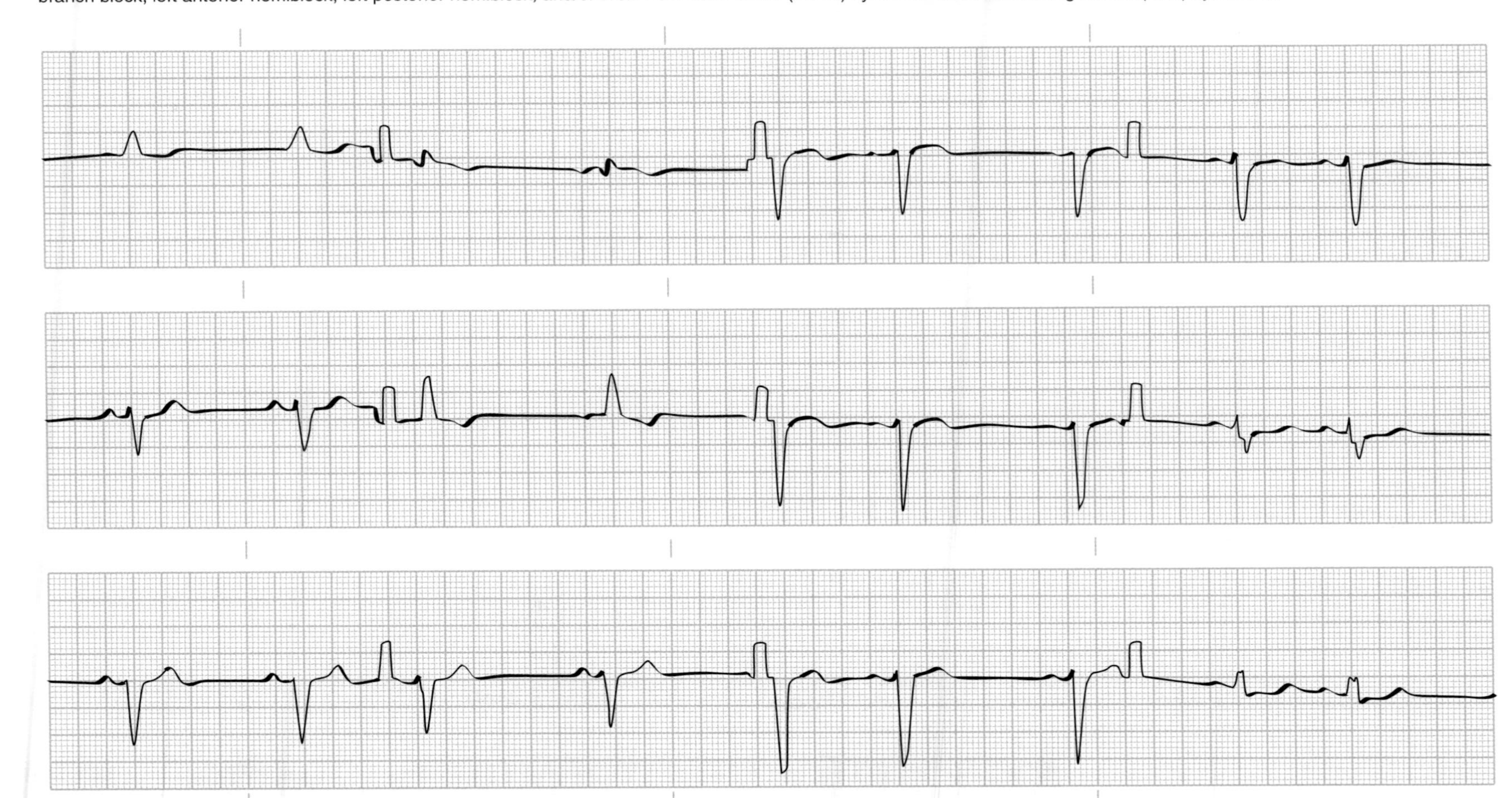

* *Note that the heart rate calculator will not be accurate with these 12-lead ECG strips.*

PRACTICE. . . MAKES PERFECT

4. For the following 12-lead ECG, identify if any of the following is present: right and/or left atrial enlargement, right and/or left ventricular hypertrophy, right or left bundle branch block, left anterior hemiblock, left posterior hemiblock, and/or Wolff-Parkinson-White (WPW) syndrome or Lown-Ganong-Levine (LGL) syndrome.

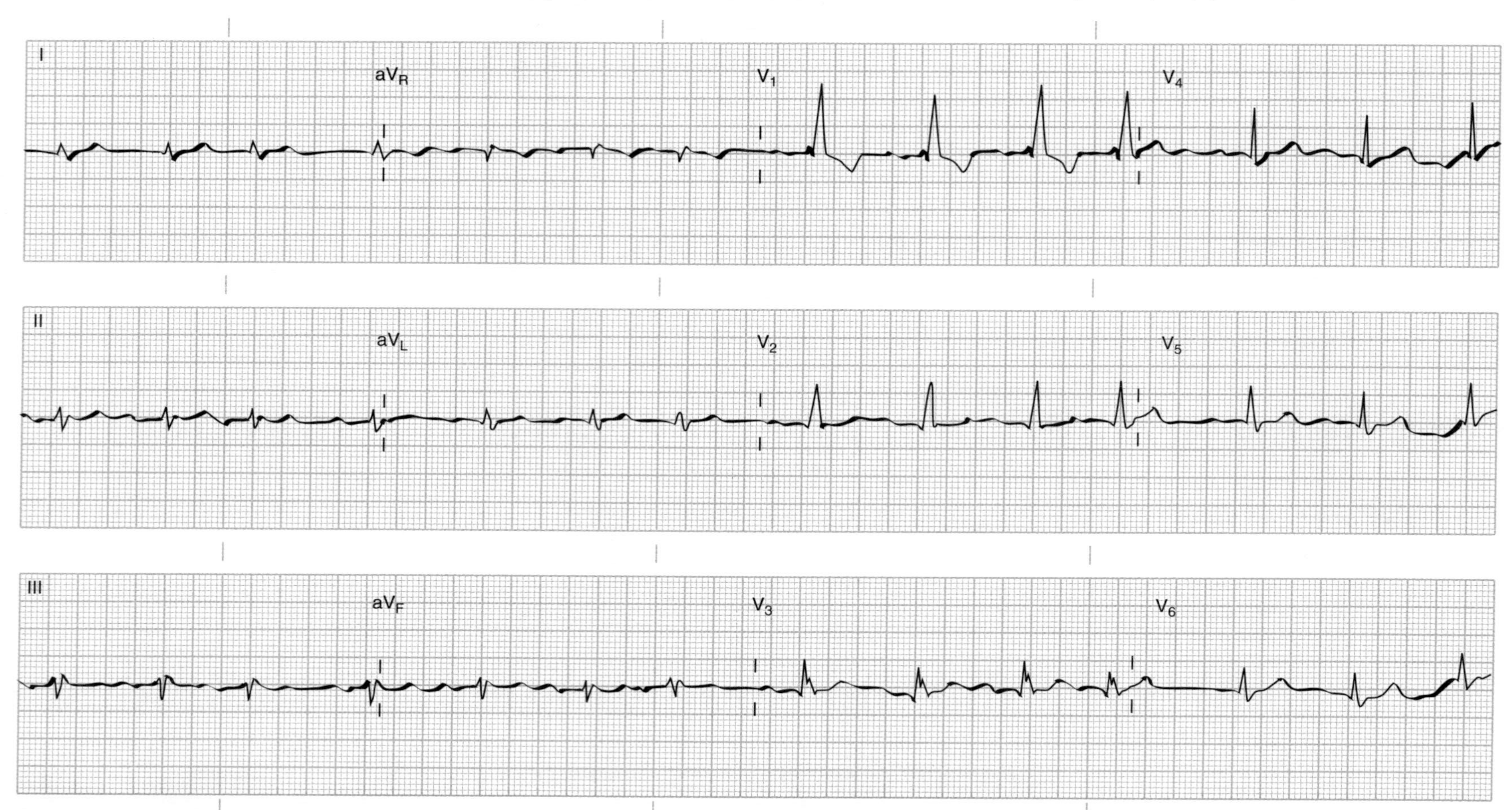

* *Note that the heart rate calculator will not be accurate with these 12-lead ECG strips.*

Key Points

- Hypertrophy is a condition in which the muscular wall of the ventricle(s) becomes thicker than normal.
- Dilation or enlargement of a chamber occurs as the result of volume overload where the chamber dilates to accommodate the increased blood volume.
- Chamber enlargement is associated with the atria (as they dilate more than they hypertrophy), while hypertrophy is associated with the ventricles.
- We look at the P wave to assess for atrial enlargement. Similarly, we examine the QRS complex to help us identify ventricular hypertrophy.
- Indicators of enlargement or hypertrophy include an increase in the duration of the waveform, an increase in the amplitude of the waveform, and axis deviation.
- The duration of the normal P wave is less than 0.10 seconds, while its amplitude should not exceed 2.5 mm.
- The first portion of the P wave represents right atrial depolarization, while the terminal portion represents left atrial depolarization.
- Leads II and V_1 provide the necessary information to assess atrial enlargement.
- The diagnosis of right atrial enlargement is made when you see an increase in the amplitude of the first part of the P wave.
- Two indicators of left atrial enlargement are increased amplitude in the terminal portion of the P wave in V_1 and increased duration or width of the P wave.
- Normally, since the V_1 electrode is positive, the wave of depolarization moving through the left ventricle will be moving away from it producing QRS complexes that are negative (very short R waves with much larger S waves).
- In the limb leads, right axis deviation is the most common characteristic seen with right ventricular hypertrophy.
- In the precordial leads, right ventricular hypertrophy causes the R waves to be more positive in the leads that lie closer to lead V_1.
- Left ventricular hypertrophy is identified by increased R wave amplitude over those precordial leads overlying the left ventricle and S waves that are smaller in the leads overlying the left ventricle (lead V_6) but larger in the leads (lead V_1) overlying the right ventricle.
- The duration of the QRS complex may be slightly prolonged in both right and left ventricular hypertrophy. However, it is rarely greater than 0.1 seconds.
- The bundle of His divides to form the right and left bundle branches. The left bundle branch then divides to form the septal, anterior, and posterior fascicles.
- The QRS complex is normally narrow—less than 0.12 seconds in duration—and the electrical axis lies between 0° and +90°.
- Bundle branch block is a disorder that leads to one or both of the bundle branches failing to conduct impulses. This produces a delay in the depolarization of the ventricle it supplies.
- In bundle branch block you will see a widened QRS complex and the R, R′ configuration in the chest leads.
- To diagnose right bundle branch block check for an R, R′ in leads V_1 or V_2.

- To diagnose left bundle branch block check for an R, R′ in leads V_5 or V_6.
- Hemiblocks cause axis deviation. Left anterior hemiblock results in left axis deviation. Left posterior hemiblock results in right axis deviation.
- Preexcitation syndromes occur when accessory conduction pathways exist between the atria and ventricles that bypass the AV node and bundle of His and allow the atria to depolarize the ventricles earlier than usual.
- Preexcitation is diagnosed by looking for a short PR interval.
- Criteria for WPW include a PR interval less than 0.12 seconds, wide QRS complexes, and a delta wave seen in some leads. Patients with WPW are vulnerable to PSVT.
- In LGL there is an intranodal accessory pathway that bypasses the normal delay within the AV node. Criteria for LGL include a PR interval less than 0.12 seconds and a normal QRS complex.

Assess Your Understanding

The following questions give you a chance to assess your understanding of the material discussed in this chapter. The answers can be found in Appendix A.

1. Hypertrophy is a condition in which the
   a. muscular wall of the ventricle becomes thicker than normal.
   b. ventricular chamber dilates to accommodate increased blood volume.
   c. heart tries to decrease its cardiac output.
   d. ECG always accurately reflects the change in muscle thickness.
2. Hypertrophy is identified by changes in the
   a. P waves.
   b. QRS complexes.
   c. T waves.
   d. PR intervals.
3. Which of the following are changes seen in the ECG that can indicate the presence of enlargement or hypertrophy?
   a. An increase in duration of the waveform.
   b. A biphasic waveform.
   c. Axis deviation.
   d. All of the above.
4. The P wave
   a. is normally 5 mm in amplitude.
   b. normally has a duration of less than 0.10 seconds.
   c. represents left atrial depolarization.
   d. is normally upright in lead V_1.
5. Which leads provide the necessary information to assess atrial enlargement?
   a. V_1 through V_6.
   b. All the limb leads.
   c. I and aV_F.
   d. II and V_1.
6. Characteristics of right atrial enlargement include
   a. the P wave appears tallest in lead II instead of lead aV_F.
   b. an increase in the amplitude of the first part of the P wave in V_1.
   c. increased amplitude of the terminal portion of the P in V_1.
   d. the terminal portion of the P wave must be at least 0.04 seconds in width.

7. With left atrial enlargement,
   a. the P wave vector swings to the right.
   b. the initial part of the P wave is enlarged.
   c. there is an increase in the duration of the terminal portion of the P wave.
   d. the P wave is taller than 2.5 mm in lead V_1.

8. The ECG evidence of atrial enlargement
   a. almost always correlates with pathologic changes in the atrium.
   b. is seen in only 10 to 20% of the patients diagnosed using other procedures.
   c. should be tempered with the patient's clinical presentation.
   d. requires careful assessment of the QRS complex in many leads.

9. To diagnose ventricular hypertrophy we assess the
   a. P waves.
   b. T waves.
   c. QRS complexes.
   d. P wave axis.

10. Normally, in lead V_1, the QRS complex will appear
   a. mainly negative.
   b. positive, with a large R wave and a short S wave.
   c. biphasic, with an R wave and an S wave of equal height.
   d. mainly positive.

11. The most common characteristic(s) seen with right ventricular hypertrophy
   a. are R waves that are more positive in the leads that lie closer to lead V_6.
   b. are S waves that are larger in lead V_1.
   c. are QRS complexes that are slightly more positive than negative in lead I and negative in lead aV_F.
   d. is right axis deviation.

12. The most common characteristic(s) seen with left ventricular hypertrophy
   a. are R waves that are more positive in the leads that lie closer to lead V_6.
   b. are S waves that are smaller in lead V_1.
   c. are R waves in lead V_2 that have an amplitude which exceeds 26 mm.
   d. is left axis deviation.

13. Below the bundle of His the conduction system divides to form the
   a. anterior and posterior fascicles.
   b. Purkinje fibers.
   c. right and left bundle branches.
   d. intranodal pathways.

14. The QRS complex
   a. is normally narrow.
   b. is greater than 0.5 seconds in direction.
   c. begins just as the impulse enters the AV node.
   d. represents ventricular repolarization.

15. With normal ventricular depolarization, the electrical axis is drawn
   a. rightward, between 0° and −90°.
   b. leftward, between 0° and +90°.
   c. upward, at +45°.
   d. downward, between 0° and +30°.

16. Bundle branch block
   a. causes narrowed QRS complexes to appear on the ECG.
   b. is a disorder in which one or both of the bundle branches fails to conduct impulses.
   c. accelerates depolarization of the ventricle it supplies.
   d. is diagnosed by analyzing only the width of the QRS complexes.

17. To diagnose right bundle branch block you check for an R, R′ in leads
    a. aV_F and aV_L.
    b. I and II.
    c. V_1 or V_2.
    d. V_3 or V_4.

18. Hemiblocks
    a. cause axis deviation.
    b. result from accessory pathways between the atria and ventricles.
    c. result in R waves being superimposed on the other.
    d. lead to a complete absence in conduction below the level of block.

19. With preexcitation syndromes,
    a. conduction of the impulse from the atria to the ventricles is delayed in the AV node.
    b. the heart is stimulated to beat faster.
    c. wide, bizarre QRS complexes are generated.
    d. impulses are conducted through accessory conduction pathways between the atria and ventricle.s

20. In WPW,
    a. the T wave is inverted.
    b. impulses bypass the AV node by traveling from the atria to the ventricles via the bundle of Kent.
    c. a small area of myocardium that is depolarized early produces a characteristic slurred initial downstroke in the QRS complex.
    d. the PR interval is prolonged.

Referring to the scenario at the beginning of this chapter answer the following questions.

21. The appearance of the QRS complex in this case indicates the presence of a(n)
    a. complete AV heart block.
    b. right bundle branch block.
    c. incomplete heart block.
    d. 1st-degree AV heart block.

22. The "rabbit ear" appearance of the QRS complex is technically referred to as
    a. QR′S.
    b. Q′R′S′.
    c. RR′.
    d. R′SR.

23. Cardiomyopathy is defined as a(n)
    a. abnormal enlargement of the heart.
    b. defect of the heart valves.
    c. weakening of the heart muscle.
    d. electrical conduction defect.

Answers to Sidebar Questions

"What do the heart's ventricles do?"

Answer: The ventricles are responsible for pumping blood through the circulatory system. The right ventricle pumps blood to the pulmonary circulation, while the left ventricle pumps blood to the systemic circulation.

"Which of the heart's atria depolarizes first?"

Answer: The right atrium depolarizes first as the SA node in which the impulse normally arises is located in the upper-right atrium.

"How many small squares on the ECG paper represent 0.10 seconds in duration? How many represent an amplitude of 2.5 mm?"

Answer: Two and a half small squares represents 0.10 seconds in duration while 2½ small squares represent 2.5 mm in amplitude.

"The QRS axis in the normal heart lies between ____________ and ____________ degrees?"

Answer: The QRS axis in the normal heart lies between 0° and +90°. This reflects the electrical dominance of the larger left ventricle over the right ventricle.

"Describe how the impulse that brings about the heartbeat is conducted from the SA node to the AV node."

Answer: The initial electrical impulse begins high in the right atrium, in the SA node. It travels through the atria via intraatrial and intranodal pathways to the AV node.

"Which side of the interventricular septum is the first to be depolarized?"

Answer: Normally, the left side of the interventricular septum is the first part of the ventricle to be depolarized. The impulse passes through the septum to the other side.

"What is the normal duration of the QRS complex?"

Answer: The normal duration of the QRS complex is less than 0.12 seconds (less than three small squares).

"Which leads are best for assessing the electrical activity in the right ventricle?"

Answer: The leads overlying the right ventricle are V_1 and V_2.

"What ECG changes tell us left axis deviation is present?"

Answer: If the QRS complex deflection is positive in both leads I and aV_F, the electrical axis is normal. If the QRS complex in lead I is upright and the QRS complex in lead aV_F has a negative deflection, then left axis deviation exists.

On the DVD

- Bundle Branch Block Lecture.

Notes

Myocardial Ischemia and Infarction

15

Case History

EMS is called to a local office building to evaluate a 46-year-old man complaining of chest pain. Upon entering the man's office the paramedics see an ashen, grey, and diaphoretic middle-aged man sitting at his desk. They notice an overflowing ashtray on the desk as they move to his side.

The paramedics perform a rapid assessment and find the patient to be hypertensive with labored respirations. High concentration oxygen is applied and an IV established. Following their cardiac protocol, the paramedics give the patient an aspirin, start him on nitroglycerin, and obtain a 12-lead ECG.

The 12-lead ECG shows 5mm of ST elevation in leads II, III, and aV_F indicating that the chest pain may be from a heart attack. The patient gives the paramedics permission to transport him to the nearest cardiac center.

The paramedics call the cardiac center and speak to the emergency medicine physician on duty. They have a diagnostic 12-lead ECG, so the physician mobilizes the cardiac team and the patient is taken immediately for emergent angioplasty. Three days later, the cardiologist tells the patient that because of the rapid care of the paramedics, combined with their ability to obtain and interpret a 12-lead ECG, he did not sustain any permanent damage to his heart and should fully recover.

Chapter Preview

- Coronary Circulation
- The ECG Waveforms
- Coronary Artery Disease
- ECG Indicators of Ischemia, Injury, and Infarction
- Identifying the Myocardial Infarction Location

KEY CONCEPT
The coronary veins return deoxygenated venous blood from the heart to the right atrium via the coronary sinus.

Coronary Veins

Deoxygenated venous blood from the heart drains into five different coronary veins that empty into the right atrium via the coronary sinus. This blood then mixes with the systemic venous return.

Deoxygenated venous blood from the heart is returned via the coronary ______________ that empty into the right atrium via the coronary ______________.

[veins] [sinus]

Increased Oxygen Needs

The resting heart extracts most of the oxygen from the coronary blood as it flows through the heart muscle. Increased oxygen demands of the myocardium that result from exercise or emotional stress can only be satisfied by increases in coronary blood flow, mostly through vasodilation.

CLINICAL MOMENT
Coronary perfusion occurs during diastole when the heart is relaxed.

The need for oxygen in local heart tissue causes the arteries to dilate, which increases blood flow. Stimulation of the sympathetic nervous system also affects coronary blood flow. The coronary blood vessels are innervated by both alpha and beta receptors. Stimulation of the alpha receptors leads to vasoconstriction, while stimulation of the beta receptors causes vasodilation.

KEY CONCEPT
Increased myocardial oxygen demands can only be satisfied by increases in coronary blood flow, mostly through vasodilation.

Increased coronary blood ______________ is needed to satisfy increased myocardial oxygen ______________. Stimulation of the ______________ receptors causes vasodilation, which increases coronary blood flow.

[flow] [demand] [beta]

The ECG Waveforms

As discussed in earlier chapters, the electrical impulse that initiates the heartbeat normally arises from the SA node. From there it travels through the atria to the AV node where there is a delay in the conduction of the impulse before it is sent to the ventricles. This delay in conduction is represented by a flat line, called the PR segment (Figure 15-2). The PR segment can be used as a baseline from which to evaluate depression or elevation, of the ST segment.

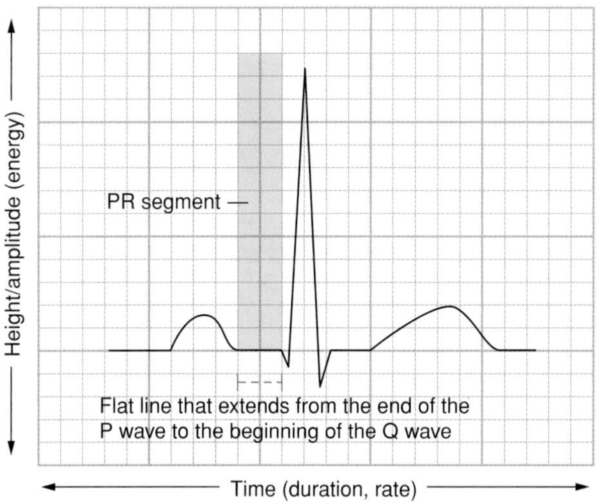

Figure 15-2
The PR segment can be used as a baseline to evaluate changes in the ST segment, such as depression or elevation.

The impulse then travels through the bundle of His, the right and left bundle branches, and the Purkinje fibers. The spread of impulse through the ventricles produces the QRS complex.

KEY CONCEPT
ST segment depression or elevation can be evaluated by comparing the ST segment to the PR segment.

We can use the ________________ segment as a baseline from which to evaluate changes in the ST segment, such as ________________ or ________________.

[PR] [depression] [elevation]

Q Waves

The Q wave is the first part of the QRS complex and represents depolarization of the interventricular septum. A tiny septal branch (fascicle) of the left bundle branch conducts the wave of depolarization to the interventricular septum. It happens so quickly that septal depolarization is not always visible on the ECG, but when it is, this small left-to-right depolarization produces a tiny, negative deflection from the baseline in one or several of the left lateral leads. This deflection is called the Q wave (Figure 15-3). It may be seen in leads I, aV_L, V_5, and V_6. Sometimes, small Q waves may be seen in the inferior leads and in V_3 and V_4. When it is present, the normal, and clinically insignificant, Q wave should have a duration of less than 0.04 seconds (1 mm or 1 small square) and be less than 25% the amplitude of the R wave in that lead.

INSTRUCTIONAL MOMENT
The intraventricular septum is the wall of muscle separating the right and left ventricles.

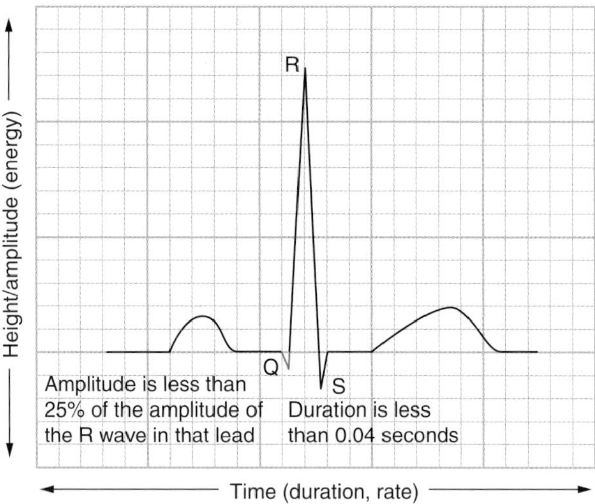

Figure 15-3
The Q wave is the first part of the QRS complex; it is a tiny negative deflection from the baseline.

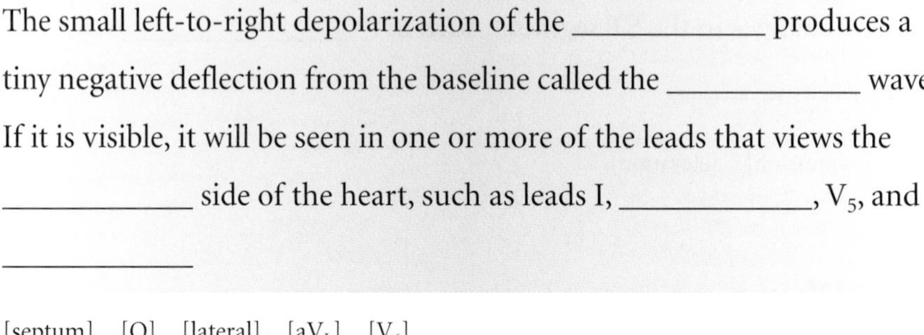
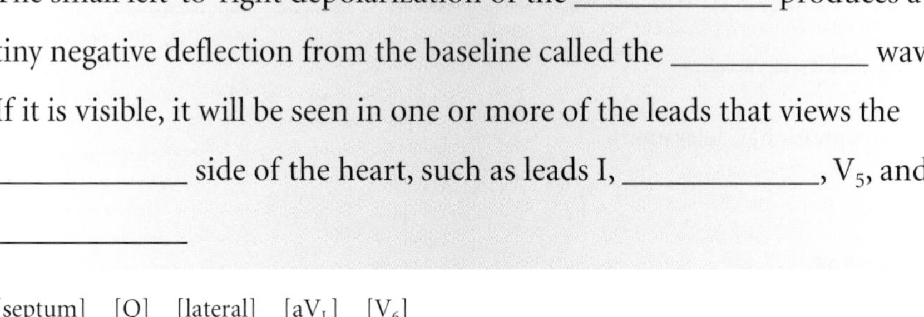

Characteristics of a Normal Q Wave

- **Small negative deflection from the baseline**
- **Duration of less than 0.04 seconds (1 mm or 1 small square)**
- **Less than 25% the amplitude of the R wave in that lead**

KEY CONCEPT
The Q wave is the first part of the QRS complex. It is the first downward, or negative, deflection from the baseline and is not always present.

The small left-to-right depolarization of the ____________ produces a tiny negative deflection from the baseline called the ____________ wave. If it is visible, it will be seen in one or more of the leads that views the ____________ side of the heart, such as leads I, ____________, V_5, and ____________

[septum] [Q] [lateral] [aV_L] [V_6]

CLINICAL MOMENT
If the first deflection following the flat line after the P wave is negative, it is called the Q wave (no matter how large).

Normal ST Segments

The ST segment is the line that follows the QRS complex and connects it to the T wave (Figure 15-4). It begins at the isoelectric line extending from the S wave until it gradually curves upward to the T wave. During the period of the ST segment, the ventricles are beginning to repolarize. Under normal circumstances, the ST segment appears as a flat line (neither positive nor negative), although it may vary by 0.5 to 1.0 mm in some precordial leads. The point that marks the end of the QRS and the beginning of the ST segment is known as the J point.

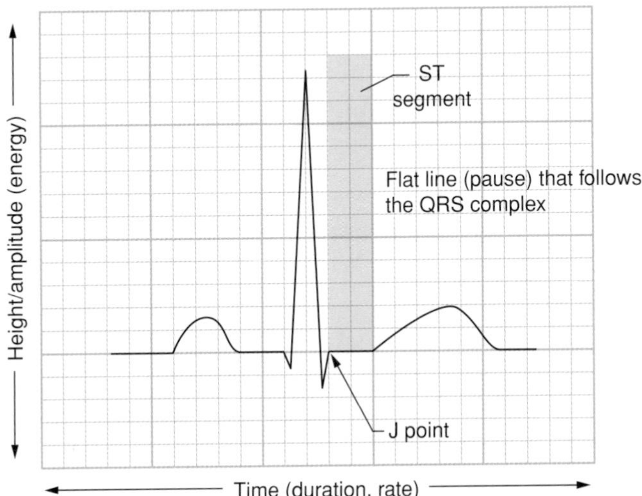

Figure 15-4
The ST segment is the line that follows the QRS complex and connects it to the T wave.

The PR segment is used as the baseline from which to evaluate the degree of displacement of the ST segment from the isoelectric line. To determine this, measure at a point 0.04 seconds (one small box) after the J point. The ST segment is considered elevated if it is above the baseline and considered depressed if it is below it.

CLINICAL MOMENT
The term ST segment is used regardless of whether the final wave of the QRS complex is an R or S wave.

Characteristics of a Normal ST Segment

- **Flat line**
- **Follows the QRS complex and connects it to the T wave**
- **Can vary by 0.5 to 1.0 mm in some precordial leads**

The ______________ line that follows the ______________ complex and connects it to the T wave is called the ST ______________. It starts at the ______________ line extending from the ______________ wave until it gradually curves upward to the ______________ wave. It contains ____ waves.

[flat] [QRS] [segment] [isoelectric] [S] [T] [no]

KEY CONCEPT
The ST segment is the flat line that follows the QRS complex and connects it to the T wave.

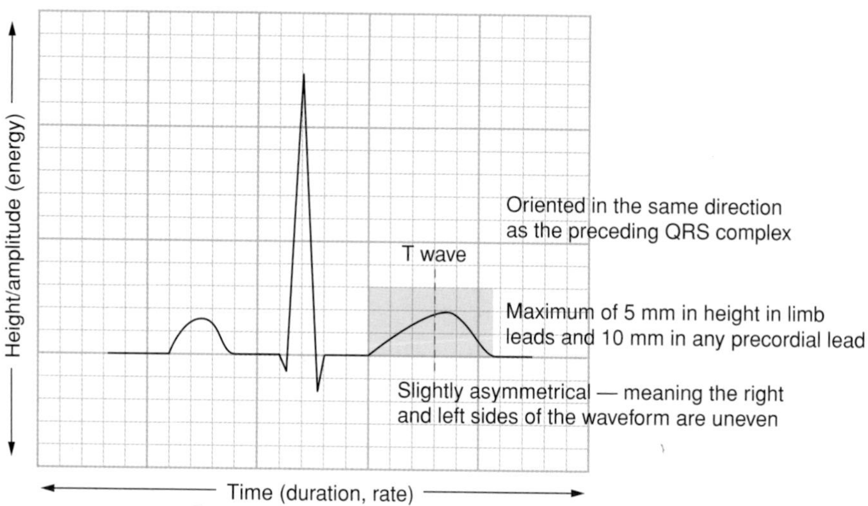

Figure 15-5
The T wave follows the ST segment and represents ventricular repolarization.

QUESTION
Why are T waves larger in the precordial leads than the limb leads? (The answer can be found on page 499.)

KEY CONCEPT
The T wave is slightly asymmetrical and oriented in the same direction as the preceding QRS complex.

CLINICAL MOMENT
Remember, atrial repolarization occurs during the QRS complex and is not visible on the regular ECG.

QUESTION
Why is the direction of the T wave the same as the QRS complex? (The answer can be found on page 499.)

Normal T Waves

Next, we should see the T wave (Figure 15-5). The T wave represents the completion of ventricular repolarization. It is larger than the P wave and slightly asymmetrical. The peak of the T wave is closer to the end than the beginning and the first half has a more gradual slope than the second half. Normally, the T wave is not more than 5 mm in height in the limb leads or 10 mm in any precordial lead. The T wave is normally oriented in the same direction as its associated QRS complex. T waves are normally positive in leads I, II, V_2 to V_6 and negative in lead aV_R. They are also positive in aV_L and aV_F but may be negative if the QRS complex is less than 6 mm in height. In leads III and V_1, the T wave may be positive or negative.

Characteristics of a Normal T Wave

- **Slightly asymmetrical**
- **Maximum of 5 mm in height in the limb leads**
- **Maximum of 10 mm in any precordial lead**
- **Oriented in the same direction as the preceding QRS complex**

The T wave is slightly ______________ and oriented in the ______________ direction as the QRS complex. Normally, it is not more than ______________ mm in height in the limb leads or ______________ mm in any precordial lead.

[asymmetrical] [same] [5] [10]

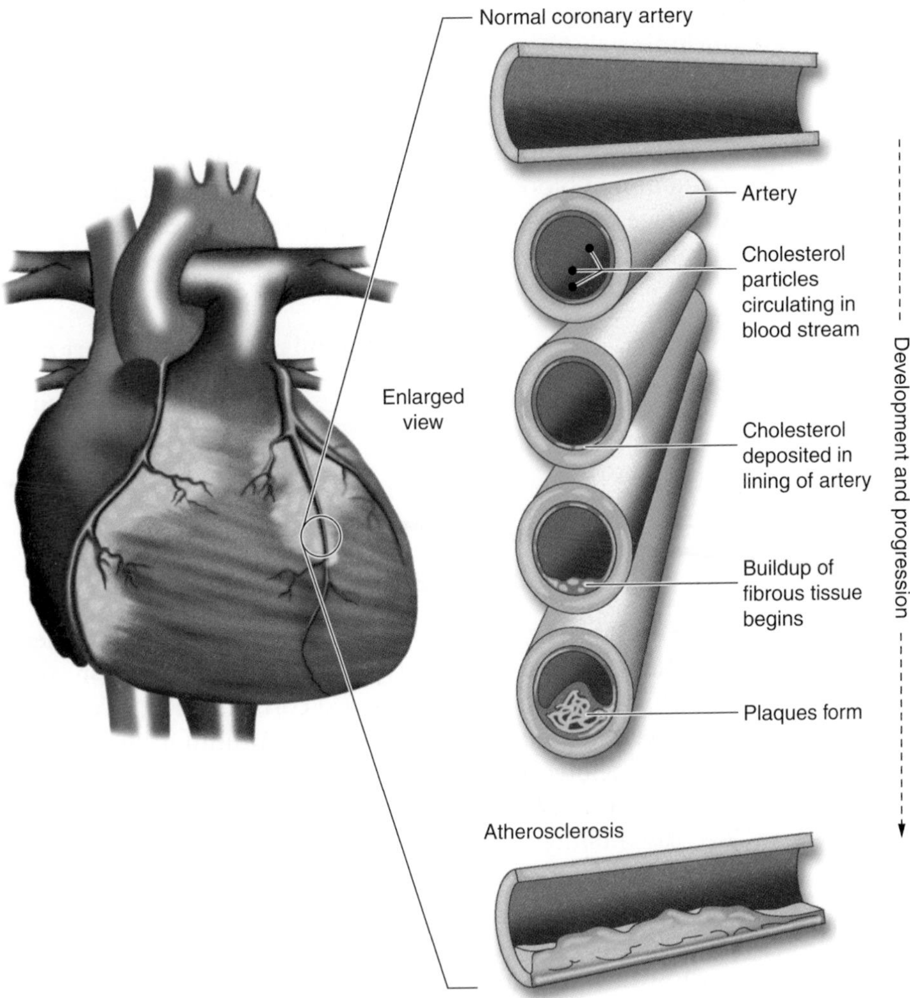

Figure 15-6
Development and progression of coronary artery disease.

Coronary Artery Disease

Any major interruption of blood flow through the coronary arteries can cause ischemia, injury, and infarction of the heart muscle. This can lead to impairment of myocardial function and sudden death.

Coronary artery disease is an umbrella term for the various diseases that reduce or stop blood flow through the coronary arteries. **Atherosclerosis** accounts for over 90% of the cases of coronary artery disease.

Atherosclerosis is a gradual, progressive process involving obstruction and hardening of the arterial wall. It begins with small deposits of fatty material, particularly cholesterol, invading the intima, the inner lining, of the arteries (Figure 15-6). This produces a nonobstructive lesion called a fatty

KEY CONCEPT
Interruption of coronary artery blood flow can lead to myocardial ischemia, injury, and infarction.

streak. Later, these areas of deposit become invaded by fibrous tissue including lipoprotein-filled smooth muscle cells; collagen; and muscle fibers; which become calcified and harden into plaques. Eventually, the plaque infiltrates the arterial wall, and the intima becomes thickened, hardened, and inelastic. This leads to narrowing of these vessels and a reduction of blood flow through them. If narrowing of the artery reaches the stage where blood flow is insufficient to meet the oxygen demands of the myocardium, coronary artery disease is said to exist.

Ischemia, _______________, and infarction of the heart muscle can result from interruption of _______________ artery blood flow.

[injury] [coronary]

Myocardial Ischemia

Myocardial ischemia is a deprivation of oxygen and nutrients to the myocardium (Figure 15-7). It typically occurs when the heart has a greater need for oxygen than the narrowed coronary arteries can deliver, or there is a loss of blood supply to the myocardium. Causes of myocardial ischemia include atherosclerosis, vasospasm, thrombosis, embolism, decreased ventricular filling time (such as that produced by tachycardia), and decreased filling pressure in the coronary arteries (such as that caused by severe hypotension or aortic valve disease).

The ischemia may be due to an intermittent shortage of oxygen to the myocardium brought on by exertion, emotional stress, or even the stress of cold weather. This ischemia produces chest pain, also known as **angina**

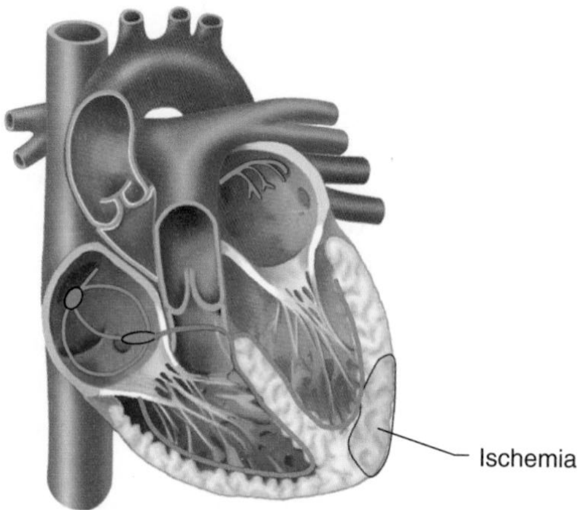

Figure 15-7
Myocardial ischemia.

or **angina pectoris.** The ischemia is usually relieved within 2 to 10 minutes of rest or by administration of a medicine, such as nitroglycerin that dilates the coronary arteries and allows the needed blood (and oxygen) to flow to the myocardium. A patient who has angina may go on to experience an infarction or may remain stable for many years. Angina is considered unstable if it is more easily provoked, becomes less predictable, and/or worsens over time.

Ischemia may also be the onset of myocardial infarction. If the blood supply is quickly restored to the ischemic tissue, permanent damage can often be avoided.

KEY CONCEPT
Decreased delivery of oxygen and other nutrients to the myocardium can result in ischemia. Ischemia can be reversed if the supply of oxygen and nutrients can be restored or increased to a level that satisfies the myocardial oxygen demand.

A lack of oxygen and nutrients leads to myocardial __________. It occurs when the need for oxygen is ________ than the narrowed coronary arteries can deliver, or there is a _____ of blood supply to the myocardium. Ischemia is reversible if the blood supply is _______ restored to the ischemic tissue.

[ischemia] [greater] [loss] [quickly]

Myocardial Injury

If the myocardial oxygen demand fails to lower, the coronary artery blockage worsens, or the ischemia is allowed to progress untreated, myocardial injury will occur (Figure 15-8). **Myocardial injury** reflects a degree of cellular damage beyond ischemia. It occurs if the blood flow is not restored (and ischemia reversed) within a few minutes. The degree of injury

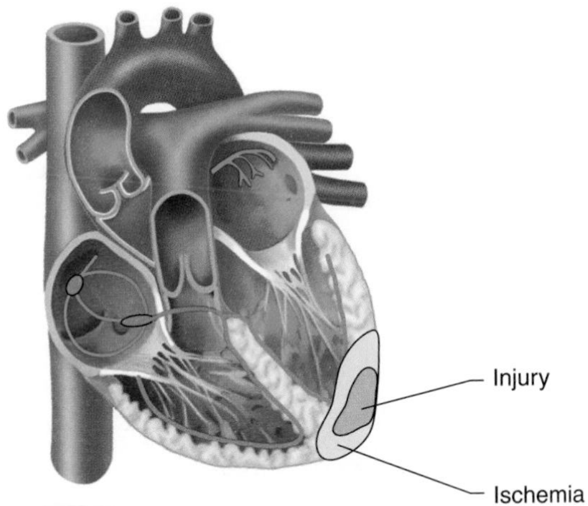

Figure 15-8
Myocardial injury.

KEY CONCEPT
Myocardial injury will likely occur if ischemia brought about by increased myocardial oxygen demands is not resolved or if the ischemia is allowed to progress untreated.

depends on if and how quickly the blood supply is restored as well as how much myocardium is involved. If blood flow is not restored to the affected area, tissue death will occur. Treatments used to restore blood flow include administration of fibrinolytic agents, coronary angioplasty, or a coronary artery bypass graft (CABG).

Myocardial injury is a degree of cellular ________________ beyond that seen with mere ________________. It occurs if the blood flow is not ________________ within a few ________________ of the onset of ischemia.

[damage] [ischemia] [restored] [minutes]

Myocardial Infarction

Myocardial infarction is the death of injured myocardial cells (Figure 15-9). It occurs when there is a sudden decrease or total cessation of blood flow through a coronary artery to an area of the myocardium. Myocardial infarction commonly occurs when the intima of a coronary artery ruptures, exposing the atherosclerotic plaque to the blood within the artery. This initiates the abrupt development of a clot (thrombus). The vessel, already narrowed by the plaque, becomes completely blocked by the thrombus. The area of the heart normally supplied by the blocked artery goes through a characteristic sequence of events described as zones of ischemia, injury, and infarction. Each zone is associated with characteristic ECG changes. There is ischemic and injured myocardial tissue surrounding the infarcted area so the size of the infarction can increase if coronary perfusion is not restored. If the patient survives an acute myocardial infarction (AMI), the infarcted tissue is replaced with scar tissue.

CLINICAL MOMENT
The cell membranes of dying myocardial cells break and leak substances into the blood. Blood tests can be used to determine the presence of these substances in the blood. These substances (called cardiac markers or serum cardiac markers) include creatine kinase (CK) MB isoforms, troponin, and myoglobin. Troponin-T and troponin-I are two tests that may be ordered for a patient with a suspected myocardial infarction. Elevated levels (positive test) indicate that myocardial infarction has occurred. The troponin-I test may have better specificity than troponin-T.

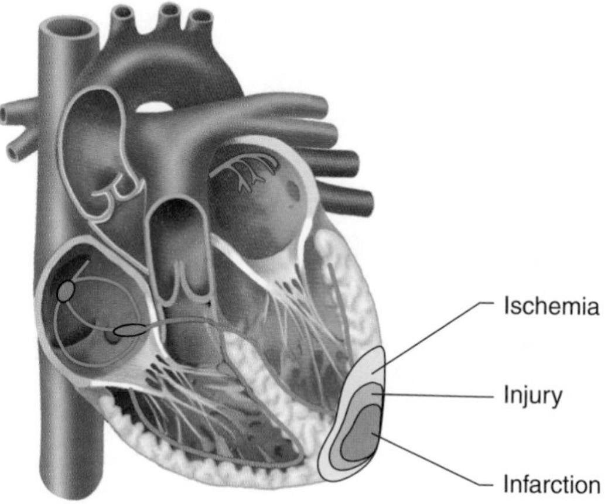

Figure 15-9
Infarction and the heart.

When blockage occurs in the left anterior descending artery it is particularly dangerous as this vessel supplies a much larger portion of the total myocardial mass than the right coronary and left circumflex arteries. Even more serious is obstruction of the left main coronary artery. Significant narrowing of this short vessel causes reduction in blood flow through both the left anterior descending and circumflex arteries. This compromises the blood supply of almost the entire left ventricle. Fortunately, obstruction of the left main coronary artery occurs in only 5% to 10% of patients with symptoms of coronary artery disease.

CLINICAL MOMENT
The diagnosis of myocardial infarction is based on the presence of at least two of the following three criteria:

- Clinical history of ischemic-type chest discomfort
- Changes on serially obtained ECG tracings
- Rise and fall in serum cardiac markers

A sudden decrease or total cessation of blood flow through a __________ artery to an area of the myocardium leads to myocardial __________. Obstruction of the __________ main coronary artery causes a reduction in blood flow through both the left anterior descending and circumflex arteries bringing about __________ blood supply in nearly the entire __________ ventricle.

[coronary] [infarction] [left] [compromised] [left]

KEY CONCEPT
Myocardial infarction is the death of injured myocardial cells.

ECG Indicators of Ischemia, Injury, and Infarction

The ECG can help identify the presence of ischemia, injury, and/or infarction of the heart muscle. It can also help identify which coronary artery or branch is occluded.

CLINICAL MOMENT
Myocardial ischemia and injury are reversible, infarction is not.

The three key ECG indicators of myocardial ischemia, injury, and/or infarction are (Figure 15-10):

- Changes in the T wave (peaking or inversion)
- Changes in the ST segment (depression or elevation)
- Enlarged Q waves or appearance of new Q waves

CLINICAL MOMENT
A *new* bundle branch block can be a fourth indicator of myocardial infarction. However, you must have access to the patient's old ECGs to confirm this.

Although the ECG usually progresses through these three indicators during an acute myocardial infarction, any one of these changes may be present without any of the others. For this reason, it is not unusual to see ST segment depression without T wave inversion. As we discuss ischemia, remember that it can be transient, such as in angina, or it can be related to myocardial infarction.

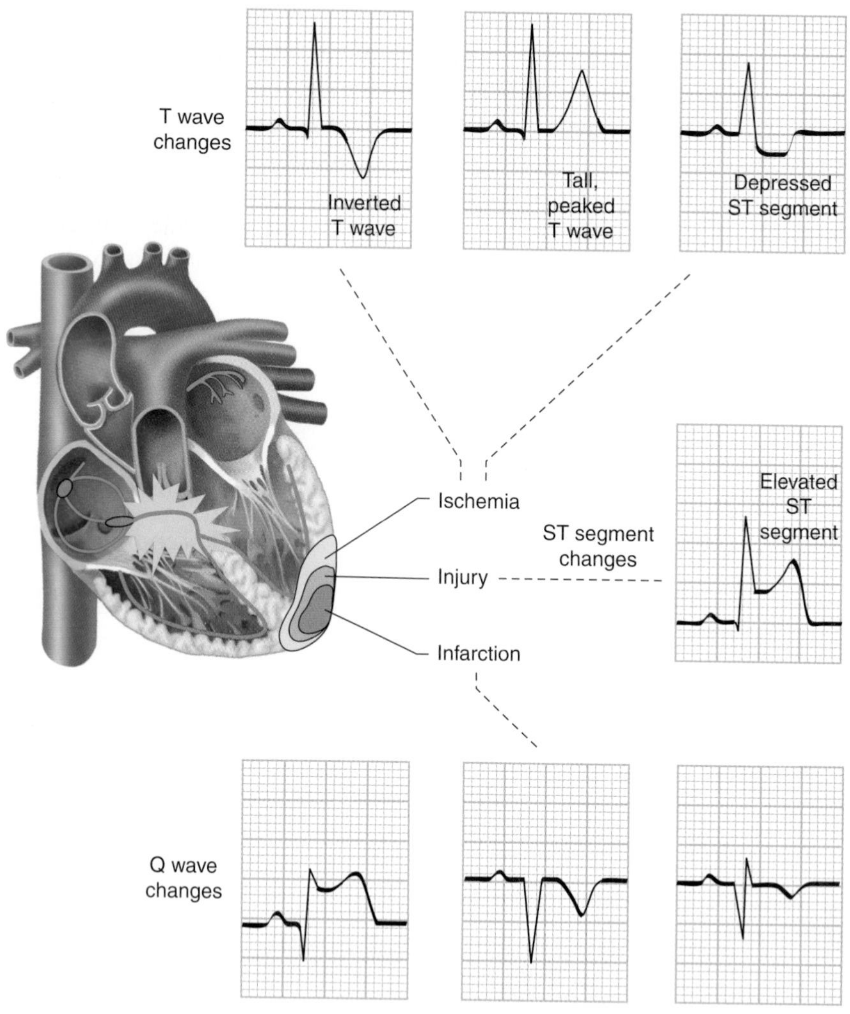

Figure 15-10
Key ECG changes with ischemia, injury, or infarction.

KEY CONCEPT
The ECG can help identify the presence of ischemia, injury, and/or infarction of the heart muscle.

The _______________ can identify the presence of myocardial ischemia, injury, and/or infarction, even to the point of revealing which coronary artery is _______________.

[ECG] [occluded]

T Wave Changes

Inverted T waves are a characteristic sign of myocardial ischemia (Figure 15-11). They invert because the lack of oxygen results in leaking of potassium from the ischemic tissue. This delays the process of repolarization. T wave inversion may be present with angina. It may also be present during a myocardial infarction as the tissue around the infarct becomes ischemic.

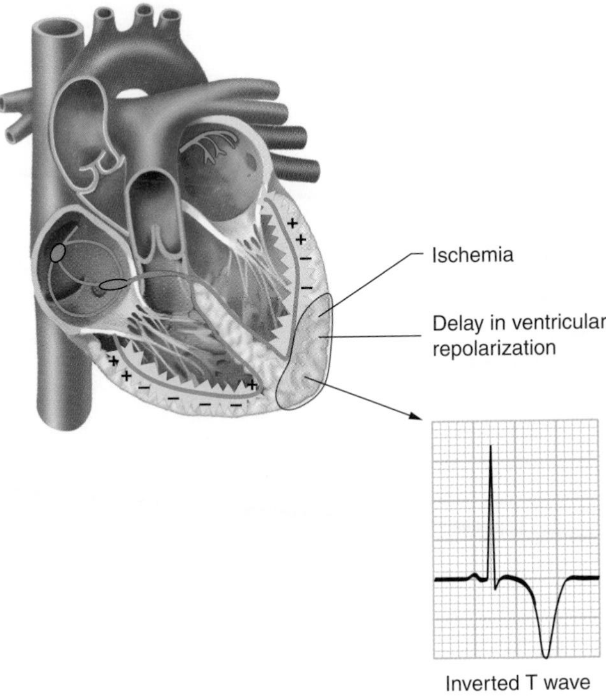

Figure 15-11
Inverted T waves are a characteristic of myocardial ischemia.

Inverted T waves associated with myocardial ischemia indicate that ischemia is present through the full thickness of the myocardium. Inverted T waves will be present in the leads facing the affected area of the myocardium. The chest leads (V_1 through V_6) are closest to the ventricles, so they are the best for checking for T wave inversion (Figure 15-12). Also, be sure to check the limb leads. The inverted T wave from ischemia is symmetrical, meaning that the right and left sides of the T wave are mirror images.

INSTRUCTIONAL MOMENT
T waves inverted in the leads where they should be positive are referred to as flipped T waves.

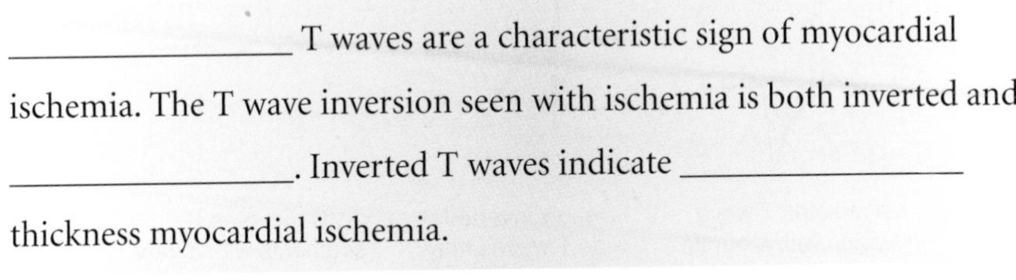

________________ T waves are a characteristic sign of myocardial ischemia. The T wave inversion seen with ischemia is both inverted and ________________. Inverted T waves indicate ________________ thickness myocardial ischemia.

[Inverted] [symmetrical] [full]

KEY CONCEPT
With myocardial ischemia, the appearance of T waves may change.

Aside from myocardial ischemia, there are many other causes of T wave inversion including pericarditis, ventricular hypertrophy, bundle branch block, shock, electrolyte imbalance, and subarachnoid hemorrhage (Figure 15-13).

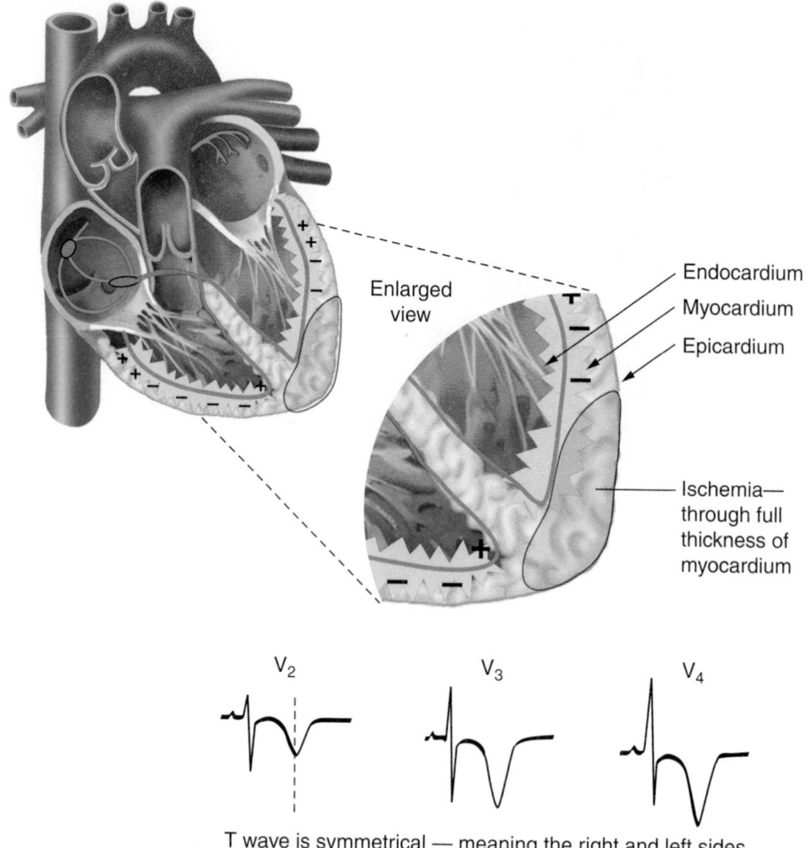

Figure 15-12
The precordial (chest) leads are best for detecting T wave inversion.

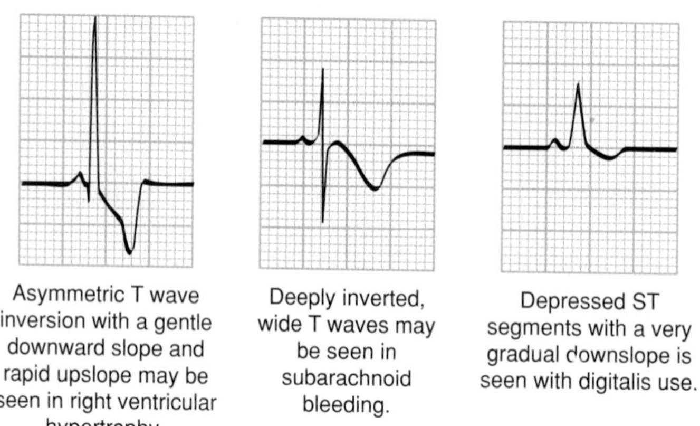

Figure 15-13
Examples of T wave inversion due to other causes.

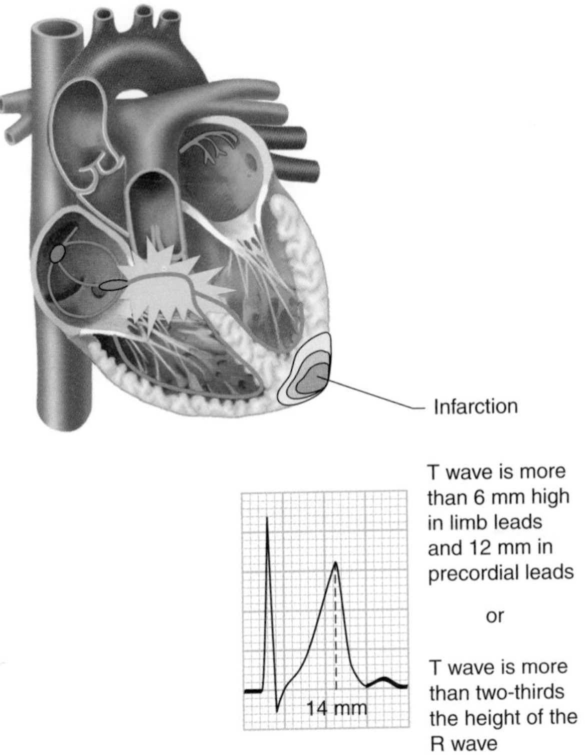

Figure 15-14
Abnormally tall and narrow T waves are another sign of acute myocardial infarction.

Inverted T waves will revert to normal if the ischemia subsides, as with angina. T wave inversion may persist from months to years after a myocardial infarction because of the damage done to the myocardium, which affects its ability to repolarize normally. Therefore, T wave inversion by itself is only indicative of ischemia if it is consistent with the patient's clinical findings and is not diagnostic of myocardial infarction.

INSTRUCTIONAL MOMENT
An indicator that helps differentiate inverted T waves associated with ischemia from inverted T waves associated with other causes is that these other causes produce asymmetrical T waves, with a gentle downslope and rapid upslope.

In the early stages of acute myocardial infarction you may first see abnormally tall and narrow T waves (Figure 15-14). This is called peaking. Within a couple of hours, the T waves invert. In general, the T wave should not be more than 6 mm high in the limb leads and 12 mm high in the precordial leads. A helpful rule to follow is if the T wave is more than two-thirds the height of the R wave, it is abnormal.

CLINICAL MOMENT
In transient ischemia, the ECG must be obtained as close as possible to the onset of chest pain; otherwise, the changes in the ECG may disappear.

 ST Segment Changes

ST Segment Depression

ST segment depression is another characteristic sign of myocardial ischemia (Figure 15-15). ST segment changes are considered significant when the ST segment falls more than 1 mm below the baseline at a point one small square (0.04 seconds) to the right of the J point and is seen in two or more leads facing the same anatomic area of the heart.

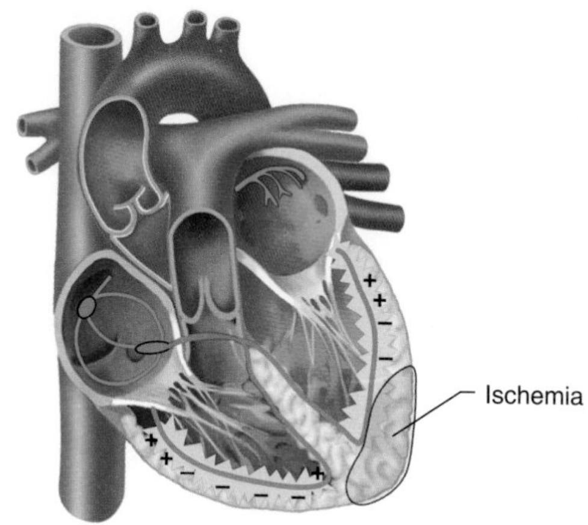

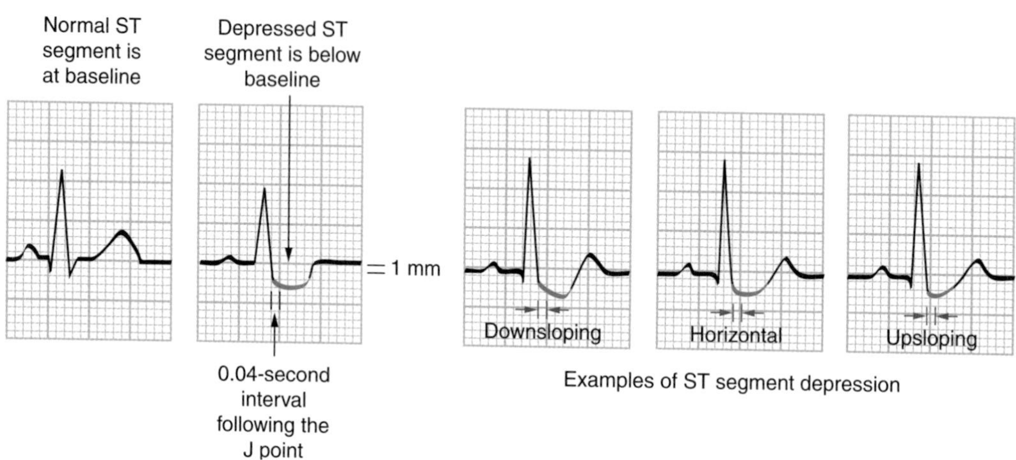

Figure 15-15
ST segment depression is another sign of myocardial ischemia.

CLINICAL MOMENT
The changes we see in the ST segment are due to ischemia delaying the process of repolarization.

KEY CONCEPT
Two characteristic signs of myocardial ischemia are inverted T waves and ST segment depression.

ST segments may be depressed and may or may not include T wave inversion (Figure 15-16).

ST segment ________________ is a characteristic sign of myocardial ischemia. ST segments may be depressed and may or may not include T wave ________________.

[depression] [inversion]

A flat depression of the ST segment occurs with subendocardial infarction (often referred to as subendocardial injury) (Figure 15-17). It may either be horizontal or downsloping in leads where the QRS complex is upright. Subendocardial infarction is an infarct that does not extend through the full surface of the ventricular wall; it involves only a small area of myocardium just below the endocardial lining.

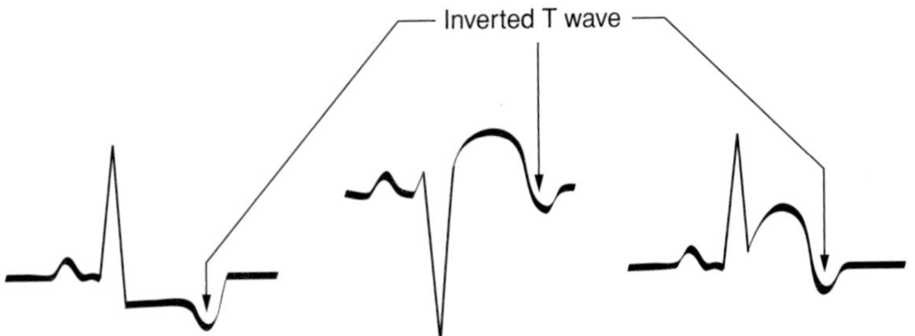

Figure 15-16
Examples of inverted T waves with ST segment depression and elevation.

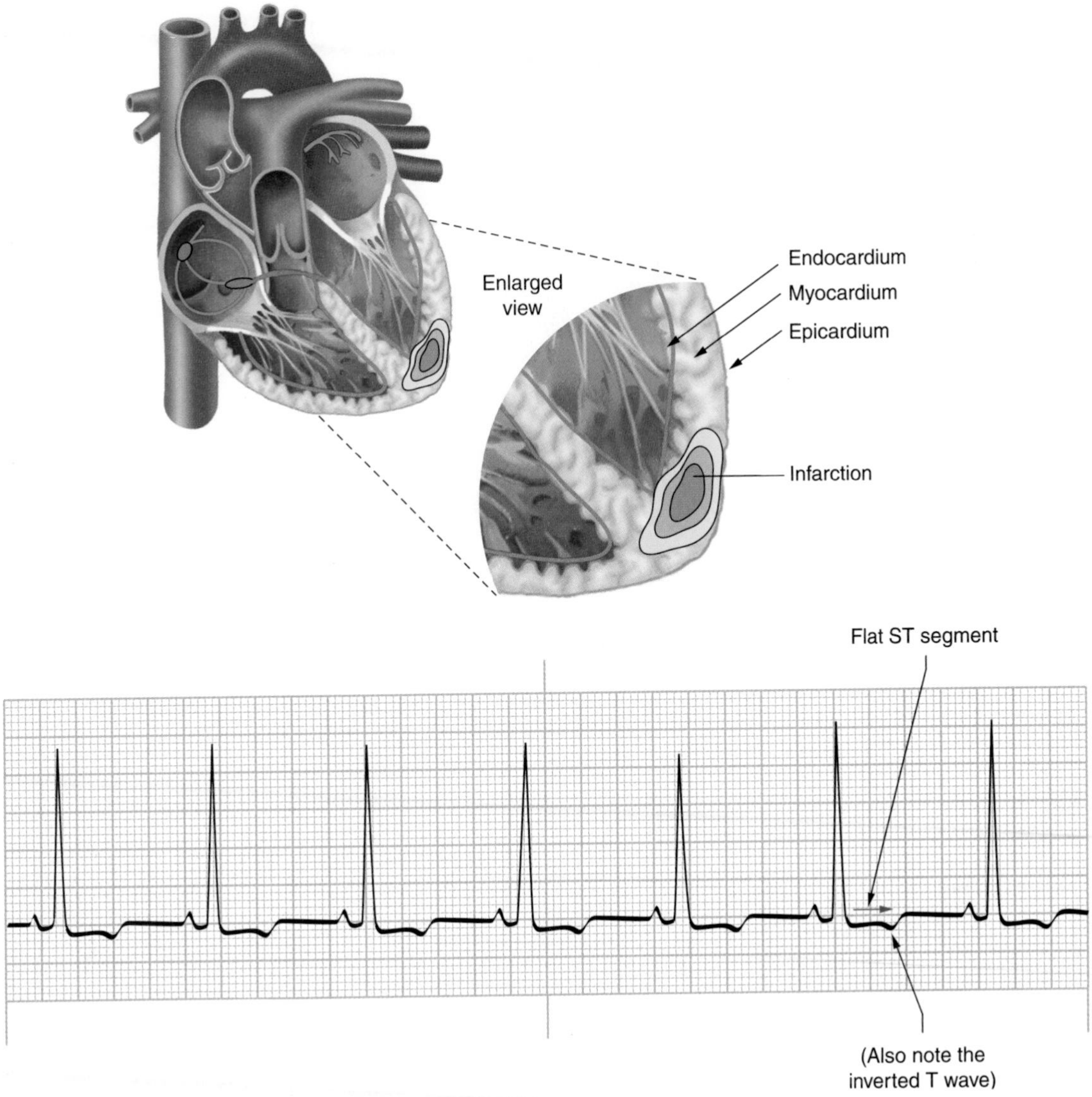

Enlarged view
Endocardium
Myocardium
Epicardium
Infarction

Flat ST segment
(Also note the inverted T wave)

Figure 15-17
The ST segment is flat (or downsloping) in subendocardial infarction.

KEY CONCEPT
Subendocardial infarction produces a flat depression of the ST segment.

Subendocardial infarction involves only a small area of myocardium just below the _______________ lining. With subendocardial infarction, the ST segment depression is _______________.

[endocardial] [flat]

ST Segment Elevation

As described earlier, myocardial injury reflects a degree of cellular damage beyond ischemia. Myocardial injury produces ST segment elevation in the leads facing the affected area (Figure 15-18). This occurs because depolarization of the injured myocardium is incomplete with the tissue remaining electrically more positive than the uninjured areas surrounding it.

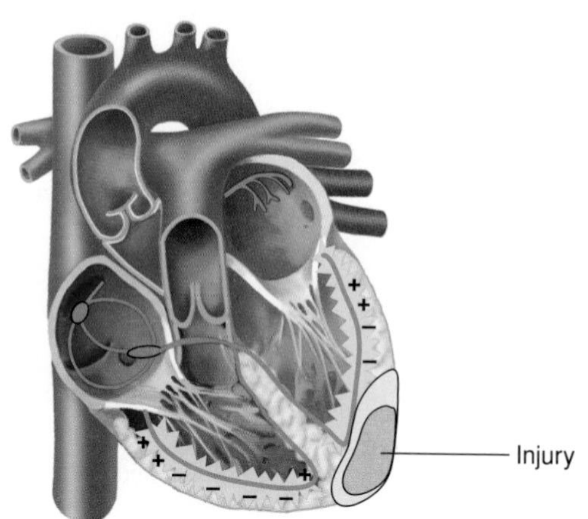

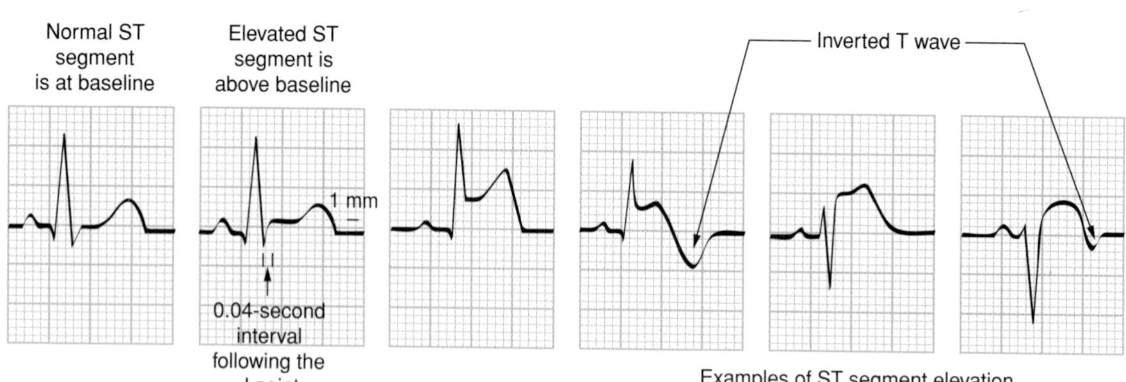

Figure 15-18
ST segment elevation is a sign of myocardial injury.

Myocardial injury produces a distinctive ST segment that bows upward and tends to merge imperceptibly with the T wave. The ST segment may be only slightly elevated or it may be elevated as much as 10 mm above the baseline. It is said to be significant when the ST segment is raised more than 1 mm above the baseline at a point one small square (or 0.04 seconds) to the right of the J point in the limb leads or more than 2 mm in the precordial leads and these changes are seen in two or more leads facing the same anatomic area of the heart. ST segment depression may be seen in the leads opposite the affected area.

CLINICAL MOMENT
A ventricular aneurysm, a weakening and bulging of the ventricular wall, should be suspected if ST segment elevation following a myocardial infarction persists.

ST segment elevation is the earliest reliable sign that myocardial infarction has occurred. It tells us that the myocardial infarction is acute.

KEY CONCEPT
ST segment elevation occurs with myocardial injury. Is the earliest reliable sign that myocardial infarction has occurred and tells us the myocardial infarction is acute.

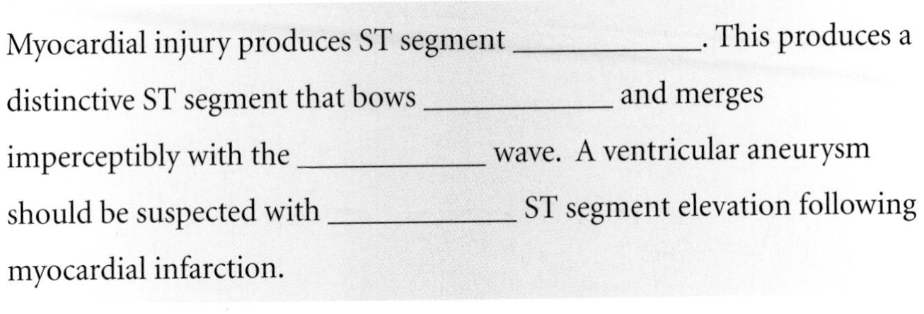

Myocardial injury produces ST segment ____________. This produces a distinctive ST segment that bows ____________ and merges imperceptibly with the ____________ wave. A ventricular aneurysm should be suspected with ____________ ST segment elevation following myocardial infarction.

[elevation] [upward] [T] [persistent]

Other than in myocardial injury, ST segment elevation may be seen in ventricular hypertrophy, conduction abnormalities, pulmonary embolism, spontaneous pneumothorax, intracranial hemorrhage, hyperkalemia, and pericarditis (Figure 15-19). With pericarditis, an inflammation of the

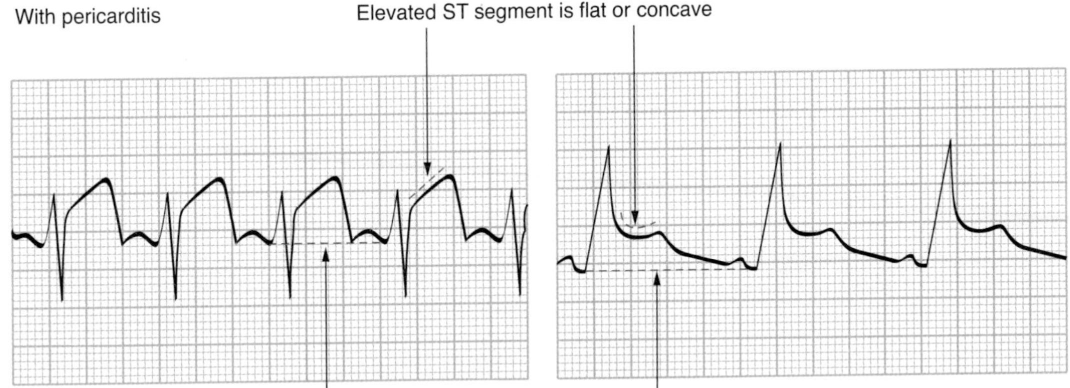

Figure 15-19
ST segment elevation may be caused by a variety of other conditions, including pericarditis.

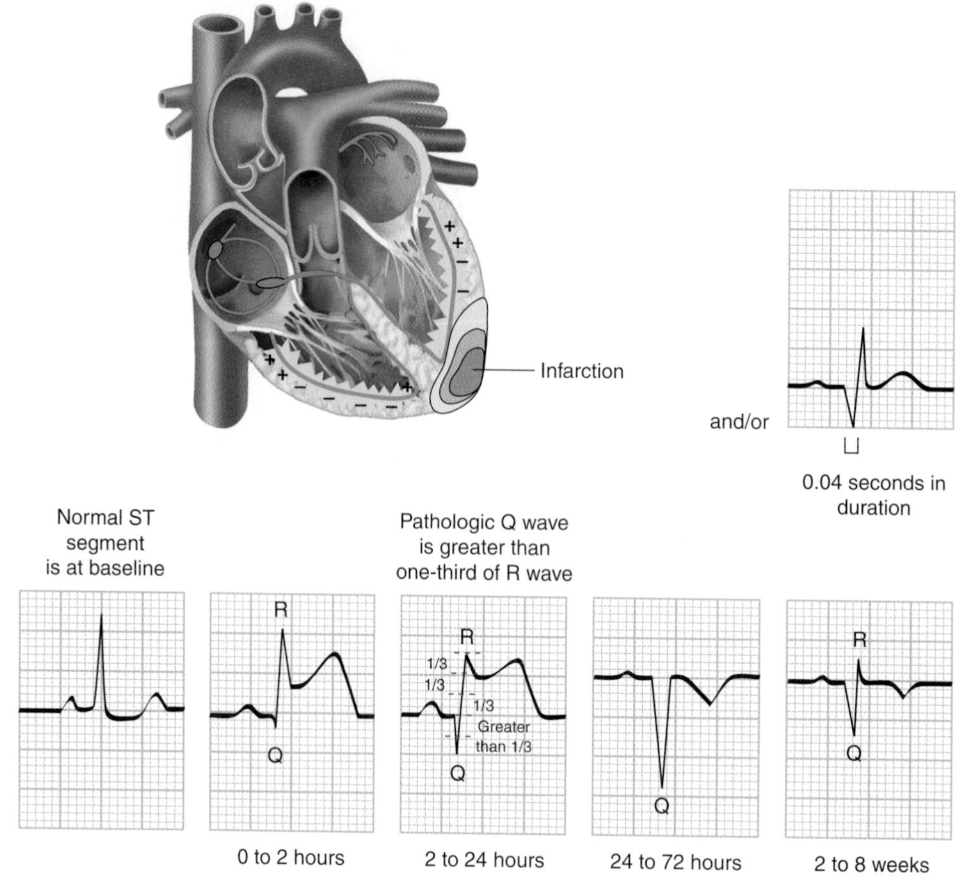

Figure 15-20
Pathological Q waves are a sign of myocardial infarction.

INSTRUCTIONAL MOMENT
To help differentiate it from other conditions, the ST segment elevation in myocardial injury is more localized and accompanied by ST segment depression in the leads opposite the injured area.

heart, the ST segment elevation is usually flat or concave (the middle sags downward) and seen in all leads except aV_R. This resolves with time. It also seems to elevate the entire T wave off the baseline, with the baseline gradually slanting back downward all the way to the next QRS complex. The P wave is often a part of this downward slanting of the baseline.

Q Wave Changes

The presence of pathologic (also called significant) Q waves indicates that irreversible myocardial damage has occurred (Figure 15-20). As the Q wave develops, the R wave disappears. While we can expect to see the Q waves within several hours of the onset of infarction, in some patients they may take several days to appear. Further, by the time the Q waves appear, the ST segment usually has returned to the baseline. Q waves often persist for the lifetime of the patient.

For the Q waves to be considered pathologic, they must

- Be greater than 0.04 seconds in duration
- Have a depth at least one-third the height of the R wave in the same QRS complex
- Be present in two or more contiguous leads (leads that look at the same area of the heart)

Q waves develop because the infarcted areas of the heart fail to depolarize producing an electrical void (Figure 15-21). As a result, the electrical

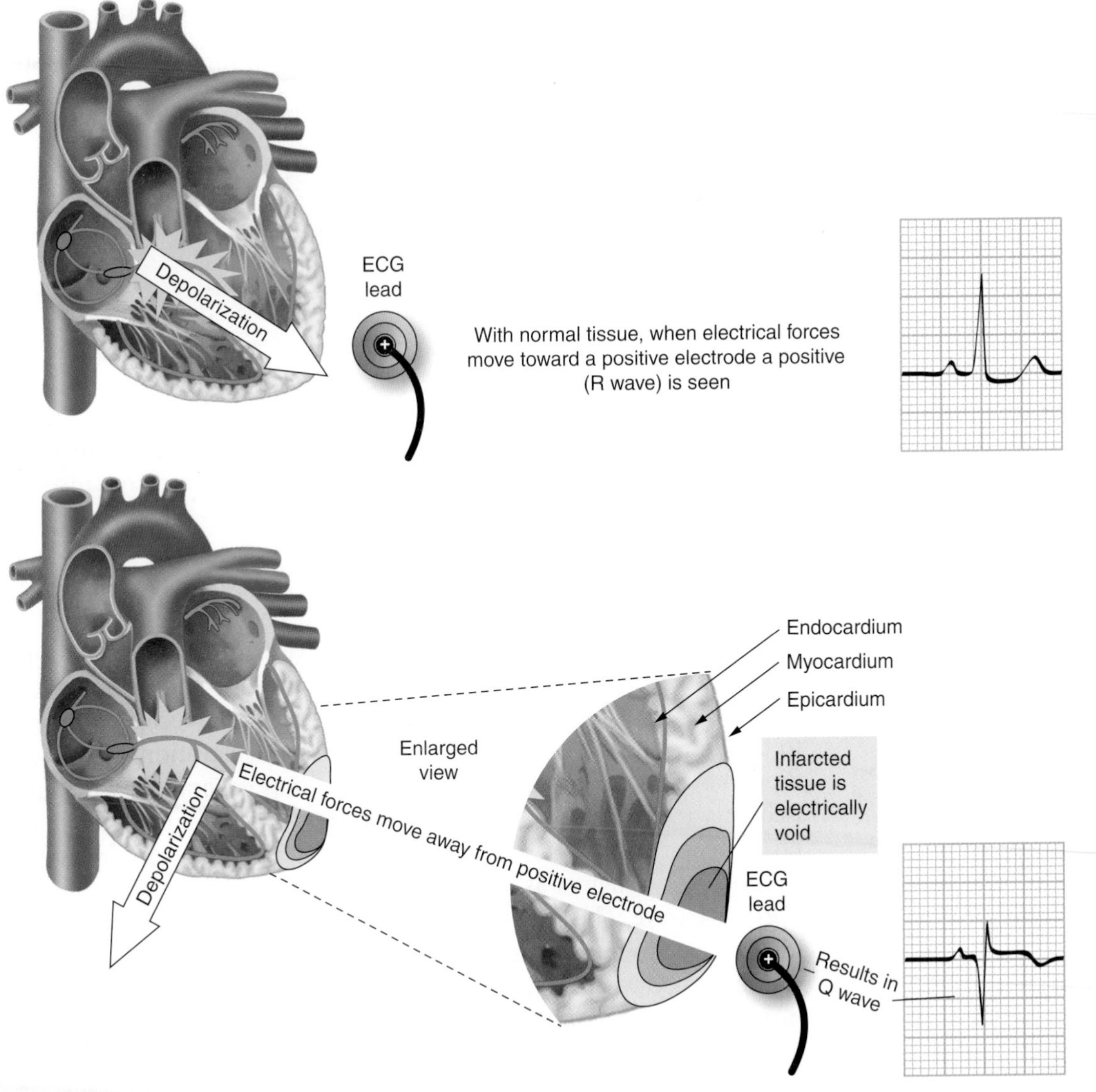

Figure 15-21
Q waves occur because infarcted tissue is electrically silent allowing the wave of depolarization moving away from the positive electrode to be seen.

CLINICAL MOMENT
Since lead aV_R normally has a very deep Q wave, due to its unique position on the frontal plane, it should not be considered when assessing possible infarction.

forces of the heart are directed away from the area of infarction. An electrode overlying the infarction therefore records a deep negative deflection, a Q wave. The electrical activity of the heart moves away from aV_R, so a Q wave is commonly seen here and therefore is not considered significant.

Non-Q Wave Infarcts

It is possible for a myocardial infarction to occur without Q waves developing. This is thought to occur when the amount of tissue infarcted is small or diffuse.

CLINICAL MOMENT
In the past, Q wave infarcts were referred to as transmural, meaning that the infarct extended completely through the myocardial wall. However, recent discoveries indicate that this is not the case and confirms that the development of Q waves has more to do with the resulting electrical void than it does the amount of tissue injured.

Pathologic Q waves indicate the presence of ______________ myocardial damage. To be considered pathologic, the Q waves must be greater than ______________ seconds in duration and have a depth at least one- ______________ the height of the R wave in the same QRS complex. They must also be present in ______________ or more contiguous leads.

[irreversible] [0.04] [third] [two]

KEY CONCEPT
Pathologic Q waves indicate the presence of irreversible myocardial damage or myocardial infarction. They tend to occur within several hours of the onset of infarction; however, in some patients they may take several days to appear.

Reciprocal Changes

The simplest explanation of reciprocal changes is that they are a mirror image that occurs when you have two leads viewing the same myocardial infarction from opposite angles (Figure 15-22).

An example is when you have a lead located over the infarcted area and a lead on the direct opposite side of the heart. The infarcted zone is electrically neutral, so the lead directly over the heart registers only an unopposed vector moving away from it. This causes the waveform to be negative, thus producing a Q wave. Next, the lead registers the other vectors contributing to the QRS and the injured tissue that causes ST elevation. The T wave is flipped because of repolarization abnormalities generated by the areas of ischemia and injury. The electrode opposite of the infarction sees an unopposed vector coming at it, giving rise to a high R wave. This lead registers the zones of ischemia as a pattern of ST depression and the injury as an upright T wave. The second lead essentially sees the mirror image of what the first electrode saw. The recording made by the lead on the wall opposite the myocardial infarction is registering the reciprocal change of that myocardial infarction. This concept is particularly important as it relates to looking for ECG changes in areas of the heart (posterior and the right ventricle) where there is not a lead directly over that area.

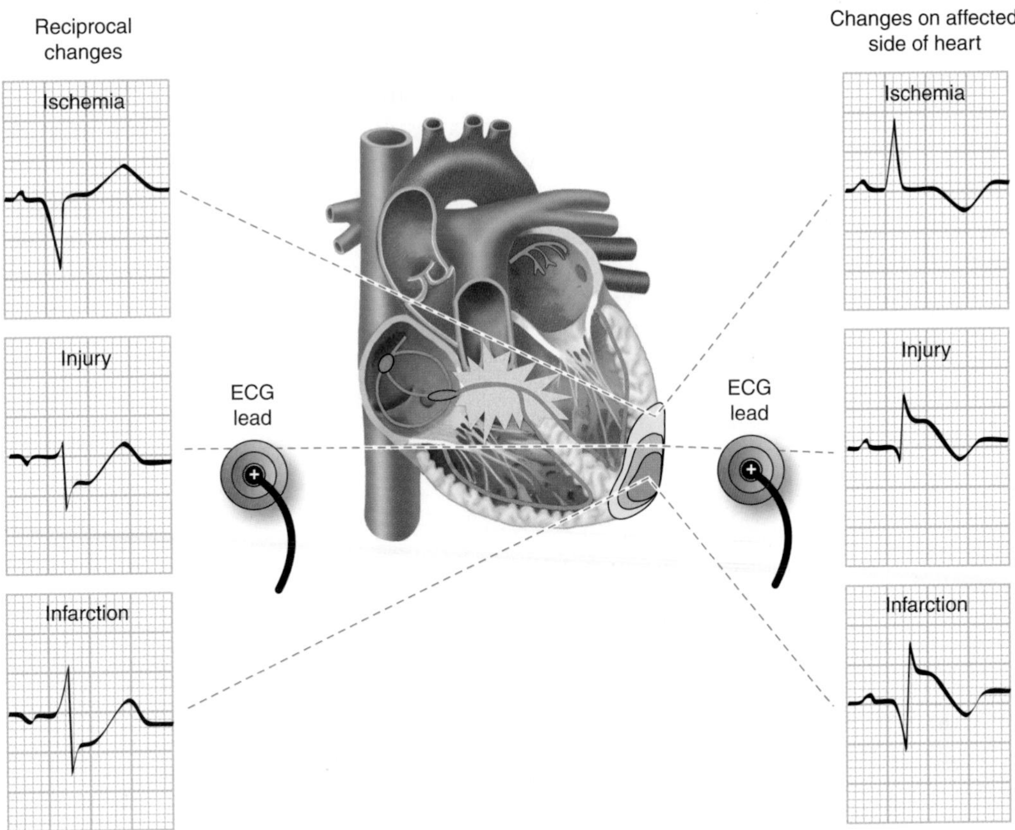

Figure 15-22
Reciprocal changes are a mirror image (opposite image) that occurs when two leads view the same infarction from opposite angles.

Identifying the Myocardial Infarction Location

As we discussed earlier, the ECG can help identify which coronary artery or branch is occluded in the presence of myocardial ischemia, injury, and/or infarction. Leads II, III, and aV_F provide a view of the tissue supplied by the right coronary artery, while leads I, aV_L, V_1, V_2, V_3, V_4, V_5, and V_6 view the tissue supplied by the left coronary artery.

When evaluating the extent of infarction produced by a left coronary artery occlusion, it is important to determine how many of these leads show changes consistent with an acute infarction. The more of these eight leads demonstrating acute changes, the larger the infarction.

CLINICAL MOMENT
Coronary artery anatomy can vary between given individuals, so the precise vessel involved is not always predictable from the ECG.

CLINICAL MOMENT
The other two precordial leads, V_5 and V_6, while located more laterally, may also help identify anterior infarction.

Anterior Infarction

Anterior infarction involves the anterior surface of the left ventricle (Figure 15-23). It may occur as a result of left anterior descending artery occlusion. Leads V_1, V_2, V_3, and V_4 are immediately over the anterior surface of the heart; therefore, they provide the best view for identifying anterior myocardial infarction. ST segment elevation, T wave inversion, and the development of significant Q waves in these leads indicate myocardial infarction involving the anterior surface of the heart.

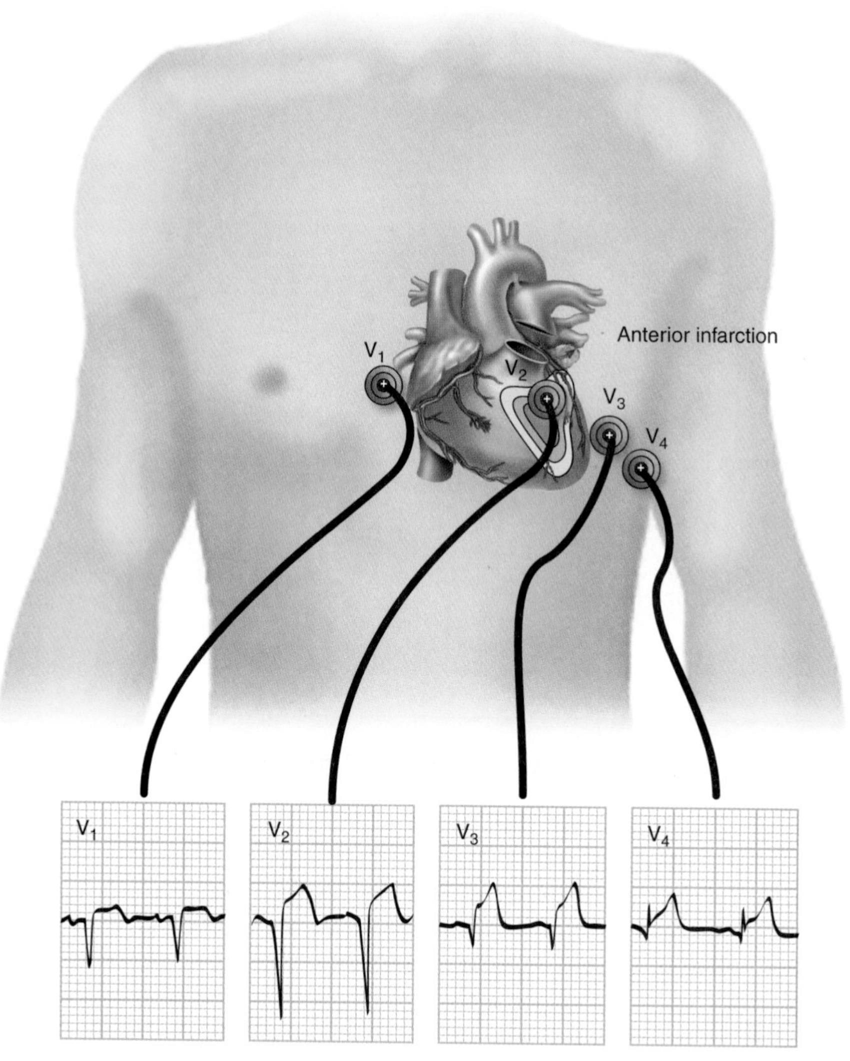

Figure 15-23
Leads V_1, V_2, V_3, and V_4 are used to identify anterior myocardial infarction.

Leads V_1, V_2, and V_3 overlie the ventricular septum, so ischemic changes seen in these leads, and possibly in the adjacent precordial leads, are often considered to be septal infarctions (Figure 15-24).

 Lateral Infarction

Infarction of the left lateral wall of the heart is referred to as a lateral wall infarction. It is often due to occlusion of the left circumflex artery. With lateral wall infarction you should see ECG changes such as ST segment elevation, T wave inversion, and the development of significant Q waves in leads I, aV_L, V_5, and V_6 (Figure 15-25).

KEY CONCEPT
Leads V_1, V_2, V_3, and V_4 provide the best view for identifying anterior left ventricular infarction. Leads V_5 and V_6, while located more laterally, may also help identify anterior infarction.

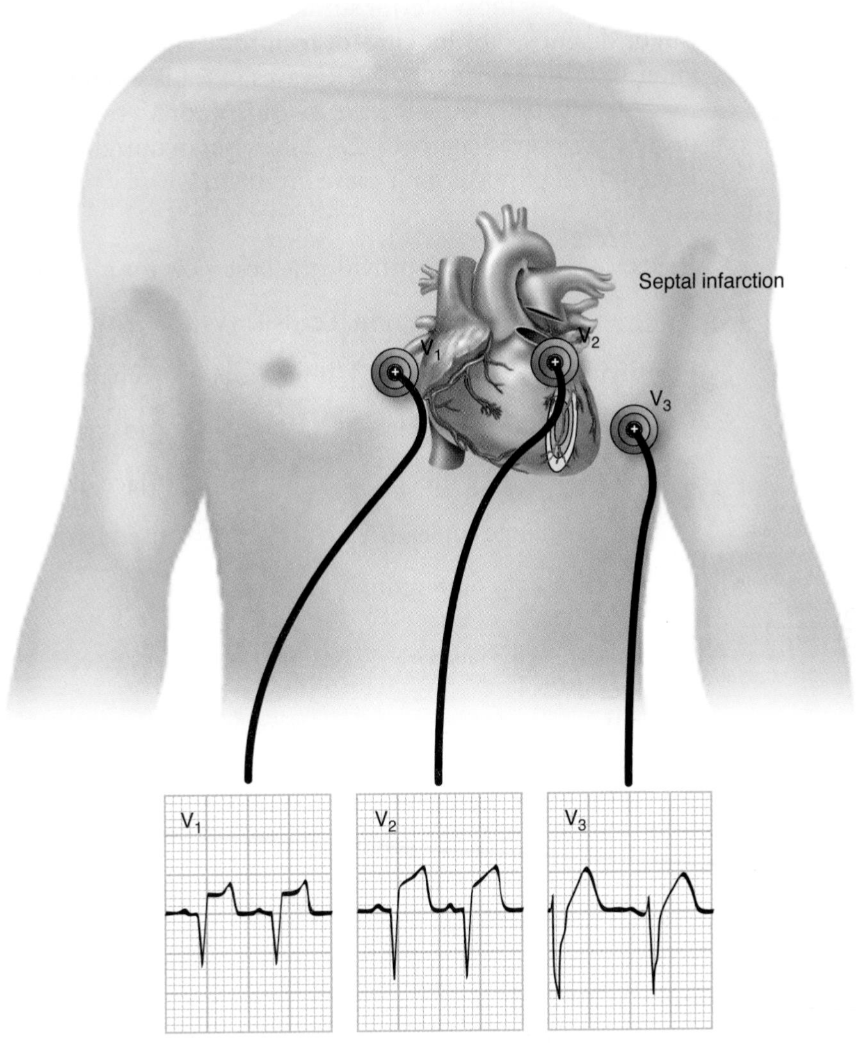

Figure 15-24
Leads V_1, V_2, and V_3 are used to identify septal myocardial infarction.

CLINICAL MOMENT
Limb leads I and aV_L and precordial leads V_5 and V_6 view the lateral surface of the heart.

 Inferior Infarction

Inferior infarction involves the inferior or diaphragmatic surface of the heart. It is frequently caused by occlusion of the right coronary artery and its descending branch. ST segment elevation, T wave inversion, and the development of significant Q waves in leads II, III, and aV_F indicate myocardial infarction involving the inferior surface of the heart (Figure 15-26).

KEY CONCEPT
ECG changes in leads I, aV_L, V_5, and V_6, such as ST segment elevation, T wave inversion, and the development of significant Q waves, indicate left lateral wall infarction.

Posterior Infarction

Posterior infarctions are usually caused by occlusion of the right coronary artery and involve the posterior surface of the heart. Since there are no ECG leads over the posterior surface of the heart, true posterior infarctions can be diagnosed by looking for reciprocal changes in leads V_1 and V_2 (the anterior leads). Normally, the R waves in leads V_1 and V_2 are mostly negative. An unusually large R wave in leads V_1 or V_2 can be the reciprocal of a posterior Q wave (Figure 15-27). Likewise, an upright T wave in these leads is reciprocal of posterior T wave inversion.

KEY CONCEPT
ECG changes consistent with myocardial infarction in leads II, III, and aV_F indicate myocardial infarction involving the inferior surface of the heart.

Leads V_1, V_2, V_3, and V_4 provide the best view for identifying _______________ infarction. Leads I, aV_L, V_5, and V_6 are best for identifying _______________ infarction. ECG changes consistent with myocardial infarction in leads II, III, and aV_F indicate myocardial infarction involving the _______________ surface of the heart. Reciprocal changes in leads V_1 and V_2 can be used to diagnose _______________ infarctions.

[anterior] [lateral] [inferior] [posterior]

KEY CONCEPT
Posterior infarctions can be diagnosed by looking for reciprocal changes in leads V_1 and V_2 (the anterior leads).

While this is useful information, remember, these guidelines are generalized as each person's ECG tracings will vary due to variances in body structure, underlying heart and lung disease, and other factors. Thus, abnormal findings may overlap somewhat in the various leads.

For each of the *Practice Makes Perfect* exercises starting on page 490 determine the area of infarction. Answers to these exercises can be found in Appendix A.

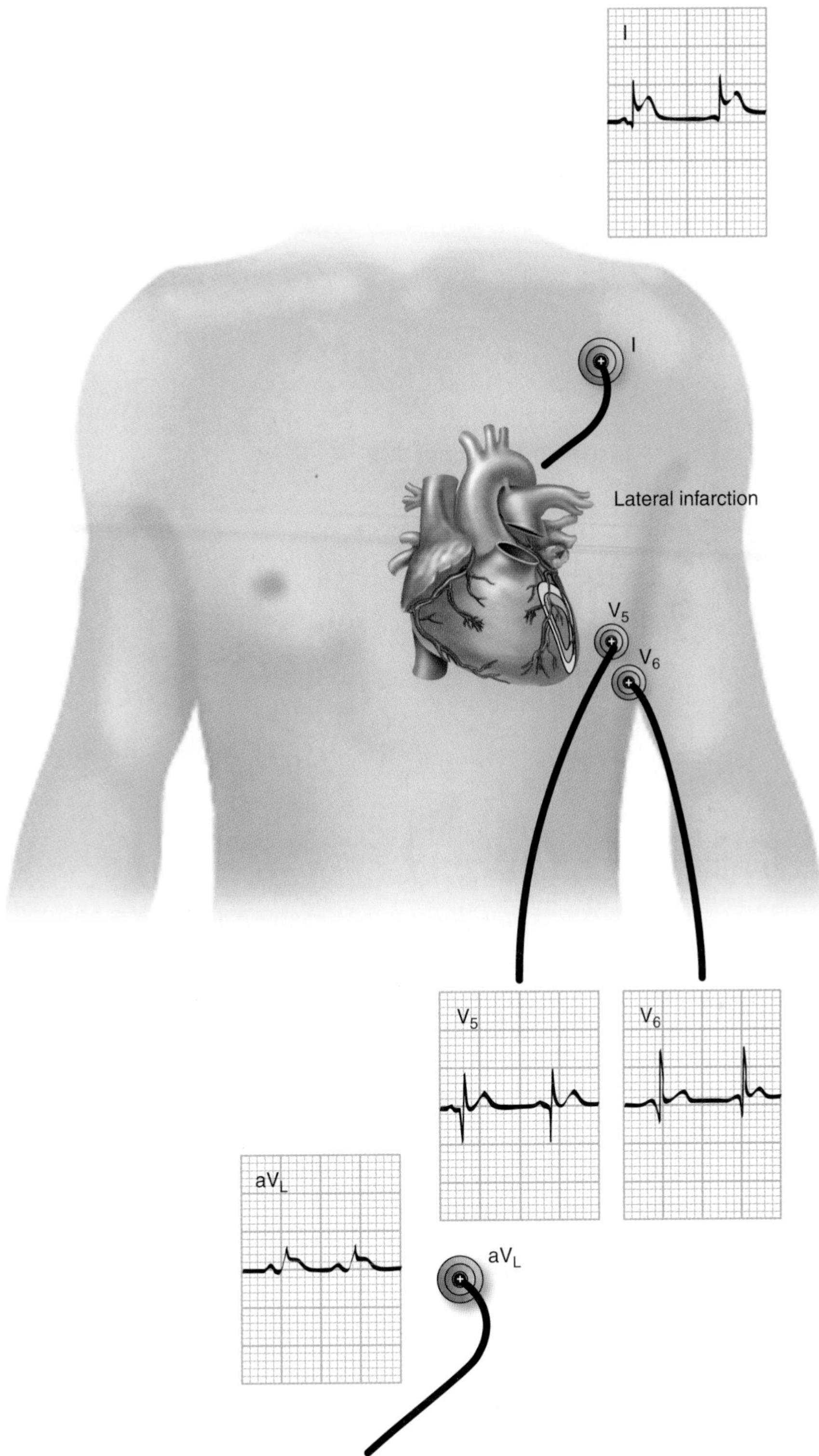

Figure 15-25
Leads I, aV_L, V_5, and V_6 are used to identify lateral myocardial infarction.

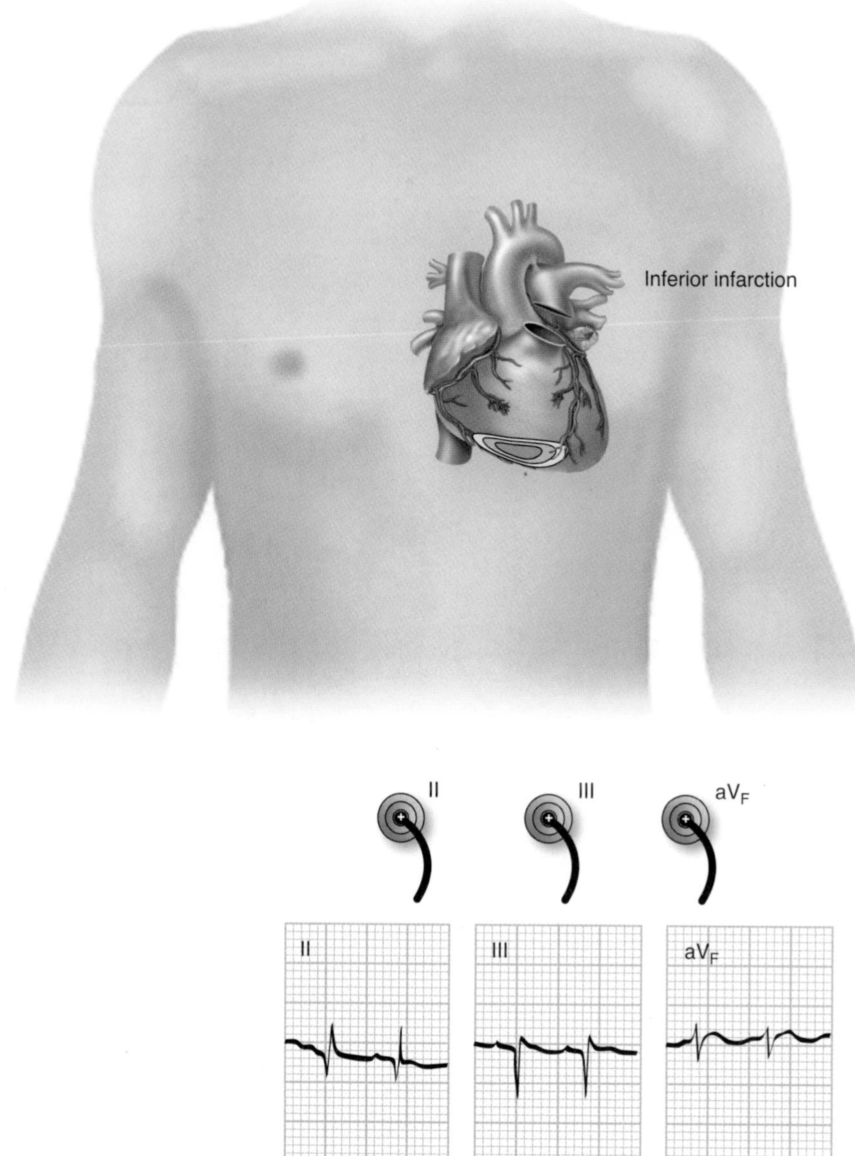

Figure 15-26
Leads II, III, and aV_F are used to identify inferior myocardial infarction.

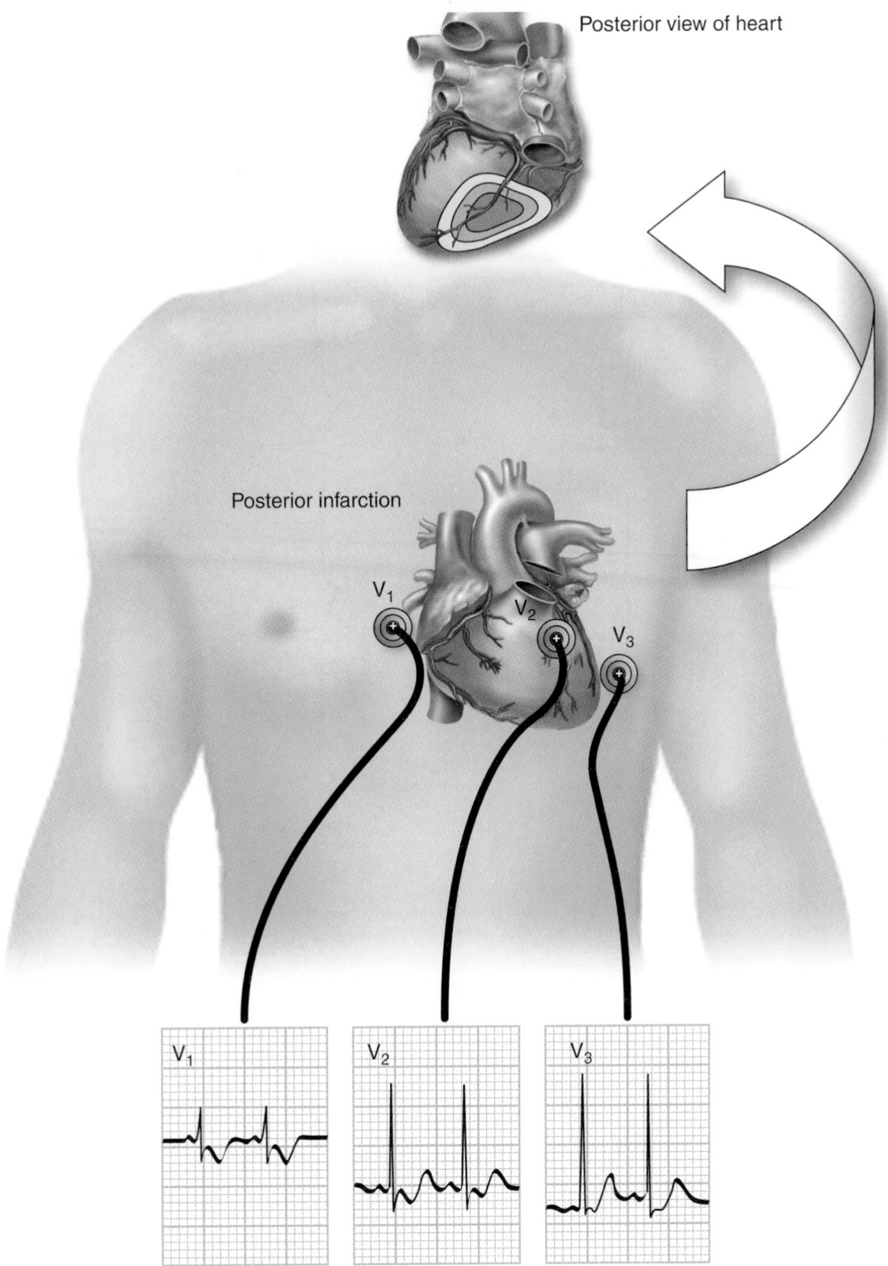

Figure 15-27
Leads V_1 and V_2 are used to identify posterior myocardial infarction.

PRACTICE. . . MAKES PERFECT

1. Identify the location where ischemia, injury, and/or infarction is likely present.

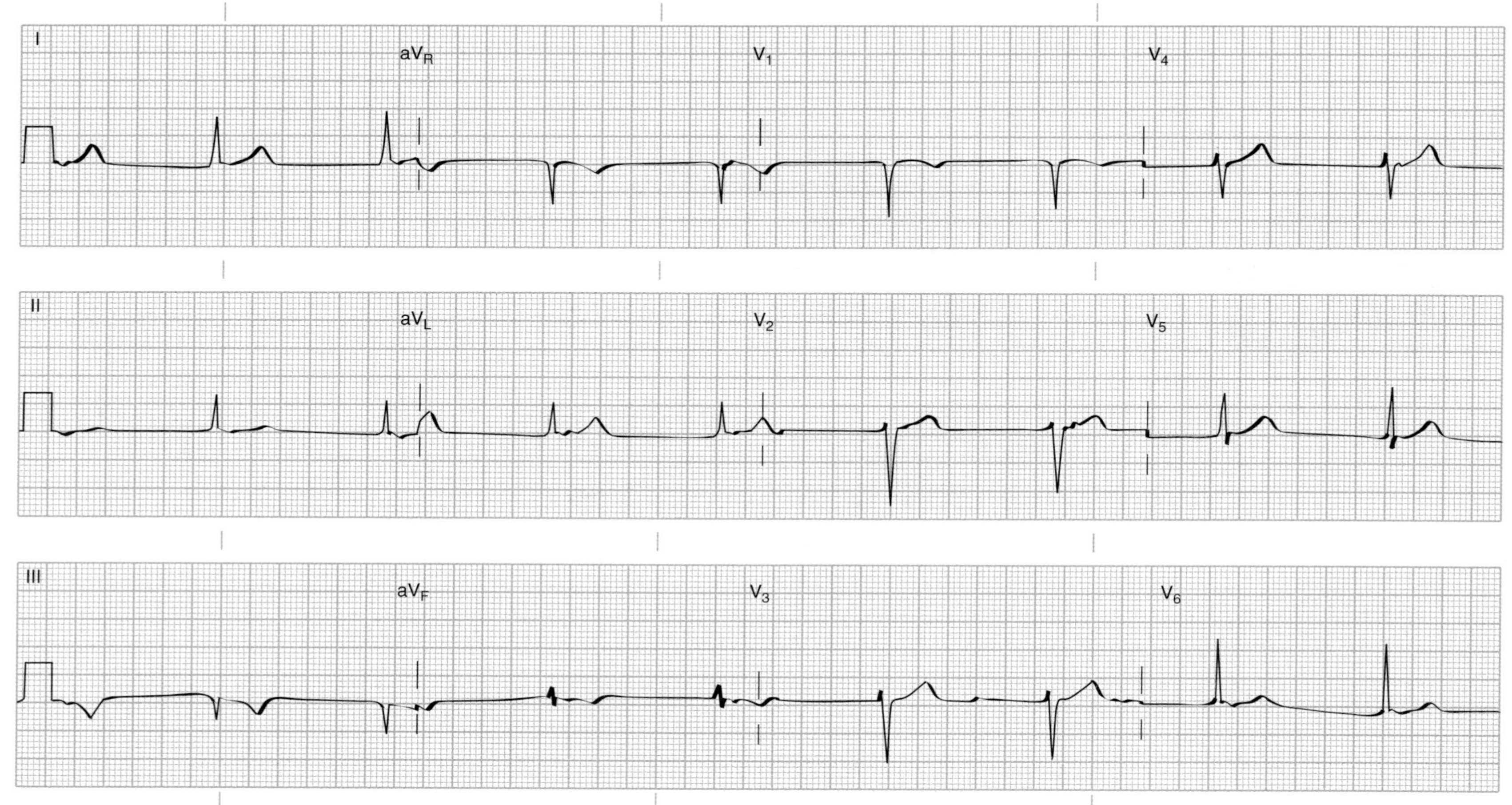

** Note that the heart rate calculator will not be accurate with these 12-lead ECG strips.*

PRACTICE. . . MAKES PERFECT

2. Identify the location where ischemia, injury, and/or infarction is likely present.

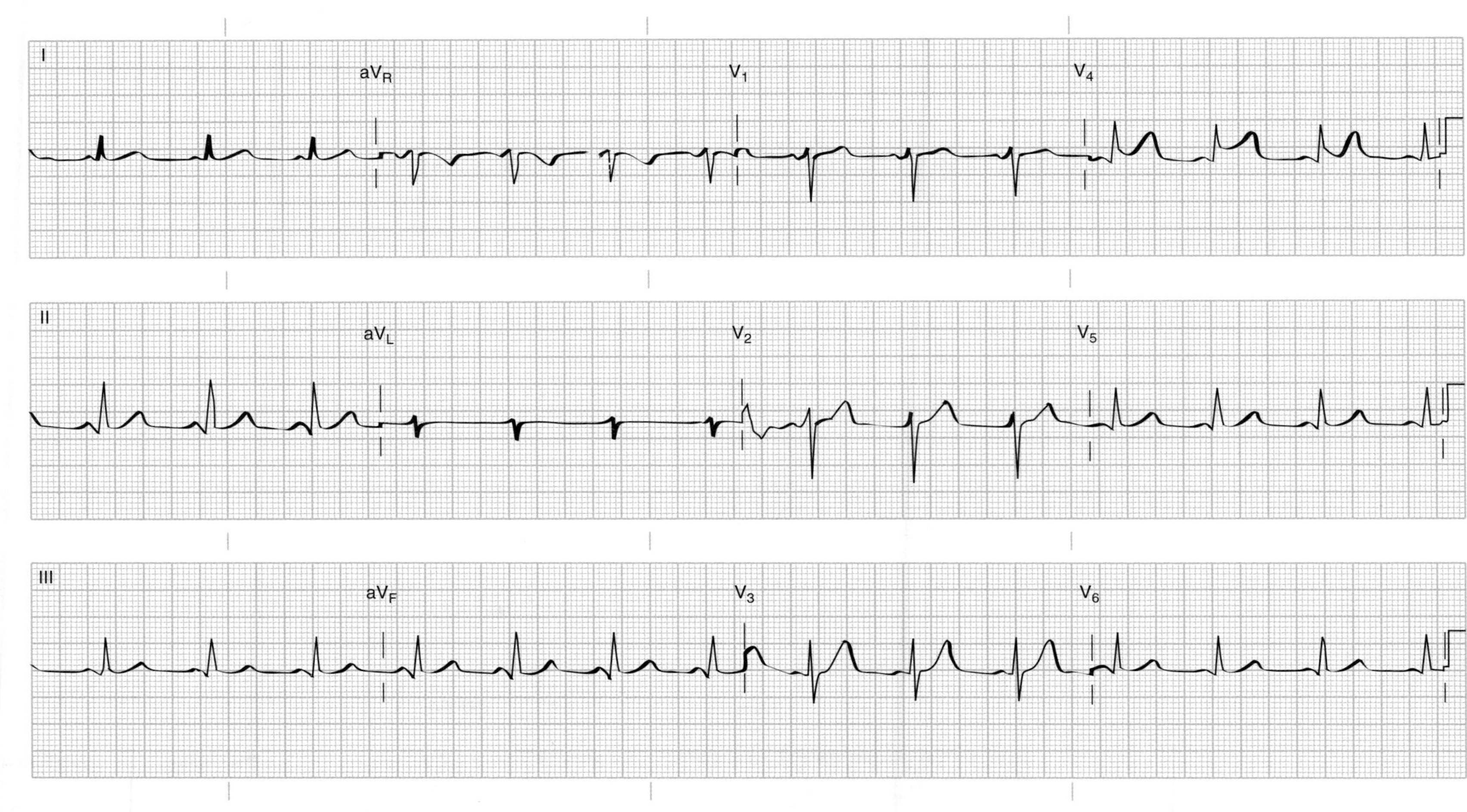

* Note that the heart rate calculator will not be accurate with these 12-lead ECG strips.

PRACTICE. . . MAKES PERFECT

3. Identify the location where ischemia, injury, and/or infarction is likely present.

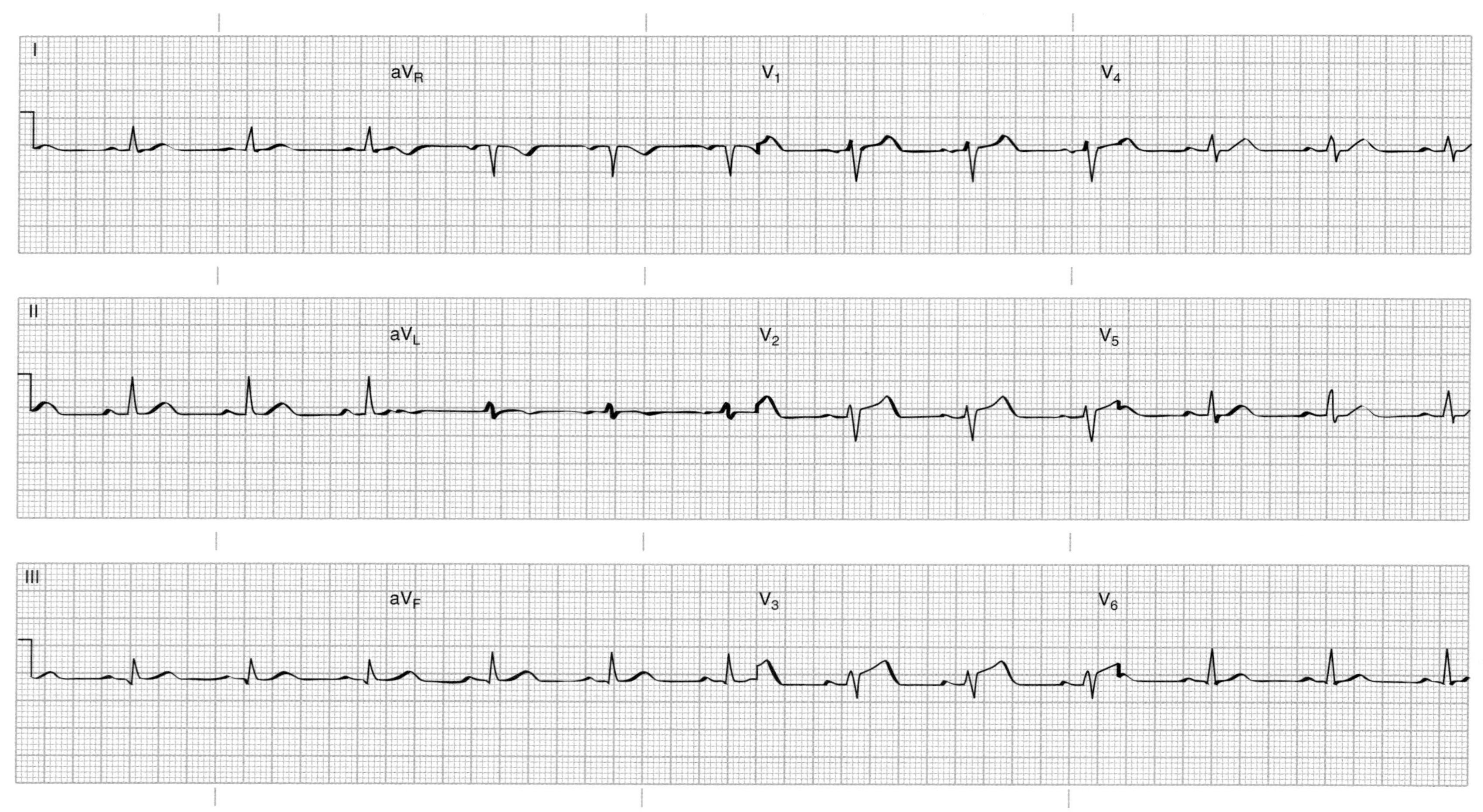

* *Note that the heart rate calculator will not be accurate with these 12-lead ECG strips.*

PRACTICE. . . MAKES PERFECT

4. Identify the location where ischemia, injury, and/or infarction is likely present.

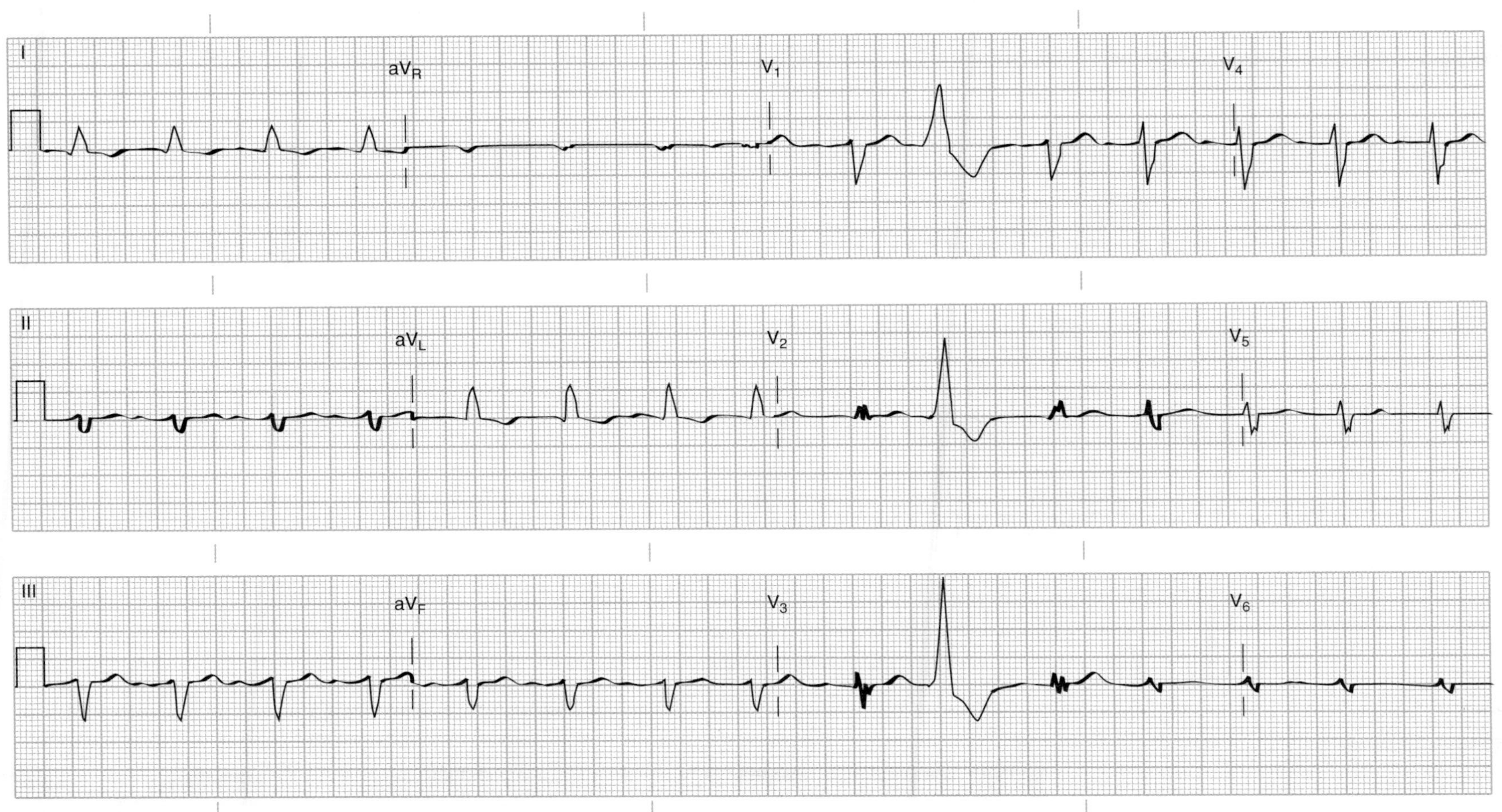

* *Note that the heart rate calculator will not be accurate with these 12-lead ECG strips.*

PRACTICE. . . MAKES PERFECT

5. Identify the location where ischemia, injury, and/or infarction is likely present.

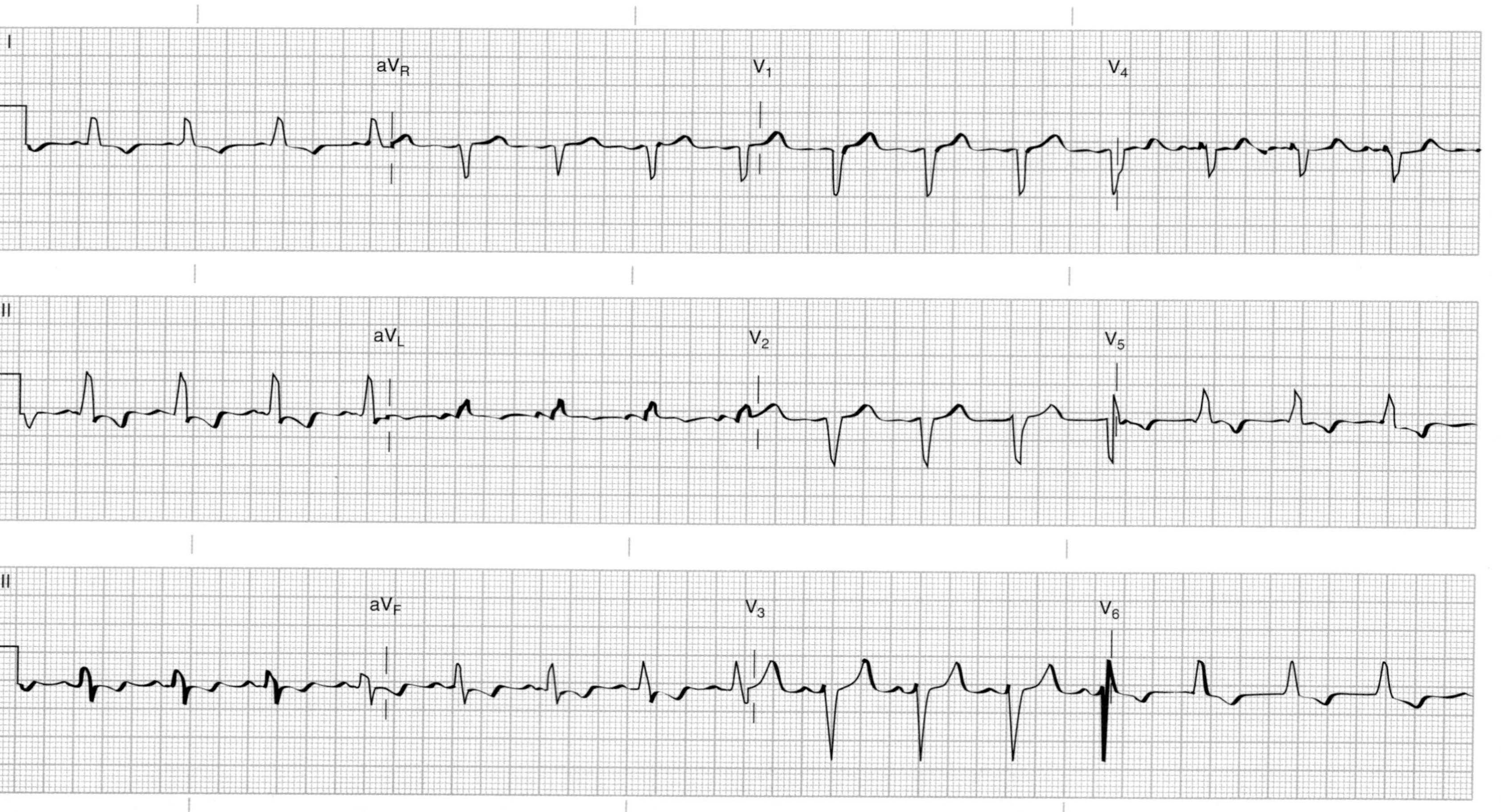

* *Note that the heart rate calculator will not be accurate with these 12-lead ECG strips.*

Key Points

- The oxygen and nutrient demand of the heart is extremely high; therefore, it requires its own continuous blood supply. The coronary arteries deliver the needed blood supply to the myocardial cells.
- The coronary veins return deoxygenated venous blood to the right atrium via the coronary sinus.
- By increasing coronary blood flow, through vasodilation, the coronary arteries satisfy increased myocardial oxygen demands.
- The ST segment can be compared to the PR segment to evaluate ST segment depression or elevation.
- The Q wave is the first part of the QRS complex. It is the first downward deflection from the baseline. It is not always present.
- The ST segment is the flat line that follows the QRS complex and connects it to the T wave.
- The T wave is slightly asymmetrical and oriented in the same direction as the preceding QRS complex.
- Myocardial ischemia, injury, and death can occur with the interruption of coronary artery blood.
- Ischemia results from decreased oxygen delivery to the myocardium. It can be reversed if the supply of oxygen is restored or increased to a level that satisfies the myocardial oxygen demand.
- Myocardial injury results if ischemia is allowed to progress untreated.
- Myocardial infarction is the death of myocardial cells.
- The ECG can help identify the presence of ischemia, injury, and/or infarction of the heart muscle.
- Inverted T waves and ST segment depression are considered two characteristic signs of myocardial ischemia.
- Subendocardial infarction results in a flat depression of the ST segment.
- ST segment elevation occurs with myocardial injury. It is the earliest reliable sign that myocardial infarction has occurred and tells us the myocardial infarction is acute.
- Pathologic Q waves indicate the presence of irreversible myocardial damage or a past myocardial infarction.
- Myocardial infarction can occur without the development of Q waves.
- Leads V_1, V_2, V_3, and V_4 provide the best view for identifying anterior myocardial infarction. Leads V_5 and V_6, while located more laterally, may also help identify anterior infarction.
- Lateral infarction is identified by ECG changes such as ST segment elevation; T wave inversion; and the development of significant Q waves in leads I, aV_L, V_5, and V_6.
- Inferior infarction is determined by ECG changes such as ST segment elevation; T wave inversion; and the development of significant Q waves in leads II, III, and aV_F.
- Posterior infarctions can be diagnosed by looking for reciprocal changes in leads V_1 and V_2.

Assess Your Understanding

The following questions give you a chance to assess your understanding of the material discussed in this chapter. The answers can be found in Appendix A.

1. The blood vessels that supply the myocardial cells with a continuous supply of oxygen and nutrients are referred to as the
   a. coronary veins.
   b. cerebral arteries.
   c. coronary arteries.
   d. carotid arteries.
2. The heart requires its own blood supply because the demand for oxygen of the myocardial cells is extremely high.
   a. True
   b. False
3. ST segment depression or elevation can be evaluated by comparing the ST segment to the
   a. Q wave.
   b. PR segment.
   c. position of the T wave.
   d. QT interval.
4. Which is true regarding the normal Q wave?
   a. It is always present.
   b. It is a small positive deflection from the baseline.
   c. It has a duration of less than 0.04 seconds.
   d. It is greater than 25% the amplitude of the R wave in that lead.
5. The ST segment
   a. contains at least two waves.
   b. begins at the peak of the R wave and gradually curves downward to the T wave.
   c. represents right and left ventricular depolarization.
   d. is the line that follows the QRS complex and connects it to the T wave.
6. The normal T wave is
   a. perfectly round.
   b. not more than 5 mm tall in the limb leads.
   c. oriented in the opposite direction of the preceding QRS complex.
   d. normally inverted in lead II.
7. Myocardial infarction
   a. is caused by coronary artery vasodilation.
   b. is also known as angina or angina pectoris.
   c. is the death of injured myocardial cells.
   d. can be reversed if the supply of oxygen and nutrients can be increased to a level that meets the myocardial oxygen demand.
8. Myocardial _______________ is the most severe result of an interruption of coronary artery blood flow.
   a. ischemia
   b. infarction
   c. injury
   d. interruption
9. The ECG can help identify the presence of ischemia, injury, and/or infarction of the heart muscle.
   a. True
   b. False
10. All of the following are key ECG indicators of myocardial ischemia, injury, and/or infarction EXCEPT
    a. inversion of the T wave.
    b. absence of Q waves in the limb leads.
    c. elevation of the ST segment.
    d. peaking of the T wave.
11. All the characteristic ECG indicators must be present to diagnose myocardial ischemia, injury, or infarction.
    a. True
    b. False

12. Match the following ECG changes with the cardiac condition in which they are seen.

ECG Change		*Myocardial Condition*
Enlarged Q waves or presence of new Q waves	___	a. ischemia
ST segment depression	___	b. injury
ST segment elevation	___	c. infarction

13. ST segment depression is considered significant when the
    a. ST segment falls more than 1 mm below the baseline at a point one small square to the right of the J point.
    b. changes are seen in at least one or more leads facing the opposite anatomic area of the heart.
    c. associated T wave is inverted.
    d. All of the above.

14. On the following illustrations, draw examples of each.
    a. Inverted T wave.
    b. Depressed ST segment.
    c. Elevated ST segment.
    d. Enlarged Q wave.

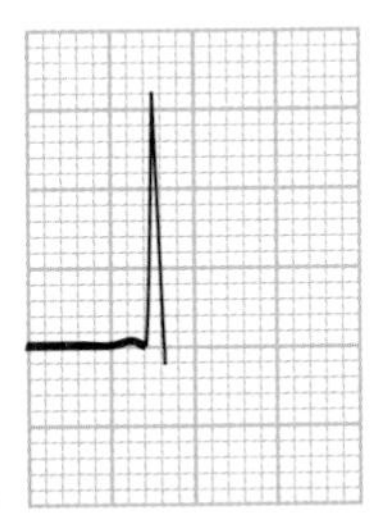
A

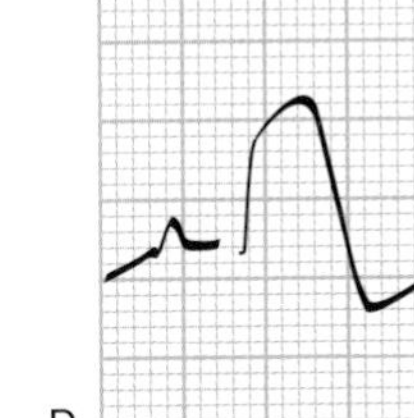
C

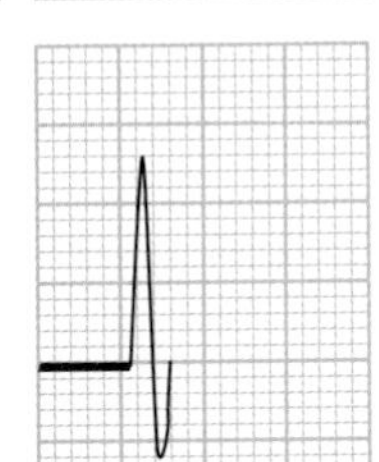
B

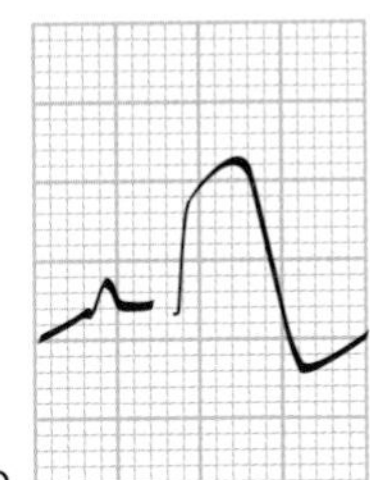
D

15. Inverted T waves associated with myocardial ischemia
    a. indicate the ischemia is present through the full thickness of the myocardium.
    b. occur just at the start of the ischemia.
    c. are asymmetrical.
    d. are observed best in the limb leads.

16. Of the following three examples of inverted T waves, circle those that are symmetrical.

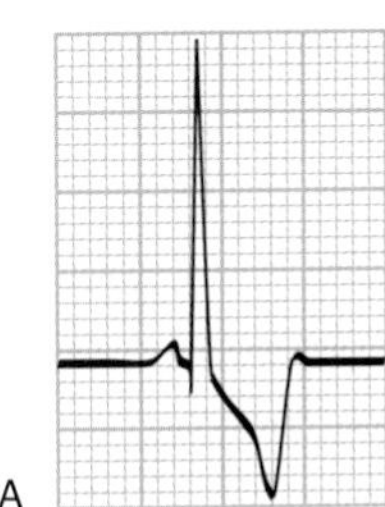
A

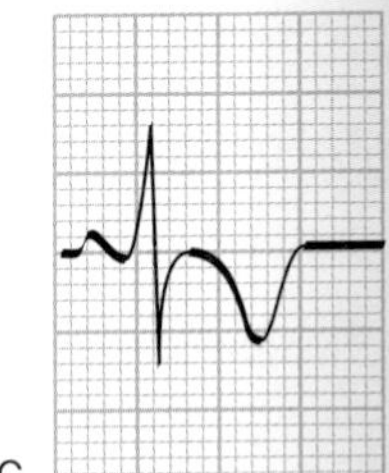
C

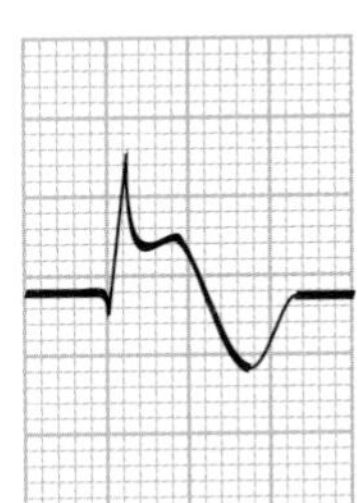
B

17. Two characteristic signs of myocardial ischemia are inverted T waves and ST segment elevation.
    a. True
    b. False

18. ST segment elevation associated with myocardial injury
    a. is usually only slight.
    b. produces a distinctive ST segment that has a sharp inclination upward and tends to merge abruptly with the T wave.
    c. occurs because there is rapid depolarization of the injured myocardium.
    d. is seen in the leads facing the affected area.

19. ST segment elevation is the earliest reliable ECG indication that myocardial infarction has occurred.
    a. True
    b. False

20. The appearance of Q waves
    a. indicates that irreversible myocardial damage has occurred.
    b. usually disappears after the myocardial infarction ends.
    a. always occurs in conjunction with ST segment elevation.
    d. is considered pathological if they are less than 0.04 seconds in duration.

21. Match the following leads where ECG changes will be seen with type of infarction.

Infarction Location		*Affected Leads*
Anterior	___	a. V_1 and V_2 (for reciprocal changes)
Inferior	___	b. II, III, and aV_F
Lateral	___	c. V_1, V_2, V_3, and V_4
Posterior	___	d. I, aV_L, V_5, and V_6

Referring to the scenario at the beginning of this chapter, answer the following questions.

22. What part of the heart was affected by the myocardial infarction?
    a. Anterior.
    b. Anteroseptal.
    c. Posterior.
    d. Inferior.

23. What is the minimum amount of ST elevation required to make the diagnosis of infarction?
    a. 1 mm
    b. 1.5–2 mm
    c. 2.5–3 mm
    d. 3.5–5 mm

24. The most important intervention the paramedics can perform to improve the patient's outcome is to
    a. apply oxygen.
    b. administer nitroglycerin.
    c. administer aspirin.
    d. rapidly transport to an appropriate facility.

Answers to Sidebar Questions

"Why are T waves larger in the precordial leads than the limb leads?"

Answer: The T waves are larger in the precordial leads than the limb leads because the precordial leads are closer to the ventricles than the limb leads.

"Why is the direction of the T wave the same as the QRS complex?"

Answer: The epicardial cells repolarize earlier than the endocardial cells so the wave of repolarization spreads in the direction opposite of depolarization. This results in the T wave being deflected in the same direction as the QRS complex.

On the DVD

- Myocardial infarction (animation).
- Myocardial ischemia and infarction lecture.
- Interpreting myocardial infarction demonstration.

Notes

Other Cardiac Conditions and the ECG

16

Chapter Preview

- Pericarditis
- Pulmonary Embolism
- Pacemakers
- Electrolyte Imbalances
- Drug Effects and Toxicity

Case History

A 52-year-old man with renal failure presents to the emergency department by ambulance for evaluation of weakness and palpitations. The physician enters the exam room and introduces himself to the patient. While doing so, he notices that the patient is in sinus rhythm on the monitor with frequent PVCs.

The patient indicates he is feeling very weak. He missed his last two dialysis appointments, and he can't seem to catch his breath. The physician examines the patient and determines that he has frothy pulmonary edema. The ECG shows runs of ventricular tachycardia and tall, peaked T-waves with a prolonged QT interval. The physician immediately summons the nurse and tells him that the patient is volume overloaded and he suspects the patient's potassium is critically elevated because he missed his dialysis appointments.

The nurse places the patient on high concentration oxygen and the physician orders blood work and 1 ampule of calcium gluconate, 2 ampules of D_{50}, 20 units of insulin, and a dose of sodium bicarbonate to be administered in fairly rapid succession.

Follow-up ECGs indicate normal T waves and diminished ectopy. The patient is taken to dialysis where the excess fluid in his system is removed.

CLINICAL MOMENT
The pericardium is a double-layered membrane that surrounds the heart. The potential space between the two layers holds 30 to 50 mL of serous, lubricating fluid.

Pericarditis

Pericarditis is another condition that can lead to changes in the ECG (Figure 16-1). Pericarditis is inflammation of the pericardium, which can produce sharp, substernal chest pain. The pain has an abrupt onset that worsens on inspiration or by movement, particularly when the individual is lying down. The pain lessens when sitting up and leaning forward. The most common causes of pericarditis are viral and bacterial infections. Other causes include uremia, renal failure, rheumatic fever, posttraumatic pericarditis, connective tissue disease, and cancer. Sometimes pericarditis can accompany an acute myocardial infarction. When pericarditis occurs in conjunction with myocardial infarction it develops several days after the infarction.

QUESTION
"What are the two layers of the pericardium?" (The answer can be found on page 525.)

Pericarditis is inflammation of the ______________. It can produce sharp ______________ pain that has an ______________ onset. The pain worsens on ______________ or with movement.

[pericardium] [chest] [abrupt] [inspiration]

KEY CONCEPT
Pericarditis is inflammation of the pericardium. It can produce sharp substernal chest pain.

ECG Changes

Initially with pericarditis the T wave is upright and may be elevated. During the recovery phase it inverts. The ST segment is elevated and usually flat or concave (sometimes described as a saggy appearance). If it is elevated it appears off the baseline, gradually sloping back down to the next QRS complex (may include the P wave). It is easy to mistake these changes for a developing myocardial infarction, given that the signs and symptoms are similar. Certain features of the ECG can be helpful in differentiating pericarditis from myocardial infarction:

- The ST segment and T wave changes in pericarditis are diffuse because pericarditis involves the whole heart. Therefore, the ECG changes will be present in all leads while those of myocardial infarction are localized to the affected myocardium.
- In pericarditis, T wave inversion usually occurs only after the ST segments have returned to baseline. In myocardial infarction, T wave inversion is usually seen before ST segment normalization.
- In pericarditis, development of a Q wave does not occur.

KEY CONCEPT
In pericarditis the T wave is initially upright and may be elevated. During the recovery phase it inverts. Also in pericarditis, the ST segment is elevated and usually flat or concave. If it is elevated, it appears off the baseline, gradually sloping back down to the next QRS complex.

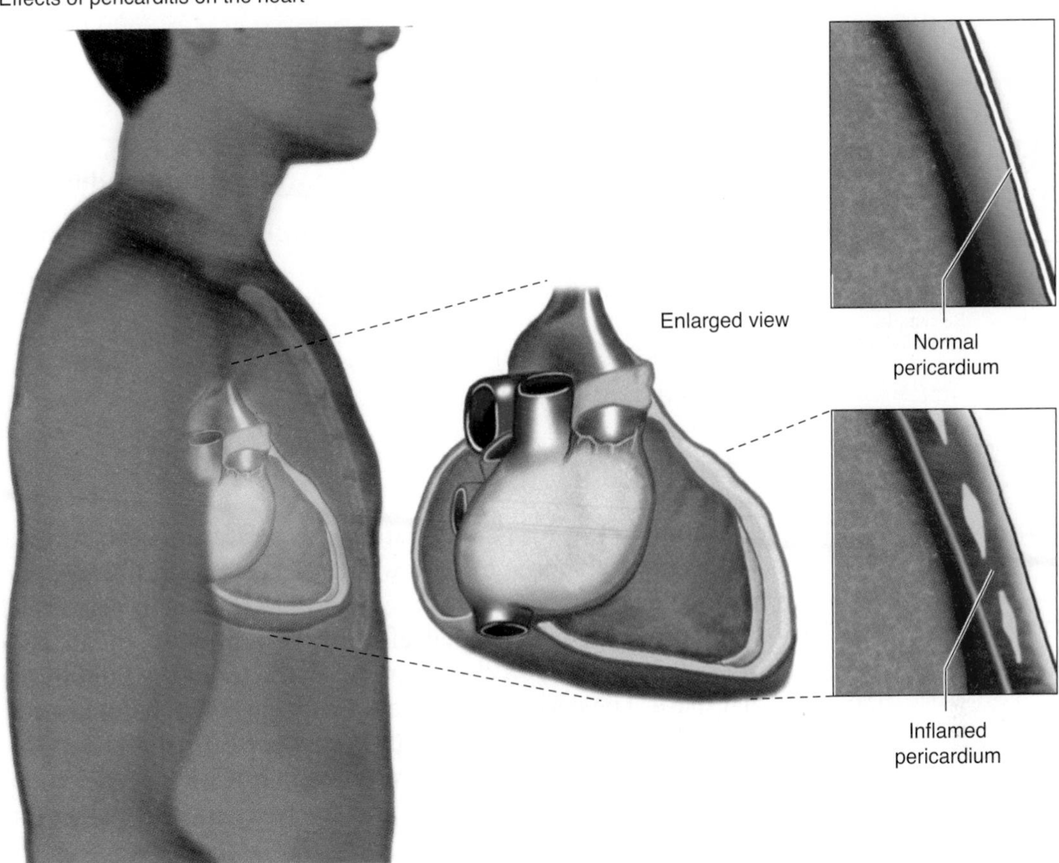

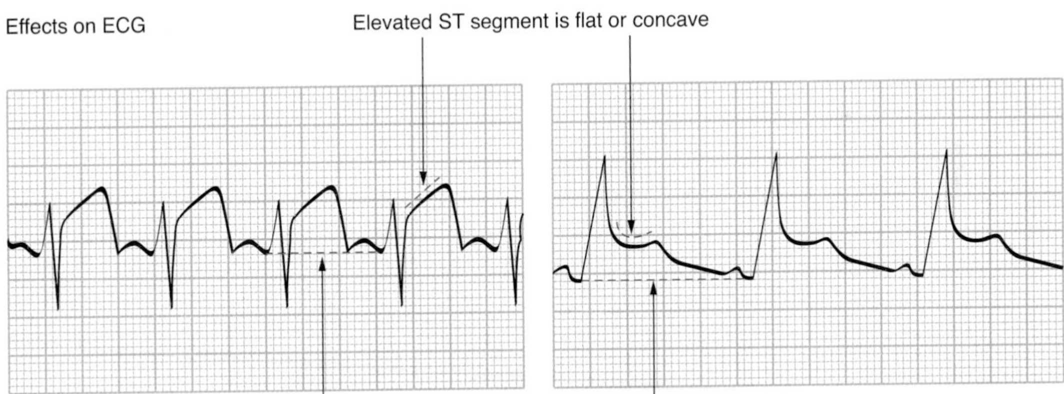

Figure 16-1
Pericarditis and ST segment elevation.

QUESTION
"What is the normal amplitude of the QRS complex?" (The answer can be found on page 525.)

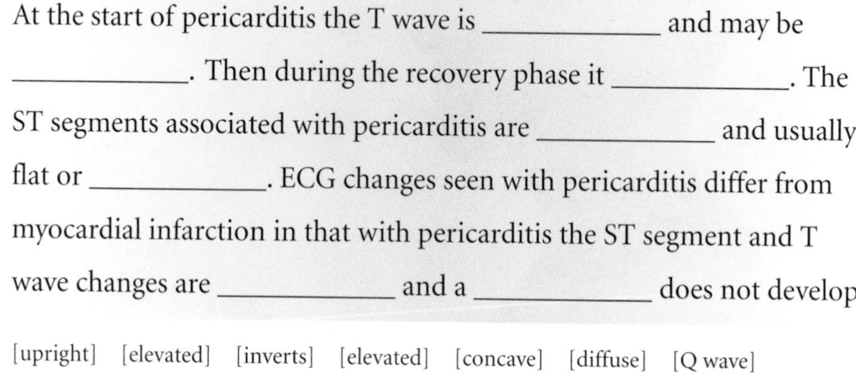

At the start of pericarditis the T wave is ____________ and may be ____________. Then during the recovery phase it ____________. The ST segments associated with pericarditis are ____________ and usually flat or ____________. ECG changes seen with pericarditis differ from myocardial infarction in that with pericarditis the ST segment and T wave changes are ____________ and a ____________ does not develop.

[upright] [elevated] [inverts] [elevated] [concave] [diffuse] [Q wave]

Pericardial Effusion

KEY CONCEPT
In pericarditis, formation of a substantial pericardial effusion causes low-voltage QRS complexes in all leads.

The inflammatory process associated with pericarditis can stimulate the body's immune response to send white cells or serous, fibrous, purulent, or hemorrhagic exudates to the area of injury leading to pericardial effusion (Figure 16-2). Pericardial effusion is a buildup of an abnormal amount of fluid and/or a change in the character of the fluid in the pericardial space. The pericardial space is the space between the heart and the pericardial sac. Formation of a substantial pericardial effusion dampens the electrical output of the heart, resulting in low voltage QRS complex in all leads. However, the ST segment and T wave changes of pericarditis may still be seen.

KEY CONCEPT
A large effusion seen with pericarditis may cause electrical alternans. This is seen on the ECG as QRS complexes that change in height with each successive beat.

____________ pericardial effusion dampens the electrical output of the heart, resulting in ____________ voltage QRS complex in all leads.

[Substantial] [low]

If an effusion is large enough, the heart may rotate freely within the fluid-filled sac. This can cause electrical alternans, a condition in which the electrical axis of the heart varies with each beat (Figure 16-3). A varying axis is most easily recognized on the ECG by the presence of QRS complexes that change in height with each successive beat. This condition can also affect the P and T waves.

CLINICAL MOMENT
The accumulation of enough fluid or exudate in the pericardial sac can lead to the development of pericardial tamponade—a condition in which the heart is compressed. This condition can cause a decrease in cardiac output.

Electrical ______________, a condition in which the electrical axis of the heart ______________ with each beat, can occur with a substantial effusion. This is recognized on the ECG by the QRS complexes that change in ______________ with each successive beat.

[alternans] [varies] [height]

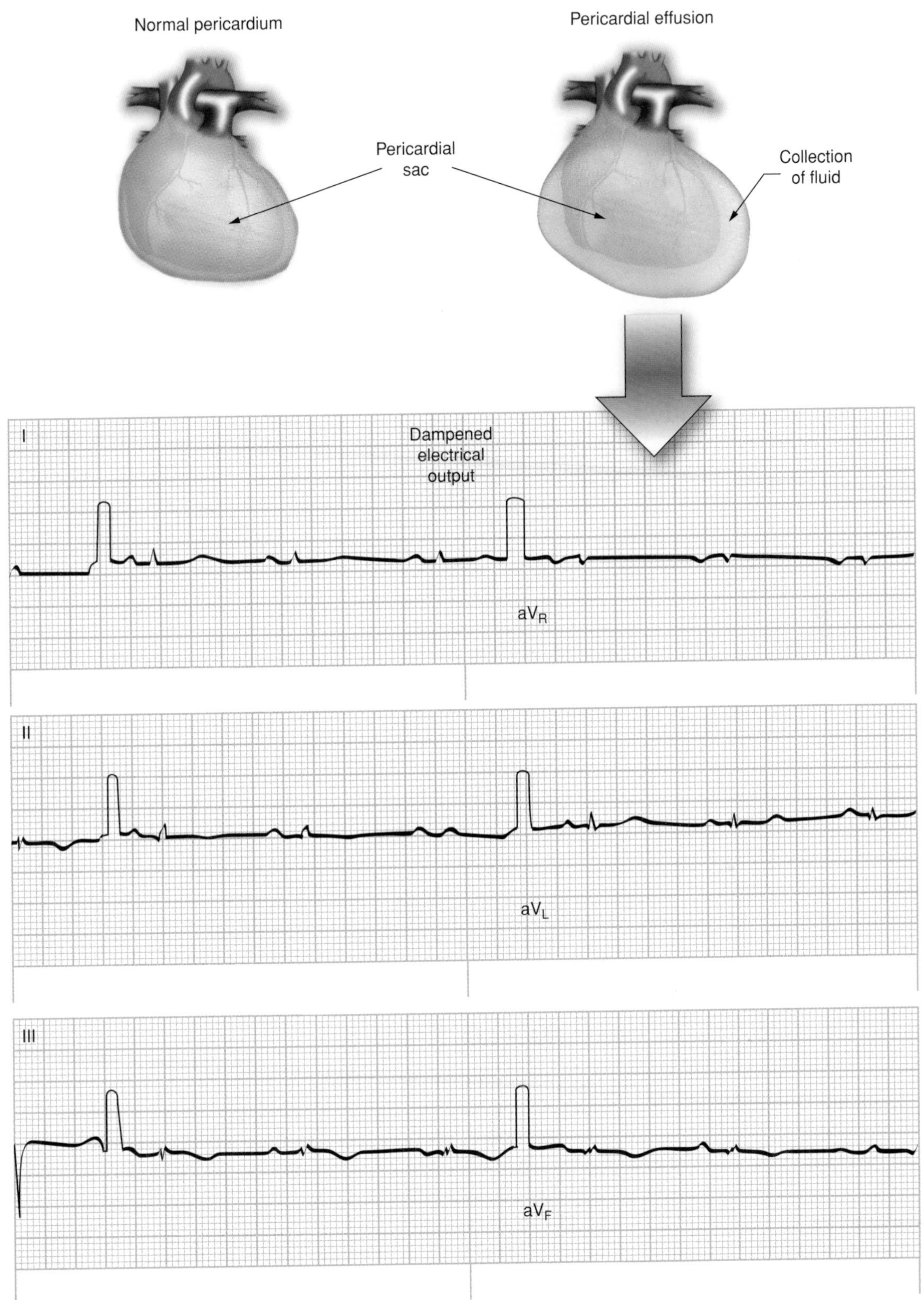

Figure 16-2
Large pericardial effusion with low-voltage QRS complexes.

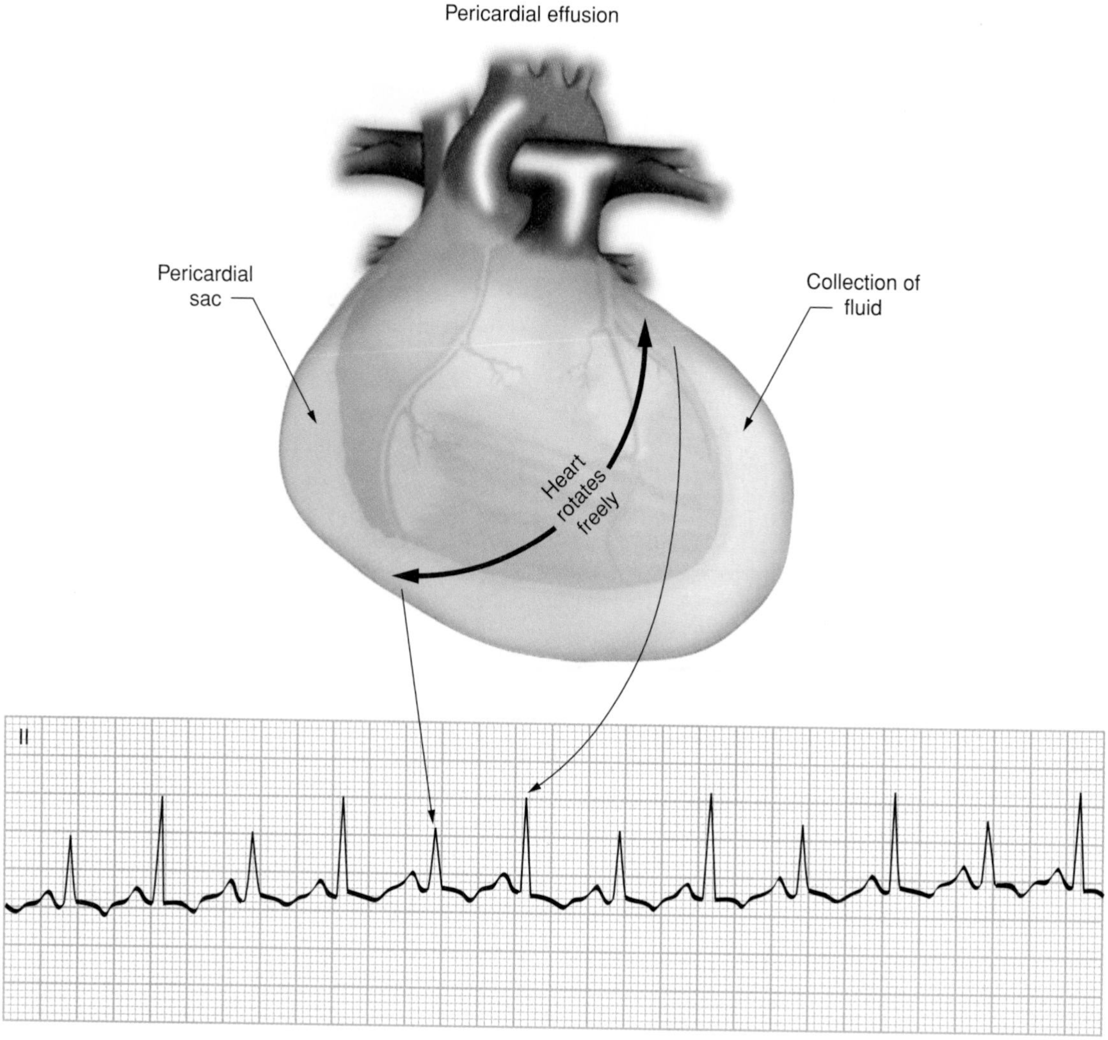

Figure 16-3
Large pericardial effusion with electrical alternans.

Pulmonary Embolism

A pulmonary embolism is an acute blockage of one of the pulmonary arteries by a blood clot or other foreign matter (Figure 16-4). This leads to obstruction of blood flow to the lung segment supplied by the artery. The larger the artery occluded, the more massive the pulmonary embolus and therefore the larger the effect the embolus has on the heart. Due to the increased pressure in the pulmonary artery caused by the embolus, the right atrium and ventricle become distended and unable to function properly, leading to right heart failure. This condition is referred to as acute cor pulmonale.

KEY CONCEPT
A pulmonary embolism is an acute blockage of one of the pulmonary arteries that leads to obstruction of blood flow to the lung segment supplied by the artery.

Massive pulmonary embolism impairs oxygenation of the blood and death may result. The most common source of the clot is in one of the

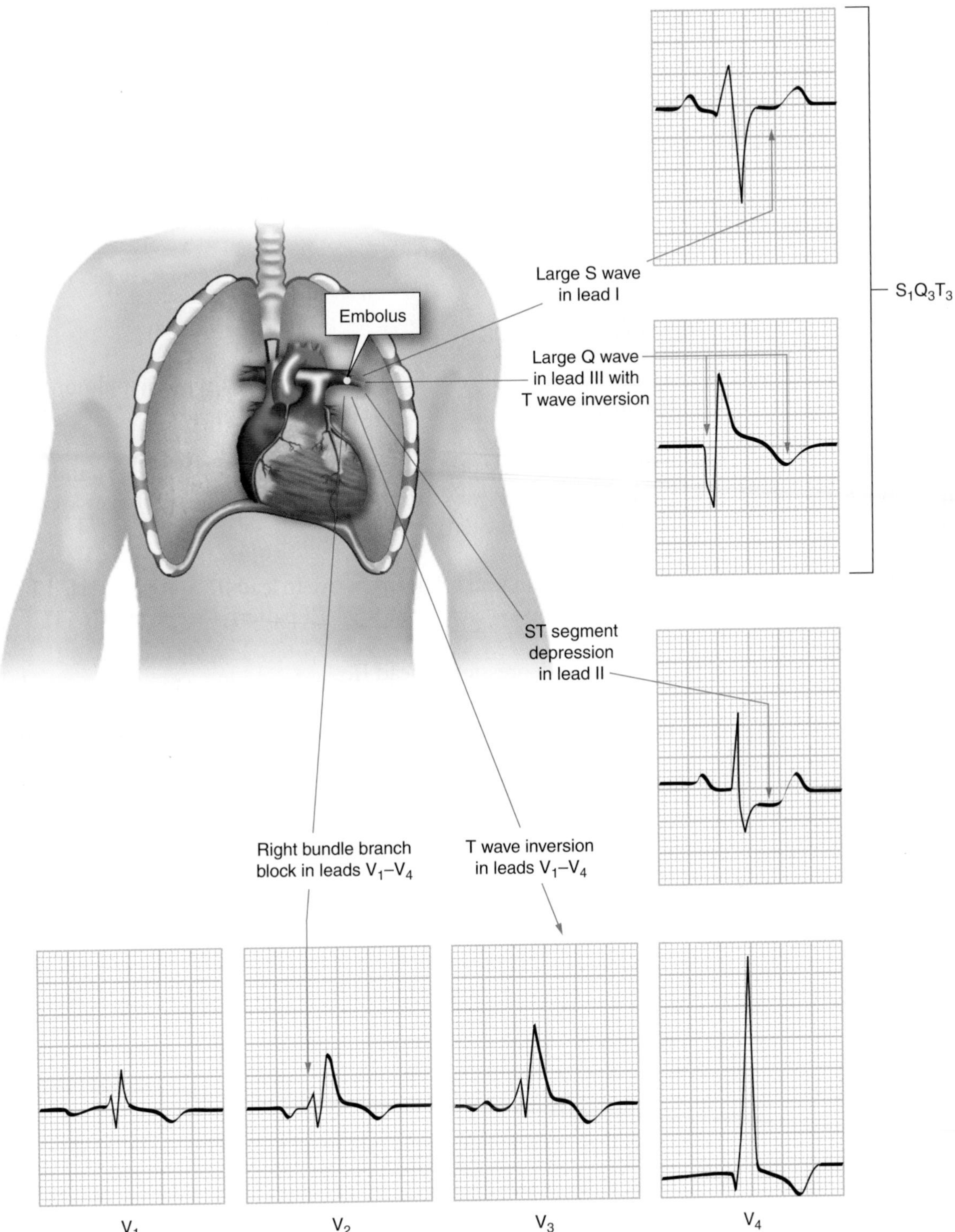

Figure 16-4
ECG changes seen with pulmonary embolism.

large pelvic or leg veins. The pain that accompanies a pulmonary embolus is pleuritic and shortness of breath is often present.

An acute blockage of a ______________ artery by a blood clot or other foreign matter is called a pulmonary embolism. This leads to obstruction of blood flow to the ______________ segment supplied by the artery.

[pulmonary] [lung]

ECG Changes

ECG changes that suggest the development of a massive pulmonary embolus include:

KEY CONCEPT
The characteristic ECG changes seen with massive pulmonary embolus include a large S wave in lead I, a deep Q wave in lead III, and an inverted T wave in lead III. This is called the S1 Q3 T3 pattern.

- Tall, symmetrically peaked P waves in leads II, III, and aV_F and sharply peaked biphasic P waves in leads V_1 and V_2. These changes are indicative of right atrial enlargement.
- A large S wave in lead I, a deep Q wave in lead III, and an inverted T wave in lead III. This is called the S1 Q3 T3 pattern (See Figure 16–4).
- ST segment depression in lead II.
- Right bundle branch block (usually subsides after the patient improves).
- The QRS axis is greater than +90° (right axis deviation).
- The T waves are inverted in leads V_1–V_4.
- Q waves are generally limited to lead III.

A number of dysrhythmias may be seen with massive pulmonary embolism, most commonly sinus tachycardia and atrial fibrillation.

In the case of a minimal or small pulmonary embolism the ECG is usually normal, or it may show a sinus tachycardia.

ECG changes seen with massive pulmonary embolus include tall, symmetrically peaked __________ in leads II, III, and aV_F, sharply peaked __________ P waves in leads V_1 and V_2, a large __________ in lead I, a deep __________ in lead III, and an inverted __________ in lead III. The QRS axis is greater than __________.

[P waves] [biphasic] [S wave] [Q wave] [T wave] [+90°]

Pacemakers

A pacemaker is an artificial device that produces an impulse from a power source and conveys it to the myocardium. It provides an electrical stimulus for hearts whose intrinsic ability to generate an impulse or whose ability to conduct electrical current is impaired. The power source is generally positioned subcutaneously, and the electrodes are threaded to the right atrium and right ventricle through veins that drain to the heart. The impulse flows throughout the heart causing the muscle to depolarize and initiate a contraction.

Pacemakers can be of tremendous clinical benefit in various circumstances including:

- 3rd-degree (complete) AV heart block.
- Symptomatic 2nd-degree AV heart block, particularly Type II.
- Symptomatic bradycardia (e.g., sick sinus syndrome).
- The sudden development of various combinations of AV heart block and bundle branch block in patients experiencing acute myocardial infarction.
- Recurrent tachycardias that can be overdriven and thereby terminated by pacemaker activity.

KEY CONCEPT
A pacemaker is an artificial device that produces an impulse and conveys it to the myocardium. The demand pacemaker is the most widely used pacemaker. The firing of a pacemaker produces one or two small spikes on the ECG.

Pacemakers are capable of responding to the immediate needs of the heart. They are programmable in terms of sensitivity, firing rate, and refractory period. They can boost the heart rate in response to motion or increased respirations for those patients who, because of either disease of the sinus node or the effects of medications, cannot appropriately increase their heart rate during activity.

The demand pacemaker is the most widely used pacemaker. It only fires when the patient's intrinsic heart rate falls below a given threshold level. For example, if the pacemaker is set at 60 beats per minute, it remains inactive until there is a pause between beats that translates into a rate below 60. The pacemaker then fires.

A ________________ is a device that produces an impulse and conveys it to the myocardium causing the myocardium to initiate ________________. The most widely used pacemaker is the ________________ pacemaker.

[pacemaker] [depolarization] [demand]

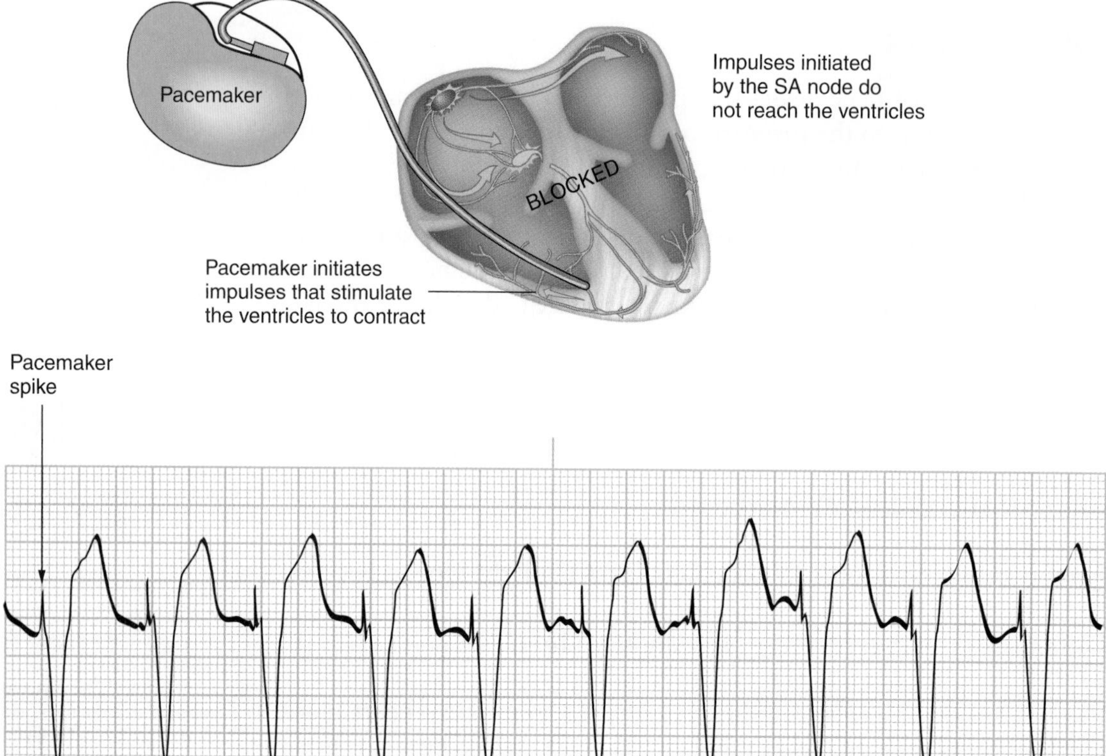

Figure 16-5
Pacemakers are used to provide electrical stimuli for hearts with an impaired ability to initiate or conduct an electrical impulse.

Pacemaker electrodes are either positioned in the atrium or ventricle alone (single-chamber pacemakers) or, more often, in both chambers (dual-chamber pacemakers or AV sequential pacemakers) (Figure 16-5).

CLINICAL MOMENT
In some patients, pacemaker spikes are not easy to see on an ECG because their amplitude is less than 1 mv. If the patient is able to communicate and is appropriately oriented, asking the question "Do you have a pacemaker?" may be of use when wide QRS complexes and left axis deviation are seen on the ECG.

The firing of a pacemaker produces a small spike on the ECG. With a ventricular pacemaker, the resulting QRS complex is wide and bizarre. Because the electrodes are positioned in the right ventricle, the right ventricle will contract first, then the left ventricle. This produces a pattern identical to left bundle branch block, with delayed left ventricular depolarization. A retrograde P wave may or may not be seen.

The firing of a pacemaker produces one or two small ______________ on the ECG.

[spikes]

An atrial pacemaker will produce a spike trailed by a P wave and a normal QRS complex. With an AV sequential pacemaker, two spikes are seen, one that precedes a P wave and one that precedes a wide, bizarre QRS complex (Figure 16-6).

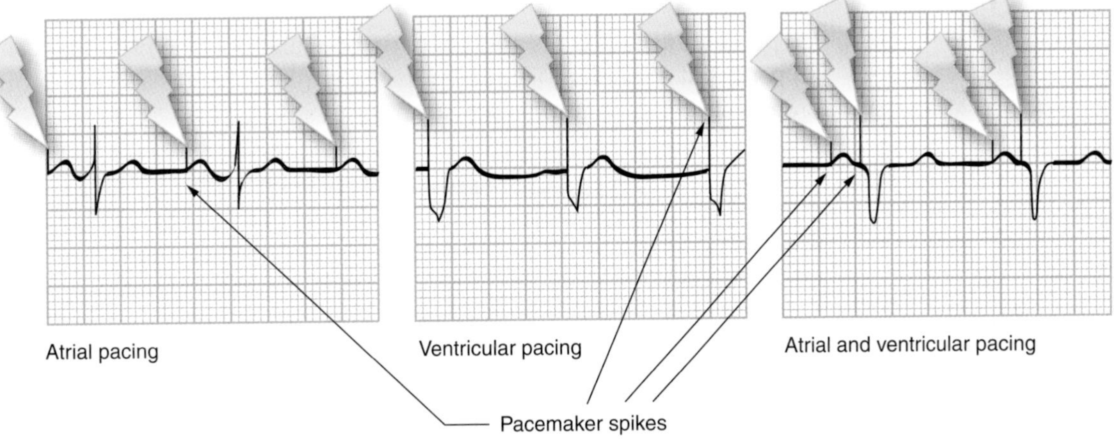

Figure 16-6
Location of pacemaker spikes on the ECG tracing with each type of pacemaker.

KEY CONCEPT
A ventricular pacemaker produces one small spike on the ECG and a wide and bizarre QRS complex. An atrial pacemaker produces a spike trailed by a P wave and a normal QRS complex. An AV pacemaker produces one spike that precedes a P wave and one spike that precedes a wide, bizarre QRS complex.

A ______________ pacemaker produces one small spike that precedes a wide and bizarre QRS complex. An ______________ pacemaker produces a spike trailed by a P wave and a normal QRS complex. An ______________ sequential pacemaker produces one spike that precedes a P wave and one spike that precedes a wide, bizarre QRS complex.

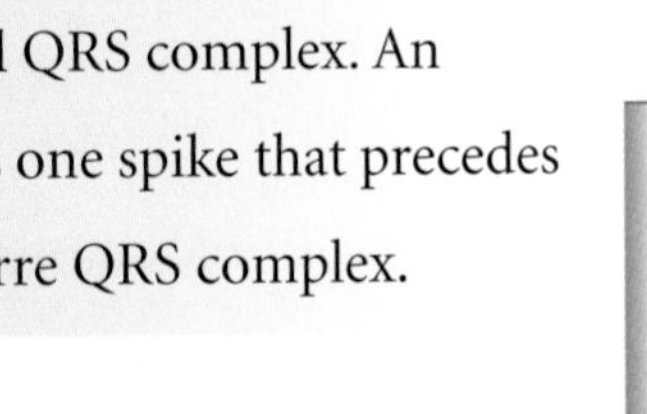

[ventricular] [atrial] [AV]

Electrolyte Imbalances

Changes in potassium and calcium serum levels can profoundly affect the ECG. Those involving potassium are the most immediately life threatening. Levels that are too high (hyperkalemia) or too low (hypokalemia) can quickly result in serious cardiac dysrhythmias. The presence of ECG changes may be a better measure of clinically significant potassium toxicity than is the serum potassium level.

________ imbalances cause ECG changes. Changes in ________ levels are the most immediately life threatening. Potassium levels that are too high are called ________ and those that are too low are called ________.

[Electrolyte] [potassium] [hyperkalemia] [hypokalemia]

QUESTION
"What role does potassium play in the generation and conduction of nerve impulses?" (The answer can be found on page 525.)

KEY CONCEPT
Increases or decreases in the potassium and calcium serum levels can have a profound effect on the ECG.

CLINICAL MOMENT
Hyperkalemia can progress to ventricular fibrillation rapidly instead of in a slow, progressive manner. For this reason you should take immediate corrective action with any change due to hyperkalemia you see on the ECG.

KEY CONCEPT
Key characteristics of hyperkalemia include T wave peaking, flattened P waves, 1st-degree AV heart block, widened QRS complexes, deepened S waves, merging of S and T waves, and sine-waves.

Hyperkalemia

Hyperkalemia generates a progression of changes in the ECG that can end in ventricular fibrillation and death (Figure 16-7). Signs and symptoms of hyperkalemia include weakness, paralysis, and respiratory failure.

T wave peaking begins as the potassium level starts to rise. You may remember from Chapter 15, peaked T waves can also be seen in acute myocardial infarction. The distinction between the two is that the changes in myocardial infarction are limited to those leads overlying the infarcted area, whereas with hyperkalemia, the changes are seen in all leads. Another distinctive feature of the hyperkalemic T wave is that both the up and down slope are concave giving the appearance of a tent. As the serum potassium increases more, the PR interval becomes prolonged, and the P wave eventually flattens and then disappears. Finally, the QRS complex widens until it blends with the T wave, forming what is called a sine-wave pattern. Idioventricular rhythm or ventricular fibrillation may ultimately develop.

ECG Changes

ECG changes seen with hyperkalemia include:

- Peaked T waves (tenting)
- Flattened P waves
- Prolonged PR interval (1st-degree AV heart block)
- Widened QRS complex
- Deepened S waves and merging of S and T waves
- Concave up and down slope of the T wave
- Sine-wave pattern

As the potassium level increases above normal, T wave ____________ begins. As the potassium level increases more, the PR interval becomes ____________, and the P wave ultimately ____________ and then ____________. Last, the QRS complex ____________ until it ____________ with the T wave. Idioventricular rhythm or ventricular ____________ may ultimately develop.

[peaking] [prolonged] [flattens] [disappears] [widens] [blends] [fibrillation]

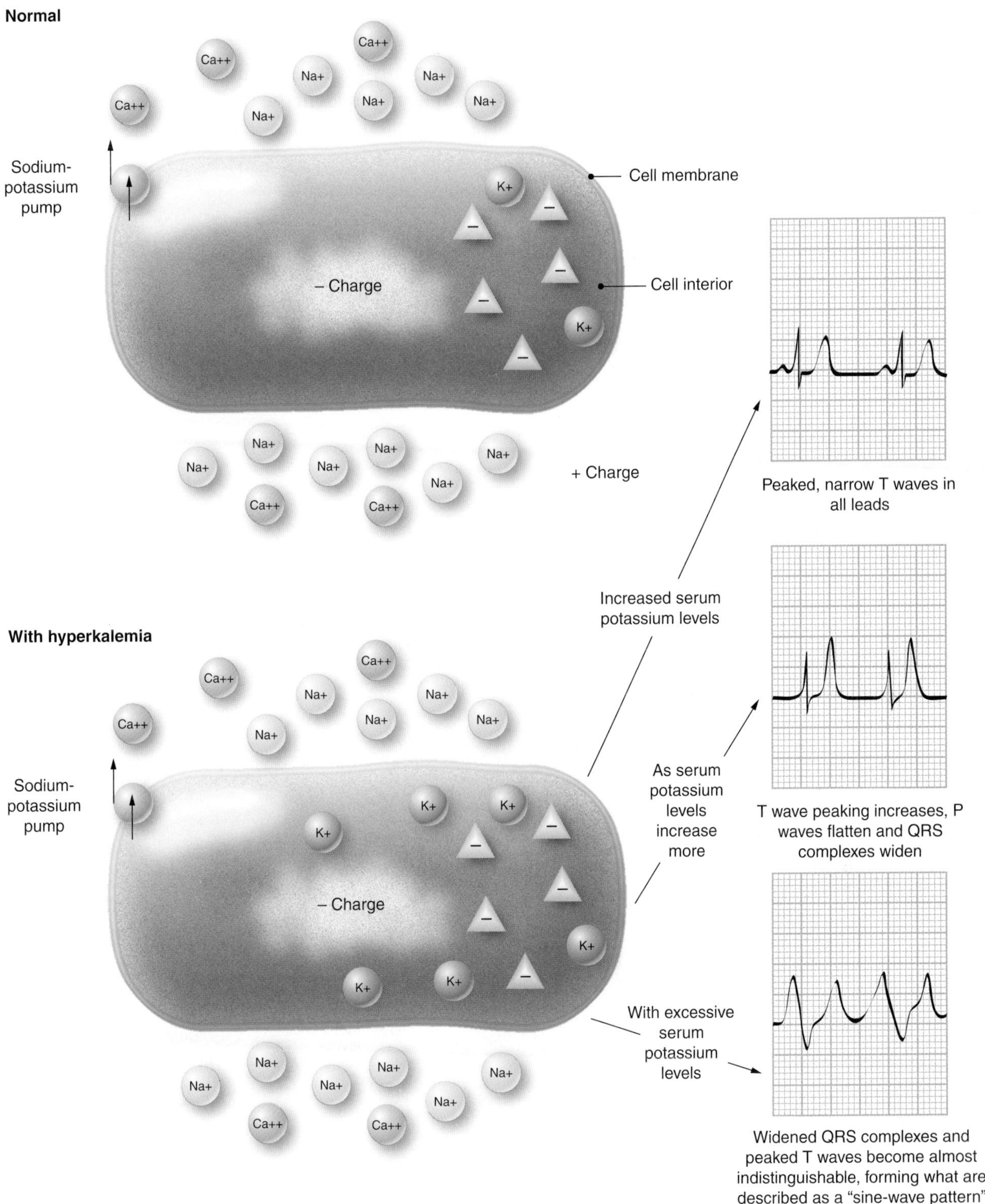

Figure 16-7
ECG changes seen in hyperkalemia.

Hypokalemia

The ECG is also an effective means of determining the presence of hypokalemia (Figure 16-8). Four key changes in the ECG can be seen with serious hypokalemia:

- ST segment depression
- Flattening of the T wave
- Appearance of U waves
- Prolongation of the QT interval

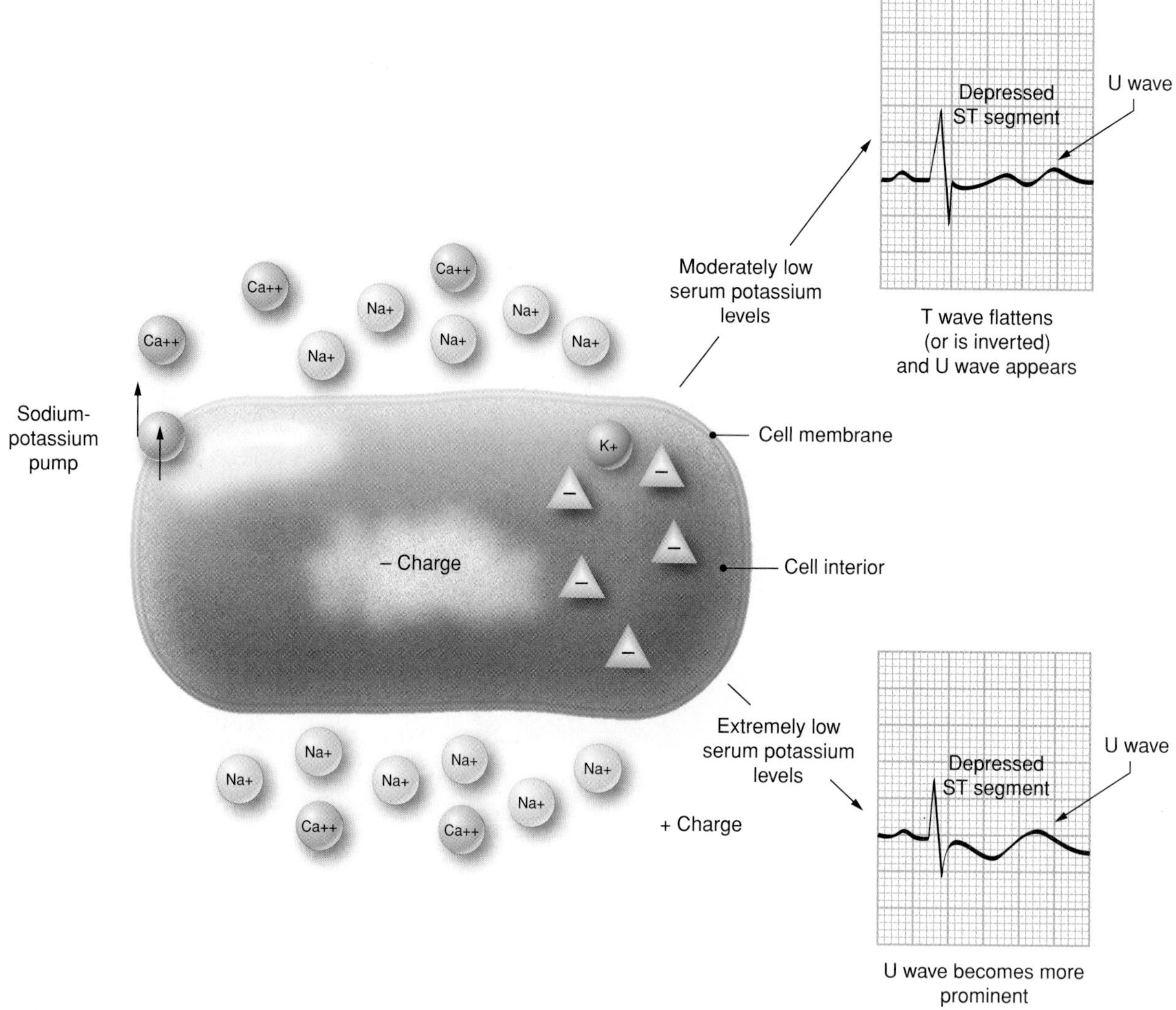

Figure 16-8
ECG changes seen with hypokalemia.

A wave that occurs after the T wave in the cardiac cycle is called a U wave. Although U waves are the most distinguishing characteristic of hypokalemia, they are not by themselves diagnostic. U waves are seen in other conditions and can sometimes be seen in patients with normal hearts and normal serum potassium levels.

CLINICAL MOMENT
Severe hypokalemia can lead to dysrhythmias and pulseless electrical activity (PEA) or asystole.

Symptoms of hypokalemia include weakness, fatigue, paralysis, respiratory difficulty, constipation, and leg cramps.

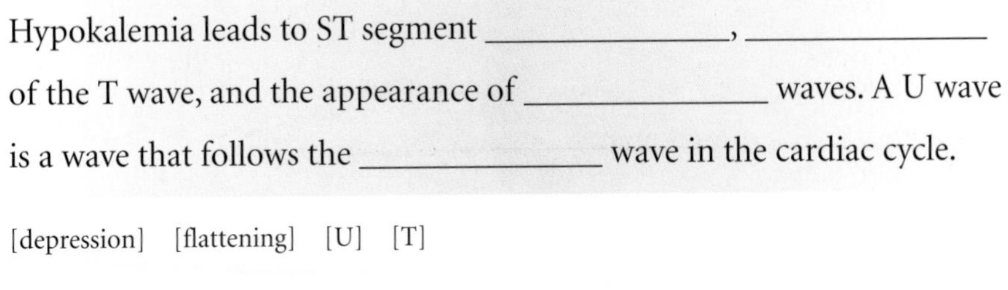

Hypokalemia leads to ST segment ____________, ____________ of the T wave, and the appearance of ____________ waves. A U wave is a wave that follows the ____________ wave in the cardiac cycle.

[depression] [flattening] [U] [T]

KEY CONCEPT
Key ECG characteristics of hypokalemia include ST segment depression, flattening of the T wave, and the appearance of U waves.

 Calcium Disorders

Calcium is needed by the myocardial cells to contract. Alterations in serum calcium levels mainly affect the QT interval (Figure 16-9). Hypocalcemia prolongs the QT interval while hypercalcemia shortens it. Torsades de pointes, a variant of ventricular tachycardia, is seen in patients with prolonged QT intervals. Hypocalcemia results in decreased cardiac contraction.

KEY CONCEPT
In hypocalcemia the QT interval is slightly prolonged.

Drug Effects and Toxicity

Some medications can have striking effects on ECG waveforms by altering the way the cells depolarize, repolarize, and innervate surrounding tissues. These changes may indicate expected, and therefore benign, effects of certain medications, as well as provide evidence of medication toxicity.

QUESTION
"What is torsades de pointes?" (The answer can be found on page 525.)

 Digoxin

Digoxin is in a class of drugs referred to as cardiac glycosides. These drugs slow the influx of sodium while allowing a greater influx of calcium during both depolarization and repolarization. This increases myocardial contractility and improves the heart's pumping ability. Digoxin can be used in heart failure to improve cardiac output.

There are two types of ECG changes seen with digoxin: those associated with therapeutic blood levels of the drug and those associated with toxic blood levels.

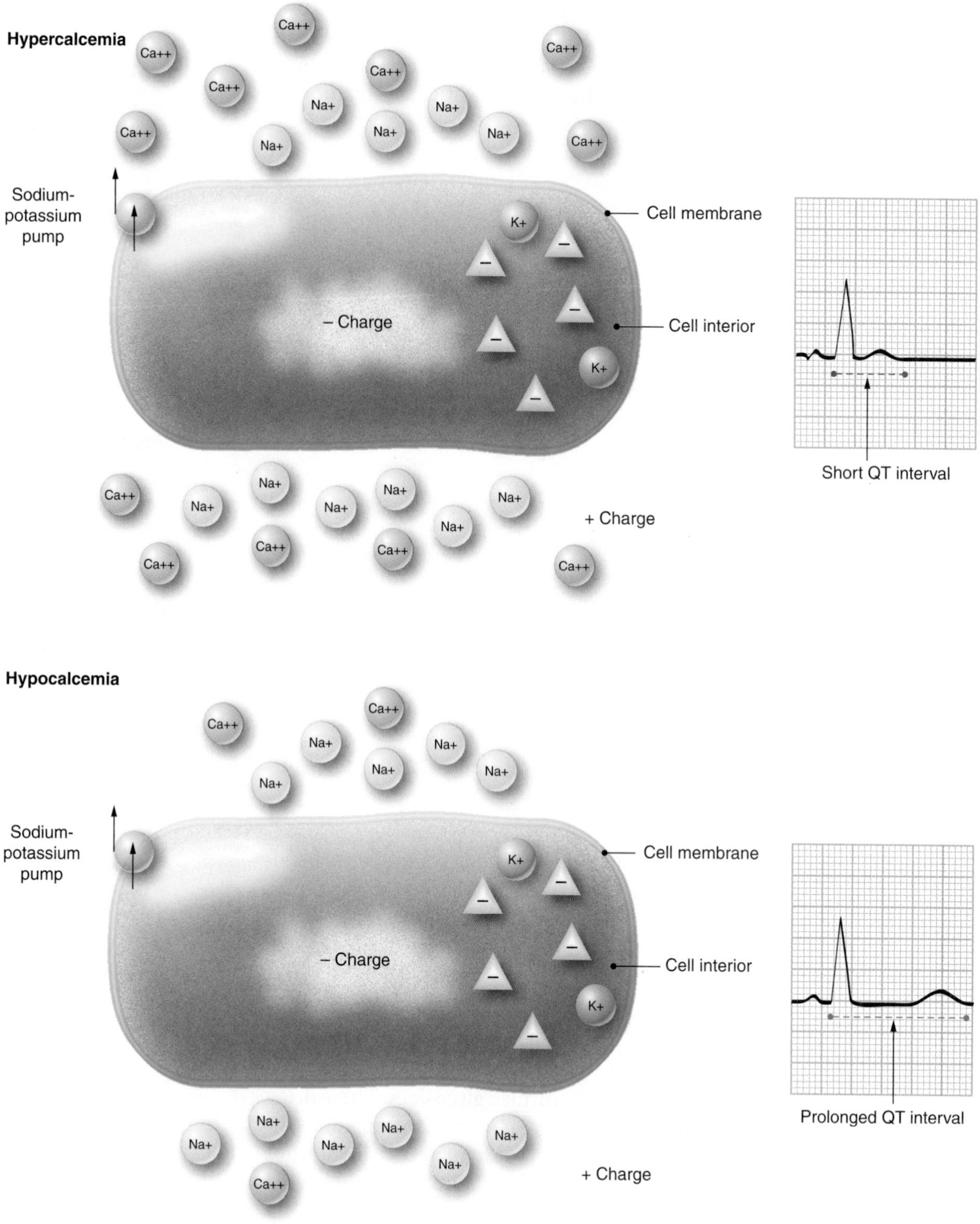

Hypercalcemia

Ca++
Na+
Sodium-potassium pump
K+
– Charge
Cell membrane
Cell interior
Short QT interval
+ Charge

Hypocalcemia

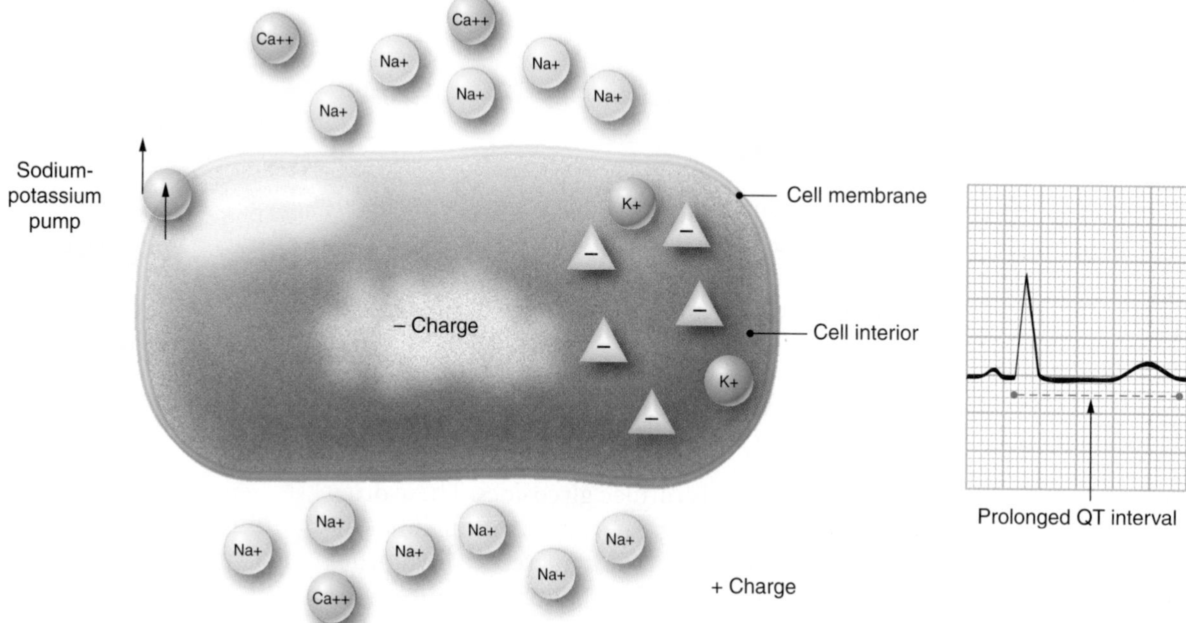

Figure 16-9
With hypercalcemia, the QT interval shortens and with hypocalcemia, the QT interval is prolonged.

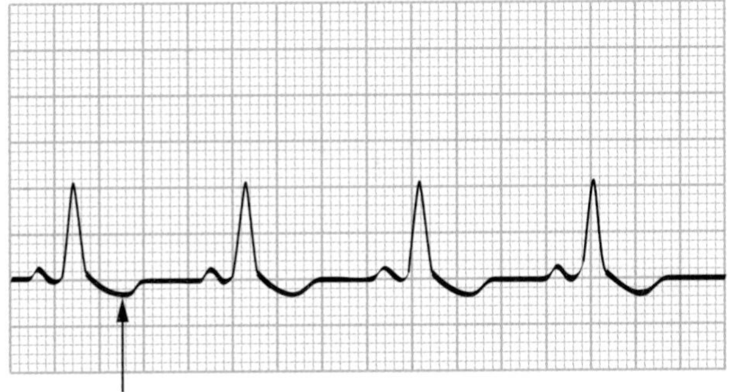

Figure 16-10
Effects of digoxin on the ECG.

In therapeutic doses, digoxin has a parasympathetic effect that slows the pacing rate of the SA node and conduction through the AV node. This effect can slow fast dysrhythmias. It also inhibits the receptiveness of the AV node to multiple stimuli, allowing fewer stimuli to reach the ventricles. This can be particularly helpful in the treatment of dysrhythmias such as atrial fibrillation and flutter. However, if the heart rate slows too much, decreased cardiac output can result.

CLINICAL MOMENT
The slowing of the heart rate is called a negative chronotropic effect while the slowing of the conduction rate is called a negative dromotropic effect.

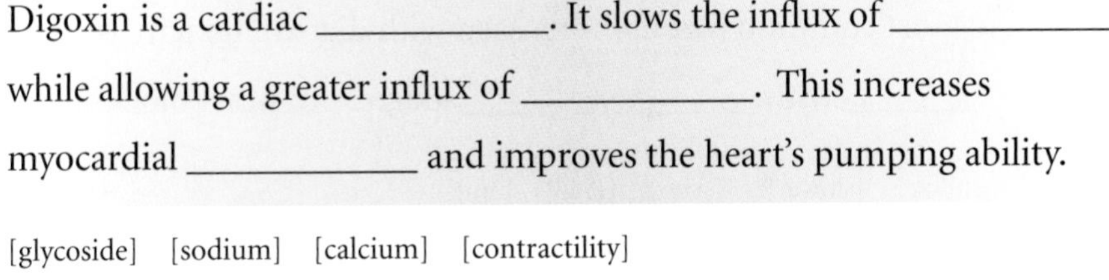

Digoxin is a cardiac ____________. It slows the influx of ____________ while allowing a greater influx of ____________. This increases myocardial ____________ and improves the heart's pumping ability.

[glycoside] [sodium] [calcium] [contractility]

KEY CONCEPT
Digoxin slows the influx of sodium while allowing a greater influx of calcium. This increases myocardial contractility and improves the heart's pumping ability. It also slows the heart rate and AV conduction making it useful in the treatment of fast atrial dysrhythmias.

Therapeutic Blood Levels—ECG Changes

Digoxin produces a characteristic gradual downward curve of the ST segment (it looks like a ladle) (Figure 16–10). The R wave slurs into the ST segment. Sometimes the T wave is lost in this scooping effect. The lowest portion of the ST segment is depressed below the baseline. When seen, the T waves have shorter amplitude and can be biphasic. The QT interval is usually shorter than anticipated and the U waves are more visible. Also, the PR interval may be prolonged.

With digoxin there is a gradual downward curve of the ____________. Sometimes the T wave is ____________ in this scooping effect. The lowest portion of the ST segment is depressed ____________ the baseline.

[ST segment] [lost] [below]

CLINICAL MOMENT
Digitalis preparations have been used to treat people since the thirteenth century. In certain circumstances or in high concentrations, digitalis can induce deadly dysrhythmias.

INSTRUCTIONAL MOMENT
The effect seen with digoxin is also referred to as a slurring of the ST segment.

KEY CONCEPT
A characteristic gradual downward curve of the ST segment is seen with digoxin. Further, the downward slope of the R wave gradually slurs as it curves downward into the ST segment.

INSTRUCTIONAL MOMENT
Digitalis is the most common, but not the only, cause of PAT with 2nd degree AV heart block.

KEY CONCEPT
Digoxin has a very narrow therapeutic margin and is excreted from the body slowly. Excessive digitalis levels can cause slower heart rates, faster heart rates, and PVCs.

Digoxin has a very narrow therapeutic margin of 0.5 to 1.5 mg/dl, and it is excreted from the body slowly. Toxic levels can occur and cause life-threatening dysrhythmias. The chance of developing toxicity is increased in hypokalemia, hypercalcemia, renal impairment, advanced age, acute hypoxia, and hypothyroidism.

Toxic Blood Levels—ECG Changes

Digoxin levels greater than the therapeutic range can cause any dysrhythmia because it increases the automatic behavior of all cardiac conducting cells causing them to act more like pacemakers. The most common dysrhythmia seen with digoxin toxicity is paroxysmal atrial tachycardia (PAT) with 2nd-degree AV heart block. The conduction block is usually 2:1 but may vary unpredictably. Other abnormal heart rhythms that may be seen include those with slower rates (junctional rhythms, heart blocks), those with faster rates (atrial, junctional, and ventricular tachycardia), and premature complexes (PACs, PJCs, and PVCs). Atrial flutter and fibrillation are least commonly seen with digoxin toxicity.

Digoxin has a very ________________ therapeutic margin, and it is excreted from the body ________________. Excessive digitalis levels can cause ________________ heart rates, ________________ atrial rates, and PVCs. The most common dysrhythmia seen with digoxin toxicity is ________________ with ________________ -degree AV heart block.

[narrow] [slowly] [slower] [faster] [PAT] [2nd]

Other Medications

Class I (specifically type IA) antidysrhythmics are a group of drugs that include procainamide, quinidine, and disopyramide. These antidysrhythmic drugs slow both atrial and ventricular rates. They do not affect rhythm but prolong AV conduction. When patients receive these antidysrhythmic drugs, the ECG may show a slight widening of the QRS complex and a lengthening of the QT interval. The increase of the QT interval is concerning as it can increase the risk of ventricular tachydysrhythmias. The QT interval must be carefully monitored in all patients taking these medications and the drug withheld if significant—usually more than 25%—prolongation occurs. Class I antidysrhythmics can also produce AV blocks, a slowed or completely blocked SA node, and other dysrhythmias.

Quinidine

ECG indicators of quinidine use include a wide, notched P wave; widening of the QRS complex; and, often, ST depression with a prolonged QT interval. The presence of U waves is typical as well. U waves represent delayed repolarization of the ventricular conduction system. These do not require any adjustment in drug dosage.

CLINICAL MOMENT

Other drugs that can increase the QT interval are other antidysrhythmic agents (e.g., amiodarone and dofetilide), the tricyclic antidepressants, the phenothiazines, erythromycin, and various antifungal medications.

Hypotension; tachycardia; widening of the QRS complex, QT interval, and PR interval; heart block; and heart failure can develop with quinidine toxicity. Episodes of torsades de pointes can also result.

Procainamide

Adverse cardiovascular effects of procainamide include bradycardia, tachycardia, hypotension, worsening heart failure, AV heart block, torsades de pointes, ventricular fibrillation, and asystole.

Calcium Channel Blockers

Calcium channel blockers primarily block the AV node, but the extent of block varies significantly within different drugs in this class. Beta-blockers slow automaticity of the SA node and the Purkinje system and block the AV node. They can have a number of effects on the cardiovascular system including bradycardia, hypotension, heart failure, chest pain, and palpitations.

You can practice identifying the various conditions detailed in this chapter in the following *Practice Makes Perfect* exercises. Answers to these exercises can be found in Appendix A.

PRACTICE. . . MAKES PERFECT

1. Identify if pulmonary embolism, low-amplitude waveforms, electrical alternans, pacemaker, electrolyte imbalance, or digitalis use are present.

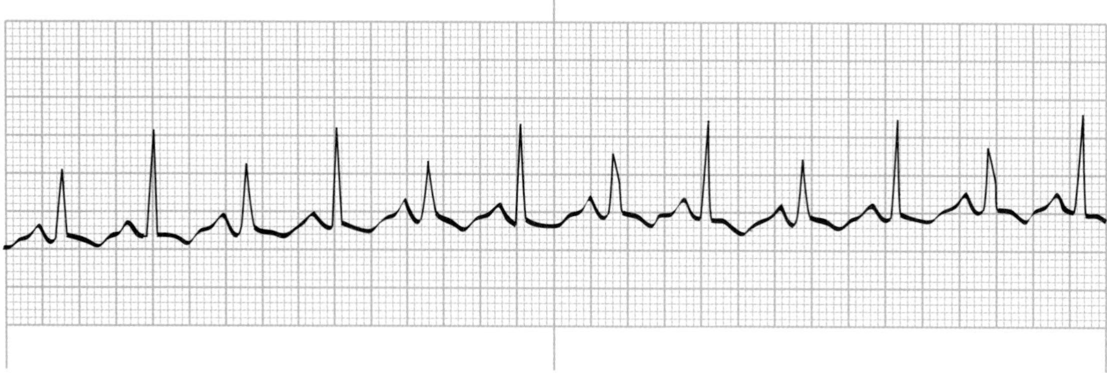

2. Identify if pulmonary embolism, low-amplitude waveforms, electrical alternans, pacemaker, electrolyte imbalance, or digitalis use are present.

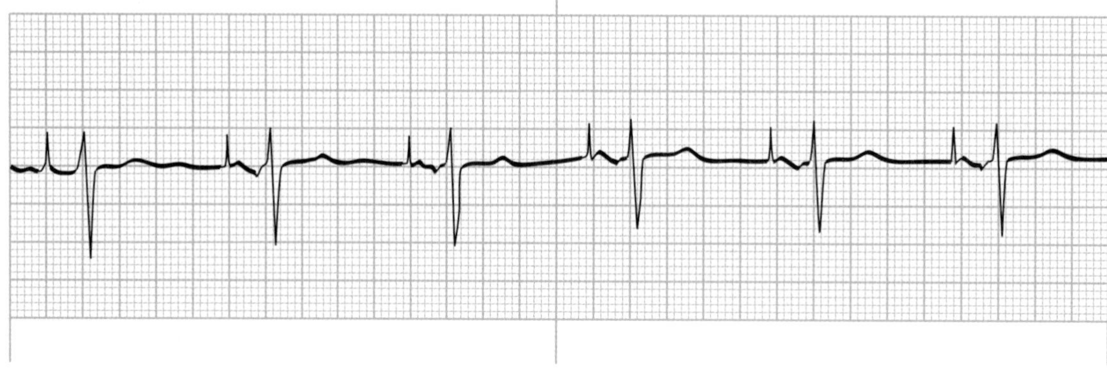

3. Identify if pulmonary embolism, low-amplitude waveforms, electrical alternans, pacemaker, electrolyte imbalance, or digitalis use are present.

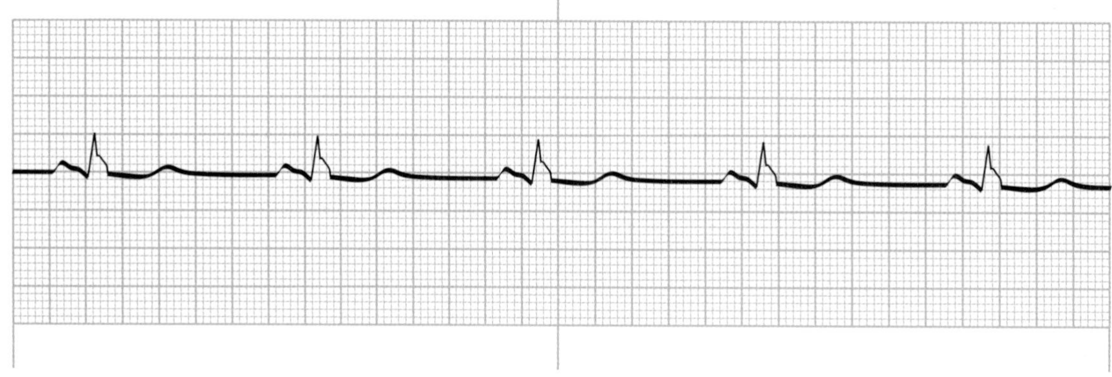

PRACTICE. . . MAKES PERFECT

4. Identify if pulmonary embolism, low-amplitude waveforms, electrical alternans, pacemaker, electrolyte imbalance, or digitalis use are present.

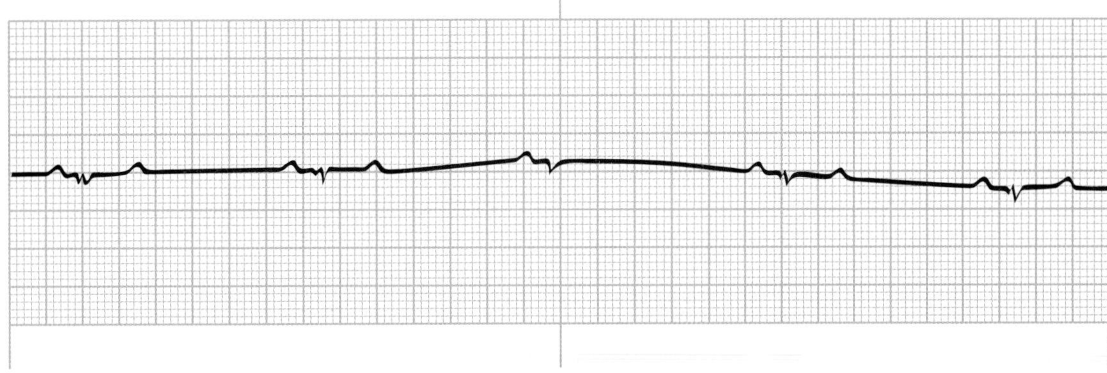

5. Identify if pulmonary embolism, low-amplitude waveforms, electrical alternans, pacemaker, electrolyte imbalance, or digitalis use are present.

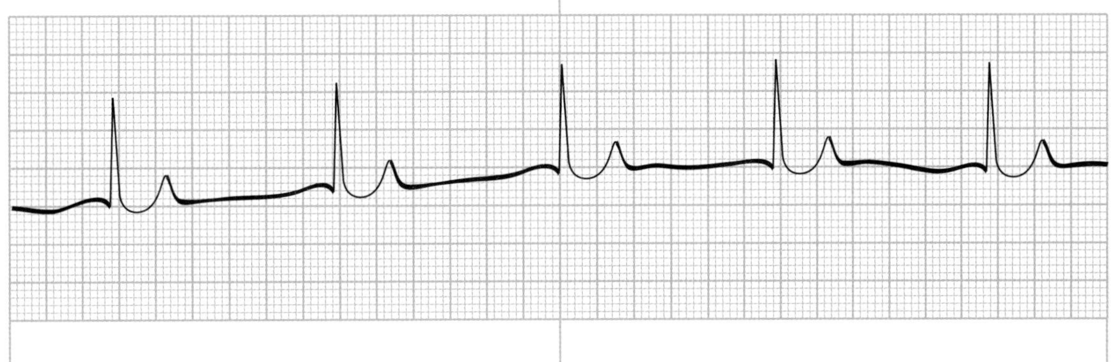

Key Points

- Inflammation of the pericardium is called pericarditis. It can produce sharp substernal chest pain that worsens with inspiration and movement, particularly when the individual is lying down.
- In pericarditis the T wave is initially upright and elevated but then during the recovery phase it inverts. The ST segment is elevated and usually flat or concave.
- A substantial pericardial effusion can occur with pericarditis. This can cause ECG changes including low-voltage QRS complexes in all leads and electrical alternans, a condition in which the QRS complexes change in height with each successive beat.
- An acute blockage of one of the pulmonary arteries that leads to obstruction of blood flow to the lung segment supplied by the artery is called a pulmonary embolism.

- The characteristic ECG changes seen with massive pulmonary embolus include a large S wave in lead I, a deep Q wave in lead III, and an inverted T wave in lead III. This is called the S1 Q3 T3 pattern.

- A pacemaker is an artificial device that produces an impulse and conveys it to the myocardium. The demand pacemaker is the most widely used pacemaker. The firing of a pacemaker produces one or two small spikes on the ECG.

- Increases or decreases in the potassium and calcium serum levels can have a profound effect on the ECG.

- Key characteristics of hyperkalemia include T wave peaking, flattened P waves, 1st-degree AV heart block, widened QRS complexes, deepened S waves, merging of S and T waves, and sine-waves.

- Key ECG characteristics of hypokalemia include ST segment depression, flattening of the T wave, and appearance of U waves.

- In hypocalcemia the QT interval is slightly prolonged.

- Digoxin slows the influx of sodium while allowing a greater influx of calcium. This increases myocardial contractility and improves the heart's pumping ability. It also slows the heart rate and AV conduction making it useful in the treatment of fast atrial dysrhythmias.

- A characteristic gradual downward curve of the ST segment is seen with digoxin. Further, the downward slope of the R wave gradually slurs as it curves downward into the ST segment.

- Digoxin has a very narrow therapeutic margin and is excreted from the body slowly. Excessive digitalis levels can cause slower heart rates, faster heart rates, and PVCs.

Assess Your Understanding

The following questions give you a chance to assess your understanding of the material discussed in this chapter. The answers can be found in Appendix A.

1. Inflammation of the pericardium is called
   a. preexcitation syndrome.
   b. myocardial ischemia.
   c. pericarditis.
   d. pulmonary embolism.

2. ECG changes seen with pericarditis include
   a. a large Q wave.
   b. an elevated ST segment, usually flat or concave.
   c. right bundle branch block.
   d. a large S wave in lead I.

3. In comparison to myocardial infarction, the ECG changes seen with pericarditis include
   a. diffuse ST segment and T wave changes.
   b. T wave inversion that usually occurs at the onset of the chest pain.
   c. development of a Q wave.
   d. the S1 Q3 T3 pattern.

4. Electrical alternans
   a. occurs with a small pericardial effusion.
   b. is a condition in which the electrical axis of the heart varies with each beat.
   c. is recognized on the ECG by QRS complexes, which change height every fifth or sixth beat.
   d. is diagnosed by analyzing just the width of the QRS complexes.

5. A pulmonary embolism
   a. is most commonly caused by a thrombus in one of the large neck veins.
   b. is an acute blockage of one of the coronary arteries.
   c. often produces chest pain unaffected by breathing efforts.
   d. can lead to acute cor pulmonale.

6. ECG changes seen with pulmonary embolism include
   a. right bundle branch block.
   b. the S1 Q3 T3 pattern.
   c. tall, symmetrically peaked P waves in leads II, III, and aV_F.
   d. All of the above.

7. A pacemaker
   a. will only generate artificial impulses at one specific preset rate.
   b. provides electrical stimuli for hearts in which there is severe myocardial damage resulting in depressed contractility.
   c. delivers defibrillation to hearts experiencing ventricular fibrillation.
   d. produces an impulse and conveys it to the myocardium.

8. An AV sequential pacemaker produces
   a. one small spike on the ECG and a wide, bizarre QRS complex.
   b. a spike trailed by a P wave and a normal QRS complex.
   c. one spike that precedes a P wave and one spike that precedes a wide, bizarre QRS complex.
   d. two spikes that precede each P wave.

9. Match the following ECG changes with the cardiac condition with which they are seen.

ECG Change		*Condition*
Peaked T waves, widened QRS complexes, and sine-waves	___	a. Hypocalcemia
Appearance of U waves, prolongation of the QT interval	___	b. Hyperkalemia
Slightly prolonged QT interval	___	c. Hypokalemia
		d. Hypercalcemia

10. Increases or decreases in the potassium and calcium serum levels can have a profound effect on the ECG.
    a. True
    b. False

11. Prolonged QT intervals are associated with
    a. atrial fibrillation.
    b. complete AV heart block.
    c. sinus bradycardia.
    d. torsades de pointes.

12. ECG changes associated with digoxin use include a(n)
    a. longer QT interval.
    b. elevated ST segment.
    c. gradual downward curve of the ST segment.
    d. shorter than normal PR interval.

13. The most common dysrhythmia seen with digoxin toxicity is
    a. 3rd-degree AV heart block.
    b. paroxysmal atrial tachycardia (PAT) with 2nd-degree AV heart block.
    c. junctional tachycardia.
    d. torsades de pointes.

14. On the following illustrations draw an example of
    a. tall T waves.
    b. sine-waves.
    c. U waves.

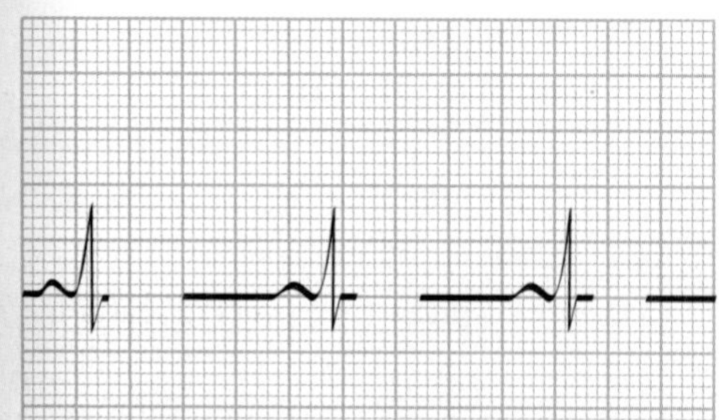
A

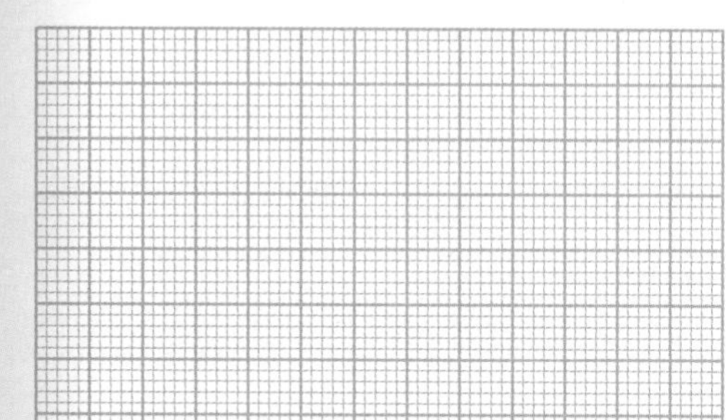
B

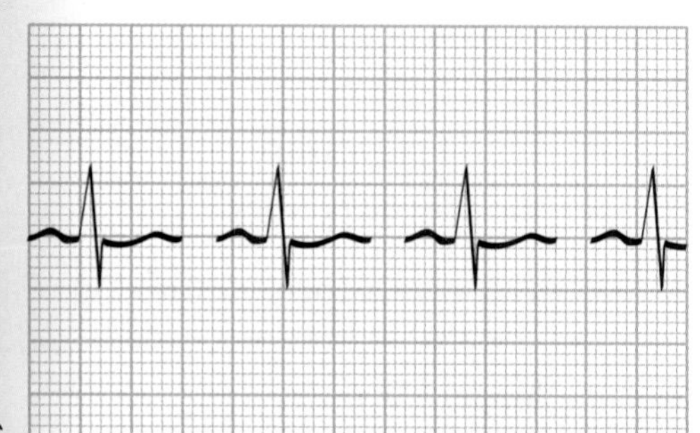
C

15. On the following illustrations draw an example of atrial, ventricular, and AV sequential pacemaker spikes.

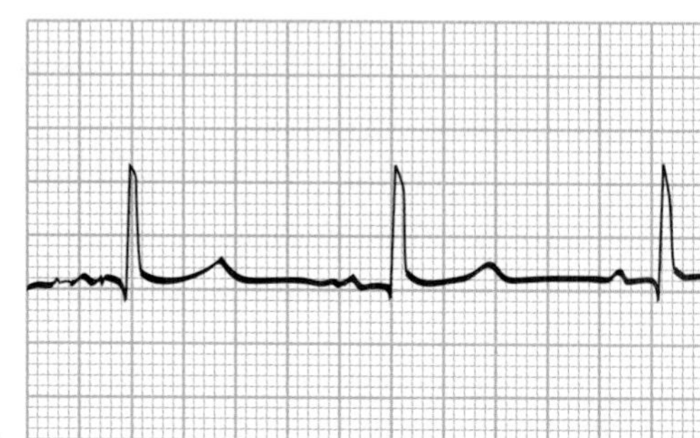
A

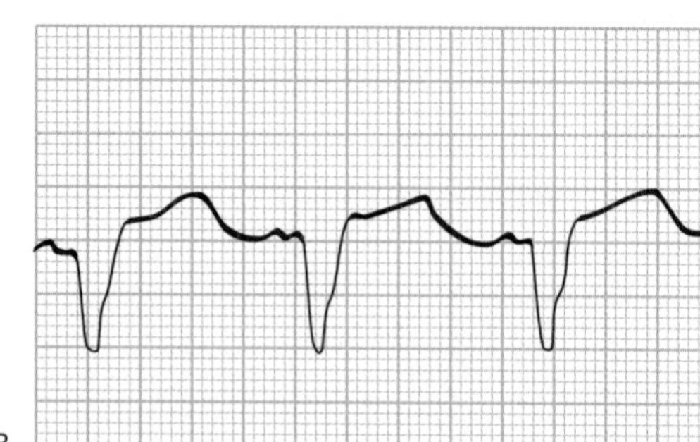
B

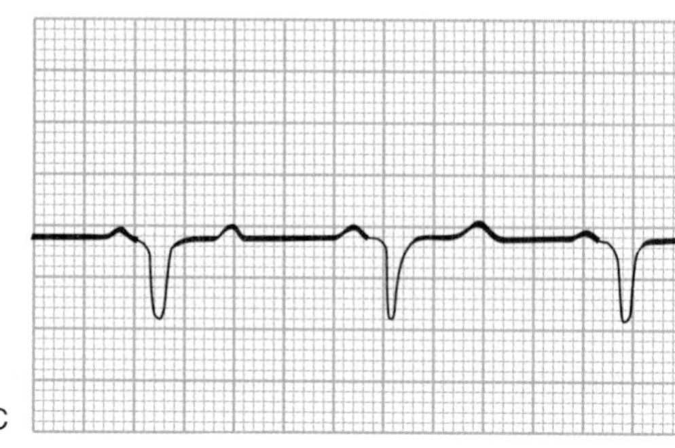
C

Referring to the scenario at the beginning of this chapter, answer the following questions.

16. What electrolyte abnormality is responsible for the patient's cardiac irregularity?
    a. Hyponatremia.
    b. Hypercalcemia.
    c. Hyperkalemia.
    d. Hypoglycemia.

17. What is characteristic of the T wave configuration in this condition?
    a. Shaped like a tent.
    b. Shaped like a mound.
    c. Notched.
    d. Round and wide.

18. What other changes to the ECG can be expected with this condition?
    a. Prolonged PR interval and widening of the QRS complex.
    b. Shortened PR interval and widening of the QRS complex.
    c. Prolonged P wave and inverted T waves.
    d. Prolonged PR interval and notching of the T waves.

Answers to Sidebar Questions

"What are the two layers of the pericardium?"

Answer: The pericardium, a double-walled closed sac, has two layers. The tough, fibrous outer layer is called the fibrous pericardium, and the inner, thin transparent lining is called the serous pericardium.

"What is the normal amplitude of the QRS complex?"

Answer: The amplitude of the normal QRS complex is 5 to 30 mm high.

"What role does potassium play in the generation and conduction of nerve impulses?"

Answer: Potassium plays a key role in repolarization of the nerve cells.

"What is torsades de pointes?"

Answer: Torsades de pointes is a unique variant of polymorphic ventricular tachycardia. It is characterized by QRS complexes that alternate (usually gradually) between upright deflections and downward deflections.

On the DVD

- Pacemakers lecture.

Notes

APPENDIX

A

Answers to Chapter Questions

Chapter 1

Answers to Assess Your Understanding

1. d: The electrocardiogram measures the heart's electrical activity. The pulse strength is measured by taking the patient's pulse while the blood pressure is measured with a sphygmomanometer.
2. b: Depolarization occurs when there is a rapid influx of positively charged ions from outside to inside the cell. During depolarization sodium enters the cells through the fast channels followed by calcium entering through the slow channels.
3. b: Nerve impulses stimulate muscle cells to contract. Without this nerve stimulation, the muscles will not contract. For this reason you can see that nerve impulse stimulation is extremely important.
4. b: The upper chambers of the heart are called the atria. The ventricles are the lower chambers of the heart.
5. a: While electrical impulses can arise from other locations in the heart, the electrical impulse that arises from the SA node normally initiates the heartbeat.
6. c: The impulse traveling through the His-Purkinje fibers generates a flat line following the P wave on the ECG.
7. b: The QRS complex represents ventricular depolarization.
8. a: Depolarization of the myocardium progresses from the atria to the ventricles in an orderly fashion. This is necessary to produce the coordinated contraction of the atria and then the ventricles.
9. c: The T wave represents ventricular repolarization.
10. b: The AV junction pacemaker cells have an intrinsic rate of 40 to 60 beats per minute. The ventricles including the His-Purkinje system have an intrinsic rate of 20 to 40 beats per minute.
11. b: The myocardium receives its blood supply via the coronary arteries. Blood flow through the coronary arteries occurs during diastole. The coronary veins return the blood to the right atrium.
12. d: Cardiac output is equal to the stroke volume (amount ejected from the ventricles with contraction) multiplied by the heart rate. A decrease in either the stroke volume or the heart rate can decrease cardiac output.
13. c: The sympathetic branch of the autonomic nervous system, also referred to as the adrenergic system, produces the "fight or flight" response. It works the opposite of the parasympathetic nervous system.
14. c: The parasympathetic nervous system is not referred to as the "adrenergic nervous system." Instead it is referred to as the "cholinergic nervous system."
15. a: Myocardial ischemia will occur if the flow of blood in the coronary arteries is diminished.
16. b: Pain causes a release of epinephrine which acts through the sympathetic nervous system to increase heart rate and blood pressure. The pain originates in the heart muscle which is starving for oxygen. Hypertension alone will not cause the heart rate to increase. Nicotine in large doses will cause the heart rate to increase but not to the level seen in this case. Parasympathetic nervous system stimulation would decrease, not increase, the heart rate.
17. d: The affected myocardial tissue becomes necrotic.

Chapter 2

Answers to Assess Your Understanding

1. a: An electrocardiogram is a graphic record of the heart's electrical activity.
2. a: Electrodes positioned on the patient's skin detect the heart's electrical activity. The ECG machine determines which electrode is positive, negative, or ground based on the lead selected.
3. b: Each small square on the ECG paper running horizontally represents 0.04 seconds in duration.

*The values listed in the following answers were determined using the heart rate calculator (supplied with this text) to determine the heart rate in regular rhythms and in irregular rhythms where there was a sufficient amount of underlying rhythm to make the determination.

The 6-second x 10 interval method was used for irregular rhythms such as totally or patterned irregularity except in the case of ventricular bigeminy—with these dysrhythmias we estimated where the normal QRS complexes would have fallen (if the PVCs were not there) and used the heart rate calculator. Alternatively, the 6-second x 10 interval method can be used to determine the heart rate.

The top portion of the heart rate calculator was used to determine the various durations. Practically speaking, your answers may differ slightly from the textbook depending on where you identify the waveform, segment or interval beginnings and endings. Small variances are not cause for concern. Helpful hints for determining the duration of the QRS complex can be found on page 176 of the text.

4. c: The larger box on the ECG paper which is made up of five small squares represents 0.20 seconds in duration.
5. b: Vertical markings on the top or bottom of the ECG paper represent 3-second intervals.
6. a: Each small square on the ECG paper running vertically represents 1 mm or 0.1 mV. Four small squares represent an amplitude of four mm or 0.4 mV.
7. a: The reference point used to identify the changing electrical amplitude on the ECG is called the isoelectric line.
8. d: Impulses that travel toward a positive electrode and away from a negative electrode are recorded on the electrocardiogram as upwards, upright, or positive deflections. Impulses traveling toward a negative electrode and away from a positive electrode are recorded as downward deflections.
9. a: Initiation of the impulse in the SA node and its movement through the atria produces a P wave. In lead II the P wave is upright and round with an amplitude not exceeding 2 to 3 mm in height and a duration of 0.06 to 0.12 seconds.
10. a: The normal PR interval is 0.12 to 0.20 seconds in duration.
11. b: The PR interval represents depolarization of the heart from the SA node through the atria and into the AV node.
12. c: The Q wave is the first negative deflection after the PR segment. It isn't always present.
13. c: Artifact may be caused by the patient moving, shivering or experiencing muscle tremors, worn out leadwires, a malfunctioning ECG machine, or the presence of 60-cycle current interference.
14. b: The frontal plane gives us a superior and inferior view of the heart's electrical activity.
15. a: The limb leads are obtained by placing electrodes on the right arm (RA), left arm (LA), and left leg (LL).
16. a: Leads I, II and III are referred to as the standard limb leads.
17. d: Leads V_1, V_2, V_3, V_4, V_5, V_6 are referred to as the precordial leads.
18. b: With lead II the positive electrode is placed on the left leg. Because depolarization of the heart flows in the same path as the negative to positive layout of the ECG electrodes the waveforms should appear upright or in a positive direction.
19. c: Lead II is a commonly used lead for continuous ECG monitoring.
20. c: With the MCL_1 lead the positive electrode is positioned on the fourth intercostal space in the right sternal border.
21. b: The ECG only measures electrical activity which we call the heart rate on the monitor. The pulse is the actual palpated beat of the heart felt at the wrist or other pressure point. It must be correlated with the ECG to ensure that every complex seen on the monitor results in a pulse. The blood pressure can only be measured using a blood pressure cuff that detects the mechanical pulse of the heart. Cardiac output can only be measured using a special device called an echocardiogram that measures the stroke volume of the contraction. Stroke volume is then multiplied by heart rate to obtain cardiac output.
22. d: Regardless of the patient's stroke volume, if the heart rate decreases significantly the cardiac output will diminish to the point the brain does not receive adequate perfusion resulting in a loss of consciousness.
23. c: The vagus nerve supplies parasympathetic tone to the heart. When it fires the heartbeat slows. When it stops firing the heart beats more quickly.

Chapter 3

Answers to Assess Your Understanding*

1. c: To analyze the ECG tracing you should use a logical and systematic approach. If a dysrhythmia or abnormality is present, this finding should be compared with your assessment of the patient.
2. b: Each dysrhythmia has specific characteristics. Successful ECG analysis is dependent on learning the characteristics or features of each normal and abnormal ECG then comparing what you see on the ECG tracing to those characteristics.
3. d: The first step in analyzing an ECG is determining the heart rate. Begin by quickly checking the ECG monitor or tracing to see if the rate is slow, normal, or fast.
4. a: The 6-second interval x 10 method can be used to estimate the heart rate in irregular rhythms.
5. d: To use the 300, 150, 100, 75, 60, 50 method locate an R wave that falls on or close to a bold line to make counting easier.
6. a: To use the 1,500 method you count the number of small squares between two consecutive R waves and divide 1,500 by that number.
7. c: The most accurate method for determining the heart rate in the regular rhythm is the 1,500 method.
8. c: Sinus bradycardia is a rhythm that arises from the SA node and has a heart rate of less than 60 beats per minute.
9. b: Tachycardia leads to decreased myocardial oxygen consumption.
10. The heart rate of this dysrhythmia is 65.
11. The heart rate of this dysrhythmia is 50.
12. The heart rate of this dysrhythmia is 130.
13. d. Because cardiac output is seriously diminished with rates higher than 250, if the patient did in fact have a pulse of 320 she would most likely have signs of shock such as an altered level of responsiveness and hypotension.
14. c: Hyperthyroidism is a condition of excess thyroxin in the blood from an overactive thyroid gland. Thyroxin acts like a sympathomimetic agent resulting in an elevated heart rate. While anxiety can produce tachycardia it rarely does so to a level of 160 beats per minute. There is no evidence that the patient is either hypoxic of abusing amphetamine.

Answers to Practice Makes Perfect Exercises

1. Heart rate = fast.
2. Heart rate = normal.
3. Heart rate = slow.

4. Heart rate = 140.
5. Heart rate = 60.
6. Heart rate = 40.
7. Heart rate = 70.
8. Heart rate = 210.
9. Heart rate = 100.
10. Heart rate = 41.
11. Heart rate = 94.
12. Heart rate = 59.
13. Heart rate = 125.

Chapter 4

Answers to Check Your Understanding

1. d: Normally the heart beats in a regular, rhythmic fashion, producing a P wave, QRS complex, and T wave with each heartbeat.
2. a: The distance between two consecutive R waves is called the R-R interval.
3. a: The second step in analyzing an ECG is checking the regularity. A regular rhythm is considered normal while an irregular rhythm is considered abnormal.
4. c: Calipers can be used to analyze an ECG by placing leg 1 on a starting point and extending leg 2 to the next consecutive waveform that is being assessed. With the calipers open in that position and keeping the point positioned over the second P wave or R wave rotate the calipers across to the peak of the next consecutive (the third) P wave or R wave. If the R-R interval or P-P interval is the same the point will be above the next R wave or P wave. If the R-R interval or P-P interval is different the point will be either before or after the identified waveform.
5. d: The paper and pen method Involves placing two marks on the paper, the first above one of the R waves on the ECG tracing and the second above the next consecutive R wave.
6. a: To use the counting the small square method you count the number of small squares between the peaks of two consecutive R waves and then compare that to the other R-R intervals.
7. c: The easiest method for determining heart rhythm regularity in which you can use supplies that are readily available is the paper and pen method.
8. a: An occasionally irregular rhythm is one that appears mostly regular but from time to time you see an area where it is irregular. A premature or early complex, also called ectopy, is a common cause of this type of irregularity.
9. b: Premature beats are also called ectopy. They cause the R-R intervals between the normal and premature beat to be shorter than normal
10. d: Sinus arrest happens when the SA node fails to initiate an impulse. It causes the R-R interval between the normal and the beat following the dropped beat to be longer than normal.
11. a: A slightly irregular rhythm is one where the P-P and R-R intervals vary somewhat. One dysrhythmia that causes a slightly irregular rhythm is wandering atrial pacemaker.
12. c: The term we use to describe sudden onset is paroxysmal.
13. d: Patterned irregularity is where the irregularity repeats itself over and over again in a cyclic fashion.
14. c: Atrial fibrillation is a chaotically or grossly irregular rhythm.
15. d: Premature complexes occuring every other (second) complex, every third complex, or every fourth complex produce a patterned irregular rhythm.
16. The heart rate is 107. This rhythm is regular.
17. The heart rate is 60. This rhythm is patterned irregularity.
18. The heart rate is 70. This rhythm is occasionalyy irregular.
19. The heart rate is 90. This rhythm is patterned irregularity.
20. The heart rate is 90. This rhythm is slightly irregular.
21. c: The only rhythm that is characterized as totally irregular is atrial fibrillation. Atrial flutter usually has a set conduction ratio of 3:1 or 4:1 and can vary slightly but overall is generally regular. Sinus dysrhythmia arrhythmia has a regular pattern to the irregularity and is associated with the respiratory rate. Ventricular fibrillation is totally chaotic and results in no cardiac output that would cause the patient to lose unconscious.
22. b: The muscle fibers of the atria, like all cardiac muscle, have the ability to spontaneously depolarize due to their level of automaticity. In atrial fibrillation, numerous areas within the atrial wall are firing simultaneously bombarding the AV node with impulses. The AV node responds to these impulses irregularly, letting some pass through while blocking others.
23. d: Due to the inefficient contraction of the atria, blood pools and clots form along the wall of the atria. Pieces of this thrombus can break off and travel to the brain and lodge in a cerebral artery causing a stroke.

Answers to Practice Makes Perfect Exercises

1. Heart rate is 125. Rhythm is regular.
2. Heart rate is 60. Rhythm is irregular.
3. Heart rate is 100. Rhythm is regular.
4. Heart rate is 58. Rhythm is frequently irregular.
5. Heart rate is 140. Rhythm is totally irregular.
6. Heart rate is 100. Rhythm is occasionally irregular.
7. Heart rate is 70. Rhythm is patterned irregularity.
8. Heart rate is 60 accelerating to 160. Rhythm is sudden acceleration.
9. Heart rate is 100. Rhythm is patterned irregularity.
10. Heart rate is 100. Rhythm is totally irregular.
11. Heart rate is 70. Rhythm is occasionally irregular.
12. Heart rate is 70. Rhythm is patterned irregularity.
13. Heart rate is 60. Rhythm is regular.
14. Heart rate is 60. Rhythm is totally irregular.
15. Heart rate is 62. Rhythm is regular.
16. Heart rate is 90. Rhythm is totally irregular.
17. Heart rate is 50. Rhythm is patterned irregularity.
18. Heart rate is 100. Rhythm is frequently irregular. It may also be described as patterned irregularity (except the portion of the middle of the tracing).

Chapter 5

Answers to Assess Your Understanding

1. c: The P waves are best evaluated by choosing the appropriate lead.
2. a: In lead aV_R the P wave is normally negative or inverted.
3. b: The third step in analyzing an ECG is looking at the P waves.
4. b: The amplitude of the P wave normally does not exceed 2.5 mm high.
5. d: An upright, round P wave (in lead II) that precedes each QRS complex indicates that the electrical impulse originated in the SA node and was carried through the atria in a normal manner.
6. d: Rounded and upright P waves are normal. P waves that follow the QRS complexes, P waves that are inverted, or P waves that are peaked or notched are considered abnormal.
7. d: Enlarged or damaged atria are among the causes that produce P waves that look different than sinus P waves.
8. c: An impulse that arises closer to the SA node produces a P wave that looks more like a normal P wave than an impulse that arises from the lower right atrium.
9. c: Premature atrial complexes may have P′ waves that are buried in the T wave of the preceding beat.
10. b: With atrial tachycardia the P′ wave looks different than P waves that arise from the SA node.
11. a: A pacemaker site that changes from location to location has P waves that continually change in appearance.
12. a: With atrial fibrillation the P waves are not discernible; instead, there is a chaotic looking baseline.
13. b: Junctional dysrhythmias have inverted P′ waves.
14. c: With junctional dysrhythmias the P′ waves may immediately precede, be buried in, or follow the QRS complexes.
15. c: More P waves than QRS complexes are seen with AV heart block.
16. Rate = 214, regular, P waves buried in T wave.
17. Rate = 78, regular, P waves vary.
18. Rate = 100, totally irregular, f waves.
19. Rate = 60, patterned irregularity, normal P waves.
20. Rate = 130, regular, F waves.
21. d: The presence of "saw-toothed" flutter "f" waves is characteristic of atrial flutter.
22. d: Since the QRS complex (ventricular firing) occurs after every fourth flutter wave (atrial firing) the atrial rate is four times the ventricular rate. $36 \times 4 = 144$/min

Answers to Practice Makes Perfect Exercises

1. 130, regular, normal P waves.
2. 75, regular, peaked P waves.
3. 100, totally irregular, chaotic baseline f waves.
4. 98, occasionally irregular, notched P waves.
5. 88, regular, biphasic P waves.
6. 78, regular, absent P waves.
7. 50, regular, normal P waves.
8. 90, totally irregular, F waves with variable conduction ratio and areas of f waves.
9. 185, regular, pointed P waves.
10. 55, regular, absent P waves.
11. 72, regular, normal P waves.
12. 140, totally irregular; chaotic baseline f waves.
13. 50, patterned irregularity, more P waves than QRS complexes.
14. 80, variable conduction ratio, F waves with variable conduction ratio.

Chapter 6

Answers to Assess Your Understanding

1. b: The lead used to assess the ECG affects the appearance of the QRS complexes.
2. b: In leads I, II, III, aV_L, aV_F, and V_4 to V_6 the deflection of the QRS complex is characteristically positive or upright.
3. c: The fourth step in analyzing an ECG is examining the QRS complexes.
4. a: The normal duration of the QRS complex is 0.06 to 0.12 seconds.
5. d: An upright (in lead II) narrow QRS complex indicates that the electrical impulse originated at or above the AV node and was carried through the ventricles in a normal manner.
6. a: The R wave is the first positive deflection in the QRS complex.
7. c: Premature atrial complexes (PACs) produce normal QRS complexes.
8. c: The amplitude of QRS complexes is higher in the precordial leads than the limb leads.
9. c: Intraventricular conduction defect is usually due to right or left bundle branch block.
10. b: Low voltage or abnormally small QRS complexes are seen in obese patients.
11. c: Bundle branch block is a cause of intraventricular conduction defect.
12. a: Bundle branch blocks may be partial or complete.
13. d: Aberrant conduction is a brief failure of one of the bundle branches conducting an electrical impulse normally.
14. c: Premature ventricular complexes produce QRS complexes that look different than those that arise above or at the AV junction.
15. a: Idioventricular rhythm has wide, bizarre-looking QRS complexes.
16. b: With ventricular tachycardia the ventricular rate is 100 to 250 beats per minute.
17. d: With 3rd-degree AV heart block the QRS complexes are slower than the P wave rate because there is complete blockage of the AV node.
18. c: Torsades de pointes has a spindle-shaped appearance.
19. b: Ventricular fibrillation is seen as a chaotic wavy line on the ECG.
20. d: Asystole is seen as a flat line on the ECG.

21. 72, occasionally irregular, normal P waves preceding each normal QRS complex, normal QRS complexes except the early beat which is wide and bizarre in appearance.
22. 105, patterned irregularity, normal P waves preceding each normal QRS complex, normal QRS complexes alternating with wide QRS complexes which are bizarre in appearance.
23. Immeasurable rate, totally chaotic, no atrial waveforms, no QRS complexes.
24. 214, regular, normal P waves preceding each QRS complex, wide QRS complexes.
25. 214, regular, no atrial waveforms, wide QRS complexes.
26. c: The extra complexes are QRS complexes without P waves and therefore originate in the ventricles and not the atria. They originate from multiple sites (foci) because each has a different shape and configuration. Therefore they are termed multi-focal premature ventricular complexes.
27. c: While pain and anxiety can result in sufficient sympathetic stimulation to cause the occasional unifocal PVC neither will cause frequent multifocal PVCs. Ischemia (tissue hypoxia) results in irritability of the cardiac muscle and increased automaticity resulting in the extra beats. The worse the ischemia the more sites are irritated and therefore the more foci of PVC generation. Infarcted muscle is dead and cannot generate an electrical impulse.

Answers to Practice Makes Perfect Exercises

1. 115, slightly irregular, varying atrial waveforms, QRS = 0.10 sec.
2. 75, regular, normal P waves, QRS = 0.08 sec.
3. 72, regular, P′ waves follow the QRS complexes, QRS = 0.08 sec.
4. 70, regular, normal P waves, QRS = 0.08 sec.
5. 136, regular, peaked P waves, QRS = 0.08 sec.
6. 60, patterned irregularity, normal P waves, normal QRS complexes = 0.08 sec, with early beats QRS complex = 0.24 sec.
7. 65, occasionally irregular, normal P waves, normal QRS complexes = 0.12 sec, with early beat the QRS complex = 0.20 sec.
8. 30, regular, absent P waves, QRS = 0.14 sec.
9. 90, patterned irregularity, normal P waves, normal QRS complexes = 0.08 sec, with early beats QRS complexes = 0.20 sec.
10. 150, regular, absent atrial waveforms, QRS complexes = 0.16 sec.
11. 70, occasionally irregular, normal P waves, QRS = 0.08 sec.
12. 65, regular, normal P waves, QRS = 0.12 sec.
13. 60, occasionally irregular, normal P waves, QRS = 0.12 sec.
14. 80, variable irregularity, F waves, QRS = 0.08 sec.
15. 120, regular, wide P waves, QRS = 0.16 sec.
16. Immeasurable rate, totally irregular, absent atrial waveforms, no QRS complexes.
17. 58, occasionally irregular, normal P waves, normal QRS complexes = 0.08 sec, with early beats QRS complexes = 0.16 sec.
18. 100, regular, normal P waves, wide QRS complexes = 0.14 sec.
19. 79, occasionally irregular, normal P waves, QRS complexes = 0.12 sec.

Chapter 7

Answers to Assess Your Understanding

1. c: The fifth step in analyzing an ECG is assessing the PR intervals.
2. b: The PR interval is the distance from the beginning of the P wave to the beginning of the Q wave.
3. d: The PR interval denotes depolarization of the heart from the SA node through the atria and AV node.
4. d: The normal duration of the PR interval is 0.12 to 0.20 seconds.
5. a: A shorter than normal PR interval is one that is less than 0.12 seconds in duration.
6. d: A rounded and upright P wave is considered normal. A P wave that follows the QRS complex, a P wave that is inverted, or a peaked or notched P wave would be considered abnormal.
7. d: PR intervals of greater than 0.20 seconds are characteristic of 1st-degree AV heart block.
8. b: With wandering atrial pacemaker the PR intervals vary.
9. d: With Wenckebach the PR intervals get progressively longer.
10. c: There is an absence of PR intervals with 3rd-degree AV heart block.
11. b: Type II, 2nd-degree AV heart block has PR intervals that are constant.
12. 72 BPM (atrial and ventricular), regular rhythm (except one small square variation between the 4th and 5th R waves), P waves are normal , QRS complexes are normal, PRI = 0.16 seconds.
13. 100 BPM (atrial and ventricular), occasionally irregular, P waves are normal (although some appear slightly biphasic), P wave of early beat is buried in T wave of preceding beat, QRS (more accurately described as QS) complexes are present, PRI = 0.18 seconds (although some appear to be 0.16 seconds).
14. 100 BPM (ventricular), greater than 350 BPM (atrial), totally irregular, indiscernible P waves – f waves are present, QRS complexes are normal , PRI is immeasurable.
15. 72 BPM (atrial and ventricular), occasionally irregular, P waves are normal , QRS complexes are normal, PRI = 0.20 seconds.
16. 60 BPM (ventricular), 80 BPM (atrial), patterned irregularity, P waves are normal although some are not followed by a QRS complex, QRS complexes are normal, PRI progressively lengthens until a QRS complex is dropped and the cycle repeats.
17. c: The rhythm has a regular irregularity to it indicating that there is a pattern to the number of P waves conducted to the AV node. Because the PR interval increases with each beat until it is too long to be conducted to the AV node this is 2nd-degree AV heart block Type I.

18. a: Death of the AV node results in total blockage of impulses from the SA node and atria. The result is complete heart block.

Answers to Practice Makes Perfect Exercises

1. 100 BPM (atrial and ventricular), regular rhythm, P waves are upright and normal, QRS complexes are normal at 0.12 seconds in duration, PRI = 0.12 seconds in duration.
2. 75 BPM (atrial and ventricular), regular rhythm, P waves are upright and normal, QRS complexes are normal at 0.08 seconds in duration, PRI = 0.16 seconds in duration.
3. 40 BPM (atrial and ventricular), regular rhythm, P waves are upright and normal, QRS complexes are normal at 0.12 seconds in duration, PRI = 0.12 seconds in duration.
4. 70 BPM (atrial and ventricular), regular rhythm, P waves are inverted, QRS complexes are normal at 0.08 seconds, PRI = 0.08 seconds in duration.
5. 60, patterned irregularity (every third beat is a premature beat - trigeminy), P waves are upright and normal but those with the premature beats differ from the P waves of the underlying rhythm, QRS complexes are normal at 0.12 seconds in duration for both the underlying rhythm and the early beats, PRI = 0.18 seconds in duration for the normal beats but varies with the premature beats between 0.16 and 0.18 seconds.
6. 56 BPM (atrial and ventricular), regular rhythm, P waves are upright and normal, QRS complexes are normal at 0.08 seconds in duration, PRI has a longer than normal duration at 0.30 seconds.
7. 100 BPM (ventricular), greater than 350 BPM (atrial), totally irregular, indiscernible P waves – f waves are present, QRS (more accurately described as RS) complexes are normal at 0.10 seconds in duration, PRI is immeasurable.
8. 56 BPM, regular rhythm, P waves are absent, QRS complexes are bizarre-looking and wide at 0.26 seconds in duration , PRI is immeasurable.
9. 100 BPM (atrial and ventricular), patterned irregularity (every other beat is a premature beat – bigeminy), P waves are upright and normal with the underlying rhythm and absent with the premature beats, QRS complexes are normal at 0.08 seconds in duration for the underlying rhythm and bizarre-looking and wide at 0.20 seconds in duration for the early beats, PRI = 0.16 seconds for the normal beats but absent with the premature beats.
10. 130 BPM (ventricular), between 250 and 350 BPM (atrial), regular rhythm, F waves are present, QRS (more accurately described as RS) complexes are normal at 0.08 seconds in duration, PRI is immeasurable.
11. 60 BPM (atrial and ventricular), regular rhythm, P waves are upright and notched, QRS complexes are wide at 0.20 seconds in duration, PRI = 0.22 seconds in duration.
12. 65 BPM (atrial and ventricular), slightly irregular rhythm (two small square variation between the 2nd and 3rd R waves, one small square variation between 3rd and 4th R waves and two small square variation between the 4th and 5th R waves), P waves are upright and normal, QRS complexes are normal at 0.10 seconds in duration, PRI = 0.16 seconds in duration.
13. 44 BPM (atrial and ventricular), regular rhythm, P waves are inverted, QRS complexes are normal at 0.08 seconds in duration, PRI = 0.16 seconds in duration.
14. 48 BPM (ventricular) 84 BPM (atrial), regular rhythm, P waves are upright and normal but there are more P waves than QRS complexes, QRS complexes are bizarre-looking and wide at 0.20 seconds in duration, PRI is immeasurable (as the P waves are not associated with the QRS complexes).
15. 120 BPM (atrial and ventricular), regular rhythm, P waves are upright and normal, QRS complexes are upright and normal at 0.08 seconds in duration, PRI = 0.20 seconds in duration.
16. 140 BPM (ventricular), greater than 350 BPM (atrial), totally irregular, indiscernible P waves – f waves are present QRS (more accurately described as RS) complexes are normal at 0.06 seconds in duration, PRI is immeasurable.
17. 60 BPM (atrial and ventricular), regular rhythm, P waves are upright and normal, QRS complexes are upright but notched at 0.10 seconds in duration, PRI = 0.20 seconds in duration.
18. 167 BPM (atrial and ventricular), regular rhythm, P waves are absent, QRS (more accurately described as RS) complexes at 0.08 seconds in duration, PRI is immeasurable.
19. 136 BPM (atrial and ventricular), regular rhythm, P waves are upright and peaked, QRS complexes are upright and normal at 0.08 seconds in duration, PRI = 0.12 seconds in duration.

Chapter 8

Answers to Assess Your Understanding

1. a: Rhythms that arise from the sinus node include normal sinus rhythm, sinus bradycardia, sinus tachycardia, sinus dysrhythmia, and sinus arrest.
2. b: Key characteristics of sinus rhythms are normal P waves, normal QRS complexes, and PR intervals that are within normal duration of 0.12 to 0.20 seconds and constant.
3. b: During normal heart activity the SA node is the primary pacemaker.
4. b: Characteristics of sinus rhythm include a rate of between 60 and 100 beats per minute.
5. c: The heart rate that is characteristic of sinus bradycardia is less than 60 beats per minute.
6. a: Sinus bradycardia often occurs naturally.
7. c: Characteristics of sinus bradycardia include a regular rhythm,
8. c: Sinus tachycardia may be caused by ingestion of caffeine or alcohol, smoking, fever.
9. b: In sinus tachycardia, the P waves, PR intervals, and QRS complexes are normal.
10. a: The type of irregularity seen with sinus dysrhythmia is called patterned irregularity.

11. d: Sinus dysrhythmia has round and upright P waves in lead II.
12. d: sinus arrest usually results in a brief pause in all electrical activity.
13. d: With sinus arrest the escape mechanism that follows the pause in electrical activity may arise from the atria, AV junction, or ventricles.
14. d: Sinus bradycardia has a rate of less than 60 beats per minute.
15. c: Sinus dysrhythmia is a dysrhythmia with patterned irregularity.
16. b: Sinus arrest occurs when the SA node transiently stops firing.
17. a: Since there is a P wave for every QRS complex and a QRS complex for every P wave, 2nd- and 3rd-degree AV heart block are excluded. Because the PR interval is normal it is not junctional, which is associated with a short PR interval and inverted P wave. Because the rhythm is initiated by a normal P wave it is a sinus rhythm and because the rate is less than 60 it is sinus bradycardia.
18. b: The vagus nerve exerts a parasympathetic stimulus to the SA node causing it to slow down.
19. a: The carotid body is a cluster of sensors surrounding the carotid artery that monitor the stretch of the carotid artery during systole.

Answers to Practice Makes Perfect Exercises

1. Atrial rate = 86 BPM, Ventricular rate = 86 BPM, regular rhythm, normal and upright P waves, notched QRS complexes at 0.10 seconds, PRI = 0.16 seconds, QT = 0.40 seconds. Normal sinus rhythm.
2. Atrial rate = 72 BPM, Ventricular rate = 72 BPM, regular rhythm, normal and upright P waves, QRS (more accurately described as RS) complexes at 0.08 seconds, PRI = 0.16 seconds, QT = 0.34 seconds. Normal sinus rhythm.
3. Atrial rate = 41 BPM, Ventricular rate = 41 BPM, regular rhythm, normal and upright P waves, Normal QRS complexes at 0.10 seconds, PRI = 0.20 seconds, QT = 0.48 seconds. Sinus bradycardia.
4. Atrial rate = 80 BPM, Ventricular rate = 80 BPM, Patterned irregularity (speeds up toward center of tracing and slows back down again), normal and upright P waves, normal QRS complexes at 0.08 seconds, PRI = 0.16 seconds, QT = 0.34 seconds. Sinus dysrhythmia.
5. Atrial rate = 125 BPM, Ventricular rate = 125 BPM, regular rhythm, normal and upright P waves, normal QRS complexes at 0.08 seconds, PRI = 0.14 seconds, QT = 0.24 seconds. Sinus tachycardia.
6. Atrial rate = 94 BPM, Ventricular rate = 94 BPM, regular rhythm, biphasic P waves, QRS (more accurately described as RS) complexes at 0.12 seconds, PRI = 0.12 seconds, QT = 0.32 seconds. Regular sinus rhythm.
7. Atrial rate = 60 BPM, Ventricular rate = 60 BPM, patterned irregularity (rate slows toward center of tracing and speeds up again), notched and upright P waves, QRS (more accurately described as RS) complexes at 0.08 seconds, PRI = 0.16 seconds, QT = 0.40 seconds. Sinus dysrhythmia.
8. Atrial rate = 40 BPM, Ventricular rate = 40 BPM, regular rhythm, normal and upright P waves, normal QRS complexes at 0.10 seconds, PRI = 0.20 seconds, QT = 0.48 seconds. Sinus bradycardia.
9. Atrial rate = 88 BPM, Ventricular rate = 88 BPM, regular rhythm, peaked P waves, QRS (more accurately described as RS) complexes at 0.12 seconds, PRI = 0.16 seconds, QT = 0.40 seconds. Normal sinus rhythm.
10. Atrial rate = 75 BPM, Ventricular rate = 75 BPM, regular rhythm, normal and upright P waves, QRS (more accurately described as RS) complexes at 0.12 seconds, PRI = 0.20 seconds, QT = 0.40 seconds. Normal sinus rhythm.

Chapter 9

Answers to Assess Your Understanding

1. a: With atrial dysrhythmias the atrial waveforms differ in appearance from normal sinus P waves.
2. c: In wandering atrial pacemaker, the pacemaker site shifts between the SA node, atria, and/or AV junction. This produces its key characteristic, P′ waves which change in appearance.
3. d: Wandering atrial pacemaker produces an irregular rhythm with normal QRS complexes and P′ waves that differ as often as from beat to beat.
4. d: Premature atrial complexes may have normal P′R intervals.
5. a: (True) A PAC arises earlier in the cardiac cycle and will interrupt the regularity of the underlying rhythm.
6. c: The heart rate characteristic of atrial tachycardia is 150 to 250 beats per minute.
7. a: The QRS complexes seen with atrial tachycardia are normally 0.06 to 0.12 seconds in duration.
8. b: With multifocal atrial tachycardia the heart rate is 120 to 150 beats per minute.
9. c: Atrial flutter has a characteristic saw-tooth pattern.
10. c: Atrial flutter has an atrial rate of between 250 and 350 beats per minute.
11. c: Atrial fibrillation has normal QRS complexes.
12. b: The atrial waveforms associated with atrial fibrillation are indiscernible and the PR intervals are nonexistent.
13. d: Atrial fibrillation has a totally irregular rhythm.
14. d: Atrial fibrillation has an atrial rate of greater than 350 beats per minute.
15. c: The saw-toothed P waves are known as flutter waves which are characteristic of atrial flutter. The QRS complex will be narrow as long as there is no conduction defect in the bundle of His and will respond in a patterned manner as a generally consistent ratio of flutter waves to QRS complexes
16. b: As the heart rate increases there is less time for the ventricles to fill between beats. The amount of blood ejected (stroke volume) diminishes and the cardiac output decreases despite the rise in heart rate. This is particularly true in the elderly who have less efficient contraction of the ventricles secondary to aging.
17. c: Cardiac output is equal to heart rate multiplied by stroke volume

Answers to Practice Makes Perfect Exercises

1. Atrial rate = 80 BPM, Ventricular rate = 80 BPM, occasionally irregular, normal and upright P waves (P′ wave of premature beat differs from P waves of underlying rhythm), normal QRS complexes at 0.08 seconds, PRI = 0.16 seconds, QT = 0.38 seconds. Normal sinus rhythm with a premature atrial complex (PAC) (7th beat).
2. Atrial rate = 80 BPM, Ventricular rate = 80 BPM, regular rhythm, varying P waves, normal QRS complexes at 0.08 seconds, PRI varies, QT = 0.32 seconds, normal. Wandering atrial pacemaker.
3. Atrial rate is greater than 350 BPM, Ventricular rate = 90 BPM, totally irregular, P waves are indiscernible – f waves are present, normal QRS complexes at 0.08 seconds, PRI is immeasurable, QT = 0.28 seconds. Atrial fibrillation.
4. Atrial rate = 300 BPM, Ventricular rate = 150 BPM, regular rhythm, atrial waveforms have saw-tooth pattern – F waves are present, normal QRS complexes at 0.12 seconds, PRI immeasurable, QT = 0.28 seconds. Atrial flutter with 2:1 conduction ratio.
5. Atrial rate = 170 BPM , Ventricular rate = 170 BPM, regular rhythm, P′ waves are upright and present, QRS (more accurately described as RS) complexes at 0.08 seconds, PRI = 0.08 seconds, QT = 0.24 seconds. Atrial tachycardia.
6. Atrial rate = 80 BPM, Ventricular rate = 80 BPM, frequently irregular (for what can be seen on this tracing), upright and normal P waves in the underlying rhythm, P′ waves of premature beats differ from the underlying rhythm (the P′ wave of the second PAC is buried in T wave of preceding beat), normal QRS (more accurately described as RS) complexes at 0.10 seconds, PRI = 0.12 seconds, QT = 0.40 seconds for the underlying rhythm. Normal sinus rhythm with 2 premature atrial complexes (PACs) (2nd and 5th complexes).
7. Atrial rate is greater than 350 BPM, Ventricular rate = 140 BPM, totally irregular, P waves are indiscernible – f waves are present, QRS (more accurately described as RS) complexes at 0.08 seconds, PRI is immeasurable, QT = 0.28 seconds. Atrial fibrillation with rapid ventricular response.
8. Atrial rate is approximately 500 BPM (quite fast for an atrial flutter), Ventricular rate = 130 BPM, regular rhythm, F waves, normal QRS complexes at 0.08 seconds, PRI is immeasurable, QT is immeasurable. Atrial flutter with 4:1 conduction ratio.
9. Atrial rate = 80 BPM, Ventricular rate = 80 BPM, occasionally irregular, normal and upright P waves in the underlying rhythm (P′ waves of premature beats differ from P waves of underlying rhythm), normal QRS complexes at 0.10 seconds, PRI = 0.16 seconds, QT = 0.40 seconds. Sinus rhythm with 2 premature atrial complexes (PACs) (3rd and 6th beats).
10. Atrial rate = 60 BPM at first then immeasurable, Ventricular rate = 60 BPM accelerating to 167 BPM, regular then sudden acceleration in heart rate, normal P waves then absent, normal QRS complexes at 0.10 seconds, PRI = 0.20 seconds, QT = 0.44 seconds. Paroxysmal supraventricular tachycardia.
11. Atrial rate = 72 BPM, Ventricular rate = 72 BPM in the underlying rhythm (60 BPM with the pause), occasionally irregular, normal and upright P waves, normal QRS complexes at 0.10 seconds, PRI = 0.16 seconds, QT = 0.40 seconds. Normal sinus rhythm with sinus arrest.
12. Atrial rate = 50 BPM, Ventricular rate = 50 BPM, regular rhythm, normal P waves, Notched QRS complexes at 0.12 seconds, PRI = 0.16 seconds, QT = 0.48 seconds. Sinus bradycardia.
13. Atrial rate = 100 BPM, Ventricular rate = 100 BPM, regular rhythm, normal and upright P waves, normal QRS complexes at 0.10 seconds, PRI = 0.16 seconds, QT = 0.38 seconds. Sinus tachycardia.
14. Atrial rate = 70 BPM, Ventricular rate = 70 BPM, patterned irregularity (speeds up toward center of tracing and slows back down again), normal and upright P waves, normal QRS complexes at 0.10 seconds, PRI = 0.12 seconds, QT = 0.36 seconds. Sinus dysrhythmia.
15. Atrial rate = 125 BPM, Ventricular rate = 125 BPM, regular, normal and upright P waves, normal QRS complexes at 0.08 seconds, PRI = 0.16 seconds, QT = 0.32 seconds. Sinus tachycardia.

Chapter 10

Answers to Assess Your Understanding

1. c: The normal PR interval is 0.12 to 0.20 seconds.
2. d: PR intervals of less than 0.12 seconds in duration are indicative of a pacemaker site that is either in or close to the AV junction.
3. c: Ectopic beats that appear with absent P waves along with a normal QRS complex are premature junctional complexes.
4. b: Junctional escape rhythm originates from the AV junction.
5. c: Junctional tachycardia has a heart rate of 100 to 180 beats per minute.
6. b: Junctional escape rhythm has a heart rate of 40 to 60 beats per minute.
7. d: Accelerated junctional rhythm has a heart rate of 60 to 100 beats per minute.
8. b: PR intervals seen with junctional rhythms will appear shorter than 0.12 seconds in duration.
9. b: Junctional escape rhythm may be preceded by an inverted P wave.
10. b: Bigeminal PJCs are PJCs that occur every other beat.
11. d: Quadrigeminal PJCs are PJCs that occur every fourth beat.
12. a: Trigeminal PJCs are PJCs that occur every third beat.
13. c: In junctional escape rhythm, the pacemaker site is in the AV junction.
14. d: Accelerated junctional rhythm has normal QRS complexes.
15. c: Paroxysmal means abruptly, without warning. Because the rhythm originates above the ventricle it is called supraventricular and because it is greater than 100 it is tachycardic.

16. b: Because the rate is so fast the P waves occur shortly after the QRS complex and are imbedded in the T wave.
17. a: PSVT occurs when an impulse originating in the atria stimulates the AV node to fire and then follows accessory pathways back to the point of origin reinitiating the impulse. This is called a "circus" impulse because it circles the atria in a self-perpetuating manner.

Answers to Practice Makes Perfect Exercises

1. Atrial rate = 80 BPM, Ventricular rate = 80 BPM, patterned irregularity, upright and normal P waves in the underlying rhythm, P′ waves associated with premature beats are absent, normal QRS complexes at 0.10 seconds, PRI = 0.16 seconds in underlying rhythm and immeasurable in the premature beats, QT = 0.40 seconds. Normal sinus rhythm with bigeminal premature junctional complexes (PJCs) (2nd, 4th, 6th and 8th complexes).
2. Atrial rate = 188 BPM, Ventricular rate = 188 BPM, regular rhythm, inverted P′ wave preceding each QRS complex, normal QRS complexes at 0.12 seconds, PRI = 0.10 seconds, QT = 0.24 seconds. Junctional tachycardia .
3. Atrial rate = 50 BPM, Ventricular rate = 50 BPM, regular rhythm, inverted P′ wave preceding each QRS complex, normal QRS complexes at 0.10 seconds, PRI = 0.10 seconds, QT = 0.58 seconds. Junctional escape rhythm.
4. Atrial rate = 92 BPM, Ventricular rate = 92 BPM, regular rhythm, P′ waves are absent, normal QRS complexes at 0.08 seconds, PRI is immeasurable, QT = 0.36 seconds. Accelerated junctional rhythm.
5. Atrial rate = 170 BPM, Ventricular rate = 170 BPM, regular rhythm, P is absent, QRS (more accurately described as RS) complexes at 0.08 seconds, PRI is immeasurable, QT = 0.24 seconds. Junctional tachycardia.
6. Atrial rate = 79 BPM, Ventricular rate = 79 BPM, occasionally irregular, upright and normal P waves in the underlying rhythm, P′ waves associated with premature beats are absent, QRS complexes are 0.10 seconds, PRI = 0.16 seconds in underlying rhythm and immeasurable in the premature beats, QT = 0.40 seconds. Normal sinus rhythm with 2 junctional complexes (PJCs) (6th and 8th complexes), this could be progressing into a junctional bigeminy.
7. Atrial rate = 30 BPM, Ventricular rate = 30 BPM, regular rhythm, inverted P′ wave follows each QRS complex, normal QRS complexes at 0.08 seconds, P′RI = 0.18 seconds, QT = 0.40 seconds. Slow junctional escape rhythm.
8. Atrial rate = 120 BPM, Ventricular rate = 120 BPM, regular rhythm, inverted P′ wave follows each QRS complex, normal QRS complexes at 0.08 seconds, P′RI = 0.16 seconds, QT = 0.36 seconds. Junctional tachycardia.
9. Atrial rate = 56 BPM, Ventricular rate = 56 BPM, regular rhythm, P′ waves are absent, normal QRS complexes at 0.10 seconds, PRI is immeasurable, QT = 0.40 seconds. Junctional escape rhythm.
10. Atrial rate = 70 BPM, Ventricular rate = 70 BPM, occasionally irregular (although the underlying rhythm is slightly irregular), upright and normal P waves in the underlying rhythm, P′ wave associated with premature beat is absent, QRS complexes are 0.10 seconds, PRI = 0.16 seconds in underlying rhythm and immeasurable in the premature beat, QT = 0.40 seconds. Normal sinus rhythm with a junctional complex (PJC) (3rd complex).
11. Atrial rate = 50 BPM, Ventricular rate = 50 BPM, slightly irregular, varying P waves, normal QRS complexes at 0.06 seconds, PRI varies, QT = 0.44 seconds. Slow (bradycardic) wandering atrial pacemaker.
12. Atrial rate = 120 BPM, Ventricular rate = 120 BPM, slightly irregular, varying P waves, normal QRS complexes at 0.12 seconds, PRI varies, QT = 0.32 seconds. Multifocal atrial tachycardia.
13. Atrial rate = 105 BPM, Ventricular rate = 105 BPM, regular, normal and upright P waves, wide QRS complexes at 0.16 seconds, PRI = 0.20 seconds, QT = 0.36 seconds. Sinus tachycardia.
14. Atrial rate = 79 BPM, Ventricular rate = 79 BPM, frequent irregularity, upright and normal P waves in the underlying rhythm, P′ waves associated with premature beats are buried in the T waves of the preceding beats, normal QRS complexes at 0.10 seconds, PRI = 0.18 seconds in underlying rhythm and 0.14 seconds in the premature beats, QT = 0.44 seconds. Normal sinus rhythm with frequent premature atrial complexes (PACs) (2nd, 5th and 7th complexes).
15. Atrial rate = approximately 250 BPM, Ventricular rate = 80 BPM, variably irregular rhythm, atrial waveforms have saw-tooth pattern – F waves are present, normal QRS complexes at 0.12 seconds, PRI immeasurable, QT immeasurable. Atrial flutter with a variable conduction ratio.
16. Atrial rate = 136 BPM, Ventricular rate = 136 BPM, regular rhythm, P waves are upright and peaked, QRS complexes are upright and normal at 0.08 seconds in duration, PRI = 0.12 seconds in duration, QT = 0.28 seconds. Sinus tachycardia.
17. Atrial rate = 70 BPM, Ventricular rate = 70 BPM, patterned irregularity, upright and normal P waves in the underlying rhythm, P′ waves associated with premature beats are absent, normal QRS complexes at 0.10 seconds, PRI = 0.14 seconds in the underlying rhythm and 0.12 seconds in the premature beats, QT = 0.40 seconds. Normal sinus rhythm with bigeminal premature atrial complexes (PACs) (2nd, 4th and 6th complexes).
18. Atrial rate is greater than 350 BPM, Ventricular rate = 90 BPM, totally irregular, P waves are indiscernible – f waves are present, QRS complexes are 0.08 seconds, PRI is immeasurable, QT = 0.36 seconds. Atrial fibrillation.
19. Atrial rate = 66 BPM, Ventricular rate = 66 BPM, occasionally irregular, normal and upright P waves (P′ wave of premature beat buried in the T wave of the preceding beat), normal QRS complexes at 0.08 seconds, PRI = 0.16 seconds, QT = 0.36 seconds. Normal sinus rhythm with a premature atrial complex (PAC) (6th beat).

20. Atrial rate = 42 BPM, Ventricular rate = 42 BPM, regular rhythm, normal and upright P waves, QRS complexes at 0.12 seconds, PRI = 0.16 seconds, QT = 0.44 seconds. Sinus bradycardia.

Chapter 11

Answers to Assess Your Understanding

1. c: Ventricular dysrhythmias have QRS complexes that are greater than 0.12 seconds in duration.
2. d: The presence of PVCs indicates irritability of the myocardium, possible hypoxia, and drug toxicity.
3. d: Premature ventricular complexes (PVCs) are followed by a compensatory pause.
4. c: PVCs that occur every other beat are called bigeminal PVCs.
5. b: PVCs that appear different from one another are called multiformed.
6. a: R-on-T phenomenon occurs when the PVC wave falls on the T wave.
7. c: Two PVCs in a row are called a couplet.
8. b: Three PVCs in succession are referred to as a run of V-tach.
9. a: Idioventricular rhythm has a rate of 20 to 40 beats per minute.
10. b: Idioventricular rhythm has wide, bizarre-looking QRS complexes.
11. d: Ventricular tachycardia has QRS complexes that are greater than 0.12 seconds in duration.
12. c: Polymorphic ventricular tachycardia has an appearance that varies considerably from complex to complex.
13. a: Ventricular fibrillation appears on the ECG monitor as having an overall pattern that appears irregularly shaped, chaotic, and lacks any regular repeating features.
14. b: With asystole there is a flat line on the ECG monitor.
15. c: Ventricular fibrillation results in chaotic impulses throughout the ventricles that do not allow the ventricle to contract at all and therefore no blood is ejected and no pulse is present.
16. a: Asystole is the absence of any electrical activity and is represented by a straight flat line on the monitor.
17. c: Defibrillation depolarizes the entire heart simultaneously resulting in asystole. Successful resuscitation from ventricular fibrillation requires one of the heart's pacemakers to begin generating impulses to the ventricles and for the ventricles to respond to this stimulation by contracting.

Answers to Practice Makes Perfect Exercises

1. Atrial rate = 86 BPM, Ventricular rate = 86 BPM, frequent irregularity, upright and normal P waves in the underlying rhythm – there are no P waves associated with premature beats, normal QRS complexes at 0.08 seconds in underlying rhythm – wide, bizarre-looking QRS complexes at 0.16 seconds in early beats, PRI = 0.12 seconds in underlying rhythm and absent in the premature beats, QT = 0.36 in the underlying rhythm and 0.40 seconds in the premature beats. Normal sinus rhythm with frequent premature atrial complexes (PACs) (2nd, 5th complexes).
2. Atrial rate = absent, Ventricular rate = 188 BPM, regular rhythm, absent P waves, QRS complexes are wide and bizarre-looking at 0.16 seconds, PRI is immeasurable, QT = 0.32 seconds. Ventricular tachycardia.
3. Atrial rate = absent, Ventricular rate = 40 BPM, regular rhythm, absent P waves, QRS complexes are wide and bizarre-looking at 0.20 seconds, PRI is immeasurable, QT = 1.12 seconds. Idioventricular rhythm.
4. Atrial rate = 60 BPM, Ventricular rate = 60 BPM, patterned irregularity (every other beat is a premature beat - bigeminy), P waves are upright and normal in the underlying rhythm but absent with the premature beats, QRS complexes are normal at 0.12 seconds in duration in the underlying rhythm but wide and bizarre in the early beats at 0.16 seconds, PRI = 0.20 seconds in duration for the normal beats but absent with the premature beats, QT = 1.00 seconds in both the underlying rhythm and the early beats. Sinus rhythm with bigeminal premature ventricular complexes (PVCs).
5. Atrial rate = 98 BPM, Ventricular rate = 98 BPM, frequent irregularity, upright and notched P waves in the underlying rhythm but P waves are absent with the premature beats, QRS complexes are normal at 0.12 seconds in duration in the underlying rhythm but wide and bizarre in the early beats at 0.14 seconds, PRI = 0.16 seconds in duration for the normal beats but absent with the premature beats, QT = 0.32 seconds in the underlying rhythm and 0.40 seconds in the premature beats. Normal sinus rhythm with frequent multiformed premature ventricular complexes (PVCs) (2nd, 4th, 7th and 9th complexes).
6. Immeasurable heart rate, totally irregular, absent atrial waveforms, no QRS complexes, PRI is immeasurable, QT is immeasurable. Ventricular fibrillation.
7. Atrial rate = 94, Ventricular rate = 94 BPM, patterned irregularity (every third beat is a premature beat – trigeminy), P waves are upright and normal in the underlying rhythm but absent with the premature beats, QRS complexes are normal at 0.08 seconds in duration in the underlying rhythm but wide and bizarre at 0.16 seconds in the early beats, PRI = 0.16 seconds for the normal beats and absent with the premature beats, QT = 0.32 seconds in the underlying rhythm and 0.36 seconds in the early beats. Sinus rhythm with trigeminal premature ventricular complexes (PVCs).
8. Atrial rate = absent, Ventricular rate = 56 BPM, regular rhythm, absent P waves, QRS complexes are wide and bizarre-looking at 0.16 seconds, PRI is immeasurable, QT = 1.00 seconds. Accelerated idioventricular rhythm.
9. Atrial rate = 74, Ventricular rate = 74 BPM, patterned irregularity (every third beat is a premature beat – trigeminy), P waves are upright and normal in the underlying rhythm but absent with the premature beats, QRS complexes are normal at 0.10 seconds in duration in the underlying rhythm but wide and bizarre in the early beats at 0.20 seconds, PRI = 0.16 seconds in duration for the normal beats but absent with the pre-

mature beats, QT = 0.40 seconds in the underlying rhythm and 0.56 seconds in the early beats. Sinus rhythm with trigeminal premature ventricular complexes (PVCs).

10. Atrial rate = absent, Ventricular rate = 188 BPM, regular rhythm, absent P waves, QRS complexes are wide and bizarre looking at 0.24 seconds, PRI is immeasurable, QT is immeasurable. Ventricular tachycardia.
11. Atrial rate is greater than 350 BPM, Ventricular rate = 110 BPM, totally irregular, P waves are indiscernible – f waves are present, QRS (more accurately described as RS) complexes at 0.08 seconds, PRI is immeasurable, QT = 0.28 seconds. Atrial fibrillation with rapid ventricular response.
12. Atrial rate = 58 BPM, Ventricular rate = 58 BPM, Regular rhythm (although there is a difference in regularity of one square between the 3rd and 4th R waves), normal and upright P waves, QRS complexes at 0.08 seconds, PRI = 0.20 seconds, QT = 0.44 seconds. Sinus bradycardia.
13. Atrial rate = 120 BPM, Ventricular rate = 120 BPM, regular rhythm, inverted P′ wave follows each QRS complex, normal QRS complexes at 0.08 seconds, P′RI = 0.16 seconds, QT = 0.36 seconds. Junctional tachycardia.
14. Atrial rate = 70 BPM, Ventricular rate = 70 BPM, patterned irregularity (slows down toward center of tracing and speeds up again), normal and upright P waves, normal QRS complexes at 0.06 seconds, PRI = 0.12 seconds, QT = 0.36 seconds. Sinus dysrhythmia.
15. Atrial rate =214 BPM, Ventricular rate = 214 BPM, regular rhythm, P is absent, normal QRS complexes at 0.08 seconds, PRI is immeasurable, QT = 0.28 seconds. Supraventricular tachycardia.
16. Atrial rate = 300 BPM, Ventricular rate = 70 BPM, variably irregular rhythm, atrial waveforms have sawtooth pattern – F waves are present, normal QRS complexes at 0.08 seconds, PRI immeasurable, QT = immeasurable. Atrial flutter with a variable conduction ratio.
17. Atrial rate = 58 BPM, Ventricular rate = 58 BPM, frequently irregular (for what you see on the tracing), normal and upright P waves (P′ waves of premature beat differ from the P waves of the underlying rhythm, and one is buried in T wave of the preceding beat), QRS (more accurately described as RS) complexes at 0.10 seconds, PRI = 0.24 seconds, QT = 0.48 seconds. Sinus bradycardia with 2 premature atrial complexes (PACs) (4th and 6th beats). There is also a 1st-degree AV heart block which we discuss in Chapter 12.
18. Atrial rate = 43 BPM, Ventricular rate = 43 BPM, regular rhythm, normal and upright P waves, QRS complexes at 0.08 seconds, PRI = 0.20 seconds, QT = 0.44 seconds. Sinus bradycardia.
19. Atrial rate = 128 BPM, Ventricular rate = 128 BPM, regular rhythm, upright and tall P waves, QRS complexes at 0.12 seconds, PRI = 0.12 seconds, QT = 0.32 seconds. Sinus tachycardia.
20. Atrial rate is greater than 350 BPM, Ventricular rate = 80 BPM, totally irregular, P waves are indiscernible – f waves are present, QRS complexes are 0.14 seconds, PRI is immeasurable, QT = 0.36 seconds (there are two T waves in the tracing that can be used to evaluate the QT). Atrial fibrillation.
21. Atrial rate = 65 BPM, Ventricular rate = 65 BPM, regular rhythm, normal and upright P waves, QRS (more accurately described as RS) complexes at 0.12 seconds, PRI = 0.20 seconds, QT = 0.44 seconds. Normal sinus rhythm.
22. Atrial rate = 60 BPM, Ventricular rate = 60 BPM in the underlying rhythm (50 BPM with the pause), occasionally irregular, normal and upright P waves, notched QRS complexes at 0.10 seconds, PRI = 0.16 seconds, QT = 0.28 seconds. Normal sinus rhythm with sinus arrest.
23. Atrial rate = 79 BPM, Ventricular rate = 79 BPM, regular rhythm, inverted P′ wave follows each QRS complex, normal QRS complexes at 0.08 seconds, P′RI = 0.44 seconds, QT = 0.36 seconds. Accelerated junctional rhythm.
24. Atrial rate = 70 BPM, Ventricular rate = 70 BPM, irregular (due to the premature beat but regularity varies slightly between the 3rd and 4th and 6th and 7th beats), normal and upright P waves (P′ wave of premature beat buried in the T wave of the preceding beat), notched QRS complexes at 0.10 seconds, PRI = 0.16 seconds, QT = 0.40 seconds. Normal sinus rhythm with a premature atrial complex (PAC) (2nd beat).
25. Atrial rate = 136 BPM, Ventricular rate = 136 BPM, regular rhythm, upright and tall P waves, QRS (more accurately described as RS) complexes at 0.10 seconds, PRI = 0.16 seconds, QT = 0.28 seconds. Sinus tachycardia.

Chapter 12

Answers to Assess Your Understanding

1. a: Heart blocks are partial delays or complete interruptions in the cardiac conduction pathway between the atria and ventricles.
2. a: With 1st-degree AV heart block the PR intervals are greater than 0.20 seconds in duration.
3. c: 1st-degree AV heart block is considered a consistent delay in conduction.
4. b: With Wenckebach not all the P waves are followed by a QRS complex.
5. a: With 2nd-degree AV heart block, Type II the P waves are all the same.
6. c: 2nd-degree AV heart block, Type II has a constant PR interval.
7. a: For the conducted beats the PR interval is constant with Type II, 2nd-degree AV heart block.
8. d: An ECG rhythm that has no correlation between P waves and QRS complexes is known as 3rd-degree AV heart block.
9. c: 3rd-degree AV heart block has P waves that seem to march through the QRS complexes.
10. b: 2nd-degree AV heart block, Type I is regularly irregular; in other words, there is a patterned irregularity to the rhythm.

11. d: With 1st-degree AV heart block it not a true block; instead there is a delay at the AV node with each impulse being eventually conducted.
12. a: With 2nd-degree AV heart block, Type I the PR interval gets progressively longer until a P wave fails to conduct, resulting in a "dropped" QRS complex. After the blocked beat, the cycle starts over again.
13. c: With 2nd-degree AV heart block, Type II some beats are conducted while others are blocked.
14. b: With 3rd-degree AV heart block there is a complete block at or below the AV node; there is no relationship between the P waves and QRS complexes.
15. c: Because the rate is normal it is neither bradycardic nor tachycardic. The rhythm originates in the SA node because the P waves are normal. However, because there are more P waves than QRS complexes there is some type of heart block. 1st-degree AV heart block has a long PR interval and there are an equal number of P waves and QRS complexes. Because the PR interval does not change it is not 2nd-degree AV heart block type I and because some of the P waves do conduct through to the AV node it is not 3rd-degree AV heart block.
16. b: The AV node has become damaged due to infarction and the resulting scar impedes its ability to sense the atrial impulse.
17. a: Because this condition can result in very slow heart rates an artificial pacemaker is required to ensure that the patient's heart rate remains in the normal range by stimulating ventricular contraction when the impulse is blocked through the AV node.

Answers to Practice Makes Perfect Exercises

1. Atrial rate = 70 BPM, Ventricular rate = 50 BPM, patterned irregularity, normal and upright P waves but not all are followed by a QRS complex, normal QRS complexes at 0.08 seconds, PRI is progressively longer until a QRS complex is dropped and then the cycle starts over again, QT = 0.28 seconds, 2nd-degree AV heart block, Type I.
2. Atrial rate = 56 BPM, Ventricular rate = 56 BPM, regular rhythm, P waves are upright and normal and each is followed by a QRS complex, QRS complexes are normal at 0.08 seconds in duration, PRI has a longer than normal duration = 0.30 seconds, QT = 0.40 seconds. Sinus rhythm with 1st-degree AV heart block.
3. Atrial rate = 94 BPM, Ventricular rate = 48 BPM, regular rhythm, P waves are upright and normal but there are two P waves preceding each QRS (in other words, not all the P waves are followed by a QRS complex), QRS complexes are normal at 0.08 seconds in duration, PRI = 0.16 seconds and is constant for the conducted beats, QT = 0.36 seconds. 2nd-degree AV heart block, Type II.
4. 50 BPM (ventricular) 84 BPM (atrial), regular rhythm, P waves are upright and normal but there are more P waves than QRS complexes, QRS complexes are bizarre-looking and wide at 0.20 seconds in duration, PRI is immeasurable (as the P waves are not associated with the QRS complexes), the P waves appear to march through the QRS complexes, QT = 0.48 seconds. 3rd-degree AV heart block.
5. Atrial rate = 60 BPM, Ventricular rate = 60 BPM, regular rhythm, P waves are upright and normal and each is followed by a QRS complex, QRS complexes are normal at 0.12 seconds in duration, PRI has a longer than normal duration = 0.30 seconds and constant, QT = 0.40 seconds. Sinus rhythm with 1st-degree AV heart block.
6. Atrial rate = 60 BPM, Ventricular rate = 50 BPM, patterned irregularity, normal and upright P waves but not all are followed by a QRS complex, normal QRS complexes at 0.08 seconds, PRI is progressively longer until a QRS complex is dropped and then the cycle starts over again, QT = 0.40 seconds. 2nd-degree AV heart block, Type I.
7. Atrial rate = 75 BPM, Ventricular rate = 36 BPM, regular rhythm, P waves are upright and normal but there are more P waves than QRS complexes, QRS complexes are bizarre-looking and wide at 0.16 seconds in duration, PRI is immeasurable (as the P waves are not associated with the QRS complexes), the P waves appear to march through the QRS complexes, QT = 0.36 seconds. 3rd- degree AV heart block.
8. Atrial rate = 94 BPM, Ventricular rate = 48 BPM, regular rhythm, P waves are upright and normal but there are two P waves preceding each QRS (in other words, not all the P waves are followed by a QRS complex), QRS (more accurately described as RS) complexes are 0.08 seconds in duration, PRI = 0.24 seconds and is constant for the conducted beats, QT = 0.36 seconds. 2nd-degree AV heart block, Type II (there is also a 1st-degree AV block).
9. Atrial rate = 115 BPM, Ventricular rate = 42 BPM, regular rhythm, P waves are upright and normal but there are more P waves than QRS complexes, QRS complexes are normal at 0.12 seconds in duration, PRI is immeasurable (as the P waves are not associated with the QRS complexes), the P waves appear to march through the QRS complexes, QT = 0.44 seconds. 3rd-degree AV heart block.
10. Atrial rate = 120 BPM, Ventricular rate = 120 BPM, regular rhythm, P waves are upright and normal, QRS complexes are upright and normal at 0.08 seconds in duration, PRI = 0.20 seconds in duration. QT = 0.30 seconds. Sinus tachycardia.
11. Atrial rate = 214 BPM , Ventricular rate = 214 BPM, regular rhythm, P′ waves are upright and present, QRS complexes at 0.06 seconds, PRI = 0.10, QT = 0.20 seconds. Atrial tachycardia.
12. Atrial rate = 45 BPM, Ventricular rate = 45 BPM, regular rhythm, normal and upright P waves and each is followed by a QRS complex, QRS complexes at 0.08 seconds, PRI = 0.44 seconds and constant, QT = 0.48 seconds. Sinus bradycardia with 1st-degree AV heart block.
13. Atrial rate = 82 BPM, Ventricular rate = 82 BPM, regular rhythm, P′ waves are absent, normal QRS complexes at 0.10 seconds, P′RI is immeasurable, QT = 0.34 seconds. Accelerated junctional rhythm.
14. Atrial rate = 125 BPM, Ventricular rate = 125 BPM, regular rhythm, upright and tall P waves, QRS com-

plexes at 0.08 seconds, PRI = 0.16 seconds, QT = 0.36 seconds. Sinus tachycardia.

15. Atrial rate = 60 BPM, Ventricular rate = 60 BPM, occasionally irregular (due to the premature beat), normal and upright P waves in the underlying rhythm, P′ wave of premature beat differs from P waves of underlying rhythm, normal QRS complexes at 0.10 seconds, PRI = 0.16 seconds, QT = 0.48 seconds. Normal sinus rhythm with a premature atrial complex (PAC) (2nd beat).
16. Atrial rate = 86 BPM, Ventricular rate = 86 BPM, regular rhythm, upright and normal P waves, QRS (more accurately described as QS) complexes at 0.08 seconds, PRI = 0.20 seconds, QT = 0.40 seconds. Sinus rhythm.
17. Atrial rate = 70 BPM, Ventricular rate = 70 BPM, patterned irregularity (speeds up toward center of tracing and slows down again), normal and upright P waves, normal QRS complexes at 0.08 seconds, PRI = 0.20 seconds, QT = 0.40 seconds. Sinus dysrhythmia.
18. Atrial rate = 65 BPM, Ventricular rate = 65 BPM, occasionally irregular (due to the premature beat), normal and upright P waves in the underlying rhythm, P′ wave of premature beat differs from P waves of underlying rhythm, notched QRS complexes at 0.10 seconds, PRI = 0.16 seconds, QT = 0.38 seconds. Normal sinus rhythm with a premature atrial complex (PAC) (2nd beat).
19. Atrial rate = 58 BPM, Ventricular rate = 58 BPM, regular rhythm, upright and normal P waves, notched QRS complexes at 0.08 seconds, PRI = 0.16 seconds, QT = 0.32 seconds. Sinus bradycardia.
20. Atrial rate = 136 BPM, Ventricular rate = 136 BPM, patterned irregularity (every fourth beat is a premature beat – quadrigeminy), P waves are upright and tall in the underlying rhythm but absent with the premature beats, QRS (more accurately described as QS) complexes are 0.06 seconds in duration in the underlying rhythm but wide and bizarre in the early beats at 0.20 seconds, PRI = 0.16 seconds in duration for the normal beats but absent with the premature beats, QT = 0.28 seconds in the underlying rhythm and 0.36 seconds in the early beats. Sinus rhythm with quadrigeminal premature ventricular complexes (PVCs).
21. Atrial rate is greater than 350 BPM, Ventricular rate = 100 BPM, totally irregular, P waves are indiscernible – f waves are present, QRS (more accurately described as QS) complexes at 0.12 seconds, PRI is immeasurable, QT is immeasurable. Atrial fibrillation.
22. Atrial rate = 130 BPM, Ventricular rate = 130 BPM, regular rhythm, upright and tall P waves, QRS (more accurately described as RS) complexes at 0.08 seconds, PRI = 0.16 seconds, QT = 0.28 seconds. Sinus tachycardia.
23. Atrial rate = 82 BPM, Ventricular rate = 82 BPM, occasional irregularity, upright and normal P waves in the underlying rhythm but P waves are absent with the premature beats, QRS complexes are normal at 0.08 seconds in duration in the underlying rhythm but wide and bizarre in the early beats at 0.14 seconds (in the 1st PVC) and 0.20 seconds (in the 1st PVC), PRI = 0.12 seconds in duration for the normal beats but absent with the premature beats, QT = 0.30 seconds in the underlying rhythm and 0.36 to 0.40 seconds in the premature beats. Normal sinus rhythm with multiformed premature ventricular complexes (PVCs) (2nd and 7th complexes).
24. Atrial rate = 375 BPM, Ventricular rate = 100 BPM, regular rhythm, atrial waveforms have saw-tooth pattern – F waves are present, , QRS (more accurately described as RS) complexes at 0.08 seconds, PRI immeasurable, QT immeasurable. Atrial flutter with a 4 to 1 conduction ratio.
25. Atrial rate = 80 BPM, Ventricular rate = 80 BPM, frequent irregularity, upright and normal P waves in the underlying rhythm but P waves are absent with the premature beats, QRS (more accurately described as QS) complexes are at 0.10 seconds in duration in the underlying rhythm but wide and bizarre in the early beats at 0.14 to 0.16 seconds, PRI = 0.16 seconds in duration for the normal beats but absent with the premature beats, QT = 0.38 seconds in the underlying rhythm and 0.40 seconds in the premature beats. Normal sinus rhythm with frequent multiformed premature ventricular complexes (PVCs) (2nd, 5th, 6th and 8th complexes) including a couplet of PVCs (5th and 6th complexes).
26. Atrial rate is greater than 350 BPM, Ventricular rate = 90 BPM, totally irregular, P waves are indiscernible – f waves are present, normal QRS complexes at 0.08 seconds, PRI is immeasurable, QT = 30 seconds. Atrial fibrillation.
27. Atrial rate = 60 BPM, Ventricular rate = 60 BPM, slightly irregular rhythm, upright and normal P waves, normal QRS complexes at 0.06 seconds, PRI = 0.12 seconds, QT = 0.36 seconds. Sinus rhythm.
28. Atrial rate = absent, Ventricular rate = 120 BPM, regular rhythm, absent P waves, QRS complexes are wide and bizarre looking at 0.14 seconds, PRI is immeasurable, QT = 0.40 seconds. Ventricular tachycardia.
29. Atrial rate = 120 BPM, Ventricular rate = 120 BPM, irregular, varying P waves, normal QRS complexes at 0.06 seconds, PRI immeasurable, QT = 0.28 seconds. Multifocal atrial tachycardia.
30. Atrial rate = 60 BPM, Ventricular rate = 60 BPM, patterned irregularity, normal and upright P waves, normal QRS complexes at 0.08 seconds, PRI = 0.20 seconds, QT = 0.40 seconds. Sinus dysrhythmia.

Chapter 13

Answers to Assess Your Understanding

1. b: The currents produced by depolarization and repolarization of the cardiac cells are called instantaneous vectors.
2. d: The electrical axis is depicted as a single large arrow.
3. a: Axis is defined in the frontal plane only.
4. c: The QRS axis is the most important and also the most frequently determined axis.
5. c: Completion of right ventricle depolarization occurs during completion of left ventricle depolarization.

6. b: The left ventricular vectors are larger and persist longer than those of the right ventricle.
7. b: The sum of all the small vectors of ventricular depolarization is called the mean QRS vector.
8. a: The center of the circle used to determine the axis of the mean QRS vector is the AV node.
9. c: The circle used to determine the axis of the mean QRS vector is divided into equal, 30-degree segments.
10. d: On the circle used to determine the axis of the mean QRS vector lead I starts at +0 degrees and is located at the 3 o'clock position.
11. c: The mean QRS axis normally points downward and to the patient's left, between 0 and +90 degrees.
12. d: Right axis deviation: +90 degrees and +180 degrees
    b: left axis deviation: 0 and −90 degrees
    c: extreme axis deviation: −180 and −90 degrees
13. If the QRS complex is positive in leads I and aV_F, the QRS axis must be normal. If the QRS complex is upright in lead I and negative in lead aV_F then left axis deviation exists. If the QRS complex is negative in lead I and positive in lead aV_F then right axis deviation exists. If the QRS complex is negative in both leads extreme right axis deviation exists.
14. Positive or upright.
15. Left half is negative, right half is positive.
16. Top half is negative, bottom half is positive.
17. a: As the mass of the left ventricle increases, the sum of the electrical forces is greater from the left side of the heart causing the axis to shift toward the left ventricle that is toward the left of normal.
18. b: As the mass of the left ventricle increases, the sum of the electrical forces is greater from the left side of the heart causing the axis to shift toward the left ventricle that is toward the left of normal.
19. d: The left ventricle must contract against a higher pressure in the aorta than the right ventricle against the pulmonary artery. Therefore, the left ventricle enlarges to a greater degree than the right.

Answers to Practice Makes Perfect

1. Left axis deviation.
2. Normal axis.
3. Left axis deviation.
4. Extreme left axis deviation.

Chapter 14

Answers to Assess Your Understanding

1. a: Hypertrophy is a condition in which the muscular wall of the ventricle becomes thicker than normal.
2. b: Hypertrophy is identified by changes in the QRS complexes.
3. d: Changes seen in the ECG that can indicate the presence of enlargement or hypertrophy are an increase in duration of the waveform, a biphasic waveform, and axis deviation.
4. b: The P wave normally has a duration of less than 0.10 seconds.
5. d: Leads II and V_1 provide the necessary information to assess atrial enlargement.
6. b: Characteristics of right atrial enlargement include an increase in the amplitude of the first part of the P wave in V_1.
7. c: With left atrial enlargement there is an increase in the duration of the terminal portion of the P wave.
8. c: The ECG evidence of atrial enlargement should be tempered with what is seen in the patient's presentation and what you know of the clinical setting.
9. c: To diagnose ventricular hypertrophy we assess the QRS complexes.
10. b: Normally, in lead V_1, the QRS complex will appear positive, with a large R wave and a short S wave.
11. d: The most common characteristic seen with right ventricular hypertrophy is right axis deviation.
12. a: The most common characteristic seen with left ventricular hypertrophy is R waves that are more positive in the leads that lie closer to lead V_6.
13. c: Below the bundle of His the conduction system divides to form the right and left bundle branches.
14. a: The QRS complex is normally narrow, between 0.06 and 0.12 seconds in duration.
15. b: With normal ventricular depolarization the electrical axis is drawn leftward, lying between 0° and +90°.
16. b: Bundle branch block is a disorder in which one or both of the bundle branches fails to conduct impulses.
17. c: To diagnose right bundle branch block, check for an R, R′ in leads V_1 or V_2.
18. a: Hemiblocks cause axis deviation.
19. d: With preexcitement syndromes impulses are conducted through accessory conduction pathways between the atria and ventricles.
20. b: In WPW impulses bypass the AV node by traveling from the atria to the ventricles via the bundle of Kent.
21. b: The fact that the QRS complex is wide and notched indicates a bundle branch block. The "rabbit ear" appearance in V_1 is diagnostic of a right bundle branch block.
22. c: The "rabbit ear" appearance refers to the notched configuration of the QRS complex of a right bundle branch block. The first wave is positive (R), the next portion is negative (S), then it ends with a second positive wave called R′ (prime).
23. c: Cardiomyopathy refers to a condition in which the heart muscle is damaged and weakened. The most common type is a congestive cardiomyopathy that results in dilation of the ventricles with a corresponding decrease in the ejection fraction.

Answers to Practice Makes Perfect Exercises

1. Left atrial enlargement (biphasic P waves in V_1).
2. Left anterior hemiblock (left axis deviation in the absence of left ventricular hypertrophy).
3. Left bundle branch block and possible ventricular hypertrophy (R wave in V_5 + S wave in V_2 = 35 mm).
4. Left posterior hemiblock (right axis deviation in absence of right ventricular hypertrophy).

Chapter 15

Answers to Assess Your Understanding

1. c: The blood vessels that supply the myocardial cells with a continuous supply of oxygen and nutrients are referred to as the coronary arteries.
2. a: (True) The heart requires its own blood supply because the demand for oxygen of the myocardial cells is extremely high.
3. b: ST segment depression or elevation can be evaluated by comparing the ST segment to the PR segment.
4. c: The normal Q wave has a duration of less than 0.04 seconds, is not always present, and is a small negative deflection from the baseline.
5. d: The ST segment is the line that follows the QRS complex and connects it to the T wave.
6. b: The normal T wave is not more than 5 mm in the limb leads.
7. c: Myocardial infarction is the actual death of injured myocardial cells.
8. b: Myocardial infarction is the most severe result of an interruption of coronary artery blood flow.
9. a: (True) The ECG can help identify the presence of ischemia, injury, and/or infarction of the heart muscle.
10. b: The absence of Q waves in the limb leads is not a key ECG indicator of myocardial ischemia, injury, and/or infarction. Inversion of the T wave, elevation of the ST segment, and peaking of the T wave are key indicators of myocardial ischemia, injury, and/or infarction.
11. b: (False) It is not necessary for all the characteristic ECG indicators to be present in order to diagnose myocardial ischemia, injury, or infarction.
12. ECG changes with type of cardiac condition with which they are seen: c. infarction: enlarged Q waves or presence of new Q waves; a. ischemia: ST segment depression; b. injury: elevation in the ST segment.
13. a: ST segment depression is considered significant when the ST segment falls more than 1 mm below the baseline at a point one small square (0.04 seconds) to the right of the J point.
14. a: Inverted T waves associated with myocardial ischemia indicate the ischemia is present through the full thickness of the myocardium.
15. a: (True) Two characteristic signs of myocardial ischemia are inverted T waves and ST segment elevation.
16. d: ST segment elevation associated with myocardial injury is seen in the leads facing the affected area.
17. a: (True) ST segment elevation is the earliest reliable sign that myocardial infarction has occurred.
18. a: The appearance of Q waves indicates that irreversible myocardial damage has occurred.
19. Leads where ECG changes will be seen with type of infarction: c. V_1, V_2, V_3, and V_4: anterior infarction; b. II, III, and aV_F: inferior infarction; d. I, AV_L, V_5, and V_6: lateral infarction; a. V_1 and V_2 (for reciprocal changes): posterior infarction.
20. d: Lead II, III, and aV_F "look" at the inferior wall of the left ventricle.
21. a: Only 1 mm of ST elevation is required to make the diagnosis of acute myocardial infarction. However, the ST elevation must be in contiguous leads that view the same portion of the heart.
22. d: The phrase "time is muscle" refers to the fact that the longer a patient delays receiving definitive care, such as angioplasty or fibrinoloytics, the more extensive the damage to the heart and the worse the outcome is to the patient.

Answers to Practice Makes Perfect Exercises

1. Inferior wall ischemia (inverted T waves in leads III and aV_F, depressed ST segment in lead II).
2. Septal injury (elevated T waves in V_3, ST segment elevation in V_4).
3. Anterior wall injury (ST segment elevation in V_2 and V_3).
4. Inferior wall ischemia (inverted T waves in leads I and aV_L)
5. Inferior-lateral ischemia (inverted T waves in leads I, II, III, aV_L, aV_F, V_5 and V_6).

Chapter 16

Answers to Assess Your Understanding

1. c: Inflammation of the pericardium is called pericarditis.
2. b: ECG changes seen with pericarditis include an elevated ST segment that is usually flat or concave.
3. a: In comparison to myocardial infarction the ECG changes seen with pericarditis include diffuse ST segment and T wave changes.
4. b: Electrical alternans is a condition in which the electrical axis of the heart varies with each beat.
5. d: A pulmonary embolism can lead to acute cor pulmonale.
6. d: All of the lists are consistent with pulmonary embolus.
7. d: A pacemaker produces an impulse and conveys it to the myocardium.
8. c: An AV sequential pacemaker produces one spike that precedes a P wave and one spike that precedes a wide, bizarre QRS complex.
9. ECG changes with type of cardiac condition with which they are seen: b. Hyperkalemia: Peaked T waves, widened QRS complexes, and sine-waves; c. Hypokalemia: Appearance of U waves, prolongation of the QT-interval; a. Hypocalcemia: Slightly prolonged QT interval.
10. a: (True) Increases or decreases in the potassium and calcium serum levels can have a profound effect on the ECG.
11. d: Prolonged QT intervals are associated with torsades de pointes.
12. c: ECG changes associated with digoxin use include a gradual downward curve of the ST segment.
13. b: The most common dysrhythmia seen with digoxin toxicity is paroxysmal atrial tachycardia (PAT) with 2nd-degree AV heart block.

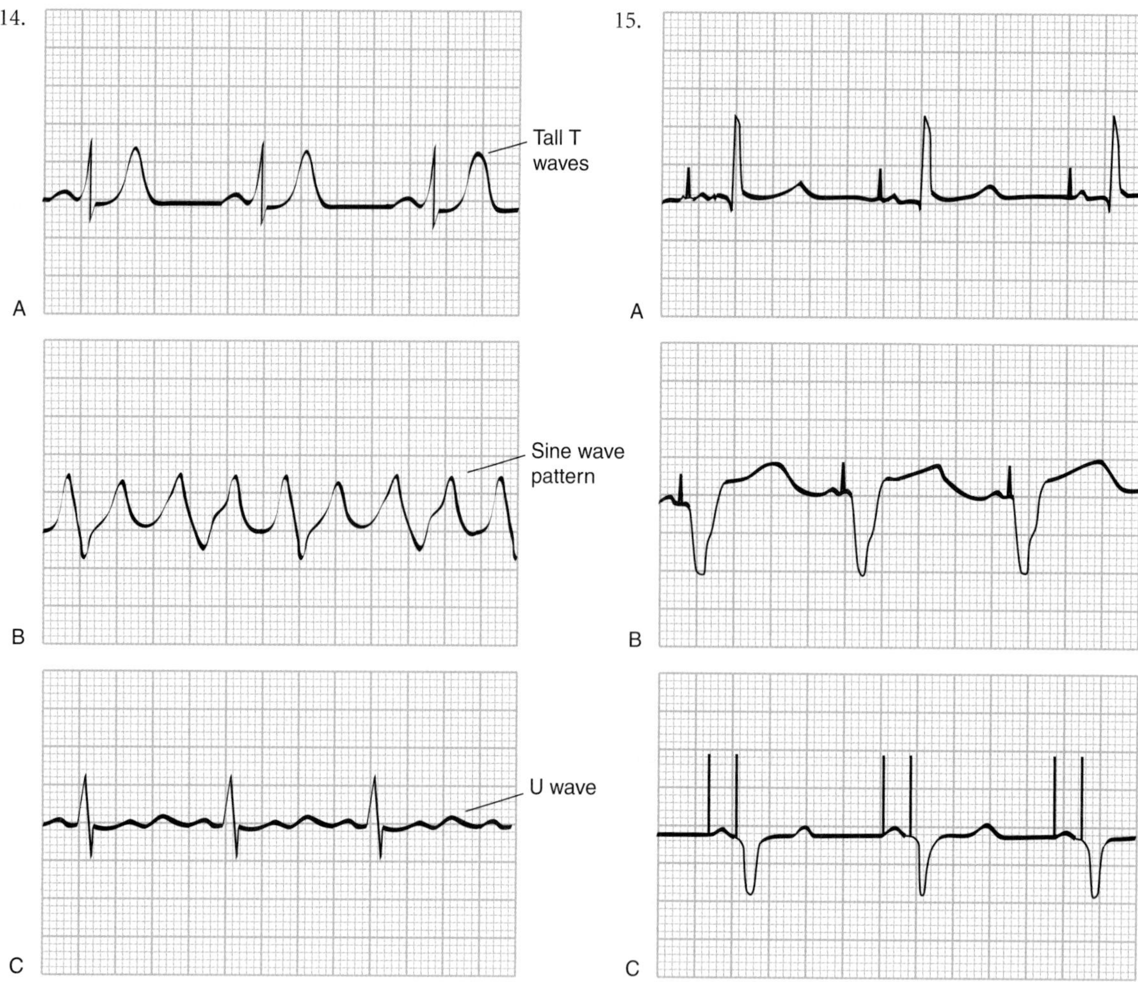

16. c: Renal failure results in abnormal retention of potassium. This elevated potassium level is called hyperkalemia.
17. a: The hyperkalemic T wave is shaped like a tent with a sharp peak and concave sides that are of equal duration.
18. a: As the potassium level increases the conduction is slowed throughout the P-QRS-T complex. The PR interval is prolonged and the QRS complex widens eventually merging into the T wave.

Answers to Practice Makes Perfect Exercises

1. Electrical alternans.
2. Pacemaker.
3. Hypocalcemia.
4. Low amplitude.
5. Digitalis effect.

Glossary

A

Aberrancy A waveform or complex that deviates from the normal or expected appearance indicating that its conduction pathway is abnormal.

Absolute refractory period The phase during repolarization during which no stimulus, no matter how strong will depolarize the cell.

Acetylcholine The chemical compound used to transmit impulses across the nerve synapse, the major neurotransmitter for the parasympathetic (cholinergic) nervous system.

Action potential The measure over time of the change in electrical charge of the cell. The action potential reflects the ability of the cell to depolarize.

Actin One of the two components of the contractile filaments involved in the muscular contraction.

Accessory pathway A conduction pathway from the sinoatrial (SA) node to the ventricles that does not pass through the normal atrioventricular (AV) node pathway.

Acute Sudden and recent onset of a condition, sign, or symptom.

Acute coronary syndrome The condition of ischemic chest pain consisting of the following conditions: unstable angina, non-ST segment elevation myocardial infarction, and ST segment elevation myocardial infarction.

Adrenalin (epinephrine) A natural catecholamine that causes bronchodilation, increased atrioventricular (AV) conduction, muscular contractility, heart rate, and vasoconstriction.

Adrenergic Nerves that release epinephrine or epinephrine-like substances.

Afterload The pressure against which the left ventricle must pump blood during contraction.

Alpha adrenergic receptors Any of the adrenergic receptor tissues that respond to norepinephrine.

Amplitude The height and depth, or waveform size, of an ECG complex.

Anemia A deficiency in the oxygen-carrying hemoglobin molecule contained in blood.

Aneurysm A pathological blood-filled dilation of a blood vessel.

Angina See angina pectoris.

Angina pectoris Chest pain resulting when the supply of oxygen and coronary perfusion is insufficient to that demanded by the heart muscle.

Antegrade Occurring or performed in a direction of the normal or forward direction of conduction or flow.

Artery A vessel that carries blood away from the heart. Arteries generally carry oxygenated blood. The exception is the pulmonary artery, which carries deoxygenated blood to the lungs.

Artifact An abnormality of the ECG arising from electrical interference unrelated to the electrical activity of the heart.

Aorta The major vessel that carries oxygenated blood from the heart to the body.

Aortic valve The valve that separates the left ventricle from the aorta.

Apex The tip of a structure that may be either at the top or bottom. The apex of the heart is the bottom of the heart.

Arrhythmia Technically speaking means the absence of a rhythm but is used synonymously with the term dysrhythmia.

Asystole Absence of cardiac electrical activity. An absence of upward or downward deflection on the isoelectric line of the ECG.

Atherosclerosis An accumulation of fat-containing deposits within the arterial wall.

Atria The chamber of the heart that collects blood returning from the rest of the body. The right atrium collects deoxygenated blood from the body and passes it to the right ventricle. The left atrium collects oxygenated blood from the lungs and passes it to the left ventricle.

Atrial kick The additional volume of blood pushed into the ventricle by the contraction of the atria.

Atrioventricular dissociation (AV dissociation) Any rhythm characterized by the atria and ventricles beating independently such as that seen in 3rd-degree AV heart block.

Atrioventricular junction (AV junction) The area of conductive tissue that includes the AV node, its atrial pathways, and the bundle of His.

Atrioventricular node (AV node) Specialized tissue at the base of the wall between the two upper heart chambers (atria). Electrical impulses pass from the SA node to the AV node then on to the bundle of His.

Augmented limb leads The limb leads aV_R, aV_L, and aV_F. The ECG waveforms produced by these leads is so small that the ECG machine enhances, or augments, them by 50% so their amplitude is comparable to other leads.

Automaticity The ability of cardiac cells to initiate spontaneous electrical impulses.

Autonomic nervous system The involuntary portion of the peripheral nervous system that regulates vital body functions. It is separated into the parasympathetic and sympathetic divisions. This system controls cardiac, smooth muscle and glandular activity.

Axis The sum of all the vectors of electrical activity associated with conduction of the action potential through the heart.

Axis deviation An abnormal shift of the normal axis of the cardiac muscle action potential often associated with ventricular hypertrophy and certain conduction defects.

B

Baroreceptors pressure sensitive nerve endings in the walls of the atria of the heart and in some larger blood vessels such as the carotid artery. Baroreceptors stimulate reflex mechanisms that allow the body to adapt to changes in blood pressure by dilating or constricting blood vessels.

Beta receptors Adrenergic receptors of the nervous system that respond to adrenaline. Activation causes relaxation of smooth muscles and increases in cardiac rate and contractility.

Bicuspid valve See mitral valve.

Bigeminy Cardiac electrical activity characterized by a pattern of one ectopic beat followed by one normal beat. These ectopic beats can be either atrial or ventricular in origin and indicate cardiac irritability.

Bipolar limb lead An ECG lead with both a positive and negative electrode. Leads I, II, and III are bipolar limb leads.

Biphasic Having two phases, one negative and one positive. A biphasic waveform has both a positive and negative deflection.

Bradycardia A heart rate below 60 beats per minute, when related to atrial or sinus rhythms.

Bundle branch Either of the parts of the bundle of His passing respectively to the right and left ventricles.

Bundle of His Specialized muscle fibers in the intraventricular septum that carry the electric impulses to the ventricles.

Burst See Salvo.

C

Calibration As it relates to the ECG machine it involves the internal regulation of the device such that 1 mV electrical signal results in a 10 mm deflection.

Catecholamine Sympathetic nervous system neurotransmitter such as epinephrine, norepinephrine, and dopamine.

Cardiac tamponade See pericardial tamponade.

Cardiac output The volume of blood pumped by the heart, usually measured in milliliters per minute. Calculated by multiplying heart rate and stroke volume.

Cardiomyopathy Any structural or functional disease of heart muscle that is marked especially by hypertrophy of cardiac muscle, by enlargement of the heart, by rigidity and loss of flexibility of the heart walls, or by narrowing of the ventricles.

Chemoreceptor A sensory nerve cell that is activated by chemicals such as the carbon dioxide detectors in the brainstem.

Cholinergic Nerve fibers that release acetylcholine.

Chordae tendineae Thin, strong strings of connective tissue that anchor the papillary muscles to the floor of the heart.

Chronotropic Affecting the rate of the heartbeat. A positive chronotropic effect increases the heart rate while a negative chronotropic effect decreases the heart rate.

Circadian rhythm The biological clock in humans based on a 24-hour cycle. At regular intervals each day, the body becomes active or tired. Some medications affect the body more at certain times during the day than others.

Compensatory pause The pause following a premature complex that allows the original rhythm to begin again at its normal rate. The compensatory pause will be exactly twice the R-R interval of the normally conducted beat, as seen following a PVC.

Contractility Ability of the cardiac muscle to contract in response to electrical stimulation.

Conductivity The ability of the cardiac muscle to transmit an electrical stimulus from cell to cell.

Coronary arteries A pair of arteries that branch from the ascending aorta and supply oxygenated blood to the myocardium.

Coronary artery disease The gradual narrowing and hardening of the coronary arteries. Usually the result of atherosclerosis.

Coronary veins Vessels that transport deoxygenated blood from the capillaries of the heart to the right atrium.

Couplet Two consecutive complexes.

Cyanosis A condition in which a person's skin is discolored to a bluish hue because of inadequate oxygenation of the blood.

D

Delta wave A slurred or widened upstroke at the beginning of the cardiac QRS complex causing prolongation of the complex. It indicates anomalous impulse conduction and is diagnostic of Wolff-Parkinson-White syndrome.

Depolarization Loss of the difference in charge between the inside and outside of the plasma membrane of a muscle or nerve cell due to a change in permeability and migration of sodium ions into the cell.

Desmosomes A specialized local thickening of the plasma membrane of myocytes that serves to anchor contiguous cells together and prevent them from pulling apart during contraction.

Diastole The period of relaxation during the cardiac cycle, when the cardiac muscle fibers lengthen, causing the heart to dilate and fill with blood. Coronary perfusion occurs during this phase.

Dilation Expansion or widening of an organ, opening, or vessel.

Dysrhythmia Any abnormality in the otherwise normal rhythmic pattern of the heartbeat.

Dyspnea Difficulty in breathing.

E

Ectopic A cardiac complex originating from somewhere other than the SA node. It may be early (premature) or late (escape) in nature.

Einthovans Triangle An electrical triangle formed by the patients' right arm, left arm, and left leg, used to position electrodes for ECG monitoring. This positioning is used to determine the direction of cardiac vectors to various leads.

Electrical axis See axis.

Electrocardiogram The tracing made by an electrocardiograph. Also known as ECG or EKG.

Electrocardiograph Device used to record electrical variation within cardiac tissue.

Electrode The electrical sensor applied to the body to record the ECG.

Electrolyte Element or compound that, when melted or dissolved in water or other solvent, dissociates into ions (atoms able to carry an electric charge). Sodium, potassium, and calcium are the primary electrolytes involved in myocardial activity.

Electromechanical dissociation (EMD) A condition characterized by seemingly normal electrical heart activity without discernible mechanical activity. This term is no longer used and has been replaced by "Pulseless Electrical Activity" (PEA).

Endocardium The serous membrane that lines the inner aspect of the four chambers of the heart and its valves.

Enlargement An increase in size.

Epinephrine See adrenalin.

Epicardium A thick serous membrane that constitutes the smooth outer surface of the heart.

Escape complex A beat that occurs after the normal pacemaker fails to fire.

Excitability The degree to which a myocardial cell is reactive to external stimuli.

Extrasystole A premature complex.

F

f waves Waves associated with atrial fibrillation. Occur at a rate of greater than 350 times per minute.

F waves Saw-toothed waves associated with atrial flutter. Occur at a rate of 250 to 350 times per minute.

Fascicle A small bundle of conducting fibers.

Fibrillation Very rapid irregular contractions of the muscle fibers of the heart resulting in a lack of synchronism between the heartbeat and pulse.

Fibrillatory A waveform associated with atrial fibrillation.

Flutter An abnormal rapid spasmodic and usually rhythmic motion or contraction of the atria.

Fusion beat Occurs when two complexes originating from different pacemakers fuse to form one complex as seen with some types of PVCs.

G

Ganglia A group of nerve cells forming a nerve center along the thoracic and sacral spine associated with the parasympathetic nervous system.

Gap junctions An area of the conducting cell that improves the rate of electrical conduction.

H

Hemiblock Failure of conduction of the muscular excitatory impulse in either of the two fascicles of the left branch of the bundle of His.

Hypertrophy Increase in bulk (as by thickening of muscle fibers) without multiplication of parts.

Hypertension A condition in which a person's blood pressure is abnormally high. For normal adults, the blood pressure should be less than 130 mm Hg systolic and less than 85 mm Hg diastolic. Pressures above 140/90 indicate a mild form of hypertension; above 180/110 is considered severe.

I

Idioventricular Relating to, or arising in the ventricles of the heart independent of the atria.

Infarction Irreversible cell death caused by prolonged obstruction of arterial blood supply to an area of the myocardium.

Inotropic Something that increases the force of contraction of the heart.

Intercalated disks The specialized regions of the cardiac muscle cells that comprise the longitudinal and end-to-end junctions between adjacent cells and that function to connect them mechanically and electrically.

Interpolated A beat that occurs between normal heartbeats without disturbing the succeeding beat or the basic rhythm of the heart.

Intraatrial pathway Electrical pathways that travel through the atria from the SA node to the AV node.

Intranodal pathway The conduction pathways through the atrioventricular (AV) node.

Ion An atom or group of atoms that carries a positive or negative electric charge as a result of having lost or gained one or more electrons.

Ischemia Local tissue hypoxia caused by an obstruction to arterial blood supply to an area of the myocardium.

Isoelectric A condition of the cell that is neither negatively nor positively charged in relation to its neighboring cells. This also refers to the baseline on the ECG that indicates neither a positive or negative deflection.

J

J point The point at which the QRS complex meets the ST segment. Also called the junction.

Junctional A cardiac rhythm resulting from impulses coming from a locus of tissue in the area of the atrioventricular (AV) node.

L

Left bundle branch The portion of the heart's conduction system that supplies the left ventricle. Composed of two fascicles; the left anterior fascicle and the left posterior fascicle.

M

M mitrale Left atrial enlargement associated with mitral valve stenosis.

Mediastinum The space in the chest between the pleural sacs of the lungs that contains all the viscera of the chest except the lungs and includes the heart, aorta, and vena cava.

Mitral valve A valve in the heart between the left atrium and the left ventricle. Prevents the blood in the ventricle from returning to the atrium during systole, and consists of two triangular flaps. Also called *bicuspid valve* or *left atrioventricular valve.*

Morphology The configuration or shape of a wave or complex on the ECG.

Multifocal Complexes that arise from different sites within the heart; usually refers to ventricular complexes.

Myocardial infarction See infarction.

Myocardial injury A degree of cellular damage beyond ischemia.

Myocardial ischemia See ischemia.

Myocardium The muscular layer of the heart.

Myocytes The individual muscle cells of the heart.

Myosin One of the two components of the contractile filaments involved in the muscular contraction.

N

Neurotransmitter A substance, such as norepinephrine or acetylcholine, used to transmit a nerve impulse across the synapse between nerve cells or to the organ being stimulated (innervated).

Noncompensatory pause The pause following a premature complex that resets the rate of the original rhythm. The R-R interval following a noncompensatory pause is less than two preceeding R-R intervals; as seen following a PAC.

Norepinephrine The chemical compound used to transmit impulses by the sympathetic nervous system. A precursor to epinephrine and referred to as noradrenaline.

O

Osborn wave A narrow, positive deflection wave at the junction of the QRS complex and the ST segment, associated with hypothermia.

Oscilloscope An instrument that displays the fluctuating electrical quantity as a visible waveform on the fluorescent screen of a cathode-ray tube.

P

P wave The electrical representation of atrial contraction. Precedes the QRS complex.

Papillary muscles The thin muscles that connect to the cusps of the mitral and tricuspid valves and contract to facilitate their ability to resist prolapsing during systole.

Pericarditis Inflammation of the pericardium.

P mitrale Right atrial enlargement associated with severe lung disease such as COPD and pulmonary hypertension.

P pulmonale Hypertrophy of the right ventricle associated with severe lung disease such as emphysema.

PR segment The isoelectric period that represents the conduction of the electrical impulse through the AV node.

Parasympathetic The part of the autonomic nervous system that contains chiefly cholinergic fibers. Tends to induce secretion, to increase the tone and contractility of smooth muscle, and to slow the heart rate.

Parietal pericardium The tough thickened membranous outer layer of the pericardium that is attached to the central part of the diaphragm and the posterior part of the sternum.

Paroxysmal An abrupt beginning and ending of an event such as a different cardiac rhythm.

PEA See Pulseless Electrical Activity.

Pericardial tamponade A condition characterized by a collection of fluid within the pericardial sac that constricts the heart and inhibits its ability to fill during diastole. Also called cardiac tamponade.

Pericardium The conical sac of serous membranes that encloses the heart and the roots of the aorta, pulmonary artery, and vena cava composed of one layer that is closely adherent to the heart while the other lines the inner surface of the outer coat with the intervening space being filled with pericardial fluid.

Polarization Refers to the cell returning to its resting state during which no electrical activity occurs and its intracellular fluid is negatively charged relative to the extracellular fluid.

PR segment The flat isoelectric line that represents the electrical impulse traveling through the His-Purkinje system.

Precordial Situated in front of the heart.

Preload The stretched condition of the heart muscle at the end of diastole just before contraction.

Pulmonic valve The heart valve that separates the right ventricle from the pulmonary artery. Also called the semilunar valve.

Pulseless Electrical Activity (PEA) A condition characterized by seemingly normal electrical heart activity without discernible mechanical activity.

Purkinje fibers Specialized heart cells capable of conducting electrical impulses and directly stimulating myocardial cells to contract.

Q

Q wave The first negative deflection of the QRS complex not following an R wave.

QRS complex The waveform that represents electrical conduction through the ventricles. Associated with ventricular contraction.

QT interval Period of time measured from the beginning of the Q wave to the end of the T wave representing the time required to depolarize and repolarize the ventricles.

Quadrigeminal Cardiac electrical activity characterized by a pattern of one ectopic beat followed by three normal beats. These ectopic beats can be either atrial or ventricular in origin and indicate cardiac instability.

R

Reentry A cardiac mechanism that is held to explain certain abnormal heart actions (as tachycardia) and that involves the transmission of a wave of depolarization along an alternate pathway when the original pathway is blocked with return of the impulse along the blocked pathway resulting in a reinitiation of the impulse.

Refractory period The phase during repolarization during which a stimulus may or may not cause the cell to depolarize. Also see relative and absolute refractory period.

Relative refractory period A later phase of repolarization during which a sufficiently strong stimulus will depolarize the cell.

Repolarization Restoration of the difference in charge between the inside and outside of the plasma membrane of a muscle fiber or cell following depolarization.

Resting membrane potential (RMP) The relative difference between the electrical charge of the inside as compared to the outside of the cell.

Retrograde Occurring or performed in a direction opposite to the normal or forward direction of conduction or flow.

Right bundle branch The portion of the heart's conduction system that supplies the right ventricle.

R-R interval The interval of time between consecutive R waves.

R wave The positive deflection in the QRS complex.

S

SA node See sinoatrial node.

Salvo A series of three or more consecutive and identical beats as in referring to a salvo of ventricular tachycardia.

Sarcolemma The plasma membrane surrounding the myocytes of the heart.

Sarcoplasmic reticulum The specialized area of the myocyte for storage of calcium required to trigger contraction of the actin and myosin filaments.

Semilunar valve See pulmonic valve.

Septum The curved slanting wall that separates the right and left ventricles of the heart and is composed of a muscular lower part and a thinner more membranous upper part.

Sick sinus syndrome A condition characterized by persistent sinus bradycardia, sinoatrial block manifested as sinoatrial Wenckebach, complete sinoatrial block, or sinus arrest.

Sinoatrial (SA) node A small mass of tissue made up of nerve fibers, which is embedded in the musculature of the right atrium. Initiates the impulses stimulating the heartbeat and is the primary pacemaker of the heart. Also called SA node, sinus node.

Sodium-potassium pump Refers to the energy-requiring process by which the cellular membrane actively moves sodium out of the cell and potassium into the cell.

ST segment Represents the phase following ventricular depolarization before repolarization begins and is helpful in assessing for the presence of cardiac ischemia.

Stroke volume The volume of blood pumped from a ventricle of the heart in one beat.

Supraventricular Relating to or being a rhythmic abnormality of the heart caused by impulses originating above the ventricles.

Sympathetic The part of the autonomic nervous system that contains chiefly adrenergic fibers. Tends to decrease glandular secretion and to speed the heart rate.

Syncytium Refers to the network of anastomosis (connections) between adjoining myocytes.

Systole The contraction of the ventricles during which blood is ejected from the ventricles into the aorta and pulmonary artery.

T

T wave Represents ventricular repolarization.

Tachycardia A heart rate greater than 100 when referring to sinus rhythms or a rate greater than is normally expected with any rhythm.

Thrombolytics Medications that attack and accelerate the body's ability to break up or lyse a blood clot (thrombus).

Torsades de pointes Ventricular tachycardia characterized by fluctuation of the QRS complexes around the electrocardiographic baseline. Typically caused by a long QT interval.

Tricuspid valve Heart valve situated between the right atrium and the right ventricle. Resembles the mitral valve in structure but consists of three triangular membranous flaps. Also called the right atrioventricular valve.

Trigeminal Cardiac electrical activity characterized by a pattern of one ectopic beat followed by two normal beats. These ectopic beats can be either atrial or ventricular in origin and indicate cardiac instability.

U

Unifocal Complexes originating from the same location (focus).

U wave A positive wave that may follow the T wave representing the final repolarization phase of the ventricles. It is rarely seen.

V

Vagus nerve Either of the pair of tenth cranial nerves that arise from the medulla and supply chiefly the heart with autonomic sensory and motor fibers.

Vector The geometric direction of travel of an electrical impulse in the heart.

Vein A vessel that carries blood toward the heart.

Ventricles The chambers of the heart that receive blood from a corresponding atrium and from which blood is forced into the arteries.

Ventricular standstill A condition where the atria continue to beat but the ventricles have stopped.

Visceral pleura The fibrous connective tissue adhering to the outer surface of an organ.

Index

A

E

F

G

H

M

N

O

P

Q

R

S

T

U

V

W